SUMMARY OF DOS COMMANDS*

COMMAND	DESCRIPTION	FORMAT	
DEBUG	Invokes the assembly-language debugging program	[D:Path]DEBUG [FileSpec] [Param1] [Param2]	625
DEL	Removes a file from the disk	DEL FileSpec[/P]	626
DIR	Lists files on a disk or in a directory	DIR [FileSpec][/P][/W]	83
DISKCOMP	Compares two diskettes	[D:Path]DISKCOMP [D1:[D2:]][/1][/8]	70
DISKCOPY	Duplicates complete diskette	[D:Path]DISKCOPY [SourceD:DestD:][/1]	63
DOSSHELL	Initiates the graphic interface	[D:Path]DOSSHELL	629
EDLIN	Line editor supplied with DOS	[D:Path]EDLIN [FileSpec] [/B]	167
ERASE	Removes a file from a disk	ERASE [FileSpec][/P]	118
EXE2BIN	Converts an .EXE file to a .COM file	[D:Path]EXE2BIN SourceFile [DestFile]	631
FASTOPEN	Speeds up file opening	[D;Path]FASTOPEN D1:[= Size][D2: = Size […][/X][D:Path]FASTOPEN D1:[= ([Size],[Buf])][…][/X]	457
FDISK	Partitions a hard disk	[D:Path]FDISK	692
FIND	Finds strings in files	[D:Path]FIND [/V][/C][/N]"String" [FileSpec…]	334
FORMAT	Prepares a disk to accept data	[D:Path]FORMATD1:[/S][/1][/4][/8][/V:label] [/B][/N:xx][/T:yy][/F:Size]	58
GRAFTABL	Displays ASCII characters on CGA	[D:Path]GRAFTABL [437¦850¦860¦863¦865¦?¦ /STATUS]	314
GRAPHICS	Enables PrtSc to print graphics screens	[D:Path]GRAPHICS [Printer Type ¦][ProfileFileSpec][/R][/B][/LCD][PB:Id]	192
JOIN	Merges two disks into one	[D:Path] JOIN [D:Path] JOIN DestD Source D:Path [D:Path] JOIN /D	447

*See Part 7, "DOS Command Reference," for a complete description of commands and their parameters.

This summary of DOS commands, plus summaries of EDLIN commands, configuration file commands, and batch-file subcommands, continues at the back of this book.

MASTERING DOS

MASTERING DOS®

Second Edition

JUDD ROBBINS

San Francisco • Paris • Düsseldorf • Soest

Cover design by Thomas Ingalls + Associates
Cover photograph by Casey Cartwright
Series design by Julie Bilski
Illustrations by Van Genderen Studio
Command-prompt screens in this book were produced with XenoFont.

To the Sennin Foundation of El Cerrito, California, and the Way of the Universe.

ACKNOWLEDGMENTS

Thanks to all the people at SYBEX who made this book much better than I ever could have alone: Fran Grimble, editor; Kay Luthin, copyeditor; Robert Campbell, technical reviewer; Paul Erickson, word processor; Charles Cowens, typesetter; Aidan Wylde, proofreader; Paula Alston, indexer; Julie Bilski, graphic artist, Rick van Genderen, illustrator; and Michelle Hoffman, screen shot producer.

Thanks also to the people who worked on this new edition of *Mastering DOS:* Vince Leone, editor; Nancy O'Donnell, copyeditor; Bob Myren and Jocelyn Reynolds, word processors; Olivia Shinomoto, typesetter; Sylvia Townsend, proofreader; Ted Laux, indexer; Eleanor Ramos, graphic artist; and Sonja Schenk, screen shot producer. Robert Campbell and Rick van Genderen repeated their roles from the original edition.

CONTENTS AT A GLANCE

TABLE OF CONTENTS

P A R T   3   COMPLETING THE FUNDAMENTALS

P A R T 6   *GOING BEYOND*

C H A P T E R 19   *WINDOWS AND DOS*   *505*

P A R T 7 **DOS COMMAND REFERENCE** ━━━━━

INTRODUCTION

You and I probably select our software based on what each package offers, and whether we need it for our business. DOS is usually a required part of your system. Just as surely as you need a printer to produce hard-copy reports and a screen to display intermediate results, you need a disk operating system (DOS) to provide the key management capabilities for your hardware. This allows each software package to deal only with its own application needs.

You may have bought DOS because you were told you had to, or simply to run your application software (Lotus 1-2-3, dBASE IV, WordPerfect, and so on). The great wealth of software being advertised, sold, and used in the business world today requires that MS-DOS, PC-DOS, or another DOS manage the overall hardware and operating environment. You will find that using DOS can be remarkably easy.

NECESSARY HARDWARE AND SOFTWARE FOR THIS BOOK

This book assumes that you have an MS-DOS or PC-DOS microcomputer. Although most of the fundamental capabilities are available in earlier versions of DOS, many of the more advanced features seen later in this book are only available to you in the most recent versions. This book uses DOS 4, although you will be told when a particular feature is unavailable in earlier versions. In fact, this book will be useful if you are using any version of DOS from 2.X upward; Versions 2.X introduced the key feature of hierarchical directories.

HOW TO USE THIS BOOK

You may have a computer with diskette drives only, or you may have a hard-disk machine. This book is appropriate for you in either case. Many examples are provided for either situation, and commands are explained in terms of what they can do on *any* disk drive. While you read through the book, you should stop as often as possible to try the commands and features on your computer. Seeing them work immediately will give you the reinforcement necessary for quickly sharpening your skills.

HOW THIS BOOK IS ORGANIZED

You don't need any background at all to get the most out of this book. As in all things, however, experience will help you to learn some things more easily and to skip other things that you already know. *Mastering DOS* is structured so that you can jump to the section or chapter that's right for you.

The first 17 chapters of *Mastering DOS* emphasize the power available to you within DOS itself, and Chapter 18 discusses various programs that fill the gaps in DOS's operations or provide capabilities that DOS lacks. The following three chapters go beyond DOS to introduce you to the multitasking capabilities of Microsoft Windows, then to the various possibilities for exceeding the 640K DOS memory limit, and lastly to the methods for running your DOS programs in an OS/2 system.

The chapters are grouped into seven parts. Part 1, "Getting Started," presents the strong foundation necessary for any user. Chapter 1 presents the fundamental pieces of hardware and software for working with a disk-operating system. Chapter 2 focuses on your first steps with the DOS diskettes, in preparation for running programs. Chapter 3 actually gets you up and running with the graphics screens of DOS 4; if you have an earlier version of DOS, you will learn how to get up and running at the DOS command prompt. Beginners must read and become comfortable with the information presented in Part 1. Those with some experience are urged to read this part to review fundamentals and to learn basic skills that might have been overlooked before.

Part 2, "Understanding the File System," is a self-contained tutorial on how DOS stores and uses information in files on disks. Chapter 4 concentrates on the DOS 4 interface and also explains the concepts of drives, directories, and files, which are generic to all DOS versions. You then learn in Chapter 5 how a directory structure is created and maintained, as well as the DOS commands for creating, naming, modifying, and manipulating your files. Chapter 6 examines how the elements of a directory system pertain to application programs. If you intend to set up your hard disk for running a word processor, a database-management system, a spreadsheet program, or almost any other application package, you should read this chapter carefully.

Part 3, "Completing the Fundamentals," rounds out your required instruction in DOS. Chapter 7 shows you how to create and modify text files using the DOS line editor, EDLIN. You will need this skill throughout the rest of the book to properly generate and update certain system files, as well as to write your own simple programs for DOS batch files. In Chapter 8, you will examine the ways you can produce printed output with your system. Lastly, in Chapter 9, you will discover how to transmit your edited files and your printed output between computers and other hardware devices. The flow of data between the central processor and peripheral devices is critical to any successful computer system. Chapter 9 provides you with the terminology and technology for data transmission, and you will also learn how to use DOS commands to control the flow of information.

Part 4, "Refining Your System," picks up the pace quite a bit. It begins the second half of the book, which is designed for those of you who want to learn more than the basics. An important, but often neglected, capability of DOS is its ability to back up and restore all or portions of your hard disk; this is discussed in Chapter 10. In Chapter 11, you will also learn how to customize your system by configuring DOS and using startup options. By customizing your DOS, you can significantly improve its performance and make it easier to use.

Unique features for using your computer internationally are presented in Chapter 12. These tools enable you to initialize your keyboard layout, printer, and screen for a foreign flair. Chapter 13 examines advanced features—pipes and filters—that give you precise control over the flow of information throughout your entire system.

Part 5, "Life in the Fast Lane," deals primarily with advanced commands and features. It explores in depth the sophisticated arena of batch files, but also presents information about third party software utilities. The information in this part is essential for an advanced user. You will learn of the possibilities and limitations of batch files in Chapter 14, and in Chapter 15 you will extend this knowledge with subcommands and parameters. You'll learn how to combine all of the elements of batch files in creative and powerful ways.

Many actual batch files and techniques are presented in Chapter 16. You can type in any of these batch files and run them immediately on your system, or you can send for a companion diskette that contains all of the batch files listed in this book. An order form for the diskette is included at the end of the book.

Chapter 17 explains the commands available to an advanced DOS user. These powerful commands can connect multiple disk drives into directory superstructures, simulate nonexistent drives with subdirectories, and reroute disk requests from one drive to another. You'll also see uncommon commands that influence the command processor itself and modify the DOS environment. In addition, you'll study a group of specialized commands that provide you with advanced techniques for manipulating your files.

The last chapter in Part 5, Chapter 18, explores the best of the add-on utility software, which can give your DOS a boost. I suggest that you seriously consider buying some of these products. Some will be useful on a daily basis; others will be critical only once in a while. When that time comes, however, you won't want to be without the right software.

Part 6, "Going Beyond," takes you further than the capabilities of DOS alone. Chapter 19 introduces you to the multitasking capabilities of Microsoft Windows, a DOS add-on program that enables several programs to run simultaneously. Chapter 20 explores the numerous ways in which programs and application environments have successfully surmounted the DOS memory limit of 640K. Finally, Chapter 21 shows you how to make a painless transition to Microsoft's powerful new operating system, OS/2. You will learn the simple procedures for running your DOS programs in the new OS/2 environment.

Part 7, "DOS Command Reference," has been included for easy access to all of DOS's commands. The first six parts of *Mastering DOS* present the most important DOS commands, leaving aside those that would impede your learning process. Chapter 22 fills in the gaps by providing you with an alphabetized reference to all commands, parameters, and possible switches. I encourage you to refer to this chapter again and again as you use DOS. A quick overview of both the usage and format of each command may be all you'll need to speed you on your way with DOS applications.

Three appendices are also included to make your use of DOS a little easier. Appendix A is a complete glossary of relevant computer terms. Appendix B is an extended table of ASCII codes, with an explanation of character sets and numbering systems. Appendix C will come in handy when you need to configure or reconfigure fixed disks.

DOS is a stable product, and it is expected to be a principal operating system for years to come. This book will be a useful companion as you learn to make effective use of your software.

ICONS USED IN THIS BOOK

Three visual icons are used in this book. The Note icon

indicates a note that augments the material in the text. The Tip icon

represents a practical hint or special technique. When you see the Warning icon

pay particular attention—it alerts you to a possible problem or offers a way to avoid a problem.

PART 1

GETTING STARTED

In Part 1, you will get a sense of what DOS is and what it can do. If you're just beginning to use DOS, you should read and become comfortable with the information presented here. Even if you have some experience, you should read Part 1 to refresh your memory and perhaps learn some basics you missed along the way.

Chapter 1 explains the fundamental pieces of hardware you will use with DOS: the central processing unit, the disk drives, hard disks and floppy diskettes, and other devices (such as printers). It introduces DOS commands and also explains how DOS stores data on disks.

In Chapter 2, you will take your first steps with DOS. You'll install, load, and start up DOS, and you'll learn how to give commands, set the system date and time, and prepare your disks for use. You'll also learn how to back up diskettes, starting with your DOS master diskettes.

Finally, Chapter 3 will get you up and running with your version of DOS. DOS 4.0 users will see and use the first graphic screen, Start Programs, for running programs and performing DOS utility operations. Users of earlier versions of DOS will also start performing similar tasks but will do so through the DOS command prompt.

THE FUNDAMENTALS
OF DOS

CHAPTER 1

EVERY COMPUTER THAT USES DISKS (HARD OR floppy) must have a master program that coordinates the flow of information from computer to disk and from disk to computer. This is called the *disk operating system,* or *DOS.* In this book, you'll learn about the operating system used on the IBM PC and compatible microcomputers. This operating system is manufactured by Microsoft Corporation and licensed to IBM and other microcomputer manufacturers. The name of this system, when purchased from Microsoft, is *MS-DOS*—that is, *Microsoft Disk Operating System.* When it is purchased from IBM, it is called *PC-DOS.*

What does all this mean? Simply that the terms *DOS, MS-DOS,* and *PC-DOS* really refer to the same thing, and in fact are often used interchangeably. In this book, the term *DOS* refers to the disk operating system used on IBM microcomputers and the wide range of IBM-compatible microcomputers.

This chapter will teach you how DOS is used and what useful functions it can perform. You will also learn about the fundamental parts of the computer sitting on your desk and about a number of computer devices (peripherals) that you might not own yet but might be interested in acquiring. You'll learn the differences between input and output devices, as well as their purpose.

Most importantly, you'll acquire an understanding of what disks and diskettes are, how they're set up, and how DOS provides you with commands to manage them. You'll see how data is organized on them, so you can make better decisions later about which disks are appropriate for your use. You'll learn a host of good techniques for caring for your disks, so you can significantly reduce the odds of losing critical data through disk failure.

Since the manufacturer of each new computer may make minor adjustments to DOS before releasing it for that machine, you may occasionally notice slight differences between your DOS's messages and those in this book. However, since DOS is virtually the same from machine to machine, you will probably never see any variation other than in the startup message.

WHAT DOS DOES

The disk operating system is assigned the task of integrating the various devices that make up a computer system. There are three major tasks the operating system must carry out. It must

- Coordinate the input and output devices, such as monitors, printers, disk drives, and modems;

- Enable the user to load and execute programs; and

- Maintain an orderly system of files on the disk.

Computer memory has one basic drawback. The area of memory in which your programs and data are stored, called *random-access memory* (*RAM*), cannot store information after the electricity has been turned off, even for a fraction of a second. To store information in the computer, you must have some means of recording it. The most common devices for this task are *disk drives,* which are devices that can read or write to magnetic disks.

Magnetic disks divide generally into two categories: *hard disks* and *floppy disks,* or *diskettes.* On a hard disk the magnetic storage medium is rigid, or hard. Hard disks are called *fixed* or *nonremovable* disks if they are built into the drive itself; they are called *removable cartridges* if they can be inserted into and removed from the disk drive. Information is stored on a disk as a collection of *characters* (see below). Hard disks usually hold at least 10 million characters, and larger models that hold 70 million characters are now available on the newest IBM Personal System/2 line of microcomputers. Each 10 million characters is roughly equivalent to 5000 pages of typed text.

Diskettes usually store less information. The most flexible and common type, the 5¼'' diskette, can store several hundred thousand characters of information, depending on the density of the magnetic material on the disk's surface. A high-capacity 5¼'' diskette can actually store 1.2 million characters. A less common but increasingly popular type, the 3½'' diskette, is often called a *microfloppy* diskette. It owes its growing popularity to higher storage densities, holding as many as 1.44 million characters. This is the largest storage capacity of any diskette; in addition, the microfloppy's small size makes it easier to store and transport.

By now you understand that different types of disks store different amounts of information. However, all disks share information in the same way—as a collection of *characters*. Any keyboard character can be stored and represented by DOS as a series of eight *bits* (of binary 0's and 1's). The eight bits can be arranged in 256 different ways, thereby representing 256 different characters. Some of these characters are the ones you can type in (A–Z, 0–9, and so on), and others are simply interpreted by DOS as *control* characters. This classification includes all special character codes that control special operations, like sounding a bell on a video monitor or performing a carriage return on a printer. See Appendix B for more details on character sets and numbering methods.

From the perspective of DOS, the term *character* is interchangeable with the term *byte*.

A series of eight bits is known as a *byte*. Approximately one thousand (actually 1024) bytes are together called a *kilobyte*, which is abbreviated as *K*. Approximately one million (actually 1,048,576) bytes are together called a *megabyte*, which is abbreviated as *Mb*.

Each complete collection of related characters is called a *file*. A disk can have many files that contain either instructions for the computer (*program files*) or data stored by the user (*data files*). A disk can contain both program files and data files. Each file must be given a unique name so that the computer can later refer to the file and load it from the disk into the computer's memory again.

DOS is responsible for managing this flow of information. As you will learn, DOS contains a host of commands and programs that enable it to store information on any disks connected to your computer. It also has full responsibility for arranging your files on these disks in ways that will contribute to easy and efficient retrieval when you need them.

WHAT YOU NEED TO KNOW ABOUT DOS

What does the average user need to know about DOS? This is a hotly debated question. Some people contend that as little time as possible should be spent on DOS. However, since DOS defines the basic structure of the computer system, you must be able to command DOS effectively to exercise full control over the computer. Knowing DOS is especially useful when something goes wrong. In this book, you will learn much about DOS that will help you to deal with both the expected and the unexpected.

THE FUNDAMENTAL HARDWARE

DOS is designed to manage the details of a variety of hardware connections and combinations. You should understand a bit about the hardware before you ever open up the DOS box and use the diskettes.

A microcomputer system is composed of a *central system unit* and a variety of *peripheral devices* (see Figure 1.1). The central system unit usually contains the primary processing chip (the *CPU,* or *central processing unit*), the main system memory (RAM), and usually one or more disk drives. The CPU is the brain of the computer. It performs the various arithmetic operations, as well as controlling the flow of data to and from the additional peripheral devices. The main memory of the computer is the place in which instructions and data are stored during program execution. Keep in mind that the amount of available and required RAM always increases as the sophistication of the programs that are run on your computer increases.

The disk drives in the minimum *configuration* (the arrangement of system components) are usually diskette drives, although a hard-disk drive is included more and more often as hardware prices continue to drop. As Figure 1.1 shows, systems that use diskettes refer to the drives as A: and B:. Systems that use one diskette drive and one hard-disk drive refer to them as A: and C:. This book will refer to these drives simply as A, B, and C.

Ordinarily, DOS limits the amount of RAM available to a 640K maximum. There are two ways around this, called extended and expanded memory. For more information, see Chapter 11.

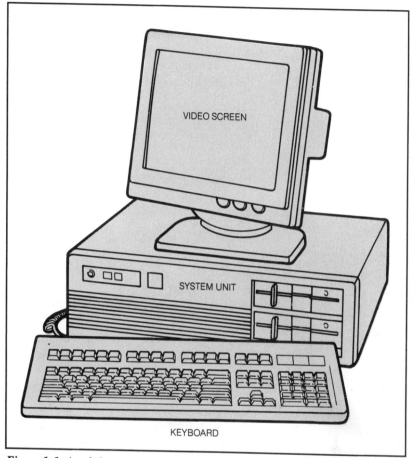

Figure 1.1: A minimum microcomputer system

The peripheral devices in the minimum configuration are the video monitor and the keyboard. The keyboard usually has one of four layouts, depending upon whether it is designed to be compatible with an IBM PC/XT, the IBM PC/AT, the IBM Personal System/2, or the IBM Convertible. There are several possible choices for a video monitor—monochrome, color graphics, or enhanced graphics are the most common. Higher-resolution monitors, although more expensive, are becoming more common in businesses using desktop-publishing and computer-aided design (CAD) software.

There is virtually no limit to the range of additional devices that can be connected to a microcomputer. Most business microcomputer systems contain more than the minimum, as Figure 1.2 shows. The various *connector ports* in the back of the computer, such as the *parallel* and *serial* ports, allow the straightforward (although not necessarily easy) connection of printers, plotters, digitizers, extra disk drives, and so on. The task of starting DOS so that it manages this hardware is consistent, no matter what hardware configuration you have.

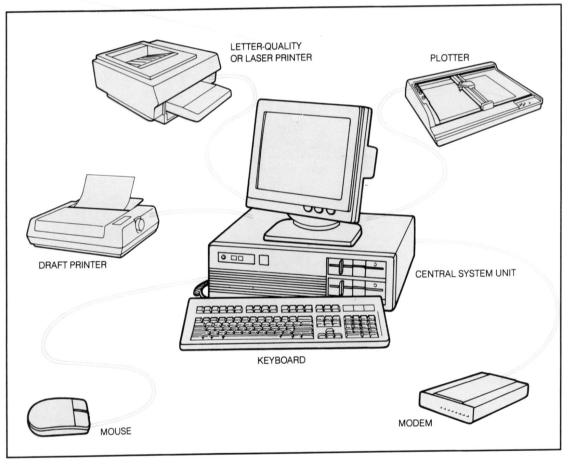

Figure 1.2: A more standard microcomputer system

INPUT AND OUTPUT DEVICES

Disk drives can be both input and output devices. Most DOS commands deal with the complex process of input from and output to the disk drives.

As you have seen, the computer you are working on is really not one machine but a group of related devices. Devices can be attached to the computer internally (inside the system unit) or externally (in separate boxes attached by cables). Some of these devices deal with the information that is input into the computer system, while other devices manage the output of information from the computer system. Some devices do both (see Table 1.1).

DEVICE	FUNCTION
Keyboard	Input only
Screen	Output only
Printer	Output only
Disks	Input and output

Table 1.1: Typical purposes of DOS devices

HOW DISKS ARE SET UP

When you buy a box of diskettes, the diskettes in that box are *not* ready to be used with your computer. In order to use them, you must prepare the diskettes with some of the special programs provided with your disk operating system. Even hard disks must be prepared. Most people never get a chance to format and set up their hard-disk drives because the dealers usually do this for them. This is not altogether an advantage, since you never learn the basics of disk setup.

This section explains how and why disk-preparation programs are used. The ideas and techniques presented here are some of the first actions you take with a new computer system. The section not only shows you what to do, it also helps you understand what is really going on when you issue these commands.

THE DISK COMMANDS

The concept of DOS is confusing for two reasons:

1. A large part of DOS is invisible to the user. DOS has two parts, one of which (the *hidden files* part) is stored on the disk but does not appear on the disk directory. The other part is a file called COMMAND.COM, which is visible on every diskette used to start up (or *boot*) the system. In DOS 4.0, COMMAND.COM occupies 37,637 bytes, while the two hidden system files together occupy another 68,794 bytes. Together these files constitute over 100K; you will pay this price in disk space on every system (boot) disk you create.

2. The actions performed by DOS are divided into two types. *Memory-resident,* or *internal, commands* are actions that DOS can always perform, no matter what disk happens to be in the computer. These commands are always in memory, and so they execute immediately when you want. *Disk-resident,* or *external, commands* are really small programs for special purposes. If you want to perform any of these actions, you must have the correct disk in the computer, or you must tell DOS where these programs are located on your disks. Since external commands are only brought into memory from a disk when you request them, it is your responsibility to ensure that they are available when needed.

On floppy-diskette systems, the DOS command files must be accessible through one of the drives. Otherwise, DOS will display an error message indicating that it can't find the requested command.

Table 1.2 shows the internal and external DOS commands. You will learn more about these commands throughout this book. For now, you will be concerned only with the fundamental disk structure that stores these commands for you and makes them available whenever you need them.

DISK ORGANIZATION

When a floppy diskette is taken out of the box, it is totally blank. So, too, is a hard disk. The primary difference between diskettes and hard disks lies only in the arrangement of the magnetic material. This material can be arranged on one or both sides of a diskette, depending on whether the diskette is single-sided or double-sided. Diskettes can also

INTERNAL COMMANDS		
BREAK	DEL	RMDIR
CHCP	DIR	SET
CHDIR	ERASE	TIME
CLS	MKDIR	TYPE
COPY	PATH	VER
CTTY	PROMPT	VERIFY
DATE	RENAME	VOL

EXTERNAL COMMANDS		
APPEND	FIND	RECOVER
ASSIGN	FORMAT	REPLACE
ATTRIB	GRAFTABL	RESTORE
BACKUP	GRAPHICS	SELECT
CHKDSK	JOIN	SHARE
COMP	KEYB	SORT
DISKCOMP	LABEL	SUBST
DISKCOPY	MEM	SYS
DOSSHELL	MODE	TREE
EXE2BIN	MORE	XCOPY
FASTOPEN	NLSFUNC	
FDISK	PRINT	

Table 1.2: Classification of DOS commands

have differing densities. The more densely the magnetic material is written onto a diskette, the more information it can hold. Hard disks, on the other hand, can have several layers of magnetic material, each with two sides, which means they can store even more information.

In order for the computer system to use any disk as a medium for storing information, the entire disk must be divided into sections organized so that every physical location on the disk has a unique address. This is the same concept as assigning ZIP code numbers to various towns and cities. When DOS assigns addresses, it then has an orderly way in which to store and then find various pieces of information.

The system of magnetic storage used by DOS is one of concentric rings (see Figure 1.3). Each ring is called a *track*. For example, there are 40 tracks (numbered 0 to 39) on each double-sided, double-density diskette, while there are twice as many tracks (numbered 0 to 79) on a high-capacity diskette. Each track is divided into smaller parts called *sectors*. Tracks and sectors are created when a disk is formatted. It is DOS's job to assign the necessary addresses for each track and sector.

The "hub hole" in Figure 1.3 is merely the center hole in a disk or diskette, which fits onto the spindle of a disk drive. Like the hole in a record and the spindle on a turntable, this hole and spindle ensure that the disk spins in a true circular path. Data can then be read from and written to consistent places on the tracks of the disk.

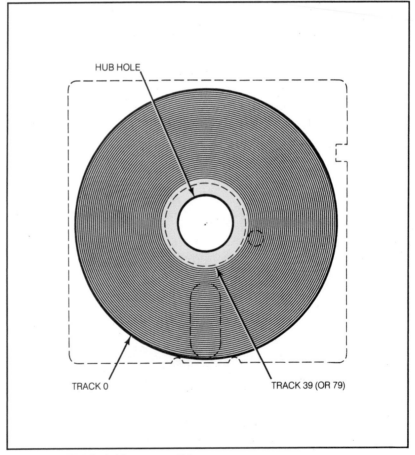

HUB HOLE

TRACK 0

TRACK 39 (OR 79)

Figure 1.3: Tracks laid out on a disk

You needn't be concerned about this addressing mechanism, since it is really only for DOS's benefit. DOS needs to know the actual disk location of your files; you only have to know their names. That's what makes the operating system such a valuable ally in running application software.

The exact number of sectors depends on what type of diskette is being formatted (see Table 1.3). Standard double-sided, double-density diskettes have 9 sectors per track, while the high-capacity diskettes available for the IBM PC-AT and compatibles have 15 sectors per track. Each sector can hold 512 bytes. The newest 3½'' diskettes containing 1.44Mb have 80 tracks per side, each track holding 18 standard 512-byte sectors.

Some of the formatted disk space is not available to you for storing data—about 6K on a 5¼'' diskette to about 18K on a 3½'' diskette. When a disk is formatted, some of the sectors are set aside for keeping track of the information stored on that disk. Every formatted disk has these areas. Together, they serve as a catalog of the contents of that disk. These areas are called the *file allocation table* (*FAT*), the *boot record,* and the *directory table.* The details of their use are beyond the scope of this book, but their impact on disk-space usage should be considered.

Standard double-density diskettes can have a maximum of 112 uniquely named files, while high-capacity diskettes can store 224 files. Hard disks can store significantly more individual files, depending on their size (20Mb, 40Mb, and so on).

Disk Structure	5¼'' Double Density	5¼'' High Density	3½'' Double Density	3½'' High Density
Number of tracks	40	80	80	80
Sectors per track	9	15	9	18
Characters per sector	512	512	512	512
Total number of sectors	720	2400	1440	2880
Total number of characters	360 K	1.2 M	720 K	1.44 M

Table 1.3: Diskette organization

TAKING CARE OF YOUR DISKETTES

If you have never dealt with diskettes before, they may look and feel flimsy. They are not as flimsy as they appear, but they are also not as durable as many users believe. In many offices, computer users seem to use their diskettes as paperweights on their desks. Sometimes people don't even keep the diskettes in the jackets they originally came in. These are usually the ones who complain most vocally about their diskettes failing several times a year.

A well-maintained diskette can easily last for years. Mishandling diskettes can have serious consequences. An accident can destroy the contents of a diskette in only seconds.

Here are some suggestions for diskette handling. Keep in mind that experience and knowledge lie behind every one of them:

- Keep your diskettes in their jackets when not in use. You never know when they may fall on the floor or when something might fall or spill on them. It's simple risk reduction.

- Don't leave your diskettes in the disk drives, especially if the computer is going to be moved. Remember, others who clean around your computer may move it to clean the table tops.

- Don't leave your diskettes in your car, where the temperature often gets high enough to warp them, making them unreadable for your computer. Also keep them away from any sources of magnetic fields, such as motors, telephone bells, and magnetic card keys.

- Don't touch the magnetic surface of the diskettes—hold them by their jackets.

- Make backup copies of all original diskettes, and keep current copies of all diskettes with important, newly created program or data files.

- Keep your backup diskette copies in a different location from the original diskette (for example, at home if your computer is at the office; at work if your computer is at home).

- Label all your diskettes, both electronically with a DOS command and with a printed, gummed label. Write on the label before you attach it to the diskette, or use a soft felt-tipped pen to write carefully on an existing label.

- Don't squeeze the last bit of space out of your diskettes. Always leave them a little empty. In the first place, you may later want to add some new files to that very diskette. You may also want to expand the size of some of the files on the diskette.

SUMMARY

This chapter introduced you to DOS—what it is, what it does, and how it is used. The chapter included the following topics:

- You learned about the fundamental pieces of hardware that make up a typical microcomputer system. This hardware constitutes the environment within which the disk operating system and all of your selected application software perform their tasks. The components are

  The central processing unit, or CPU, which performs analytic or computational tasks.

  The disk drives, which work with disks to store your data and program files.

  Disks and diskettes. There are two types of hard disks, fixed and removable, each storing from 10 to 70 megabytes of data. There are two classes of floppy diskettes, 5¼'' (which can store from 180K to 1.2Mb of data) and 3½'' microfloppy diskettes (which can store from 720K to 1.44Mb of data).

  The system console, consisting of a video monitor for output displays and a keyboard for the input of data and commands.

  Other devices such as modems, mice, digitizers, plotters, and a wide range of printers.

- You learned that the primary means of communicating with your computer is with input and output devices. The principal input device is your keyboard, and the principal output device is the video screen. Most printed copy (hard copy) is generated on a printing device, such as a dot-matrix, letter-quality, or laser printer.

- You learned that DOS has two types of commands, resident and transient. Resident commands reside in a portion of memory reserved by DOS and are always available. Transient commands reside in files on your system disk and must be read into memory before being executed.

- You learned that information is stored on a disk in circular patterns called tracks, which are broken up into easily addressable, 512-byte portions called sectors.

- You learned that DOS arranges and maintains the physical and logical arrangement of information stored on the disks. Your programs and data are stored on the disk in collections of bytes called files.

- You learned that you must treat your diskettes with care.

Now that you've learned the fundamentals of DOS, Chapter 2 will help you begin to actually use your computer. Get ready to take those important first steps with DOS disks and DOS commands.

YOUR FIRST STEPS
WITH DOS

CHAPTER 2

YOUR FIRST STEPS WITH DOS HAVE LITTLE TO DO with the software itself. Instead, they involve acquiring the right pieces of hardware, turning the computer on, and preparing the disks for use. In this chapter you will concentrate on installing DOS itself on your computer, preparing your disks properly, and taking the first few critical steps toward becoming a proficient user of this powerful operating system.

You will learn in this chapter how to get your DOS going and, consequently, how to get going with any application program you will be running. You'll learn how to set the time and date correctly if your system doesn't have a built-in clock and calendar. When daylight saving time comes around, you'll know how to make the necessary adjustments to your system.

In this chapter you'll also learn how to issue DOS commands, either through the graphic interface of DOS 4 or through the command prompt of earlier versions. You'll learn how to correct any errors you make quickly and efficiently. Since you may change your mind about a command you've given to DOS, you'll also learn how to tell DOS about your changes.

In addition, you'll learn to prepare disks for storing your valuable data and file information, as well as for booting up your system. Backing up your disks and exploring the status of a disk are necessary skills you'll also acquire here. In short, this chapter starts to "teach you the ropes" of DOS.

INSTALLING DOS 4 ON YOUR COMPUTER SYSTEM

Preparing DOS properly requires a different sequence of steps for diskette and hard-disk installation. The DOS 4 installation process is automatic in all cases, assuming that you turn on your computer with the DOS 4 INSTALL diskette in your A drive. If you have an earlier version of DOS, refer to your individual disk and DOS manuals for the proper installation procedure on your computer. Appendix C offers instructions on the specific task of hard-disk partitioning. This is a required preparatory step for installing any version of DOS on a hard disk, but most dealers actually perform this step for you when they prepare and check out your hardware.

This section will guide you through a typical installation sequence for DOS. The sample sequence used assumes that you are installing DOS 4 on a hard disk. However, minor differences in installation between 5¼'' and 3½'' diskettes and between the different storage sizes on these media will not be emphasized. Instead, you'll concentrate on the flow of questions and answers that the DOS 4 installation sequence will typically present, regardless of individual disk differences.

When you boot up your system, using the DOS 4 INSTALL diskette, the actual program that controls the installation procedure is called SELECT. It displays information and requests entries from you. Its first display is shown in Figure 2.1.

This entire selection process can be used later on your own to install DOS 4 on a different hard disk, or another set of diskettes, by simply rerunning the SELECT program. Chapter 6 explains how to run this and any other application program under DOS 4.

Pressing Return to continue the process brings up the screen shown in Figure 2.2, which informs you of the requirements for different kinds of diskettes.

If you do not have the appropriate number of diskettes ready, you should press the Escape key now to terminate the installation process. Otherwise, you can press Return to continue installing DOS 4. Notice that your primary key options are displayed at the bottom of the screen. At this point, they are the Return (Enter) key and the

Figure 2.1: Initial SELECT screen

Figure 2.2: Diskette requirements of DOS 4

Escape (Esc = Cancel) key. Later on, other appropriate key alternatives will be displayed.

Other keys on your keyboard play special roles during installation. Although you will recognize many of these keys if you have used other microcomputer software, they are not all intuitively obvious. The next screen displayed by SELECT is in fact a list of all the keys with special purposes (see Figure 2.3).

Most of these keys do standard jobs. For example, you press Return to accept the current entry and proceed to the next installation step. The key assignment that calls for special attention is the Tab key. As you'll see in some screens, SELECT displays more than one entry field. Pressing Tab is necessary to switch from one field to another so that you can make or adjust an entry. A common mistake would be to type in an entry and then press Return, expecting to move to the next field on the screen. However, this would actually move to the next SELECT screen, leaving all other entry fields on the previous screen incomplete. You'll see how this works when you enter the date and time.

Press Tab to move from one entry field to another on the same screen. Press Return when all fields on one screen have been completely specified.

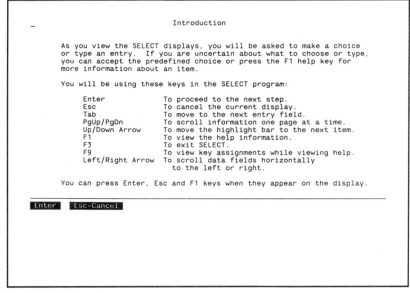

Figure 2.3: Special key assignments during SELECT

The next screen appearing in this installation process is shown in Figure 2.4. In this screen you can allocate some of the memory in your system. The three options here represent a balancing act between various internal DOS capabilities, which require the assignment of memory space, and the memory that remains after DOS 4 consumes what it needs. Table 2.1 lists all the various parameter values and initialization conditions affected by your choice on this screen.

As you can see, more DOS 4 features are built into your installed system if you take choice 2 or 3, a balanced or maximal DOS-function system. For example, GRAPHICS Print Screen support (see Chapter 8) and extended display support (see Chapter 11) are included only with choice 2 or 3. However, the DOS SHELL default is always included. Space for the File Control Blocks (see Chapter 22) is only taken in a maximal DOS configuration, while memory space for the BUFFERS (see Chapter 11) is increased uniquely for choices 2 and 3.

Some settings are set by SELECT depending on your responses to specific questions. For instance, if you select a country and keyboard other than the United States, then memory is reserved for *code-page switching* (see Chapter 12). Other options are automatically set based on your hardware configuration. For instance, if you are installing

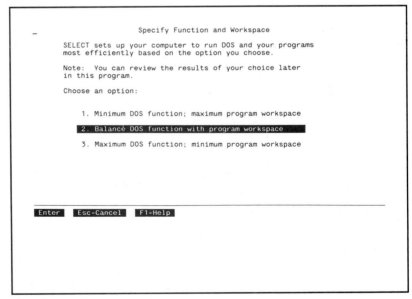

Figure 2.4: Assigning memory in DOS 4

DOS FUNCTION	MINIMAL DOS; MAXIMAL WORKSPACE	BALANCED DOS AND WORKSPACE	MAXIMAL DOS; MINIMAL WORKSPACE
AUTOEXEC.BAT DEFAULTS			
Code-Page Switching	No	No	No
GRAFTABL display support	No	No	No
GRAPHICS PrtSc support	No	Yes	Yes
DOS SHELL	Yes	Yes	Yes
CONFIG.SYS DEFAULTS			
Extended display support (ANSI.SYS)	No	Yes	Yes
Virtual disk support (VDISK.SYS)	No	No	No
BREAK	On	On	On
BUFFERS	–	20	25,8
FCBS	–	–	20,8
FILES	8	8	8
LASTDRIVE	E	E	E
STACKS	–	–	–
VERIFY	Off	Off	Off
– indicates that no explicit value is set. DOS will decide the value at boot time.			

Table 2.1: Default values for DOS 4 function and workspace balancing

DOS 4 on a system with a color graphics adapter (CGA), then GRAFTABL display support (see Chapter 12) is installed for you.

After deciding on the balance between the memory for DOS and the workspace, you are asked by SELECT to choose a country and keyboard combination. The default country is the United States; this also means that code-page support for international operations is not installed. The next screen displays this default status and presents an opportunity to select a different country or keyboard:

Choose an option:

1. Accept predefined country and keyboard

2. Specify a different country and keyboard

If you take choice 2, then you successively receive the screens shown in Figures 2.5 and 2.6. Use your cursor keys to highlight the desired country on the first screen, then press Return. Then use the cursor keys to highlight the particular keyboard layout you intend to use and press Return.

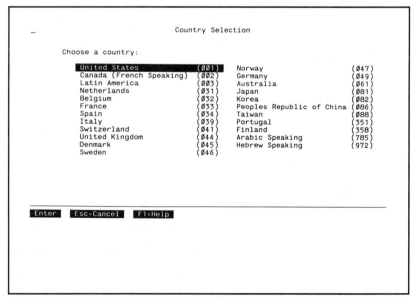

Figure 2.5: Selecting a country code for DOS 4

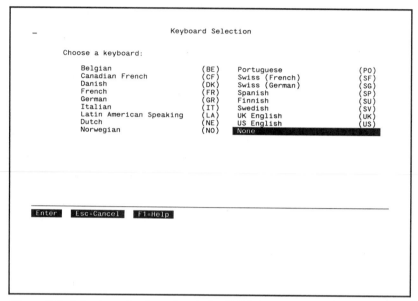

```
                    Keyboard Selection
 _

     Choose a keyboard:

          Belgian                    (BE)   Portuguese          (PO)
          Canadian French            (CF)   Swiss (French)      (SF)
          Danish                     (DK)   Swiss (German)      (SG)
          French                     (FR)   Spanish             (SP)
          German                     (GR)   Finnish             (SU)
          Italian                    (IT)   Swedish             (SV)
          Latin American Speaking    (LA)   UK English          (UK)
          Dutch                      (NE)   US English          (US)
          Norwegian                  (NO)   None

     _____
     Enter     Esc=Cancel    F1=Help
```

Figure 2.6: Selecting a keyboard code for DOS 4

At this point, SELECT has most of the information needed to install DOS 4. It now must be told whether to install the resulting system on a hard disk or on a set of floppies. SELECT checks your available hardware and displays the possible drives to install DOS on. You simply choose which drive will receive the complete set of DOS 4 files.

If you are installing DOS 4 on a hard disk, you receive another screen prompt at this point. The DOS utilities can be installed in a directory of the hard disk. The default directory displayed is the standard C:\DOS directory. Unless you have a good reason for doing otherwise and already know what you are doing, you should simply press Return to accept this default value.

This screen, seen in Figure 2.7, is the first example of an entry screen with multiple fields. The top field on the screen allows you to enter a revised directory name, and the bottom field allows you to select an action.

Select choice 1 to update all system files on your hard disk and copy all DOS 4 files to the specified directory. Select choice 2 to copy the nonsystem files to your alternate directory. After pressing Tab to move to the Options field, highlight the choice you want and press Return to continue the installation process.

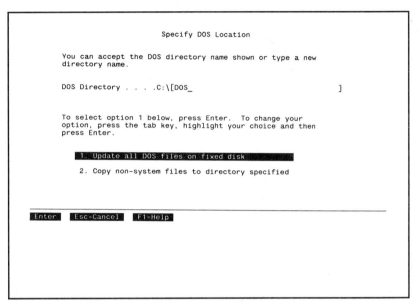

Figure 2.7: Installing DOS in a hard-disk directory

Next comes the specification of the number and type of printers in your DOS 4 setup. First, you are asked for the number of printers:

How many printers do you have? . . . . **[0] (0–7)**

You can specify a configuration consisting of no printers or as many as seven printers. To change the number 0, type over it, then press Return. If you indicate any printers at all, SELECT will then display a screen similar to Figure 2.8.

A variety of special-purpose printers are displayed. Highlight your printer and press Return. If your printer is not listed here, highlight the generic type of printer you have. If you indicated more than one printer, this screen and all other printer query screens will be repeated for each printer.

Once again, SELECT checks your hardware configuration. If you chose a parallel printer, SELECT displays a list of your hardware's parallel ports, showing at least LPT1. Highlight the port to which your printer is connected, then press Return to select it. If you chose a serial printer, you are shown a similar list of your hardware's serial ports. Highlight and select the port to which the printer is connected.

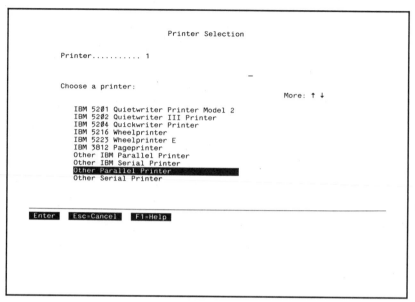

Figure 2.8: Selecting a DOS 4 printer

For serial printers, you are also asked if you wish to refer to the serial printer as a parallel printer. If so, you can select any of DOS 4's three possible parallel port labels: LPT1, LPT2, or LPT3.

You're basically done at this point. SELECT now asks if you are satisfied with all of your answers and would like to complete the automated installation process. SELECT also offers you the opportunity to revise your previous choices with the following prompt:

Choose an option:

1. Accept configuration and continue with installation

2. Review, change, or add installation choices

If you choose number 2, you can correct earlier entries and elaborate on some of the DOS-function variables. For example, you could explicitly request virtual disk support (VDISK.SYS) and enter any desired parameters. You can also modify any of the default values for BUFFERS, FCBS, etc.

If you choose number 1, DOS displays the screen shown in Figure 2.9, which facilitates your initial setup of a built-in calendar and

If your system uses a mouse other than the IBM PS/2 mouse, you must change installation choices in order to install the correct mouse driver.

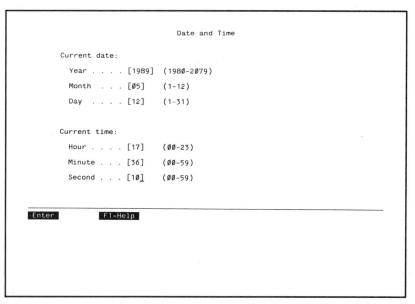

Figure 2.9: Initializing the current date and time of day

clock. Remember to press Tab between each field entry; only press
Return after you have entered all startup values correctly.

Only one possible step remains before SELECT copies all
required files to the disk drive that you specified for the installed copy
of DOS. If this target disk is not formatted, SELECT will now automatically format it. This may happen if your dealer (or you) followed
the steps in Appendix C, but neglected to format the disk after partitioning it. SELECT is even smart enough to recognize the existence
of additional logical drives in an extended DOS partition. If the disk
hasn't yet been formatted, you will be shown a screen that gives you
the option of formatting any existing logical drive at this time, or
skipping it and beginning the final copying of the DOS files.

Several screens ensue now, depending on what type and size disk
media you are using to install DOS 4. You are successively prompted
to insert the different DOS disks into your A drive. SELECT copies
the appropriate files from them to the target disk(s). Once all the
disks have been copied, you have finished installing DOS 4 on your
hard disk (see Figure 2.10) or on several floppy disks.

The screen seen in Figure 2.10 varies slightly depending on whether
you have just installed DOS 4 on a fixed disk or on floppies. It also varies

```
                              Installation Complete

    _


               Installation of IBM DOS 4.00 is complete.

               The files AUTOEXEC.400 and CONFIG.400 have been
               copied to your fixed disk.  The files contain the
               options selected for DOS 4.00.  To get the options
               selected, update your AUTOEXEC.BAT and CONFIG.SYS
               files.  Refer to the "Getting Started with DOS 4.00"
               book for information on updating these files.

               FOR INFORMATION ON USING THE DOS SHELL, REFER TO
               THE "GETTING STARTED WITH DOS 4.00" BOOK.


          Remove all diskettes.  Press Ctrl+Alt+Del to start DOS.
```

Figure 2.10: Final SELECT installation screen

depending on whether your installation updates an existing version of DOS or is completely new. In either case, you are done with the installation. Remove the DOS diskettes from drive A and reboot your computer with your newly installed DOS 4. If you installed DOS on your hard disk, you press Ctrl-Alt-Del to reboot. If you installed DOS on diskettes, you place the diskette labelled STARTUP in drive A and then press Ctrl-Alt-Del to reboot.

The installed versions of two critical files, AUTOEXEC.BAT and CONFIG.SYS, contain the necessary setup information resulting from your answers in the prompted installation process. Assuming this is your first installation, you are ready to go now. However, if your disk already contained versions of these files, the new versions created by SELECT are named AUTOEXEC.400 and CONFIG.400. You can give your original files new names, then rename the .400 files to .BAT and .SYS, respectively. Or, you can just study the .400 files and edit the desired new lines into your existing AUTOEXEC.BAT and CONFIG.SYS files.

GETTING STARTED

Your first task after turning on your computer, once DOS 4 has been installed, is to load the required DOS files from your disk(s) into your computer's memory. If you installed DOS on a hard disk, you simply turn the power on to start up your DOS. You can also do this by restarting your system from the hard disk by pressing Ctrl-Alt-Del. If you installed DOS on floppies, you need to restart your system to load DOS. To do this, place your STARTUP DOS 4 system diskette (or an earlier DOS version SYSTEM diskette) in drive A, close the door, and then press Ctrl-Alt-Del. (Drive A is usually on the left side of most computers; however, some computers place it at the top when the drives are located one on top of the other.)

The computer will go through a process called *booting* or *bootstrapping*. This process loads DOS into the memory of the computer and is necessary before the computer can be used. Once DOS is in memory, you can begin to work.

SETTING THE DATE AND TIME AT STARTUP

You will first learn how to set the date and time on your system, using all versions of DOS earlier than 4. This section will then show you how to perform the same task with DOS 4. In this way, you will understand the approach needed to obtain any of DOS's system services, regardless of which version you are running.

SETTING THE DATE AND TIME IN DOS 3.X
If your version of DOS is earlier than DOS 4, it will display the following message after the computer tests its internal hardware:

```
Current date is Tue 1-01-1980
Enter new date (mm-dd-yy):_
```

January 1, 1980, is the default startup date each time you bring DOS up on your system. Assuming you do not have an automatic clock in your system, you will see this message each time DOS starts up. Normally, you enter the correct date at this point. However, if your system is configured with additional hardware that includes a battery-powered clock, you won't have to enter the date each time. The additional hardware comes with instructions on avoiding the standard DOS request for correcting the date, as well as on dealing with the subsequent request for the time of day:

Current time is 0:02:47.82
Enter new time:_

DOS keeps track of time in standard military format, so if you want to enter 10:30 A.M., you simply enter 10:30. However, if you wanted to enter 3:30 P.M., you would have to enter 15:30.

After you've entered the correct date and time, you're on your way. DOS will display a version of the following text, although the actual wording will vary slightly from computer to computer. In some versions of DOS, you will receive the following copyright notices *before* the date and time request:

DOS version 3.3
Copyright Matsushita Electric Industrial Co., Ltd 1987
Copyright Microsoft Corporation 1981, 1987
A>_

Since in this example the system diskette has been loaded in drive A, the DOS A> prompt now appears. As you will see throughout this book, when versions of DOS earlier than 4 are installed on a hard disk, the typical "DOS is ready" prompt is C>, indicating that DOS is installed on drive C and is waiting for your instructions.

SETTING THE DATE AND TIME IN DOS 4   When DOS 4 starts up, the appearance of the screen is considerably different. Figure 2.11 represents the first screen seen by a typical DOS 4 user.

The primary difference that you'll notice between DOS 4 and earlier DOS versions is the graphic shell shown in Figure 2.11. All commands are accessible from this point. From now on, I will focus on how to access the DOS 4 commands, but I will also explain the simple parallel entry method for obtaining the same command capabilities from an earlier DOS version.

The DOS 4 shell is nothing more than a graphic interface that has been added to give users a simpler means to explore and use many of the features built into DOS. In addition, it incorporates some new

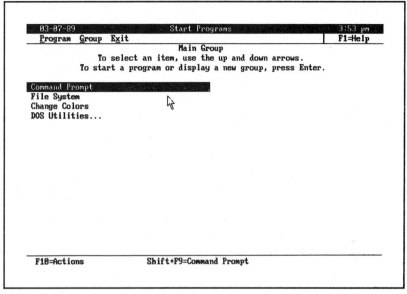

```
03-07-89                    Start Programs                    3:53 pm
Program  Group  Exit                                          F1=Help
                            Main Group
               To select an item, use the up and down arrows.
            To start a program or display a new group, press Enter.

Command Prompt
File System                              ⤷
Change Colors
DOS Utilities...




F10=Actions              Shift+F9=Command Prompt
```

Figure 2.11: First DOS 4 screen display

capabilities not found in earlier versions of DOS.

For now, concentrate on the different appearance of the DOS 4 graphic interface for the date and time functions. Contrast this to what you have just seen for DOS 3.3 and earlier. It is only the date and time functions' appearance that has changed; their functionality is the same.

To reach DOS 4's date and time functions, first select the fourth menu choice, DOS Utilities, from the Main Group; you will then see the DOS Utilities submenu shown in Figure 2.12. You will further explore the remaining utilities on this submenu in Chapter 3. For now, select the Set Date and Time choice to produce the screen shown in Figure 2.13.

This display of a small secondary window in the middle of your screen is the standard method for submitting commands in DOS 4. To tell DOS 4 to process a command, like DATE, you first select an English-language choice from a menu. DOS 4 then displays the secondary screen window which prompts you for any required additional parameters or data.

In the DOS 4 graphic interface, you press certain keys to choose the next step. For instance, while the Set Date and Time Utility window is being displayed, you can press the Return key to submit your

To select a choice on a menu, use the ↑ or ↓ key to move the highlighting to your choice, and press Return. If you have a mouse, you can select an item by moving the mouse pointer to it and double clicking the mouse's first button.

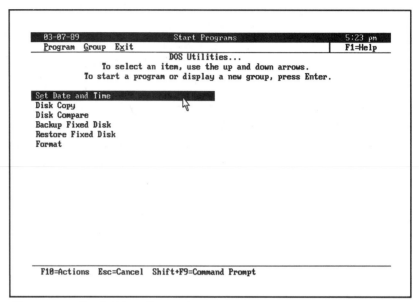

Figure 2.12: The DOS Utilities submenu

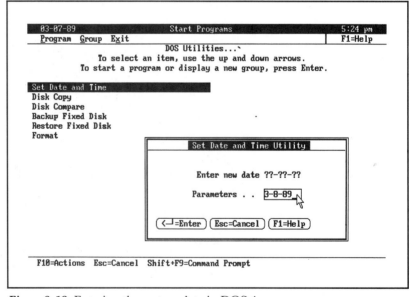

Figure 2.13: Entering the system date in DOS 4

newly typed-in date (for example, 3-8-89 in Figure 2.13), the Esc key to cancel the operation completely (thereby retaining the current system date), or the F1 key to obtain an additional window containing help information. You'll explore all of these possibilities in more depth in Chapter 3.

After you have entered the date, another window appears (see Figure 2.14) that prompts you to enter the correct time.

If you press Return without typing in new values for the date or time, DOS 4 merely switches to the command line that you saw in the preceding section on DOS 3.3. You will then be expected to either enter a new date or time or press Return to retain the previous value.

In Chapter 3 you will explore the principal commands available from the main menu of the Start Programs screen in DOS 4. Right now, you'll learn some more required fundamental skills associated with your first and continuing steps with DOS.

HOW DOS GETS GOING

You may wonder how DOS gets into the computer. A small part of it is already in the computer memory. Intelligent bootstrapping

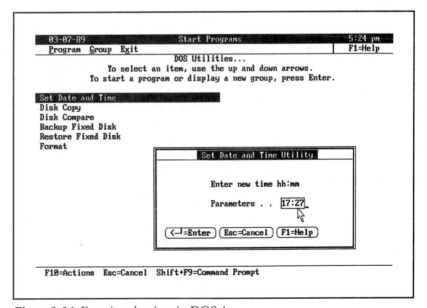

Figure 2.14: Entering the time in DOS 4

logic ensures that the rest of it is loaded automatically from the disk when you turn on the computer. That is why, on floppy-disk systems, a diskette must always be present in drive A before you turn on the computer. If you have a hard disk, it is always ready and takes the place of the diskette in drive A. After it is loaded, DOS shares the computer memory with the programs you run and the data those programs use (see Figure 2.15).

To let you know that DOS is active, the computer displays its readiness in different ways, according to your version of DOS and your system configuration. In DOS 4, you see the graphic shell shown in Figure 2.11. In all earlier versions, you receive a blank screen except for a prompting line that looks like this:

    A>

This DOS prompt is a simple way of asking you for your instructions. Unless you deliberately change this prompt, it always has two characters: a letter and a greater-than sign (>). The letter indicates the drive that is currently active; unless otherwise specified, all commands will affect data on that drive only. If you are using a two-drive system, the letter will be A (for the left drive) or B (for the right drive).

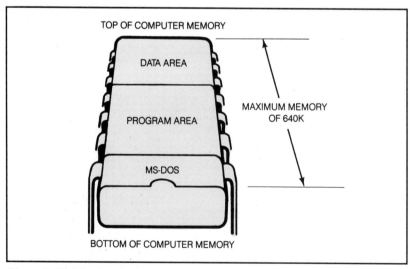

Figure 2.15: Memory map

Hard-disk users will usually see the letter C, which indicates the standard hard-disk drive.

Whenever you see the A> or C>, it means that DOS is ready to accept a command from you. It also tells you that you are not working in any other program.

GIVING COMMANDS TO DOS

You can control what DOS will do for you and when DOS will do it. In this book, you will learn many instructions (commands) that you can give to DOS. In DOS 3.3 and earlier, nearly all of these commands must be entered at the DOS prompt. The equivalent prompt for commands in the DOS 4 graphic shell is introduced in Part 2.

When the blinking cursor is positioned at the DOS prompt, all you need to do is type in a valid DOS command and press the Return key. (The cursor always indicates the position of the next character to be typed.) DOS does not process your request until it determines that you have actually pressed the Return key. Some DOS computers label the Return key RETURN; others label it ENTER; still others only label it with the ◄┘ symbol. All are equivalent. I will use the term *Return key* to indicate the key that you should press on your keyboard to do this job.

In the next chapter, you'll discover how to switch from the DOS 4 graphic-shell screens to the former standard command-prompt interface. The information about command and parameter entry presented in the next few pages applies to you whether you completely specify the command at a prompt, or whether you select a command from a DOS 4 shell screen and then enter the parameters in a displayed window, which we'll call a *dialog box*.

The additional qualifications for command requests are called *parameters* or *arguments*. (I'll use the term *parameter*.) In general, parameters can be thought of as placeholders for data that you will type in when you execute the actual command. The data is called the *value* of the parameter. I will use descriptive terms in italic type—for example, *FileName*—to represent parameters. You'll learn the most important examples of all of these modifiers in the context of the appropriate commands.

You must press the Return key after almost every command in DOS. I will not specify so after each command; instead, you should learn to use the key as an automatic end to each of your commands. Should you *not* be required to press Return for a command, I will clearly state so at the appropriate point.

Modifying a DOS
command with a
parameter or a switch is
analogous to modifying a
verb in a sentence with an
adverb.

Many DOS commands permit the specification of *switches*. A switch slightly changes how the command executes. *What* the command does remains the same; only *how* the command executes its task changes because of the added switch. As you learn new commands in this book, you'll also learn the most important and useful switches available with each command. In some cases, other switches exist, but their purpose is either obscure or not frequently needed. Chapter 22 provides you with an exhaustive list of additional switches.

EDITING CONTROLS

Several keys on the keyboard perform special tasks. The location of these keys differs, depending on whether you are using a keyboard that is compatible with the IBM PC/XT, the PC/AT, the Personal System/2, or the PC Convertible. Figures 2.16 through 2.19 show the complete layouts of these keyboards. Several key combinations also are interpreted in particular ways by programs like DOS. The following sections show you how to save energy and time by using these keys.

CORRECTING MISTAKES

What happens if you make a mistake? There are a few editing controls in DOS that you may find handy. The most common one is the

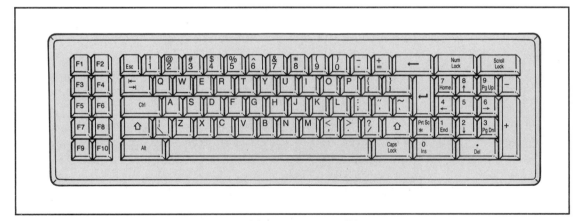

Figure 2.16: Keyboard layout for the IBM PC/XT and compatible computers

Backspace key, often seen as a ← symbol on your keyboard just above the Return key. If you type the characters

B:*.COM

as part of a command entry but do not press Return, your cursor will be on the space just beyond the last character you typed. To erase that

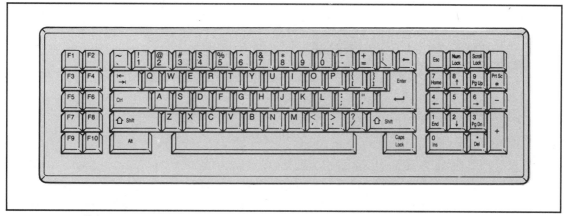

Figure 2.17: Keyboard layout for the IBM PC/AT and compatible computers

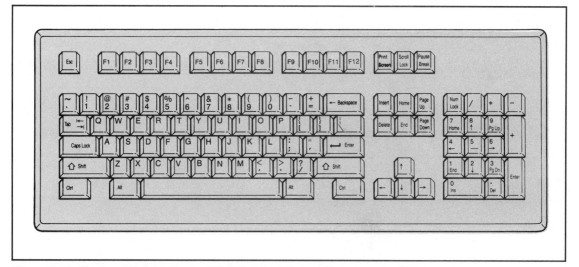

Figure 2.18: Keyboard layout for the IBM Personal System/2 and compatible computers

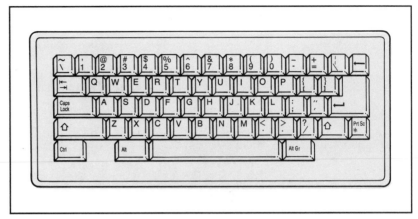

Figure 2.19: Keyboard layout for the IBM PC Convertible and compatible
computers

character, you press the Backspace key. The M disappears and the cursor moves one space to the left. To erase the next character, the O, you would again press the Backspace key. Continuing to press this key would remove the entire character sequence, keystroke by keystroke. In DOS 3.3 and earlier, since you type in the command as well as the parameters, you can backspace over the command itself. From a DOS 4 graphic screen, you can only backspace over the attached parameters.

CANCELING A COMMAND

Suppose that you entered a command and decided before you pressed the Return key that you wanted to cancel it. You may have changed your mind, or you may have realized that you simply entered the wrong request; you may even have become confused and need to reconstruct the request completely. In DOS 3.X, you could use the Backspace key to remove all the characters.

A better way, however, is to use the Esc key (short for Escape) to cancel the entire line with a single keystroke. If you entered a typical command like

DIR B:*.EXE

you could cancel the entire command by pressing Esc. Similarly, if you select a command in DOS 4, such as the TIME command shown in Figure 2.14, pressing the Escape key has the same result. Alternatively, you can use your mouse to point to and select the small button in the dialog box labeled Esc = Cancel. In the DOS 4 shell, the dialog box will then disappear, leaving you with the preceding screen (in this case, the DOS Utilities submenu screen). In earlier versions of DOS, a backslash mark (\) appears on the line you typed, and the cursor moves to the next line. This indicates that the entire command will be ignored. For example,

    DIR B:*.EXE\
    –

Note that the command is not erased from the screen; it is only ignored. The cursor moves to the next line, and you can enter your next DOS command.

REPEATING A COMMAND

DOS 3.3 and earlier versions of DOS hold the last command you issued in its memory. If you press the F3 function key, your last command will automatically be retyped for you. The function keys are usually located on the left side or top of your keyboard.

Suppose you needed to locate a particular file called 89BUDGET.WK1 on one of several diskettes. You could place the first possible diskette in drive A or B and enter the command

    DIR 89BUDGET.WK1

If you don't see the file listed, you could remove the first diskette, place the second possible diskette in the drive, and press F3. Your original DIR command is retyped for you on the line. Pressing Return again will execute this DOS command for the second diskette.

Whenever you have to perform the same DOS request multiple times (whether for several diskettes, several files, or several directories), using the F3 key can often save you much time by retyping the command line for you. DOS 4 users can use this F3 key to resubmit a command only when the command prompt is active.

CORRECTING PART OF A COMMAND

Once again, when a command prompt is active, you have the opportunity to correct and resubmit a command without having to retype it completely. Suppose you entered the command

        DOR B:*.COM

DOS responds with the message "Bad command or file name." This makes sense; the command should have been entered as DIR, not DOR. You might think that the only way to correct this mistake is to retype the entire command. However, DOS provides a better way to edit the most recently entered command. The F1 key will recall one letter at a time from the previous command. With this example, pressing F1 will make the D appear. Now you can type the correct letter, I. To recall the rest of the command line, which was entered correctly, you press F3. The corrected command is then ready to be executed. Pressing Return will execute the line as if you had retyped the entire line.

The F1 and F3 keys are handy tools to learn how to use. Although other function-key capabilities exist, you won't use them very often; you can explore their usage later on your own. Table 2.2 summarizes the editing keys used at the command prompt in all versions of DOS.

CLEARING THE DISPLAY

As you work at the command prompt, you may at times want to clear the current screen display and begin again with a clean screen. DOS contains a command to do this. Entering

        CLS

and pressing Return will clear the screen and then redisplay the current DOS prompt at the top of the screen with the cursor beside it, awaiting your next command. Note that clearing the screen has no effect on either disk files or programs in computer memory. It simply clears the display of text or output left over from previous commands.

KEY NAME	FUNCTION
F1	Retypes one character at a time from the last command entry
F2	Retypes all characters from the last command entry up to the one identical to your next keystroke
F3	Retypes all remaining characters from the last command entry
F4	Retypes all characters beginning at the first match with your next keystroke and ending with the last character from the last command entry
F5	Permits direct editing of all the characters from the entire last command
F6	Places a special end-of-file code at the end of the currently open file; sometimes referred to as a CTRL-Z or ^Z end-of-file code
Ins	Permits insertion of characters at the cursor
Del	Permits deletion of the character to the left of the cursor
Esc	Abandons the currently constructed command without executing it

Table 2.2: DOS editing keys

SUMMARY

This chapter contains specific information to guide your first steps with your new operating system. You discovered many important facts about DOS.

- DOS 4 has a completely automated installation process, managed by a program called SELECT. Your DOS 4 INSTALL diskette automatically invokes this important utility.

- Once installed, DOS gets going automatically when it is booted. The startup procedure reads the first sectors on a system disk to bring the DOS hidden files into memory. This loading process in DOS 3.3 and earlier versions ends with the DOS prompt, which indicates that DOS is waiting for your command request. The same loading process in DOS 4 results in the first DOS shell screen, the Start Programs screen.

- You can set the system date and time at startup with the DATE and TIME commands. DOS 4 users can set both via a menu choice on the DOS Utilities screen.

- Entering and editing commands at the DOS prompt is as simple as typing the command itself, along with any necessary parameters or switches, and pressing Return. Submitting commands in DOS 4 requires that you first select the command from the DOS 4 menu system. Then you enter any required data through a dialog box. Chapter 3 explores this procedure in more depth.

- Parameters are merely placeholders for the actual entry values you will type when you give the command.

- Switches modify the operation of a DOS command, giving you the same sophisticated control over DOS commands as adverbs give you over verbs when you construct a sentence.

- The function keys are simple one-keystroke tools that make formulating commands easier and less time-consuming. DOS uses function keys F1 through F6 for specific command-line editing purposes. The most commonly used function keys are F1, which retypes one character at a time from the last command, and F3, which retypes all remaining characters from the last command.

- At the command prompt, you can correct mistakes immediately by pressing the Backspace key or cancel a command completely with the Esc key.

- You can erase the entire command-prompt screen with the CLS command.

In Chapter 3, you'll complete your introduction to the fundamentals of DOS by learning how to run critical utility commands. DOS 4 users will also learn the primary menu options shown in the Start Programs screen.

UP AND RUNNING

CHAPTER 3

YOU'VE DISCOVERED WHAT OPERATING SYSTEMS
are. You've also installed DOS on your own computer system and
taken your first few simple steps with it. Now it's time to take a few
larger steps. You must learn how to perform some essential system
operations, such as copying your original DOS diskettes to protect
them. In the process, you'll explore the major possibilities open to
you when you first get your system up and running each day.

USING YOUR MOUSE
OR KEYBOARD IN DOS 4'S MENUS

If your DOS 4 system is installed, this is a good time to bring it up
on your machine and try the various things discussed in this section.
Moving the cursor, changing selections, and actually making choices
are all simple chores. Reading about the necessary steps is actually
more time-consuming than just doing them. Using your keyboard or
mouse when you read something here will assure that you immediately understand what is explained.

For example, after the initial Start Programs screen appears (Figure 3.1), press the up or down arrow (↑ or ↓) key five times. You'll see
how the four items are successively highlighted. After the top or bottom item on the list is highlighted, pressing an arrow key once more
merely begins the highlighting process again at the other end of the
list. This is called *wrapping around* the list. Do not press the Return key
yet. This will actually complete your selection, and begin the program or next operation selected. Be patient; that will come later in
this section.

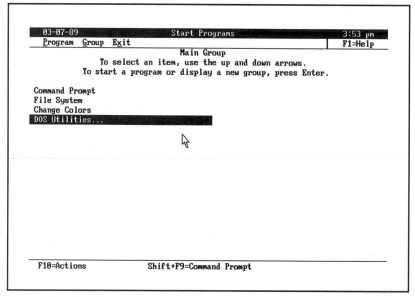

```
 03-07-89                     Start Programs                   3:53 pm
  Program  Group  Exit                                        F1=Help
                              Main Group
            To select an item, use the up and down arrows.
            To start a program or display a new group, press Enter.

 Command Prompt
 File System
 Change Colors
 DOS Utilities...

                                         ▷

 F10=Actions              Shift+F9=Command Prompt
```

Figure 3.1: Main Group choices on the Start Programs screen

The mouse pointer appears as an outline of an arrowhead if your screen is in graphics mode and as a solid moveable rectangle if your screen is in text mode.

If you have a mouse on your system, you move it to move the mouse pointer on the screen. As you can see in Figure 3.1, the mouse pointer is symbolically represented by an arrowhead. If you want to highlight something on the screen with your mouse rather than your keyboard, you first move the mouse pointer to the desired item, then press button one on the mouse. Try selecting each of the four items in the Main Group by using your mouse now.

As you've already learned, some special keystrokes such as F1 (Help) are always available to you in the DOS 4 shell. Other keystrokes are optionally available to you at different times. (You'll learn these at the appropriate times.) Here, at the first Start Programs screen, you can see on the bottom line of your screen that pressing F10 will automatically move the selection cursor from the Main Group of menu choices to the action bar. The *selection cursor* is the extended highlight on a screen item; it is typically a reverse-video cursor.

Press F10 repeatedly. You'll see how the selection cursor switches from the Main Group items to the action bar and back again. Actually, what you see is the first item (Program) in the action bar being highlighted. To highlight Program with a mouse, you can simply move the mouse pointer to the Program choice on the action bar and press button one. Once you have moved the selection cursor to the action bar, you can use the left and right arrow (← and →) keys to successively highlight each of the three choices on the action bar.

In addition to moving the mouse pointer directly to the action bar to make a choice, you can also move it to the F1 = Help phrase in the upper-right corner of the screen or to the F10 = Actions phrase on the bottom line, and press button one. This is the mouse equivalent of pressing those keys on your keyboard.

Now that you know how to move the selection cursor around the screen, with a mouse or with individual keystrokes, you will want to know how to tell DOS to actually perform the selected operation. Once something is highlighted, a keyboard user need only press the Return key. DOS will then perform the action specified. This action, of course, varies according to which item or screen choice is highlighted when you press the Return key.

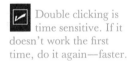 Double clicking is time sensitive. If it doesn't work the first time, do it again—faster.

Mouse users have an advantage in controlling operations in DOS 4. A special technique called *double clicking* enables you to simultaneously highlight and select an operation. After moving the mouse pointer to a desired location on your screen, press button one on your mouse twice very quickly. This procedure is called double clicking, and assumes that you want to highlight an item and request DOS to go ahead with the action or choice at the same time.

UNDERSTANDING THE DOS 4 START PROGRAMS SCREEN

In the previous chapter, you saw the introductory Start Programs screen displayed by DOS 4 (see Figure 3.1). This screen differs from the one seen in Figure 2.11 only in that DOS Utilities is highlighted, instead of Command Prompt.

In this section, you should concentrate on understanding the various portions of the Start Programs screen. The top line is called the title bar; it contains a brief title for the screen contents, as well as today's date and time. Whenever a rectangularly shaped window of information is displayed for you (such as the Set Date and Time Utility dialog box seen in the previous chapter), it is always displayed with its own title bar containing an identifying label for the window.

The line below the title bar on this Start Programs screen contains what is known as the action bar. This line lists single words (Program, Group, and Exit) that indicate which major actions can be taken while this screen is displayed. When selected, each of these actions displays a special secondary menu of choices. You will learn how to use these so-called *pull-down menus* (vertical submenus displayed directly below the action word selected) in Chapter 6.

Also visible on the right side of the title-bar line is the reminder (F1 = Help) that pressing F1 at any time will display a help screen of relevant text. As you'll discover in a subsequent section about online help, the information window displayed always contains text appropriate to the currently highlighted item or area of your screen. Other available keys, both here and on other DOS 4 screens, are discussed in the following section.

The third line of this Start Programs screen merely identifies this first screen as containing the Main Group of programs that can be started from this screen. The four possible choices that appear when DOS 4 begins are Command Prompt, File System, Change Colors, and DOS Utilities. Each choice either begins a program immediately or displays another group of choices. You'll explore these possibilities in more detail here and in succeeding chapters.

INITIATING THE DOS COMMAND PROMPT

If you have a mouse and DOS 4, try the double-clicking method now to activate the Main Group choice called Command Prompt. If you only receive the highlighting and nothing else happens, try it again but reduce the time between the two clicks. Double clicking is time dependent; you must click twice in a very short time interval for it to be recognized as a double click. Otherwise, it may be misinterpreted as button one pressed twice successively, which is a technique that serves another purpose.

If you just have a keyboard or simply wish to explore the alternate method of selecting items, use the down or up arrow key to highlight

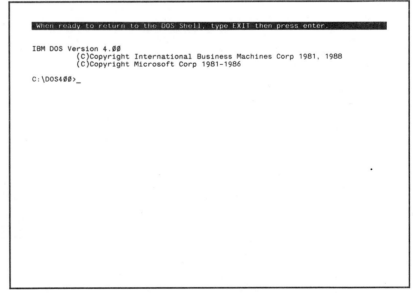

Press Shift-F9 to switch to the command prompt from DOS 4's menu system.

Command Prompt. Remember that you first will need to press F10 to return the selection cursor back to the Main Group choices if one of the items on your action bar is currently highlighted. Once Command Prompt is highlighted, you only need to press the Return key to activate it. Since IBM anticipates that you may want to switch to the command prompt often, they created a key combination, Shift-F9, that you can use to do this quickly.

When the command prompt is activated by any of these methods, you receive the screen seen in Figure 3.2. At this point, you can issue any of the commands I present in this book. DOS 3.X users receive this type of command prompt automatically when DOS is booted up. In these earlier versions, you always remain at the command prompt. In DOS 4, however, you can return to the graphic shell interface by entering the EXIT command at the command prompt. Although you can change the command prompt (see Chapter 11), it is shown here as C >.

In DOS 4, you have a choice between the new graphic shell interface, which is the default, and the old command prompt interface. If you are an experienced user of an earlier version of DOS, you may want to switch to the command-prompt interface to do things that you know how to do until you become comfortable with the graphic shell. As you

Figure 3.2: The DOS 4 command prompt

read more chapters, you will have less and less need to use this older interface. Because I assume that DOS 4 users will be using the graphic interface, I will usually refer to earlier versions of DOS when explaining how to do something at the command prompt. Just remember that DOS 4 users can also use the command prompt.

CHANGING THE COLOR OF YOUR SCREEN

Returning to the Main Group screen of Start Programs (Figure 3.1), you can make three other choices besides the command prompt. The File System option is such a significant part of DOS that I devote Part 2 of this book to the many aspects and possibilities available when you choose this option from the Main Group screen.

For now, let's move to the third choice, Change Colors. Making this selection brings up Figure 3.3. Depending on the type of monitor you own, the appearance of the screen shown in Figure 3.3 will vary in color, resolution, and emphasis. Therefore, this figure merely represents the general appearance your DOS 4 screens will take on if you select a different color combination.

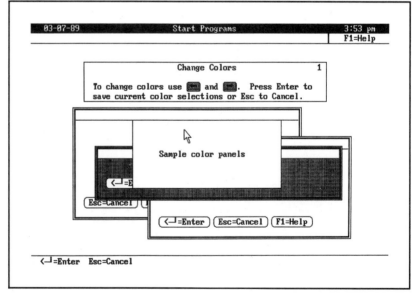

Figure 3.3: Changing your screen colors in DOS 4

The topmost window in this screen is labeled Change Colors, and in Figure 3.3, it has the number 1 in its upper-right corner. This number represents the first of four possible color combinations. Successively pressing the right or left arrow key will redisplay your screen using these four different combinations of colors. Try this now to see the resulting effects on your screen. Press Return when and if you find a color combination more pleasing than the default one you've been looking at up to now. Press the Escape key if you're only experimenting and do not wish to make any changes to your screen's color patterns.

OBTAINING ONLINE HELP

The final choice in the Start Programs main group is DOS Utilities. You first saw this option in Chapter 2 when you entered or adjusted your system's date and time. Selecting DOS Utilities on the Main Group screen brings up a screen that lists a secondary group of possibilities beginning with Set Date and Time.

You saw in Chapter 2 that selecting this first choice on the DOS Utilities screen allows you to enter the date and time to your system. In fact, you successively receive two dialog boxes for entering new values for the date and time in your system. Make these selections on your system now, bringing your screen to the point where you are being prompted to enter a new date.

When the main group or any subgroup of choices is visible on your screen, you can always press F1 to display a help window containing context-sensitive information. This means that the help text will be relevant to the group item, or action-bar item, that is highlighted when you pressed F1. If you have activated some program or process that displays a subordinate window, such as is done with the Set Date and Time choice, then pressing F1 brings up a window containing helpful text for that process.

Figure 3.4 provides an example of what is shown when you press F1 during the setting of the date and time. The new window, whose title bar contains Help, is displayed overlapping the existing Set Date and Time Utility window. As with all windows, this Help window has its own additional set of special keystrokes. Pressing Esc will erase the help window itself, restoring you to the point you were at when you were setting the date and time. Since pressing F1 always displays a help screen about the currently selected item, pressing it now produces another help window containing explanatory information about the help window you are looking at.

F11 is important in that it provides you with a list of all DOS 4 help topics. Even if you are not in the middle of a particular system activity, you can view this alphabetical listing for all system functions and select the desired topic from it.

Figure 3.4 has more text to display than fits in the size window being shown, and a *scroll bar* therefore appears on the right side of the window. Keyboard users can simply press the down arrow key to scroll down the text and view all the additional information. Naturally, you can scroll upward by pressing the up arrow key.

Mouse users have additional control over the display of additional information. Placing the mouse pointer on the down arrow symbol at the bottom of the scroll bar, and pressing button one has the same effect as pressing the down arrow key on your keyboard. Putting it on the double arrow symbols and pressing button one is the same as pressing the conventional PgUp and PgDn keys on your keyboard.

On a system with an installed mouse, you have another visual element. The *slider box* appears as a vertical white rectangle inside the

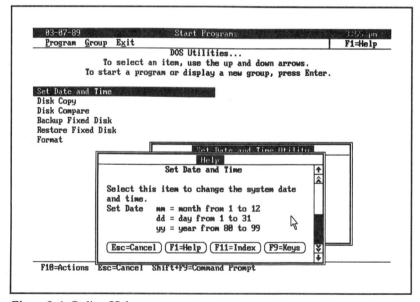

> Whenever information does not fit into its window, DOS 4 provides a vertical *scroll bar* on the right side of the window.

Figure 3.4: Online Help screen

scroll bar, located between the up and down arrow symbols. Figure 3.5 shows the same Help window after the text has been scrolled downward several lines—notice the position of the slider box.

The slider box moves inside the scroll bar proportionately to the window's text, showing you how far along in the entire contents you've progressed. The size of the slider box changes to give you an idea of how much information there is to scroll through. Think of the box as representing the current window and the dark area of the scroll bar as representing the total amount of information to scroll through—therefore, if the slider bar fills half the dark area, the current window contains roughly half of the information to scroll through.

You use this slider box by positioning the mouse pointer over it, pressing button one, and then moving the mouse without releasing the button. When you finally release button one, the window is redisplayed at the new position in the text.

All help screens operate this way, offering you a consistent interface to be used with either the keyboard or the mouse. In fact, you use a similar scroll bar in many other DOS 4 operations that involve the display of more information than can be fit into one graphic window.

Slider boxes do not appear when your shell has been installed in text mode.

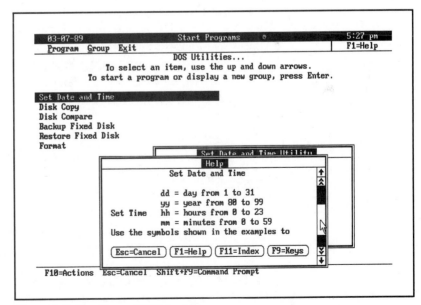

Figure 3.5: Scrolling a DOS 4 window

EXPLORING THE PRIMARY DOS UTILITIES

DOS 4 incorporates several key operations in the DOS Utilities subgroup of programs. These have direct DOS 3.X equivalents that will be presented in the appropriate sections below. You should use some of these commands immediately. You will probably use others often enough to justify their inclusion here. As you will learn in Chapter 6, you can easily add commands to this list or remove utilities that you don't use very often.

CHANGING THE SYSTEM DATE AND TIME

In Chapter 2, you investigated how to set your system's date and time when you first install and begin to operate it. If your system does not have a built-in, battery-powered clock, you are automatically prompted by DOS to enter the correct date and time each time you start up. However, even if your system does have the hardware for keeping track of the date and time, there may be times when you need to correct one or the other. For instance, in most of the United States, Daylight Savings time requires you to adjust all clocks by one hour twice a year.

To change the system time in DOS 4, you select DOS Utilities from the main Start Programs group, then select Set Date and Time from the displayed secondary group. You then follow the graphic prompts to correct the existing values for the date and time. In DOS 3.31 and earlier, you enter the TIME command at the DOS prompt anytime you want to see the current system time or change it:

```
C>TIME
Current time is 11:09:14.05
Enter new time:_
```

At this point, you could press Return to keep the current time, or you could enter time in the standard format of *hours*:*minutes*:*seconds*.

Occasionally, you may want to run a program that is date-stamped for a day other than the actual day it is run. As an example, consider the case of the paymaster of a large computer company who wanted to run an end-of-quarter report two days early. The quarter actually ended on Saturday, and he wanted to be off skiing that weekend.

Unless you are running DOS 3.3X or DOS 4, the changed time or date is only retained until DOS is rebooted or the system shuts down. Earlier versions of DOS require the Diagnostics program from the Utilities disk to make this permanent update. Systems containing add-on clock and calendar cards or boards also require you to run special utility programs supplied with them.

What did this creative manager do? He changed the system date with the DATE command from Friday, 12-30-88, to Sunday, 1-1-89. Then, after running the report dated for that coming Sunday, he changed the date back for the remainder of Friday's work. (He assumed that no other transactions would be received and processed in the remaining days of the quarter.) Although his approach is not necessarily advisable, having the command does give you this capability.

In a more serious vein, the testing of newly developed financial programs, for example, often requires data to be 30, 60, or 90 days old. Instead of creating different data all the time, you could use the same data and change the system date for each test. This would allow you to make your data appear to be 30, 60, and 90 days old so you could test the program easily.

PREPARING YOUR DISKS FOR USE

If you don't need to boot your system from the disk you are formatting, make it a *data disk*. All possible disk space is then available for your program and data storage.

As you learned in Chapter 1, all disks must be prepared correctly before you can use them. This goes for hard disks, regular and high-density diskettes, and microfloppy diskettes. All disks, once formatted, can store any information you like. If you also want a disk to be able to start your system (in other words, boot it), then you must include special DOS files on that disk, and you must prepare it in a special way. Once you've followed these steps, the disk is called a *system disk*. However, there is now less room remaining on the disk to store data for or from your application programs. Nonsystem disks are called *data disks*.

There are three main types of disk preparations:

1. *Formatting a data diskette.* This process is used to create a diskette that will operate in the computer but will not contain information initially. You use such diskettes to receive and store data.

2. *Creating a system diskette.* This process is most often used when you receive a new software package. Most programs are not ready to be run when purchased; you must usually perform this process in order to get a working copy of the program.

3. *Backing up a diskette.* This process makes an exact copy of another diskette. The DISKCOPY command is used; it is the fastest way for DOS to copy an entire diskette.

The next sections will teach you how to perform these three processes. The FORMAT command is the primary means of preparing disks. In DOS 4, the Format choice on the DOS Utilities group actually runs the FORMAT command. As you'll see, you simply use different switches for this command to tell DOS whether you want to create a blank data diskette or a system diskette. A number of other switches allow you to specify different diskette densities and layouts (see Chapter 22). They are less frequently needed, so I won't go over them here.

FORMATTING A DATA DISKETTE   Use a *scratch diskette* to try the following preparation commands. A scratch diskette is one that is fresh out of the box from your local computer store or is any old diskette that contains information you don't care about. If you do not have one, you should get one before you continue reading.

For users of DOS 3.31 and earlier, your computer screen should have the A> prompt on the screen (or C> if you are a hard-disk user). Place the scratch diskette in drive B (or drive A, often the only diskette drive on a typical hard-disk system). Now you are ready to format the diskette. Enter the command

FORMAT B:

for a dual-diskette system, or enter

FORMAT A:

for a hard-disk system.

DOS 4 users select Format from the DOS Utilities group. You then receive the dialog box shown in Figure 3.6. In this example, with DOS 4 running on a hard-disk computer with only one floppy-disk drive, the *a:* parameter is automatically inserted into the dialog box entry field. If you booted DOS 4 from a floppy disk in drive A, you probably intend to format disks using your B drive. You must ensure that the parameter entered in the dialog box is *b:*. Do this by simply typing over the *a:* with a *b:*.

Simply pressing Return now will invoke the FORMAT command with one parameter, the value of the drive (A) containing the diskette to be formatted. The only difference between the processing of DOS 4 and

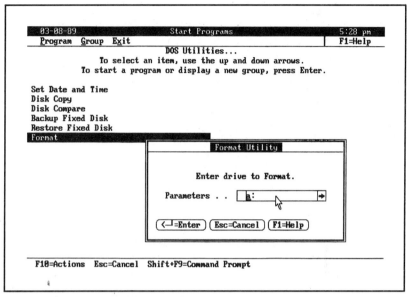

Figure 3.6: Format Utility in DOS 4

earlier versions is that DOS 4 helps you submit the proper syntax for the command.

Once this command begins, the FORMAT utility program will ask you to place a diskette in the drive you've specified. For example, you will see the following prompt:

Insert new diskette for drive A:
and press ENTER when ready...

⊙ When you format a disk, any information stored on that disk is destroyed. Make sure that the disk you format does not contain valuable information.

If you have not done so already, place the diskette in the drive at this point. When you are ready to begin the formatting process, press Return. DOS will take over and erase any data on your diskette. It electronically lays down a pattern of marks, which makes up the tracks and sectors you learned about in Chapter 1.

You can rename your FORMAT command (see Chapter 5) so that unauthorized users can't do any disk formatting. This helps guarantee that disks with valid data will not be formatted (and zapped). DOS 4 users can go even further by password protecting the Format choice on the DOS Utilities screen (see Chapter 6).

Diskettes can be formatted as many times as you like. You can even format some diskettes that were used previously by another

Be sure to use disk-
ettes with the proper
density format.

computer. Of course, any information stored by the other computer on that diskette will be wiped out.

The number of seconds it takes to format the diskette varies, depending on the size of the diskette (double-density, high-capacity, etc.). The default size for formatting is established by the disk drive used, and not the diskette placed in that drive.

DOS 4 users are next automatically prompted to enter a textual label for this newly formatted diskette:

Volume label (11 characters, ENTER for none)?

Earlier versions of DOS left this labeling as a user option, specified by the /V switch entered after the drive identifier.

When the formatting process is done, DOS shows you how much room for your files is available on the diskette you have just format-ted. This will be 362,496 bytes on a double-sided, double-density diskette or 1,213,952 bytes on a high-capacity diskette. DOS 4 users are also told how many bytes exist in each physical block on the disk (often called a cluster; now called an *allocation unit*), and how many of these blocks are available on this disk. DOS 4 also assigns a unique serial number to each formatted diskette and writes that number on the first (reserved) sector of the diskette. For example,

1213952 bytes total disk space
1213952 bytes available on disk
512 bytes in each allocation unit
2771 allocation units available on disk

Volume Serial Number is 1550-0BFF

The computer will then ask you if you want to format another diskette. If you enter Y for Yes, the process will begin again, and you will be prompted to insert another diskette in your selected drive. If you are done, you enter N for No. The FORMAT command will end, return-ing you to the DOS prompt (in earlier versions) or to the DOS 4 shell. DOS is now ready for your next command, and your formatted disk-ettes are ready to accept information.

MAKING A SYSTEM DISKETTE   You come now to the last type of disk setup procedure. This technique requires you to understand the difference between a system disk and a nonsystem disk. A system disk is one that contains three special files. Their most common names are listed in Table 3.1. If you want to boot up DOS with a disk, that disk must have these system files stored in reserved sectors in its first track. Only if this is true can the DOS boot-up program find them, load them, and bring up DOS properly.

Only COMMAND.COM is visible to the user; the other two files, IBMBIO.COM and IBMDOS.COM, are hidden. This does not mean that they do not take up space on the disk—they do. It means that their names do not appear on any directory listing. These hidden files contain most of the information that you have been calling DOS. When you turn on the computer, one of the first things it does is seek the information in these files and read it into memory. The appearance of the DOS 4 shell or the command prompt indicates that these files have been read and stored in the computer's internal memory.

What would happen if you turned on the computer and the boot drive did not contain these system files? The computer would not load DOS and would therefore not be capable of using the disk drives. You would then receive a message requesting that a DOS system diskette be placed in the boot drive. To correct the situation, you would place a diskette that has the DOS files on it in the drive and reboot the system.

You can see that having DOS on a disk is important. When you used the FORMAT command previously, you created a totally blank diskette. This was not a system diskette, because it did not have the three DOS files on it. Now you will learn how to format a diskette and copy the system's files to it at the same time.

At any command prompt, you can enter the following command:

FORMAT B:/S

MS-DOS SYSTEMS	PC-DOS SYSTEMS
IO.SYS	IBMBIO.COM
MSDOS.SYS	IBMDOS.COM
COMMAND.COM	COMMAND.COM

Table 3.1: DOS system file names

> IBMBIO.COM file contains the software programs for sending data to and receiving data from peripheral devices like printers and disks. The IBMDOS-.COM file contains the logic and routines for managing the data organization itself. In essence, the file system is controlled by logic in IBM-DOS.COM, and the more nitty-gritty signal and data communications are handled by routines in IBMBIO.COM.

/S (the System switch) tells the computer to add the DOS files to the diskette in drive B to complete the formatting process. To begin this formatting process, you simply press Return after making sure you have the right diskette in drive B.

In DOS 4, you would simply type /S on the Parameters line in the dialog box shown in Figure 3.6. Pressing Return then invokes the FORMAT command with B: as the drive identifier and /S as the switch requesting that a system disk be prepared. When the process is done, DOS tells you how much space on this disk it uses and how much remains available for your use. In this example, the diskette in drive B is now a system disk. You can use it to get the computer started.

> You set up a diskette with only the DOS files so that you can transfer program files from another disk to it.

Usually, you must transfer a new software program to your own system disk; most programs do not come on a system diskette. Although you can sometimes put DOS on your newly purchased application program diskette, it is usually preferable to follow these steps:

1. Format a system disk.

2. Copy your new program files to that disk.

3. Use this disk both to boot the computer and to run the application program.

4. Put your application software's original diskettes in a safe place.

Here's an example of a situation in which you might need to prepare a system disk. Imagine that you want to place BASICA.COM from your DOS Supplemental diskette (DOS 3.3) or from your Operating/Working diskette (DOS 4) on a self-booting disk. Your ultimate goal will be to automatically initiate the BASICA program when you start up the system (see Chapter 14). Feel free to follow the steps below, substituting an alternate application program, if you wish, for BASICA.COM. I actually performed this process, substituting EDITOR.EXE for BASICA.COM, so that my copy of XyWrite III Plus would automatically come up after my DOS 4 diskette booted up.

First, select a scratch diskette and format it. Next, follow the appropriate steps for your own system's needs. DOS 4 users should perform these steps from the command prompt. You'll learn in Part 2 how to run these copying operations through the DOS 4 shell.

For Dual-Diskette Systems   To prepare a system disk and copy the BASICA program to it on your dual-diskette system, follow these steps:

1. Place the scratch diskette in drive B and use the command

    FORMAT B:/S

2. Then copy the BASICA.COM file from drive A to the new system diskette in drive B by using the COPY command:

    COPY BASICA.COM B:

Your diskette is now prepared to receive any other application programs (with the COPY command) as well as to boot DOS.

For Hard-Disk Systems   To prepare a system disk in your hard-disk system, follow these steps:

1. Place the scratch diskette in drive A and use the command

    FORMAT A:/S

2. Then copy the BASICA.COM file from drive C to the new system diskette in drive A by using the COPY command:

    COPY BASICA.COM A:

Your diskette is now prepared to receive any other application programs (with the COPY command) as well as to boot DOS.

BACKING UP A DISKETTE   Now you will see how the DISK-COPY command can be used to precisely duplicate the contents of one diskette on another. You do not have to format the target diskette when using the DISKCOPY command, since DISKCOPY automatically formats it if necessary.

In this section you'll see how to make duplicate (backup) copies of your DOS diskettes so that you can then employ the backup diskettes, while carefully storing and protecting the originals.

The procedure is slightly different if you have a one-diskette or two-diskette system. You may have one diskette drive in your system because that is all you have, or you may have one diskette drive because your system has a hard disk. In either case, you will use the DISKCOPY command to create an exact copy of each DOS diskette. You will need as many diskettes for this purpose as your version of DOS comes with.

In this section I explain the process for copying any single diskette. Table 3.2 lists the quantity and names of the DOS diskettes that you need to copy to produce backup versions of your original DOS disks. The instructions in this section apply for all versions of DOS.

DOS prompts you several times during the disk-copying operation, referring to your original diskette (which you are copying) as the *source* diskette, and referring to the new blank diskette (to which you are making your copies) as the *target,* or *destination,* diskette (see Figure 3.7).

For One-Diskette Systems   DOS 4 users should first select Disk Copy from the DOS Utilities screen. You will see the Diskcopy Utility dialog box shown in Figure 3.8.

The source diskette is the disk you are copying, and the target diskette is the disk that will contain the backup version.

VERSION	NUMBER OF DISKS	DISK LABELS
4	2	Install and Operating/Working (3½'') media
	5	Install, Select, and Operating 1/2/3 (5¼'' media)
3.3X	1	Startup/Operating (3½'' media)
	2	Startup and Operating (5¼'' media)
Earlier	2	System and Supplemental (5¼'' media)

Table 3.2: Comparing disks in DOS 4

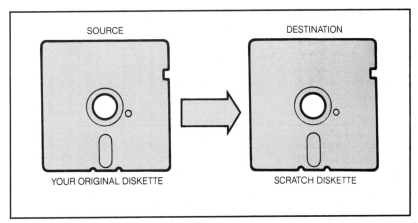

Figure 3.7: Copying diskettes with the DISKCOPY command

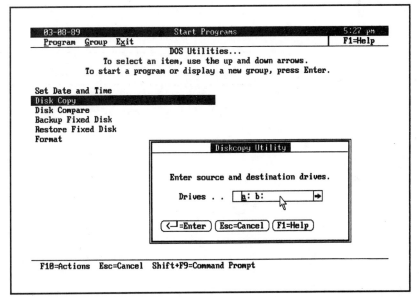

Figure 3.8: Copying diskettes in DOS 4

DOS 4's default parameter line is labeled Drives and contains both a: and b:. You can backspace over the *a:* and *b:* if you are making a copy using only one drive (the A drive). Pressing Return here has the same result as entering

    DISKCOPY

or

    DISKCOPY A:

at a command prompt. When the DISKCOPY command executes, DOS will prompt you like this:

    Insert source diskette in drive A:
    Press any key to continue...

The individual prompting messages during operations like DISKCOPY vary slightly between versions. This does not affect the actual operation.

    In this single-diskette environment, DOS will actually ask you to place first the source diskette and then the destination diskette into drive A (see Figure 3.9).

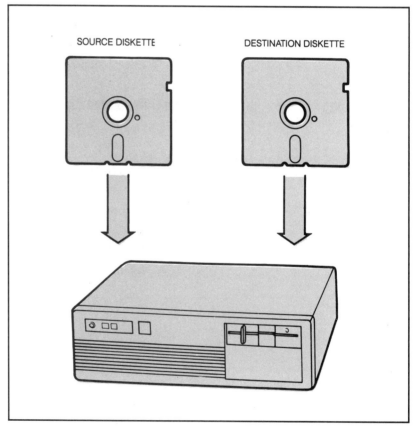

Figure 3.9: Copying diskettes using only one disk drive

Assuming your DOS diskette is still in drive A, press the Return key to begin the DISKCOPY operation. DOS will give you an informative message as it copies your diskette. This message will vary according to the diskette's storage density and its number of sides. For example,

Copying 80 tracks
15 Sectors/Track,2 Side(s)

When DOS has read as much as it can from the diskette, it will prompt you to

Insert target diskette in drive A:
Press any key to continue...

At this point, take a label and write on it the name of the original disk you are copying. Then place this label on one of the blank diskettes. Place this blank diskette in drive A and press Return. DOS will then copy to the blank diskette whatever part of the original DOS diskette it was able to read in its first pass. When it has finished copying this information to your new diskette, it may prompt you to again place the original DOS diskette in drive A. This will depend on the total size (in bytes) of your source diskette, and whether it can be completely read into memory and then copied in only one pass. If it can't, DOS will prompt you to

Insert source diskette in drive A:
Press any key to continue...

If you receive this message, you should remove your blank diskette and put the original DOS diskette in, so that DOS can continue reading information from it. At some point, it will prompt you to again insert the destination diskette in drive A. This is your cue to take out the original diskette and place your newly labeled diskette in drive A. Depending on the amount of memory you have on your computer and the version of DOS you are using, this juggling of diskettes will continue until all of the information from the original diskette is read, and all of it can be written to the destination diskette.

At the end of this cycle, DOS asks if you would like to copy another diskette. If your version of DOS has more than one diskette, you should answer Y (for Yes), since you need to copy all remaining original DOS diskettes. Label each additional blank diskette to reflect the name of the original DOS diskette that is being copied to it. Repeat this DISKCOPY process until all your originals have been copied.

For Dual-Diskette Systems   If your system has two compatible diskette drives, copying the diskettes can go much faster because no juggling is required. Assuming you have your original DOS diskette in drive A, label your blank diskette and place it in drive B. Then, for versions of DOS prior to 4, type the following command at the DOS prompt:

DISKCOPY A: B:

DOS 4 users need only select Disk Copy from the DOS Utilities screen. This brings up the screen seen in Figure 3.8; you just press Return at this point, since the default is for a source diskette in drive A and a destination diskette in drive B. This version of DISKCOPY tells DOS to read everything from the diskette in drive A and write it to the diskette in drive B (see Figure 3.10). DOS will prompt you as follows:

Insert source diskette in drive A:
Insert target diskette in drive B:
Press any key to continue...

> To protect you original DOS source diskettes, place write-protect tabs over each diskette's write-protect notch *before* beginning the DISKCOPY procedure.

Double-check that your original DOS diskette is in drive A and that your blank diskette, which is to become the copy of the DOS system diskette, is in drive B before you press the Return key. Pressing Return will then initiate the operation to completely copy the contents of the one diskette to the other. While DOS makes the copy, you will be informed as to what type of diskette it believes it is copying (single- or double-sided, the number of sectors to a track, and so on). For example,

Copying 80 tracks
15 Sectors/Track,2 Side(s)

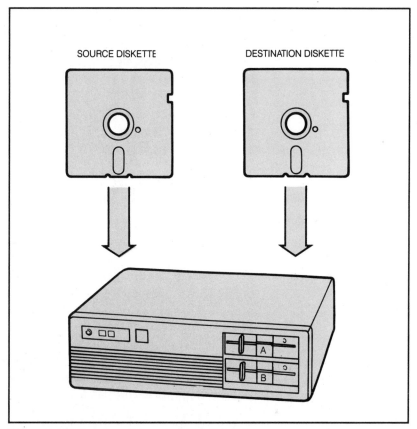

Figure 3.10: Copying disks using two disk drives

When it has finished copying the source diskette, DOS will ask you if you want to copy another one:

Copy another diskette (Y/N)?

You should typically answer Y for Yes. You will then be prompted to place the source diskette (your next DOS diskette) in drive A and insert the target diskette (another blank, newly labeled diskette) in drive B. Then—and only then—should you press the Return key to initiate the new process of copying the original diskette's files onto your new backup diskette.

When you have run through this DISKCOPY process for each of your original DOS diskettes, you can answer N for No to the question about copying another diskette. When the DOS command prompt or the DOS 4 shell returns, you are ready to continue using DOS in earnest.

The procedure you have just followed to back up the DOS diskettes can also be used to safely back up copies of most of your application software. However, certain copy-protected programs cannot be backed up in this fashion.

Copy-Protected Diskettes   Diskettes that are *copy-protected* cannot be copied by DOS accurately. DOS expects all diskettes to have the same basic setup in terms of tracks, sectors, directories, and so on. If a diskette is organized at all differently, then the DISKCOPY command will not work.

Copy protection was originally designed to prevent users from making inexpensive copies of expensive software. These cheap copies often prevented original manufacturers from receiving all their due income. However, after several legal battles (over the right of users to make legitimate backup copies for themselves) and several marketing battles (over large corporations refusing to buy copy-protected products that could not be placed on hard disks without continued diskette handling), the current trend has been away from copy-protected programs.

It is possible to purchase programs like COPY II PC that can decipher most of the special codes used by copy-protected software. By using this type of program, you can make backup or archival copies of your protected software. Since DOS can't do this, such a package is a good investment if your software collection includes copy-protected software.

UNDERSTANDING THE REMAINING DOS 4 UTILITIES

One of the remaining utilities listed on the DOS Utilities screen is the Disk Compare choice, which simply invokes the standard DOS utility command, DISKCOMP. You can use this choice after any disk-copying procedure, such as the ones you performed in the preceding sections. A copy operation is not guaranteed to produce an completely accurate disk copy because reading and writing of electromagnetic information can be adversely affected by a number of physical factors, such as the condition of the disk's surface. Using the Disk Compare utility can assure you that the resulting disk copy is a correct replica of the original disk. Invoking this operation in DOS 4 produces the screen shown in Figure 3.11.

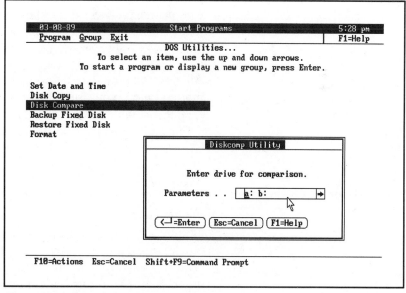

Using a DOS 3.X DISKCOMP utility to compare two disks formatted with DOS 4's FORMAT command will produce a comparison error in the boot sector.

The equivalent entry for earlier versions of DOS is the following command:

DISKCOMP a: b:

The DISKCOMP command makes a detailed comparison of all tracks and sectors on the two disks in drives A and B. Since DOS 4 stores a volume serial number in the boot sector of each disk, and this number is necessarily unique, it is not compared when you use DOS 4's DISKCOMP utility.

There are many remaining DOS utility commands. They will be presented throughout the book in context of the appropriate chapters.

Figure 3.11: Comparing disks in DOS 4

SUMMARY

The DOS 4 Start Programs screen represents merely a new graphic interface to all of DOS 4's commands and utilities. You learned in this chapter how to access all features of DOS 4 from this initial Start Programs screen. You have also explored the relationship between DOS 4 and earlier versions of DOS.

- Selecting Command Prompt from the startup DOS 4 screen displays the command-line prompt familiar to users of earlier DOS versions.

- All of DOS 4's features and functions are available through the new graphic windowing interface, either by keyboard controls or with an installed mouse.

- If you have a color monitor, you can change the DOS 4 shell color combinations easily and quickly from the main screen.

- You can always press F1 to get online help, which is information that is relevant to the currently selected screen item.

- The primary DOS utility operations are available from the DOS Utilities menu. You will learn in Chapter 6 how to add other DOS utility programs to this default list.

- All disks, whether hard, floppy, or microfloppy, must be formatted before you use them. You've seen how to prepare a scratch or blank diskette for storing files with the FORMAT command. This diskette can also be used to boot the system when you add the /S switch to the FORMAT command. However, this does cost you storage space on the diskette; less space is then available for your files.

- A working system disk can be created for most software packages by a simple procedure. First, you prepare a blank system disk; then you copy the appropriate files from your required software to it to create a self-booting system disk that contains your application software.

- You use the Disk Copy, or DISKCOPY, command which automatically formats your target disks as needed to make copies of your DOS diskettes. In fact, you can also use it to back up your other disks.

- The Disk Compare, or DISKCOMP, command makes a detailed track and sector comparison between two diskettes.

PART 2

UNDERSTANDING THE FILE SYSTEM

In Part 2, you will learn how to make DOS do much more for you. Chapter 4 will teach you the commands and features that you need to access your data on different drives, in different directories, and in individual files. You will discover how to obtain directory listings in DOS 4 and earlier versions. In Chapter 5, you will learn how to perform various file manipulations such as copy, move, delete, and rename.

Chapter 6 is a special look at using directory structures and grouping programs on a hard disk. First, you will discover how to create, move between, and delete directories and subdirectories. You will then learn how to set up your hard disk for three types of application programs: a word processor, a spreadsheet, and a database-management system. You will learn how to prepare and run any other programs you plan to use regularly. You will learn how to incorporate your own programs and groups of programs into DOS 4's graphic menu structures.

INTRODUCING
THE FILE SYSTEM

CHAPTER 4

BY NOW, YOU'VE LEARNED THE FUNDAMENTALS
of DOS, and you've seen what it can do. You've entered simple commands and prepared your disks. In this chapter, you will learn about
directories and how to access your files.

When you work with DOS, you will always deal with files of one sort
or another. Program files you purchase must be stored in some portion
of your disk; data files you create must be stored in another portion. The
more practiced you become at defining and accessing these disk portions, or directories, the more success you will have with DOS.

The DOS 4 File System is your primary connection to DOS directories, DOS files, and application programs. This chapter introduces
you to the File System of DOS 4, showing you how to access your
computer's various drives, directories, and files. You will also learn
the parallel commands and operations available to you in earlier versions of DOS. If you have DOS 3.X, go directly to the section "The
Nature of DOS Files."

UNDERSTANDING
THE DOS 4 FILE SYSTEM SCREEN

Chapter 3 introduced you to the Start Programs screen, which is
the first screen that appears after DOS 4 boots up. Selecting the Main
Group choice called File System from this menu brings up the screen
seen in Figure 4.1. (Your system will have different directories listed
in the window on the left.)

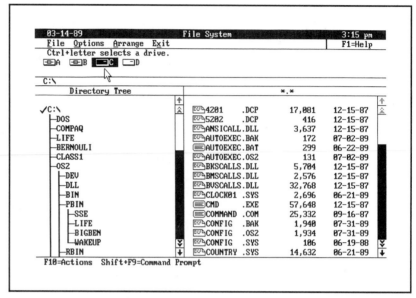

Figure 4.1: The main File System screen

Although this screen is slightly more complex than anything you've seen so far, it is very clearly organized. In essence, it is a full-screen window, containing a title bar on the top line and showing the currently available principal keystrokes on the bottom line. Just below the title bar is the action bar, containing four primary actions labeled File, Options, Arrange, and Exit. Chapter 5 focuses on the range of File System operations accessible from these action choices. When you select one of these actions, you can perform many operations by choosing commands from the pull-down menus that appear.

Below the action bar are three other primary portions of the screen. In these three areas you specify the disk drive you want to work on, the group of files you want to work with (the directory), and the individual file names you want to access.

You can switch among each of these areas by successively pressing the Tab key on your keyboard. Try it now on your DOS 4 system. Pressing Tab once will switch the highlight from the Drive area below the action bar to the Directory Tree area of your screen. This is the lower-left portion of the screen, containing a graphic rendition of the directory structure for the currently selected disk drive.

Press Tab again to switch the highlight to the File area on the right side of the screen, highlighting the first file (4201.DCP) in the list. Press Tab again to bring the highlight up to the action bar, and press it one last time to move the highlight back to the Drive area.

There are four key areas on your screen, and you move among them by pressing the Tab key an appropriate number of times. When you've switched to an area, you move your highlight within the area by pressing the arrow keys on your keyboard. For example, you press the left or right arrow key when you are in the action bar or the Drive area. You press the up or down arrow key when you are in the Directory Tree or the File area. Try these different possibilities now, even if your system has a mouse.

Mouse users can switch areas more easily. You need only move the mouse pointer to any area and press button one. Not only does that automatically switch areas, but it also simultaneously selects an entry in the area. Use your mouse now to successively point to and select a different drive, a different directory, and a different file.

SWITCHING YOUR CONTROL FOCUS

When the File System screen first comes up (Figure 4.1), the boot drive is automatically selected. Notice that the symbol, or *icon,* that represents the C drive is initially highlighted. You can switch your attention to the data on another drive by simply pointing to one of the other displayed drive icons and pressing button one. To use the keyboard to switch drives, you press the left or right arrow key until the desired drive letter is highlighted, and then press Return. Alternatively, you can simply press Ctrl-X, where X is the drive letter, to quickly change drives at this point as well. Try each method now on your system. The number and letters of the drive icons will vary according to the hardware you've installed on your system.

Directories are groups of files.

Once you've selected the correct drive, you will want to find the file grouping, or *directory,* containing the files you're interested in. Switch to the Directory Tree area of the screen and highlight the directory you want. Use the keyboard or mouse techniques to do this.

As you can see in Figure 4.2, or on your own system if you are trying these techniques while you read, the file names displayed on the right side of the screen are those contained in the directory you've selected on the left side of the screen.

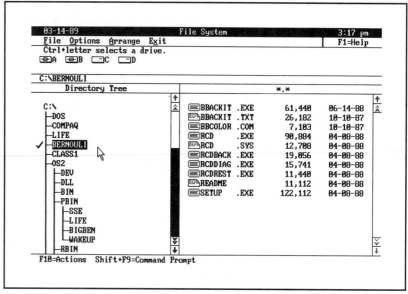

```
┌──────────────────────────────────────────────────────────────────┐
│ 03-14-89                  File System                   3:17 pm    │
│ File  Options  Arrange  Exit                          │ F1=Help   │
│ Ctrl+letter selects a drive.                                       │
│ ⊟A   ⊟B   ⊟C   ⊟D                                                  │
│                                                                    │
│ C:\BERNOULI                                                        │
│     Directory Tree                            *.*                  │
│                                     ┌───┐                 ┌───┐     │
│   C:\                             ▲ │ ↑ │ ▤BBACKIT .EXE  61,440  06-14-88 │ ↑ │ ▲ │
│   ├DOS                              │ ⌃ │ ▨BBACKIT .TXT  26,182  10-10-87 │ ⌃ │    │
│   ├COMPAQ                           │   │ ▤BBCOLOR .COM   7,103  10-10-87 │   │    │
│   ├LIFE                             │   │ ▤RCD     .EXE  90,884  04-08-88 │   │    │
│ ✓ ├BERNOULI      ▯                  │   │ ▨RCD     .SYS  12,708  04-08-88 │   │    │
│   ├CLASS1                           │   │ ▤RCDBACK .EXE  19,056  04-08-88 │   │    │
│   ├OS2                              │   │ ▤RCDDIAG .EXE  15,741  04-08-88 │   │    │
│   │ ├DEV                            │   │ ▤RCDREST .EXE  11,440  04-08-88 │   │    │
│   │ ├DLL                            │   │ ▨README        11,112  04-08-88 │   │    │
│   │ ├BIN                            │   │ ▤SETUP   .EXE 122,112  04-08-88 │   │    │
│   │ ├PBIN                           │   │                                 │   │    │
│   │ │ ├SSE                          │   │                                 │   │    │
│   │ │ ├LIFE                         │   │                                 │   │    │
│   │ │ ├BIGBEN                       │ ⌄ │                                 │ ⌄ │    │
│   │ │ └WAKEUP                     ▼ │ ↓ │                               ▼ │ ↓ │    │
│   │ └RBIN                           └───┘                                 └───┘     │
│ F10=Actions  Shift+F9=Command Prompt                               │
└──────────────────────────────────────────────────────────────────┘
```

Figure 4.2: Selecting a different directory

Notice that the current directory is highlighted only when the screen focus is in the Directory Tree area, as it is in Figure 4.2. At all times, however, a check mark appears beside the directory name you've chosen. For example, in Figure 4.1 the screen focus was in the Drive area, and only the check mark indicates that the root directory (C:\) was chosen. C:\ is also displayed on the line above the Directory Tree area. This line changes whenever you select a different directory.

Notice that the arrows at the top of the scroll bar for the directory window are grayed, indicating that going up is not an option available to you at this moment. Using the mouse or keyboard to move the Directory Tree display to its lowest point brings up the screen shown in Figure 4.3. Because you can now go no further down, the bottom arrows on the scroll bar become grayed. Notice that no slider box appears and all up and down arrows are grayed in the File area's scroll bar because all the file names for the selected directories fit within the window.

To select multiple files with a mouse, you point to each file name and press button one for it. If you change your mind, simply point to a selected file name and press button one again. This will deselect the file.

All unavailable options in DOS 4 are always grayed, whether they represent pull-down menu items or scroll-bar directional arrows.

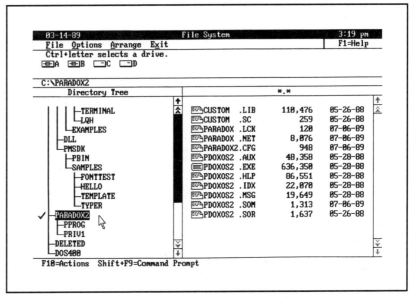

```
 03-14-89                    File System                  3:19 pm
    File Options Arrange Exit                            F1=Help
    Ctrl+letter selects a drive.
    ⊟A   ⊟B   ⊐C   ⊐D

 C:\PARADOX2
         Directory Tree                          *.*
                                        ↑  ▱CUSTOM   .LIB  110,476  05-26-88
            ├─TERMINAL               ⊼  ▱CUSTOM   .SC       259  05-26-88
            └─LQH                       ▱PARADOX  .LCK      120  07-06-89
           └─EXAMPLES                   ▱PARADOX  .NET    8,076  07-06-89
         ├─DLL                          ▱PARADOX2 .CFG      948  07-06-89
         ├─PMSDK                        ▱PDOXOS2  .AUX   48,358  05-28-88
          ├─PBIN                        ⬡PDOXOS2  .EXE  636,350  05-28-88
          └─SAMPLES                     ▱PDOXOS2  .HLP   86,551  05-28-88
              ├─FONTTEST                ▱PDOXOS2  .IDX   22,070  05-28-88
              ├─HELLO                   ▱PDOXOS2  .MSG   19,649  05-28-88
              ├─TEMPLATE                ▱PDOXOS2  .SOM    1,313  07-06-89
              └─TYPER                   ▱PDOXOS2  .SOR    1,637  05-26-88
 ✓ ─PARADOX2            ▱
       ├─PPROG      ⬚
       └─PRIV1
      ├─DELETED                      ⩔
      └─DOS400                       ↓
    F10=Actions  Shift+F9=Command Prompt
```

Figure 4.3: Scrolling through the directories in drive C

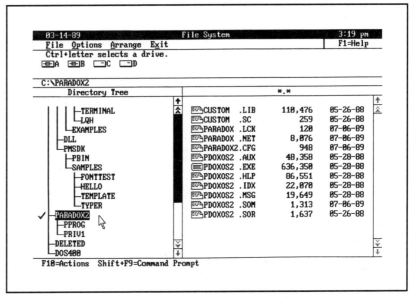 If you inadvertently press Return when selecting a file, DOS will attempt to open or start it. To stop DOS from doing this, simply press the Escape key.

If you don't have a mouse, you select a file by pressing the space-bar when the file name is highlighted. Pressing the spacebar once when the highlight is on a selected file will deselect it.

Take a look at Figure 4.4. In it, you see that the small icons located to the left of the BBACKIT.TXT and README files have been highlighted. This is the way that DOS indicates that you've selected files. The extended cursor highlight has been moved to another file (SETUP.EXE) in the directory, but it is not currently selected.

Regardless of whether you select one file or fifty-one files, the next operation you ask DOS to execute will be performed for each selected file. You might select these two files, for example, to then ask DOS to print them.

The rectangular paper icon indicates a data file, and the lined octagonal icon indicates a program file.

Notice that two different types of file icons are used by DOS. A rectangle with one corner turned over represents a data file, symbolizing the data on a piece of paper. An octagonal icon marks a program or file that can be executed, symbolizing a signpost containing the name of a command or application program.

An executable program or command always has an extension of .COM or .EXE, while an executable batch program always has an

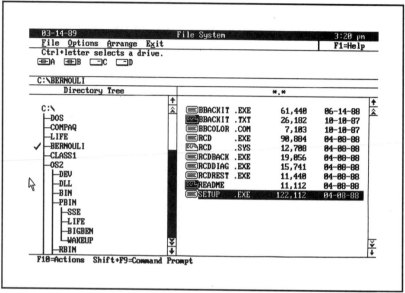

Figure 4.4: Selecting multiple files

extension of .BAT. Only files with these three extensions are symbolized by the octagonal icon. All other files are represented by the paper icon. When you select a file, its icon is switched to reverse video.

THE NATURE OF DOS FILES

Now that you know how to maneuver about the File System screen, you can take a closer look at the concepts behind its major areas. First, let's explore the information being displayed in the File area. You use this area to see a listing of all the files contained in each directory of the disk drive.

On diskettes, at least, you could read the printed disk label, although the label may not have the correct information on it. Also, it rarely contains all the information that is available electronically in DOS. The only way to be sure of what is really on any disk is to have DOS display a directory of the files on that disk.

Before storing each diskette you use, print a directory listing of its contents using the techniques described in Chapter 8. To print a sorted listing, use the techniques in Chapter 13.

DISPLAYING INFORMATION ABOUT YOUR FILES

In DOS 4, you are presented with a listing of files in the File area of your File System screen. When you highlight a directory in the Directory Tree area of this screen, DOS then lists the files contained in this particular directory. In earlier versions of DOS, you had to invoke the DIR (Directory) command from the command prompt to display a listing of your files. For example, if you enter the command

        DIR

the computer will display a listing of all the files found in the current directory on the currently active drive. If you are using an earlier version of DOS, simply enter DIR and view the results on your screen. You'll see that they are similar to what you see in the File area of DOS 4's File System screen. The key difference is that DOS 4 displays an icon to the left of the file name.

Each line that appears in the list of files describes a file that is stored on the disk. Versions of DOS earlier than 4 display four pieces of information about each file: the file name, the file size, and the date and time of its creation or last update. For example,

BBACKIT.EXE	61,440	06-14-88	03:00p
(File Name)	(Size)	(Date)	(Time)

In addition to the icon, file name, file size, and date information, DOS 4 can also display the file's time information when you switch to a screen display that contains all files on the selected drive. The Directory Tree area is suppressed, and the extra space is used to display the time data. This alternative display option is presented in Chapter 5.

When using earlier versions of DOS, which do not offer the convenience of the scroll bar, you can still control the listing of files on the screen by using a *Ctrl-key combination*. To do this, you hold the Ctrl key down and then press another key at the same time. When you issue the DIR command for a directory that has more than a screenful of files, the file listing will simply scroll off the screen. However, pressing the key combination Ctrl-S (^S) freezes the screen and stops any automatic scrolling. Press the same combination to start the screen

Press Ctrl-S to stop a directory listing that is scrolling off the screen. Press Ctrl-S again to continue the listing.

output going again. This type of key combination is called a *toggle*.

If you haven't already done so, and you have an earlier version of DOS, try the DIR command now on each of the drives in your own system. For example:

```
DIR A:
DIR C:
```

If you have other drives, try the command on them. If you accidentally try the command with a drive letter that doesn't exist, DOS will tell you so. You'll receive the error message "Invalid drive specification," and then a new DOS prompt will be displayed. However, if you ask for a directory listing on a drive that *does* exist on your system, but the drive isn't ready (the drive door isn't closed or the diskette hasn't been inserted), you'll receive an error message: "Abort, Retry, Fail" in DOS 3.3, or "Abort, Retry, Ignore" in versions of DOS earlier than 3.3.

If you've really made a mistake, simply type the letter A to abort the request; if the diskette wasn't ready, prepare it and then type R to retry the DIR request. In general, you should only select the FAIL option if you are a DOS programmer and understand the nature of the internal system call that has failed, and how to proceed in the program.

Compared to previous DOS versions, DOS 4 handles errors considerably better. If the drive is not ready when you request a directory listing for it in DOS 4, you will receive a dialog box containing the following message:

```
Drive not ready

1. Try to read this disk again
2. Do not try to read this disk again
```

CONSTRUCTING DOS FILE NAMES

Each file name has two principal parts:

1. A base name

2. An extension (optional)

The general form of every DOS file name is as follows:

BaseName.Ext

where *BaseName* represents the base name, which can be up to eight characters long. *Ext* represents an optional file-name extension that comprises no more than three characters and is separated from the base name by a period. Figure 4.5 illustrates the general form.

DOS may display a file name in a different way than you entered it. For instance, in Figure 4.4 you can find a file named RCD.EXE listed. The base name is only three letters long, but there are five additional spaces displayed before the period separator symbol. This is done to align the column of names. When you use this name at a command prompt, or in the parameters entry box of a DOS 4 command, you must enter it as RCD.EXE. You enter the period immediately after the base name and then type the three-character extension. Note that DOS does not care if the letters are uppercase or lowercase. However, you cannot enter spaces as part of a file name, even though that is the way it appears in the directory listing.

DOS checks for invalid characters when you enter a base name, and you can use any characters except the following:

$$. " / \ [ ] \mid < > + : = : ,$$

In addition, all DOS control codes (see Appendix B) are also invalid. For the sake of readability as well as typeability, use only alphabetic and numeric characters in your file names.

> DOS is not case sensitive. For example, to DOS Rcd.exe, rcd.exe, and RCD.EXE are all the same file.

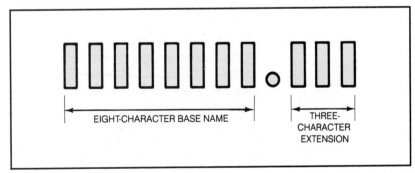

EIGHT-CHARACTER BASE NAME   **THREE-CHARACTER EXTENSION**

Figure 4.5: File-name structure in DOS

The following base name would not be acceptable to DOS because it contains a space:

MY FILE

However, this would be acceptable:

MY_FILE

The space has been replaced with an underscore, which is a legal character. Many people use this character to simulate a space, since it is visually unobtrusive. Use it if you like, but it always slows down the typing of the name; using the name MYFILE with neither a space nor an underscore would be quicker and easier.

The same rules on invalid characters in the base name apply to the extension as well.

Take a look at the following list of file names:

A:LETTER.TXT

SAMPLE DAT

X

MY:FILE

msdos.les

Sample.File

C.test.doc

b:user.fil

Do you know which of these are valid and which are not? If not, reread the preceding section before going on. The valid file names are A:LETTER.TXT, X, msdos.les, and b:user.fil. The others are all constructed incorrectly.

SAMPLE DAT is not acceptable because it contains a space. MY:FILE is unacceptable because two characters precede the colon. In DOS command-prompt entries, the drive, directory, and file name can all be combined. In this way, you can establish with one expression exactly which file(s) you are interested in, which directory they appear in, and the location of that directory (its *path*). MY:FILE is incorrect because colons cannot appear in a base name; a colon can *precede* the base name if a drive identifier is specified. However, a drive identifier can only be a single letter.

The file name Sample.File is invalid because a file extension can contain at most three characters. (In fact, DOS will accept this entry and treat it as if Sample.Fil had been typed; the ending "e" will be ignored.) The last invalid example, C.test.doc, will not work because a drive specification must be followed by a colon. Also, only one period can appear in a file name.

Drive specifications and extensions are optional. The usual purpose of an extension is to group together files of the same type. Traditionally, file extensions such as .BAS (for BASIC language programs), .COM (machine-language command files), and .DAT (data files) have been used to identify the type of information contained within certain files.

Tradition is not the only reason for following naming conventions. They also make it easier to see, group, and access all files of the same type. When you look at the files contained in any new application package, for example, you can often understand what many of them are used for simply by noting their extension names (.HLP for help files, .TXT for text files, .OVL for overlay files, and so on). See Table 4.1 for commonly used extensions.

VIEWING LONG DIRECTORY LISTS

In DOS 4, you needn't worry about directory lists that are too long for your screen. You have your scroll bar to manage the display of the list. However, earlier versions of DOS do need some additional help. There are two alternative ways to list a directory if it is too long to be displayed on a single screen at one time. Naturally, these techniques will work at the command prompt in DOS 4 as well. In earlier versions of DOS, enter

DIR/W

The resulting directory listing is called a *wide directory,* because the files are listed horizontally instead of vertically, which means that more names can fit on a single screen. In this display, however, DOS no longer lists the size, date, and time of each file, which saves space. /W is an example of a switch; it modifies the way the DIR command executes.

FILE EXTENSION	TYPE OF FILE
.BAK	Backup copies of files
.BAS	BASIC programs
.BAT	Batch files
.BIN	Binary object files
.COM	Simple executable programs (like DOS commands)
.DAT or .DTA	Data files
.DBF	Database files
.DRV	Device driver files
.EXE	Executable programs, usually larger than 64K and more sophisticated than .COM programs
.NDX	Index files
.OVR	Overlay files
.PRG	dBASE program files
.SYS	DOS device drivers
.TXT	Plain ASCII text files
.WKS or .WK1	Worksheet (spreadsheet) files

Table 4.1: Commonly used file-name extensions

Here's another variation on the DIR command. In this case, /P is the switch, and it modifies the result of the command in a different way. If you enter

DIR/P

the screen fills and the list pauses until you press another key. If you then press Return again, the next screenful of file names is displayed. This is somewhat akin to the Ctrl-S combination you saw earlier, except the listing breaks at precise places depending on how many directory entries it takes to fill the screen.

In summary, there are three styles of command-prompt directory listings:

DIR   Full listing of all files, including size, date, and time

DIR/W   Wide directory; file size, date, and time not shown

DIR/P   Directory listing pauses when one screen is filled; size, date, and time shown

REFERRING TO FILES ON OTHER DRIVES

In versions of DOS earlier than 4, you can specify another drive's directory by following the DIR command with the letter that indicates the drive. If you type

DIR B:

on a dual-diskette system with a diskette in the second drive, the computer will display the list of files on the diskette in drive B. You could also get a wide display of the list for drive B by entering

DIR B: /W

CHANGING THE DEFAULT DRIVE

The A> prompt indicates that DOS will work with the diskette in drive A unless you specify otherwise. Thus, if this is the prompt you see on your system, then drive A is considered the *default* drive for all commands. All commands will act on files located on the default drive unless you specifically include another drive name as part of the command or file name. You can change the default drive simply by typing in the letter for the desired new default drive. Entering

B:

would change an A> prompt to B>. Note that drive names must be followed by a colon when you enter them at a command prompt. Entering the DIR command now would cause the red light on drive B to light, since it is now the default drive; DOS would also tell you this by changing its prompt to B >. At this point, you could still get a listing of drive A by entering

DIR A:

EXPLORING THE DISK DIRECTORY STRUCTURE

Now that you understand more about files, you'll learn more about the concepts of directories and subdirectories. If you have DOS Version 2.X or later, every disk in your system can be logically split up into directories and subdirectories. This ability to create and maintain purposeful groupings of files is the most powerful organizational tool in DOS.

DISTINGUISHING BETWEEN DIRECTORIES AND SUBDIRECTORIES

Directories are like separate drawers in a filing cabinet. Subdirectories are like the labeled categories within each drawer. Files are stored in subdirectories and isolated from other files. Just as a well-organized filing cabinet promotes efficiency in the office, a well-organized set of DOS directories and subdirectories enables you to quickly and easily store and retrieve your program and data files.

As Table 4.2 shows, a hard disk will store many times the amount of data or number of files that can be stored on a floppy diskette. For example, if the average size of your files is 20,000 bytes, then a 10-megabyte hard disk would hold approximately 500 uniquely named files. If the average file is smaller (say, 10,000 bytes), then you could have 1,000 different files on the disk. This raises the problem of keeping order among a huge list of files. DOS allows you to create subdirectories—units of organization that divide the hard disk into sections to solve this problem.

In this book, the word *subdirectory* refers to any directory on a disk other than the root directory.

The words *directory* and *subdirectory* are often used interchangeably in DOS. Both are correct. *Subdirectory* is a relative term; any directory is a subdirectory of another directory, with the exception of the root directory. I use the word *subdirectory* for any directory on a disk other than the *root* (main) directory. I use the word *directory* to refer to either

TYPE OF DISK	TOTAL STORAGE (BYTES)	NUMBER OF 20K FILES
5¼" floppy	360K	18
High-capacity 5¼" floppy	1.2Mb	60
Double-sided 3½" floppy	1.44Mb	72
Hard disk	10Mb	500
Hard disk	20Mb	1,000

Table 4.2: Potential files on disks of different sizes

the root or any one of the many possible subdirectories extending from it.

While subdirectories are usually associated with hard disks, DOS can just as easily create subdirectories on floppy diskettes. They function exactly the same on diskettes as they do on hard disks, differing only in the volume of data they are capable of holding. You'll learn in Chapter 6 how to create new directories within existing directories on your disks.

CHANGING THE DEFAULT DIRECTORY

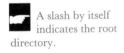 A slash by itself indicates the root directory.

Just as DOS allows you to select a default drive, it also allows you to select a default directory for a disk. When you first log on a disk, the root directory of that disk is the assumed default directory. That is why C:\ was the directory whose file contents were displayed in Figure 4.1 when you first logged on the File System of your DOS 4 system. When a slash symbol is used alone, it indicates the root, or first, directory on a disk drive.

Having a default directory allows you to work with only the files contained within that subdirectory. For example, if you are in the root directory and want to see a listing of the files in a subdirectory, you must enter DIR followed by a backslash and the name of the subdirectory for command-prompt versions of DOS. On the other hand, if you make the subdirectory the default directory (rather than the root), simply entering DIR at the command prompt will give you the listing.

The command used to change directories in command-prompt versions of DOS is the CHDIR or CD command. For example, entering

CD \UTIL

makes the UTIL subdirectory the current DOS default whenever you make references to files on the current disk drive. Naturally, in DOS 4, you change directories by simply selecting a different directory from the Directory Tree portion of the File System screen.

SUMMARY

To use your computer effectively, you need to understand how data, programs, and information of any sort are stored in files and how to properly manage these files. In this chapter, you learned the following:

- The DOS 4 File System screen provides you with complete graphic access to files, directories, and drives.

- You can easily switch the command focus between drive controls, directory alternatives, and individual files with either special keystrokes or the mouse.

- You can easily select individual or multiple file entries by pressing your mouse button or your spacebar. All pull-down menu choices for file operations then apply to the selected file(s).

- The DOS directory contains a listing of all base names and extensions for each separate file in it. It also may contain their sizes and the dates and times these files were created. DOS 4 also displays a selection icon next to each file name.

- The DIR (Directory) command permits you to obtain listings of each directory's contents at the command prompt. Certain switches modify the DIR command request. More files can be listed on the screen with the /W switch, and information can be presented one screenful at a time with the /P switch.

- In DOS 3.3 and earlier versions, file references apply typically to the current default drive. However, by preceding the file name with a drive identifier, like A: or C:, you can reference files on different drives.

In the next chapter, you'll take a closer look at the pull-down menus in DOS 4. You'll learn about the various actions you can initiate in DOS 4 while you explore the range of commands for managing files in all versions of DOS.

MANIPULATING FILES
AND DIRECTORIES

CHAPTER 5

LEARNING MORE ABOUT FILES AND DIRECTORIES will give you more confidence and control over your system. You will learn how to display the contents of text files, how to erase old files that you no longer need or that are occupying too much space, and how to make copies of any files onto 5¼'' or 3½'' diskettes so you can free disk space for new work.

As an aid in keeping your work organized, you will see how to easily rename files. If simple renaming isn't enough, you will learn to rapidly move and regroup files between disk drives and between directories.

DOS 4 users will also discover the myriad of new possibilities for graphic display of your disk's files, none of which exist in earlier versions of DOS. I also will explain new DOS 4 options for file selection and presentation.

MANAGING YOUR SCREEN DISPLAY

First, you should learn how to manage your display screen more effectively. To that end, DOS 4 users should select the Options choice from the File System action bar. The pull-down menu shown in Figure 5.1 appears, displaying three choices.

The first choice, Display options, enables you to specify which subset of files are to be displayed from each directory you select, and what order they are to be displayed in. You can ask DOS to display

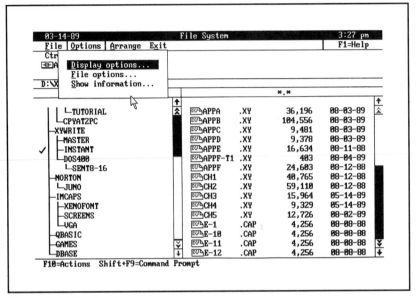

Figure 5.1: The Options menu

files according to any of the following:

- their base name

- their file extension

- their date of creation or last modification

- their byte size

- the order they are actually stored on your disk

This last choice is the only way in which file names are displayed in earlier versions of DOS.

Figure 5.2 shows the dialog box which appears after you select Display options from the Options pull-down menu. There are two primary portions to this dialog box. First, the Name area is at the upper-left portion of the window; your cursor is here by default when the window first appears. The *.* in the Name entry field represents DOS's method of identifying all files in the directory. You can change this *.* indicator to another expression if you want to restrict which file names are displayed.

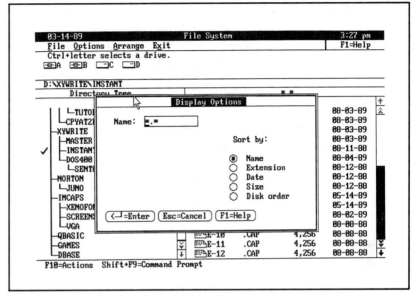

Figure 5.2: The Display Options dialog box

LIMITING THE FILE DISPLAY

Although the DOS 4 File area (or the DIR command in earlier versions) is useful for displaying the names of files, some practical problems require other techniques. For example, you might want to know if the current drive or the current directory contains a file called TRADEMRK.XY. If you simply scan the list of file names, or enter the DIR command in earlier DOS versions, you might be hard pressed to locate TRADEMRK.XY. This is especially true if you have hundreds of files to review, as you might on a hard disk. It might be better to narrow down the display to just the files that have the extension .XY. This would make it much easier to find the file you want.

DOS allows you a certain degree of ambiguity in asking for files. This means that you can ask for different groupings of files from the directory. The asterisk is used as a wild-card symbol to indicate your criteria. For example, if you want to list all files ending with the extension .XY, you enter *.XY in the entry field, as shown in Figure 5.3. To specify this restriction in earlier DOS versions, you enter the

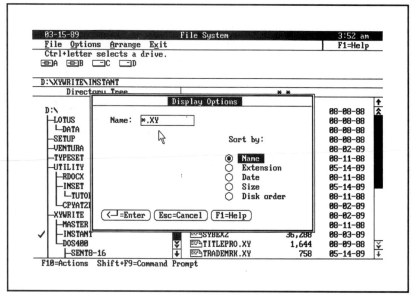

Figure 5.3: Restricting the display of file names

following DIR command:

    DIR *.XY

You can now easily determine if TRADEMRK.XY is in the current directory, because DOS has displayed a smaller number of files—only those that end in .XY.

You can use wild cards to select listings of files by their base names as well as by their extensions. Suppose you want to list all of the files on the current disk that started with the letters CH. Since you do not care what letters come after CH, you use asterisks for the rest of the base name and the extension. In DOS 4, simply enter CH*.* in the Name entry field. In earlier versions, you enter

    DIR CH*.*

DOS will then list all the files that begin with the letters CH.

Another way to search for names is to use the ? symbol. The question mark is a wild-card symbol for one character, as opposed to the asterisk symbol, which stands for a number of characters. For example, entering APP?.XY in the Display Options dialog box would result in a display containing APPA.XY, APPB.XY, APPC.XY, and APPD.XY. In other words, all four letter .XY file names that start with APP and have an .XY extension are displayed. Users of earlier versions would enter the command

DIR APP?.XY

to restrict the directory listing to those files that have four-character base names, with the first three characters being APP. Only files with an .XY extension are included.

The next file specifications combine the * and ? wild cards:

??S?????.*
??S*.*

Both of these specifications have the same effect: they tell DOS to list only those files that contain the letter S as the third character in their names. (Remember that a DOS file name is limited to a maximum of eight characters for its base plus an optional extension.)

What type of files does the following specification identify?

S???.COM

Put your DOS 4 Operating diskette in drive A, and try this specification to see which files meet it. See if your prediction is correct. Take a few moments now to experiment with both the * and the ? wild cards. Through practice you will be able to use wild cards to effectively manage your groups of files.

SPECIFYING THE SORTING ORDER FOR THE FILES

The Display Options dialog box provides you with another way to control the file listing with its column labeled Sort by (see Figure 5.3). DOS 4 offers you the ability to sort the directory file listing by one of the following:

- base name
- extension

- date

- size

- order on the disk

None of the first four options are available in earlier DOS versions, which automatically use the order the files are stored on the disk.

After limiting which file names are to be displayed, you can switch to the Sort by column. Remember to press the Tab key to switch over to this dialog-box entry area, then use the arrow keys to change the order of display. Or, you can simply point your mouse to one of the selection circles next to the ordering choices and press button one.

After you've specified any changes to the Name field and indicated which sorting order to follow, simply press Return, or click your mouse on the Enter at the bottom of the Display Options dialog box. For example, if you specified a sorting order based on Size for the .XY files, you would receive the screen seen in Figure 5.4.

Notice that the sizes are shown in descending order. If more files that meet the display specification exist than can be shown in the File area of the screen, the scroll bar becomes active and a slider box appears for you to use. Also notice that the active file specification is displayed just above

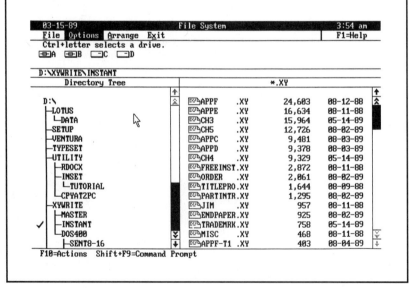

Figure 5.4: Ordering by file size

the File area. Up to now, this has been *.*, but in Figure 5.4 the current and more restrictive *.XY specification is shown.

If you select Date as the sorting order, DOS 4 displays files in reverse chronological order, beginning with the one that was worked on most recently. Choosing Extension sorts the files alphabetically by their extensions, which have zero to three letters. If you select Disk order, the files are listed in the order DOS actually stores them in its directory tables on the disk. (This is how they are displayed in earlier DOS versions.) Sorting by Name, which is the automatic default in DOS 4, alphabetizes the file names using the base names and extensions.

SETTING UP SPECIAL FILE-ACTIVITY OPTIONS

Selecting the File Options choice on the Options menu produces the screen seen in Figure 5.5. Notice that I've reset the file specification to *.* and sorted it by Date.

All three choices in this dialog box are available only to DOS 4 users. You select or deselect options in the standard way, with your mouse button one, or with the arrow keys and spacebar on your keyboard. In Figure 5.5 the first two options have been selected, while the third one is not currently activated.

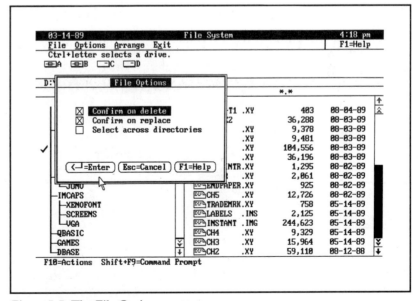

Figure 5.5: The File Options menu

Both deleting and replacing (discussed later in this chapter) can be dangerous activities. You can lose quite a bit of work by accidentally erasing a file from the disk or overwriting it with data from another file. When you select the first two options on the File Options menu, DOS 4 will automatically prompt you to confirm the selected file deletion or replacement before completing it.

If you issue a deletion request and the Confirm on delete option is set on, then DOS 4 displays a *confirmation box* on the screen. This box warns you that the file will be deleted and prompts you to confirm your request or withdraw it. Since deleting a file is no longer a single step operation, it requires a few extra seconds to do. However, these few extra seconds may be all you'll need to realize that you made a mistake; withdrawing the request is simple, requiring no time-consuming recovery operations. You'll see examples of confirmation boxes later in this chapter.

The Confirm on replace choice is necessary for moving and copying files, two operations that can also involve the deletion of files. As you'll see later in this chapter, you can ask that an existing file be copied from one place to another on your disk. You can also move a file from one place to another. In each operation, the new site for the file may have a file with the same name already. This existing file will be obliterated by the file you've explicitly asked DOS to place there. This confirmation setting protects you by displaying a confirmation box on your screen and prompting you to ask that the requested operation be completed.

The third choice on the File Options menu is very powerful. Selecting across directories means that you can choose files to be copied, erased, moved, etc., from any directory. Even though DOS 4 selection procedures are already more powerful than in earlier versions of DOS, they typically occur within the confines of a single directory. When Select across directories is turned on, however, you can choose files for an operation from as many different directories as you like.

Select across directories is an extraordinarily useful feature. With it, you can easily issue single commands which can act on files located in multiple places. For example, you can regroup miscellaneous files scattered among your disks into one directory. Merely turn on this selection switch, then move to the various directories to mark all desired files. Then with one single MOVE command, you assemble all the files in one directory.

DISPLAYING DETAILED DRIVE, DIRECTORY, AND FILE INFORMATION

The last choice on the Options menu is called Show information. When you select this Show information choice, your entire current system status is displayed (see Figure 5.6). The File area in Figure 5.6 shows only one selected file (the icon for C16.XY is in reverse video). In fact, the Show Information box displayed on the left side of the screen verifies that C16.XY is the current file. However, this information box also indicates that three other files on drive D, and none from drive C, have also been selected.

As you can see in Figure 5.6, the total size of the four selected files is 128,507 bytes. The current directory is MASTER, which contains 1,415,192 bytes spread among 74 files. The current drive is D, whose volume label is DRIVE D. Only about one-fourth of the disk's total space is unused and currently available; the other three-fourths is consumed by 24 directories and 882 files.

Selecting the Show information option is valuable whenever you want to learn more about how a particular disk is being used. It is particularly important when you need to quickly get a sense of the available space on a drive, and it is invaluable when you've made

Use the Show information choice when selecting files for transfer to a diskette to ensure that the total number of bytes to be transferred does not exceed the available space on the diskette.

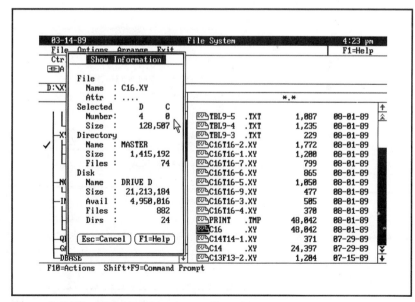

Figure 5.6: The Show information option

multiple file selections and need some visible feedback about how far along in your selection process you've gone.

Note that the four files selected in this example could conceivably be located within the MASTER directory, or, if Select across directories was on, they could be anywhere on your system.

TAKING ADVANTAGE OF FILE-DISPLAY ARRANGEMENTS

Another significant improvement of DOS 4 is the Arrange pull-down menu seen in Figure 5.7. You use this menu to make screen-arrangement choices.

The Single file list option is the default method, and it is the one you've been seeing so far in this chapter. Only one directory is highlighted at a time, and the files contained in that directory are shown on the right side of the screen. In Figure 5.7, the second choice, Multiple file list, has been previously selected. As a result, the screen is split in two, giving you the ability to simultaneously view and select files in two directories at once. Notice that when the Multiple file list

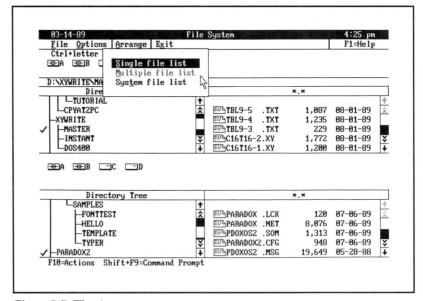

Figure 5.7: The Arrange menu

option is active, as in Figure 5.7, the Multiple file list choice is grayed. This is reasonable, since the only possibilities at this point are either to switch back to Single file list or to switch to the System file list, which is discussed below.

The MASTER directory from drive D has been chosen in the top Directory Tree section, and the files in that directory are shown on the right. Both the Directory Tree and the File area have active scroll bars, since the display window is now less than half of its former size.

In the bottom Directory Tree section, the PARADOX2 directory has been selected. Notice that just above the bottom Directory Tree is the familiar line of disk drive icons, which means that you can select a different drive for this second Directory Tree. In this way, you can view two directories that are situated on different drives. In each half of the screen, you simply select one of the drive icons, then move into the Directory Tree area to highlight the desired directory. Lastly, of course, you can move into each File area to select one or more files for a particular DOS operation.

The third choice on the Arrange menu is System file list, and the effect of this unique DOS 4 feature can be seen in Figure 5.8.

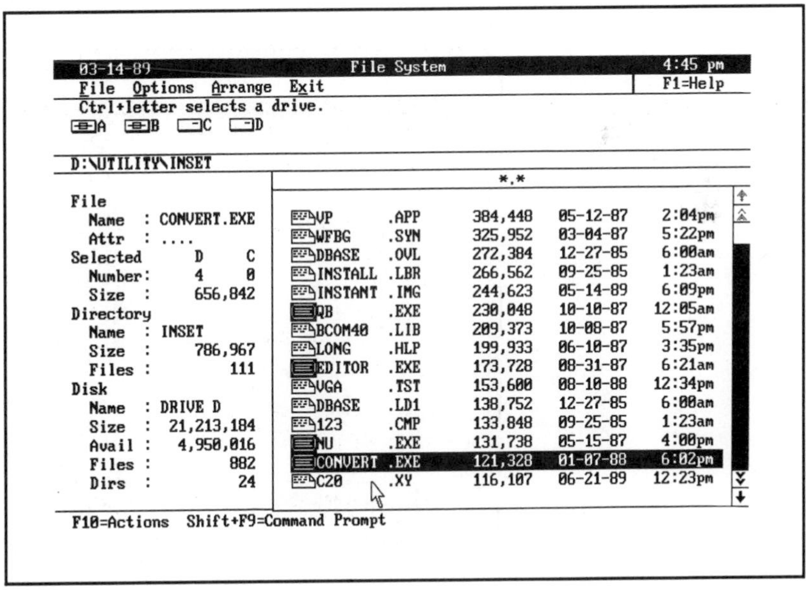

The Tab key switches the control focus from area to area on a DOS 4 screen even when the screen contains many separate window areas.

In each half of the screen, the independently selected directory is indicated by a check mark to the left of the directory's name.

Figure 5.8: Viewing a System file list

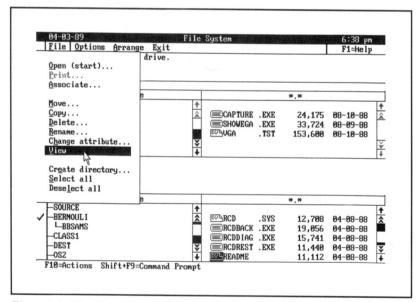 Use System file list (with Name ordering) to quickly find a file. Also use it to identify files with identical names that are located in different directories. The duplicate names will appear together.

In this special view of your files, you can scroll continuously through *all* files on your selected disk drive. Since all files are basically lumped together, you have no need for the Directory Tree portion of the display. Consequently, it is replaced by the Show Information display that you saw earlier. As you highlight and/or select different files, the information displayed on the left changes accordingly.

The files are all displayed according to the sorting order that is currently selected on the Options menu. You can see in Figure 5.8 that the files are now sorted by size, in descending order.

PERFORMING THE MAJOR FILE OPERATIONS

Figure 5.9 shows the primary pull-down menu that appears when you select File from the action bar. Depending on which files are selected when you pull down this menu, some of the file-operation choices may be grayed, indicating that they are currently unavailable. In this particular display, for example, a single text file

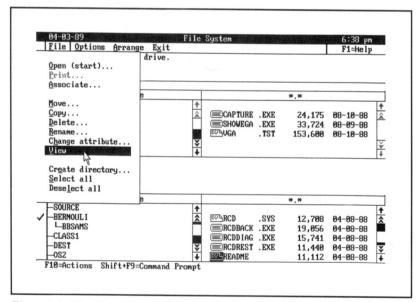

Figure 5.9: The File menu

(README) has been selected in the lower display window (directory BERNOULI) and all the file menu choices are available.

VIEWING THE CONTENTS OF A FILE

Selecting the View choice on the File menu results in Figure 5.10. If you had selected more than one file and then pulled down the File menu, the View choice would have been grayed. Only one file may be selected for viewing at a time.

As the notice at the top portion of the screen indicates, you can move through a large file by successively pressing the PgUp or PgDn key.

The TYPE command is the easiest way to read a file in earlier versions of DOS. To use it, enter

TYPE *FileName*

MOVING FILES
BETWEEN DRIVES AND DIRECTORIES

DOS 4 lets you move files between locations in a single operation. (Users of earlier versions must follow the steps explained in the sections following this one.) Coupled with DOS 4's ability to select one

You can only view one file at a time.

Remember to use the Ctrl-S key combination to stop and start the display of the contents of a file.

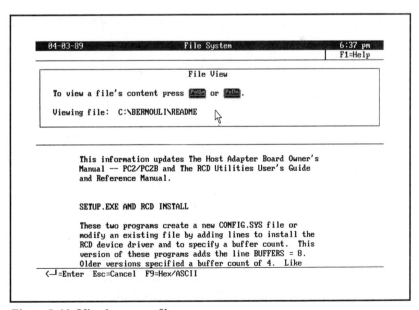

```
 04-03-89                    File System                   6:37 pm
                                                          F1=Help

                            File View

  To view a file's content press PgUp or PgDn.

  Viewing file:  C:\BERNOULI\README

  ────────────────────────────────────────────────────────────

        This information updates The Host Adapter Board Owner's
        Manual -- PC2/PC2B and The RCD Utilities User's Guide
        and Reference Manual.

        SETUP.EXE AND RCD INSTALL

        These two programs create a new CONFIG.SYS file or
        modify an existing file by adding lines to install the
        RCD device driver and to specify a buffer count.  This
        version of these programs adds the line BUFFERS = 8.
        Older versions specified a buffer count of 4.  Like
  ─────────────────────────────────────────────────────────────
  ◄─┘=Enter  Esc=Cancel  F9=Hex/ASCII
```

Figure 5.10: Viewing a text file

or more files from different directories, you now have a powerful and simple way to reorganize your disk. Building on what you've learned so far, take a look at Figure 5.11.

In this figure, you're using the split screen to verify the status of the disk before and after the move operation. Two files (C19F19-2.GRA and C19F19-1.GRA) are selected from the SCREENS directory in the top display window. The destination directory is checked in the bottom window.

Selecting the Move choice from the File menu brings up the dialog box shown in Figure 5.12. This dialog box is representative of what you'll see during many similar file operations. The currently selected file names are displayed for you in the From entry field. You cannot type in this field. You must select all desired files before invoking a particular file operation. If more names have been selected than are displayed in the From field, you can scroll the From field from left to right to see them.

The To field initially contains the root directory of the currently selected drive. You are expected to type in the desired destination directory. I typed in the name of the MASTER directory, specifying that it is located on the D drive in the XYWRITE directory. Once

You cannot enter text directly into a From field.

You can move files across drives by specifying the destination drive.

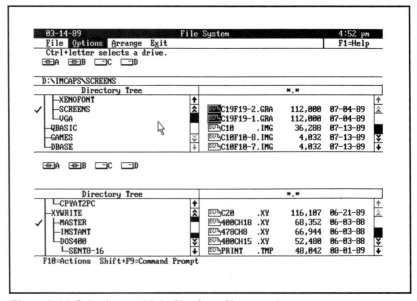

Figure 5.11: Selecting multiple files for a file operation

again, keyboard users press the Tab key to switch between the From and To fields. Pressing Return, or clicking Enter in the dialog box with your mouse, initiates the Move operation. The results can be seen in Figure 5.13.

As you can see, the listing of the SCREENS directory at the top no longer contains the two C19 files, while the MASTER directory at the bottom of the screen now displays them. In fact, during a Move operation, the selected files are first copied to the destination location (the To directory); after being copied, they are deleted from their original location (the From directory).

Each of these subordinate operations (Copy and Delete) can be performed individually. As you'll see below, selecting them from the File menu generates dialog boxes similar to the one you just saw for the Move operation.

COPYING FILES

Making copies of files is a very common and important operation. In this section I'll show you how to copy files for a variety of purposes.

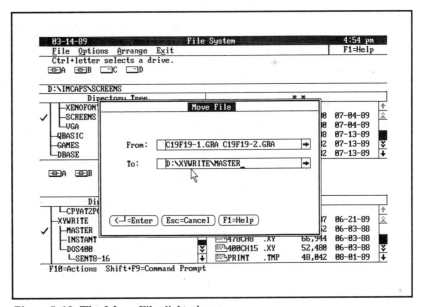

Figure 5.12: The Move File dialog box

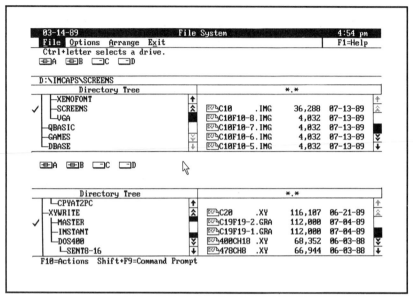

Figure 5.13: Results of a Move operation

COPYING FILES ACROSS DIRECTORIES Whether you create
a new directory (see the next chapter) or use an existing one, you can
use it to store files. The basic file-operation commands (COPY,
ERASE, RENAME, and so on) in all versions of DOS will work
with any directories. As you just saw with DOS 4's Move command,
the source files are simply the ones you select before choosing Move.
If you had previously activated Select across directories from the
Options pull-down menu, your source files could have been from
directories other than the current one.

The Copy command works in a similar way to the Move command. In Figure 5.14 three files had been selected in the TYPESET
directory (see the check mark next to it in Figure 5.14) when Copy
was chosen as the desired operation.

As noted earlier, you can see that the three file names do not completely fit into the From field. That's okay; DOS keeps track of all
selected names. To see the rest of the file names in the From field,
you would simply move your cursor or mouse pointer to it and use
the right arrow to scroll right.

Once again, you are expected to enter the destination directory. I've
typed D:\XYWRITE into the To field to indicate where these selected

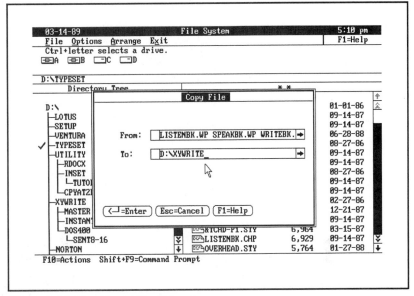

Figure 5.14: The Copy File dialog box

word-processing files are to be copied. Since this is a Copy operation, the three source files will still exist in the From directory after new copies of them have been added to the XYWRITE directory.

Earlier versions of DOS require you to use the COPY command at the command prompt. However, it is not as powerful at specifying multiple source files as DOS 4's Copy feature. For example, you might have to make three separate command entries to accomplish the previous Copy operation:

```
COPY LISTENBK.WP D:\XYWRITE
COPY SPEAKBK.WP D:\XYWRITE
COPY WRITEBK.WP D:\XYWRITE
```

Note that you can use wild cards to enter just one command. For example, you can enter

```
COPY *.WP D:\XYWRITE
```

but this will copy more than just the three desired files if there are other .WP files in the source directory. Naturally, if you bring up the command prompt in DOS 4, you can still enter these same commands. Chapter 22 shows the complete and detailed syntax available to users of earlier DOS versions.

At any command prompt, the general form of the COPY command is

COPY *OldFile(s) NewFile(s)*

The first field after the COPY command itself is the name of the file(s) to copy (the From field in DOS 4's Copy File dialog box). The second field contains the name of the new file(s) to be created, or the name of the directory into which the old files are copied. When the COPY command is done, both files (or sets of files) will contain the same information.

You will find many uses for the COPY command. You might want to make a secondary copy of a file you are working on, or you might want to make a backup copy of a file on another disk for precautionary reasons. You might want to make a replica of several files at the same time, perhaps from someone else's disk to yours. The following sections explore these and other uses of the COPY command.

MAKING SECONDARY COPIES   A second working copy of a file can be made easily with the COPY command. You can retain the original while working on and modifying the copy. To create the secondary copy, enter

COPY BUDGET.TXT BUDGET.BAK

In DOS 4, you would select BUDGET.TXT before choosing the Copy command (BUDGET.TXT would then appear in the From field), and then enter BUDGET.BAK in the To field. In DOS 4, you must precede the destination file name (e.g., BUDGET.BAK) with the names of the appropriate drive and directory. After the copying operation is completed, a listing of your current directory would show two files where there had previously been only one, since the new copy (BUDGET.BAK) would be created in the same directory as the source file (BUDGET.TXT).

MAKING BACKUP COPIES   With COPY, you can make a backup copy on another disk. Suppose that you want to copy your PHONES.DAT file to the diskette in drive B. You could do this by entering

COPY PHONES.DAT B:

DOS 4 users would, of course, first select PHONES.DAT for the From field and enter B: in the To field. Invoking the command creates a copy of PHONES.DAT on the diskette in drive B, using the same name. Put this backup diskette away to protect yourself against when your original file or disk is inadvertently lost.

MAKING MULTIPLE COPIES   Multiple files can be simultaneously copied by using wild cards with the COPY command. If you need to copy all files with an .SYM extension to the B drive, you enter

COPY *.SYM B:

DOS 4 users have to select all the .SYM files, which are then displayed in the From field when Copy is chosen from the File menu, and then enter B: in the To field. New users frequently ask if two copies of a file can be created on a disk by copying it twice to the same disk location. The answer is no; there is only one copy. DOS will not allow two files to have exactly the same name on the same diskette. If a file is copied to a diskette that already has a file with that name, DOS erases the old file and then copies the new file to that file name.

In earlier versions of DOS, you receive no warning of this. DOS 4 can prompt you to confirm that you want this overwriting to occur. Remember that this is controlled by the Confirm on replace choice on the File Options menu reached through the Options menu.

Thus, in earlier versions of DOS, you are much more likely to erase all the information contained in a file by accidentally copying another file of the same name to that disk. When this happens, the old file is *overwritten* by the new file, and you are *in big trouble!* However, since there can be different directories on a disk, you can have two matching file names on the same disk if the two files are located in different directories.

DOS 4 users should always have the Confirm on replace option set on to protect against accidentally overwriting files.

If you have an earlier version of DOS and you're not completely confident that a wild-card COPY command will copy over only the files you want, use a DIR command first with the same wild-card specification on the destination drive. Check the results of this directory listing to ensure that no unexpected duplicate file names will be accidentally overwritten. If you discover a file that you weren't trying to specify, either change its name or give a different name for the COPY command's destination file (COPY *OldFile* B:*NewName*).

Take a moment to practice with the COPY command. If a colleague or friend has some spreadsheet or database files or even games that you've been wanting to take a look at, now's the time. Of course, you should only make copies if there will be no copyright violation involved.

MAKING COMPLETE DISK COPIES   One of the most common uses of the COPY command is to copy all the files from one diskette to another. This is necessary because diskettes can become worn out from use over a long period of time. Copying the files to a new diskette will solve this problem. Also, keeping multiple copies of important files protects you against computer problems, human errors, or accidents such as fires.

You've already been introduced to the DISKCOPY command for making a complete copy of one disk to another disk. Why should you consider using a version of the COPY command? It's difference is subtle. DISKCOPY copies the original disk exactly, *retaining all noncontiguity*. The COPY command will usually rewrite files to contiguous tracks and sectors on the new disk, improving future disk-access speed. The net result is that the performance or responsiveness of all your programs may improve.

To copy all the files from the diskette in drive A to that in drive B, you should enter

COPY *.* B:

Of course, DOS 4 users must first select all files in the current directory before issuing a Copy request. Perhaps the most obvious way to obtain the equivalent of a *.* entry in the Copy File dialog box is to select each file individually. However, DOS 4 offers an easier way to do this; it is the Select all choice on the File menu. When

If the destination diskette (in drive B in this example) already contains some files, it may not have enough space for all its existing files as well as the new files from A. If this occurs, DOS will display the message "Insufficient Space." The best solution is to use a freshly formatted diskette or to erase files on the destination diskette before issuing the COPY command to ensure that there is enough space for the source diskette's files.

you choose this option, all icons in the displayed directory are switched to reverse video. You can then choose Copy from the File menu and enter B: in the To field of the Copy File dialog box to complete the copy operation. The File menu also provides a means of turning off Select all with its Deselect all choice.

SOME FINE POINTS ABOUT COPYING FILES　In most of the cases so far, the new file created in the destination directory received the same name as the original file. When necessary, you can direct DOS to assign new names as part of the COPY procedure. For example, the command

```
COPY *.DBF \BACKUP\*.BAK
```

will make backup copies of all .DBF (database) files in the current directory. The new copies will appear in the BACKUP directory with the extension .BAK.

By specifying *.DBF for your source files, you are assuming that all the .DBF files are on the current drive and in the current directory. Since you specify the destination directory (BACKUP) without a drive, you are assuming that it is on the current drive. For anything other than the default, you must specify either the drive, the directory, or both.

USING COPY TO CREATE, VIEW, AND PRINT FILES　There will be times when you will be working in DOS and need to save a few lines of text for later use. Usually you will want to continue with your work and won't want to waste time switching to a line-editing or word-processing program. You can keep working in DOS and create a text file by using DOS's COPY command. When you use COPY to create a file, you are actually copying information from the keyboard to a disk. I will first show you how to create a file with the COPY command at the command prompt, and then you'll see how this command can also be used to send the file's text to other devices, such as your monitor and printer.

When you specify CON as the source in the COPY command, you can use the keyboard to enter text into a disk file. CON stands for console, which comprises the keyboard and monitor.

The colon (:) after a device name (as in CON:) is not strictly necessary, since DOS will figure out what you mean. However, it's good form to enter the colon, if only for consistency with the way you enter drive identifiers (such as A: and C:).

To do this, enter the following command:

COPY CON: TEXT1.DAT

The cursor moves to a new line in which nothing else—not even the DOS prompt—appears. This indicates that you are no longer at the system level. DOS will now allow you to enter text directly from the keyboard, and anything that you type will eventually be stored in the file TEXT1.DAT. For example, you could enter

This is an example of keyboard entry into a text file.

or any other text lines, pressing Return after each line. You would then need to enter the character that DOS uses to mark the end of a file, a Ctrl-Z, which is sometimes shown as ^Z. You obtain this unusual character by holding down the Ctrl key and pressing the letter Z. The symbol ^Z will then appear on the screen.

To complete the file, press Return. The disk drive will spin and all the lines of text that you typed at the keyboard will be saved as a file. This is a convenient method for creating small text files quickly. For large files you use a line editor (like EDLIN, which is contained in your DOS software and is described in Chapter 7) or a word processor (which offers much more in the way of text manipulation).

To see the data, you can simply reverse the items in the COPY command and enter

COPY TEXT1.DAT CON:

followed by Return. The destination device CON now stands for the monitor. DOS 4 users can use the View choice on the File menu to display the contents of any text file like this. The text will be displayed just as it was typed in.

You can also print the file with the COPY command. If you want to have a hard copy of the file for reference, enter the following command:

COPY TEXT1.DAT LPT1:

Using LPT1 as the destination tells DOS to send the file to your printer. It will then be printed, and you can continue working at the command prompt.

COMBINING FILE COPIES   COPY can also be used at a command prompt to join two or more files together, which allows you to gather up small data files into a single large file. This is useful when you have created several small documents, all of which need to be word processed. To see how this is done, you could enter

COPY CON: TEXT2.DAT

then enter

This is additional text that is stored in another text file
^Z

pressing Return after each line. You would then use the COPY command to join the TEXT1.DAT and TEXT2.DAT files. This is sometimes called *concatenation*. The general form of the command is the following:

COPY FirstFile + SecondFile + etc. CombinationFile

The + sign is used to indicate the joining of text from two or more files. If you want to combine two existing files like TEXT1.DAT and TEXT2.DAT, you enter the following command:

COPY TEXT1.DAT + TEXT2.DAT COMBO.DAT

To see the results, you enter

COPY COMBO.DAT CON:

The destination file, COMBO.DAT, would contain all the text lines from both of the two source files:

This is an example of keyboard entry into a text file.
This is additional text that is stored in another text file.

You can even use the wild-card characters in your COPY commands to join text files. For example, if you want to join together all the .DAT files into one text file, you enter

COPY *.DAT ALL.TXT

This form is simpler than typing "*file1* + *file2* + *file3* + ..."; however, it is only quicker when all the files to be joined have the same extension. This is a good example of how you can save time and effort by intelligently giving similar files the same extensions.

REMOVING AND RENAMING FILES

There are just a few more file-operation commands that you should know about to aid your activities at this point. Of course, many other commands exist, but you'll only need them in more advanced situations, which are covered later in this book. You should now become comfortable with deleting and renaming files.

DELETING FILES AND DIRECTORIES

Suppose you had copied LISTENBK.WP, SPEAKBK.WP, and WRITEBK.WP (three files used in an earlier section of this chapter) from TYPESET to XYWRITE for some temporary purposes. After editing these copies, you may reasonably decide to erase them. After all, the original files still remain untouched in the TYPESET directory.

Select the three files from the XYWRITE directory, then issue the Delete command from the File menu. This brings up the dialog box seen in Figure 5.15. You must now explicitly press Return or select Enter with the mouse to ask DOS 4 to complete the deletion request.

All DOS users can erase files from a command prompt by simply specifying the file(s) to be deleted. For example,

ERASE LISTENBK.WP

would immediately erase LISTENBK.WP from your disk (provided that you were in the same directory as LISTENBK.WP). However, DOS 4 users have a prompting switch they can activate at the command prompt. This /P switch gives you a chance to individually confirm or withdraw your deletion request for each file. For example,

ERASE *.WP /P

causes DOS 4 to display the name of each file in the current directory with a .WP extension. After each name is displayed, you will be

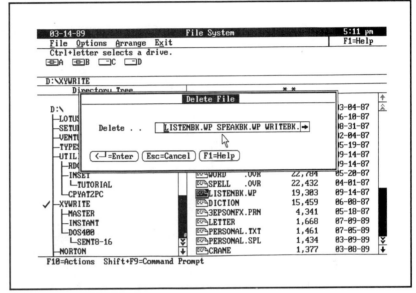

Figure 5.15: The Delete File dialog box

prompted to confirm what you want to do with that file:

LISTENBK.WP,   Delete (Y/N)?

If you originally requested the deletion from the DOS shell (and earlier selected Confirm on delete from the File Options menu), you will receive a Delete File confirmation box, which displays the name of the file to be deleted and asks you to select one of two options:

1. Skip this file and continue
2. Delete this file

With this feature, you could conceivably select all the files in a directory and then delete just the particular files (three in Figure 5.15) that you no longer need. This box also displays how many files meet the criteria and which file will be affected next. Figure 5.16 shows an example of a Delete File confirmation box.

In Figure 5.16, a series of files in the TYPESET directory with the extension .CHP were selected, each of which also has an ampersand (&) as the first character in its name. There are 19 of these files, and

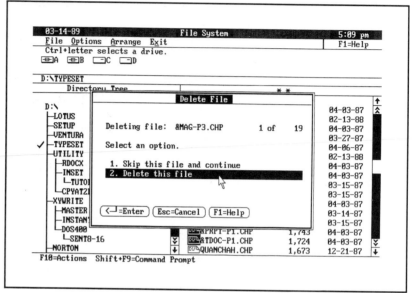

Figure 5.16: The Delete File confirmation box

each one of them will require explicit confirmation of the deletion request.

The most common use for the ERASE command is to clean up disks that have been in use for a while. Old versions of data files often proliferate; early copies of memos and other word-processed documents always seem to expand to fill any available space on your disk. If you have a disk that fits this description, now is a good time to use ERASE and clean it up.

You cannot delete (remove) a directory that still contains files.

If you try to erase all files in a directory by selecting the directory and then Delete in DOS 4, you will receive the confirmation box shown in Figure 5.17. Choice 2 will not work, however, because DOS will not let you delete a directory that contains any files. If you want to remove the directory itself, you must erase or move all of its files and then come back to this box.

If you accidentally choose Delete without having selected any files, you will also receive this confirmation box. In this case, you didn't intend to delete an entire directory, and you would select choice 1, Do not delete this directory.

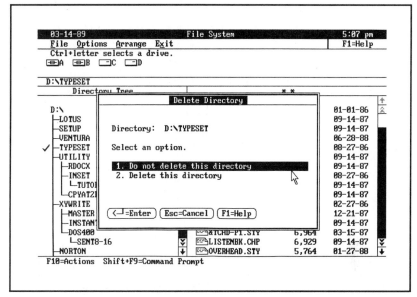

Figure 5.17: The Delete Directory confirmation box

The equivalent DOS 3.3 command for deleting an entire directory is the RMDIR, or RD, command. You always have to specify the directory name. In this case, you would enter

RD TYPESET

Of course, regardless of which DOS version you are using, you cannot delete a directory that still contains files. Every version of DOS will prompt you with an error message when it receives your request to delete a directory that is not empty.

CHANGING THE NAME OF A FILE   You can change the name of a file without affecting its contents. There may be times when you want to change some file names so that you can use the ? or * wild card to manage blocks of files.

Remember that you must select one or more files before choosing an operation for them from the File menu. After selecting the three files in the JUNO directory with a Select all command, I chose the

Rename option. As Figure 5.18 demonstrates, whenever a series of files is selected, a file-operation dialog box will display each one in turn, showing its place in the series and the total number of files selected. In the Rename File dialog box, you would enter a new file name for each of the three files.

DOS 4 automatically submits three RENAME commands when you enter the three new file names. It is actually DOS's standard RENAME command that operates behind the scenes. You would have to submit three separate RENAME commands yourself to rename each individual file in earlier DOS versions. The general form of this command is

RENAME *OldName NewName*

The first file name is the old name you want to change. The file name that follows is the new name the file will receive.

In this example, entering

RENAME CONFIG.JJJ CONFIG.BAK

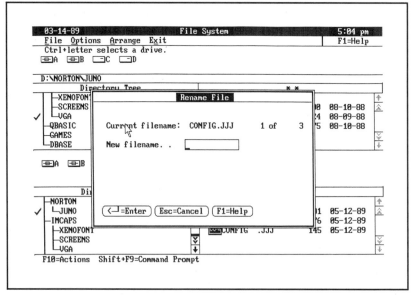

Figure 5.18: The Rename File dialog box

You can only use the RENAME command for renaming files on a single disk drive. You *cannot* use the RENAME command to simultaneously copy a file from one disk to another while renaming it—use the COPY command to do that particular chore. RENAME only changes the name of the file, whereas COPY creates an entirely new file. With COPY, you begin with one file and end up with two; with RENAME, you begin with one file and end up with the same file.

changes the first file, CONFIG.JJJ, to CONFIG.BAK.

You can also use the * and ? wild cards with the RENAME command. For example, if you want to change all files that have an extension of .CMD to files that end in .PRG, you can do so by entering the following command at the command prompt:

RENAME *.CMD *.PRG

This sort of operation is sometimes required when you switch from one system to another, or when a software manufacturer significantly changes its naming conventions.

The RENAME command also offers a limited degree of protection. You may not be the only person with access to your computer and disks. In that case, you may want to safeguard some of your data files. You can rename an obvious file like BUDGET.WK1 to TEMP.NDX, a clearly misleading name. Prying eyes are not as likely to notice the renamed file.

Take a moment now to try this renaming technique on any files for which you'd like to restrict access. But be careful: first, don't forget the new file name you choose; second, don't select a dispensable name (like TEMP.NDX) if anyone else using your disk is at all likely to delete files.

SHUTTING DOWN THE DOS 4 FILE SYSTEM ACCESS

The final pull-down menu in the File System is the Exit menu shown in Figure 5.19. You will typically select the Exit File System choice only when you are done manipulating all your files and directories. At that point, the File System screen will disappear and the Start Programs screen will reappear. You can quickly obtain the same result by simply pressing F3.

Press Escape or select the Resume File System choice if you reached this Exit menu in error, or if you changed your mind.

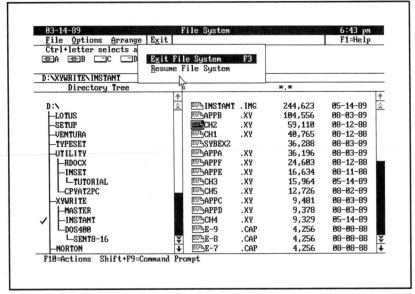

Figure 5.19: The Exit menu

SUMMARY

In this chapter, you have examined the pull-down menus of DOS 4's File System. You learned the following things:

- The Display options choice enables you to specify which files will be displayed for each directory. It also allows you to indicate a sorting order for the file entries.

- The File options choice enables you to have a confirmation box displayed before you delete or replace files. This is a new protection mechanism available only in DOS 4.

- Selecting across directories is another powerful new feature in DOS 4. You can select any number of files from any number of directories if the Select across directories choice is set on. Then you can later choose any of the file-operation commands to act on those files. In earlier versions of DOS, you can only use the * and ? wild-card characters to select multiple files for file operations.

- DOS 4's Show information option displays system-wide summary data, including byte totals for the drive, directory, and selected files.

- You can request DOS 4 to display file names in several screen arrangements, including a single-directory display, a split-screen display of two directories, and a system-wide display that lists all file names on a drive, cutting across directory distinctions.

- Files can be easily moved into and among various disk directories with the COPY command. The COPY capability in DOS is one of its most powerful features, spanning many standard application needs.

- DOS 4 offers a combined COPY and ERASE command called Move on the File menu.

- The RD (Remove Directory) command removes empty directories from your hierarchical structure. DOS 4 users can use the Delete choice on the File menu to delete either files or directories. However, DOS will only delete a directory if there are no other directories or files of any sort remaining in it.

- Files can be easily typed out on your console with the TYPE command, or with DOS 4's View option on the File menu.

- Any file can be quickly renamed on its drive by using the Rename option on the File menu or the RENAME command.

In the next chapter, you will continue your study of DOS 4's File System, particularly in the context of selecting, grouping, and running DOS commands and application programs on your hard disk.

RUNNING PROGRAMS ON A HARD DISK

CHAPTER 6

RUNNING PROGRAMS ON A HARD DISK IS MUCH more convenient than using diskettes, but to take full advantage of a hard disk you must learn how to organize it. I'll show you how to arrange and manage your disk so that you can simplify your work and get the most out of your programs.

Running programs and setting up DOS 4 program groups is the major subject of this chapter. You'll use the appropriate directory commands to set up your hard disk for three common and very popular types of programs: a word processor, a spreadsheet, and a database-management system. You'll also discover how to add selected DOS commands as well as your own utility and application programs to DOS 4's menus. With the techniques you learn here, you will be able to set up your hard disk for any application software.

THE BASICS OF THE DIRECTORY STRUCTURE

This chapter will give you the complete understanding of the disk and directory structure that you need to run your application programs and utilities. You'll also learn that many program files need to navigate the directory structure in order to access the relevant files, and I'll show you how to make this work.

CREATING AND DELETING DIRECTORIES

It is always a good idea to create a separate directory for files that are related to one another. Having similar and related files together makes it easier and faster to use them.

Selecting the Create directory choice on the File menu in DOS 4's File System tells DOS to make a new directory. Figure 6.1 shows the dialog box that appears when you choose this menu option. Notice that in the Directory Tree window behind this dialog box the check mark is beside the name LOTUS, indicating that this is the current directory.

All you are required to do at this point is to type in a new name for the directory that you have asked DOS to create. In this example, I typed in DATA and pressed Return. The immediate result is seen in Figure 6.2.

The graphic Directory Tree is instantly updated to show drive D's added directory. You can now do what you like with the new directory, treating it like any other one on your disk. If you try to do anything with it before you actually transfer some files into it, you'll receive the message that there are "No files in selected directory."

In earlier versions of DOS, you can only create a directory by using the MKDIR (or MD) command. For instance, to create the same DATA directory in DOS 3.3, you would have to submit the command

MD DATA

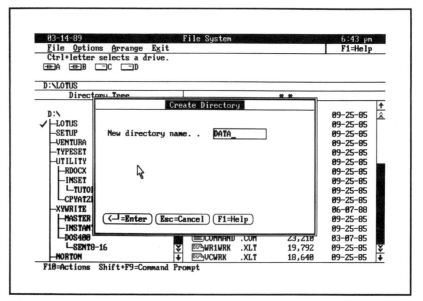

Figure 6.1: The Create Directory dialog box

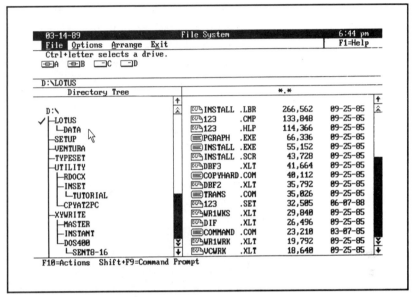

```
┌──────────────────────────────────────────────────────────────────────┐
│ 03-14-89                    File System                        6:44 pm │
│  File  Options  Arrange  Exit                                │ F1=Help │
│ Ctrl+letter selects a drive.                                           │
│ [═]A   [═]B   [─]C   [─]D                                               │
│ ──────────────────────────────────────────────────────────────────────│
│ D:\LOTUS                                                               │
│    Directory Tree                                      *.*            ↑ │
│                                  ┌─┐                                 ┌─┐│
│    D:\                           ↑ │  INSTALL .LBR    266,562 09-25-85 ↑│
│  ✓ ├─LOTUS                         │  123     .CMP    133,848 09-25-85  │
│    │  └─DATA                       │  123     .HLP    114,366 09-25-85  │
│    ├─SETUP              ▯          │  PGRAPH  .EXE     66,336 09-25-85  │
│    ├─VENTURA                       │  INSTALL .EXE     55,152 09-25-85  │
│    ├─TYPESET                       │  INSTALL .SCR     43,728 09-25-85  │
│    ├─UTILITY                       │  DBF3    .XLT     41,664 09-25-85  │
│    │  ├─RDOCX                      │  COPYHARD.COM     40,112 09-25-85  │
│    │  ├─INSET                      │  DBF2    .XLT     35,792 09-25-85  │
│    │  │  └─TUTORIAL                │  TRANS   .COM     35,026 09-25-85  │
│    │  └─CPYAT2PC                   │  123     .SET     32,505 06-07-88  │
│    ├─XYWRITE                       │  WR1WKS  .XLT     29,840 09-25-85  │
│    │  ├─MASTER                     │  DIF     .XLT     26,496 09-25-85  │
│    │  ├─INSTANT                    │  COMMAND .COM     23,210 03-07-85  │
│    │  └─DOS400                   ⊻ │  WR1WRK  .XLT     19,792 09-25-85 ⊻│
│    │     └─SENT8-16              ↓ │  VCWRK   .XLT     18,640 09-25-85 ↓│
│ F10=Actions  Shift+F9=Command Prompt                                   │
└──────────────────────────────────────────────────────────────────────┘
```

Figure 6.2: The Directory Tree is immediately updated.

This command creates the DATA directory in your current directory, which should be the LOTUS directory. If it is not, you must prefix the new directory's name in the MD command as shown here:

> MD \LOTUS\DATA

Furthermore, if the current drive is not the one containing the LOTUS directory, then you must even preface this expression with the drive identifier:

> MD D:\LOTUS\DATA

Since you can always see the current directory and drive in DOS 4's graphic shell, managing your directories in DOS 4 is much easier to do.

DELETING DIRECTORIES As you saw in Chapter 5, if you want to delete a directory from a disk, you must first remove all its files. When the directory is empty, select it, and then select Delete from the File menu. If you had previously selected Confirm on delete from the

Options menu, the confirmation box shown in Figure 5.17 would now come up and wait for your next action. Select choice 2. If you had not previously selected Confirm on delete, the current directory will be removed immediately after you select Delete from the File menu.

UNDERSTANDING PATHS

The combination of a prefix and the destination directory or file, as in

D:\LOTUS\DATA

is called a *path name*. DOS attaches path names to subdirectories and files so that it can keep track of them. A *path* is a linked series of directories that leads to a subdirectory or file. For example, in order to get to the DATA directory, you must first pass through the LOTUS directory. This requirement to follow a path to any particular directory can be compared to climbing a tree. To get to any particular branch you have to first climb past the larger branches leading to it. Any branch on the tree is analogous to a DOS directory or subdirectory.

Each branch of a tree can have new branches, or subdirectories, growing from it. Just as each branch may also have fruit or leaves on it, each subdirectory may have program or data files stored in it.

In DOS 4, the full path name to the files in the current directory is always displayed just above the Directory Tree portion of the screen. Thus, in Figure 6.2 every file in the LOTUS directory has a path-name prefix of D:\LOTUS. Similarly, each file later placed in the new DATA directory would have a prefix of D:\LOTUS\DATA. If this is not totally clear, take a moment to look back at the screen examples in the previous chapter. Nearly all of them illustrate what path names are.

Most of the files used in the commands in Chapter 5 are two levels deep in the directory structure. For example, in Figure 5.3 you can find the file TRADEMRK.XY in D:\XYWRITE\INSTANT. This path-name prefix indicates that the file is actually in a directory called INSTANT, which in turn is in another directory called XYWRITE, which in turn is in the root directory of drive D.

The path system in DOS subdirectories allows you to create increasingly complex but organized groupings. By taking advantage of this system, you can easily manage several levels of subdirectories.

VIEWING THE STRUCTURE

Naturally, the Directory Tree graphic display of DOS 4 provides you with a clear visual representation of a disk's directory structure. If you are at the command prompt, however, in any version of DOS, you can use the TREE command to get a summary of the directories and subdirectories on a disk.

TREE is an *external* command. This means that it will not work in every circumstance. TREE is really a program file provided with DOS. This file, TREE.COM, must be present on one of the disks in your system, or you cannot execute the TREE command. If your system is installed on a hard disk, then TREE.COM must be in an accessible directory. The usual place for this and other DOS utilities is the DOS directory, located in the root.

Entering

TREE

will list the volume label (and serial number in DOS 4) of the disk in the current default drive as well as all its directories and any subdirectories. You can specify a drive parameter if you want to see the tree structure of another drive without changing the current default drive. For example, entering

TREE B:

will display information about all the directories on the diskette in drive B.

In DOS 4, TREE produces a completely graphic rendition of the disk's structure, like the Directory Tree seen in the File System screens. Earlier versions of DOS only show a text screen that lists the directory names, and, if requested by switch setting, the file names contained in those directories.

In all DOS versions, you can get a more detailed tree display that lists the specific files in each subdirectory by entering

TREE/F

It's sometimes difficult to view an entire TREE listing on your monitor, because it is usually longer than one screen. If you have a printer, you can get a printed copy of the screen display by entering

A:TREE /F > PRN

This command uses a special feature called *redirection* (see Chapter 13).

SETTING UP FOR THE STANDARD SOFTWARE APPLICATIONS

Now that you know how to make directories and view your directory structure, I'll show you how to set up your hard disk for software applications. As an example, I'll use the three most common types of business-oriented software, which are word processors, spreadsheets, and database-management systems. For convenience, I will place the three sample applications in directories on the C drive.

Each of the examples in this section are purposely general. They may be different from your particular software package. However, the following setups represent three different styles. The style shown under the word-processing example, for instance, may be appropriate for your spreadsheet software. Or vice versa. You should simply strive to understand the demonstrated options. Then you can select the one best suited to your application and system.

LOADING YOUR WORD PROCESSOR ONTO THE HARD DISK

In this section, you'll set up your hard disk to store all your word-processing files in a particular directory. To do this, you must have a copy of the program already on a floppy diskette. I am assuming that your word processor is not copy-protected. If it is, you'll need to follow the special instructions in its user's manual.

Although your word processor may be different from the example given here, the process of setting up your hard disk will be similar. You'll still need to take the following steps:

1. Create a subdirectory for the word processor on your hard disk.

DOS 4 users only need to highlight the desired disk structure location of the new directory. Then, select the Create directory choice on the File menu.

Users of earlier versions of DOS must use the MD command to create the new directory. For example,

MD \WP

2. Copy the word-processing files from the floppy diskette(s) to the subdirectory you just created.

Sometimes, your new word-processing program diskette will have a prewritten installation program to do all of the required steps. Use it. You can always redo things in your own way later, after you've worked with your directory structure. In either case, the next step that either you or the installation program should follow is to place the word-processing master diskette in drive A and copy it to your hard disk.

To do this, DOS 4 users need to log onto the A drive from the File System screen, choose Select all from the File menu, and then choose Copy.

Users of earlier versions of DOS use the COPY command with the following wild cards to copy all the files:

COPY A:*.* C:\WP

During the copying process, DOS lists the names of the files as they are copied. If your word processor is on more than one diskette, copy each diskette.

3. Change the default directory to the word-processing directory, then run the program.

Naturally, DOS 4 users only need to highlight the new WP directory, then select and run the word-processing main program. Users of earlier versions of DOS must change the default directory to WP and type the name of the main program. To do so, you enter

CD \WP

Then enter the base name of the program itself. For example, Word-Star users enter

WS

while WordPerfect users enter

WP

The opening screen of your word processor will appear. Now you can proceed to create and edit documents, referring to your word processor's user's manual as needed.

LOADING YOUR SPREADSHEET PROGRAM ONTO THE HARD DISK

Loading a popular spreadsheet like Lotus 1-2-3 onto a hard disk is not much different from working with a word processor like Word-Star or WordPerfect. Although the procedure will be similar if you have a different spreadsheet program, the example presented here uses 1-2-3 Version 2 because it contains a copy-protection mechanism (unlike the word-processing example of the previous section). This special situation requires some discussion.

All the information necessary to run copy-protected programs cannot be directly transferred to the hard disk. For example, if you simply copy all the Lotus files to the hard disk, 1-2-3 still needs to access the original floppy diskette in order to run.

The most recent versions of many copy-protected programs, including 1-2-3, allow you to install the software on the hard disk permanently. Even though a program is copy protected, it is still worthwhile to copy the files to the hard disk for two reasons:

- The program will load more quickly.
- All of the Lotus 1-2-3 system files can be placed in a single subdirectory, thus requiring no future juggling of all the Lotus diskettes.

MAKING SUBDIRECTORIES FOR PROGRAMS   Most newer software packages like 1-2-3 allow you to store work and access files in different directories. With earlier and still popular versions of programs like WordStar, all of the data files you create must occupy the same subdirectory as the program.

1-2-3 can switch from one data subdirectory to another while the program is operating. This allows you to group together related

1-2-3 program files, separating them from worksheet files. As you'll soon see, you can use the DOS directory structure more effectively by maintaining directories for groups of worksheets, separate from the main LOTUS directory of program files.

The first step is to create a directory for all of the Lotus system files. DOS 4 users use the Create directory choice on the File menu to create a LOTUS directory. Users of earlier versions of DOS must enter

    MD \LOTUS

at the command prompt. Then copy the programs in the Lotus package to that directory. DOS 4 users can select drive A at the File System screen, then select all files on the diskette in drive A, and copy them to the new LOTUS directory on the hard disk. Users of earlier versions of DOS must enter

    COPY A:*.* C:\LOTUS

at the command prompt. These steps must naturally be performed for all diskettes in your spreadsheet software package. Now that the 1-2-3 files have been copied, you can run the program.

To do this, DOS 4 users highlight the LOTUS directory, then select the main LOTUS.EXE program, and choose Start from the File menu. Users of earlier DOS versions first change the default directory to the LOTUS directory and then enter the name of the main program by using the following commands:

    CD \LOTUS
    LOTUS

When LOTUS begins, it prompts you with a menu of LOTUS system programs. If you select the main 1-2-3 spreadsheet program and have not yet installed it permanently according to the manufacturer's instructions, 1-2-3 will check the copy-protection scheme on the diskette in drive A. Once the copy-protection scheme has been checked, you no longer need to have the floppy diskette in drive A.

CONFIGURING PROGRAMS   When you copy a program to a hard disk from a floppy diskette, the program is not necessarily *configured*. Configuration is the setup process that gives the program all of the information unique to your system, such as what type of screen display and printer are being used. In addition, some programs require you to specify the default data drive and directory. 1-2-3 is one of those programs.

Just because the program was copied to the hard disk, it does not follow that 1-2-3 knows what drive you want to use for data. When 1-2-3 is copied to a hard-disk drive, it will by default attempt to store data on drive B. To change the default disk and directory for any program like this, there is usually some command in the software that can be invoked. You should refer to your software's users' guide to discover it. In 1-2-3, it is the /WGDD command.

CREATING MULTIPLE SUBDIRECTORIES FOR YOUR DATA FILES   Since 1-2-3 allows you to change the subdirectory used to store program data, you can create a separate directory for your spreadsheet files. In fact, if you work in an office where more than one person uses the computer, each person's work can be stored in a different subdirectory. You can also store work related to different projects in separate subdirectories if that suits your office better.

To see how this works, you must return to DOS. Since subdirectories are organized in a hierarchical order, LOTUS, which is a subdirectory of the root, can also have subdirectories of its own.

Suppose that in your office, three people, Sue, Harry, and Alice, will be working with 1-2-3. To keep their work from getting confused, it might be useful to separate and store their files into unique subdirectories. In DOS 4, you simply select LOTUS from the Directory Tree window, then run the Create directory command three times, specifying the name for the subdirectory each time. In a command-prompt DOS version, you create individual directories for each of these people by entering the following commands:

```
MD \LOTUS\SUE
MD \LOTUS\HARRY
MD \LOTUS\ALICE
```

Your hard disk will then be structured as shown in Figure 6.3. Figure 6.4 shows another way to visualize the directory structure.

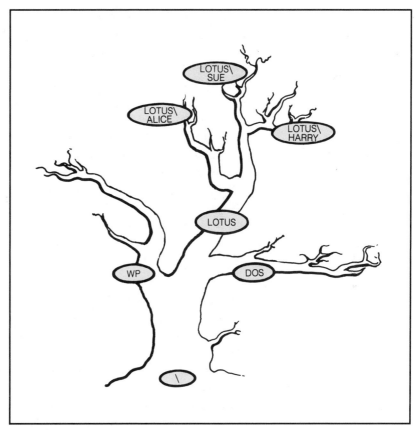

Figure 6.3: DOS directory structure (tree view)

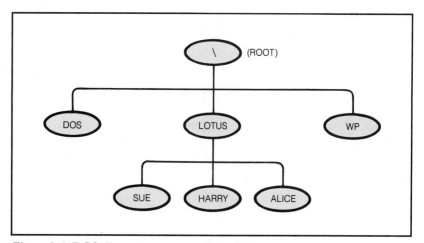

Figure 6.4: DOS directory structure (line view)

RUNNING PROGRAMS IN SUBDIRECTORIES   At this point you have set up a directory that contains the main program files and subdirectories for its data files (you could use this setup for your word processor as well.) To run the program, you would change the current directory to LOTUS, start the program, and then tell the program in which subdirectory you wish it to work. This type of request from within a program varies with each program, but the concept remains the same.

In 1-2-3, the command to change default subdirectories is the File Directory command (/FD). The program will first display the current directory setting. Because you started 1-2-3 when you were in the main LOTUS directory, 1-2-3 automatically sets the default to C:\LOTUS. To change directories, you would enter the full path name of the subdirectory that you want to use. If you were Alice, for instance, you would specify to 1-2-3 that you want it to use your directory. Including the drive as well, you would submit the following at the 1-2-3 entry line:

> C:\LOTUS\ALICE

All files would then be saved in or retrieved from the subdirectory LOTUS\ALICE. In this way, Alice can have her work separated from Harry's and Sue's. If Harry or Sue later logged on, they could go through the same sequence to ensure that they had access to the files in their respective subdirectories.

> Because every program has different assumptions about default directories, you may at times try to retrieve a file and not find it. Check the default directory. The solution is often as easy as resetting it to the directory that you regularly use for file work.

RUNNING YOUR DATABASE-MANAGEMENT SYSTEM

As a last example, let's create a directory for a DBMS (database-management system). Suppose you intend to use a package like dBASE IV for several purposes. You may plan to write your own customized accounting program to manage your entire inventory system; you may even plan to manage your company's personnel records with the software.

You can use DOS's now familiar directory creation commands to create a DBMS directory containing three subdirectories (ACCOUNTS, INVNTORY, and PRSONNEL). The results are shown in Figure 6.5. As you can see, you've set up a directory structure that is organized by application purpose rather than by user, as

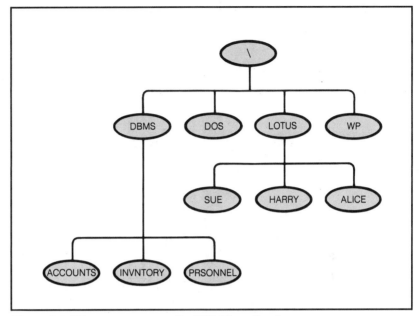

Figure 6.5: Directory structure for DBMS applications

you did with LOTUS in the previous example. It's always up to you to decide on the grouping of your files.

Of course, now you probably want to run your DBMS program. If you are a dBASE IV user, you could simply change the current directory to DBMS, then start the dBASE program. The next section describes this and other methods of running programs.

RUNNING PROGRAMS FROM THE FILE SYSTEM

There are many ways to initiate a program under DOS, regardless of which DOS version you are using. DOS 4 also provides you with a few extra methods. In this chapter, I demonstrate all of the possibilities; you can select the ones that will work best for you. I use DOS's CHKDSK program in my first examples, since it is a utility that will come in handy when you set up and work with your directory structure.

RUNNING COMMANDS
AND UTILITIES DIRECTLY

As you know, you can start up a program by simply typing its name at the command prompt. For example, entering

CHKDSK

will initiate DOS's CHKDSK program if it is in the current directory, or if you had previously used the PATH command to specify its location. (PATH commands are discussed later in this chapter.)

Even if you have not set up a PATH command, you can still run a program located in another directory or on another disk by prefixing the file name with a complete path name and drive identifier. For example, if you enter

D:\DOS400\CHKDSK A:

DOS will find the CHKDSK program in drive D's DOS400 directory, then run it for the diskette in drive A. The normal output of the CHKDSK is a full-screen display, as seen in Figure 6.6. When you

```
When ready to return to the DOS Shell, type EXIT then press enter.

IBM DOS Version 4.00
        (C)Copyright International Business Machines Corp 1981, 1988
        (C)Copyright Microsoft Corp 1981-1986

C:\DOS400>CHKDSK A:

Volume MASTERDOS4   created 03-16-1989 7:43a

   1213952 bytes total disk space
   1213952 bytes available on disk

       512 bytes in each allocation unit
      2371 total allocation units on disk
      2371 available allocation units on disk

    655360 total bytes memory
    519312 bytes free

C:\DOS400>_
```

Figure 6.6: CHKDSK output for a diskette in drive A

use the full path name for a program, it doesn't matter what directory you are in.

DOS 4's File System provides you with three additional ways to initiate the CHKDSK program. All three methods require that the program's location, the DOS400 directory, be selected in the Directory Tree.

First, you can highlight CHKDSK.COM in the File area with your keyboard using the Tab and arrow keys. You would then press Return to initiate the program. Second, you can use your mouse to run CHKDSK by simply double clicking on the line containing the name CHKDSK.COM. Lastly, you can select CHKDSK.COM with either the mouse (single click) or the keyboard (Tab and spacebar). Then you would choose File from the action bar (see Figure 6.7). Since the CHKDSK.COM program is already selected, it will be run if you simply choose Open (start) from the File menu.

DOS 4 displays a dialog box when you initiate a program from the File System. You use the dialog box to include any desired parameters (see Figure 6.8). Hence, running CHKDSK this way and entering the drive identifier in the Options field will obtain an output screen representing that drive's disk.

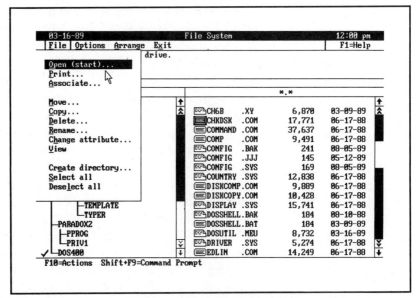

Figure 6.7: Running CHKDSK from the File System screen

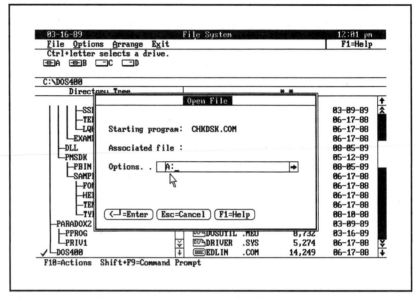

Figure 6.8: The Open File dialog box for a DOS 4 executable program

Figure 6.9 shows the standard output for a CHKDSK command on a hard disk (drive C). In a CHKDSK output screen, the total space on the hard disk is followed by an indication of how many hidden files exist, and how much space they take up. Having three hidden files in DOS 4 is fairly typical; they contain the system information (IBMBIO.COM and IBMDOS.COM) and the volume ID entry. Sometimes, other hidden files appear, representing one of several methods used for copy protection or file security.

The number of directories and files, and how many bytes they consume, is presented next. The consumed space is subtracted from the total disk size to come up with the number of bytes available to you for other files.

The last two lines of the CHKDSK output really have little to do with the disk itself. Instead, they indicate how much conventional memory exists on your system and how much of it is available at the moment you run the CHKDSK command. The space taken up usually represents what DOS itself uses, but it could also include how much memory is consumed by internal programs (see Chapter 18) or by secondary command processors (see Chapter 17).

```
Volume ROBBINS C    created Ø6-16-1988 7:57p

 21256192 bytes total disk space
    55296 bytes in 3 hidden files
   11Ø592 bytes in 53 directories
 19812352 bytes in 766 user files
  1277952 bytes available on disk

     2Ø48 bytes in each allocation unit
    1Ø379 total allocation units on disk
      624 available allocation units on disk

   65536Ø total bytes memory
   52536Ø bytes free
Press any key to continue . . .
_
```

Figure 6.9: CHKDSK output for a hard disk

The DOS 4 version of CHKDSK also outputs several additional lines concerning the allocation units on your disk (see Figures 6.6 and 6.9). An allocation unit, which is sometimes called a cluster, represents the number of bytes that are treated as a minimum size unit during the assignment of disk space to files. CHKDSK indicates how many bytes exist in each of these allocation units, how many units there are, and how many remain available for use by files. It's simply another way of assessing the space consumption and availability on your disk.

RUNNING PROGRAMS AUTOMATICALLY

One of the most common parameters entered after a program name is the name of a data file to be used by the program you are running. For example, if I include a data file as an optional parameter for my word-processing program (EDITOR.EXE), then that file is automatically loaded into memory, ready to be used in the word processor. In other words, entering

EDITOR TRADEMRK.XY

at the command prompt will start up my word processor and also load the TRADEMRK.XY text file. Remember that this file-name reference will only work when both program and data files are in the current directory, or when you have properly set the PATH list.

DOS 4 users have an additional method of running programs automatically. You can associate a program like EDITOR.EXE with one or more standard extensions, such as .TXT, .XY, or .WP. In this way, whenever you select a text file that has one of these extensions from the File System, DOS 4 will automatically run the associated program file. It will then also automatically load the selected data file.

Take a look at Figure 6.10, in which text file CH3.XY has been selected. The File menu is displayed, and the Open choice is about to be made.

Normally, selecting and opening a data file will have no effect on program files. However, because I have established an association between the text file's extension and a program file, selecting Open results in the screen shown in Figure 6.11. Pressing Return now initiates the EDITOR.EXE program, using CH3.XY as the first data file to edit.

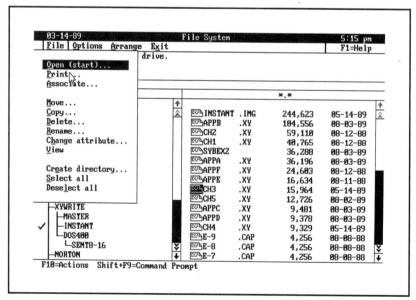

Figure 6.10: Selecting a data file runs the associated program.

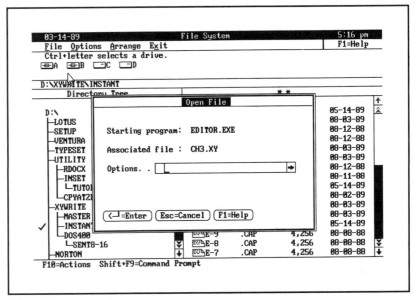

Figure 6.11: The Open File dialog box for associated programs

As you'll see in the following section, you can control whether this dialog box appears. You can load the program and the associated data file, with no prompting box for options (i.e. switches or parameters) if you like. If this box is displayed, you can enter any of the required or optional switches and parameters. All programs and commands have their own unique set of possible parameters and switches (see Chapter 22).

HOW TO MAKE ASSOCIATIONS Establishing an association between an executable program and the data files' extensions is straightforward. First, you select the executable program you'll want to run. Then, you pull down the File menu and select Associate. Lastly, you tell DOS 4 the extensions you want it to associate with that executable program.

For example, I wanted DOS to automatically run my word-processing program whenever I selected any text file, whether its extension is .XY (my own specifier), .TXT (fairly common standard), or .WP (used by other text processors on my system).

Figure 6.12 depicts the sequence that I followed. First I selected the XYWRITE directory from the Directory Tree. Next I chose the EDITOR.EXE program from the file listing. Lastly, I pulled down the File menu and selected Associate. DOS 4 then displayed the Associate File dialog box seen in Figure 6.12.

The entry window in this dialog box is initially blank. You must enter the extensions that you wish to associate with a program as I did here. Press Return when you've typed in all the possible extensions. After you specify the extensions during this setup process, DOS then asks you if you want prompting to occur when the specified program later runs:

1. Prompt for options
2. Do not prompt for options

Your response here will govern how an associated program file will later execute—with a pause for option entry, or not. If you choose to be prompted, the dialog box shown in Figure 6.11 will appear when you open a file that is associated with a program.

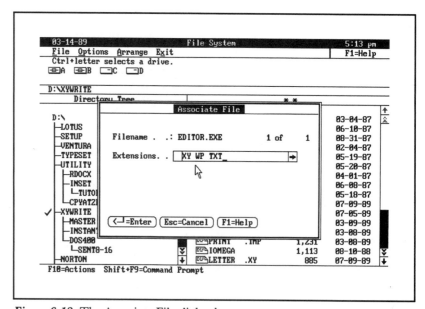

Figure 6.12: The Associate File dialog box

RUNNING PROGRAMS FROM YOUR DEFAULT DIRECTORY

Usually you set the working directory to the one you are in; related files are then read from and written into that directory. Sometimes, you will want to run a utility program that is in another directory. For instance, you may want to run the CHKDSK program in the DOS400 directory, or a special hard-disk management program like Q-DOS II, located in the UTILITY directory.

Most of the time, you do not want to leave the current directory and go through the hassle of resetting to another directory. In fact, more and more programs are allowing you to run other programs while the original program is still active (see the discussion on secondary command processors in Chapter 17). Therefore, you will want to avoid changing the current working directory. The PATH and APPEND commands are your best solution. (APPEND, however, is only available to DOS 3.3 and DOS 4 users.)

Suppose that after copying all the necessary database programs to your DBMS subdirectory, you made it your current directory and you now want to see how much space is left on your hard disk. If you enter

    CHKDSK

to analyze the disk, you will get the message ''Bad command or file name'' because DOS will look only in the current directory for that program.

As you saw in the previous section, the CHKDSK program is stored in the DOS400 subdirectory. How can you tell DOS to check the DOS400 subdirectory if it can't find the requested program in the current directory? Instead of specifying the path name every time you want to run a program, you can set up a PATH command. It tells DOS what subdirectories, in addition to the current one, it should check whenever you enter a program to run.

To open a path to the DOS400 subdirectory, you would enter the following command at a command prompt:

    PATH \DOS400

The CHKDSK command would now execute properly, because the path to the correct subdirectory is open.

Do not leave any spaces between the entries on the path list. DOS stops reading the line when it comes across the first space on the list.

You can open a more complex path by separating a list of directory names with semicolons. For this example, enter

PATH \DOS400;\WP;\LOTUS;\DBMS

If the program you specify can't be found in the current default directory, DOS will first look for it in the DOS400 subdirectory. If it isn't there, DOS will then successively look in the WP, LOTUS, and DBMS subdirectories. DOS will only return the "Bad command or file name" message to you if it doesn't find it in any of these directories.

By prefacing all entries in a path with their drive designator, you can execute the desired program from any logged drive.

By opening a PATH command, you can set the default directory before you start up your main program. You can then request the program from the default directory. Whenever your program reads or writes files, it will use the default directory. For example, to do database work with the accounting files, you could set the DOS default to the DBMS\ACCOUNTS directory and the PATH to DBMS, and then invoke the database-management program (in this case, dBASE IV) by entering

CD \DBMS\ACCOUNTS
PATH \DBMS
DBASE

DOS 4 users can change the current directory and call up dBASE from the File System screens. The PATH command, however, must be previously set from the command prompt.

The default directory is now ACCOUNTS, so dBASE will expect to find all databases (.DBF) and program (.PRG) files in that directory. It will hunt for its own management programs along the directories specified on the path, finding them in DBMS.

NAVIGATING THE DOS DIRECTORY STRUCTURE

While subdirectories are essential for good organization, they can nevertheless be confusing at times. DOS provides the PATH and APPEND commands to help you maneuver through the complex tangle of directories.

SEARCHING PATHS

There will be instances when you will need to reach a file in a directory other than the one you're in (that is, the default directory). For example, in the drive D that I use in these chapters, I switch among EDITOR.EXE, the main word-processing program located in the D:\XYWRITE directory, the DOS utilities, which are located in the D:\DOS400 directory, and the data file in the D:\XYWRITE-\DOS400 directory that contains the chapter you are now reading.

Now, let's move to the root directory of drive D. In DOS 4, you would get there by highlighting the D:\ line in the Directory Tree. In earlier versions of DOS, you would enter

The PATH command does not change the active directory. It simply tells DOS to search another directory if the program requested is not in the active directory.

    CD \

You are now at the beginning of the path for all the directories and files on drive D. Suppose you want to run the CHKDSK.COM program. As you learned in the previous sections, you can run CHKDSK.COM from the current directory when it is in another directory by using the PATH command and specifying which directory should be checked. In this case, the CHKDSK.COM program is in the DOS400 directory. To create a path from the current working directory (the root) to the DOS400 directory, you enter

    PATH \DOS400

This command establishes a path between the root directory and the directory containing CHKDSK.COM. You can now run the program from the root because DOS will find it through its specified search path.

SETTING UP A COMPLEX PATH

As you saw in the "Running Programs from Your Default Directory" section, you can open a path to several directories at once by entering a series of path names separated by semicolons (and no spaces). For example, if DOS can't find the program you ask for in your default directory, you could ask it to search the UTIL directory first and then UTIL\SPECIAL by entering

    PATH \UTIL;\UTIL\SPECIAL

Notice that if you simply entered

PATH \UTIL\SPECIAL

only UTIL\SPECIAL, and not UTIL, would be searched. Multiple paths allow you to access programs in several directories without having to constantly revise your PATH command.

Let's take a look at another example. Assume that you have an application program called IMSHOW.EXE located in the \UTIL\SPECIAL directory in drive C. How would you set the PATH in DOS to run this program if your current default directory is still the root? For example, which of these commands would you use?

1. PATH \UTIL;\SPECIAL;\FINAL

2. PATH \UTIL\SPECIAL

3. PATH UTIL\SPECIAL

Many people are uncertain about the use of *delimiters,* which are simply characters that separate one computer term from another. How and when they are used is always critical. A space separates the PATH command itself from the list of directory names. The backslash symbol, as you know, separates directory names in a single path. The semicolon separates different *complete* directory names in the same PATH listing and tells DOS to successively search each of the named directories until the desired program file is found. If DOS does not find the program in the current directory or in any of the directories listed in the PATH command, it displays the ''Bad command or file name'' message.

Choice 2 above is the correct one. PATH \UTIL\SPECIAL is the full path name from the root to the directory containing the desired program. The semicolons make choice 1 incorrect—this PATH specifies three independent directories and indicates that they are all immediate subdirectories of the root. None of them contains the IMSHOW.EXE file, indeed, the SPECIAL directory does not even exist at this level.

Choice 3 is wrong *most* of the time. Because the lack of a leading backslash causes the path to branch off the current directory, this choice is correct only if the current directory is the parent directory of UTIL. Since the UTIL is a subdirectory of the root, the syntax in choice 3 will work only if the root is the current directory.

LIMITATIONS OF THE PATH COMMAND

You may want to redefine the directory path for certain applications. The more often DOS has to resort to the path to find files, the longer it will take and the slower the system's response time will be.

If you find that DOS generally takes a while to locate your programs, you may want to redefine your PATH command for those files. Since DOS searches the path in the order in which you list directory names, you should list the directories in the order most likely to succeed.

For now, you should at least consider using a single PATH command that enables DOS to hunt for and find all of your main programs:

PATH \DOS400;\UTIL;\LOTUS;\WP;\DBMS

Only program files that can be run under DOS (.COM, .EXE, files, or .BAT files) can be found via PATH.

You can only use the PATH command to search for files with the extensions .COM, .EXE, and .BAT. The first two types are executable programs, and the last is a DOS batch file. (See Chapters 14 through 16 for more on batch files.) As DOS will not search the path directories for files with other extensions, you cannot use it to access data files not found in the current directory.

Some programs, such as WordStar 3.3, require special *overlay* files that are usually not loaded into memory until they are needed, and the PATH command itself will not enable DOS to locate and load these files. Some of the newest programs requiring overlays are able to run because they are smart enough to use DOS's PATH information themselves to locate their overlay files. If you are using one of the older programs, you may have to run it from within the directory that contains both the main and overlay files.

DOS 3.3 and DOS 4 contain the APPEND command, which can be used to find nonexecutable files. APPEND enables you to set up a path to overlay files and data files, effectively removing DOS's former inability to locate these files. To create an APPEND command, you list the directory names containing the files you want DOS to find after the command name itself. For instance,

APPEND \WP;\DBMS\DATA

establishes another searching path that DOS will use to locate overlay files for a word processor and database files for your database-management system. As you'll see in Chapter 17, the DOS 4 APPEND command is even more powerful and does some of the work of the PATH command.

CHECKING THE PATH

After working in several different directories, you may not be sure which is the current directory. You may also not be sure which path DOS will take to search for files not found in the current directory. If this is the case, you can see what the current path is by entering

   PATH

at the command prompt. DOS then lists the current path, which is also known as opening the path. To close the path, enter the PATH command with a semicolon (;) alone as follows:

   PATH;

The semicolon indicates that the path is once again reset to the current working directory only. In this way, you control whether any other directories are searched for executable files. If you run the PATH command listing any directories, you establish the PATH list. If you later decide *not* to search these other directories, then running PATH with only a semicolon once again restricts the search to only the current directory. After you've entered this command, asking DOS for the current path will produce the message ''No Path.''

SETTING UP DOS 4 MENUS AND PROGRAM GROUPS

You've seen now how to run programs from both the File System window of DOS 4 and the command prompt in all DOS versions. As you know, you initiate the File System itself by choosing it from the Main Group menu on the Start Programs screen. The Main Group menu also contains a DOS Utilities option, which you have selected in previous chapters to then initiate one of its utilities.

Since you are now familiar with these screens, I will show you how the Main Group and DOS Utilities screens can be modified to extend DOS's Start Programs capability. You will learn how to add your own program names or DOS utilities to these group menus. You will even discover how to define your own completely new program group menu, listing your favorite and most commonly run programs. By creating your own program menu, you can initiate programs quicker than if you used the File System screens.

ADDING PROGRAMS TO A MENU GROUP

Let's take a closer look at the DOS Utilities menu on the Start Programs screen. From this screen, you can select the Program choice from the action bar, pulling down its menu. This results in the screen shown in Figure 6.13.

The Start choice on the Program menu is similar to the Open (start) choice on the File menu in the File System; it enables you to initiate whichever program you had selected before choosing Start. The difference here is that the Start Programs list contains brief phrases for the program names that are easier to understand than the .EXE or .COM file names in a directory list.

You can add other utilities to this list quite easily. You first select Add, to bring up the Add Program dialog box seen in Figure 6.14.

You can now give DOS the name of the file to run and the more understandable menu phrase or expression to display for users. For

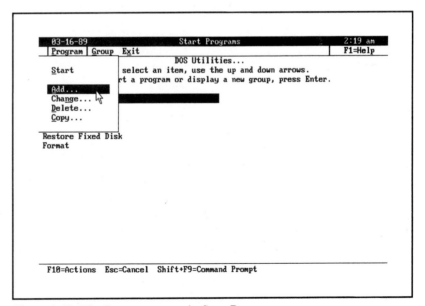

Figure 6.13: The Program menu in Start Programs

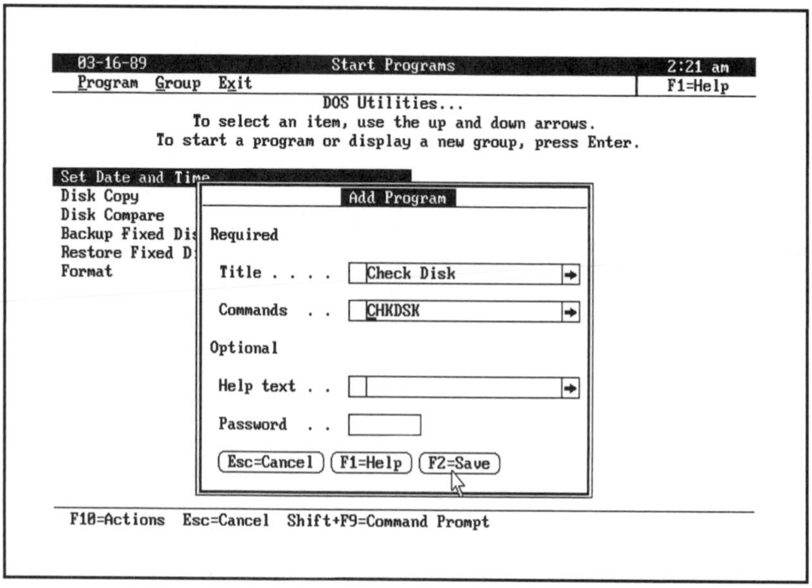

Figure 6.14: The Add Program dialog box

instance, suppose you want to run the CHKDSK.EXE program but want it to be listed in the menu as Check Disk. You would fill in the two required fields as shown in Figure 6.14 and then press Return. The title, which will be displayed on the DOS Utilities menu (see Figure 6.15), will be Check Disk, and the underlying program that will automatically be run will be CHKDSK. If you have DOS 4, you should try this on your system now.

If you actually add this new Check Disk entry to your screen, you will be slightly disappointed when you run the utility. Although the result will be what you requested—the screen will clear and the CHKDSK output will be displayed—the DOS Utilities screen menu will immediately redisplay, erasing the all-too-briefly displayed CHKDSK results. The next section will explain how to correct this problem.

As it stands now, the CHKDSK program will run with no additional parameters; therefore, only the boot drive will be checked.

CHANGING THE WAY PROGRAMS RUN

The first step toward solving the problem with CHKDSK is to pull down the Program menu and select Change. This will bring up the dialog box shown in Figure 6.16.

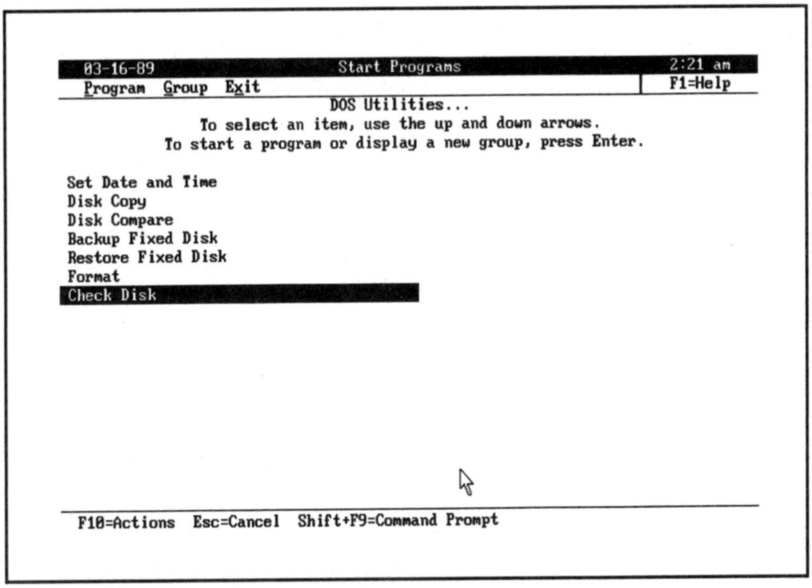

Figure 6.15: Adding other utilities to the DOS Utilities menu

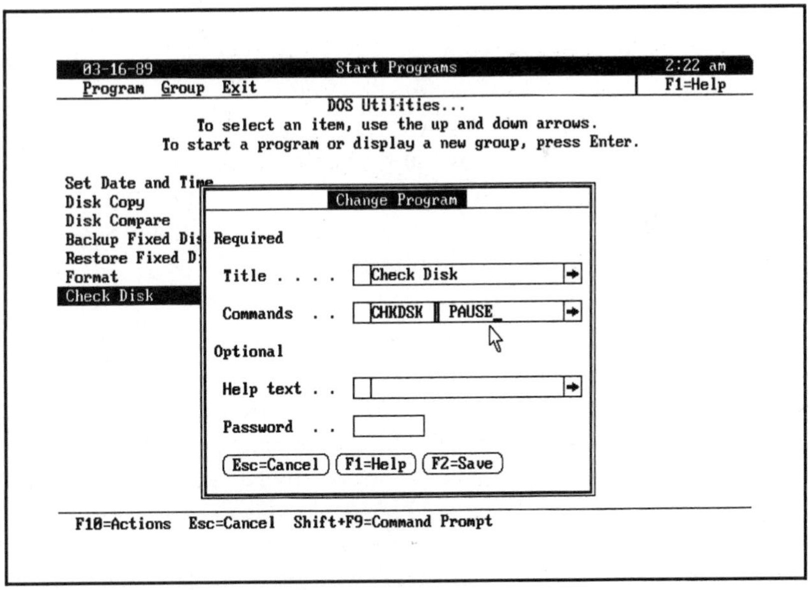

Figure 6.16: The Change Program dialog box

The F4 key separates program-startup commands from one another in the Start Programs screens.

Press the Tab key to move from the Title field to the Commands field. Move the cursor to the right of the CHKDSK command, press the F4 function key, then type in the secondary command PAUSE. Pressing F4 will instruct DOS to treat the horizontally entered commands as if they were entered separately and sequentially on separate lines at the command prompt. The PAUSE command will cause the output display of CHKDSK (or any command) to remain on the screen until you remove it. To do so, just press any key. The previous screen will then be redisplayed.

The commands you enter in this overall field are called *program-startup commands*. As you'll discover, this field enables you to input command options that will be executed one after the other whenever you select your newly installed menu choice.

DELETING AND COPYING MENU CHOICES

The Delete choice in the Program menu enables you to remove any menu choice at some later point. For example, you may decide to remove one of the initially standard entries, such as the Backup or Restore option. Both of these options would be unnecessary on your system if you use special tape-backup software to back up and restore your files.

You will not need the Copy choice very often, so I won't discuss it in detail here. You only use it after you've set up several groups of menu listings and want to quickly copy a complete entry from one group to another, without having to reenter the entire Add Program field information.

REORDERING MENU CHOICES

In addition to copying and deleting menu choices; you can also reorder them. To rearrange the order in which the choices are displayed, you use the Reorder option seen on the Group menu in Figure 6.17.

As an example, suppose you want to make your new entry, Check Disk, the first entry on the list. You need to first highlight Check Disk, then pull down the Group menu, and select Reorder. Next, move the highlight to the desired new location (the top of the list) and press Return. The selected entry (Check Disk) is then placed in this new entry location, and it will be redisplayed there every time you select DOS Utilities. Figure 6.18 shows the new order of the DOS utilities.

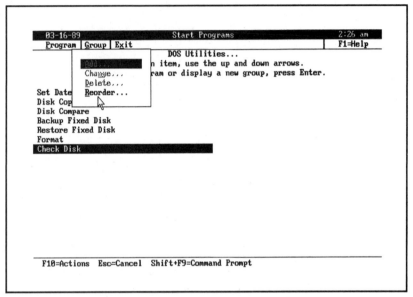

Figure 6.17: Reordering a group's menu entries

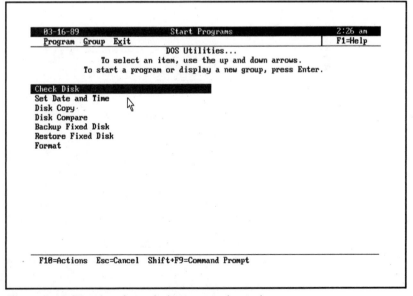

Figure 6.18: Results of reordering a menu's entries

DEFINING YOUR OWN PROGRAM GROUPS

Notice that the three Group choices of Add, Change, and Delete are grayed in Figure 6.17. This is because adding a new group of program choices is possible only when you are at the Main Group screen. This explains why Group's Add, Change, and Delete choices are activated (not grayed) when you pull the Group menu down from the Main Group screen. At this point, you can select Add to obtain the dialog box shown in Figure 6.19.

Entering APPLICATIONS in the Title field directs DOS to display that term on the Main Group menu of the Start Programs display. In the Filename field, you enter a base name for the file that will contain all information about this new group and its subordinate program entries. For example, APPLICS has been specified as the file's base name in Figure 6.19.

You can enter any amount of textual help information you like into the Help text field. Users will be able to read this text when they select APPLICATIONS from the Main Group screen and press F1 for help.

What you enter in the Title field does not have to be all uppercase—you can capitalize your menu choices any way you want.

When you enter help text for a menu option, type an ampersand (&) at the end of each phrase. DOS will then insert a carriage return there when it displays the text in the Help window.

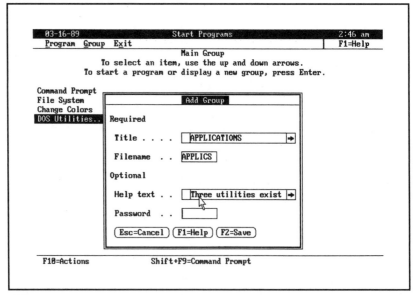

Figure 6.19: Adding a new group of menu choices

Figure 6.20 shows the new Main Group menu with its added APPLICATIONS group. Since the new group has been selected, pressing F1 displays the Help window containing help information about it (see Figure 6.20). The Help window's standard pushbutton keys and scroll bar are activated for you to peruse the help text. (Notice that ampersands were inserted before the two numbered items so that each item would begin on a new line.)

When you first select a newly defined group item, like APPLICATIONS, a screen with the group's title appears, along with a message that the "Group is empty." Your task then is to pull down the Program menu and select Add to add your first program to this group (see Figure 6.21).

In Figure 6.21, I added a menu choice entitled Norton Utilities, and specified its primary utility, NU.EXE, as the program that will run. Additionally, I chose to protect this utility with a password. Any program group or menu choice can be password protected. You do not need a password to select the APPLICATIONS group, but running the powerful Norton program, one of the APPLICATION menu choices, will now require you to enter 9-26-70 as its password.

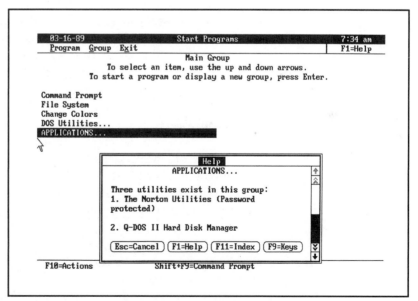

Figure 6.20: Personalized help for the APPLICATIONS group items

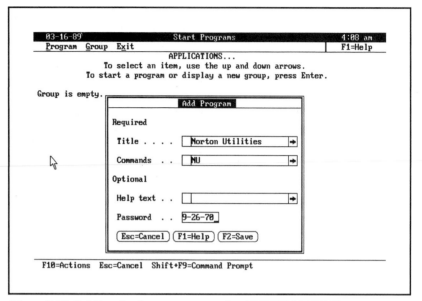

Figure 6.21: Adding the first program to the APPLICATIONS group

Without the correct password, you will be denied access to the program. Whenever you select Norton Utilities from the APPLICATIONS menu, you will receive the password verification window seen in Figure 6.22. When you type the password, the characters that you type will not appear on the screen. If you type the correct password at this point, the NU.EXE program will be loaded and the Start Programs screen will only return when you exit NU. If your password is not correct, you will receive a warning box on your screen that contains a simple ''Password incorrect'' message. You will then be returned immediately to the previous Start Programs screen.

I followed this procedure several more times to add other customized applications to the APPLICATIONS group. You can see my completed APPLICATIONS menu in Figure 6.23.

At this point, I have added a hard-disk-management program (QD2.EXE) and a program to provide advanced backup (BACK-IT.EXE). I have also installed Ventura Publisher to the APPLICATIONS program group.

When you originally install Ventura Publisher on a hard disk, it goes through an installation process and creates a special batch file called VP.BAT. You must execute this batch file whenever you want

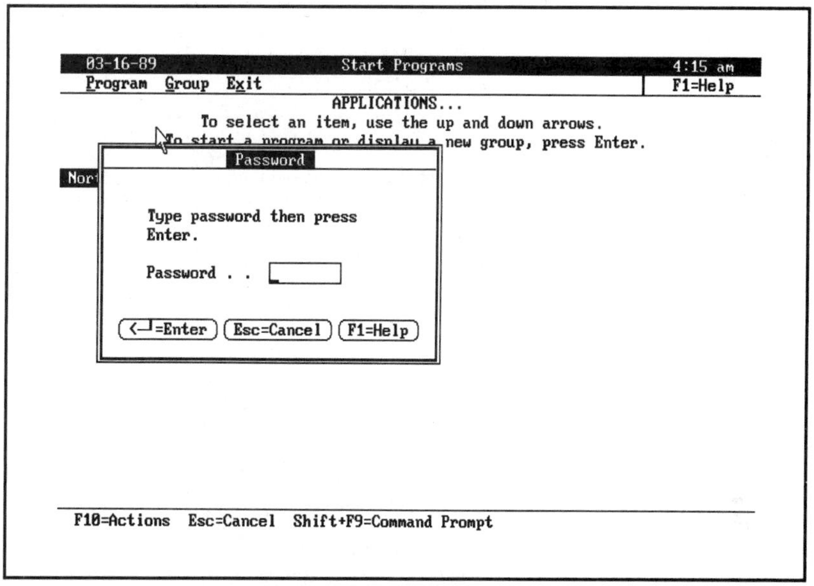

```
 03-16-89                 Start Programs              4:15 am
  Program  Group  Exit                                F1=Help
                        APPLICATIONS...
               To select an item, use the up and down arrows.
               To start a program or display a new group, press Enter.
 ┌─────────────────┤ Password ├─────────────────┐
 │Nor                                            │
 │                                               │
 │      Type password then press                 │
 │      Enter.                                    │
 │                                               │
 │      Password . . [        ]                  │
 │                                               │
 │                                               │
 │    (<─┘=Enter) (Esc=Cancel) (F1=Help)         │
 └───────────────────────────────────────────────┘




   F10=Actions  Esc=Cancel  Shift+F9=Command Prompt
```

Figure 6.22: The Password dialog box

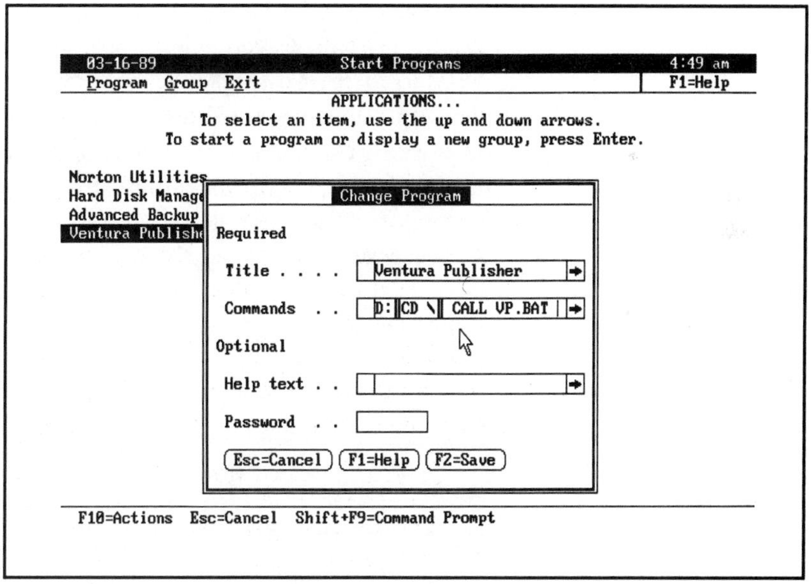

```
 03-16-89                 Start Programs              4:49 am
  Program  Group  Exit                                F1=Help
                        APPLICATIONS...
               To select an item, use the up and down arrows.
               To start a program or display a new group, press Enter.

 Norton Utilities
 Hard Disk Manage┌────────┤ Change Program ├────────┐
 Advanced Backup │                                  │
 Ventura Publishe│ Required                         │
                 │                                  │
                 │ Title . . . .  [Ventura Publisher]→│
                 │                                  │
                 │ Commands  . .  [D:][CD \][CALL VP.BAT]→│
                 │ Optional                         │
                 │                                  │
                 │ Help text . . [            ]→    │
                 │                                  │
                 │ Password  . . [        ]         │
                 │  (Esc=Cancel) (F1=Help) (F2=Save)│
                 └──────────────────────────────────┘

   F10=Actions  Esc=Cancel  Shift+F9=Command Prompt
```

Figure 6.23: Running batch files from a group screen

to run Ventura. In previous versions of DOS, you do this by simply typing VP and pressing Enter. In the DOS 4 graphic shell, you can use the Change Program box to tell DOS to run VP.BAT whenever you select Ventura Publisher from the menu.

In Figure 6.23, you can see that I highlighted Ventura Publisher, selected Change from the Program menu, and then added three commands. Remember that you press F4 to separate the commands. When listed on separate lines, these commands look like this:

> Use CALL to invoke .BAT files that you install under selections in your program groups.

```
D:
CD \
CALL VP.BAT
```

These commands make D the current drive, change the current directory to the root, and call up the VP.BAT batch file (which initiates the Ventura program). If I did not use the CALL command here, the batch file would still run Ventura, but I would not be able to return to the graphic shell when I finished a Ventura session. I would end up at the command prompt instead.

SUMMARY

In this chapter, you have explored the many ways you can run programs in DOS. All versions of DOS share certain common techniques for setting up hard-disk structures and initiating programs. DOS 4 offers additional ways to start programs from its graphic display screens.

You have learned the following methods of working with directory structures and running programs:

- You know how to use the Create directory choice or the MD command to make a subdirectory in any existing directory.

- You learned how to set up your hard disk for a word processor, a spreadsheet, and a database-management system. Using these examples, you should be able to set up an efficient directory structure for all your application software systems.

- You can run programs by selecting them directly from the DOS 4 File System screens.

- You learned how to associate data and text files with program files, such as word processors and database managers, so that you can automatically run the program by simply selecting its associated file.

- You can use the PATH command to direct DOS to search through a specified series of directories for .EXE, .COM, and .BAT files that are not located in the current working directory.

- With DOS 3.3 and later versions, you can use the APPEND command to tell DOS to search through a specified series of directories for data and overlay files that are not located in the current working directory.

- You can now set up your own customized menus of program files to be initiated from DOS 4's Start Programs screen. You then run a sequence of commands automatically by selecting your prepared menu choice.

- When you set up your menu choice, you can also create a related help window for it. You can also password protect each menu or menu option individually.

In Part 3, I will teach you how to control the flow of information to the screen (Chapter 7), to the printer (Chapter 8), and even to other devices through the DOS communications ports (Chapter 9). You will also learn how to edit standard text files, which is crucial for effectively managing the DOS configuration and control features that I will discuss in later chapters.

PART 3

COMPLETING THE FUNDAMENTALS

Part 3 rounds out your education in the basics of using DOS. Chapter 7 teaches you how to create and modify text files using the DOS line editor, EDLIN. You will use EDLIN throughout the rest of the book to generate and update system files, as well as to write your own simple programs (called batch files). In Chapter 8, you will learn how to send your work to the printer. Chapter 9 describes communications terminology and technology, and shows you how to control data transmission with DOS commands. You can then transmit the files you prepared in Chapter 7 to other computers.

USING THE DOS EDITOR

IN ADDITION TO THEIR ABILITY TO PROCESS NUMBERS and large amounts of data, computers are exceptionally good at manipulating text. It comes as no surprise, then, that there are so many different programs available to do this.

The advantages of using a computer instead of a typewriter are many. Text can be manipulated on the screen, changed, and corrected before it is printed out. Also, whole documents and reports can be stored on disk for later use. This means you can type in half a report, go away for a week, and then come back and finish it. You can also create a rough draft and later make corrections to it in minutes, without having to retype everything.

There are two primary kinds of programs that allow you to create and manipulate text. The first kind is a line editor like the DOS EDLIN editor. With a line editor, you work with a line of text at a time. Line editors number each line and reference each line by these numbers. You can make corrections to only one line at a time.

The second kind of program, a word processor, shows you a full screen of text. You can move the screen cursor to any character position on any line and make changes anywhere on the screen. Word processors usually support such features as multiple fonts, boldfacing, and underlining.

Naturally, it's up to you to choose the kind of program you want. You may want to use both, at different times. The DOS line editor is approximately 14K in DOS 4, and half that size in earlier versions, so it can comfortably fit on most application diskettes in diskette-based systems. This means that you won't need to juggle diskettes often. On the other hand, you may feel much more comfortable using the more extensive set of commands available with most word processors. You might also prefer to edit any character on any line in the full-screen mode of a typical word processor. However, word processors usually require tens of thousands of bytes of disk space merely to contain them, and they have more extensive RAM requirements than line editors. In addition, you must usually purchase them, whereas EDLIN is available in your DOS system at no additional charge.

The EDLIN program is so small that you can keep a copy of it on each of several diskettes for rapid and easy file editing. Most advanced word processors are too large to fit on diskettes that contain any other sophisticated software.

DOS provides the EDLIN.COM program as part of your system. It is disk-resident and acts like any other external command. You can use EDLIN to create and edit text files, which are files that contain standard letters, numbers, and punctuation symbols. Except for the special codes indicating carriage returns, line feeds, and the end of a file (Ctrl-Z), these files have no control codes for such features as underlining on a printer or high intensity on a display. Remember that you can easily display any text file on your monitor with DOS 4's View command (on the File menu) or with the TYPE command at the DOS command prompt. In short, EDLIN works with whole lines of text, but you cannot use it to change fonts or to produce bold-face or underlined text. EDLIN can, however, manipulate text files, and it contains search and replace functions and standard text-editing features.

GETTING EDLIN STARTED

EDLIN is started from the DOS prompt with the command

EDLIN *FileSpec*

where *FileSpec* is the drive, path, file name, and extension of the file to be created or edited. You must use the full file name, including any extension. As always, EDLIN must either be resident on the disk you are using, in the current default directory, or on the path to be searched by DOS.

In DOS 4, you have several additional methods for starting the EDLIN program. These methods of running programs were all discussed in the preceding chapter. Figure 7.1 shows the Open File dialog box that you see when starting EDLIN.COM from DOS 4's File System. To create a text file, you simply enter the file name (and its path if you don't want it to be in the current directory) in the Options

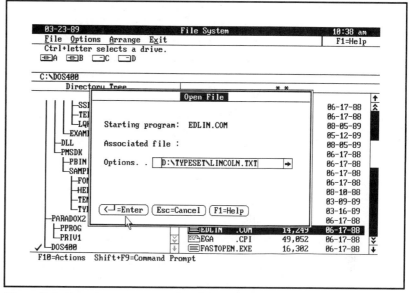

Figure 7.1: Creating a new text file with EDLIN in DOS 4

field. In this example, the LINCOLN.TXT file will be created in the TYPESET directory on drive D.

STARTING A NEW FILE

If EDLIN is invoked with a *FileSpec* value for a file that does not currently exist, it will respond with the following message and prompt:

New file
*_

EDLIN is giving you a clean slate, awaiting your commands. Table 7.1 summarizes the commands you can use with EDLIN, their actions, and their general formats. You will learn about each of these as you work through this chapter.

CHANGING AN EXISTING FILE

Invoking EDLIN with the *FileSpec* of an existing file will yield the following:

End of input file
*_

The optional /B switch (short for Binary) can be used with this EDLIN command when the file you will be working on contains Ctrl-Z markers other than the end-of-file marker. As you'll learn later in this chapter, you can use EDLIN to incorporate and then edit control characters in a text file.

COMMAND	ACTION	GENERAL FORMAT
A	Appends lines	[*Num*]A
C	Copies lines	[*Line*],[*Line*],*Line*[,*Count*] C
D	Deletes lines	[*Line*][,*Line*] D
—	Edits line	[*Line*]
E	Updates and exits	E
I	Inserts lines	[*Line*]I
L	Lists lines	[*Line*][,*Line*] L
M	Moves lines	[*Line*],[*Line*],*Line* M
P	Displays full page	[*Line*][,*Line*] P
Q	Aborts and exits	Q
R	Replaces globally	[*Line*][,*Line*] [?] R[*String*][^Z*NewString*]
S	Searches globally	[*Line*][,*Line*] [?] S[*String*]
T	Merges files	[*Line*] T [*FileSpec*]
W	Writes lines	[*Num*] W

Table 7.1: Summary of EDLIN commands

EDLIN tries to load your entire text file into available memory (RAM). When it tries to load a file that is longer than 75 percent of the currently available RAM, it will load only the first part of that file and will use only 75 percent of the available memory. The message just shown will not appear, but the prompt will. You may then edit the lines that were loaded. When you are done editing these lines, you can use EDLIN commands to write the edited lines out to a diskette and then bring in additional text lines to edit.

BRINGING NEW TEXT INTO MEMORY

The command needed to add new, unedited lines of text from a disk file is the Append command, abbreviated as the single character

A. This command is only used when you have loaded a file that is larger than 75 percent of current memory. Entered at the EDLIN * prompt, its general format is

[*Num*]A

This command loads *Num* lines from the rest of the file (where *Num* is the number of lines to load), provided there is room. If there is insufficient room to load any more lines from your file, the command will not load anything. You must then use the W command (described shortly) to write some of your edited lines from EDLIN to disk.

If you successfully load the rest of the file into memory, the following message will appear:

End of input file

You can then continue editing using any of the EDLIN commands.

COMBINING SEPARATE TEXT FILES

The Transfer command (T) is used to combine two text files: one in memory and another somewhere else. When you specify the file to be transferred into the middle of your current file (*FileSpec*), the whole file is read in and inserted before the line number specified by *Line:*

[*Line*] T *FileSpec*

If *Line* is not specified, the file's contents are inserted before the current line.

This command can be quite useful. For example, suppose you have the following two files:

File1	File2
1: Line 1, File 1	1: Line 1, File 2
2: Line 2, File 1	2: Line 2, File 2
3: Line 3, File 1	3: Line 3, File 2
4: Line 4, File 1	4: Line 4, File 2

If File1 is the current file being edited in memory, and you enter the following command:

3 T FILE2

The brackets around parameters in this chapter indicate that these EDLIN parameters are optional for a command. The brackets themselves are not entered as part of the command.

the result is a new combined file, which looks like this:

```
1:  Line 1, File 1
2:  Line 2, File 1
3:*Line 1, File 2
4:  Line 2, File 2
5:  Line 3, File 2
6:  Line 4, File 2
7:  Line 3, File 1
8:  Line 4, File 1
```

Note that the current line is now the first line of the transferred file, as indicated by the EDLIN * prompt.

MAKING SPACE FOR LARGE FILES

The Write command (W), like the Append command, is only needed when your file is too large to fit in 75 percent of available memory. In that situation, only 75 percent of your file will have been loaded. If you want to edit the rest of the file, you need to make some room. You must transfer lines from the file in memory to disk, thus freeing up enough space to let more if not all of the rest of the file be loaded. The general format of this command is

[*Num*] W

where *Num* is the number of lines to be written. After you execute this command, you can load the rest of the file with the A command.

If you do not specify the number of lines to be written, the W command will keep writing lines to the disk, starting with line 1, until 75 percent of available memory is free. If there is already 75 percent of available RAM freed for EDLIN text lines, then no lines will be written to disk. If, for example, the first 200 lines were written to disk, then line 201 of the total file would become line 1 of the memory portion being worked on by EDLIN. For example, the command

200 W

would cause the first 200 lines of the current file to be transferred to disk, and line 201 would be numbered line 1. You could then read in additional text lines from the disk file with the A command.

DISPLAYING EDLIN FILES

Perhaps the most common activity you'll ask your line editor to perform will be to show you the text in your file. EDLIN offers two commands for this purpose: the L command for listing any range of lines, and the P command for rapidly looking at complete screenfuls of your file.

LISTING YOUR TEXT FILE

Since line numbers change each time you add or delete a line, the List command (L) will probably be your most frequently used command. You will always want to see the new numbers assigned to each of your text lines before you execute new line-oriented commands.

You can list a block of lines in a variety of ways. If you don't provide explicit line numbers for starting and stopping, EDLIN will attempt to display 23 text lines—a screenful. The size of the display range can extend from 11 lines before the current line to 11 lines after the current line.

Perhaps the most common format for this command is to specify the precise line numbers at which to begin and end the listing. For example,

6,19L

displays lines 6 through 19 on your screen and then redisplays EDLIN's prompt.

Simply typing L with no line-number specification will display the 11 lines preceding the current line, then the current line, and then the 11 lines after the current line. If your file does not have 23 lines, the entire file will be listed.

LISTING YOUR TEXT FILE RAPIDLY

The Page command (P) is like the L command, except that it redefines the current line number to whatever line has been displayed last on the screen. This command provides you with a rapid way to list all the lines in your text file, a screenful at a time.

Entering a line number alone, as in

17 P

will display up to 23 lines starting with line 17. The last line listed becomes the current line. You can also display a specified range of lines and make the last line the current line, as in

14,28 P

If you simply enter P, EDLIN will make its standard assumptions, giving you a 23-line display, starting with the line after the current line and making the last line displayed the new current line.

EDITING EDLIN FILES

As you have worked through the previous sections on getting EDLIN started, you have seen that EDLIN is *command-oriented;* that is, it does not display menus, but rather expects you to enter individual commands. Because of this, you can move around and do things in EDLIN much more quickly than you could with a menu system, but you must know the commands in order to execute them quickly.

You have also seen the EDLIN prompt, the asterisk symbol. Whenever you see this on the screen with a blinking cursor next to it, EDLIN is prompting you for a command. This prompt also shows you the current line of the file being edited, which is the default line being worked on. Any EDLIN command you enter will deal with the text on this particular line (and possibly others as well). You can move a certain number of lines forward or backward from the current line, and you can insert, edit, or delete in relation to it.

Here are some useful tips to keep in mind as you work with EDLIN:

- Most commands can be entered using just the first letter of the command. When you are performing an operation on a specific line or group of lines, specify the line numbers first.

- The EDLIN letter commands can be entered in uppercase, lowercase, or a combination of the two.

- Line numbers can be specified in a number of ways; however, they must be whole numbers between 1 and 65529. When you enter more than one line number, you must separate them with commas. If you enter a line number higher than the highest line number in memory and you are going to add a line, the line will be added after the highest line number.

- You can refer to the as-yet-nonexistent line following the highest line number in memory by using the number sign (#).

- You can use a period to specify the current line.

- The Plus and Minus keys can be used to specify lines *relative* to the current line number. For example,

      − 20, + 5D

  will delete the 20 lines preceding the current line number, the current line number, and 5 lines after the current line number. If the current line number was 50, lines 30 through 55 would be deleted.

- You can enter more than one command on a line. If you do this, separate each complete command by a semicolon (;).

- It is possible (although not often necessary) to enter a control character into your file. To do this, you must press Ctrl-V first and then the desired control character (in uppercase).

- If you are displaying a lot of data, you can pause the screen output by pressing the Break key, Ctrl-ScrollLock. Press Ctrl-ScrollLock again to restart the output. Note that the processing of the command will have stopped also.

Now let's take a look at the editing tasks you'll want to do with EDLIN, and the commands that perform these tasks.

INSERTING NEW LINES

The Insert command (I) is used to insert lines. Its general format is

[*Line*]I

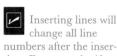 Inserting lines will change all line numbers after the insertion. For example, if you insert new text at line 3, remember that all line numbers after 3 have been changed. It's best to do a new listing (L) to discover the new numbering before issuing any new commands.

Again, *Line* may be specified as either a specific or a relative line number. Not including *Line* will result in lines being added before the current line. If you created a new file called LINCOLN.TXT by calling up EDLIN, you would use the I command to insert text for the first time at line 1. Entering 1I at the EDLIN * prompt like this:

    *1I

would yield

    1:*_

which places you in insert mode. As you can see in Figure 7.2, EDLIN shows you each line number as you type it.

Notice the ^C on line 4. This is EDLIN's response when you press Ctrl-C during text insertion. Use the Ctrl-C key combination to exit from text insertion and return to the EDLIN prompt.

The I command can also be used to insert new text before any existing text line in the file. Simply specify the line number in the file before which you want the new text to be placed.

```
New file
*1I
        1:*Four score and seven months ago (approximately),
        2:*DOS's forefathers brought forth upon this nation
        3:*a new operating system (more or less).
        4:*^C

*_
```

Figure 7.2: Inserting text for the first time

CHANGING EXISTING LINES

Editing a line merely means that you are changing the information on the line, *not* adding or deleting a line. If no line number is specified (in other words, you have simply pressed Return), then you will start editing the line after the current line. If the current line is the last line in the file, pressing Return will do nothing but produce another * prompt. Usually, however, you can enter any line number to put you into edit mode for that line. You may also use relative line numbers to edit a line.

When you are put into edit mode (for example, by entering 3 and pressing Return), the display looks something like this:

```
3:*a new operating system (more or less).
3:*_
```

The arrow keys or any of the function keys will work as they do at the DOS prompt. For example, pressing F3 will do the following:

```
3:*a new operating system (more or less).
3:*a new operating system (more or less)._
```

The original line 3 is completely retyped, with the cursor waiting at the end of the line for additional input.

While editing any line, pressing the right arrow key will move the cursor one character to the right and display the character it was on (or under). Pressing Esc-Return or the Break key combination anywhere on the line will take you out of edit mode and leave the line unchanged.

If you want to add something to the end of the line, simply press F3 and start typing. You will automatically be put into insert mode. If your cursor is located anywhere else on the line, you must press the Ins key to enter insert mode, and press it again to leave that mode. In Figure 7.3, you can see how line 3 of our example was changed. F3 was pressed, the Backspace key was used to erase the period, and then the new characters '', dedicated'' were typed. After the change, the L command was used to list the current contents of the file.

The edit to line 3 is only the first step in a common sequence, as shown in Figure 7.4. A change is made, followed by a listing of the

```
New file
*1I
      1:*Four score and seven months ago (approximately),
      2:*DOS's forefathers brought forth upon this nation
      3:*a new operating system (more or less).
      4:*^C

  *3
      3:*a new operating system (more or less).
      3:*a new operating system (more or less), dedicated
  *L
      1: Four score and seven months ago (approximately),
      2: DOS's forefathers brought forth upon this nation
      3:*a new operating system (more or less), dedicated
  *_
```

Figure 7.3: Making corrections to a line

```
*1I
      1:*Four score and seven months ago (approximately),
      2:*DOS's forefathers brought forth upon this nation
      3:*a new operating system (more or less).
      4:*^C

  *3
      3:*a new operating system (more or less).
      3:*a new operating system (more or less), dedicated
  *L
      1: Four score and seven months ago (approximately),
      2: DOS's forefathers brought forth upon this nation
      3:*a new operating system (more or less), dedicated
  *4I
      4:*to the proposition that all computers (with the same
      5:*microcomputer chip) are created equal.
      6:*^C

  *L
      1: Four score and seven months ago (approximately),
      2: DOS's forefathers brought forth upon this nation
      3: a new operating system (more or less), dedicated
      4: to the proposition that all computers (with the same
      5: microcomputer chip) are created equal.
  *_
```

Figure 7.4: Adding new lines at the end of a file

file. Then another editing command follows (in this case, a new text insertion at the end of the file), and yet another L command is used to verify the results of the last edit. Continuing this process and adding still more text (with a correction to line 10 along the way) results in the 12-line text file shown in Figure 7.5.

MOVING LINES (CUTTING AND PASTING)

The Move command (M) allows you to move one line or a body of lines in a file to a new location in the file. (A group of lines to be moved is called a *block*.) For example, entering

```
9,12,6 M
L
```

at the EDLIN prompt will move lines 9 through 12 in the file shown in Figure 7.5 to a new position—in front of line 6, as shown in Figure 7.6. This is commonly called *cutting and pasting*. Naturally, when the operation is completed, all affected lines are renumbered. Notice that the current line has moved to the new sixth line, since this was the first line in the block that was moved.

```
            7:*wars. It is altogether fitting and proper (some may
            8:*disagree) that we should do this.
            9:*Now, we are engaged in a great computer war (more
           10:*have fallen than have risen), testing whether this DOS
           11:*or any other DOS so conceived and so dedicated, can
           12:*long endure.
           13:*^C
    *10
           10:*have fallen than have risen), testing whether this DOS
           10:*have fallen than have risen), testing whether this DOS,
    *L
            1: Four score and seven months ago (approximately),
            2: DOS's forefathers brought forth upon this nation
            3: a new operating system (more or less), dedicated
            4: to the proposition that all computers (with the same
            5: microcomputer chip) are created equal.
            6: We are met today to chronicle a part of these DOS
            7: wars. It is altogether fitting and proper (some may
            8: disagree) that we should do this.
            9: Now, we are engaged in a great computer war (more
           10:*have fallen than have risen), testing whether this DOS,
           11: or any other DOS so conceived and so dedicated, can
           12: long endure.
    *_
```

Figure 7.5: Intermediate version of the text file

```
        3: a new operating system (more or less), dedicated
        4: to the proposition that all computers (with the same
        5: microcomputer chip) are created equal.
        6: We are met today to chronicle a part of these DOS
        7: wars. It is altogether fitting and proper (some may
        8: disagree) that we should do this.
        9: Now, we are engaged in a great computer war (more
       10:*have fallen than have risen), testing whether this DOS,
       11: or any other DOS so conceived and so dedicated, can
       12: long endure.
    *9,12,6M
    *L
        1: Four score and seven months ago (approximately),
        2: DOS's forefathers brought forth upon this nation
        3: a new operating system (more or less), dedicated
        4: to the proposition that all computers (with the same
        5: microcomputer chip) are created equal.
        6:*Now, we are engaged in a great computer war (more
        7: have fallen than have risen), testing whether this DOS,
        8: or any other DOS so conceived and so dedicated, can
        9: long endure.
       10: We are met today to chronicle a part of these DOS
       11: wars. It is altogether fitting and proper (some may
       12: disagree) that we should do this.
    *_
```

Figure 7.6: Cutting and pasting text

COPYING LINES

The Copy command (C) is used to copy blocks of lines to other places in a file. It is similar to the M command, although not as frequently used. When you use the C command, the original lines are not bodily moved to a new place in the file; instead, they are replicated in the new place, leaving the original lines intact. After the copy has been made, all line numbers will be recalculated, and the first line that was copied will become the new current line.

There are three versions of the C command. In the first, you can make a replica of the current text line anywhere else in the file. The copy of the current line will be inserted in front of the line specified by *Line:*

,,*Line*[,*Count*] C

The commas represent placeholders for values that haven't been entered by you; the default (that is, the current line) is used. The optional *Count* parameter can be used to specify the number of times the operations should be repeated.

You can also copy multiple lines at once using the C command. The following format causes all of the lines from *Line1* through the current line to be copied to the position before *Line2:*

> *Line1,,Line2[,Count]* C

The third possible format of the C command allows you to explicitly specify the range to be copied:

> *Range,Line3[,count]* C

In any EDLIN command that allows the specification of multiple lines, the beginning line number must be less than or equal to the ending line number. EDLIN cannot work backwards.

Range represents a pair of delimited line numbers. This version of the C command is similar to the previous version, except that in *Range* you specify the last line number to be copied, instead of defaulting to the current line number.

Here's an example of using the *Count* parameter with the C command. If you were editing any text file of at least five lines and executed the following:

> *1,4,5,3 C

you would be telling EDLIN to make a copy of lines 1 through 4 in your file at a point just before line 5, and then to repeat this operation twice more (a total of 3 for *Count*).

SEARCHING FOR TEXT STRINGS

The Search command (S) locates lines. You can ask EDLIN to carry out the search over a variety of ranges. The general format of this command is

> *[Scope] [?] S[String]*

Scope can be defined as any of the following parameters:

- *Line* causes the search to start at *Line* and stop at the end of the file;

- *,Line* causes the search to start at the line after the current line and end at *Line;*

- *Line1,Line2* causes the search to cover only the lines within the block between *Line1* and *Line2*.

- Not using the *Scope* parameter results in the search starting at the line after the current line and ending at the last line in the file.

The *String* parameter specifies the text that you are looking for. The first character of this text should immediately follow the S. If *String* is not included on the command line, the search string last used in a Search or Replace command is used. If no Search or Replace command has yet been used in the session, then the message ''Not found'' will be displayed.

If you specify ? in this command, EDLIN will stop each time it locates the specified string, and it will ask you for confirmation that the string is the correct one.

As an example of using the Search command, let's look for all occurrences of the word *is* in the following file:

```
1: This is the first line
2: of a test file to demonstrate
3: the use of the Search command.
4: It is included for your own
5: information.
```

You would enter the following command:

```
*1,5 ? Sis
```

You would then see

```
 1: This is the first line
O.K.? n
 4: It is included for your own
O.K.? n
Not found
*_
```

You can see that line 4 has become the current line, as it was the last line to contain a match with *String*. Notice that line 1 only came up once in the search. This is because the search finds a whole line with a

The Search and Replace commands are case sensitive—they will look for *exactly* what you type. For example, the S command will consider *Judd* and *judd* to be two different words because of the different capitalization.

match on it. If there is more than one match, it's a waste of time to successively redisplay the same line.

SEARCH AND REPLACE CAPABILITIES

R is the Replace command. It gives you the ability to search through any specified range of lines and replace every occurrence of specific text (*String*) with new replacement text (*NewString*).

The general format for the R command is

[*Scope*] [?] R[*String*][Ctrl-Z*NewString*]

The *Scope* and *String* parameters are the same as those for the Search command. If you are going to enter replacement text (*NewString*), end *String* by pressing Ctrl-Z. (This is optional, since you may only want to search for and remove the specified string wherever it is found.)

NewString is the text that will replace *String*. It does not need to be the same size as *String,* since it will be inserted after *String* has been deleted. If *NewString* is left out, then *String* will be deleted in the specified block. If *String* is left out as well, EDLIN will use the *String* value from the last Search or Replace command, and the *NewString* value from the last Replace command. If Search and Replace have not been used during the current session, you will get the message "Not found."

When ? is specified in this command, EDLIN will display the replaced or modified line and ask whether you wish to confirm the changes that were made ("O.K.?"). You should answer Y or press Return if you want the changes to become permanent.

Once an occurrence of *String* has been found and you have accepted or not accepted the change, the search will continue in the specified block. Multiple occurrences on the same line are included in the replacements.

Let's try this command with the example you worked with earlier in this chapter. You can quickly ask EDLIN to search in the file for each occurrence of the text string *DOS*. When found, the command will replace *DOS* with *MS-DOS* (see Figure 7.7).

In this example, you specified that all occurrences in lines 1 through 12 are to be acted upon. You can see by the EDLIN prompt that line 10 has become the current line, since it was the last line changed. Notice also that each line that contained the sought-after string of characters was displayed after the change was made (lines 2, 7, 8, and 10). As shown in the figure, you usually execute the L command to verify the results of your command request.

```
         7: have fallen than have risen), testing whether this DOS,
         8: or any other DOS so conceived and so dedicated, can
         9: long endure.
        10: We are met today to chronicle a part of these DOS
        11: wars. It is altogether fitting and proper (some may
        12: disagree) that we should do this.
    *1,12RDOS^ZMS-DOS
         2: MS-DOS's forefathers brought forth upon this nation
         7: have fallen than have risen), testing whether this MS-DOS,
         8: or any other MS-DOS so conceived and so dedicated, can
        10: We are met today to chronicle a part of these MS-DOS
    *L

         1: Four score and seven months ago (approximately),
         2: MS-DOS's forefathers brought forth upon this nation
         3: a new operating system (more or less), dedicated
         4: to the proposition that all computers (with the same
         5: microcomputer chip) are created equal.
         6: Now, we are engaged in a great computer war (more
         7: have fallen than have risen), testing whether this MS-DOS,
         8: or any other MS-DOS so conceived and so dedicated, can
         9: long endure.
        10:*We are met today to chronicle a part of these MS-DOS
        11: wars. It is altogether fitting and proper (some may
        12: disagree) that we should do this.
    *_
```

Figure 7.7: Search and replace operation

DELETING LINES

Deleting lines causes all lines after the deletion to be renumbered. Even if you do not request a listing of the lines (with L), they are still renumbered. For example, if you execute the command 1D twice, you will have deleted lines 1 and 2.

The Delete command (D) is used to delete one or more lines from the file. Its general format is

   [*Line*],[*Line*]D

The *Line* parameters specify the line or lines that you want to delete.

Suppose you had written some new text and added it to the current file beginning at line 13 (see Figure 7.8). Then you decided (either immediately or later) that this new text was not appropriate, so you needed to delete it with the D command. Figure 7.9 shows the results of deleting the lines and then listing the remaining file.

ENDING THE EDITING SESSION

There are two ways to exit EDLIN, depending on whether you want to save the changes you've made to the file or not. You can

```
        8: or any other MS-DOS so conceived and so dedicated, can
        9: long endure.
       10:*We are met today to chronicle a part of these MS-DOS
       11: wars. It is altogether fitting and proper (some may
       12: disagree) that we should do this.
 *13I
       13:*The world will little note (not counting book reviewers,
       14:*of course) nor long remember what we say here, but you
       15:*can never forget what you learn here (who could possibly
       16:*forget such drama, not to mention irreverence?).
       17:*^C

 *L
        6: Now, we are engaged in a great computer war (more
        7: have fallen than have risen), testing whether this MS-DOS,
        8: or any other MS-DOS so conceived and so dedicated, can
        9: long endure.
       10: We are met today to chronicle a part of these MS-DOS
       11: wars. It is altogether fitting and proper (some may
       12: disagree) that we should do this.
       13: The world will little note (not counting book reviewers,
       14: of course) nor long remember what we say here, but you
       15: can never forget what you learn here (who could possibly
       16: forget such drama, not to mention irreverence?).

 *_
```

Figure 7.8: Additional text entries

```
        6: Now, we are engaged in a great computer war (more
        7: have fallen than have risen), testing whether this MS-DOS,
        8: or any other MS-DOS so conceived and so dedicated, can
        9: long endure.
       10: We are met today to chronicle a part of these MS-DOS
       11: wars. It is altogether fitting and proper (some may
       12: disagree) that we should do this.
       13: The world will little note (not counting book reviewers,
       14: of course) nor long remember what we say here, but you
       15: can never forget what you learn here (who could possibly
       16: forget such drama, not to mention irreverence?).
 *13,16D
 *L
        2: MS-DOS's forefathers brought forth upon this nation
        3: a new operating system (more or less), dedicated
        4: to the proposition that all computers (with the same
        5: microcomputer chip) are created equal.
        6: Now, we are engaged in a great computer war (more
        7: have fallen than have risen), testing whether this MS-DOS,
        8: or any other MS-DOS so conceived and so dedicated, can
        9: long endure.
       10: We are met today to chronicle a part of these MS-DOS
       11: wars. It is altogether fitting and proper (some may
       12: disagree) that we should do this.

 *_
```

Figure 7.9: Multiple lines deleted

abort the entire editing operation and restore the file to its original condition, or you can save all your edits to the disk file, permanently engraving those changes in the original file.

QUITTING THE EDITING SESSION WITHOUT SAVING

Entering the Quit command (Q) all by itself is one way of getting out of EDLIN and back to DOS without saving all of the work you have just done. EDLIN will ask you if you are sure you wish to leave without saving your file. Anything other than an answer of Y will abort the Q command, and you will be back at the EDLIN prompt.

This exit path usually is used when you have made a mistake. Suppose, for example, that you changed your mind about the deletion of lines 13 to 16 done in the last section. You've decided to keep those lines in the text after all. You could type them in all over again; or, if there are no other edits at stake, you could abort the entire editing process, go back to DOS, and then call up the text file for editing once again. Since you made other edits in LINCOLN.TXT, entering the Q command is a mistake. To return to the file instead of quitting and losing your changes, enter N at the Quit command's prompt (see Figure 7.10). You can then retype the lines that were mistakenly deleted.

If you are willing to give up all the editing you did in this particular EDLIN session, then you could enter Y to quit. This returns you to the command prompt or to DOS 4's File System, depending on which way you originally intiated the EDLIN program.

Make sure that there is enough room on your disk for the file to be saved. If there is not, the part of the file that *can* fit will be saved with an extension of .$$$. The original file will be retained on the disk, no new .BAK file will be created, and the part of the edited file not saved will be lost.

SAVING YOUR WORK AND EXITING TO DOS

The usual way to exit EDLIN and save your changes is to use the End command (E). With this command, the file you originally named when you started EDLIN will be given a .BAK extension; the edited file will retain the original extension. If you created a completely new file, no .BAK file would be created.

At the end of the file, EDLIN will insert a carriage return and line feed if they are not already there. It will also insert a Ctrl-Z code to be used for an end-of-file marker.

EDLIN will *not* prompt you to make sure you want to leave. Entering E followed by a press of the Return key is all you need to save all of your editing changes and return to DOS (see Figure 7.10).

SUMMARY

In this chapter, you've learned about the commands available in DOS's line editor, EDLIN, for creating and manipulating text files, as well as for modifying the text within them. Here is a brief review:

- All of EDLIN's capabilities are accessible with simple one-letter commands. These commands act on one or more lines within the text file, and act on the text within those lines.

- You can create a new file simply by typing EDLIN *FileSpec* at the command prompt or by selecting EDLIN and specifying *FileSpec* in DOS 4's File System. The file will be created and you can execute any of EDLIN's editing commands by typing in the appropriate command at the asterisk prompt.

```
          12: disagree) that we should do this.
     *Q
     Abort edit (Y/N)? N
     *13I
          13:*The world will little note (not counting book reviewers,
          14:*of course) nor long remember (a new DOS version is always
          15:*on its way) what we say here. But you will not forget
          16:*the lessons learned here; who could possibly forget such
          17:*irreverence?
          18:*^C

     *L
           7: have fallen than have risen), testing whether this MS-DOS,
           8: or any other MS-DOS so conceived and so dedicated, can
           9: long endure.
          1Ø: We are met today to chronicle a part of these MS-DOS
          11: wars. It is altogether fitting and proper (some may
          12: disagree) that we should do this.
          13: The world will little note (not counting book reviewers,
          14: of course) nor long remember (a new DOS version is always
          15: on its way) what we say here. But you will not forget
          16: the lessons learned here; who could possibly forget such
          17: irreverence?
     *E
     Press Enter (<——⌐) to return to File System. _
```

Figure 7.10: Ending the Editing session

- If the available memory in your system is not sufficient to hold your entire text file, you can use the Write command with the Append command to write edited lines to disk and then add unedited lines to memory.

- You can enter new text with the Insert command. The Break key allows you to terminate the data entry.

- You can list any or all text lines with the Line command. You can also list the entire file, a screenful at a time, with the Page command.

- Once entered, text can be modified in a variety of ways. The DOS function keys can be used to modify any line once you've brought up that line by typing its number.

- You can move one or more lines around in the file with the Move command. You can also leave those lines in place, while making a complete copy of them elsewhere with the Copy command.

- Besides the Move and Copy commands, which manipulate large blocks of text, the Transfer command can insert one complete text file into another.

- What goes in can always come out. The Delete command can remove one or more text lines—permanently.

- Any text string can be searched for with the Search command. The even more powerful Replace command can search for any text string and replace it with another string. If you like, the Replace command can be used to replace one string with *nothing*, effectively creating a large-scale (global) deletion capability.

- You can end your EDLIN editing session with the End command, which saves your edited work under the original file name and then returns you to the DOS command prompt or DOS 4's File System. Or you can abort the entire editing session with the Quit command, which, after confirming that you really mean to do it, restores your file to its original condition.

Now that you know how to create and modify text files with EDLIN, you should turn to Chapter 8. Having beautifully sculpted text on a disk may be satisfying, but printing it out on paper is even better. You will find that it's much better to read the entire file from a printed manuscript than from one 23-line display at a time.

PRINTING

CHAPTER 8

COMPUTERS CAN DO MANY MARVELOUS THINGS, AND do them all at lightning speeds. However, the magic of the computer would be all for naught if there were no way to see the results.

We often take output for granted. Yet, you know by now that without a DIR, TYPE, or COPY command, you'd never be able to see the results of your work. In this chapter, you'll learn a wide range of output capabilities in DOS. You'll discover some easy methods, some "quick-and-dirty" techniques, and some sophisticated commands for controlling when output will occur, where it will go, and what it will look like. You'll also learn why these alternatives work as they do.

Printing simple screen images of both text and graphics screens is the easiest kind of output to master quickly, so you'll learn that right away. Since printing onto paper is unquestionably the standard method for obtaining hard-copy results from programs, the principal focus of this chapter will be on producing printed output.

Indirect printing plays a very important role in more and more systems. The last section in this chapter will take an in-depth look at this feature. With indirect printing, you can continue to work on your computer while it sends output to a printer. This is DOS's first step into the world of multitasking and multiprocessing, where more than one program can execute at one time and more than one user can share the system's capabilities. The full potential of this power will not be realized until the next generation of hardware and software becomes available. For now, however, it can provide a significant improvement in system performance, allowing printing to occur simultaneously with other computing tasks.

PRINTING SCREEN IMAGES

A Color Graphics Adapter (CGA) monitor can generate graphics images using an array of pixels (dots) that is 640 pixels wide by 200 high. This density— 128,000 pixels—is acceptable for most applications, although many programs produce more pleasing and detailed results using denser output screens. An Enhanced Graphics Adapter (EGA) monitor has a density that is twice that of the CGA. Its graphics mode produces an array of 640 × 350 pixels, while its successors, the Professional Graphics Adapter (PGA) and the Video Graphics Array (VGA), produce 640 × 480. The VGA has several additional display modes, a popular one being 720 × 400 resolution for increasing the number of text lines displayed. The top of the line in graphics capabilities on the new Personal System/2 machines features a 1024 × 768 pixel addressability.

It's often easier to generate results on the video screen than on any other output device. However, as you'll learn in this chapter, anything that can be displayed on your video screen can also be transferred to your printer.

All printers can create an exact replica of any text that appears on a screen. With DOS commands, you can easily obtain hard copies of any important data that is being displayed on your monitor. This may be all you ever need to be satisfied with printed output from your computer system. In fact, many users never need to print anything with DOS commands—their application programs have built-in commands for managing output printing. To accurately replicate an image on the screen that was created in graphics mode instead of text mode, however, you must have a printer capable of creating graphics.

If neither you nor your dealer has yet connected your printer, you should do so now. If you need to do more than simply connect your printer and cable to the appropriate ports, consult Chapter 9, which covers communications in detail.

DOS requires you to press the keystroke combination Shift-PrtSc to print a copy of whatever is on the screen. The Shift-PrtSc key combination will work on any video monitor if the information being displayed is in standard text characters. To see how it works, turn on your computer and bring up any program at all, or just use a simple directory listing. Turn on your printer and press Shift-PrtSc. It's as simple as that to obtain hard copy.

Assuming you have a printer capable of generating graphics images, you can also create printed images of graphics by following a simple preparatory procedure. The GRAPHICS command in DOS is a disk-resident program that enables the same Shift-PrtSc combination to capture a graphics screen image for printing if you have an IBM- or Epson-compatible printer. You must invoke this command *before* attempting to print a graphics screen.

The simplest form of the command is invoked by typing

GRAPHICS

at the command prompt. In DOS 4, you can start the GRAPHICS program from the File System (see Chapter 6). Invoking GRAPHICS causes future presses of the Shift-PrtSc combination to reproduce on your printer all screen images, including graphics images. Graphics images cannot be printed without taking this crucial step.

If you have a graphics program or an integrated package that includes graphics, try running it now and printing one of the resulting graphics images. First try it without executing GRAPHICS. Then go back to DOS and run the GRAPHICS command. Return to your program, and try Shift-PrtSc with the same graphics image.

The GRAPHICS command has some flexibility when it comes to output appearance. Its general form is

GRAPHICS *PrinterType* /B /R

where *PrinterType* is one of the possible parameter values defining printer type, as shown in Table 8.1. /B and /R are switches you can use for background color and reverse video, as you will see shortly. As always, if the GRAPHICS.COM file is not in the current directory, you should precede the GRAPHICS command with the drive and directory where it can be found. When you run the GRAPHICS

PARAMETER	PRINTER TYPE
COLOR1	For a color printer with a black ribbon (prints up to 19 shades of grey) or for any color printer when your video monitor is monochrome
COLOR4	For a color printer with a red/green/blue ribbon
COLOR8	For a color printer with a cyan/magenta/yellow ribbon
GRAPHICSWIDE	For printers with wide 13½'' carriages
GRAPHICS	For the IBM Graphics printer, as well as for a variety of IBM- and Epson-compatible graphic printers
THERMAL	For the IBM PC Convertible printer

Table 8.1: PrinterType parameters for the GRAPHICS command

command from your DOS or DOS400 directory in DOS 4's File System, you enter *FileSpec,* and if desired, the /R and /B switches, in the Options field.

The GRAPHICS command in DOS 4 has been dramatically enhanced. See Chapter 22 for a listing of all the new switches and options and refer to the DOS user's manual for further details.

Figure 8.1 shows a typical graphics screen. If you try to print this screen with the Shift-PrtSc combination without first running the GRAPHICS command, the result will be unsatisfactory, as you see in Figure 8.2. However, if you use the GRAPHICS command with the default graphics *PrinterType* by first typing

> ### GRAPHICS

then pressing Return, and *then* using Shift-PrtSc, the printed result will be what you want to see, as shown in Figure 8.3.

If you specify *PrinterType* as COLOR4 or COLOR8, you have the option of printing the background screen color. You then use the /B switch when you invoke the command by typing, for example,

> ### GRAPHICS COLOR4 /B

> Printing a screen that contains only text with Shift-PrtSc is reasonably quick (under a minute for most microcomputer printers). Printing a screen containing graphics will take several minutes, depending on the graphics resolution and screen contents, as well as the speed of your printer.

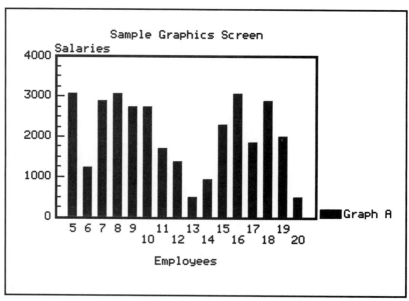

Figure 8.1: A typical graphics screen on a video display

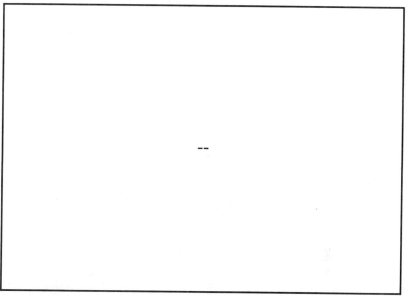

Figure 8.2: Figure 8.1 printed with the Shift-PrtSc combination

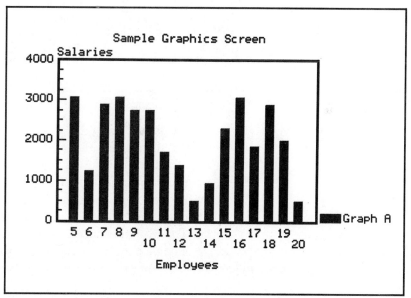

Figure 8.3: Figure 8.1 printed with GRAPHICS and Shift-PrtSc

As an alternative, the /R switch with this command produces a striking *reverse-video* image (white letters on a black background). For example, typing

GRAPHICS   COLOR4   /R

would produce the reverse-video printing shown in Figure 8.4.

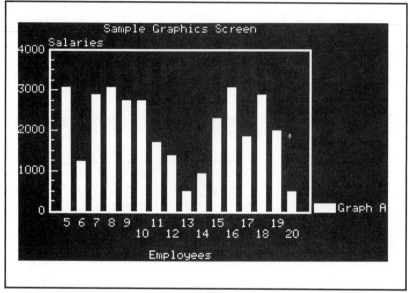

Figure 8.4: Reverse-video printout of Figure 8.1

Finally, you should know that the graphics mode of your video display will affect the printed image. If your screen is in high-resolution mode (640 columns by 200 rows), then the printed image will be rotated 90 degrees on the paper. This is often called a *horizontal landscape* image. If the screen is in medium-resolution mode (320 columns by 200 rows), the printed image will be printed as you see it. This is called a *vertical portrait* image. The resolution affects color printouts as well as displays; it is possible to obtain four colors in medium-resolution mode, but only two different colors in high-resolution mode.

PRINTING FILES

Creating exact replicas of displayed data with the Shift-PrtSc command and the GRAPHICS command is easy, but it is limited to one

Keep in mind that if a file is stored in some special format (as it is for spreadsheet programs, database programs, and many word-processing programs), you will need to use a special output printing sequence for the appropriate program to obtain a printed copy.

You cannot print files in DOS 4 by using the Copy choice from the File menu.

screenful of information at a time. There will be many times when you need a printed copy of an entire data file. Most files are created as standard ASCII files, which usually contain standard letters, numbers, and punctuation. In addition, each line of an ASCII file has a carriage return and line feed (CR/LF) at the end of it, but no other special control characters are embedded within the file. An ASCII file can be printed in several ways, as you will see in the following sections.

PRINTING FILES WITH THE COPY COMMAND

At the command prompt, the simplest way to print one or more data files is to use the COPY command. The general form of the COPY command is

COPY *FileName(s) DeviceName*

where *FileName(s)* is the name of the file (or files) and the destination, *DeviceName,* is the printer's *reserved device name.* (You will learn about these names in Chapter 9.) DOS reserves several special names like LPT1 or COM1 for the hardware ports to which printers are connected.

If the file you want to print is called KEYS.DTA, then it can be printed simply by specifying either of the following two commands:

COPY KEYS.DTA LPT1:
COPY KEYS.DTA PRN:

In these commands, LPT1 is a name for the first parallel printer port (see Chapter 9) and PRN is the standard default device name for the first connected printer. The printer will be engaged immediately, and the entire file will be printed. You will now have to wait until the printout is completed before the DOS prompt will return. Nothing else can be done by your DOS system or by you until the printing terminates.

As you learned in Chapter 5, you can copy multiple files with one command by using a wild-card specification. In this situation, you can also initiate the printing of multiple text files with one statement. For instance, you could initiate the printing of all the .BAT files in the LOTUS directory by entering

COPY \LOTUS*.BAT PRN:

DOS will respond to this request by successively echoing on the screen the name of each .BAT file. After echoing a name, it will transmit all the contents of that file to the printer and move on to the next file in the LOTUS directory that meets the .BAT file specification. Once again, you will not regain control at the DOS prompt until all of the specified files have been printed.

INDIRECT PRINTING AND SPOOLING

In the previous section, the COPY command allowed you to transfer files to a printer. However, COPY will not relinquish control of the system until the print transfer is complete. Since the DOS prompt does not reappear, you are unable to enter any other DOS command or do anything else while the printing proceeds.

The PRINT command is DOS's solution. Unlike the COPY command, which directly prints to your printer, the PRINT command causes printing to occur indirectly. PRINT sends information out to a disk file to indicate which data files are to be printed. Then, later, while you are doing other work, DOS will independently read this disk file to discover which data files should be printed. The printing will occur simultaneously with other work you may then be doing with DOS and your computer system.

Indirect printing is often called *spooling,* an acronym for "*s*imultaneous *p*eripheral *o*perations *on-l*ine." Spooling is the only form of limited multitasking available in the current versions of DOS. (Multitasking is the apparent simultaneous operation of different programs or computer tasks.)

Switches and wild cards, when used intelligently, can also help you control the flow of information and files from one place to another—in this case, from a disk to a printer. The biggest complaint about system performance centers is the long waiting time for slow peripheral devices like printers and plotters, and the PRINT command and switches help to address that complaint.

Use the .PRG files seen in the DBASE\ADMIN\EXPERT directory of Figure 8.5 as you work through the following sections.

```
C>DIR/W \DBASE\ADMIN\EXPERT\*.PRG

   Volume in drive C is ROBBINS
   Directory of  C:\DBASE\ADMIN\EXPERT

ARCHIVE  PRG     COLPRINT PRG     COMM     PRG     DATE     PRG     DELAY    PRG
DIR      PRG     DISKRPT  PRG     DUPLICAT PRG     GETSPACE PRG     LOWER    PRG
MAIL     PRG     MENU     PRG     MESSAGE  PRG     MODIFY   PRG     PRINT    PRG
PRINTER1 PRG     PRINTER2 PRG     PRINTER3 PRG     RUNDIR   PRG     SBENTRY  PRG
SBREPORT PRG     SBUPDAT2 PRG     SBUPDATE PRG     SNAP     PRG     STATS    PRG
STRIP    PRG     TIME     PRG     VALIDATE PRG     WASH     PRG     WINDEMO  PRG
WINDOW   PRG
        31 File(s)   1212416 bytes free

C>_
```

Figure 8.5: The DBASE\ADMIN\EXPERT directory

PRINTING FILES WITH THE PRINT COMMAND

The PRINT command is functionally similar to COPY. You could enter the following to print files on a standard system printer:

COPY *FileName(s)* **PRN:**

You could also enter just

PRINT *FileName(s)*

⊙ The DOS 4 Print option on the File menu is only available after the print spool has been set up by invoking a single PRINT command at the command prompt. It is easiest to do this from your AUTOEXEC.BAT file (see Chapter 14).

To send files to your printer and continue working in DOS 4, you can use the File System (see Figure 8.6). In this example, I selected four .PRG files before pulling down the File menu and choosing the Print option.

Unlike the COPY command, which has to be told a printing destination such as PRN, PRINT *knows* that its job is to send the specified file names to a printer. You can use one of the special switches, discussed later in this section, to indicate which printing device the files

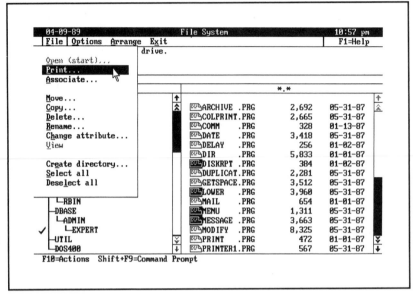

Figure 8.6: Using the print spool in DOS 4

are to be printed on, but it's not really necessary. If you haven't specified the switch, DOS will ask you for a destination the very first
time you invoke the PRINT command:

Name of list device [PRN]:

At this point, you could just press Return to accept the displayed default
device name of PRN, or you could enter a specific reserved device name
(like COM2) for your system. You must run the PRINT command
once from the command prompt, or from a batch file such as your
AUTOEXEC.BAT, in order to activate DOS 4's Print option. In either
case, it is very important to run the PRINT command *before* the DOS 4
shell is activated or *after* you have terminated the shell. If you want to terminate the shell in order to run PRINT, do so by pressing F3 (except
when you are in the File System). *Do not* press Shift-F9 or use the Command Prompt menu choice.

Stop now briefly and try the PRINT command to print any text files
(.TXT, .BAT, .DTA, and so on) you have on your system. Just enter
the PRINT command at the DOS prompt, followed by a list of the file
names you want to print. Use two or three names the first time; then,

If you want to exit the
shell to run PRINT
for the first time, be sure to
press F3. Using other
methods will not remove
the shell sufficiently from
memory to prevent mem-
ory conflicts.

when DOS asks you for the name of the list device (the destination), just press Return. If you are a DOS 4 user, try sending files to the printer a second time by using the Print option on the File menu.

DUAL TASKING WITH PRINT

The major difference between PRINT and COPY is apparent immediately after you specify the file names to print and answer any questions PRINT may ask you the first time you use it. The DOS prompt returns right after PRINT begins its work. You can invoke other programs or commands while PRINT prints your files. The effect is apparently simultaneous action: the CPU seems to be managing the printing job at the same time it is responding to your new requests at the DOS prompt for nonprinting work. The indirect printing, or spooling, is called a *background task,* while your principal new work (if any) is called the *foreground task.*

This dual-tasking technique is actually electronic chicanery—a silicon sleight-of-hand. A DOS computer has only one central processing chip (CPU), and it can really only do one thing at a time. However, it *can* do things very quickly. In any given period of time, a CPU can rapidly shift its processing attention from a slow printer to a slow typist to a not-really-so-fast disk drive.

If an operating system were advanced enough to manage all this shifting of attention from one operation to another and from one device to another, you would see a true multitasking environment. However, DOS is only advanced enough to play this juggling game between two things: printing and, at most, one other activity.

Figure 8.7 shows a request for the printing of a single text file, MAIL.PRG, as a background task. In this example the PRINT command has been invoked for the first time since DOS was brought up. When DOS prompted me for the name of the desired printer (by using the formal specification "list device"), I entered LPT1.

Notice that a message appears informing you that the resident part of PRINT has been installed. PRINT expands the resident memory requirements of DOS when it runs. Although the extra memory requirement reduces the memory remaining for your primary application program, this cost is a small price to pay for the ability to

```
C>PRINT  \DBASE\ADMIN\EXPERT\MAIL.PRG
Name of list device [PRN]: LPT1:
Resident part of PRINT installed

    C:\DBASE\ADMIN\EXPERT\MAIL.PRG is currently being printed

C>_
```

Figure 8.7: First use of PRINT for background printing

Just as you must run PRINT once at the command prompt before running DOS 4's shell and using the Print option, so must you use the command prompt to first run any program or DOS command that installs itself as a TSR (terminate-and-stay-resident) routine before you run the program from the shell. (See Chapter 22 to find out which DOS commands are TSRs.) If you do not take this precaution your system may develop serious memory conflicts and could crash.

continue using your computer while printing proceeds. PRINT also displays a message stating that the requested file is currently being printed. Then the standard DOS prompt reappears. If you now initiate any other command or program, DOS will simply shift its processing power back and forth between the new job and the currently running print job.

Depending on how much slack time exists in your new program (for example, keyboard or disk waiting), the new program may not get held up to any noticeable extent. Usually, however, the print job can never run as fast as it could if it were not contending with a foreground task for the processor's attention. DOS will do its best to efficiently juggle the time-sharing between tasks.

USING SWITCHES WITH PRINT

DOS provides you with certain switches that give you performance controls for indirect printing. Detailed analysis of these switches is beyond the scope of this book. In fact, using these switches at all may be unnecessary for the average user. If future versions of

DOS permit multitasking, these parameters will be more useful for fine-tuning advanced DOS.

In the example seen in Figure 8.7, no switches were specified. DOS set its own intelligent initial values for the performance parameters. However, you can specify other values for these parameters. The memory-resident setup will follow defaults unless you specify other values by switches. Some of these switches can only be used the first time PRINT is invoked. These switches and their parameters are shown in Table 8.2.

The only one of the six initialization switches that you might want to consider setting consistently is /Q, the Queue switch, which indicates how many separately named files can be managed by the PRINT command. A *queue* is just a waiting line, like a line of people waiting for a bus or bank service. In this context, a queue is a list of files to be printed. DOS allows ten file names in the queue as a default maximum, but you can adjust that value with the /Q switch.

Figure 8.8 shows what happens if you try to print more files than there are queue entries. As you can see, I tried to queue up thirty-one files at the command prompt. Even though there are 31 files that match the wild-card specification (*.PRG), only the first 10 are accepted for printing into the queue. Since the /Q switch has not been used, the default assumption of ten slots was taken by PRINT.

In this situation, DOS displays several messages. It first indicates that the PRINT queue is full. Next, it indicates that the first file, ARCHIVE.PRG, is currently being printed. Messages also appear indicating that each of the other nine files is currently in the queue. Figure 8.9 portrays how this queueing works.

The remaining 21 .PRG files that were not accepted into the queue for printing will have to be queued up with other PRINT commands after these 10 finish printing. At best, other PRINT commands that are issued when some of the ten slots open up will fill the open slots. However, the total number of queued files can never exceed the maximum queue size. Trying to queue more than 10 files in DOS 4 produces a screen such as the one seen in Figure 8.10. Selecting choice 1 will cause DOS to skip the listed file or directory and attempt to load the next in line. Selecting choice 2 will immediately resubmit a Print request. This will work since some of the queue entries probably will have freed up.

SWITCH AND PARAMETER	EFFECT
/D:*Device*	Specifies the device to which print output is to be sent (COM1, LPT2, and so on)
/Q:*QueueSize*	Specifies how many files can be accepted by the PRINT command at one time for background printing. Maximum number is 32, and the default value is 10
/M:*MaxTicks*	Specifies the maximum of CPU clock ticks to be used by the PRINT command each time it is given control by the CPU. Range of allowable values is 1 to 255, with a default value of 2
/B:*BufferSize*	Specifies the number of bytes in memory to be used for data to be printed. 512 bytes is standard, but it can be increased in 512-byte increments
/U:*BusyTicks*	Specifies how many clock ticks to wait for a printer that is still busy with earlier printing. Allowable range is 1 to 255, with a default value of 1
/S:*TimeSlice*	Specifies how long PRINT waits prior to getting its share of the CPU. Range is 1 to 255, with a default value of 8

Table 8.2: Switches and parameters for the first PRINT command

If you know that you will frequently need to queue up more than ten files at a time, you can type your very first PRINT request as

PRINT *FileName(s)* /Q:32

```
C>PRINT  \DBASE\ADMIN\EXPERT\*.PRG
PRINT queue is full

    C:\DBASE\ADMIN\EXPERT\ARCHIVE.PRG is currently being printed
    C:\DBASE\ADMIN\EXPERT\COLPRINT.PRG is in queue
    C:\DBASE\ADMIN\EXPERT\COMM.PRG is in queue
    C:\DBASE\ADMIN\EXPERT\DATE.PRG is in queue
    C:\DBASE\ADMIN\EXPERT\DELAY.PRG is in queue
    C:\DBASE\ADMIN\EXPERT\DIR.PRG is in queue
    C:\DBASE\ADMIN\EXPERT\DISKRPT.PRG is in queue
    C:\DBASE\ADMIN\EXPERT\DUPLICAT.PRG is in queue
    C:\DBASE\ADMIN\EXPERT\GETSPACE.PRG is in queue
    C:\DBASE\ADMIN\EXPERT\LOWER.PRG is in queue

C>PRINT /T
PRINT queue is empty

C>_
```

Figure 8.8: Partial PRINT queue

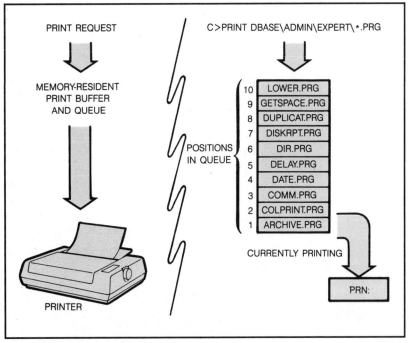

Figure 8.9: How the PRINT queue works

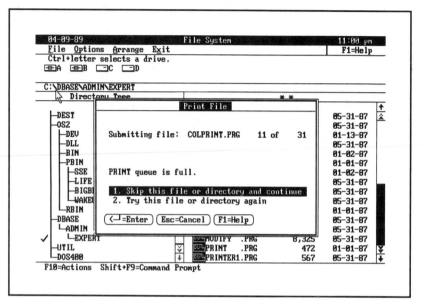

Figure 8.10: Queuing files in DOS 4

Although each increase in queue size takes up additional memory, you should use this command if you frequently need to print many files.

Three other switches are always available to you for management of the queue and its entries. As you can see in Table 8.3, they are /P (Print), /C, (Cancel printing), and /T (Terminate all spooling). These can be used each time PRINT is invoked, although you'll usually prefer to simply list the files you want to print.

You'll probably use /P least often, since it is already the system default. When you select the .PRG files and the Print option as shown in in Figure 8.6, DOS 4 queues up the chosen files, assuming that there are enough available slots in the queue. In earlier DOS versions, you invoke the PRINT command and specify the files to be printed, as in

PRINT DISKRPT.PRG LOWER.PRG MENU.PRG MESSAGE.PRG

The /P switch is assumed by DOS; it is not necessary to enter it specifically. You will only need to use it when you construct more complicated PRINT requests.

Switch and Parameter	**Effect**
/P:*FileName(s)*	Prints the file(s) specified; this is the default
/C:*FileName(s)*	Cancels the printing of the file(s) specified
/T:*FileName(s)*	Terminates the printing of all specified file(s) in the PRINT queue

Table 8.3: Switches and parameters for any PRINT command

When specifying file names in a PRINT command, you can list several separately named files on the same PRINT request line.

To cancel print requests or see a PRINT queue's status when you are in DOS 4's File System, press Shift-F9 to bring up the command prompt. You can then enter the appropriate commands.

If you want to cancel the printing of one or more files already in the queue, you can do so at the command prompt with the /C switch. For instance, to remove the DIR.PRG and DATE.PRG entries from the queue, effectively canceling the former print request for those two files, enter

PRINT DIR.PRG /C DATE.PRG

Notice that the /C switch applies to the file name immediately preceding the switch in the command line and all files listed after it (up until the next switch). This allows a complex but useful construction in which you simultaneously add and remove queue entries. In the next example, LOWER.PRG and DUPLICAT.PRG are removed from the queue with /C, while STATS.PRG is added with /P:

PRINT LOWER.PRG /C DUPLICAT.PRG STATS.PRG /P

Like the /C switch, the /P switch applies to the file name immediately preceding it on the command line.

If the file you wish to cancel is currently printing, the printing will stop and you will receive a message to that effect. If the file you cancel is elsewhere in the queue, it will be removed, and the new status of the PRINT queue will be displayed on your monitor. In fact, you can always see the current queue status by simply entering the PRINT command at the DOS prompt with no parameters or switches. Figure 8.11 demonstrates a status request issued partway through the printing of the .PRG files.

```
C>PRINT

    C:\DBASE\ADMIN\EXPERT\DISKRPT.PRG is currently being printed
    C:\DBASE\ADMIN\EXPERT\DUPLICAT.PRG is in queue
    C:\DBASE\ADMIN\EXPERT\GETSPACE.PRG is in queue
    C:\DBASE\ADMIN\EXPERT\LOWER.PRG is in queue

C>_
```

Figure 8.11: Current status of the PRINT queue

If you use a plotter and your software allows off-line plotting (that is, the software doesn't have to control the plotting process directly), you can use the PRINT command to queue several plots at once. Refer to your plotting program's documentation for further details.

Finally, the /T switch will cancel all file names in the queue. Perhaps the paper has jammed, or an ink-jet cartridge has run dry while the printing continues. In these cases, you may like to cancel all outstanding print requests and then restart the output spool, naming specific files in your desired order. Simply enter the command

PRINT /T

DOS will print the message ''All files canceled by operator'' on the printer. It will also display on the screen a message stating that the PRINT queue is empty.

SUMMARY

Printed output from your system is fundamental for nearly all software applications. This chapter has presented a variety of methods for obtaining printed output for both simple screen images and files:

- You can easily obtain hard-copy printouts of screen images consisting solely of text characters by using the Shift-PrtSc key combination.

- You can generate printed images of graphics screen images with the same Shift-PrtSc combination, provided that you first run the GRAPHICS command.

- You can use GRAPHICS at the command prompt, or run the GRAPHICS program from DOS 4's File System, with two useful switches for "special effects." The /B switch prints a separate background screen color if you are using multi-color printer ribbons. The /R switch produces the dramatic effect of white letters on a solid black background.

- You can use COPY to print text files that don't fit on one screen, by simply copying the files to a printer instead of to another file. However, you cannot use the Copy option, DOS 4's menu version of the COPY command, to print files.

- You can use PRINT to print files indirectly while you work at the same time with other DOS programs or commands. After you have invoked PRINT from the command prompt once, you can print files indirectly with DOS 4's Print option. This works for plotters as well as printers.

- You can control the files placed into the PRINT queue for output spooling by means of switches. You can initially configure the queue to hold up to 32 files with the /Q switch, and you can control how much time and memory DOS will reserve for spooling operations with the /M, /B, /U, and /S switches.

- You can add more files to the PRINT queue with the /P switch, remove files from the queue with the /C switch, and terminating all spooling operations by removing all files from the queue with the /T switch.

Now that you've learned several methods of printing with DOS, you can extend these techniques with the information in the next chapter. Printing is only one form of data communications. Chapter 9 will take you on an extended tour of other DOS communications capabilities, which permit information to be transferred to many other output devices besides printers.

COMMUNICATIONS

CHAPTER *9*

PRINTING IS ONE FORM OF SYSTEM COMMUNICATIONS; you learned about it first in Chapter 8 because of its central role in any computer system. This chapter concentrates on the speaking and listening that goes on between computer devices. As you'll see, there are many other devices to understand besides printers in any complete computer system. Beyond simply connecting these devices, you will learn in this chapter how to get them started and how to transfer information to and from them. Learn this information well, and you will no longer be at anybody else's mercy when it comes to buying and hooking up new equipment.

This chapter will help you understand the differences between parallel and serial communications, so you can make intelligent decisions about which is right for you. You will also learn enough about the various aspects of these two kinds of communications to use the DOS communications setup commands properly.

One major DOS command in particular, the MODE command, is central to an understanding of data transfer to printers, serial ports, and the video display. You'll learn what it can do for you and when to use it. It will give you control over

- Your printer (for improving the appearance of your hard-copy output),

- Your video screen (for enhancing all displayed information),

- Your keyboard (for getting more out of each key than simply what is printed on the key), and

- Just about any additional device at all that connects to one of the communications ports (plugs) in the back of your computer. This includes such devices as plotters, modems, and digitizers.

SYSTEM COMMUNICATIONS IN GENERAL

To understand computer communications, you need to understand the concept of data structure and storage. When you enter keyboard characters into programs, either as data or instructions, you enter them as numbers, letters, or punctuation marks, as represented on the face of the key. Each of these keystrokes is interpreted by the computer as a well-defined string of *binary digits,* the 0's and 1's you may already know about.

A computer and all its connected devices (*peripheral* devices) can be thought of simply as a large collection of very tiny electronic parts. Each of those parts can receive—or *not* receive—a small voltage, according to the logic built into the computer. The voltages affect the bits of magnetic material that store data for you or store instructions for the computer itself. If a bit is energized with a small voltage, it has a value of 1. If it receives no voltage, it has a value of 0. The word *binary* means two; as you see, a single bit has two possible values, 0 or 1.

You may not realize it, but in communicating with others, you usually perform a variety of tasks based on simple yes/no answers or simple directives. Everything can be broken down into smaller and smaller components, from hitting a baseball properly, to conducting an interview, to carrying out a superior's orders. Similarly, in a computer system, everything can be broken down into component bits. Complex logic and decision making are broken down into sequences of bits that either receive voltage or do not receive voltage—values of 1 or 0. Perhaps this is not as rich an alphabet as A through Z, but it serves the same purpose.

Communication between people is a sequence of sentences, which consist of a sequence of words, which in turn consist of a sequence of letters. These sequences are broken up by verbal pauses or inflections, or written punctuation marks, intended to help the listener (or reader) better understand the speaker (or writer). Pauses and punctuation, therefore, help to *synchronize* the communication of information. To synchronize computer communications, a sequence of 0's and 1's is grouped into seven or eight data bits, each group representing a character. Characters can be letters (A–Z), numbers (0–9), or special symbols or codes (* # % " : > ? and so on).

To understand why some communications use seven data bits while others use eight, let's briefly look at the binary number system. One bit can have the value 0 or 1. Therefore, two bits in a row have four possible combinations of values, since each bit has two possible values:

- 0 followed by 0, or 00
- 0 followed by 1, or 01
- 1 followed by 0, or 10
- 1 followed by 1, or 11

Taking this a step further, three bits in a row can have eight possibilities:

- 0 followed by 00, or 000
- 0 followed by 01, or 001
- 0 followed by 10, or 010
- 0 followed by 11, or 011
- 1 followed by 00, or 100
- 1 followed by 01, or 101
- 1 followed by 10, or 110
- 1 followed by 11, or 111

As you can see, the binary system is based on powers of the number 2. With one data bit, there are two possibilities (2^1); with two data bits, there are four possibilities (2^2); and with three data bits, there are eight possibilities (2^3). Continuing this progression will result in the following:

- Four data bits = 16 possibilities (2^4)
- Five data bits = 32 possibilities (2^5)

- Six data bits = 64 possibilities (2^6)
- Seven data bits = 128 possibilities (2^7)
- Eight data bits = 256 possibilities (2^8)

The standard keyboard and ASCII character set is more than covered by the 128 possibilities contained in seven data bits. However, there are additional characters (graphics characters, foreign-language characters, and so on) that constitute what is called the *extended ASCII set*. When these additional characters must be transmitted, the eight-bit form of data communications is used. Appendix B covers this issue more fully. You will usually see characters represented as eight bits, and communicated as such. This conventional eight-bit unit is a byte, the fundamental storage and data unit you deal with throughout DOS.

The groups of bits we have been examining represent either data or controlling information. In a conversation, you gain someone's attention by saying their name or saying something like "Hey, you." Computer communications use special groups of bits to gain the attention of another device. Once the attention is obtained with this *control code,* or special sequence of bits, the actual data transmission can begin.

Computers also use additional bits to ensure synchronization. *Stop bits* follow each unique character code (string of bits) to set it off from other transmitted information. In order to minimize sending or receiving errors, a *parity bit* is also sent after the data bits. This bit is used by both the transmitting and receiving equipment, but how it is computed and used is beyond the scope of this book.

PARALLEL VERSUS SERIAL COMMUNICATIONS

When you type a capital J from the keyboard, a code is sent to the computer's input routines, which translate it into the binary digits 01001010. The letter itself is echoed back to the video screen to confirm what you typed (see Figure 9.1). Remember that the video screen is part of the system's console; the keyboard is the input part of the console and the video screen is the output part. The passing of information between these parts is called data transmission.

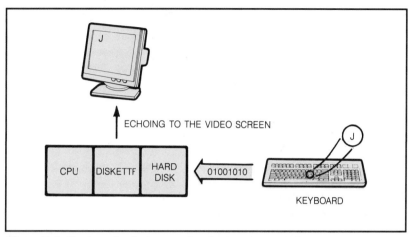

Figure 9.1: Keyboard echoing—a simple data transmission

Serial communications are often referred to as *asynchronous communications,* because the sending and receiving devices do not send and receive simultaneously, or synchronously. Instead, each uses an agreed set of electrical signals to indicate when to stop and start actual data transmission (see the MODE command later in this chapter).

There are two methods of data transmission: parallel and serial. Nearly all DOS microcomputers are connected with peripheral devices using one of these two communication techniques. Although most printers use the parallel method of data transmission, some use the serial method. Other peripheral devices like plotters, digitizers, modems, and mice usually transmit data serially.

If a peripheral device is connected to a serial port and is designed for serial transmission, each bit will be sent to or received from the central processing unit one bit at a time, and only one transmission wire will be used. If the peripheral device is connected to a parallel port and is designed for parallel transmission, then eight separate bits will be transmitted simultaneously over eight separate wires. (In both cases, other wires are used for additional purposes, such as the synchronization of signals or grounding; however, it's sufficient in this context to understand the concept in terms of one wire versus eight.)

Consider a simple analogy. In Figure 9.2 an airport's baggage terminal has eight conveyor belts, and passengers' suitcases are unloaded from eight flights simultaneously. In Figure 9.3, however, the airport has only one conveyor belt. The baggage from all eight flights is unloaded onto it. The passengers in this situation have to wait eight times as long as those in the first airport, and they probably won't be happy about it. Then again, the airline officials may not mind, since they spent one-eighth the amount of money on the conveyor mechanism and the ongoing expenses for maintenance and

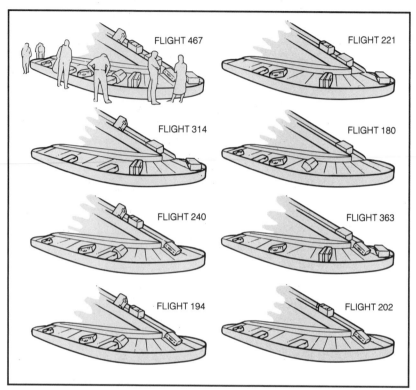

Figure 9.2: Unloading luggage with multiple conveyor belts

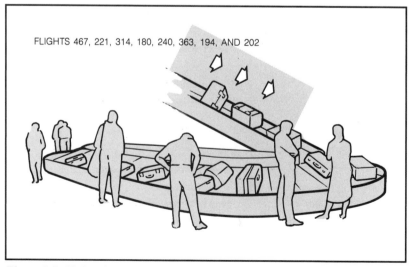

Figure 9.3: Unloading luggage with one conveyor belt

terminal space rental. It's a tradeoff of time versus money. In this analogy, you are the airline officials. You make the decision about what equipment you buy and use, deciding whether to spend more money on parallel connections or less money on serial connections, which require more waiting time for certain peripheral devices.

Let's return to the example of keyboard data transmission. Say you type in the word JUDD and you want the CPU to send it to a peripheral device. Your keystrokes will be translated into the ASCII character codes shown in Table 9.1.

Figure 9.4 shows a parallel transmission of these characters. As you can see, eight wires are used. A serial transmission of the same characters would require only one wire, as you can see in Figure 9.5.

LETTER	BINARY DIGITS
J	01001010
U	01010101
D	01000100
D	01000100

Table 9.1: ASCII codes for the letters J, U, D, and D

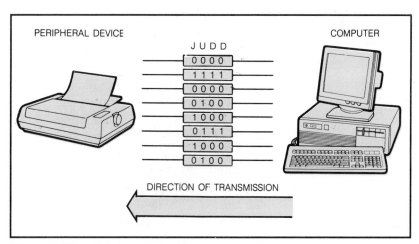

Figure 9.4: Parallel data transmission

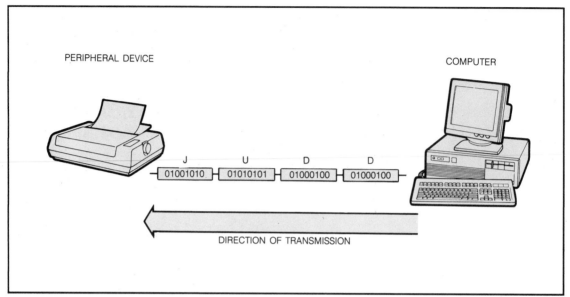

PERIPHERAL DEVICE

COMPUTER

J   U   D   D

01001010   01010101   01000100   01000100

DIRECTION OF TRANSMISSION

Figure 9.5: Serial data transmission

However, the transmission of data would be much slower. This explains why virtually all printers that print faster than several hundred characters per second *must* use parallel transmission and be connected to a computer correctly for parallel transmission.

DOS DEVICES VERSUS FILES

Operating systems treat devices that represent either the source of data or the destination for data in a consistent manner. As you've seen many times already, you specify the source and destination of the data in your software commands. The consistency with which you can reference hardware devices (like the console) or software ''devices'' (like a disk file) makes it easy to learn both new commands and new concepts. Commands like COPY work in precisely the same way for a data transfer from a CPU to a disk file or a data transfer from a CPU to a peripheral device (a printer).

DOS is designed to understand and permit the referencing of certain typical peripheral devices. Unlike file names, which you can make up yourself (as long as you obey certain rules), device names are restricted to certain reserved names, shown in Figure 9.6. DOS

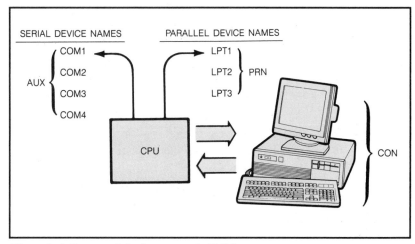

Figure 9.6: Reserved device names in DOS

allows only three specific parallel device names (LPT1, LPT2, and LPT3) and four serial device names (COM1, COM2, COM3, and COM4). Versions of DOS earlier than 3.3 only allowed two serial device names, COM1 and COM2.

The additional device names in Figure 9.6, AUX and PRN, are called standard device names. They are used to communicate with the first connected serial and parallel ports, respectively. You can use these nonspecific device names if you don't want to be bothered with the details of which communications port is connected to your printer or device. Programs don't necessarily have to know which device is connected to which port. They can simply reference PRN, and the output will be routed to the first connected parallel port; or they can reference AUX, and the output will be routed to the first connected auxiliary communications (serial) port.

Keep in mind that you must purchase the actual hardware to make the proper connections. In other words, DOS may understand what it means to send data to a serial port called COM1, but you must have a serial connector on your system, and it must be connected to a serial device, or the request is meaningless.

Even if you have purchased various pieces of peripheral equipment and sufficient add-in boards to connect them, DOS may not be able to address all of them. For instance, if your setup is like that in Table 9.2, there are no more reserved names available if you decide

Like the drive names in previous chapters (A, B, C, and so on), reserved device names should be followed by a colon in your commands. This lets DOS know when the device name ends and the sequence of parameter values begins.

You can improve the flexibility of your system design by using PRN and AUX as port device names. AUX can refer to any one of the four serial ports, COM1 to COM4. Later, you can easily change your hardware connections without having to make any changes to your software references.

to buy another serial device (perhaps an inexpensive networking alternative). In this case, you would have to buy some form of switch. You would need to connect the switch to one port (say, COM1) and then connect the two peripherals (the mouse and the modem, for example) to the switch.

Once all this hardware has been connected, you still must exercise great care to ensure that your software will work. The key to this is to make sure that two or more devices connected to the same switch do not try to transmit data at the same time. Your first reaction may be that this isn't a complication you expect to run into very often. On the other hand, you may have a computer with only one serial port (COM1), and you might want to use a graphics package that requires a mouse for input and a plotter for output. In this case, short of buying another serial-port connector, you can run your software by using a switch for the two devices. You might not think that there will be any problem with both devices trying to use the same serial line simultaneously, but what actually happens is that you become impatient with the slowness of the plotter, and long to regain control of the computer while the plot progresses independently.

When you are using the same serial line for two purposes, one operation must wait for the other to finish. If you are plotting, you cannot throw the switch to activate the mouse until all the plotting data has been transmitted to the plotter. When you are using the mouse to control cursor movement and menu selections, you cannot switch over to the plotter for output until all mouse movements have been completed.

INITIALIZING DEVICES AND PORTS

Different peripheral devices, when connected to the computer, require special setup sequences. The MODE command permits you

DOS RESERVED NAME	DEFINITION	SAMPLE CONNECTION
LPT1	First parallel port	Fast draft printer
LPT2	Second parallel port	Letter-quality printer
LPT3	Third parallel port	Laser printer
COM1	First serial port	Modem
COM2	Second serial port	Plotter
COM3	Third serial port	Mouse
COM4	Fourth serial port	Digitizer

Table 9.2: A sample port configuration

Installing memory-resident programs while in the DOS 4 File System can crash your system. Since some forms of the MODE command install such programs, it is safest to run MODE from a command prompt *before* invoking the DOS 4 shell.

to initialize aspects of your printers and your serial-port devices, as well as to redirect output between parallel and serial ports, and even to control some features of your video display. Other capabilities of MODE for the support of foreign-language characters will be discussed in Chapter 11. Figure 9.7 depicts the capabilities of the MODE command that you'll explore in this section.

Since the syntax of some of the optional parameters changed in DOS 4, I use the newer syntax here. If you have an earlier version of DOS, you should refer to your DOS user's manual. Since I discuss only the principal parameters in this section, you should refer to Chapter 22 to learn about the many optional parameters that are only infrequently needed.

In all four situations, the MODE command is invoked like any other disk-resident DOS command. Simply typing MODE at the DOS prompt, preceded by any drive or path-name specification, will initiate the MODE operations. Assuming MODE is either in the current drive and directory or on the path you have specified, you would enter

MODE *Parameters*

In DOS 4, *Parameters* represents what you enter in the Options field after you select MODE.COM in the File System, as seen in Figure 9.8. In the remainder of this chapter, I'll show you the command-prompt syntax of the MODE command.

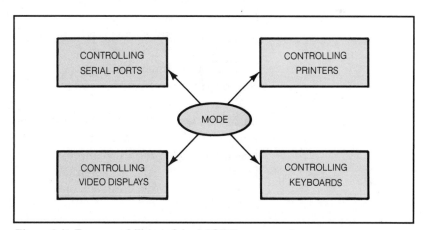

Figure 9.7: Four capabilities of the MODE command

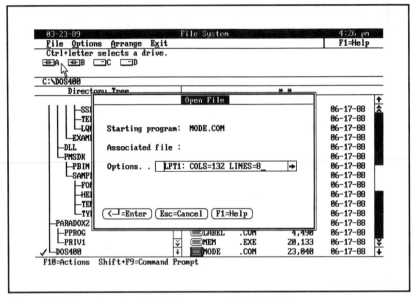

Figure 9.8: Running the MODE command in DOS 4

Depending on what parameters you specify, one of the four versions of this command will be activated. The four major versions of this command almost act as four separate commands.

CONTROLLING THE PRINTER   An operation that is often desired by users is to turn on *compressed print*. Wide spreadsheets and database records are often hard to read when the number of characters per line exceeds the standard 80 characters. Most printers assume a normal default of 80 characters, because most programs generate data using an 80-column video screen. Printers also assume a default value of 6 lines per vertical inch, but you can control that as well.

Programs that can scroll left and right, like spreadsheets and database management programs, can generate more than 80 columns on a line. The following version of MODE gives you a simple way to instruct DOS to send the printer the necessary control codes requesting it to squeeze up to 132 characters on a line, or to squeeze up to 8 lines of output per vertical inch on the paper. The general form of this MODE command is

MODE *PrinterPort CharsPerLine LinesPerInch*

⊙ This version of the MODE command assumes you are using the most common kind of printer: an EPSON MX series, an IBM graphics printer, or a compatible. Any other printer may require different control codes, making this DOS command useless to you.

Filling in the parameters with values, you could issue the following command to initialize the printer port to LPT1, the characters per line to 132, and the lines per inch to 8:

MODE LPT1: COLS = 132 LINES = 8

Figure 9.9 demonstrates what a sample text file would look like if it was printed after this command was executed. Figures 9.10 through 9.12 show the other variations on the two parameters controlling characters per line and lines per inch.

```
      This line and the next are limited to 80 characters or less.
      ........10........20........30........40........50........60........70........80
      This next line typifies wide spreadsheet rows or data base records (and 'wraps around' in 80 column mode)
1"    ........10........20........30........40........50........60........70........80........90.......100.......120.......132..
      These next four lines take up 1/2" vertically
      when lines per inch (LPI) is set to 8,
      and take up 2/3" when LPI = 6,
      regardless of how the characters per line is set.
```

Figure 9.9: Output of MODE LPT1: COLS = 132 LINES = 8

```
      This line and the next are limited to 80 characters or less.
      ........10........20........30........40........50........60........70........80
      This next line typifies wide spreadsheet rows or data base records (and 'wraps a
1"    round' in 80 column mode)
      ........10........20........30........40........50........60........70........80
      ........90.......100.......120.......132..
      These next four lines take up 1/2" vertically
      when lines per inch (LPI) is set to 8,
      and take up 2/3" when LPI = 6,
      regardless of how the characters per line is set.
```

Figure 9.10: Output of MODE LPT1: COLS = 80 LINES = 6 (the DOS default)

```
      This line and the next are limited to 80 characters or less.
      ........10........20........30........40........50........60........70........80
      This next line typifies wide spreadsheet rows or data base records (and 'wraps around' in 80 column mode)
1"    ........10........20........30........40........50........60........70........80........90.......100.......120.......132..
      These next four lines take up 1/2" vertically
      when lines per inch (LPI) is set to 8,
      and take up 2/3" when LPI = 6,
      regardless of how the characters per line is set.
```

Figure 9.11: Output of MODE LPT1: COLS = 132 LINES = 6

```
      This line and the next are limited to 80 characters or less.
      ........10........20........30........40........50........60........70........80
      This next line typifies wide spreadsheet rows or data base records (and 'wraps a
1"    round' in 80 column mode)
      ........10........20........30........40........50........60........70........80
      ........90.......100.......120.......132..
      These next four lines take up 1/2" vertically
      when lines per inch (LPI) is set to 8,
      and take up 2/3" when LPI = 6,
      regardless of how the characters per line is set.
```

Figure 9.12: Output of MODE LPT1: COLS = 80 LINES = 8

The MODE command has limited capability for sending control codes to printers. Some applications like Lotus 1-2-3 and Framework II let you send control codes directly to a printer. In fact, you can use EDLIN or your own word processor to include a sequence of control codes in a file (say, CTRLCODE.TXT) and then send the file directly to a printer with the simple instruction COPY CTRLCODE.TXT PRN.

With these MODE commands for compressed print, DOS will respond to your command entry with statements similar to the following:

```
LPT1: not rerouted
LPT1: set for 132
Printer lines per inch set
No retry on parallel printer time-out
```

The first and fourth lines of these DOS messages refer to other versions of the MODE command, which you'll see shortly. The second and third lines indicate the horizontal and vertical printer settings, respectively. DOS 4 users will then be prompted to "Press Enter to return to File System."

Dot-matrix printers make the horizontal compression occur by printing the dots closer together. Letter-quality printers create the same effect by leaving less space between characters. Compressing the print on letter-quality printers usually requires you to change the print wheel or thimble so the resulting squeezed printout is readable.

INITIALIZING SERIAL COMMUNICATIONS PORTS　Synchronization is a difficult problem when serial devices are connected to computers. For example, if a computer sends data out to the serial port at a rate of 1200 bits per second, any printer connected to that port must be set (by means of hardware switches or software initialization) to receive this information at the same rate. This requirement also works in reverse.

A second version of the MODE command allows you to correctly set a number of parameters for this and other aspects of serial communications. The general form of this MODE command is

Don't bother initially with this version of the MODE command; follow the initialization instructions in your software program's manual or in your serial device's instruction book. This usually is all you need for success—only if this fails will you need to understand these MODE parameters more fully.

MODE *SerialPort BaudRate, Parity, DataBits, StopBits, Retry*

The parameters have the following meanings:

- *SerialPort* indicates which one of the four possible peripheral connectors is being used by DOS for a particular device.

- *BaudRate* sets the speed at which data bits will be transmitted through the serial port.

- *Parity* represents the number of binary 1's, if any, that are used in a data transmission; this is used for error detection.

- *DataBits* specifies the number of bits used to represent actual transmitted data.

- *StopBits* represents the one or two bits used at the end of the data bits to indicate that end.

- *Retry* indicates how MODE is to respond to another system request for the serial port.

Table 9.3 contains the allowable values for these parameters.

As an example, the following command issued at the DOS prompt would set the second serial port to transmit at 1200 baud, with no parity, using eight data bits with one stop bit:

MODE COM2: BAUD = 1200 PARITY = N DATA = 8 STOP = 1 RETRY = R

DOS 4 users will find that the RETRY = R setting is the most compatible with earlier DOS versions.

The last parameter value, RETRY = R, requests that DOS automatically try again to send data to a busy communications port. This is necessary when the first request is met by a control signal indicating that the device is still busy processing the last transmission. This setting is particularly useful with printers, which process data significantly slower than the computer's central processing unit.

This version of the MODE command is disk-resident, but it does require that a permanent part of physical memory be reserved for its

PARAMETER	POSSIBLE VALUES
SerialPort	COM1, COM2, COM3, or COM4
BaudRate	110, 150, 300, 600, 1200, 2400, 4800, 9600, or 19200
Parity	(none, odd, even, mark, or space)
DataBits	5, 6, 7 or 8
StopBits	1, 1.5, or 2
Retry	E (the default) returns an error to a busy port's status check. B returns a busy signal to a busy port's status check. R returns a ready signal to a busy port's status check.

processing and buffering chores. This means that when you run the command for the first time, it will take up a small additional amount of memory, extending the memory requirements of your DOS's memory-resident portion. A message to that effect is issued by DOS at the same time as confirmation is made of the port settings:

Resident portion of MODE loaded
COM2: 1200,n,8,1,r

Normally, serial devices are accompanied by instruction manuals that describe the required settings. The best advice is to follow scrupulously the suggested settings for connection. Switches often have to be set on or in the printer, as well as on the board that is controlling your serial port itself. In addition, the software product you are using might need to be initialized as well, since it may send its data directly to the port.

All of these locations and parameters are opportunities for error or frustration in connecting serial devices to computers. Unfortunately, there is no consistent standard for serial communications as there is for parallel communications. You must determine the characteristics of your serial device and issue the proper MODE command *before* using the port in any way. Good luck!

CONNECTING A SERIAL PRINTER TO A COM PORT   In the specific case where the serial device you have connected to a COM port is a printer, an additional version of the MODE command is required. Printed output usually goes to a PRN device (usually a parallel port like LPT1), so you must redirect that output to a COM port with the command

MODE LPT*Number:* = COM*Number*

The *Number* parameter should hold the specific number of your chosen port.

Assuming that you have first initialized the communications parameters for the port so that the device and the CPU are synchronized, as in the last section, you can redirect the LPT1 port to the COM2 port with

MODE LPT1: = COM2

DOS will confirm the redirection for all succeeding print output requests with the following:

LPT1: rerouted to COM2:

CONTROLLING THE MODE OF THE VIDEO DISPLAY Certain video characteristics can be controlled with the final version of the MODE command. This version is used most often when you purchase nonstandard equipment and when you connect multiple monitors to your computer. The command is used to tell DOS which monitor is receiving the video-display request; it also allows you to adjust the video image in a horizontal direction.

The command has at most three parameters, of which the first is the most often used:

MODE *VideoType, Direction, TestPattern*

The three parameters can take on the values shown in Table 9.4.

PARAMETER	POSSIBLE VALUES
VideoType	MONO (for IBM monochrome display)
	CO80 (for color 80-column display)
	CO40 (for color 40-column display)
	BW80 (for black-and-white, 80-column display; this disables color on a normal color monitor)
	BW40 (for black-and-white, 40-column display)
	80 (adjusts to 80-column display; does not change the color status)
	40 (adjusts to 40-column display; does not change the color status)
Direction	R or L (for right or left)
TestPattern	T (if a test pattern is to be shown)

Table 9.4: Video-display values for MODE parameters

The simplest form of this version of the MODE command only involves the *Video Type* parameter. Setting the display mode to 40 or 80 characters is as simple as entering

MODE 80

or

MODE 40

80-column mode is the standard for business applications, although some games reset the mode to 40 columns. Naturally, 40-column mode produces larger, more legible characters on the video monitor. Figures 9.13 and 9.14 demonstrate the same directory display in 80- and 40-column modes.

Entering a parameter value of 40 or 80 for *Video Type* will not affect the current status of the monitor's color. Assuming the monitor is controlled by a CGA (color graphics adapter) or an EGA (extended graphics adapter), you can explicitly enable or disable color by preceding the column number by CO (to enable color) or BW (to disable color, leaving a black-and-white image). If you have an IBM monochrome display, the proper parameter value is MONO. In fact, if

```
C>DIR

    Volume in drive C is ROBBINS
    Directory of  C:\UTILITY\XENO

    .            <DIR>      5-02-86    1:17p
    ..           <DIR>      5-02-86    1:17p
    XENOCOPY EXE     83968  8-17-87    6:18p
    README           5067   8-21-87   12:35p
    XDEF     OPT     1221    8-25-87   10:06a
    SYBEX    OPT     1221    8-25-87   10:07a
         6 File(s)     634880 bytes free

C>_
```

Figure 9.13: Directory display after a MODE 80 command

your system has both a monochrome *and* a color monitor, you can switch output between them by simply entering

MODE MONO

to switch output to the monochrome monitor, or

MODE CO80

to switch output to the color monitor, using 80 columns with color enabled.

Some monitors need a certain amount of horizontal adjustment. You may not need to adjust yours very often, but if you do, the *Direction* and *TestPattern* parameters will come in handy. You can shift the display to the right or to the left by entering an R or an L as the *Direction* parameter. In either case, you can display a test pattern on the screen to help with the adjustments by entering a T as the *TestPattern* parameter. Entering

MODE 80, L, T

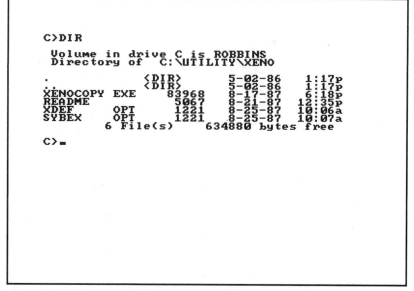

Figure 9.14: Directory display after a MODE 40 command

produces the screen shown in Figure 9.15.

If you answer N (for No) to the question on seeing the rightmost 9, DOS will shift the entire screen image to the left by one character (if the display mode is 40 columns) or by two characters (if it is 80 columns). You will then be asked the same question, and you can shift the display until all 80 characters are visible—when the rightmost 9 can be seen.

SETTING YOUR KEYBOARD'S TYPEMATIC RATE This keyboard repetition feature is only available to DOS 4 users. A new variation of the MODE command enables you to set both the rate at which a keystroke is repeated as you hold a key down and the delay time before the repetitions begin.

You can submit the MODE command using the special RATE and DELAY optional parameters:

MODE CON *SetRate SetDelay*

You should consult your DOS user's manual for a detailed listing of all

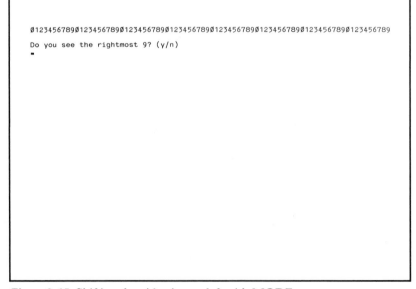

```
0123456789012345678901234567890123456789012345678901234567890123456789012345678901234567890123456789
Do you see the rightmost 9? (y/n)
```

Figure 9.15: Shifting the video image left with MODE

possible settings for these parameters. As a simple example, the following entry will set the typematic rate to two repetitions per second:

MODE CON RATE = 1

The *SetRate* parameter actually ranges from a value of 1 (standing for 2 repetitions per second) to a value of 32 (standing for 30 repetitions per second).

You control the auto-repeat delay time with the second parameter. You can set a 1 second delay by entering:

MODE CON DELAY = 4

The range of values for the *Set Delay* parameter varies from 1 to 4, standing for delay times of 1/4, 1/2, 3/4, and 1 second. Naturally, you can combine these two optional parameter settings into one command entry.

SUMMARY

This chapter covered important communications aspects of DOS. Output from your system is fundamental to effectiveness, and in this chapter, you learned quite a bit about data transfer and system output in general. Here is a brief review:

- Files and hardware devices share certain similarities, which permits you to use them interchangeably in a number of commands.

- Devices communicate with the central processing unit of your computer in one of two ways: by parallel or serial data transmission. Parallel communications send data bits out to a device on separate wires simultaneously. Serial communications send the same data bits out to a device on a single wire successively, using additional control characters and bits to help distinguish when and where the transmission and characters begin and end.

- Each bit of magnetic memory—data bit—can be either energized with a voltage or not energized, with a value of 1 or 0, respectively. Eight bits make up the proverbial byte, and each byte can represent up to 256 different codes. These codes can represent either standard letters, numbers, and punctuation, or special control codes, foreign-language characters, and graphics characters.

- DOS can send and receive bytes of information to and from three parallel devices connected to hardware ports. These devices and their parts are addressed by programs as LPT1, LPT2, and LPT3.

- DOS 3.3 and later versions also can send data to and accept data from as many as four separate devices connected to four communications ports. These serial ports are addressed by the names COM1, COM2, COM3, and COM4. Earlier versions of DOS only allowed the first two COM ports to be referenced.

- The MODE command is the principal DOS command for controlling serial communications. It handles both the setup and status of certain serial and parallel output devices. It is also required to properly initialize the communications between a computer and a printer or plotter. Several parameters defining the command must be carefully set in order to synchronize the CPU and the device, or the data transfer may not work at all. The parameters include the baud rate, the parity of the transmission, the number of data bits and stop bits, and the transmission instructions for busy ports. DOS's MODE command also lets you set the keyboard repetition (typematic) rate and the delay time before automatic repetitions begin.

- Another version of the MODE command allows you to control multiple display monitors, which can be either color or black-and-white and can display either 40 or 80 columns across.

- DOS 4's MODE command also lets you set the keyboard repetition (typematic) rate and the delay time before repetitions begin.

By now you've certainly learned many new things about DOS and have no doubt begun to use your disk and hardware capabilities more efficiently. This is a good time to step back and consider the work invested in your system. The next chapter emphasizes the protection of this investment—it shows you how to back up and restore your files.

PART 4

REFINING YOUR SYSTEM

In Part 4, you will learn advanced techniques that are normally overlooked by many beginning and intermediate DOS users. Chapter 10 shows you how to protect your files by backing them up and how to restore backed-up files if the originals are lost. In Chapter 11, you will start learning how to customize your DOS. You will find out how to create and use a RAM disk, use expanded memory in DOS 4, control the screen display, and redefine keys. Chapter 12 explains how to customize your system for working with a foreign language. The customization techniques include adapting your keyboard, screen display, and printer. Finally, Chapter 13 teaches you how to use pipes, filters, and redirection to control input and output in your computer system.

BACKUPS AND RESTORATIONS

Experience seems to be the best teacher in all things, and most people who back up files regularly do so because they have experienced an uncomfortable loss of data at some point. The more data they lost, the more frequently they now back up.

ONE OF THE DISADVANTAGES OF HARD DISKS IS THAT when and if they fail, or crash, all the information stored on them can be lost. Much more is at stake than just one floppy diskette's worth of contents. Back up your hard disk regularly or run the constant risk of losing your data!

Of course, you can also rewrite backed-up versions of files back onto your hard disk; this is usually done when the hard-disk version has been deleted, destroyed, or corrupted. You may never need to restore a file, but your backup files will provide you with some inexpensive protection against either hardware or software failure.

This chapter describes in depth how to protect your programs—and more importantly, your data—from loss due to operator error or hardware failure. However, you must remember to back up your files on a regular basis to keep the backup floppy diskettes up-to-date with the changes you've made on your hard disk. Depending on how frequently you generate new data files or update old ones, you may want to back up your disk every week or every month (or more or less frequently).

In fact, other than the regular backups you are going to make, there are three times when you should back up your hard disk:

1. Your computer is going to be moved. Especially if your computer will be traveling long distances in airplane cargo holds or in shipper's trucks, you should back up your data before the trip. Your hard disk may not survive the physical handling (or occasional abuse).

2. You are running out of space on your hard disk, and you decide to take an hour or two to delete some files, consolidate some directories, and create new branches in your directory

tree since you now feel much more comfortable using the DOS directory structure. With such a massive project, you should protect yourself against your own enthusiasm and fatigue by doing a backup.

3. You are going to run a fragmentation elimination program like VOPT. You will learn more in Chapter 18 about how programs like this can reorganize all the files on your disk, providing improved system performance afterwards. During the reorganization, your entire hard-disk contents are liable to loss in the event of a power failure. Do a complete disk backup just prior to running such a program.

SPECIAL COMMANDS FOR YOUR DISKS

If you're using a dual-diskette system, you can easily use DISKCOPY, COPY, or even XCOPY (see Chapter 17) to back up diskette files onto another diskette. Protecting yourself from the major trauma of losing an entire hard disk, however, requires more effort than that. DISKCOPY is designed for diskette copies, and the COPY and XCOPY commands have a fundamental weakness: the destination for your copied files is limited to what can be stored on that one drive. If the directory you're in contains more files than can fit on one destination diskette, or even if it contains one extremely large file that exceeds the capacity of the backup floppy, the COPY and XCOPY commands simply can't handle the job.

In order to allow you to back up files onto a series of floppy diskettes or another fixed (hard) disk, DOS provides a special command called BACKUP. With BACKUP you can make copies of the files on any of your disks. This command is usually used to back up the files from a hard disk and spread them, if necessary, over a series of floppy diskettes.

The BACKUP command does not work for copy-protected diskettes. As you will learn in Chapter 18, utility programs like COPY II PC allow you to back up diskettes that are copy-protected.

HOW BACKUP FILES ARE STORED

The files placed on a diskette by the BACKUP command are not stored as standard DOS files. In Figure 10.1, I used the DOS 4 Show Information window to present the directory listing of the sample .XY files to be backed up. Figure 10.2 shows the directory listing of the diskette in drive A after I completed the backup procedure. Compare these two figures. You'll see that the original files have not been backed up in their original format.

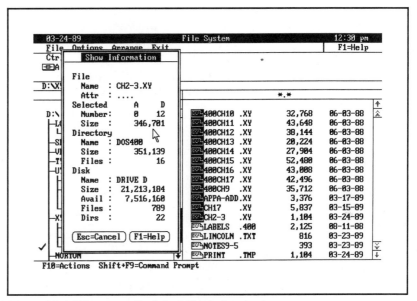

Figure 10.1: Directory of original files before backup

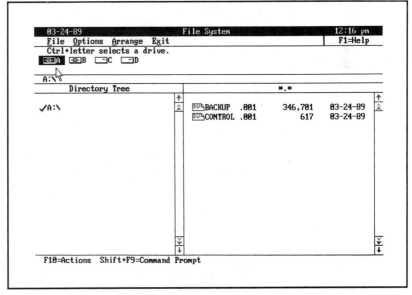

Figure 10.2: First backup diskette after completion

Figure 10.3 shows you the manner in which the files have been backed up. These original files have been combined efficiently into one single file, called BACKUP.001, which contains only the original data. A separate control file, called CONTROL.001, contains the actual file names and their lengths, as well as the source directory from which these files were obtained. As you can see in Figure 10.1's Show Information window, the twelve selected .XY files comprise a total of 346,701 bytes. This same number of bytes is written to the BACKUP.001 data file on the diskette.

This backup procedure was first implemented in DOS 3.3. If you have an earlier DOS version, your backup diskette will be quite different. It will have *file versions* (not replicas) of each of your original files, as well as an additional entry in the directory listing called BACKUP.@@@, with a length of 128 bytes. If you have a disk with this entry, it indicates that the files stored on that disk have been put there with an earlier DOS version of the BACKUP command.

Files stored with earlier versions of BACKUP *appear* to be independently accessible, but they cannot be read meaningfully with any of DOS's other commands, like the COPY command. In earlier versions of DOS, BACKUP changes the actual file contents, whereas in DOS 3.3 and later versions, it compacts the files into one file. You

The DOS 3.3 and DOS 4 versions of BACKUP are faster than previous versions, while requiring less disk space to store the original files. The primary reason for this is that each file does not waste extra disk cluster space during the storage process. The compaction technique uses both space and time more efficiently.

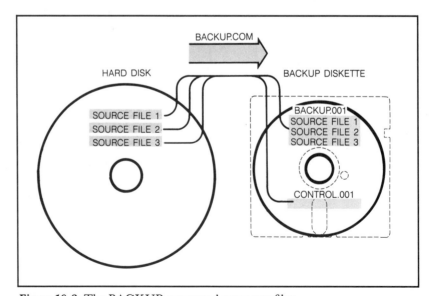

Figure 10.3: The BACKUP command compacts files

can only use these files again by restoring them to their original condition with the RESTORE command.

MAKING BACKUP COPIES OF YOUR FILES

When you format a diskette for use during the backup process, it is not necessary to use the /S switch. In fact, it is inadvisable: using /S will make less space available for the backup files on floppy diskettes.

You can back up a hard disk either onto diskettes or onto another hard disk. When you back up a hard disk onto diskettes, you also need to format enough diskettes before you begin. If you are using DOS 3.3 or a later version, you will be able to format them during the backup process. If you are using an earlier version of DOS, however, you should prepare in advance enough formatted destination diskettes to hold all of your data, since you cannot back up onto unformatted disks. (Only the DISKCOPY command can do that.) You will have to stop the backup process (or borrow someone else's computer) if you run out of formatted disks in the middle of backing up your files.

Backing up files from one hard disk to another is much faster than backing them up onto a collection of diskettes. It is also easier, since you don't have to insert and remove successive diskettes; the backup process between hard disks can proceed unattended.

If your system has an extra hard disk for backup, make sure that it has enough space to hold all the backup files. If it doesn't, the entire process will terminate, and you'll have to make space on the backup disk by deleting some files.

Before you start backing up files, you should learn how to use the DOS VERIFY command. VERIFY controls the degree of error checking performed by DOS after all disk-write operations. When you execute the command

VERIFY ON

the verification mode is turned on. Each disk write will be followed by a confirmation procedure verifying that the data just written can be read without error. It is a good idea to execute this command just prior to running a backup; it increases the likelihood that your backup files will be written accurately. Although data errors occur infrequently, a backup file is the worst place for such an error to occur. After your backup operation, you can execute VERIFY OFF at the DOS prompt to restore normal read/write operations. When the verification mode is on, overall DOS operations are significantly slowed down.

BACKING UP A COMPLETE DIRECTORY

The general form of the BACKUP command has two parameters:

BACKUP *SourceFile(s) DestinationDrive*

SourceFile(s) is the standard path name plus any specific file names you wish to select for backup. *DestinationDrive* is the letter identifier of the disk drive that will receive the file copies.

DOS 4 users can invoke the BACKUP command from the DOS Utilities menu seen in Figure 10.4. You then enter the appropriate source and destination values in the dialog box's Parameters field. When the Backup Utility dialog box appears, its Parameters field contains the following entry:

c:*.* a: /s

You can type over these default values with anything else. You will shortly learn the meaning of these specific values as well as the range of possible alternatives. In the rest of this chapter, I will use the command-prompt format for all command examples. Remember

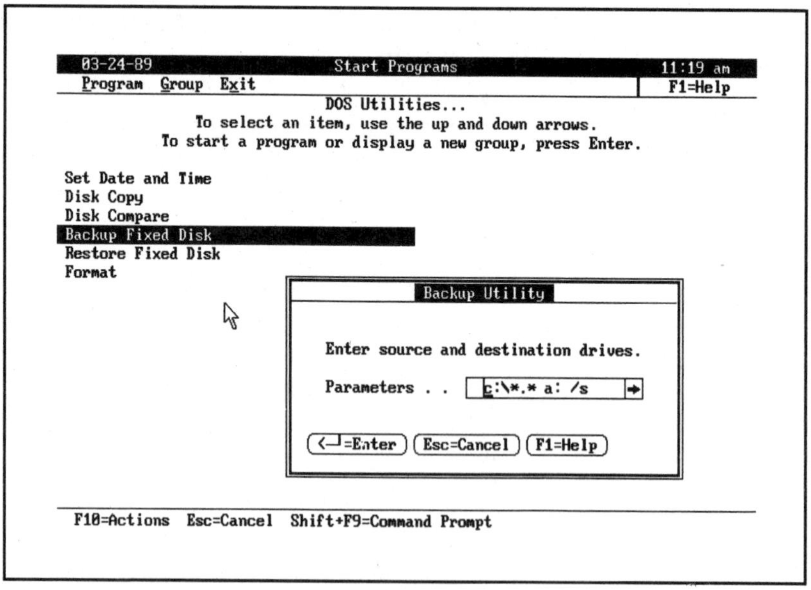

```
┌──────────────────────────────────────────────────────────────┐
│  ┌────────────────────────────────────────────────────────┐  │
│  │ 03-24-89              Start Programs           11:19 am │  │
│  │ Program  Group  Exit                          │ F1=Help │  │
│  │                   DOS Utilities...                        │
│  │         To select an item, use the up and down arrows.   │
│  │        To start a program or display a new group, press Enter.│
│  │                                                          │
│  │  Set Date and Time                                       │
│  │  Disk Copy                                               │
│  │  Disk Compare                                            │
│  │  Backup Fixed Disk                                       │
│  │  Restore Fixed Disk                                      │
│  │  Format                                                  │
│  │                    ┌─────────────Backup Utility────────┐ │
│  │                    │                                    │ │
│  │                    │  Enter source and destination drives.│
│  │                    │                                    │ │
│  │                    │  Parameters . . │c:\*.* a: /s │ ▶ │ │
│  │                    │                                    │ │
│  │                    │  (◄─┘=Enter) (Esc=Cancel) (F1=Help)│ │
│  │                    └────────────────────────────────────┘ │
│  │                                                          │
│  │  F10=Actions  Esc=Cancel  Shift+F9=Command Prompt        │
│  └────────────────────────────────────────────────────────┘  │
└──────────────────────────────────────────────────────────────┘
```

Figure 10.4: The Backup Utility dialog box

that if you run the command from a DOS 4 screen, you only need to enter the parameters (and any possible switches).

Suppose that you wanted to back up all the files in your D:\XYWRITE\DOS400 directory. You would simply specify the name of the desired directory as the first parameter. When you do not specify any specific files, DOS selects and copies all files in the directory to the backup drive (A).

> BACKUP D:\XYWRITE\DOS400 A:

DOS displays the message

> Insert backup diskette 01 in drive A:
>
> Warning! Files in the target drive
> A:\ root directory will be erased
> Press any key to continue. . .

This warning gives you a chance to verify that you put the correct diskette into drive A, before DOS overwrites everything on it. Presumably, you are placing a blank diskette into the destination drive to receive the source files. You could, of course, be reusing a previously used diskette containing files you don't mind writing over.

Pressing Return at this point will begin the backup process. All the files in the named directory will now be copied over to your backup diskette (or your backup hard disk, if your destination drive is another hard disk). DOS will list all the files in this directory as they are being backed up to the specified disk drive.

BACKING UP A PARTIAL DIRECTORY

You can also perform selective backups—for example, backing up only the .XY files from the D:\XYWRITE\DOS400 directory. Simply specify the names of the files you wish to back up. To back up all .XY files in the D:\XYWRITE\DOS400 directory, enter

> BACKUP D:\XYWRITE\DOS400*.XY A:

As always, DOS will list the files while it writes the backup copies (see Figure 10.5).

```
Insert backup diskette 01 in drive A:

WARNING! Files in the target drive
A:\ root directory will be erased
Press any key to continue . . .

*** Backing up files to drive A: ***
Diskette Number: 01

\XYWRITE\DOS400\400CH10.XY
\XYWRITE\DOS400\400CH11.XY
\XYWRITE\DOS400\400CH12.XY
\XYWRITE\DOS400\400CH13.XY
\XYWRITE\DOS400\400CH14.XY
\XYWRITE\DOS400\400CH15.XY
\XYWRITE\DOS400\400CH16.XY
\XYWRITE\DOS400\400CH17.XY
\XYWRITE\DOS400\400CH9.XY
\XYWRITE\DOS400\APPA-ADD.XY
\XYWRITE\DOS400\CH17.XY
\XYWRITE\DOS400\CH2-3.XY
Press any key to continue . . .
_
```

Figure 10.5: DOS lists file names as files are backed up

Files created by the BACKUP command may not be deleted; they are created with an attribute indicating that they are read-only, which means that you cannot erase them (see the ATTRIB command in Chapter 17). In order to regain the disk space on this diskette, you will have to reformat it with the FORMAT command.

If DOS runs out of room on your first diskette, you will be prompted like this:

> Insert backup diskette 02 in drive A:
>
> Warning! Files in the target drive
> A:\ root directory will be erased
> Press any key to continue. . .

DOS will continue to copy backup versions of your files onto this second diskette. The process will continue with additional diskettes, as necessary, until all your requested files have been copied.

OTHER TYPES OF BACKUP PROCESSING

You may often need to do more than back up to a blank diskette all or some of the files in a DOS directory. For example, you might want to add additional files to a backup set to maintain some grouping and organization in your backups. You might also want to include files in the directory tree *below* the main directory you've just specified. Then again, you might want to combine these possibilities with selection criteria that go beyond simple wild-card specifications. You might want to back up files that have changed since your last backup, and not want to spend time backing up unchanged files when they are already on a perfectly good backup disk. Or, you might want to back up only those files created or modified since a certain date or even after a certain time on a certain day.

All of these options can be invoked by using one or more of the DOS switches for the BACKUP command (see Table 10.1). These switches are described in the following sections. You will concentrate in this chapter on the most important ones; the others are presented more fully in Part 7, the command-reference section of this book.

⊙ If you already know how to use some advanced commands like SUBST, JOIN, APPEND, or ASSIGN (see Chapter 17), do not have these commands active when you issue the BACKUP command. They're difficult enough to use properly; it would not be possible for DOS to later restore files properly if these commands were active in a different way when you ran the BACKUP command.

ADDING FILES TO AN EXISTING BACKUP

The /A switch tells DOS not to erase (write over) any existing files stored on the floppy diskette, but to add the newly backed-up files to that disk. For example, Figure 10.5 depicts the backup of the .XY files from the DOS400 directory. At some point, you might also want to back up files in another directory (in this example, the INSTANT directory). Although you could back them up to a separate diskette, you might logically want to add these additional files to the same

Switch	Result
/A	Adds files to a backup disk
/S	Backs up subdirectories
/M	Backs up modified files only
/D	Backs up files by date
/T	Backs up files by time on the date specified by /D
/F	Formats the destination diskette if necessary
/L	Creates a log file for the files contained in the compacted backup file

Table 10.1: Switches for the BACKUP command

backup set. You could do this—even if more than one diskette is required—by using the /A switch. Figure 10.6 shows the backing up of the five .XY files in the INSTANT directory. The form of the BACKUP command you need to use to add these files to your backup diskette is the following:

BACKUP D:\XYWRITE\INSTANT\CH?.XY A:/A

This adds the new files to the BACKUP.001 file on the diskette in drive A. It also updates the CONTROL.001 file with information about the newly added files. Figure 10.7 portrays this process. Compare it to the original portrayal in Figure 10.3.

The resulting backup diskette (see Figure 10.8) now contains all the originally backed-up files, as well as the newly added ones. The sizes of both the BACKUP.001 and CONTROL.001 files increase. This represents the augmentation of the BACKUP.001 file with the contents of the five INSTANT files, and the addition of information about the files to the CONTROL.001 file.

```
Insert last backup diskette in drive A:
Press any key to continue . . .

*** Backing up files to drive A: ***
Diskette Number: Ø1

\XYWRITE\INSTANT\CH1.XY
\XYWRITE\INSTANT\CH2.XY
\XYWRITE\INSTANT\CH3.XY
\XYWRITE\INSTANT\CH4.XY
\XYWRITE\INSTANT\CH5.XY
Press any key to continue . . .
_
```

Figure 10.6: Adding files to an existing backup set

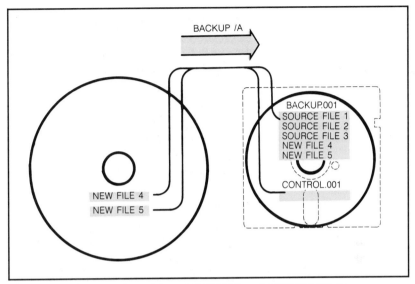

Figure 10.7: Adding files updates BACKUP and CONTROL files

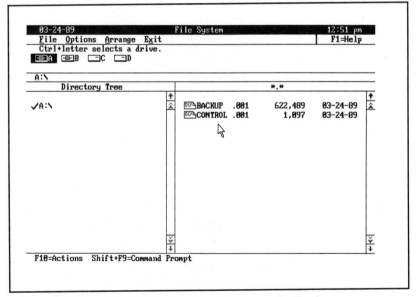

Figure 10.8: Augmented disk directory after successive backups

If the existing backup required multiple diskettes, you would be prompted to insert the last backup diskette before the actual backup copies would be written to the backup set:

Insert last backup diskette in drive A:
Press any key to continue. . .

Let's put some of these skills to work on your system. First, select two separate sets of files on your disk that need to be backed up. Try choosing files in two separate but important directories. Next, prepare several formatted diskettes to receive your selected files.

In order to decide how many diskettes you need, use the DIR command (or use the Directory Tree in DOS 4's shell) to display the names of all the files you plan to back up. Add up all the file sizes for your selected diskettes, and then divide by the number of bytes on each of your backup diskettes. This number represents how many diskettes you'll need. For example, if you were backing up onto double-density, double-sided diskettes (360K), your calculations might go like this:

1. Total size of all selected files: 3Mb

2. Number of bytes per diskette: 360K

3. 3,000,000 divided by 360,000: 9 diskettes

DOS makes it easy for you to back up a variable amount of file information. If you add an /F switch to a BACKUP command, DOS will automatically format any diskette being used that is not already formatted. This relieves you from having to calculate how many diskettes you'll need and formatting them. Using this switch requires that the FORMAT.COM command file be available either in the current default directory or somewhere along the DOS path.

This calculation is only approximate for two reasons. First, 360K is really not 360,000 bytes. (Since a kilobyte equals 1024 bytes, 360K equals 360 × 1024, or 368,640 bytes.) The approximation is close enough, however, since the CONTROL.001 file takes up a variable number of bytes, depending largely on how many files are backed up. Performing the same type of calculation for the other types of diskettes supported by DOS would give the results seen in Table 10.2.

Once you have calculated the correct number of diskettes and formatted them, issue the correct BACKUP command to back up all the files in your first selected directory. Then issue a second BACKUP command to append the files from the second directory you chose onto the first backup-diskette set. Use the /A switch.

Finally, issue one or more DIR commands for the backup diskettes to verify that all the original files were successfully copied. To do this, you need to compare the size of the BACKUP.001 file with the total

Description	Capacity	Required Diskettes To Back Up 10M
5¹/₄'' single-sided	160K	63
5¹/₄'' single-sided	180K	56
5¹/₄'' double-sided	320K	32
5¹/₄'' double-sided	360K	28
5¹/₄'' high-capacity	1.2Mb	9
3¹/₂'' double-sided	720K	14
3¹/₂'' double-sided	1.44Mb	7

Table 10.2: Calculating the number of required backup diskettes

size of all your original files. In DOS 4, you can avoid the drudgery of adding up file sizes by simply choosing Select across directories from the Options menu, selecting all the files you just backed up, and then using the Show Information window to see the total size of the selected files.

BACKING UP SUBDIRECTORIES

The /S switch tells DOS to copy the files contained in any sub-directories of the directory being backed up. This switch is extremely powerful with the BACKUP command, on par with the ability of the XCOPY command to move automatically through the directory tree structure. For example, if you started the backup in the root directory (C:\), specified all files (*.*), and used the /S option:

```
BACKUP C:\*.* A: /S
```

DOS would attempt to back up the entire hard disk. This is the default parameter setting you see when you initiate the BACKUP command with DOS 4's Backup Fixed Disk option (see Figure 10.4). The /S switch tells DOS first to back up all data and program files in the root directory and then to go to each subdirectory in the root. DOS backs up all files in each subdirectory and then proceeds to do the same for each subdirectory of that subdirectory.

If you wanted to back up just a portion of your hard-disk tree structure, you would just specify the main branch to begin with. Assuming a tree structure like the one in Figure 10.9, you could back up all the files in the DBASE branch by entering

BACKUP C:\DBASE A: /S

DOS would first back up the files in the DBASE directory. Then it would proceed to the next directory in that portion of the tree (DB3PLUS) and copy the files located there. It would then continue on through each of the other subdirectories (CLASSES and ADMIN) in the tree structure, copying all the files in them. DOS will prompt you to enter additional backup diskettes as each one fills up.

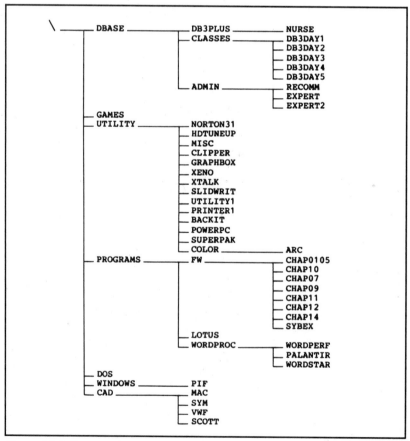

Figure 10.9: Sample directory structure

PERFORMING MULTIPLE OPERATIONS WITH ONE COMMAND

As in most DOS commands, multiple switches can be used simultaneously as long as it makes sense to do so. The /A and /S switches can work together for some useful purposes. You might be interested in locating and backing up all the BASIC program files (*.BAS) on your entire disk. Using the /S switch will allow the BACKUP command to look successively into each subdirectory you specify.

The following command will locate and back up all .BAS files anywhere on the disk:

BACKUP C:*.BAS A: /S

This works because you've specified the root directory with which to begin (C:\), the wild card for finding BASIC files only (*.BAS), and the subdirectory search switch (/S).

As you know, changing the starting directory can limit the portion of the directory tree that is searched. The following command will find only .BAS files located in the UTILITY subdirectory and in all subdirectories located below it in the directory structure:

BACKUP C:\UTILITY*.BAS A: /S

The addition of an /A switch to the preceding examples will add all the files found to the existing backup disk:

BACKUP C:\UTILITY*.BAS A: /S /A

BACKING UP MODIFIED OR NEW FILES

The /M option tells DOS to back up only files that have not already been backed up or that have been modified since the last backup. DOS is able to do this because it marks each file on the disk as it is backed up. This mark—actually a bit stored by DOS for every file—is called the *archive bit*. Whenever a file is modified or a new file is created, DOS changes the mark to indicate that the file will need to be backed up later. This archiving feature allows the backup process to skip files that have not been changed since the last backup. When any file is newly created in DOS, its archive bit is set to indicate that it should be treated like any other existing file that has undergone some changes.

As an example, suppose that you have a GAMES directory in which you keep your children's favorite computer games. Naturally, you need to safeguard your sanity in the event of a disk crash. You may suffer more if all these games are lost than you would if your business files were lost. Of course, neither situation will faze you if you've been conscientiously backing up your files.

Assume that you recently backed up all your files in this example directory. Your children then bring home two new games, HEAD-ROOM.COM and MADMAX.EXE. You can add these to your existing GAMES backup set with the /M and /A switches:

BACKUP C:\GAMES A: /M /A

The /A switch tells DOS to add all selected files to an existing backup, while the /M switch selects only the two new files from the much larger collection of unchanged files.

Immediately attempting to back up the very same files again would result in a message stating that no files were found to back up. This is because the archive bit was changed to indicate that the two files had already been backed up.

BACKING UP BY DATE AND TIME

DOS allows you to specify by date, and by time on that date, the files to be backed up. When you enter a date, DOS will back up only files that possess the same date or a more recent date.

Let's look at an example. In my word-processing directory named DOS400, there are a total of 16 files (see Figure 10.10). Some of these are temporary files, some are text from chapters being written, and one contains notes to my editor. Assume that all the files dated earlier than March 22, 1989, are on backup disks already. You can selectively back up only the four files created in this directory since March 22 by using the /D switch:

BACKUP D:\XYWRITE\DOS400 A: /D:3/22/89

As usual, the first parameter selects the directory or the set of desired files, the second parameter indicates the destination drive,

If you are using a date format for a different country, as discussed in Chapter 12, you should revise the form of the date used here. For example, European countries usually use dates in the form *day/month/year*, so a selection of files on or after March 22, 1989, would require /D:22/3/89 to be entered for the switch.

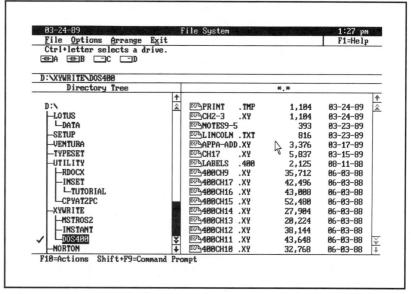

Figure 10.10: Backing up files by date

and the final entry on the line is the switch. Notice that the /D switch is followed by a colon, which is followed immediately by the specific date on or after which you want the new and updated files to be selected for backup.

Another switch you can use with BACKUP is /T, which allows you to control backups by the time of day. In general, /D is more practical than /T.

CREATING A LOG FILE OF THE FILES BACKED UP

Since all the files you back up are compacted into a single backup file, it's a good idea to simultaneously ask DOS to create a log file for you. This file will store the date and time of the backup, as well as the full path and file name of each backed-up file. It will have the extension .LOG. Also, DOS will indicate which of the possible backup diskettes each particular file was stored on.

To use this feature you need to add another switch to your BACKUP command. The /L switch alone will cause DOS to create the log file under the name BACKUP.LOG; it will store this file in the root directory of your source drive. If you would like to give the log file another name, the switch format to use is

/L:*LogFileName*

As an example, if you wanted to generate a log file for the previous presented backup of word-processing files, you would add an /L switch to the complete BACKUP command:

BACKUP D:\XYWRITE\DOS400 A: /D:3/22/89 /L

If you preferred to store the log-file information in a file in the original source directory, you could do so by making the /L switch more specific:

BACKUP D:\XYWRITE\DOS400 A: /D:3/22/89
/L:\XYWRITE\DOS400\MAR22.LOG

The results of running this BACKUP command switch can be seen in Figure 10.11, which represents what DOS displays on the screen during the logging operation.

```
    Insert backup diskette Ø1 in drive A:

    WARNING! Files in the target drive
    A:\ root directory will be erased
    Press any key to continue . . .

    *** Backing up files to drive A: ***
    Diskette Number: Ø1

    Logging to file C:\DOS4ØØ\MAR22.LOG

    \XYWRITE\DOS4ØØ\LINCOLN.TXT
    \XYWRITE\DOS4ØØ\CH2-3.XY
    \XYWRITE\DOS4ØØ\NOTES9-5
    \XYWRITE\DOS4ØØ\PRINT.TMP
    Press any key to continue . . .
    _
```

Figure 10.11: DOS messages during logging operation

Figure 10.12 shows the contents of the log file (MAR22.LOG) itself. Using logging again during file-adding operations (/A) will add the newly backed-up files, along with their full path names, to this log file. This parallels the adding of file data and controlling information to the BACKUP and CONTROL files on the backup disk.

RESTORING FILES FROM A BACKUP DISK

The RESTORE command is used to bring files from a backup-diskette set (or a fixed disk) back onto a hard drive. It can be the original source hard-disk drive for the files, or it can be another hard-disk drive onto which you want to place the files.

The general form of the RESTORE command is

RESTORE *BackupDrive Destination*

Restoring files is almost the reverse of backing them up, with fewer switches and options for restoration. Unfortunately, there is one

The RESTORE command is the only way to properly copy files from a backup diskette. Neither the COPY nor the XCOPY command will accomplish this task correctly.

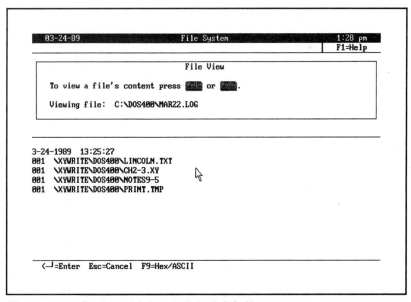

Figure 10.12: Contents of the MAR22.LOG file

point of potential confusion. Contrary to what you might expect, RESTORE does not work in exact reverse of the BACKUP command. With BACKUP, you can specify a directory name alone, indicating you want to back up all files in the directory. With RESTORE, it's a little trickier. The second parameter, *Destination*, is the problem. If you do not specify a destination at all, the restoration is made to the current directory. However, in such a case, the current directory must be the same directory as the original source of the files on the backup disk. Otherwise, you'll receive the possibly misleading message "No files were found to restore." It isn't even sufficient to specify the correct directory as the *Destination* parameter for the RESTORE command (the Restore Fixed Disk choice on the DOS utilities menu).

You must specify the full path name for the files to be restored (*Destination*). Figure 10.13 shows the result of restoring the four files previously backed up by date. I used the following command to do this (remember you only add the parameters to DOS 4's Restore Utility dialog box):

RESTORE A: D:\XYWRITE\DOS400*.*

```
Insert backup diskette 01 in drive A:
Press any key to continue . . .

*** Files were backed up 03-24-1989 ***

*** Restoring files from drive A: ***
Diskette: 01
\XYWRITE\DOS400\LINCOLN.TXT
\XYWRITE\DOS400\CH2-3.XY
\XYWRITE\DOS400\NOTES9-5
\XYWRITE\DOS400\PRINT.TMP

Press any key to continue . . .
—
```

Figure 10.13: RESTORE requires a complete path name

RESTORING ONLY SOME
OF YOUR BACKED-UP FILES

As always, DOS provides a variety of very useful switches for commands like RESTORE. There are two principal switches presented here that will be quite useful to you at various times. Other possible switches are presented in Chapter 22.

If you have backed up an entire directory tree or any subdirectory tree, you will need to use the /S switch to restore the subdirectory tree structure. Also, if you have made changes to any of the previously backed-up files, you should use the /P switch to ensure that the old version does not overwrite the new version.

The ability to select the files you want restored can be very useful. It can also cut down on the time required to restore files by restoring only those files you actually need.

RESTORING DIRECTORY STRUCTURES
The /S switch on the RESTORE command is the exact reverse of the /S switch on the BACKUP command. When used with BACKUP, /S allows you to search through a directory and all of its subdirectories for files to back up. When used with RESTORE, /S ensures that the backed-up files are restored to their proper subdirectories.

In fact, if DOS discovers that a subdirectory is missing during the restoration process, it will automatically recreate that subdirectory before copying the backed-up files to it. Your destination directory may be missing for a variety of reasons. Your entire disk may have crashed or have been erased inadvertently. More likely, you may have erased the directory and file contents, after backing them up, in order to reclaim the disk space for other purposes. Or you may simply be restoring the directory structure and files to a different computer and hard disk.

PROTECTING AGAINST ACCIDENTAL OVERWRITING
The /P switch is extremely useful if you're not completely sure of yourself or if a good deal of time has elapsed between the backup and restoration. When this switch is specified, DOS will ask you during the restoration if you really mean to restore an old version and overwrite an existing disk file. It will do this when the existing disk file has been updated since the earlier backup version, or if the disk file has been marked as read-only. (The latter situation almost never occurs, so you needn't worry about it; you will learn about read-only files in Chapter 17.)

As a last example of RESTORE, I'll show you how to selectively restore files in DOS. Adding the /P switch to the previous RESTORE command ensures that any files modified on the hard disk since the previous BACKUP are not accidentally overwritten. For example,

RESTORE A: D:\XYWRITE\DOS400*.* /P

gives the results shown in Figure 10.14.

The /P switch enabled RESTORE to note that one of the files (CH2-3.XY) has been changed since it was backed up. The RESTORE command checks each file before restoring it. When it checked CH2-3.XY, I was warned that the file had changed since it had last been backed up. I could then choose which version (the older one on the backup disk or the newer one on the hard disk) I wanted to keep.

Now test your understanding of the RESTORE process. First back up any selected set of text files. If you completed the earlier exercises using BACKUP, you can use the resulting diskette if it contained text files. Otherwise, choose some files from your word-processing (or other text-oriented) directory.

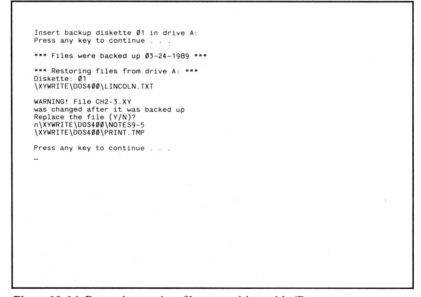

```
Insert backup diskette 01 in drive A:
Press any key to continue . . .

*** Files were backed up 03-24-1989 ***

*** Restoring files from drive A: ***
Diskette: 01
\XYWRITE\DOS400\LINCOLN.TXT

WARNING! File CH2-3.XY
was changed after it was backed up
Replace the file (Y/N)?
n\XYWRITE\DOS400\NOTES9-5
\XYWRITE\DOS400\PRINT.TMP

Press any key to continue . . .
_
```

Figure 10.14: Protecting against file overwriting with /P

Make some textual change to one of the text files by using your word processor or DOS's EDLIN (see Chapter 7). Next, restore the backed-up files to their original directory. Use the /P switch so you do not overwrite the newly changed text files. Use your text-editing program to verify that the old versions of the changed files were not rewritten onto your disk.

SUMMARY

This chapter has taught you how to back up your disks. Power failures do occur in businesses, brownouts occur even more frequently, and a multitude of other incidents can cause the intermittent loss or corruption of important files. Therefore, making backups is critical for avoiding disaster. This chapter has presented the following backup information:

- You should back up your files before moving your computer, when you are close to filling up your hard disk, and just before running a fragmentation reduction program.

- The BACKUP command can make a complete copy of all the files in a directory when you simply specify the directory name and the disk drive to receive the backup copies.

- Backup copies of files are written into a compacted file on each backup diskette. The compacted file is called BACK-UP.*xxx,* where *xxx* is the number of the backup disk.

- Each BACKUP.*xxx* file is accompanied by a file called CONTROL.*xxx* (again, *xxx* is the disk number). This file contains such controlling information as the names and lengths of the files compacted into the BACKUP.*xxx* file.

- With the BACKUP command you can make selective backups of some of the files in a directory by using appropriate switches. For instance, you can make backups of files that have changed since the last backup was performed by using the /M switch.

- The /D switch permits the backup of files that have changed or that have been created since a certain date.

- The /T switch permits the backup of files based on the time of creation or modification.

- Adding a new set of files to a backup set is easily done by using the /A switch.

- The powerful /S switch allows you to back up files located deep within the directory tree.

- Automatic formatting of the destination diskettes for the BACKUP command will be done by DOS whenever you specify the /F switch.

- All backup processing can be recorded in a log file by using the /L switch. You can specify your own path and file name to receive the logging information; otherwise, a BACKUP.LOG file is created in the root directory of the source drive.

- The RESTORE command allows you to write files and directories from the backup-diskette set back to a hard disk—either the original or a new one. The /S switch permits restoration of the treelike directory structure. The /P switch allows you to complete this process safely in the event that existing disk versions of any files are newer and should not be overwritten.

In Chapter 18, you'll learn about several additional utility programs that you can purchase for backing up your files; they go beyond the power and flexibility of the DOS BACKUP command. For example, hard-disk backup programs like BACK-IT give you much more flexibility and convenience in including and excluding sets of files during the backup process. Naturally, these programs cost extra money, while DOS's BACKUP and RESTORE commands are free.

In the next two chapters, you'll look at more precise control over DOS's internal setup and system configuration. In Chapter 11, you'll learn how to initialize several key DOS parameters and how to exploit the power of DOS drivers. In Chapter 12, you'll revisit the MODE command in yet another one of its significant roles—support for foreign-language characters, graphics characters, and multiple keyboard layouts.

CUSTOM CONFIGURATIONS OF DOS

SO FAR, EVERYTHING YOU'VE SEEN ABOUT DOS HAS been clearly defined. Every feature has had a concrete definition and strict limits on how it could be used and what results you could expect. Behind the scenes, however, there are several additional aspects to DOS itself that have considerable flexibility, and that you can control.

DOS is like your home: you can walk in and accept everything as it is, or you can adjust the environment to your liking. In your home, you can open some windows or close others; you can turn the lights on or off; you can set the thermostat to a different temperature; you can even rearrange the furniture. DOS, too, also has a certain way in which it appears when you "walk in," or start it up. This internal configuration, and how you can adjust it, is the subject of this chapter.

In DOS, you can customize your system in many ways. Chapters 14, 15, and 16 concentrate on the batch-file mechanism for complete on-line adjustments. Here, you'll focus on customizing some of the inner workings of DOS itself.

Two principal mechanisms exist for the internal setups: the CONFIG.SYS file and the PROMPT command. Using the CONFIG.SYS file, you can specify the number of internal DOS buffers. You can also use CONFIG.SYS to load additional drivers such as ANSI.SYS, which enables you to redefine keys and control the display. DOS has another driver you can load to create a RAM disk. DOS 4 users also have access to two special drivers for managing expanded memory and expanded-memory emulation. In this chapter, you'll learn all these customization methods.

USING THE CONFIG.SYS FILE

When a microcomputer is turned on, it runs through a built-in bootstrap program. The time-consuming part of a typical bootstrap is a memory test. The more memory you have, the longer the test will take; if you ever expand the memory of your system, you will probably notice the difference.

Following the memory test, the bootstrap attempts to find the disk-resident portion of DOS on one of the drives in the system, usually beginning with drive A. That is why the light on drive A comes on before the hard drive is accessed, even if you have a hard disk. It is also why anyone can circumvent a menu system set up on your hard disk—one can always place a DOS system disk in drive A, boot the system from that disk, and then access any files on the hard disk.

When the system drive is found (the one that has a copy of the DOS files on it), the computer reads the information into its memory. The next thing DOS does is to scan the root directory of the drive from which it has read the DOS files for a special file called CONFIG.SYS. If this file is not present, DOS initializes your system according to built-in default values. If a file called AUTOEXEC-.BAT exists (see Chapter 16 for a detailed explanation of this file), DOS then proceeds with the instructions in that file and displays the DOS prompt (usually A> or C>, depending on which drive contained the system files).

If a CONFIG.SYS file is present in the root directory DOS scans, it will contain a list of special statements that define a nonstandard system configuration. Figure 11.1 shows a sample CONFIG.SYS file actually used on a typical 640K DOS system. You'll learn in this chapter what each line of this file represents.

CONFIG.SYS is unique in the following ways:

- It can alter the internal setup of DOS itself.
- It can only be activated by booting or rebooting the computer.
- It can contain only a limited set of commands.

Since the CONFIG.SYS file is a standard ASCII text file, you can create and modify it with a text editor like EDLIN (see Chapter 7) or

```
FILES=20
BUFFERS=15
DEVICE=C:\DOS\ANSI.SYS
DEVICE=C:\DOS\VDISK.SYS 120
```

Figure 11.1: A typical CONFIG.SYS file

your own word processor. Each line in this file has the form

Command = Value

The commands you'll learn about in this chapter are the most important and useful ones. They are FILES, BUFFERS, and DEVICE. (You can refer to the Part 7 command reference for other possibilities.) Let's look at each of these.

SPECIFYING THE NUMBER OF ACTIVE FILES

More and more frequently, users are running sophisticated programs like dBASE IV, Framework III, and XyWrite. These programs can work with several files at the same time, so they require the installation of a special CONFIG.SYS file. This usually requires you to change the normal DOS default value for FILES.

The default value set by DOS is only eight files. This means there are eight places reserved by DOS inside its own memory space to track information about open files. DOS itself uses three of these, and every running application program, overlay file, RAM-resident program, and so on, may use additional places out of the eight.

> The value used for FILES includes all files open in your system. This includes files used by foreground programs (like CHKDSK) and background programs (like PRINT or any network program).

Most popular application programs recommend that you set the FILES value to 20 in your CONFIG.SYS file, although some programs recommend higher or lower settings. Unless you're willing to run extensive performance tests in your system environment, just follow the software manufacturer's instructions for setting the value of FILES. However, you might be using several different software application packages. For example, you may be using a computer-aided design package that recommends the setting FILES = 20, and you may also be using a database management package that recommends FILES = 15. Take the larger value. Although it will cost you some additional memory space when DOS boots up, it won't be much (48 bytes per open file), and at least you'll guarantee that your software will run.

SPECIFYING THE NUMBER OF INTERNAL DOS BUFFERS

The BUFFERS command refers to the way DOS manages the input and output of data to and from the disk drives. When a command is issued by a program to read information from a file, DOS really serves the role of an intermediary by loading the information into a reserved buffer area. Figure 11.2 presents a visual interpretation of this activity.

Efficiency is the primary reason that operating systems use buffers. Imagine yourself in the role of an operating system. Then imagine that someone (an application program) wants to give you something, while someone else (a disk file) wants to get that same thing. If you act as a buffer by accepting the object with one hand and then hold it until you can locate the receiving person, the transaction will be fairly straightforward. However, if you try to do this procedure without using your hands or moving around, getting the giver together with the receiver in the same room, you've made your job much more difficult. In addition, you would not be able to do much else until the two-person operation was completed. DOS uses buffering to make transactions efficient.

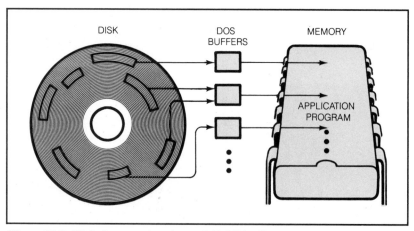

Figure 11.2: Disk data passing through DOS buffers

When a disk request is made, DOS checks the information in its buffer before it tries to read the disk. This can sometimes eliminate the need to actually read the disk; DOS may find that the requested file data is already in the buffer—if, for instance, the file has recently been called up by another program or DOS request. (This is, in part, the principle behind disk-buffering programs like Lightning, discussed in Chapter 18.) The result is that some programs will perform certain operations faster.

Each buffer in DOS can hold 528 bytes. If you increase the number of buffers, the memory-resident requirements for DOS itself will increase. This will decrease the available memory for any application program, as well as for any memory-resident program you wish to use during your main program's execution. Sophisticated programs like Framework III, which has its own buffer management and configuration file and therefore uses memory intensively, will suffer greatly from too large of a BUFFERS value.

DOS 4 provides two additional capabilities in its BUFFERS command. The command syntax is shown in Chapter 22. In essence, by adding a second parameter, you can improve throughput by reserving several buffers to be used for read-ahead purposes. When files are processed sequentially (as in a record-by-record database summation), DOS can read several sectors ahead to have the required data in memory when needed. Since this reduces the input/output waiting time, the program executes faster.

You can also add DOS 4's /X switch to the BUFFERS command in the CONFIG.SYS file. The /X switch directs DOS to use any available expanded memory for the buffers; this retains more low memory for programs, thereby using the memory more efficiently. In many cases, this technique will even enable programs that would otherwise require more physical memory to run in your available memory.

A law of diminishing returns is at work here. Up to a point, more DOS buffers means faster performance for your system. On the other hand, too many buffers means DOS may spend more time looking through its buffers than it would spend to just go to the disk and read the necessary data. Unless you have a good reason, use the software manufacturer's recommended setting for BUFFERS. A common setting is a value of 15.

DOS 4 users can use the /X switch to free up low memory, which provides more memory for some programs' internal processing. This potentially means that larger spreadsheets or word-processing documents can be handled by memory-limited programs. More available memory also means faster processing by those programs that can swap to disk, since the extra memory enables you to swap data to and from disks less frequently.

USING DEVICE
DRIVERS TO CUSTOMIZE DOS

The CONFIG.SYS file is also used to load additional software drivers into DOS. Software drivers are special-purpose programs whose only responsibility is to control specific peripheral devices (see Chapter 12 for an additional discussion of device drivers). DOS can't be responsible for knowing all the control codes for all possible external devices; operating systems in general leave the details of communicating with and controlling these devices to the special driver programs.

Device drivers extend the command range of DOS. Naturally, they also take up more memory, which is one reason why they are optional. A special driver called ANSI.SYS extends the functions of DOS to include reprogramming or redefinition of keys and screen colors in DOS. You'll look at that feature more closely in the following section.

DOS also has a driver that is used to create a *RAM disk* (sometimes called a *virtual disk*). The RAM disk is not really a disk—it is an area in memory that simulates the operations of an additional disk drive. A critical aspect of this mechanism is that any files placed on the RAM disk are really memory resident. They can therefore be retrieved at the speed of memory, which is usually microseconds or nanoseconds. Files on actual mechanical disk drives are slower, usually in the millisecond range.

Memory reserved for use as a RAM disk is no longer available for internal use by programs. If you take up too much space with a RAM disk or any other memory-resident software, there may not even be enough remaining memory to load your main application software.

If you have expanded or extended memory that can be allocated for RAM disk space, you can use it to reserve your low memory for your programs (discussed in the next two sections). If you do not have expanded or extended memory, you must do a bit of calculating to figure out how much memory is available for your RAM disk. Simply subtract the memory required by your version of DOS from your total physical memory (640K, 512K, or whatever). Then subtract the memory requirements of your particular application program from the remaining number. This tells you the maximum remaining memory that could be allocated for a RAM disk. For example, if the total physical memory of your system is 640K, the space required by your DOS version is 45K, and the space required by your application program is 384K, you have 211K remaining for your RAM disk (640 − 45 − 384 = 211).

Use only as much memory for your RAM disk as you need. You should know in advance how you plan to use this space.

There are a few other things you must consider. The size of your version of DOS varies according to the values of FILES, BUFFERS, and any other CONFIG.SYS parameters. It also varies according to how many additional DOS programs you run, which require extra memory (like the MODE command of Chapter 9 and the KEYB command of Chapter 12). Naturally, if you run any memory-resident programs like Sidekick, you need to subtract their memory requirements as well.

CREATING A RAM DISK

You know that DOS maintains a directory and a file allocation table on each disk, along with the actual data and program files. In order to simulate this structure in memory, a special piece of software is required. This software is included in your DOS in a file called either VDISK.SYS (for PC-DOS) or RAMDRIVE.SYS (for MS-DOS).

If you are using a version of DOS for any machine other than an actual IBM computer, you will need to substitute RAMDRIVE.SYS wherever you read VDISK.SYS in this text.

The simulated RAM disk seen in Figure 11.3 can be implemented simply by including the following values in your DEVICE specification:

DEVICE = C:\DOS\VDISK.SYS 120

If you don't have AT extended memory, you can place your RAM disk in *expanded* memory, such as Intel's Above Board. Expanded memory, specially configured according to the "LIM standard," works in regular PCs and XTs, as well as ATs. It actually overcomes the DOS 640K limit, so many programs are written to use it for data just like regular memory.

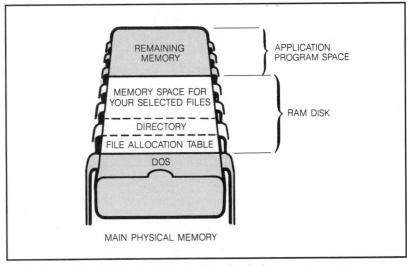

Figure 11.3: RAM disk simulation using physical memory

This DEVICE setting brings into memory the VDISK (virtual or RAM disk) driver.

In this example, the VDISK.SYS file itself is located on drive C in the DOS directory. The parameter value of 120 indicates that a total simulated disk of size 120K should be created from the available physical memory (640K or whatever you have in your system).

If you have an IBM PC/AT or a compatible computer, you should know about a switch you can use when you set up a RAM disk. The /E switch will use *extended memory*—extra memory above the conventional 1Mb of addressable memory—if your machine has this additional memory installed. The previous example could be modified to generate a 120K RAM disk in extended memory like this:

DEVICE = C:\DOS\VDISK.SYS 120 /E

DOS also allows you to have multiple RAM disks simultaneously. Just as you can use different physical devices to protect files from one another by separating them on different drives, you can do the same with the much faster RAM disks. Each RAM disk will be given a new single-character drive identifier by DOS.

All you need to do to create multiple RAM disks is have multiple copies of the DEVICE command. DOS knows what physical drives exist in your system, and it creates the additional drives using the next available letters. For instance, if your system had one or two diskette drives and two logical drives (C and D), then adding the following two statements to your CONFIG.SYS file would create the RAM disks E and F with sizes of 512K (see Figure 11.4) and 1024K (see Figure 11.5):

DEVICE = C:\DOS\VDISK.SYS 512 /E
DEVICE = C:\DOS\VDISK.SYS 1024 /E

> If you intend to create and use disk drives with drive identifiers beyond the letter E, DOS 3.2 and above will permit you to do so but will require another statement in your configuration file. This additional statement must be of the form LASTDRIVE = *x*, where *x* is the last valid alphabetic character DOS will use for a drive identifier.

Note that the /E switch has been specified in each of these two DEVICE statements. This directs DOS to install both RAM disks in extended memory.

There are other methods for creating RAM disks. These usually require software that comes with enhancement boards like AST's Six-Pak Plus or Quadram's Quadboard, or they require add-on boards that act as dedicated RAM disks. Some of these have their

```
C:\>CHKDSK E:

Volume VDISK  V4.Ø created 12-Ø6-1984 12:ØØp

    518912 bytes total disk space
    518912 bytes available on disk

       256 bytes in each allocation unit
      2Ø27 total allocation units on disk
      2Ø27 available allocation units on disk

    655360 total bytes memory
    526560 bytes free

C:\>_
```

Figure 11.4: A 512K RAM disk

```
C:\>CHKDSK F:

Volume VDISK  V4.Ø created 12-Ø6-1984 12:ØØp

   1Ø42944 bytes total disk space
   1Ø42944 bytes available on disk

       512 bytes in each allocation unit
      2Ø37 total allocation units on disk
      2Ø37 available allocation units on disk

    655360 total bytes memory
    526560 bytes free

C:\>_
```

Figure 11.5: A 1024K RAM disk

None of the
CONFIG.SYS file's
settings take effect until
the DOS system is booted
up. Remember this if you
make any changes to
your CONFIG.SYS
file—you must reboot
before the changes take
effect.

own power supplies and battery backups, which means no data loss
will occur during power outages. Another benefit of this type of add-
on is that no system memory is used up by the device driver that
manages the RAM disk. Installing a RAM disk with software packages or add-on boards requires a different procedure; you should follow the manufacturer's instructions.

USING A RAM DISK

Now that you know how to create a RAM disk, you should also
know how to use what you've created to its best advantage. Here are
some suggestions for using your RAM disk.

Place a copy of your DOS system's primary disk-resident program, COMMAND.COM, on your RAM disk. Then employ the
following special instructions to inform DOS that all future references to COMMAND.COM can locate it on the RAM disk, not on
the boot disk. Assuming your RAM disk is on drive E (substitute the
appropriate letter on your system), you should enter the following
command at the DOS prompt:

SET COMSPEC = E:\COMMAND.COM

This will speed up all programs that invoke DOS from within themselves, such as Framework III or QDOS II. These programs work by
loading a second copy of the command processor (COMMAND-
.COM) from a RAM disk. This command will also speed up application software that overwrites the command-processor portion of
DOS and then requires its reloading before the software can restore
DOS and its prompt.

Load the files for frequently referenced DOS commands, like
CHKDSK.COM and FORMAT.COM, onto your RAM disk;
also load EDLIN.COM if you use EDLIN often to edit small text
files (see Chapter 7). In fact, load any text files that are run frequently, like batch files.

Load any large support files (like spelling dictionaries or a thesau-
rus file) that your word processor or integrated software may need.
Also place index-type files (generated by many database management systems) on the RAM disk for much more rapid accessing of
data records, especially if you must search through many records in
large data files.

Place your favorite disk-resident utility programs (shareware, public domain, or purchased, like the Norton Utilities) on the RAM disk if you use them frequently. Also place overlay files on your RAM disk for improved execution of your software. These overlays contain the portion of your application program that couldn't fit into memory and is normally read into a special part of memory only when needed. The overlay features of your software will operate at rapid RAM speeds if you place them on your RAM disk. Note that you will need to make your RAM disk the default DOS disk before invoking your application program so it will look for the overlay file on the RAM disk and not on the standard drive.

Remember to set your path properly so DOS can find main programs. Set the RAM disk near or at the front of the PATH specification so that the file copies on the RAM drive are accessed first, not the original files that may also be accessible from directories on the path.

Before you follow these suggestions for using your RAM disk effectively, you should learn how to use it safely. As you know, using a RAM disk is much faster than using real disks. Programs that formerly took hours to run may take minutes, minutes can become seconds, and waiting time can disappear. When RAM disks are used improperly, however, hours of work can disappear in seconds.

Since a RAM disk is created in memory, any information stored on it will vanish when the computer is turned off. You gain great advantage by storing and accessing the right files on a RAM disk, but you must remember that these files are destroyed when you turn off the power or a power failure occurs, if there's a brownout in your building, if your computer plug comes out of the wall, or if you reboot your system with Ctrl-Alt-Del.

Back up the files in a RAM disk to a real disk frequently.

If you place and update important data files on a RAM disk for the sake of rapid access, save copies of them to a real disk before you turn off the power. Also back up copies of them to a real disk at frequent intervals to avoid losing all your work.

MANAGING EXPANDED MEMORY IN DOS 4

Chapter 20 explains how expanded memory can overcome DOS's 640K memory limit. DOS 4 is the first version of this popular operating system that includes drivers to support this increasingly important technique.

The DOS 4 drivers for expanded memory must be included in your CONFIG.SYS to have any effect in your system. The first, and more common, driver is the XMA2EMS.SYS. This driver assures that programs running under DOS 4 can be supported by the Lotus, Intel, Microsoft (LIM) Expanded Memory Specification (EMS) 4.0 discussed in Chapter 20.

To use the XMA2EMS.SYS driver, you must have one of the following hardware adapters (or any other adapter that conforms to the LIM 4.0 specification) installed in your system:

1. IBM 2Mb Expanded Memory Adapter

2. IBM PS/2 80286 Expanded Memory Adapter/A

3. IBM PS/2 80286 Memory Expansion Option

Furthermore, to use the IBM PS/2 Model 80 or any other 80386 system, you must have both the XMA2EMS.SYS and the XMAEM-.SYS drivers installed.

You should refer to the DOS 4 user's manual if you have any memory conflicts after installing these drivers.

The following DEVICE commands represent some typical examples you can use to install your drivers. Refer to your manual for more details.

For example, to install expanded memory pages P0, P1, P2, and P3 at the memory location D000 hexadecimal, enter

DEVICE = C:\DOS\XMA2EMS.SYS FRAME = D000

By default, the FRAME parameter specifies four contiguous pages for use in DOS 4. The beginning address in this example is D000, which is the default; however, you can set the individual addresses to any available pages within the hexadecimal range C000 to E000. If you do not specify the /X parameter, then DOS assigns as many 16K chunks of memory as are available.

Suppose you want to allocate 1.5Mb of expanded memory. This represents ninety-six 16K pages. To do this, you enter

DEVICE = C:\DOS\XMA2EMS.SYS FRAME = D000 /X:96

DOS then assigns 16K to each of the 96 pages. Taking this one step further, you can also set aside two specific pages in expanded memory for special DOS purposes. Page number 254 (P254) can be reserved for data to be used by VDISK.SYS and FASTOPEN.EXE (see Chapter 17). Similarly, page 255 (P255) can be reserved for use by the BUFFERS command. To reserve these two pages, you specify the XMA2EMS.SYS driver with the P254 and P255 identifiers and use the /X switch. For example,

DEVICE = C:\DOS\XMA2EMS.SYS FRAME = D000 P254 = C000
P255 = C400 /X:96

The DEVICE statement for the XMAEM.SYS driver must precede the DEVICE statement for the XMA2EMS.SYS driver.

If you have an 80386-based computer, you can still take advantage of the XMA2EMS.SYS expanded-memory driver by first emulating expanded memory. This technique is also discussed in detail in Chapter 20. DOS 4's XMAEM.SYS driver uses the 80386 memory-map registers with extended memory to specifically emulate the IBM PS/2 80286 Expanded Memory Adapter/A. If you wish to use extended memory for the purpose of emulating expanded memory, you must install this XMAEM.SYS driver before installing the XMA2EMS.SYS driver. For example, you could use all available extended memory for emulation purposes by simply including the following in your CONFIG.SYS:

DEVICE = C:\DOS\XMAEM.SYS

Should you wish to retain some of your extended memory for other purposes, you can limit the amount used for emulation by specifying a size parameter. This value represents the number of 16K pages used in the emulation. For example, to use 512K of extended memory to emulate expanded memory, enter the following command:

DEVICE = C:\DOS\XMAEM.SYS 32

This size specification will override your /X parameter in the DEVICE statement for the XMA2EMS.SYS driver, which follows the XMAEM.SYS DEVICE statement.

INSTALLING MEMORY-RESIDENT FEATURES IN DOS 4

DOS supports a number of advanced commands that remain in memory during their operation. These programs are called *Terminate and Stay Resident* (TSR). After they are run a first time, they continue to reside in memory to be used as needed.

In earlier versions of DOS, four of these commands can be initiated at the command prompt or in a batch file (see Chapter 16). With DOS 4, you have a new INSTALL command that enables you to install these four when you configure your system.

Just as the CONFIG.SYS file can contain several DEVICE commands, so can it contain several INSTALL commands. You can have up to four INSTALL statements in your configuration file. The four TSR commands that you can use with INSTALL are discussed elsewhere in this book as follows:

COMMAND FILE	*CHAPTER DISCUSSED IN*
FASTOPEN.EXE	Chapter 17
KEYB.COM	Chapter 12
NLSFUNC.EXE	Chapter 12
SHARE.EXE	Chapter 22

Installing any one of these command files requires that you specify the same set of parameters that you would enter if you ran the same command at the command prompt or in DOS 4's shell. For instance, to install the FASTOPEN feature for drive C using its standard default values, enter

```
INSTALL = C:\DOS\FASTOPEN.EXE  C:
```

Using INSTALL to specify a DOS feature requires that you specify the full path and file name, including the extension.

As with any other file name specified in a CONFIG.SYS, you must enter the complete file name, including the extension. Now that you have your CONFIG.SYS set up for RAM disks, expanded memory, and memory-resident commands, you'll explore customizing your system for your screen and keyboard.

ADDING POWER WITH THE ANSI SYSTEM DRIVER

The ANSI (American National Standards Institute) system allows you to modify the default setup of your screen and keyboard. For example, you can change the characteristics of the screen, including both the cursor position and screen colors (with a color monitor, of course). You can also redefine the expected value of keys on your keyboard, so you can customize the use of your function keys, as well as how the Ctrl, Shift, or Alt key affects them.

In order to obtain any of these customizing capabilities, you must have the ANSI.SYS driver installed in your system. The third line of CONFIG.SYS (see Figure 11.1) does just that:

DEVICE = C:\DOS\ANSI.SYS

Some special-purpose application programs like PreCursor, a hard-disk management program, and SuperKey, a keyboard redefinition program, require that you include this type of command in your CONFIG.SYS specification. Of course, you should specify the full path name to the ANSI.SYS file; in this example, ANSI.SYS is located in the DOS directory on drive C.

Even if you are not yet using application software that requires the ANSI.SYS driver, the possibilities in the next section will probably inspire you to include this line in your CONFIG.SYS specification all the time.

ANSI.SYS AND THE PROMPT COMMAND

The PROMPT command is used to enter ANSI commands. You use it to control the screen's appearance when at the DOS command prompt. Remember that you can also change graphic screen colors from DOS 4's main Start Programs menu. Since you are already familiar with the DOS 4 menu method, I'll now show you how to customize your screen from the command prompt in any DOS version. For example, the form of the PROMPT command used to change the color of the screen is

PROMPT $e[*aaaa*m

The letter m in the PROMPT escape sequence signifies the end of your sequence of attribute settings. It must be lowercase.

where *aaaa* represents screen attributes or colors (shown in Table 11.1). Separate these values with semicolons if you use more than one. $e is a special symbol combination (the dollar sign $ followed by the letter e), recognized by DOS as an equivalent of the Esc key. The ANSI driver is

ATTRIBUTES	
0	All attributes off
1	Bold
4	Underline (on IBM-compatible monochrome monitors only)
5	Blinking
7	Reverse video

COLORS	FOREGROUND	BACKGROUND
Black	30	40
Red	31	41
Green	32	42
Yellow	33	43
Blue	34	44
Magenta	35	45
Cyan	36	46
White	37	47

Table 11.1: Video-screen color and attribute codes

invoked when an escape sequence is received, which is any series of keystrokes begun with the Esc key; therefore, $e invokes the ANSI driver. There is no limit to the number of attributes you can enter between the left bracket [and the letter m.

CONTROLLING THE SCREEN DISPLAY

It's up to you to decide if you like the standard white letters on a black background (even if you've bought a color monitor), or if you prefer something flashier. Using the attribute and color codes shown in Table 11.1, along with the PROMPT command, you can customize things as you like.

To switch the display to dark letters on a light background (see Figure 11.6), you would use an attribute value of 7 for reverse video:

PROMPT $e[7m

All future output on your screen will now appear as reverse video—black on white. Notice that in Figure 11.7, the DIR/W itself is displayed in reverse video after the PROMPT command has been executed.

To return to normal video (see Figure 11.7), you would use an attribute value of 0, which turns off all special attributes:

PROMPT $e[0m

USING META SYMBOLS

Notice that there appears to be no visible prompt at the bottom of the screens just shown. This is because the PROMPT command was used to set video attributes only. Various other possibilities can be

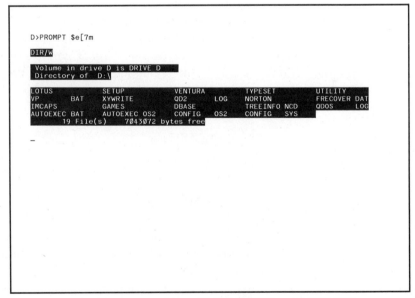

Figure 11.6: Setting reverse video with PROMPT and ANSI.SYS

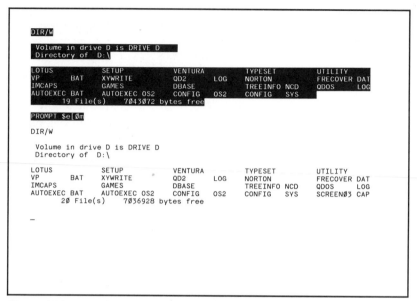

Figure 11.7: Resetting to default video attributes

combined with these attributes by stringing them together. You can create a wide range of output possibilities by using symbolic replacements, called *meta symbols,* for the desired output result. Table 11.2 lists the single-character meta symbols that can be used in conjunction with the $ character to influence the output of the PROMPT command.

For instance, to display the current directory, you would enter

    PROMPT $p

To display the current directory and the > symbol, you would enter

    PROMPT pg

To display the current directory and the > symbol, *and* to set to boldface all future video output, you would enter

    PROMPT pg$e[1m

The results of this command are shown in Figure 11.8.

Symbol	Meaning
e	The Esc key
p	Current directory of the default drive
g	The > character
n	Default drive identifier
d	System date
t	System time
v	Version number
l	The < character
b	The ¦ character
q	The = character
h	A backspace
_	The carriage-return/line-feed sequence

Table 11.2: Meta symbols for the PROMPT command

```
    Volume in drive D is DRIVE D
    Directory of  D:\

LOTUS            SETUP           VENTURA             TYPESET            UTILITY
VP        BAT    XYWRITE         QD2         LOG     NORTON             FRECOVER DAT
IMCAPS           GAMES           DBASE               TREEINFO NCD       QDOS     LOG
AUTOEXEC BAT     AUTOEXEC OS2    CONFIG      OS2     CONFIG   SYS       SCREEN03 CAP
       20 File(s)    7036928 bytes free

PROMPT $P$G$E[1m

D:\>DIR/W

    Volume in drive D is DRIVE D
    Directory of  D:\

LOTUS            SETUP           VENTURA             TYPESET            UTILITY
VP        BAT    XYWRITE         QD2         LOG     NORTON             FRECOVER DAT
IMCAPS           GAMES           DBASE               TREEINFO NCD       QDOS     LOG
AUTOEXEC BAT     AUTOEXEC OS2    CONFIG      OS2     CONFIG   SYS       SCREEN03 CAP
SCREEN04 CAP
       21 File(s)    7030784 bytes free

D:\>_
```

Figure 11.8: Combinations in the PROMPT command

COMBINING MULTIPLE ATTRIBUTES

All of the preceding possibilities can be combined to create more complex prompt effects. The simplest combinations only involve two attributes at once. For example, to create a reverse-video display that blinks, you can combine the codes for blinking (5) and reverse video (7):

PROMPT $e[5;7m

Future output will be seen as black characters that blink on a light background. To set things back to normal again, you would enter

PROMPT $e[0m

You can enter text into your prompt by simply typing it with no special meta symbols; text can also be embedded between any special-purpose meta symbols. For example, you can change the prompting message to "Your Command?" and display it in high intensity with the following:

PROMPT $e[1mYour Command?$e[0m

The beginning $e[1m turns high intensity on for the phrase "Your Command?" and the ending $e[0m turns it off.

Color monitors present other interesting alternatives. Using the color codes of Table 11.1 and the meta symbols of Table 11.2, it's easy to set any desired combination for foreground and background colors. For example, the following command will set a three-line prompt. The first line will contain the current directory (p). The carriage-return/line-feed sequence (_) ensures that the system date (d) appears on the next line. The time (t) and the > character (g) will be on the third line, and all succeeding text (including the future prompting strings) will be displayed as blue characters on a yellow background:

PROMPT p_d_tg$e[34;43m

A slight change to this command could give you similar information, while using reverse video for the special information only. In

Complicated or long screen prompts can wrap around to a second screen line as you type them in, but you should not press the Return key to get to the second line. The Return key terminates your prompt-string input; DOS will wrap a multiple-line command request on its own.

this way, the same PROMPT command could be used for both color and monochrome monitors. Notice in Figure 11.9 that the display of commands and output is in normal video, since the reverse-video code is reset immediately after the > symbol is output:

PROMPT $e[7m$p$_$d$_$tge[0m

You may not like the multiline appearance of this information. You could just as easily put the same information on one line with the following variation:

PROMPT $e[7m$p $d tg$e[0m

The spaces in this command are critical to the separation of the directory name, date, and time. The results are shown in Figure 11.10.

There are many more fanciful things you can do with the PROMPT command to control the video display. The codes required would go well beyond the scope of this book, but you can manipulate the cursor and its location in a variety of ways.

Use the PROMPT command now to redefine your DOS prompt to provide more information. Issue the proper command to display

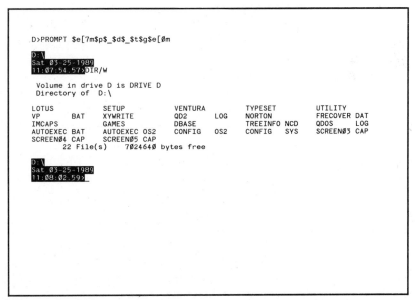

Figure 11.9: A three-line, reverse-video prompt

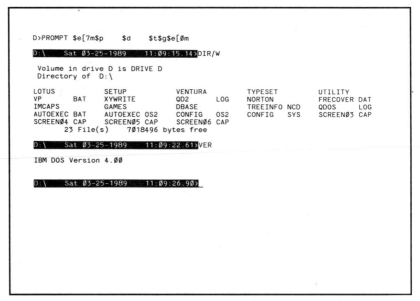

Figure 11.10: A one-line, reverse-video prompt

the DOS version number on one line, the system date on the next line, and the current directory on the third line of this multiline prompt. On a fourth line, generate the text string

Enter next command, please :

If you have a monochrome monitor, have this message appear in reverse video. Remember to reset the video attribute so that the rest of the video display appears in normal video. If you have a color monitor, have this message appear as white letters on a red background.

REDEFINING KEYS

As well as changing screen colors, you can use the ANSI system to reprogram some of your keys to type out commands or phrases. You can define any of the ASCII keys or the extended keyboard keys (F1–F10, Home, End, and so on). Some people have even used this technique to redefine individual keys to represent other individual keys, so that the keyboard assumes a different layout.

Like screen attributes, key reassignment begins with the special symbol for the Esc key ($e) and continues with the left bracket ([). If you want to assign new values to a normal key like the "a" key or the = key, you enter the ASCII value of the key, like 96 for the letter a or 61 for =. However, if you want to reassign values to the special keys on your keyboard (which is a more common goal), you must begin the key assignment with a zero and then follow it with the special code given the key by DOS (see Table 11.3).

FUNCTION KEY	REDEFINITION CODE	FUNCTION KEY	REDEFINITION CODE
F1	59	Ctrl-F1	94
F2	60	Ctrl-F2	95
F3	61	Ctrl-F3	96
F4	62	Ctrl-F4	97
F5	63	Ctrl-F5	98
F6	64	Ctrl-F6	99
F7	65	Ctrl-F7	100
F8	66	Ctrl-F8	101
F9	67	Ctrl-F9	102
F10	68	Ctrl-F10	103
Shift-F1	84	Alt-F1	104
Shift-F2	85	Alt-F2	105
Shift-F3	86	Alt-F3	106
Shift-F4	87	Alt-F4	107
Shift-F5	88	Alt-F5	108
Shift-F6	89	Alt-F6	109
Shift-F7	90	Alt-F7	110
Shift-F8	91	Alt-F8	111
Shift-F9	92	Alt-F9	112
Shift-F10	93	Alt-F10	113

Table 11.3: Function-key redefinition codes

For example, F10 has the reassignment code 68. Suppose that you wanted to have the F10 key automatically type the command DIR/W. You would enter

PROMPT $e[0;68;"DIR/W";13p

First, $e[tells DOS that an ANSI command is being entered. Next, 0 tells DOS that the key to be redefined is part of the extended keyboard. The 68 selects F10 as the key to be redefined. "DIR/W" is the text of the command. (Note that these text characters are enclosed in quotation marks to indicate that they are not codes for ANSI.SYS to interpret.) 13 is the code for the Return key, which is required after the DIR/W command, just as it would be if you typed in DIR/W at the keyboard yourself. The last character in a key redefinition is always p, just as the last character in the video redefinition was an m.

Try out this technique now. Use the ANSI.SYS system to program your F7 function key to perform a CHKDSK command. Don't forget to make sure you have a CONFIG.SYS file in your root directory, and be sure it contains a DEVICE specification that loads the ANSI.SYS driver.

Finally, some very fancy custom menu systems can be set up simply with the PROMPT command and a well-thought-out group of function-key assignments. There are ten function keys (F1–F10), ten shifted function keys, ten Ctrl–function-key combinations, and ten Alt–function-key combinations. These provide 40 assignment possibilities. The extended code numbers for redefining these keys are also shown in Table 11.3.

The following PROMPT commands redefine several keys. The first will cause the shifted F4 key to type FORMAT A:. The second will cause the Ctrl-F6 combination to type CHKDSK, and the third will cause the Alt-F8 combination to type CD \:

PROMPT $e[0;87;"FORMAT A:";13p
PROMPT $e[0;99;"CHKDSK";13p
PROMPT $e[0;111;"CD \";13p

You must assign a key its original code value in order to reset it. The following sequence will reset all three of the example function-key sequences:

PROMPT $e[0;87;0;87p$e[0;99;0;99p$e[0;111;0;111p

Some programs reset the function-key definitions when they begin, and you will not be able to use the PROMPT command for key redefinition. When you encounter such a situation, the best solution is to purchase and use a keyboard redefinition program like Keyworks (see Chapter 18), which will allow you to redefine any key while another program is operating.

The nicest thing about all these possibilities is that they are cumulative—that is, you can issue any number of key redefinition requests and they will accumulate. Until you reset each one, they will retain their new definitions while you are at the DOS prompt level.

SUMMARY

In this chapter, you've learned some very powerful methods in DOS to customize your system for both power and convenience:

- The CONFIG.SYS file permits you to initialize several internal DOS system variables at bootup time.

- The BUFFERS command defines precisely how many internal buffers DOS will use.

- The FILES command specifies the maximum allowable number of open files that DOS will understand and support while DOS and your application programs run.

- The DEVICE command allows you to incorporate any number of specialized peripheral device drivers into your DOS configuration.

- A RAM disk is a memory-resident simulation of a typical mechanical disk. It offers you increased system performance and speed.

- The ANSI.SYS device driver provides extraordinary controls over both the video monitor and the keyboard. It provides a number of special codes, which give you the ability to redefine any keys and to control the video output. Using these codes with the PROMPT command allows you to make your system more intelligent, useful, and fun to operate.

In the next chapter, you'll learn about another type of system configuration: initializing your keyboard and monitor to understand and display international character sets.

INTERNATIONAL SETUP
OF DOS

DIFFERENT COUNTRIES USE DIFFERENT SYMBOLS TO represent their own systems. For example, currency symbols differ among countries—the $ in the USA, the DM in Germany, and the F in France. Time formats also vary: the separator symbol between the hour and minutes is a colon in the U.S., but a period in Norway. Decimal numbers are also punctuated differently; in the U.S., they contain a period, but in Spain they contain a comma. You'll learn in this chapter how to set up your version of DOS to understand the default values for symbols used in different countries.

Different countries also employ different keyboard layouts. If you learned to type in the U.S. and then tried typing on a French typewriter or keyboard, you would type the letter A each time you meant to type a Q, and vice versa. This is because the key labeled A on an American keyboard is labeled Q on a French keyboard. You'll also learn in this chapter about the differences between keyboard layouts in different countries and how you can easily ask DOS to redefine all the keys properly. In addition, you'll learn how to rapidly switch between the various possible layouts.

This chapter presents the international language-support features found in DOS 3.3 and DOS 4 only. You may need to make some adjustments to your system to improve the display and printout of foreign characters; the required steps will be presented later in this chapter.

If you're a foreigner in the U.S., you can easily switch between the U.S. default key values and your own. In this way, you can avoid learning the U.S. keyboard layout in order to work on computers here. The same is true in reverse for Americans working abroad. This feature is explained in detail later in this chapter.

CHARACTER SETS FOR DIFFERENT COUNTRIES

The group of characters used in a country or on a computer composes the character set of that country or computer. Most countries, like the United States and Great Britain, share a common set of characters. However, some countries have enough different characters and symbols to justify creating a special character set just for them.

Along with the different character sets comes different placement of the characters on a computer keyboard, which makes sense—commonly used elements must be easy to use. For example, on a French keyboard certain American keys are reversed, and other keys are for accented letters.

ASCII CODES

A computer does not interpret letters as letters per se, but assigns an ASCII code to each letter. These codes range from 0 to 255, representing the 256 possible combinations of binary digits contained in an eight bit byte.

Codes 0 through 31 are usually reserved for control codes, the codes that do not produce a visible character but perform some particular action. For example, printing the code 7 on most computers causes the computer to beep, and code 13 causes a carriage return. These codes control the functions of the hardware.

Codes 32 through 126 are standard characters and symbols (see Table 12.1). The capital alphabet starts at code 65, and the lowercase alphabet starts at code 97. Code 127 represents the deletion symbol. The control codes and the standard character codes together make up an entire set (from 0 to 127) called ASCII codes. The computer translates characters into these codes, and so does any other device using the characters. When a computer sends ASCII 65 to the printer, it expects an A to be printed out, so the printer must also translate from code 65 to A. You can see why it is important for these codes to be standardized; many pieces of equipment rely on the same code.

Codes 128 through 255 are computer/printer specific. IBM uses codes 128 through 255 for some graphics characters, while Epson, on some of its printers, uses them for italics.

Hex Digits	1st	0-	1-	2-	3-	4-	5-	6-	7-
2nd									
0					0	@	P	'	p
1				!	1	A	Q	a	q
2				"	2	B	R	b	r
3				#	3	C	S	c	s
4				$	4	D	T	d	t
5				%	5	E	U	e	u
6				&	6	F	V	f	v
7				'	7	G	W	g	w
8				(	8	H	X	h	x
9				)	9	I	Y	i	y
A				*	:	J	Z	j	z
B				+	;	K	[	k	{
C				,	<	L	\	l	¦
D				-	=	M	]	m	}
E				.	>	N	^	n	~
F				/	?	O	_	o	△

Table 12.1: Standard ASCII characters and symbols

The extended ASCII codes also represent certain specialized keys or key combinations, such as Alt-C or F1. These codes are defined by first sending an ASCII null character (code 0) to the device, and then another code. For example, sending code 0, then code 59 would have the same effect as pressing the F1 key.

The combinations of all these codes produce the complete visual and printed output you are used to seeing. Depending on where you live and work, however, you may have altogether different characters in your language and keys on your keyboard.

WHAT COUNTRY DO YOU CALL HOME?

When DOS boots up, the system date and time are queried. Everybody agrees that any given date has a month, a day, and a year, but not everyone agrees on that order. In the U.S., dates are shown with the month first, the day next, and the year last. In Europe, the day is shown first, the month next, and the year last. In the Far East, the year is first, the month next, and the day last. Hence, 11/04/07 can mean November 4, 1907; April 11, 1907; or April 7, 1911. It depends on who's writing the date *and* who's reading it. Again, that's why standards are so important.

The DATE function in DOS will display the system date according to the accepted custom in a specific country. Table 12.2 shows the countries currently understood by DOS, along with their country and keyboard codes. You'll learn later in this chapter how to set up your version of DOS to understand which country or keyboard is in use.

The order of the month, day, and year fields is only one of many things that differ among countries. Separator symbols between the month, day, and year values also vary from country to country. In fact, there are a host of special symbols that vary among countries: time separators (a colon or a period), list separators (a semicolon or a comma), decimal separators (a period or a comma), thousands separators (a comma or a period), and currency symbols ($, F, Fr, MK, DKR, and others). The U.S. shows time in 12-hour A.M./P.M. format, while most other countries use a 24-hour display. Most countries show two decimal places of accuracy in currency displays, while Italy shows none.

DOS maintains internal tables of these differing values according to which country has been set up as the system default. If you do nothing, the U.S. will be assumed to be the standard. However, if you wish to customize the system for some other country, you can simply use the proper country code from Table 12.2 to add a line to your CONFIG.SYS file:

COUNTRY = *Code*

Figure 12.1 shows the results of DOS date and time requests after the system CONFIG.SYS file was changed to a default of Switzerland

COUNTRY	COUNTRY CODE	KEYBOARD CODE
Arabic	785	–
Australia	061	US
Belgium	032	BE
Canada (Eng.)	001	US
Canada (Fr.)	002	CF
Denmark	045	DK
Finland	358	SU
France	033	FR
Germany	049	GR
Hebrew	972	–
Italy	039	IT
Japan	081	–
Korea	082	–
Latin America	003	LA
Netherlands	031	NL
Norway	047	NO
Portugal	351	PO
Simplified Chinese	086	–
Spain	034	SP
Sweden	046	SV
Switzerland (Fr.)	041	SF
Switzerland (Ger.)	041	SG
Traditional Chinese	088	–
United Kingdom	044	UK
United States	001	US

Table 12.2: International DOS country and keyboard codes

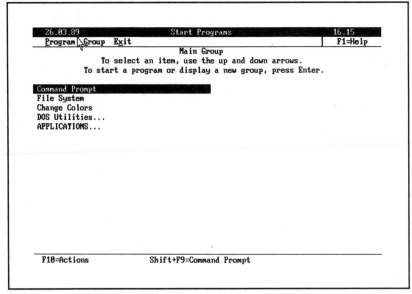

Figure 12.1: Date and time formats for COUNTRY = Switzerland

(code 041). Notice the changed format for the date and time in the upper-left and upper-right corners of the DOS 4 screen. The date now reflects the European standard of *dd-mm-yy*, while the time is shown in the common 24-hour format.

Getting the date and time was easy in this example. The real value of the COUNTRY code in CONFIG.SYS can only be realized fully by programmers using specialized assembly-language techniques. Thus, only a programmer can really obtain the specialized symbol and separator information necessary to customize an application program to the country it may run in. However, you can make a reasonable amount of adjustment yourself.

UNDERSTANDING CODE PAGES

DOS provides a complex ability to redefine its understanding of the keyboard you use. This is based on its feature called *code pages*. Code pages represent some complicated concepts, but with a little help and some extra knowledge, they can easily be understood. Let's start with the keyboard.

THE KEYBOARD TRANSLATION TABLE

The keyboard is simply a segregated group of buttons, monitored by a microprocessor that sends a signal to DOS when any key is pressed. The signal that goes to DOS is called a *scan code*. A scan code is not a letter or an ASCII code, but simply a code that tells DOS which key has been pressed. It has nothing to do with what is printed on the physical key, but merely with the physical location of the key.

At any time, whether DOS is busy or not, something will happen inside the computer when you press a key. This "something" is called an *interrupt*. One kind of interrupt occurs when a hardware device asks for the attention of the CPU. In the case of a keyboard, a small electrical signal—a scan code—is sent to DOS, indicating which key was pressed. The part of DOS that takes in the interrupt and processes it is called a *device driver* (or sometimes an *interrupt handler*).

When the keyboard device driver receives a signal, it processes the scan code to determine which key was pressed *and* to convert the scan code back into an ASCII code. This translation is done through a table in memory that compares scan codes and ASCII codes. Figure 12.2 diagrams this process.

During the entire process of handling each keyboard interrupt, DOS does not treat a scan code as any particular letter or symbol (such as the letter A), but simply as an ASCII code (such as 65).

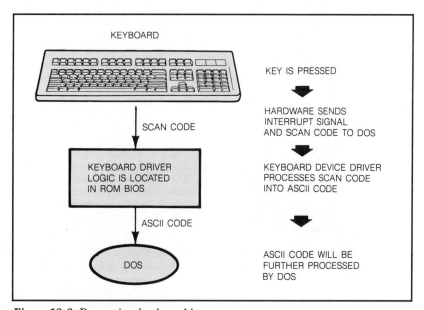

Figure 12.2: Processing keyboard interrupts

Take a look at the two different Personal System/2 keyboards used in the United States and France, shown in Figures 12.3 and 12.4. There are more than fifty other keyboard layouts in use on different computers in different countries. All of these are understood by DOS; the complete layouts for these alternatives are displayed in your DOS user's manual.

On a U.S. keyboard, if you press A, its scan code will be translated into ASCII code 65. However, if you hit the same key on a computer

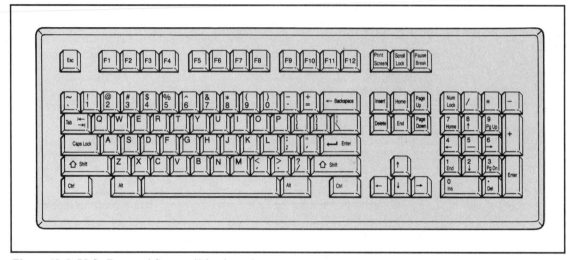

Figure 12.3: U.S. Personal System/2 keyboard

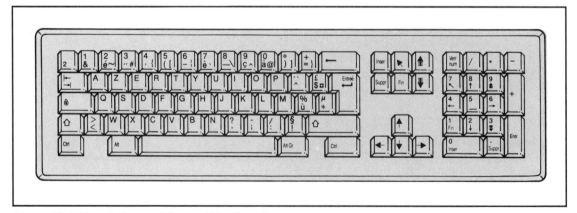

Figure 12.4: French Personal System/2 keyboard

with a French keyboard translation routine embedded in the device driver, the same scan code will be converted to ASCII code 81, or the letter Q.

If a key combination such as Alt-Ctrl-2 is pressed with the U.S. translator installed, not much will happen, because the U.S. keyboard translator does not have an entry in its table for this scan code. However, if you press this key combination on a computer with the French keyboard translator in effect, you will get the @ symbol. The French translator understands this scan code and will match it up. The ASCII code generated will be 64, which is the same code generated by pressing Shift-2 with a U.S. keyboard translator. Both yield the same @ symbol. The two keyboard translation tables translate different keyboard scan codes to the same ASCII codes, allowing countries with different keyboards to use all the same characters, even though the keys are labeled differently. Countries that have different keyboard layouts but still use the same character set are grouped into the same code page.

CODE PAGES

After interpreting what key was pressed on the keyboard and converting the scan code into an ASCII code by means of a translation table, DOS next determines where the ASCII code should go. If it goes to a disk drive, it is simply routed there and stored on the disk. If, however, it is destined for a monitor or printer, it is first processed by a code page. A code page is yet another translation table that converts an ASCII code into a printable or displayable character.

There are five code pages available in DOS. The standard code page (numbered 437 in DOS) for the United States can be seen in Table 12.3. (Refer to Appendix B for a complete explanation of the hexadecimal system shown in this table, as well as other number systems.) The other principal code page is the Multilingual code page, numbered 850 (see Table 12.4). It contains a host of international characters.

You'll soon learn how to use and switch between these code pages, as well as the other three code pages also available in DOS (Portugese, Norwegian, and Canadian French). See your DOS user's manual for the precise layouts of these remaining code pages.

Hex Digits 1st / 2nd	0-	1-	2-	3-	4-	5-	6-	7-	8-	9-	A-	B-	C-	D-	E-	F-
0		►		0	@	P	`	p	Ç	É	á	▓	└	╨	α	≡
1	☺	◄	!	1	A	Q	a	q	ü	æ	í	▒	┴	╤	β	±
2	☻	↕	"	2	B	R	b	r	é	Æ	ó	▓	┬	╥	Γ	≥
3	♥	‼	#	3	C	S	c	s	â	ô	ú	│	├	╙	π	≤
4	♦	¶	$	4	D	T	d	t	ä	ö	ñ	┤	─	╘	Σ	⌠
5	♣	§	%	5	E	U	e	u	à	ò	Ñ	╡	┼	╒	σ	⌡
6	♠	▬	&	6	F	V	f	v	å	û	ª	╢	╞	╓	µ	÷
7	•	↨	'	7	G	W	g	w	ç	ù	º	╖	╟	╫	τ	≈
8	◘	↑	(	8	H	X	h	x	ê	ÿ	¿	╕	╚	╪	Φ	°
9	○	↓	)	9	I	Y	i	y	ë	Ö	⌐	╣	╔	┘	Θ	∙
A	◙	→	*	:	J	Z	j	z	è	Ü	¬	║	╩	┌	Ω	·
B	♂	←	+	;	K	[	k	{	ï	¢	½	╗	╦	█	δ	√
C	♀	∟	,	<	L	\	l	|	î	£	¼	╝	╠	▄	∞	ⁿ
D	♪	↔	-	=	M	]	m	}	ì	¥	¡	╜	═	▌	φ	²
E	♫	▲	.	>	N	^	n	~	Ä	₧	«	╛	╬	▐	ε	■
F	☼	▼	/	?	O	_	o	△	Å	ƒ	»	┐	╧	▀	∩	

Table 12.3: Code page 437 for the United States

Hex Digits 1st / 2nd	0-	1-	2-	3-	4-	5-	6-	7-	8-	9-	A-	B-	C-	D-	E-	F-
0		►		0	@	P	`	p	Ç	É	á	▓	└	ð	Ó	-
1	☺	◄	!	1	A	Q	a	q	ü	æ	í	▒	┴	Ð	ß	±
2	☻	↕	"	2	B	R	b	r	é	Æ	ó	▓	┬	Ê	Ô	=
3	♥	‼	#	3	C	S	c	s	â	ô	ú	│	├	Ë	Ò	¾
4	♦	¶	$	4	D	T	d	t	ä	ö	ñ	┤	─	È	õ	¶
5	♣	§	%	5	E	U	e	u	à	ò	Ñ	Á	┼	ı	Õ	§
6	♠	▬	&	6	F	V	f	v	å	û	ª	Â	ã	Í	µ	÷
7	•	↨	'	7	G	W	g	w	ç	ù	º	À	Ã	Î	þ	¸
8	◘	↑	(	8	H	X	h	x	ê	ÿ	¿	©	╚	Ï	Þ	°
9	○	↓	)	9	I	Y	i	y	ë	Ö	®	╣	╔	┘	Ú	¨
A	◙	→	*	:	J	Z	j	z	è	Ü	¬	║	╩	┌	Û	·
B	♂	←	+	;	K	[	k	{	ï	ø	½	╗	╦	█	Ù	¹
C	♀	∟	,	<	L	\	l	|	î	£	¼	╝	╠	▄	ý	³
D	♪	↔	-	=	M	]	m	}	ì	Ø	¡	¢	═	¦	Ý	²
E	♫	▲	.	>	N	^	n	~	Ä	×	«	¥	╬	Ì	¯	■
F	☼	▼	/	?	O	_	o	△	Å	ƒ	»	┐	¤	▀	´	

Table 12.4: Code page 850 for multilingual operations

Special code pages exist for Hebrew and for Asian languages in DOS 4. However, their use requires special supplemental software and hardware.

Code pages are simply character sets. As you saw in the last section, one character set (code page) can satisfy the needs of several different countries. Countries with significantly different character sets and keyboards are grouped into other code pages. The 25 different country codes (shown in Table 12.2) correlate altogether with, at most, five different character sets, so only five different code pages are needed. Remember, a code page has 256 entries, so even if in the U.S. you rarely use an accented e, it is included in one of the extra spaces in the U.S. character set.

After the scan code has been translated into an ASCII code, it is matched to the currently active code-page translation table. Now you're into the output side of DOS management. The device driver responsible for the output device now uses built-in logic to send a sequence of control instructions to the output device. These instructions describe precisely how to display the character that was represented by the ASCII code. The process by which DOS and the output device drivers convert the ASCII code to visual output is shown in Figure 12.5.

DEVICES AND THEIR DRIVERS

All output consists of sequences of codes being sent to an output device like a monitor or printer. Unfortunately, not all monitors or printers act the same, have the same features, or can be controlled by the same device driver. In fact, sometimes the device driver consists of software instructions residing in your computer's main memory, while at other times these instructions reside in special memory built into the output device. Microsoft provides device drivers for the IBM Proprinter and Quietwriter printers, as well as device drivers for the PC Convertible display (LCD) and the Enhanced Graphics Adapter used on the PC/XT, PC/AT, and Personal System/2 displays.

Each output device driver translates the requested output data into the specific commands needed to form the character for each device. Figure 12.6 shows this part of the process. As the figure suggests, you must have one of the special monitors or printers to access any special additional symbols available in any non-U.S. code page.

TRANSLATION TABLES AND DEVICE DRIVERS

DOS supports more than 50 different keyboard layouts and 11 languages. Microsoft has supplied all of the necessary keyboard

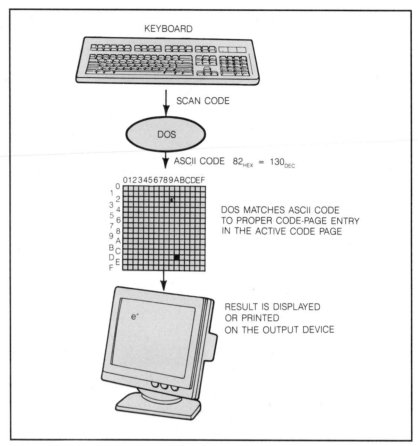

Figure 12.5: Code pages and device drivers control output

Some computers manufactured solely for foreign use have the foreign character set built in, as well as a keyboard with the appropriate key labels in place. These computers will not respond at all when you try to switch keyboard layouts with either the KEYB command or the Ctrl-Alt-function key combinations. No logic has been included to load in additional keyboard tables, since the necessary non-U.S. tables are already there.

translation tables in a file called **KEYBOARD.SYS**, which is loaded into the computer by using the KEYB command at the DOS prompt.

The output device drivers are loaded into memory from individual files. They are contained on the IBM Startup disk (DOS 3.3) or the IBM Install disk (DOS 4) in the files 4201.CPI, 4208.CPI, 5202.CPI, EGA.CPI, and LCD.CPI. CPI stands for code-page information; 4201 and 4208 refer to different models of IBM Proprinters, while 5202 refers to the IBM Quietwriter III printer. EGA refers to both the standard Enhanced Graphics Adapter and the IBM Personal System/2 display types, while LCD will drive the IBM Convertible's LCD screen.

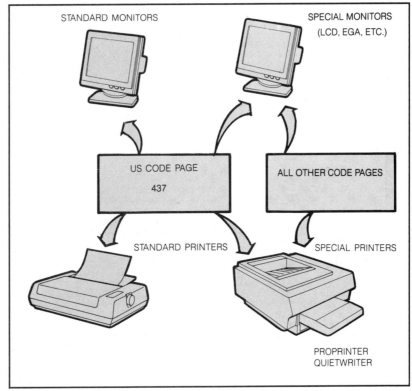

Figure 12.6: Sending output to standard and special devices

As you know, a DOS device driver can have up to nine different code pages to choose from. Each of these is referred to by a unique number, as shown in Table 12.5. Since code page 437 is the standard U.S. code page that is used with any monitor, 437 is the default when DOS boots up. This is the only code page that can be used with devices other than the printers and monitors supported by special-purpose drivers included in your DOS version.

Figure 12.7 ties all of the preceding sections together. It shows the entire process of moving information from beginning to end—from the keyboard interrupt to the final display or printed output.

Let's quickly run through a last example of the process. Assume you've loaded the Canadian French keyboard translation table into the computer (you'll learn how to do this in the next section). You've also loaded code page 863 and the 4201.CPI device driver, as you

LANGUAGE	CODE PAGE
Standard Code Pages	
United States	437
Multilingual	850
Portuguese	860
Canadian French	863
Norwegian and Danish	865
DOS 4 Code Pages Requiring Extra Hardware and Software	
Hebrew Speaking	862
Japan	932
Korea	934
Simplified Chinese	936
Traditional Chinese	938

Table 12.5: Code-page identification numbers

wish to print a character on the Proprinter. The character you want to print is the 3/4 symbol, which is not included in the normal ASCII character set of U.S. computers or printers. The 3/4 symbol on the Canadian keyboard can be printed by using the key combination Alt-Shift- = .

When this key combination is pressed, a scan code is sent to the keyboard device driver, which routes the scan code to the keyboard translation table. Here, the scan code is matched against the ASCII table, and an ASCII code (in this case, 173) is sent back to DOS. DOS sees that this character was destined for the printer and sends it on its way. The code is now processed by the Proprinter, which uses the installed code page. The Proprinter's driver now translates ASCII 173 to a set of hardware instructions that describe how to print a 3/4 symbol.

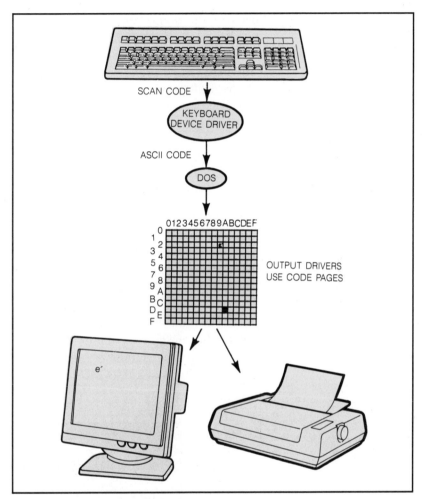

Figure 12.7: The overall code-page process

WORKING WITH CODE PAGES

Now that you understand how code pages are used, you must learn the required sequence of DOS commands necessary to implement them. You first need to learn how to tell DOS that you will be

using the national language-support scheme (NLS), which is just
another name for the code-page mechanism. You also need to learn
how to prepare, select, and switch between the various code pages.
The following sections will teach you the mechanics of the process.
Figure 12.8 provides an overview of the DOS command sequences
necessary for a complete international setup, which you will explore
in this chapter.

LOADING CODE-PAGE SUPPORT ROUTINES

NLSFUNC (short for national language-support functions) is a
DOS command that allows for the use of the new extended country
information provided with DOS 3.3 and later versions. This command will load in all of the required country-specific information. It
must be run *before* you attempt to select any code page other than the
default (437). As part of the format for the NLSFUNC command,
you must tell DOS where you've placed the COUNTRY.SYS file.
This file contains information that defines the country standards,
such as the date and time format, the rules of capitalization, and special symbol usage for each of the 25 available country codes (see
Table 12.2). U.S. standards will be assumed if you neglect to specify
the location of the COUNTRY.SYS file.

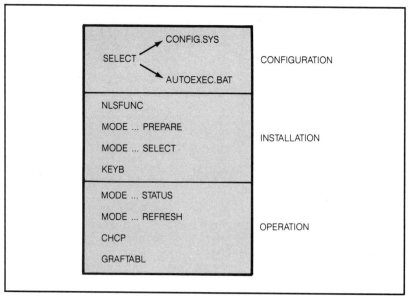

Figure 12.8: Command overview for international DOS operations

Assuming you have placed COUNTRY.SYS in the DOS directory, the command can be invoked as simply as

NLSFUNC \DOS\COUNTRY.SYS

The code-page support routines will be loaded into memory. No direct action or messages will be shown on the screen.

LOADING SPECIFIC CODE PAGES

After preparing DOS for national language-support operations, you can select specific code pages to use. The primary command for this purpose is a familiar one: MODE. This command has several versions. They all have a similar format:

MODE *DeviceName* CODEPAGE *Clause*

DeviceName is any valid DOS output reserved name, such as CON or LPT2. *Clause* represents a parameter you can use with several different values:

In all versions of the MODE command, CODEPAGE can be contracted to CP. In addition, PREPARE can be abbreviated to PREP, SELECT to SEL, REFRESH to REF, and STATUS to STA. You can reduce your typing burden by using these abbreviations, as well as saving time and reducing the likelihood of errors. The full spelling is shown in this chapter for the sake of clarity only.

- With a PREPARE parameter, you specify which code pages you want to be available for output operations.

- Use the SELECT parameter to choose which of the code pages is to be the active one for a particular output device.

- Use the /STATUS parameter to display the status of all code pages and connected output devices supporting code-page operations.

- For advanced output devices that retain code-page information in memory located within the device itself (as opposed to main memory), use the REFRESH parameter to restore the information in case the device is turned off or loses power.

Let's discuss the processing managed by the MODE command in a bit more depth. You first use the PREPARE parameter to install the code-page information necessary for the output drivers to handle the special international characters. With the SELECT parameter you then select the code page to be activated on the specified device. This means you can have several code pages loaded into the device at once, but only one can be active at any one time. At any time, you can use the /STATUS parameter to display the active code page and all of the other code pages available. Finally, with REFRESH you can reinstall the currently active output driver in the specified device if it was erased due to power loss.

With the PREPARE parameter, you can load one or several code pages for a device with one MODE command. This requires that you specify the device's reserved name, the list of allowable code pages (one or more), and the file containing the output driver. Code page 437 is the default code page; it is automatically loaded into the device. 437 is also the only code page that can access a nonspecified device (that is, one that IBM has not specifically written drivers for).

Think of it this way. A small buffer is set up for each device, and into this buffer you can enter a numeric list of code-page designations, one of which is active at a time. For example, entering

```
MODE CON CODEPAGE PREPARE = ((850,437)
C:\DOS\EGA.CPI)
```

will load the code-page information file EGA.CPI, specify that code pages 850 and 437 be selected for possible activation, and attach these code-page values to the EGA display.

Suppose that later you decide that you want to replace 850 with 863, and that also you want to make code page 865 available. You would enter

```
MODE CON CODEPAGE PREPARE = ((863,,865)
C:\DOS\EGA.CPI)
```

The two commas hold the place of the second code page, thereby leaving 437 (the U.S. code page) as the second code page. If you had specified ((,850,437) instead, then the first code page would have been saved and the second and third written over and reset to 850 and 437.

If you execute this command and the requested device is unavailable (not hooked up), you will get the message

Codepage operation not supported on this device

Assuming you really do have a device that supports code-page operations, check to see that it is connected properly to your system, that it is powered up, and that it is on-line.

The next parameter for the international version of the MODE command can only be used after you have properly prepared your code pages with PREPARE; the SELECT parameter will only work if the requested code-page device driver has been loaded. SELECT activates the specified code page on the specified device. For example, entering

> MODE CON CODEPAGE SELECT = 850

will make code page 850 the active code page for the console or the display device. Using this parameter in the previous example would make 850 active for an EGA display.

When you want to see information on the currently active code page, as well as a list of selectable code pages for a specific active device, you only need to enter

> MODE CON CODEPAGE /STATUS

DOS will display information about the current code page assigned to the monitor and keyboard.

The last parameter, REFRESH, is very useful if for some reason you need to turn your printer off. The output device drivers stay resident inside the device they drive. The available code pages and their related information are available through DOS, which is resident in your computer. So, when a device driver is installed, a copy is made of the code-page information in the computer and loaded into the memory of the device. If the device is turned off, then its memory is lost, and hence its modified driver. However, the original copy is still in the computer's memory. Instead of having to load the code page again with PREPARE, REFRESH just makes another copy and sends it out to the device's memory.

For example, suppose you've entered the following sequence of commands:

> MODE LPT1 CODEPAGE PREPARE = ((850,437)
> \DOS\4201.CPI)
> MODE LPT1 CODEPAGE SELECT = 850

If the device driver for your output device is resident in hardware, using PRE-PARE is unnecessary, since it will overwrite the hardware page. See your DOS user's manual for more detail on hardware code pages.

This means you have installed code-page information for an IBM Proprinter model and that you have two code pages to choose from, with 850 the currently active code page. Selecting a code page (with SELECT) causes the code-page driver to be copied to the hardware device (in this case, the printer connected to LPT1). Now, if you decide to turn the Proprinter off and then back on (perhaps to reset some switches), it would lose its local memory copy of the code-page information. To reload the code-page driver without spending the system's time to retrieve it from the disk, you would issue the command

MODE LPT1 CODEPAGE REFRESH

LOADING A KEYBOARD TRANSLATION TABLE

You have properly prepared your system to use national language support with the NLSFUNC command. You have also correctly installed the desired code-page information with MODE's PREPARE parameter, and you have selected a specific code page to use with MODE's SELECT parameter. The next step involves the KEYB command. This command is used to load in a new keyboard translation table for a specific country. In fact, it loads in a complete replacement for the keyboard driver resident in your computer's hardware (ROM BIOS). You can now select from the 21 different country codes you saw in Table 12.2.

If you were using alternate character sets in previous versions of DOS, then you need to use code page 850, since the character sets and keyboard layouts of the previous versions are incompatible with DOS 3.3 and DOS 4 (see Table 12.6).

The Multilingual code page (850) can support the primary character symbols used by all countries. If you switch between documents from different countries, it would be a good idea to load code page 850 in addition to your native code page so that you can view these other documents.

The general format for the KEYB command is

KEYB *KeyCode, CodePage, FileSpec* **/ID:***zzz*

where *KeyCode* is one of the two-letter country codes in Table 12.2, *CodePage* is one of the five three-digit code-page numbers, *FileSpec* is

Country	Keyboard Code	Existing Code Page	New Code Page
Australia	US	437	850
Belgium	BE	437	850
Canada—English	US	437	850
Canada—French	CF	863	850
Denmark	DK	865	850
Finland	SU	437	850
France	FR	437	850
Germany	GR	437	850
Italy	IT	437	850
Latin America	LA	437	850
Netherlands	NL	437	850
Norway	NO	865	850
Portugal	PO	860	850
Spain	SP	437	850
Sweden	SV	437	850
Switzerland—French	SF	437	850
Switzerland—German	SG	437	850
United Kingdom	UK	437	850
United States	US	437	850

Table 12.6: Old versus new code-page conversion table

KeyCode entry. However, for countries that use more than one keyboard layout, you add the /ID switch to the KEYB command; the *zzz* the full path name to the keyboard definition file KEYBOARD.SYS, and the optional /ID switch is used to specify the keyboard layout. Most countries use only one keyboard, which you identify with your

parameter specifies which layout to use. For example, France (120, 189), Italy (141, 142), and the United Kingdom (166, 168) all have two common keyboard alternatives.

You can create a KEYB command for the Netherlands, a country that uses just one keyboard layout, with the following command:

    KEYB NL, 850, \DOS\KEYBOARD.SYS

This will load the Netherlands keyboard translation table, based on code page 850, which is contained in the KEYBOARD.SYS file. Located in the DOS directory, the KEYBOARD.SYS file contains all of the keyboard translation tables for all possible countries.

Once you complete this initialization, the keys on the keyboard will no longer necessarily result in the letter, number, or character shown on the key. The assumption is that you will be using one of the scores of different keyboard layouts, each with its own key labels. In fact, if you're taking advantage of the keyboard reconfiguration capability but you are still using your original keyboard, it's a good idea to get new key labels, switch the key labels around, or simply to put new labels on the keys that have been changed.

There are often more accented characters than there are possible keys to assign. In this case, DOS understands special two-key sequences to represent the specially accented character. For instance, certain foreign letters require a circumflex over them. On the French keyboard, this symbol looks like the control, or "hat," symbol located over the 6 on the top row of a U.S. keyboard. In order to create this particular language-dependent effect, you must press the lowercase key just to the right of the letter p and *then* press the letter you want to put the circumflex over. In other words, you must employ a two-keystroke sequence to generate the two-part character symbol.

The set of these special keys that initiate a two-part character sequence are referred to as *dead keys* in DOS. If you make a mistake in typing the sequence, DOS will usually beep at you, show the erroneous result, and require you to erase the error and reenter the proper dead-key sequence. In this way, DOS provides yet another time-saving capability with the KEYB command, which saves you from having to touch up your text results with added accents and other special marks after the fact.

You can have up to two keyboard translation tables in memory at one time, but one of these must always be the standard U.S. table. To switch between the U.S. and another translation table, use these key combinations:

- Ctrl-Alt-F1 for the standard U.S. translation table
- Ctrl-Alt-F2 for a non-U.S. translation table

SWITCHING BETWEEN AVAILABLE CODE PAGES

Now that your system is prepared for code pages and you've selected one to be active, there may be times when you'd like to switch to a different code page. You'll need to do this when you are switching between documents written by personnel either in or for different countries. The CHCP command allows you to change the currently loaded code page. It is a very simple command to use. By issuing the command

CHCP 850

If you only want to change the code page on a particular device, use the MODE command with SELECT. Use the CHCP command to change all prepared code-page devices at once.

you can replace the currently active code page with code page 850. Any of the other four possible code-page numbers can be used if they have been properly prepared with the MODE command first.

The CHCP command does not have a parameter indicating which output device is being selected. That's because CHCP works on all prepared output devices, changing the active code page on all of them to the requested number.

ASSIGNING FOREIGN CHARACTERS ON A U.S. KEYBOARD

Now you understand how to load various code pages into your system and how to access characters via their table value (000 to 256 decimal or 00 to FF hexadecimal). I'll now show you another important technique. Often, you will have one code page loaded and a specified keyboard that does not have keys assigned for all possible characters. You can assign to unused keys these foreign or graphic characters and incorporate them into your work without changing your code page each time.

To do this, you only need to run the PROMPT command (discussed in the last chapter) one or more times to redefine the keys to your needs. For instance, suppose that you are writing a French manuscript about the British economy, and your analysis requires some Greek mathematical equations. You may want the Alt-F8 key to represent the French letter *e* with an accent grave (è), the Alt-F9 key to represent the Greek Sigma (Σ), and the Alt-F10 key to represent the British pound sign (£). By using the function-key redefinition codes in Table 11.3, you can make all three key assignments with the following PROMPT command:

PROMPT $e[0;111;"è"p$e[0;112;"Σ"p$e[0;113;"£"p

As I explained in the previous chapter, the $e[0; tells DOS that an extended key redefinition follows. The 111, 112, and 113 codes stand for the Alt versions of F8, F9, and F10. Following each of the three-digit codes are quotation marks, which enclose the character to be assigned. You create each of these characters by holding the Alt key down on your keyboard and typing the decimal equivalent of key's ASCII code on the numeric keypad.

In other words, the è is created by holding down the Alt key, pressing 138 (8A hex) on the numeric keypad, and then releasing the Alt key. Continue typing the PROMPT statement. When you reach the character inside the second pair of quotation marks, use the combination Alt-228 (E4 hex) for the Σ symbol. Lastly, press Alt-156 (9C hex) to obtain the £ sign inside the third pair of quotation marks. Make sure you type the entire PROMPT command carefully, noting especially the semicolons and the lowercase *p*, which are critical separators in this single PROMPT statement.

DISPLAYING EXTENDED ASCII CODES ON A COLOR GRAPHICS ADAPTER

A CGA monitor shows less detail than EGA, PGA, and VGA monitors because it has fewer pixels. When your CGA monitor is in graphics mode, you must use the GRAFTABL command in order to display the nonstandard characters with ASCII codes above 128. Entering

GRAFTABL 860

will load the Portugese code page and display the following message:

Portugese Version of Graphic Character Set Table has just been Loaded.

This means that the characters—whether graphics symbols or national symbols—that occupy the ASCII codes above code 128 will be accessible, and the ones displayed will be those from the special Portuguese code page.

To dramatize the necessity of this command, Figure 12.9 shows the extended ASCII codes for the U.S. code page when a CGA monitor is in graphics mode. As you can see, the characters are indecipherable. After GRAFTABL 437 is executed, however, the codes are displayable, as shown in Figure 12.10.

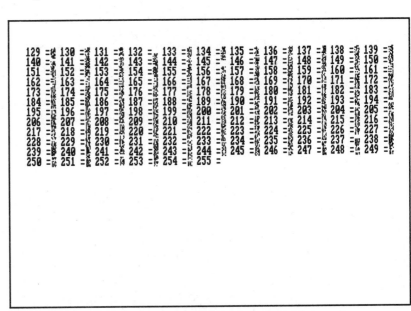

If you use this command, make sure that the path is set properly for finding it. Also make sure that you run the GRAFTABL command *before* invoking the programs that use the CGA graphics mode. Naturally, if you will be facing this problem on a regular basis, you should add the GRAFTABL command to your AUTOEXEC.BAT file (you will learn how later in this chapter).

You should only consider using the GRAFTABL command if you run programs that set the video mode to graphics. Otherwise, you lose the memory occupied by the alternate character set and gain nothing in return.

Figure 12.9: Extended ASCII codes before GRAFTABL is used

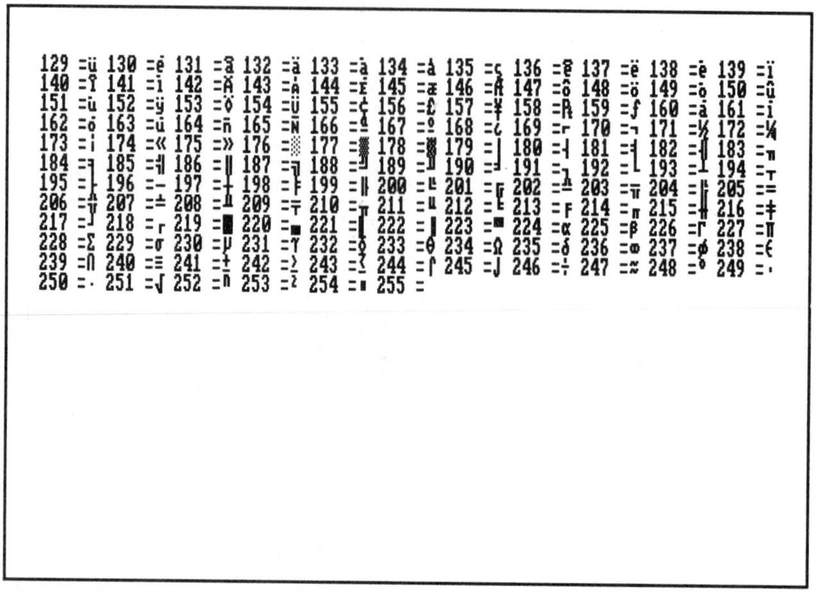

Figure 12.10: Extended ASCII codes after GRAFTABL is used

PREPARING AN INTERNATIONAL DOS SYSTEM DISK

DOS provides a special command, SELECT, which can save you a good deal of trouble if your principal goal is to have a system disk that supports code-page switching. With the following methods and commands, the delimiter format and keyboard information for each country can be installed permanently on a disk.

INSTALLING COUNTRY AND KEYBOARD INFORMATION

DOS 4 users have the luxury of a full-screen version of SELECT; you saw how it worked in Chapter 2 when you installed DOS 4 on your system. DOS 3.3 users have to do somewhat more work themselves. This section explains how you prepare a diskette for international use in DOS 3.3.

The SELECT command expects to read all the necessary DOS information from your startup and operating disks, now located on a diskette on drive A or B. It will manage the formatting of the destination disk and the copying of all necessary DOS files to this other disk. (The destination disk must not be the same as the source disk.) You must specify the desired three-digit country code and the two-letter keyboard code, both from the list in Table 12.2.

The required format of the SELECT command is

SELECT *Source Destination xxx yy*

Source is either A or B; it must contain the KEYBOARD.SYS, COUNTRY.SYS, FORMAT.COM, and XCOPY.EXE files. *Destination* is the drive and path to which the DOS command files will be copied. (The root directory is the default, but if you use the SELECT command to set up a hard disk, I recommend you create a subdirectory to hold the appropriate files.) The *xxx* is the country code, and the *yy* is the keyboard code. Since the U.S. keyboard file is resident in the computer's memory, it does not need to be on the source disk.

When you first execute SELECT, the following message appears on the screen:

SELECT is used to install DOS the first time. SELECT erases everything on the specified target and then installs DOS.
Do you want to continue (Y/N)?

Entering Y will start the process, while N will abort it.

Here is an example of the SELECT command. Entering

SELECT B: C:\JUDD 001 US

will format and copy the DOS commands files from drive B to drive C, directory JUDD, and install drive C with the U.S. rules for the date, time, and so on.

The SELECT command will also create two files on the destination disk. These are an initial AUTOEXEC.BAT file:

PATH \;\JUDD;
KEYB US 437 \JUDD\KEYBOARD.SYS
ECHO OFF
CLS
DATE
TIME
VER

If you are using a high-density drive as the destination drive for the SELECT command, you *must* use high-capacity diskettes. Also, since the SELECT command uses the FORMAT command, anything on the destination disk will be destroyed during the preparation of the disk. If you prepare a hard-disk drive in this way, you must be careful.

and the CONFIG.SYS file:

COUNTRY = 001,437,\JUDD\COUNTRY.SYS

The next section provides more details about these two files. SELECT will also copy all of the contents of the source disk, including COM-MAND.COM, into the specified directory. The six files that must be accessible on your source drive for this command to work are COM-MAND.COM, FORMAT.COM, SELECT.COM, XCOPY.EXE, KEYBOARD.SYS, and, finally, COUNTRY.SYS.

MODIFYING THE REQUIRED SYSTEM FILES YOURSELF

The CONFIG.SYS and AUTOEXEC.BAT files can contain statements that will automate some of this setup for you if you don't want to rely on SELECT alone. You've already read about using CONFIG.SYS, and you'll read about AUTOEXEC.BAT in more detail in Chapter 16. You can make these adjustments with your own word processor, with DOS's EDLIN editor, or by using the COPY command. COPY can be used to add a line (say, *FileName*) to any ASCII file in the following way. At the command prompt, you can type the command

COPY *FileName* + CON

When you are done entering lines to be added, press Ctrl-Z and Return. You will now be back at the DOS prompt.

UPDATING THE CONFIG.SYS FILE FOR INTERNATIONAL SUPPORT

The DEVICE configuration command in CONFIG.SYS can be used to load the various drivers needed for code-page switching. Assuming you have typed the above command or are in an editor and are creating or modifying a CONFIG.SYS file, adding the following lines will install the various required drivers. In these cases, you need a different DEVICE line in your CONFIG.SYS for each different printer and display device.

The sample entry

DEVICE = *D:*\DISPLAY.SYS CON: = (*Type,Hwcp,x*)

in your CONFIG.SYS file loads the specialized display device drivers. *D* is the location of the DISPLAY.SYS file. *Type* is either LCD or EGA, depending on the display being used. *Hwcp* is the code-page number(s) supported directly by the hardware device, and *x* is how many code pages will be added. The value for *x* should be 1 if 437 is the current code page, and 2 if it isn't.

This entry loads the specialized device drivers supporting the Proprinter and Quietwriter:

DEVICE = *D:*\PRINTER.SYS LPT1: = (*Type,Hwcp,x*)

The parameters are the same as those just described, except that *Type* can be 4201, 4202, or 5202.

The IBM Proprinter models reserve a hardware memory area in their own read-only memory (ROM) specifically for code-page information. The IBM Quietwriter III Printer Model 5202 uses hardware font cartridges to perform the same support purpose.

You can also have the country automatically set at the time your system boots up. The line to add to your CONFIG.SYS file is

COUNTRY = *xxx*

where *xxx* is the appropriate country code.

UPDATING YOUR AUTOEXEC.BAT FILE

Commands can be added to the AUTOEXEC.BAT file in the same way as they are for the CONFIG.SYS file. Including the KEYB command in the AUTOEXEC.BAT file lets the keyboard translation table and country codes be loaded in automatically. For example, adding the following line to your AUTOEXEC.BAT file:

KEYB FR 033

will automatically load the keyboard and country information for France.

You can also include versions of the NLSFUNC, MODE, and CHCP commands, which will work in conjunction with the CONFIG.SYS statements. As an example, the following lines included in your AUTOEXEC.BAT file would initialize national language-support operations, prepare code pages 863, 437, and 850, load the keyboard information file for France, and then select 850 as the active code page for both output devices:

```
NLSFUNC
MODE CON: CP PREPARE = ((863,437,850) \DOS\EGA.CPI)
MODE CON: CP PREPARE = ((863,437,850) \DOS\4201.CPI)
KEYB FR 033
CHCP 850
```

SUMMARY

Along with the PC family of computers, DOS has been a worldwide phenomenon. Recognizing this international influence, DOS provides certain features that allow you to customize your operating version. Although the specific commands and functions for national language support will be used primarily by only a small percentage of users, you may be one of that small group. This chapter is then critical to understanding the intertwined requirements of DOS setup.

- DOS supports many different languages and countries. DOS 3.3 supports five different groups of 256-character ASCII codes, called code pages. DOS 4 supports an additional five code pages, which are available only when special hardware or software is included with your system.

- There are scores of different languages, countries, and keyboard layouts. More are added with each new version of DOS. DOS supports them all with a series of specialized commands.

- The code page is the fundamental table of information available to device drivers. Device drivers manage input from the keyboard (KEYBOARD.SYS) and output to printers and monitors (DISPLAY.SYS).

- Special identification codes exist in DOS for each country and for each keyboard used in those countries.

- Keyboard device drivers convert scan codes, which represent the key that was pressed, to ASCII codes. The precise ASCII code depends on which of five code pages is active.

- Output drivers for the IBM Quietwriter III Printer Model 5202 and the line of IBM Proprinter models support printing of any of the specialized code-page symbols. Also available to support international output are the output drivers for the Enhanced Graphics Adapter, the IBM PC Convertible LCD display, and the IBM Personal System/2 displays.

- The DOS NLSFUNC command loads national language-support functions. It is an essential first command for installing international operations.

- Different versions of the MODE command allow you to prepare an output device for code-page use, select a specific code page for a particular display or printer, present the current code-page status of a device, and restore the code page in the hardware of certain output devices.

- The KEYB command is needed to specify which country and keyboard combination is to be activated for keyboard input, once your national language-support operations have been fully installed.

- Certain keys on some foreign keyboards understand two-key sequences to implement accents. The first key selects the accent mark, but displays nothing; it is called a dead key. The second key selects the character to be accented and displayed.

- Code pages can be activated or changed for all connected and prepared output devices by specifying a CHCP command along with the number of the desired code page.

- The PROMPT command allows you to assign foreign or graphic characters to unused keys. With this option, you can create a keyboard layout tailored to your work needs.

- You may not have a fancy new monitor, but you may want to display the extended ASCII characters (codes 128–255) on your CGA monitor when it is in graphics mode. You can do that by loading in an alternate character set with the GRAF-TABL command.

- The SELECT command prepares a system disk that is properly configured for international operations. If you specify the desired code pages and the proper country code, DOS will create a system disk with all necessary files on it.

- SELECT also creates the useful CONFIG.SYS and AUTOEXEC.BAT files with the necessary initial lines for national language-support operations.

- You can adjust your own CONFIG.SYS file with the appropriate DEVICE command for required keyboard and display output device drivers.

- You can update your own AUTOEXEC.BAT file to include the necessary NLSFUNC, MODE, KEYB, CHCP, and GRAFTABL commands for your system.

In the last three chapters, you've learned a good deal about customizing DOS. From controlling backups, to creating customized configurations and international layouts, you've done a good deal of work. The next chapter will present the last major subject in the ''Refining Your System'' part. It will focus on DOS's ability to redirect and filter all input and output information.

REDIRECTING THE ACTION

CHAPTER 13

IN THIS CHAPTER, YOU'LL CONCENTRATE ON THREE
related features: redirection, filters, and pipes. These features offer
you additional ways to control input and output in your system, as
well as new ways to process your information. They are of great
interest to programmers designing automated applications for DOS
systems; they are also of practical value for anyone using DOS.

CONTROLLING THE FLOW OF INFORMATION BY REDIRECTION

Redirection refers to the ability of a program or a DOS command to
choose an alternative device for input or output. As you know, most
programs and commands have a default device. For example, when
you enter the DIR command, the computer assumes that you want a
directory to be displayed on the screen. This is because the default for
DIR is the console (CON), which consists of the screen as the output
device and the keyboard as the input device. Your normal "interface" with the microcomputer system is through the system console.

SENDING SCREEN OUTPUT TO THE PRINTER

You often need a hard-copy printout of the information that
appears on your computer screen. As you learned in Chapter 8, the
Ctrl-PrtSc key combination is limited to only one screenful of information at a time. However, it is often useful to send the complete output from a command such as DIR to another device, such as the

printer. DOS has a simple way of redirecting the complete output, no matter how many screenfuls of data are involved.

Following a command with >PRN tells DOS to redirect the output to the printer. Think of the > sign as an arrow pointing to the destination. Entering the following command will redirect the standard DOS directory listing to the printer (PRN), instead of to the video screen:

DIR >PRN

DOS 4 users should try this at the command prompt. When the File System is up in DOS 4, you can always see the file listing for the currently selected directory. Although using the Shift-PrtSc key combination will print the screen image, it won't print all the file names if they don't fit within the 16-name limit of this DOS 4 window. Using the above DIR command at the command prompt will print the entire listing regardless of how many files are in the directory.

The same principle of redirection applies to any DOS command that sends data to the screen. Entering

CHKDSK >PRN

will generate a status check of disk and memory and send it to the printer rather than to the video screen.

STORING SCREEN OUTPUT IN A DISK FILE

DOS can also direct the output to a text file. This means that the information displayed on the screen can be sent to a file on the disk. Screen displays are temporary; if a directory display is captured and stored in a file, however, its information can be used at a later time.

This redirection technique has many practical uses. If you're in a hurry and don't want to wait for printed output, you can quickly send the information to a disk file and then peruse it at your leisure. You can read it into your word-processing program and make modifications to it, or include it in reports. You can read it with a database-management program and perform file-management functions based on the information sent by DOS into the disk file.

An excellent use of redirection is to create a file that is a catalog of the contents of several diskettes. If you were working with a word processor or a database program, you could then get a master listing of all the files you have stored on all your working diskettes. If you were working with a hard disk, you could make a catalog of your backup disks.

The first step in creating your own diskette catalog is to decide where the master list will be placed. Let's assume you want to place the data in a file called CATALOG. The first cataloged directory will be that of the diskette in drive A. Entering

DIR A: > CATALOG

at the DOS command prompt produces no visible result on the screen. You told DOS not to display the directory on the screen, but rather to store the information in a file called CATALOG. If you were watching, you would have seen the A drive light come on as the CATALOG file was being written.

To check the results of this command, you can ask DOS to type the contents of the CATALOG file:

TYPE CATALOG

The directory will be displayed just as if you had typed in the DIR command. However, this printout represents the directory when the original CATALOG file was created by DOS; it is like a snapshot of the original directory. It contains only the directory information that existed when the file was created.

Redirecting DOS output to a disk file can be misleading. Remember that the information contained in that file will not be current and will not be updated automatically to reflect any future changes to your system.

Try the following sequence now to reinforce your understanding of redirection. Redirect the output from the DIR and CHKDSK commands at the DOS prompt to a disk file. You can call this file CATALOG, or you can give it a name of your own. Then use the TYPE command to verify that the output was generated properly.

Later on, you can see that the contents of this file are unchanging. After doing some other work with the system, issue a DIR or CHKDSK command at the DOS prompt again. Then compare the results to the snapshot contained in your CATALOG file.

ADDING OUTPUT TO AN EXISTING FILE

Redirection also allows you to add the directory display of another drive to the CATALOG file. This requires a slightly different command. Look at the following two commands:

```
DIR A: > CATALOG
DIR A: >> CATALOG
```

What is the difference?

The first command simply replaces the old CATALOG file with a new one. The second command, on the other hand, causes the output from the DIR command to be *appended* to (added to) the existing CATALOG file. The directory listing of the new diskette placed in drive A will be appended to the directory listing of the diskette previously placed in drive A.

You can continue this process by placing other diskettes in drive A and repeating the >> command. CATALOG will grow as you store your diskette directories on it. If you are a hard-disk user, you can place your diskettes in A, and your CATALOG file will be updated on drive C.

To see the contents of this file in DOS 4, you can use the View command on the File menu. In earlier DOS versions, you can simply enter

```
TYPE CATALOG
```

The result will be a consolidated directory that spans the contents of a number of diskettes.

If you need a hard copy of the directories, you can redirect the data to your printer and use the TYPE command:

```
TYPE CATALOG > PRN
```

You can edit this command's output with your word processor, print the results on gummed labels, and attach them to your original diskettes. Some companies sell programs for $50 that do this simple task.

Try the redirection feature yourself right now. Create your own CATALOG file, listing all the file names on several diskettes. If you're interested only in the names themselves and not in the size or date and time information, use a DIR/W command to direct the output to your CATALOG file. Remember to use a single > sign to create the file and a double >> sign to append new directory output to it. Dual-diskette users should place the diskettes to be cataloged into drive B, creating the CATALOG file on drive A. Hard-disk users should place their diskettes into drive A, creating the CATALOG file on drive C.

RECEIVING INPUT FROM TEXT FILES

DOS can receive input from a text file. This means that instead of waiting at the console to enter data, make responses, or otherwise generate input for a DOS command or a program, you can type your responses in advance. DOS will then take each response from the input file as it is needed. Let's look at a simple example.

Input from a file is more unusual than output. In the normal course of computer use, most users will not take advantage of the feature described here. However, it can be useful.

You may have noticed that some DOS commands require the user to enter additional keystrokes after the program has begun. For example, the FORMAT command will always pause and ask you to press any key before actual formatting takes place. This safety precaution protects you from errors, giving you a moment to take a deep breath (and to check the disk in the drive) before actually committing yourself to the formatting process.

You could avoid that extra keystroke by creating an input file to be used with the FORMAT command. The input file would contain any keystrokes that you wanted typed in while the program was running. In this case, a simple press of the Return key will do. To create a file containing a Return character, you could use a word processor, or you could create the KEYS file from the DOS prompt using the COPY command you saw earlier. Enter

COPY CON: KEYS

and press Return. Then press Return again. Enter

N

and press Return. Then enter

^Z

and press Return. The KEYS file now contains the keystroke for the Return key. It also contains the No response (N) to the FORMAT command's request "Do you want to format an additional diskette?"

To indicate that these responses are coming from a file and not from you at the keyboard, the < symbol is used:

FORMAT B:/S < KEYS

When you enter this command, the formatting does not pause—the Return keypress has been input from the KEYS file. When the single disk is completely formatted, the N tells FORMAT you're done, and the DOS prompt reappears. As you can see, this kind of feature can save you time and effort, and can be useful in many situations.

PROCESSING YOUR FILE INFORMATION WITH DOS FILTERS

Another powerful feature of DOS is its use of *filters* to process data directly. Just as a camera filter changes what you see through the lens, a DOS filter can process in unique ways any data that passes through it and can change what you see on the screen. There are three filters included in DOS: SORT, FIND, and MORE. They are stored on disk as the SORT.EXE, FIND.EXE, and MORE.COM files.

ARRANGING YOUR DATA WITH THE SORT FILTER

Let's look first at one of the most useful filters, the SORT filter. SORT rearranges lines of data. Take a look at the sample data files in Figures 13.1 and 13.2. These lists could have been prepared with a word processor, a database manager, a spreadsheet, or even with DOS itself. Lists like these usually grow in size, with the new entries added chronologically as your business acquires new clients or as you make new friends and acquaintances.

Every once in a while, you probably rewrite your own personal phone list. You usually want the list in last-name order, but you might want a special printout in nickname or first-name order. Even more

```
┌─────────────────────────────────────────────────────────────────┐
│ ▐03-27-89▌              File System              8:10 am         │
│                                               ┌─────────┐        │
│                                               │ F1=Help │        │
│   ┌──────────────────────────────────────────┴─────────┴──┐     │
│   │                      File View                         │     │
│   │                                                        │     │
│   │  To view a file's content press ▐PgUp▌ or ▐PgDn▌.      │     │
│   │                                                        │     │
│   │  Viewing file:  D:\XYWRITE\DOS400\BUSINESS.TXT         │     │
│   └────────────────────────────────────────────────────────┘     │
│                                                                   │
│   Cantonese Imports   134  Roberts   Joseph 212/656-2156         │
│   Brandenberg Gates   754  Bennett   Mary   415/612-5656         │
│   Sole Survivor,Inc.  237  Evans     Gail   415/222-3514         │
│   Presley Plastics    198  Presley   Robert 716/245-6119         │
│   Plymouth Granite Co 345  Williams  Peter  617/531-6145         │
│   Bucket Dance Wear   276  Lewis     Ann    415/635-2530    ▷    │
│   Intelli-Strategies  743  Griffiths Robert 415/362-9537         │
│   Benicia Balloons    983  Franklin  Marie  212/524-4157         │
│   Standard Shelters   690  Rucker    Sally  415/532-1107         │
│   Panama Rain Corp.   576  Cook      Freda  408/534-9739         │
│                                                                   │
│                                                                   │
│   ←┘=Enter  Esc=Cancel  F9=Hex/ASCII                             │
└─────────────────────────────────────────────────────────────────┘
```

Figure 13.1: A business contact list

```
┌─────────────────────────────────────────────────────────────────┐
│ ▐03-27-89▌              File System              8:10 am         │
│                                               ┌─────────┐        │
│                                               │ F1=Help │        │
│   ┌──────────────────────────────────────────┴─────────┴──┐     │
│   │                      File View                         │     │
│   │                                                        │     │
│   │  To view a file's content press ▐PgUp▌ or ▐PgDn▌.      │     │
│   │                                                        │     │
│   │  Viewing file:  D:\XYWRITE\DOS400\PERSONAL.TXT         │     │
│   └────────────────────────────────────────────────────────┘     │
│                                                                   │
│   Klaar     Wim     213-968-2345  Ready                          │
│   Torrance  Stan    415-567-4534  Stan                           │
│   Quilling  Alan    415-526-4565  Al                             │
│   Keepsake  Alice   415-249-3498  Jala                           │
│   Bentley   Robert  415-654-4864  Speed         ▷                │
│   Hendley   Candice 415-212-3434  Candy                          │
│                                                                   │
│                                                                   │
│                                                                   │
│   ←┘=Enter  Esc=Cancel  F9=Hex/ASCII                             │
└─────────────────────────────────────────────────────────────────┘
```

Figure 13.2: A personal phone list

often, businesses need to reprint their client list in some usable order. Perhaps the telephone receptionist needs an updated list in company-name order. The marketing department may need the same list printed in telephone-number order. Then again, the accounts payable department may want the list in customer ID order. All of these are very easy to obtain with the SORT filter.

Using the redirection concept presented in the previous section, you can take each of these representative lists and rearrange the data to suit your needs. One form of filtering is to enter the following command at the DOS prompt:

SORT < BUSINESS.TXT

DOS 4 users can also start the SORT command by entering the appropriate parameters in the Options field (see Figure 13.3).

Remember that you have the choice of using the command prompt in any DOS version or using a dialog box in DOS 4. I present the main parameter options for the commands in this chapter. You can then choose how to enter them, according to your version of DOS. The sample screens all represent DOS 4 outputs.

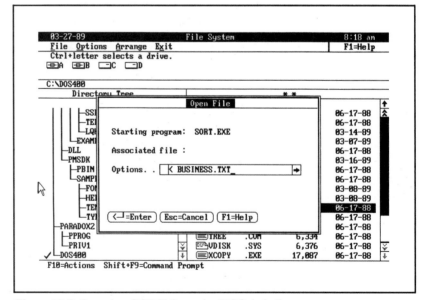

**Figure 13.3:** Running SORT from the DOS 4 shell

Sorting the BUSINESS.TXT file results in the list ordered by company name as shown in Figure 13.4.

A similar arrangement of your personal phone list can be obtained by entering

SORT < PERSONAL.TXT

These lists are sorted by whatever data comes first on the line. Later in this chapter, you'll learn how to use SORT to arrange the data based on other information in each line.

In this case, the arrangement is by last name (see Figure 13.5).

In both examples just given, the .TXT files were directed to be *input* to the SORT command—the < arrowhead points to SORT. Since there was no redirection specified for output, the sorted results appeared on the video screen. Each of these commands could also specify an output redirection that would place the sorted results in a disk file. You could then work with the sorted file as you liked, perhaps delaying the printing until a convenient time.

The two sorted lists could be saved in the files CLIENTS.TXT and PHONES.TXT with the following commands:

SORT < BUSINESS.TXT > CLIENTS.TXT
SORT < PERSONAL.TXT > PHONES.TXT

```
Benicia Balloons      983  Franklin  Marie   212/524-4157
Brandenberg Gates     754  Bennett   Mary    415/612-5656
Bucket Dance Wear     276  Lewis     Ann     415/635-2530
Cantonese Imports     134  Roberts   Joseph  212/656-2156
Intelli-Strategies    743  Griffiths Robert  415/362-9537
Panama Rain Corp.     576  Cook      Freda   408/534-9739
Plymouth Granite Co   345  Williams  Peter   617/531-6145
Presley Plastics      198  Presley   Robert  716/245-6119
Sole Survivor,Inc.    237  Evans     Gail    415/222-3514
Standard Shelters     690  Rucker    Sally   415/532-1107




    Press Enter (<──┘ ) to return to File System.
```

Figure 13.4: Sorting by company name

```
Bentley    Robert   415-654-4864   Speed
Hendley    Candice  415-212-3434   Candy
Keepsake   Alice    415-249-3498   Jala
Klaar      Wim      213-968-2345   Ready
Quilling   Alan     415-526-4565   Al
Torrance   Stan     415-567-4534   Stan




Press Enter (<—┘ ) to return to File System.
```

Figure 13.5: Sorting by last name

Figures 13.6 and 13.7 show the verification of these results with the TYPE command. Figure 13.8 shows how the SORT filter works.

PERFORMING TEXT SEARCHES WITH THE FIND FILTER

When you are doing character searches in DOS or any other processing language, the case (upper or lower) of the characters is critical. You must always specify the character string *exactly* as you expect to find it in the file.

Let's look at another DOS filter, the FIND command. It permits you to scan any text file for a series of text characters and to locate any lines in the file that contain the specified characters. For instance, let's take the business contact list from Figure 13.1 and try to find all clients located in the area code 415:

FIND "415" BUSINESS.TXT

This command will locate all lines in the specified text file (the second parameter) that contain the specified character string (the first parameter). Figure 13.9 shows the DOS 4 version of this command request, while Figure 13.10 demonstrates the results.

```
When ready to return to the DOS Shell, type EXIT then press enter.

IBM DOS Version 4.00
        (C)Copyright International Business Machines Corp 1981, 1988
        (C)Copyright Microsoft Corp 1981-1986

C:\DOS400>SORT < BUSINESS.TXT > CLIENTS.TXT

C:\DOS400>TYPE CLIENTS.TXT
Benicia Balloons     983  Franklin  Marie   212/524-4157
Brandenberg Gates    754  Bennett   Mary    415/612-5656
Bucket Dance Wear    276  Lewis     Ann     415/635-2530
Cantonese Imports    134  Roberts   Joseph  212/656-2156
Intelli-Strategies   743  Griffiths Robert  415/362-9537
Panama Rain Corp.    576  Cook      Freda   408/534-9739
Plymouth Granite Co  345  Williams  Peter   617/531-6145
Presley Plastics     198  Presley   Robert  716/245-6119
Sole Survivor,Inc.   237  Evans     Gail    415/222-3514
Standard Shelters    690  Rucker    Sally   415/532-1107

C:\DOS400>
```

Figure 13.6: Sorted client list in text file

```
When ready to return to the DOS Shell, type EXIT then press enter.

IBM DOS Version 4.00
        (C)Copyright International Business Machines Corp 1981, 1988
        (C)Copyright Microsoft Corp 1981-1986

C:\DOS400>SORT < PERSONAL.TXT > PHONES.TXT

C:\DOS400>TYPE PHONES.TXT
Bentley    Robert   415-654-4864   Speed
Hendley    Candice  415-212-3434   Candy
Keepsake   Alice    415-249-3498   Jala
Klaar      Wim      213-968-2345   Ready
Quilling   Alan     415-526-4565   Al
Torrance   Stan     415-567-4534   Stan

C:\DOS400>
```

Figure 13.7: Sorted phone list in text file

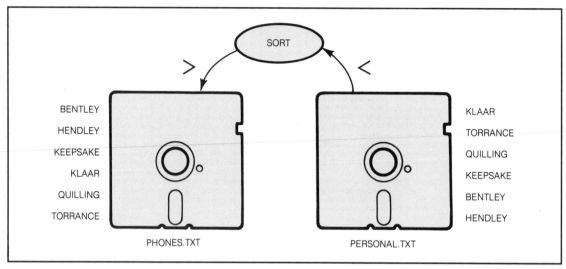

Figure 13.8: The SORT filter at work

The quotation marks around your character strings are delimiters. You must use them. They assist DOS in distinguishing a character string from the command line's other characters, which represent commands, file names, or parameters.

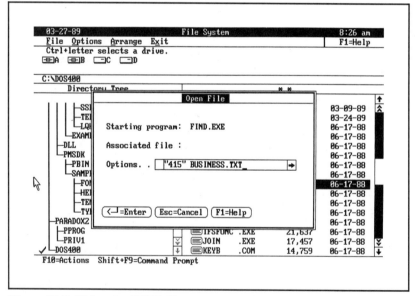

Figure 13.9: Using the FIND filter to extract data

Note that the first line of the output identifies the input text file.

This is a typical database extraction request that has been handled by DOS *almost* satisfactorily. Notice that the Benicia Balloons

```
---------- BUSINESS.TXT
Brandenberg Gates   754  Bennett    Mary    415/612-5656
Sole Survivor,Inc.  237  Evans      Gail    415/222-3514
Bucket Dance Wear   276  Lewis      Ann     415/635-2530
Intelli-Strategies  743  Griffiths  Robert  415/362-9537
Benicia Balloons    983  Franklin   Marie   212/524-4157
Standard Shelters   690  Rucker     Sally   415/532-1107




            Press Enter (<──┘ ) to return to File System.
```

Figure 13.10: Results of the search for ''415''

company has been included in the results, even though its area code is not 415. You asked DOS to find every line in the file that included 415 anywhere in the line, and 415 is in the last four digits of that company's telephone number (524-4157). Therefore, the line was filtered into the resulting selection.

To solve this problem, you can specify '' 415'' as the character string. By including the extra space before the digits 415, you will be sure to extract only the telephone numbers that begin with the desired digits. Enter

FIND '' 415'' BUSINESS.TXT

Figure 13.11 shows the results. Your command has selected the correct lines from the file.

You can also name more than one file as input to the FIND filter. With the command shown in Figure 13.12, you could quickly see if any of your area code 212 business clients appeared on your personal phone list as well.

Make sure your specified character string is unique enough to find only the data you're looking for. The fewer characters in your string, the greater the likelihood that DOS will find lines containing those characters.

```
When ready to return to the DOS Shell, type EXIT then press enter.

IBM DOS Version 4.00
        (C)Copyright International Business Machines Corp 1981, 1988
        (C)Copyright Microsoft Corp 1981-1986

C:\DOS400>FIND " 415" BUSINESS.TXT

---------- BUSINESS.TXT
Brandenberg Gates    754   Bennett   Mary    415/612-5656
Sole Survivor,Inc.   237   Evans     Gail    415/222-3514
Bucket Dance Wear    276   Lewis     Ann     415/635-2530
Intelli-Strategies   743   Griffiths Robert  415/362-9537
Standard Shelters    690   Rucker    Sally   415/532-1107

C:\DOS400>
```

Figure 13.11: Making sure your character string is sufficient

```
When ready to return to the DOS Shell, type EXIT then press enter.

IBM DOS Version 4.00
        (C)Copyright International Business Machines Corp 1981, 1988
        (C)Copyright Microsoft Corp 1981-1986

C:\DOS400>FIND "212" BUSINESS.TXT PERSONAL.TXT

---------- BUSINESS.TXT
Cantonese Imports    134   Roberts   Joseph 212/656-2156
Benicia Balloons     983   Franklin  Marie  212/524-4157

---------- PERSONAL.TXT
Hendley    Candice 415-212-3434    Candy

C:\DOS400>
```

Figure 13.12: Filtering multiple files

In these sample situations, business and personal lives have been kept apart. The FIND command could just as easily have been used with two different business mailing lists, as in Figure 13.13, in order to identify duplicate entries that should be removed from data lists. This is an example of how DOS can help you weed out extra entries.

The example in Figure 13.13 requires you to specify a FIND character string like " 617". Therefore, only duplicates for the 617 calling area will appear; you would have to respecify more area codes to be complete. However, other tools that you've learned about can do the job even better. First use the COPY command to join the two business files into one temporary file, which you can delete later; then use SORT to filter the resultant file.

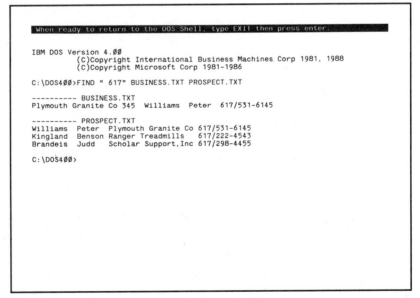

When you are joining two files to create a third, or when you are creating any temporary file, make sure your disk has enough space on it for the operation.

Using TYPE with the sorted file would now show you all possible duplicates. You could proceed to find any subset of records of interest (for example, the 617 calling area) with FIND. In each case, you would not have to look back and forth between two lists. Duplicates would appear one right after the other in the output listing.

```
When ready to return to the DOS Shell, type EXIT then press enter.

IBM DOS Version 4.00
        (C)Copyright International Business Machines Corp 1981, 1988
        (C)Copyright Microsoft Corp 1981-1986

C:\DOS400>FIND " 617" BUSINESS.TXT PROSPECT.TXT

---------- BUSINESS.TXT
Plymouth Granite Co 345  Williams  Peter  617/531-6145

---------- PROSPECT.TXT
Williams  Peter  Plymouth Granite Co 617/531-6145
Kingland  Benson Ranger Treadmills   617/222-4543
Brandeis  Judd   Scholar Support,Inc 617/298-4455

C:\DOS400>
```

Figure 13.13: Finding duplicate entries in multiple lists

CONNECTING DOS OPERATIONS WITH PIPES

You've seen how the SORT and FIND filters can work with data files as input. Now you'll explore how filters can work in connection with other programs or DOS commands. When these connections are made, they are called *pipes*. Earlier in this chapter, you saw how you could change DOS's default input and output devices using redirection. Pipes allow you to combine the power of redirection with that of filters. You can simultaneously change (filter) your data while it is being moved (redirected) from one location to another.

Even with the redirection techniques you have learned so far in this chapter, if you want to do several things in a row, you might still have quite a bit of work to do. You might need to run one program, send its results to a disk file, and then run another program to process the resulting data. Then you might have to take the next program's input from that disk file to continue the processing chain, perhaps creating several intermediate files before getting the final result. Piping allows you to take the output of one command or program and make it the input of another command or program. You can do this several times in a row. An entire series of programs that generate intermediate output for one another can be automated by using the sophisticated combination of filters and pipes.

COMBINING PIPING AND SORTING

As you know, the SORT filter can be used to create a sorted directory listing. By adding pipes, you can use any column that appears in a directory listing as the criterion for a sorting order. This is very helpful, because a normal directory display does not arrange the files in any particular order. Using the SORT filter, you can produce your directory listings in order of file name, file extension, file size, date of creation, or even time of creation. As you'll see, you can take any text file and arrange it in any way you like as well.

Pipes are created by using the vertical bar symbol (¦). Entering the command

    DIR ¦ SORT

sends the output of a DIR command to the SORT filter before it is sent to the screen. The filtered result is a sorted directory display. Figure 13.14 shows a standard directory listing before sorting. Figure 13.15 shows the SORT processing operation itself, and Figure 13.16 presents the sorted results.

This procedure required only a single piping sequence. Previously, you would have had to redirect the results of the DIR command into a disk file and then redirect the disk file so that it would be the input of the SORT filter. The pipe was created automatically by DOS to handle this job.

Note that the first three lines have also been sorted:

```
17 File(s)    821248 bytes free
Directory of A:\
Volume in drive A is PIPING DEMO
```

The "17 File(s)" line is indented seven spaces beyond the "Directory" and "Volume" lines, which themselves are indented one space. The file names that follow are not indented.

Two extra files, 09010315 and 0901041F, appear in the sorted listing. These files are temporary work files created during the sorting

```
A:\>DIR

 Volume in drive A is PIPING DEMO
 Directory of  A:\

COMMAND  COM     37637 06-17-88   12:00p
COUNTRY  SYS     12858 06-17-88   12:00p
VDISK    SYS      6376 06-17-88   12:00p
MODE     COM     23040 06-17-88   12:00p
FIND     EXE      5983 06-17-88   12:00p
SHELL    CLR      4438 06-17-88   12:00p
SHELL    HLP     66977 06-17-88   12:00p
SHELL    MEU      4588 06-17-88   12:00p
PCMSDRV  MOS       961 06-17-88   12:00p
EGA      CPI     49052 06-17-88   12:00p
XMAEM    SYS     19312 06-17-88   12:00p
XMA2EMS  SYS     29236 06-17-88   12:00p
SELECT   DAT     22453 06-17-88   12:00p
SELECT   EXE     99791 06-17-88   12:00p
TREE     COM      6334 06-17-88   12:00p
       15 File(s)       822272 bytes free

A:\>
```

Figure 13.14: Unsorted directory listing

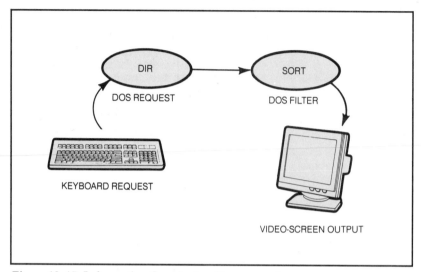

Figure 13.15: Information flow during filter operation

```
A:\>DIR | SORT


        17 File(s)      821248 bytes free
 Directory of  A:\
 Volume in drive A is PIPING DEMO
0901Ø315             Ø  Ø3-27-89     9:Ø1a
09Ø1Ø41F             Ø  Ø3-27-89     9:Ø1a
COMMAND   COM    37637  Ø6-17-88    12:ØØp
COUNTRY   SYS    12838  Ø6-17-88    12:ØØp
EGA       CPI    49Ø52  Ø6-17-88    12:ØØp
FIND      EXE     5983  Ø6-17-88    12:ØØp
MODE      COM    23Ø4Ø  Ø6-17-88    12:ØØp
PCMSDRV   MOS      961  Ø6-17-88    12:ØØp
SELECT    DAT    22453  Ø6-17-88    12:ØØp
SELECT    EXE    99791  Ø6-17-88    12:ØØp
SHELL     CLR     4438  Ø6-17-88    12:ØØp
SHELL     HLP    66977  Ø6-17-88    12:ØØp
SHELL     MEU     4588  Ø6-17-88    12:ØØp
TREE      COM     6334  Ø6-17-88    12:ØØp
VDISK     SYS     6376  Ø6-17-88    12:ØØp
XMA2EMS   SYS    29236  Ø6-17-88    12:ØØp
XMAEM     SYS    19312  Ø6-17-88    12:ØØp

A:\>
```

Figure 13.16: Sorted directory listing

operation by DOS on the default drive. They will be erased automatically after the piping operation is complete. Their obscure file names are based on the date and time of the actual SORT operation. They will always be different.

The default drive must not be write-protected—DOS needs to create temporary files while it is performing its filtering job. In addition, the default drive must have sufficient available space to create the temporary files. Otherwise, the automatic piping process will be unable to continue.

You can ignore these files completely if you wish. However, you may not want to have them appear in your sorted output—their inclusion may simply confuse others who read your output listing. To avoid this, you should set the default drive to a drive other than the one you want sorted. You can then use the PATH command to tell DOS where to find the SORT.EXE file. On a dual-diskette system, you might set the path to drive A; on a hard-disk system, you might set the path to the DOS directory on drive C.

Look at Figure 13.17 for further clarification. In this case, you first make drive C the default. The temporary files will be written on this new default drive. Then you ask for a directory listing of drive A, telling DOS to direct the DIR command's output to the SORT command for filtering. The sorted directory listing is then displayed, and the two temporary files are saved to the DOS400 directory.

CUSTOMIZING YOUR DOS SORTS

Let's explore piping a little further, and in the process, look at some additional capabilities of DOS filters. The SORT filter allows

```
A:\>C:

C:\DOS400>DIR A: | SORT


        15 File(s)       822272 bytes free
   Directory of  A:\
   Volume in drive A is PIPING DEMO
COMMAND   COM    37637 06-17-88   12:00p
COUNTRY   SYS    12838 06-17-88   12:00p
EGA       CPI    49052 06-17-88   12:00p
FIND      EXE     5983 06-17-88   12:00p
MODE      COM    23040 06-17-88   12:00p
PCMSDRV   MOS      961 06-17-88   12:00p
SELECT    DAT    22453 06-17-88   12:00p
SELECT    EXE    99791 06-17-88   12:00p
SHELL     CLR     4438 06-17-88   12:00p
SHELL     HLP    66977 06-17-88   12:00p
SHELL     MEU     4588 06-17-88   12:00p
TREE      COM     6334 06-17-88   12:00p
VDISK     SYS     6376 06-17-88   12:00p
XMA2EMS   SYS    29236 06-17-88   12:00p
XMAEM     SYS    19312 06-17-88   12:00p

C:\DOS400>
```

Figure 13.17: Creating automatic piping files on the default drive

you several different ways to sort. For example, the /R switch tells the program to sort in reverse (descending) order. Entering

DIR A: ¦ SORT /R

produces a directory listing in reverse alphabetical order (see Figure 13.18).

SORT also allows you to specify the column on which you want the sorting to take place. Normally, SORT begins with the first character in the line. However, you can tell SORT to sort from another position in the data line, which allows you to sort your directory in a variety of ways. The following command will sort by file extension rather than by file name (see Figure 13.19):

DIR A: ¦ SORT / + 9

The +9 in this command tells DOS to sort based on the ninth character space. Since DOS uses eight-character file names, the

```
C:\DOS400>DIR A: ¦ SORT /R
XMAEM     SYS     19312 06-17-88  12:00p
XMA2EMS   SYS     29236 06-17-88  12:00p
VDISK     SYS      6376 06-17-88  12:00p
TREE      COM      6334 06-17-88  12:00p
SHELL     MEU      4588 06-17-88  12:00p
SHELL     HLP     66977 06-17-88  12:00p
SHELL     CLR      4438 06-17-88  12:00p
SELECT    EXE     99791 06-17-88  12:00p
SELECT    DAT     22453 06-17-88  12:00p
PCMSDRV   MOS       961 06-17-88  12:00p
MODE      COM     23040 06-17-88  12:00p
FIND      EXE      5983 06-17-88  12:00p
EGA       CPI     49052 06-17-88  12:00p
COUNTRY   SYS     12838 06-17-88  12:00p
COMMAND   COM     37637 06-17-88  12:00p
 Volume in drive A is PIPING DEMO
 Directory of  A:\
       15 File(s)      822272 bytes free


C:\DOS400>
```

Figure 13.18: Directory sorted in reverse alphabetical order

```
C:\DOS400>DIR A: ¦ SORT /+9

SHELL     CLR      4438 06-17-88  12:00p
TREE      COM      6334 06-17-88  12:00p
MODE      COM     23040 06-17-88  12:00p
COMMAND   COM     37637 06-17-88  12:00p
EGA       CPI     49052 06-17-88  12:00p
SELECT    DAT     22453 06-17-88  12:00p
FIND      EXE      5983 06-17-88  12:00p
SELECT    EXE     99791 06-17-88  12:00p
SHELL     HLP     66977 06-17-88  12:00p
SHELL     MEU      4588 06-17-88  12:00p
PCMSDRV   MOS       961 06-17-88  12:00p
VDISK     SYS      6376 06-17-88  12:00p
COUNTRY   SYS     12838 06-17-88  12:00p
XMAEM     SYS     19312 06-17-88  12:00p
XMA2EMS   SYS     29236 06-17-88  12:00p
     15 File(s)     822272 bytes free
Volume in drive A is PIPING DEMO
Directory of  A:\

C:\DOS400>
```

Figure 13.19: Sorting by file extension

ninth character space is always blank (to separate the base name from the extension). Beginning the sort here sorts on the following three characters, the extension.

Of course, DOS 4 users can easily create these sorted directory listings by using the Options menu in the File System. However, the SORT filter method gives you precise control over any data, enabling you to arrange it based on any column in the data lines. You can use the SORT filter for data that you create at the console or for data in a file.

By choosing the sixteenth character space in a directory listing, you could just as easily sort the directory by file size (see Figure 13.20). Character space 16 gets you past the base name and extension, allowing sorting to begin with the file-size numbers.

DIR A: ¦ SORT / + 16

COMBINING
REDIRECTION WITH FILTERS AND PIPES

To make your job easier and quicker, a filter can also be combined with a redirection command. To print a sorted directory listing, you

```
C:\DOS400>DIR A: ! SORT /+16

PCMSDRV   MOS        961  06-17-88   12:00p
SHELL     CLR       4438  06-17-88   12:00p
SHELL     MEU       4588  06-17-88   12:00p
FIND      EXE       5983  06-17-88   12:00p
TREE      COM       6334  06-17-88   12:00p
VDISK     SYS       6376  06-17-88   12:00p
COUNTRY   SYS      12838  06-17-88   12:00p
XMAEM     SYS      19312  06-17-88   12:00p
SELECT    DAT      22453  06-17-88   12:00p
MODE      COM      23040  06-17-88   12:00p
XMA2EMS   SYS      29236  06-17-88   12:00p
COMMAND   COM      37637  06-17-88   12:00p
EGA       CPI      49052  06-17-88   12:00p
SHELL     HLP      66977  06-17-88   12:00p
SELECT    EXE      99791  06-17-88   12:00p
 Directory of  A:\
 Volume in drive A is PIPING DEMO
        15 File(s)      822272 bytes free

C:\DOS400>
```

Figure 13.20: Sorting by file size

could enter

DIR A: ¦ SORT > PRN

As Figure 13.21 shows, the output of the DIR command is piped forward to become the input to the SORT command; the SORT command's output is then redirected from the screen to the printer.

As another example, you can create a text file containing a sorted directory listing by entering

DIR A: ¦ SORT > SORTDIR

As Figure 13.22 shows, this is similar to the previous example, except that the final sorted directory listing is not sent to the printer but is instead redirected to the SORTDIR disk file. To see the contents of the SORTDIR file, you could use the TYPE command or the View option from DOS 4's File menu.

With pipes and filters, you can also reference files located elsewhere within the DOS directory structure. As an example, Figure 13.23 shows a file called CAD.KEY that is contained in the

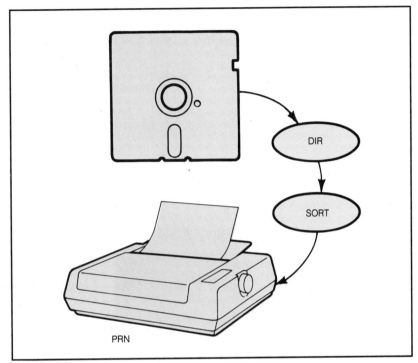

Figure 13.21: Combining pipes, filters, and redirection

CAD\VWF directory. CAD.KEY lists the internal macros (mini-programs) of a computer-aided design (CAD) program. It contains three columns of information: the numeric key code, an ASCII indication of which key on the keyboard invokes the macro, and the name of the file containing the macro instructions.

The list of macro keys appears in the order in which the keys were created during previous use of the CAD program. Even with only a handful of possibilities, it is difficult to see which keys are taken and which are still available for macro assignment. A simple use of the SORT filter can rearrange the file lines within the same file, as shown in Figure 13.24. The command to use is

SORT < \CAD\VWF\CAD.KEY > \CAD\VWF\CAD.KEY

Figure 13.25 shows the results of this simple sorting.

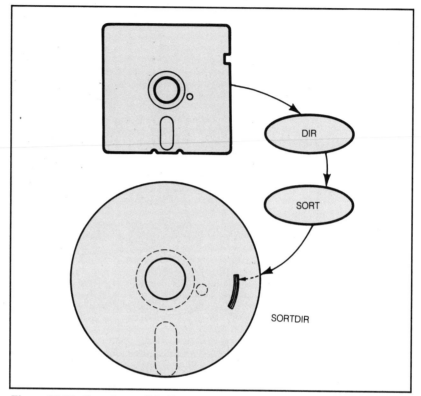

Figure 13.22: Creating a disk file by combining commands

Test your understanding now of filters, pipes, and redirection. Select any subdirectory of interest on your hard disk, or put any diskette of interest into a disk drive. Construct and enter the proper command to ask DOS to produce a directory listing, sort it by file size, and then print the sorted results on your printer.

SAVING TIME BY COMBINING FILTERS

Once you are comfortable with DOS filters, you can save yourself both typing time and waiting time. You don't need to wait for the SORT filter to finish its work before you ask the FIND filter to begin. For example, you might want to obtain a sorted listing of all the .EXE files on a disk. By using the SORT and FIND filters together,

```
C>TYPE \CAD\VWF\CAD.KEY
 316   F2  CLEARALL.MAC
  86    V  VERTSNAP.MAC
 318   F4  EXAMPLE2.MAC
  79    O  SNAPOFF.MAC
  71    G  SNAPGRID.MAC
  66    B  BACKUP.MAC
  76    L  LINE.MAC
  49    1  ALAN1.MAC
  65    A  ALAN2.MAC
  80    P  PLOTFIT.MAC
  51    3  ALAN3.MAC
  52    4  alan4.mac
 317   F3  EXAMPLE4.MAC

C>■
```

Figure 13.23: List of macro codes for a CAD program

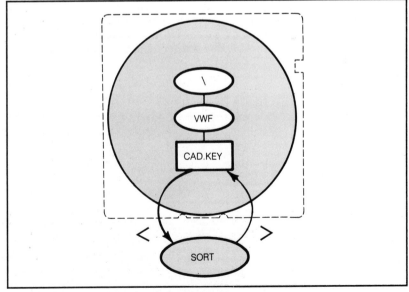

Figure 13.24: Sorting a file back into itself

```
C>SORT    <   \CAD\VWF\CAD.KEY    >   \CAD\VWF\CAD.KEY

C>TYPE   \CAD\VWF\CAD.KEY
    49     1  ALAN1.MAC
    51     3  ALAN3.MAC
    52     4  alan4.mac
    65     A  ALAN2.MAC
    66     B  BACKUP.MAC
    71     G  SNAPGRID.MAC
    76     L  LINE.MAC
    79     O  SNAPOFF.MAC
    80     P  PLOTFIT.MAC
    86     V  VERTSNAP.MAC
   316    F2  CLEARALL.MAC
   317    F3  EXAMPLE4.MAC
   318    F4  EXAMPLE2.MAC

C>■
```

Figure 13.25: The sorted directory structure

you can tell DOS to execute both filters, one after the other. Enter

DIR A: ¦ SORT ¦ FIND ".EXE"

DOS will then sort the files in the A drive and display just the sorted
.EXE files.

You have probably seen advertisements for sorting programs that
promise to sort your files by any field within them. You can do all of
that kind of sorting with simple DOS commands now. You've
learned how to use switches on the SORT command to arrange your
directory lines by categories other than the first category. You've also
learned how to send the sorted results from one filter to another
through piping.

For another example of sophisticated DOS manipulation, you
could now take the original business contact list shown in Figure
13.1, sort it by telephone number, pipe the results into the FIND
filter to extract the 415 area code entries, and finally pipe the results
back into the SORT command to be rearranged alphabetically:

SORT /+43 < BUSINESS.TXT ¦ FIND " 415" ¦ SORT

Figure 13.26 demonstrates the results of this example. Notice that the first sort takes place using character space 43, the first space containing the phone number. If there were several contacts from the same company, their entries would appear in phone number order for each alphabetized company.

This is another example of how a well-written DOS command can save you the purchase of a functionally simple piece of additional software. In the next chapter, you'll see an example of how you can set up a batch file to provide yourself with this kind of capability.

CONTROLLING SCREEN OUTPUT

The last filter available in DOS is named MORE. It causes the screen display to pause, just as the /P switch does with the DIR command. Why not just use the /P with the SORT filter? Try it, and see what happens. If you enter

DIR A:/P ¦ SORT

you'll only get a blinking cursor if your directory required more than one screenful of information. This is because of the way the filter

```
 When ready to return to the DOS Shell, type EXIT then press enter.

IBM DOS Version 4.00
         (C)Copyright International Business Machines Corp 1981, 1988
         (C)Copyright Microsoft Corp 1981-1986

A:\>SORT /+43 < BUSINESS.TXT ¦ FIND " 415" ¦ SORT
Brandenberg Gates   754  Bennett   Mary    415/612-5656
Bucket Dance Wear   276  Lewis     Ann     415/635-2530
Intelli-Strategies  743  Griffiths Robert  415/362-9537
Sole Survivor,Inc.  237  Evans     Gail    415/222-3514
Standard Shelters   690  Rucker    Sally   415/532-1107

A:\>
```

Figure 13.26: Sorting, extracting, and sorting again

works. When data is filtered, it is stored in a temporary file; only then is the output filtered. Since the output is to be filtered, it's not sent to the screen. However, the now inappropriate pause required by the DIR A:/P command occurs anyway, so the computer is forced to pause when a screenful of information is sent *into* the pipe. This is not what you really want.

The proper way to handle pauses with filters is to use the MORE filter, like this:

DIR A: ¦ SORT ¦ MORE

The MORE filter works because it pauses the output of the SORT filter, rather than pausing the input from the DIR command. This sequence will only display one screenful at a time from the sorted directory listing, signaling you with the "More" message that more output remains to be viewed. Pressing Return will display the next screenful of information. The command

DIR ¦ MORE

will create a directory display like the one in Figure 13.27.

```
    Volume in drive C is ROBBINS C
    Directory of  C:\DOS400

    .            <DIR>       08-10-88    3:00p
    ..           <DIR>       08-10-88    3:00p
CONFIG   SYS        169  08-05-89    2:22p
ANSI     SYS       9148  06-17-88   12:00p
COMMAND  COM      37637  06-17-88   12:00p
DOSSHELL BAK        184  08-10-88    3:25p
COUNTRY  SYS      12838  06-17-88   12:00p
DISKCOPY COM      10428  06-17-88   12:00p
DISPLAY  SYS      15741  06-17-88   12:00p
DRIVER   SYS       5274  06-17-88   12:00p
FASTOPEN EXE      16302  06-17-88   12:00p
FDISK    COM      70151  06-17-88   12:00p
FORMAT   COM      22923  06-17-88   12:00p
IFSFUNC  EXE      21637  06-17-88   12:00p
KEYB     COM      14759  06-17-88   12:00p
KEYBOARD SYS      23360  06-17-88   12:00p
MODE     COM      23040  06-17-88   12:00p
PRINTER  SYS      18946  06-17-88   12:00p
REPLACE  EXE      17199  06-17-88   12:00p
SELECT   DAT      22453  06-17-88   12:00p
-- More --
```

Figure 13.27: The MORE filter

Remember that you use this MORE filter for directory displays at the command prompt only. However, as with the SORT filter, MORE is useful for more than just listing files. For instance, you could insert MORE in the DOS 4 program-startup command sequences discussed in Chapter 6. Whenever you install a program that generates more than a screenful of data, you may be able to use the MORE filter to control the output.

PIPES, FILTERS, AND REDIRECTION: AN EXAMPLE

Filters can help you overcome missing features in existing programs. One common problem is knowing how to sort a mailing list created by a word processor that does not contain a sorting feature. By planning a bit, you can get the SORT filter to help you out.

Here is a typical mailing list, which uses commas to separate the name, address, and city fields (categories of information). WordStar uses a file arranged like this to produce MailMerge letters.

```
Smith,John, 12 Main St., Oakland
Gable, Nina, 10 Maple Dr., WC
Omney, Diana, 1 Nut St., Pinole
```

Assume that this information is stored in a file called NAMES.TXT. The file could be created with the text mode of any word processor; in WordStar, you should use the nondocument mode to enter data for this special purpose. The data could also be entered using the COPY command, as you've seen earlier:

```
COPY CON: NAMES.TXT
Smith,John, 12 Main St., Oakland
Gable,Nina, 10 Maple Dr., WC
Omney,Diana, 1 Nut St., Pinole
^Z
```

To sort this file by last names, you would enter

```
TYPE NAMES.TXT ¦ SORT > LIST.TXT
```

This would create a new file, called LIST.TXT, that would contain the sorted list of names. To see the contents of LIST.TXT, you could enter

TYPE LIST.TXT

The list would appear after the command as shown in Figure 13.28. Since it is already sorted, it could now be used more readily by your word-processing program or any other application program.

The FIND filter can also be used to select entries based on some common text. For example, you could select all the people in your mailing list that live in a certain city. Look at the following command:

TYPE LIST.TXT | FIND "Pinole" > RESULTS.TXT

This selects only those lines in LIST.TXT that contain the characters "Pinole". (Remember, the string of characters to be matched must be entered in the same case in which the original text was entered.) The results of this selection are then redirected to RESULTS.TXT, the output disk file. RESULTS.TXT will contain only one of the mailing-list entries—the one containing "Pinole", as shown in Figure 13.28.

```
When ready to return to the DOS Shell, type EXIT then press enter.

IBM DOS Version 4.00
            (C)Copyright International Business Machines Corp 1981, 1988
            (C)Copyright Microsoft Corp 1981-1986

D:\XYWRITE\DOS400>TYPE NAMES.TXT
Smith,John, 12 Main St., Oakland
Gable,Nina, 10 Maple Dr.,WC
Omney,Diane, 1 Nut St.,Pinole

D:\XYWRITE\DOS400>TYPE NAMES.TXT | SORT > LIST.TXT

D:\XYWRITE\DOS400>TYPE LIST.TXT
Gable,Nina, 10 Maple Dr.,WC
Omney,Diane, 1 Nut St.,Pinole
Smith,John, 12 Main St., Oakland

D:\XYWRITE\DOS400>TYPE LIST.TXT | FIND "Pinole" > RESULTS.TXT

D:\XYWRITE\DOS400>TYPE RESULTS.TXT
Omney,Diane, 1 Nut St.,Pinole

D:\XYWRITE\DOS400>
```

Figure 13.28: Mailing list sorted by filters and redirection

As in the earlier examples, this method is not a substitute for a real data management program. For example, if someone lived on Pinole street in Richmond, they too would appear on this DOS-generated "Pinole" list. However, features like FIND and SORT can be of great value, even to a new computer user. As you'll continue to learn in the next chapters on batch files, you can do many things with DOS alone that you otherwise would spend considerable money on.

SUMMARY

In this chapter, you've learned about powerful DOS features for specialized utility operations. You've seen that redirection allows you to specify alternative input and output devices for DOS commands. Pipes enable you to direct the flow of information with precision from one command to another. Filters permit you to process the data as it flows through your central processing unit under your direction. The chapter presented the following important points:

- Special symbols are used by DOS during redirection operations. The > sign indicates a new output device, and < indicates a new input source. If you use the >> sign, the output is appended to the specified file.

- Certain DOS commands can filter data. This data can be input at the keyboard, from an existing file, or even from another program or command.

- The SORT filter can easily arrange the lines of output from any command or data file. Optional switches add significant power to this command: /R produces a reverse-order listing, while / +n sorts the file by the nth character space instead of the first. This allows you to sort your data in meaningful orders.

- The FIND filter displays lines that contain the specified characters.

- The MORE filter performs the simple task of making the display pause when output fills the screen. This gives you the opportunity to read the complete display before continuing the processing.

- Pipes are preceded by the ¦ symbol. They transmit the output from one command to another, in effect making one command's output the next command's input.

- Pipes can be combined with both filters and redirection in sophisticated ways to produce powerful results.

The examples in this chapter should serve to spark your imagination—you can now create your own useful utility extensions. In Chapter 18, you'll learn about a number of utility programs that you can purchase to extend the power of DOS. With the tools from this chapter alone, however, you can develop your own programs for file sorting, text searching, and diskette cataloging.

PART 5

LIFE IN THE FAST LANE

Part 5 deals primarily with advanced commands and features. Chapters 14, 15, and 16 teach you how to use batch files to execute groups of DOS commands automatically, which saves you time. Chapter 14 describes the basic features and limitations of batch files and gives you practice in building simple batch files. Chapter 15 extends your knowledge by teaching you the DOS batch-file subcommands and parameters, enabling you to build more complex batch files. In Chapter 16, you will find many batch files and techniques that you can use immediately.

In Chapter 17, you will learn a number of advanced DOS commands for manipulating your files and directories, for managing the DOS command processor, and for modifying the DOS environment. Lastly, Chapter 18 presents an overview of numerous utility programs that you can purchase and use to enhance the power of DOS.

THE POWER OF DOS
BATCH FILES

IN THIS CHAPTER, YOU WILL BEGIN TO LEARN ABOUT batch files. you've already learned several DOS features that give you added power. Batch files can multiply the power of DOS dramatically, not just add to it. This chapter will show you what batch files are, and how they can be created and used. You will learn why they are so important to you and to your effectiveness as a DOS user.

Up to this point, you've learned quite a bit about individual DOS commands. You know that when you want to execute a DOS command, you type in the command at the prompt or invoke it in the DOS 4 shell. When the command is complete, DOS displays the prompt or shell again; then you can enter another command. You've seen that when you work with DOS, you must enter these commands one at a time.

Batch files allow you to enter a *group* of DOS commands automatically. A batch file is a series of ordinary DOS commands that the computer can execute automatically as a group (a *batch*) instead of one at a time.

You create batch files to automate DOS activities that require more than one DOS command. As you will see, this simple idea has some unexpected benefits. DOS's ability to understand simple batch files allows you to create sophisticated DOS programs, which are more complex batch files containing a series of commands and also special elements called variables, conditional statements, and subroutines.

BUILDING A BATCH FILE

Batch files can be as simple or complex as you want them to be. Let's take a simple task first. Assume you're working on a hard disk and would like to find out what .COM and .EXE files are available to you in the latest version of DOS installed on your disk. You would first need to change the active directory to the directory that contains the DOS files. As you know, you could then use DOS 4's Display Options menu to specify that only *.EXE files are to be displayed. Then you can have DOS display only *.COM files. At the command prompt, you would successively enter each of the following DOS commands to obtain the same result:

```
CD \DOS400
CLS
DIR/W *.COM
DIR/W *.EXE
```

(Clearing the screen with CLS lets you compare the two listings easily.) The result of this sequence would be the screen shown in Figure 14.1.

```
C:\DOS400>DIR/W *.COM

 Volume in drive C is ROBBINS C
 Directory of  C:\DOS400

COMMAND  COM    DISKCOPY COM    FDISK    COM    FORMAT   COM    KEYB     COM
MODE     COM    SYS      COM    ASSIGN   COM    BACKUP   COM    CHKDSK   COM
COMP     COM    DISKCOMP COM    EDLIN    COM    GRAFTABL COM    GRAPHICS COM
LABEL    COM    MORE     COM    PRINT    COM    RECOVER  COM    RESTORE  COM
SHELLB   COM    TREE     COM
        22 File(s)    8124416 bytes free

C:\DOS400>DIR/W *.EXE

 Volume in drive C is ROBBINS C
 Directory of  C:\DOS400

FASTOPEN EXE    IFSFUNC  EXE    REPLACE  EXE    SELECT   EXE    XCOPY    EXE
SHELLC   EXE    APPEND   EXE    ATTRIB   EXE    FILESYS  EXE    FIND     EXE
JOIN     EXE    MEM      EXE    NLSFUNC  EXE    SORT     EXE    SUBST    EXE
BACKIT   EXE    QD2      EXE    BASICA   EXE
        18 File(s)    8124416 bytes free

C:\DOS400>
```

Figure 14.1: DOS program-file listings

To complete the task, you had to issue four commands. If this were a task that you did often, you could automate the task with a batch file containing the commands. To do so, however, you'd need to know the rules for building batch files.

RULES FOR BATCH FILES

In order for DOS to properly recognize and process a file as a batch file, there are several rules you must follow. These rules apply to

- File type
- Naming conventions
- Limitations of the batch-file mechanism
- Running and stopping batch files

BATCH FILES MUST BE ASCII TEXT FILES Standard text files contain normal ASCII characters, and each line ends with a carriage return (CR) and a line feed (LF). This definition may not mean much to novice computer users; it is more important to know how to produce such files.

You can create a batch file using the DOS COPY CON command, the EDLIN line editor, or a word-processing program that can create an ASCII standard file or convert its files to ASCII standard. You can use the following word-processing programs to produce ASCII files directly:

- WordPerfect, using TEXT IN/OUT
- WordStar in nondocument mode or with the UNFORM format
- Microsoft Word, saving the file as UNFORMATTED
- DisplayWrite 4, using ASCII COPY TO FILE
- Framework III, using DISK EXPORT ASCII

You can use the following programs to convert files to DOS standard text files after they have been saved as word-processing files:

- MultiMate, running the CONVERT program
- Samna, using the DO TRANSLATE ASCII command
- Symphony, using the PRINT FILE command

The best way to create and manipulate your batch files is to use one of these word processors, because a word processor offers the greatest range of commands for manipulating text. The next best way is with EDLIN; while it is less flexible than a word processor, EDLIN does have the advantage of being available with DOS. The "least-best" way is to use COPY CON, because it only allows text entry; it does not permit any manipulation of already entered text.

Because you may not have a word processor, this book assumes you are using EDLIN to create your batch files. If you need to refresh your memory on EDLIN, refer to Chapter 7.

BATCH FILES MUST BE NAMED IN ACCORDANCE WITH CERTAIN CONVENTIONS

You've probably noticed by now that there are certain classes of files on your system: .COM and .EXE program files, .BAS BASIC language files, .WK1 spreadsheet files, .DBF database files, and probably many others. DOS must be able to distinguish a batch file from these other types of files on your system.

You can give a batch file almost any name you like, as long as you use the .BAT extension. Of course, the name must adhere to standard DOS file-naming rules, with no more than eight letters or numbers in the base name. SIMPLE.BAT and START.BAT are examples of acceptable batch-file names.

You should never create a batch file that has the same name as a DOS command (for example, DIR.BAT or FORMAT.BAT). If you do, DOS can become confused as to whether you wanted to execute the command with that name or the batch file with that name. DOS always assumes you want to execute a DOS command first; only if it can't find a DOS command (or any .EXE or .COM files) will it look to see if there is a batch file with the name that you typed

Batch-file names should be unique. Never give a batch file the same name as either a DOS command or a program name (that is, the name of an .EXE or .COM file).

in. DOS expects you to enter the command or batch-file name without typing the extension. Thus, you could create a file named DIR-.BAT, but you could never use it—DOS would always assume when you entered DIR that you wanted the Directory command, not the DIR.BAT file.

BATCH FILES HAVE CERTAIN LIMITATIONS Only commands that work at the DOS prompt can be included in a batch file. You'll soon see that there are some additional controlling commands (called subcommands) that can be used in a batch file; you can also use variable input parameters, which will be covered in detail later in this chapter. However, the main commands that do something for you are always going to look just as they would if they were typed at the DOS prompt.

RUNNING AND STOPPING BATCH FILES Executing all the instructions within a batch file is as simple as typing the name of the .BAT file containing those instructions. As with commands and programs, however, if you don't precede the batch-file name with a drive identifier and a directory name, the assumption will be the current drive and current directory.

You can run any batch program in DOS 4's File System by simply selecting it from the File area. If you or other users will use the batch programs repeatedly, you may want to install them in one of the Start Programs menus (see Chapter 6).

You can stop batch-file execution at any time by pressing the Break key combination (Ctrl-ScrollLock). DOS will ask you if you want to terminate the batch job. Usually, you answer Y for Yes, since that's why you pressed the Break combination in the first place. However, if you have a change of heart and answer N, the current step in the batch file will be ignored and the rest of the commands will be executed.

Users of diskette systems should be aware that exchanging a diskette containing an executing batch file for another diskette will force DOS to stop after it completes the current instruction and prompt you to reinsert the original diskette. Only then can the next instruction in the batch file be executed properly.

CREATING YOUR FIRST BATCH FILE

Take a moment now to create your first batch file. Create your own version of SIMPLE4.BAT, including all the statements seen in

Figure 14.2. Use the EDLIN program unless you are familiar with an available word processor and plan to use it for all your batch-file work.

When you enter

EDLIN SIMPLE4.BAT

DOS will create a file called SIMPLE4.BAT. Remember that when you use EDLIN, you are entering text into a file. This means that nothing appears to happen when you type in a command. Only after the SIMPLE4.BAT file has been written can you tell DOS to read, process, and execute the instructions contained in it.

Write the file now using EDLIN's I (Insert) command. Leave insertion mode by pressing Ctrl-C and then enter E to end the edit. The DOS prompt returns, and you are ready to execute the batch file by typing in its name *without* the .BAT extension:

SIMPLE4

The results of typing in this one-word command are the same as those produced when all four commands were typed in separately.

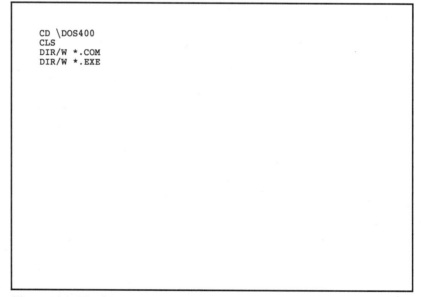

```
CD \DOS400
CLS
DIR/W *.COM
DIR/W *.EXE
```

Figure 14.2: The SIMPLE4.BAT file

DOS executes each of the commands automatically, one after the other, without further assistance from you.

Like programs or disk-resident DOS commands, batch files can be located on any disk and in any directory, and they can be referenced by simply specifying the full path name to them. For example, if SIMPLE4 were located in a directory called UTILITY\MISC on drive C, you could execute it by entering

C:\UTILITY\MISC\SIMPLE4

Remember that you can stop the execution of the batch instructions by pressing the Break key combination.

EDITING A BATCH FILE

You will notice that the batch file you just wrote displays the command lines contained within it as each one executes. This echoing of the commands to the screen is controlled by the ECHO command. The default status of ECHO is ON, which means that DOS commands executed from a batch file are displayed as they are executed. However, output results are sometimes more attractive or readable if the commands are *not* displayed. Let's add a line to the batch file that will set ECHO to OFF.

Bring up EDLIN again, specifying the full name of the file you want to edit, SIMPLE4.BAT. Use the I command to enter

ECHO OFF

as the new line 1. To list the resulting file, enter the L command and press Return. EDLIN will display your batch file:

```
*L
1: ECHO OFF
2: CD\DOS400
3: CLS
4: DIR/W *.COM
5:*DIR/W *.EXE
```

Now use the End command to save the file and return to DOS.

If you use EDLIN to edit your batch files, you will notice an extra DOS prompt on your screen after a batch file completes. This second prompt appears because EDLIN has inserted a carriage return before the end-of-file marker in SIMPLE4.BAT. Don't be concerned; it won't cause any harm.

Now you can try the modified batch file. As before, just enter

SIMPLE4

That's all it takes to execute all the individual DOS commands contained within the SIMPLE4.BAT file. Note that since ECHO is OFF, only the results of the commands, not the commands themselves, will be displayed (see Figure 14.3).

```
    Volume in drive C is ROBBINS C
    Directory of  C:\DOS400

    COMMAND   COM    DISKCOPY COM     FDISK    COM    FORMAT   COM    KEYB     COM
    MODE      COM    SYS      COM     ASSIGN   COM    BACKUP   COM    CHKDSK   COM
    COMP      COM    DISKCOMP COM     EDLIN    COM    GRAFTABL COM    GRAPHICS COM
    LABEL     COM    MORE     COM     PRINT    COM    RECOVER  COM    RESTORE  COM
    SHELLB    COM    TREE     COM
            22 File(s)      8118272 bytes free
    Volume in drive C is ROBBINS C
    Directory of  C:\DOS400

    FASTOPEN EXE     IFSFUNC  EXE     REPLACE  EXE    SELECT   EXE    XCOPY    EXE
    SHELLC    EXE    APPEND   EXE     ATTRIB   EXE    FILESYS  EXE    FIND     EXE
    JOIN      EXE    MEM      EXE     NLSFUNC  EXE    SORT     EXE    SUBST    EXE
    BACKIT    EXE    QD2      EXE     BASICA   EXE
            18 File(s)      8118272 bytes free
    C:\DOS400>
```

Figure 14.3: Results of running SIMPLE4.BAT

VARIABLES IN BATCH FILES

Until now, you've only seen batch files that have been designed for a specific use: for example, a batch file that quickly and easily lists all the .COM and .EXE files in the DOS directory. In such cases, the batch file works with constant values (*.COM or *.EXE). If batch files could accept variables, as more sophisticated programming languages do, they could be much more flexible.

You can create DOS batch files that will do just that. Variables in any language allow you to construct programs that differ in a well-defined way each time the program is run. In other words, the program stays the same, but the value used by the program to complete its tasks varies. You can consider the DOS batch-file feature to be a simple programming language.

Let's take a moment to look at the terminology involved. As you have seen throughout this book, many DOS commands accept a variety of parameters. These parameters are just additional pieces of information needed by DOS to clarify the task specified in the command. For example, the command COPY REPORT.DOC FEBRUARY.DOC contains the COPY command, and the REPORT and FEBRUARY documents are its respective source and destination parameters. Next month, however, you might want to run the COPY command again, with the REPORT.DOC file as the source and the MARCH.DOC file as the destination. Thus, the second parameter can be considered a variable parameter, since it needs to be changed each month.

Batch files can accept variables as easily as they can accept DOS commands. Variables always begin with a percentage sign (%) and are followed by a number from 0 to 9. Thus, DOS allows variables named %0, %1, %2, and so on.

To see how this system works, create a simple batch file called DEMO4.BAT, consisting of the following three lines:

```
CLS
CD %1
DIR *.%2
```

Note that instead of entering a specific directory name to change to, you used the variable expression %1. This means that %1 can stand for any directory you like. Similarly, the variable %2 is used to stand for a file extension, like EXE, COM, or BAT. Each time you run this batch file, you specify which directory %1 stands for and which extension %2 represents.

Here's how the % symbol works. When you type in any DOS command, DOS assigns variable names to each section of that command. You might invoke this batch file by entering

```
DEMO4 \DBASE COM
```

DOS would then internally assign %0 to the first phrase (DEMO4), %1 to the second phrase (\DBASE), %2 to the third phrase (COM), and if there were other parameter entries on the line, % values up to %9. Since the batch file contains the variable names %1 and %2, it will use whatever phrases you enter after DEMO4 on the command line. Thus, if you execute the command line above, the

    CD %1

in the batch file will execute as if you had actually typed

    CD \DBASE

and the next line in the batch file,

    DIR *.%2

will execute as if you had actually typed

    DIR *.COM

When the batch program runs, it will clear the screen, change the current directory to \DBASE, and then display all files with a .COM extension. Figure 14.4 shows the running of this batch file from DOS 4's File System. Users of earlier DOS versions can simply enter the parameters after the batch-file name on the same command-prompt line, as you have seen. With either method, you get the same results (see Figure 14.5).

Running the batch file again with different values for the two variable parameters will generate different results. For instance, entering

    DEMO4 \BERNOULI EXE

produces a listing of all the .EXE files in the \BERNOULI directory.

This technique is called *deferred execution,* since the decision as to what parameter will be used is deferred until the time of batch-file execution. In this example, two directory-oriented commands will be executed, but the decision as to what specific directory listing will be produced is deferred until the batch file has actually been called and the %1 and %2 parameters have been specified after the batch-file name.

As you'll see in later examples, you can use a variable parameter (%1, %2, and so on) repeatedly in one batch file.

03-29-89 File System 11:40 am
File Options Arrange Exit F1=Help
Ctrl+letter selects a drive.
A B C D
D:\XYWRITE\DOS400
Open File
Starting program: DEMO4.BAT
Associated file :
Options. . \DBASE COM
<┘=Enter Esc=Cancel F1=Help
F10=Actions Shift+F9=Command Prompt

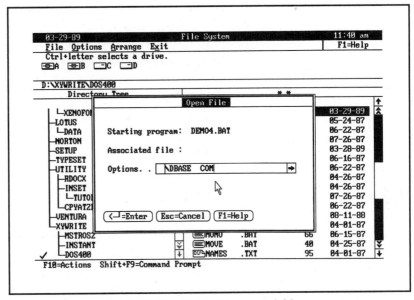

Figure 14.4: Running DEMO4.BAT with two variable parameters

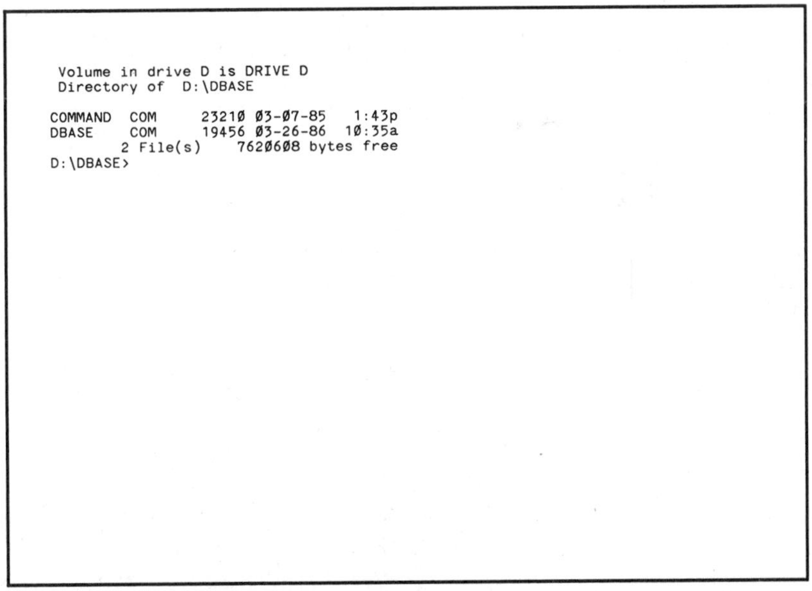

Volume in drive D is DRIVE D
Directory of D:\DBASE
COMMAND COM 23210 03-07-85 1:43p
DBASE COM 19456 03-26-86 10:35a
2 File(s) 7620608 bytes free
D:\DBASE>

Figure 14.5: Results of running DEMO4.BAT using \DBASE (%1) and COM (%2)

Let's look at another example of a batch file using variable parameters. This time, you'll create MOVE.BAT, a batch file whose purpose will be to move files from one drive or directory to another. As you know, you must do two things to move a file:

1. Copy the file to the destination drive or directory.

2. Erase the file from the source drive or directory.

Your task is to create a batch file that will issue all the necessary commands, so that you only need to supply the file names to be moved and the identifier of the new drive.

DOS 4 users, of course, can use the Move option on the File menu to move files. However, it can sometimes be time-consuming to have to change directories, select files, and then execute the Move command. After writing the MOVE batch file, you can install it on DOS 4's Start Programs menu, then run it whenever you like from any directory (see Chapter 6).

The batch file MOVE.BAT requires two variables, %1 and %2. The first one will be a file name or a wild card to use for selecting a file or files. The second variable will be the letter specifying the destination drive. For example, you might want to move all the .EXE files from the current directory to drive B. To do that, you could enter the following four lines at the DOS prompt:

```
CLS
COPY *.EXE B:
ERASE *.EXE
DIR/W B:
```

Then again, you might want to move all the .PRG files from your DBASE\TEST subdirectory on drive C to the ACTIVE directory on drive C:

```
CLS
COPY C:\DBASE\TEST\*.PRG  C:\ACTIVE
ERASE C:\DBASE\TEST\*.PRG
DIR/W C:\ACTIVE
```

There will probably be many occasions when you need to perform this operation between drives, between directories, or both, so this is

> Although this MOVE batch file is just an extra convenience in DOS 4, it is invaluable in earlier DOS versions, which do not have a comparable command.

Be very careful when you set up and run the MOVE batch file because the ERASE command deletes your original files. If the COPY command in the batch file fails—because the destination disk is full, for example—you will have lost your files. Always back up your files before moving them to avoid this problem.

a perfect opportunity to use variables. Write a batch file called MOVE.BAT, which contains these lines:

```
CLS
COPY %1 %2
ERASE %1
DIR/W %2
```

This batch file issues the proper commands for you if you merely indicate the desired file source and destination. For example,

```
MOVE *.EXE B:
```

will move all the .EXE files from the current directory to drive B.

```
MOVE D:\IMCAPS\*.CAP  D:\IMCAPS\SCREENS
```

will move all the *.CAP files from the IMCAPS main directory on drive D to its SCREENS subdirectory. The results are shown in Figure 14.6.

```
D:\IMCAPS\SCREENS>COPY  D:\IMCAPS\*.CAP  D:\IMCAPS\SCREENS
D:\IMCAPS\F14-Ø4.CAP
D:\IMCAPS\F14-Ø5.CAP
D:\IMCAPS\F14-Ø1.CAP
D:\IMCAPS\F14-Ø3.CAP
D:\IMCAPS\F14-Ø6.CAP
        5 File(s) copied

D:\IMCAPS\SCREENS>ERASE D:\IMCAPS\*.CAP

D:\IMCAPS\SCREENS>DIR/W D:\IMCAPS\SCREENS

 Volume in drive D is DRIVE D
 Directory of  D:\IMCAPS\SCREENS

.            ..            C19F19-1 GRA    C19F19-2 GRA    C1Ø      IMG
C1ØF1Ø-Ø IMG    C1ØF1Ø-1 IMG    C1ØF1Ø-2 IMG    C1ØF1Ø-3 IMG    C1ØF1Ø-4 IMG
C1ØF1Ø-5 IMG    C1ØF1Ø-6 IMG    C1ØF1Ø-7 IMG    C1ØF1Ø-8 IMG    CH17--39 CAP
CH17--4Ø CAP    CH17--Ø1 CAP    CH17--Ø2 CAP    F14-Ø4   CAP    F14-Ø5   CAP
F14-Ø1   CAP    F14-Ø3   CAP    F14-Ø6   CAP
        23 File(s)    7696384 bytes free

D:\IMCAPS\SCREENS>
D:\IMCAPS\SCREENS>
```

Figure 14.6: Running the MOVE.BAT file

The same batch file can be used to move the files the other way. Simply reverse the parameters. Entering

    MOVE B:*.EXE C:

will move all the .EXE files from drive B to drive C. (Substitute A for C in this command if you are using a dual-diskette system.)

Variable parameters are a mainstay of batch-file creation. You should stop here for a while and try out these new tools. Create a batch file called PARA.BAT that uses three variables: %1, %2, and %3. Have this program make a new directory (MD) using the first variable as the complete path name and directory name. Have it use the second variable as a wild-card file name. Then have it copy all file names meeting the wild-card specification in the current directory to the directory specified in %1. The batch file should do a DIR/W on this new directory after the transfer, and should end with a CHKDSK on the disk drive specified in the third variable, %3. For example, if you wanted the following lines to be executed in your batch file:

    MD \TRIAL
    COPY EX*.COM \TRIAL
    DIR/W \TRIAL
    CHKDSK B:

you should be able to invoke your batch file as follows:

    PARA \TRIAL EX*.COM B:

SUMMARY

In this chapter, you took your first look at the DOS batch-file mechanism. It extends the power of your operating system by allowing you to build your own new set of commands. The new set of commands can be used just like any existing DOS command, except that it is your customized batch file that executes when requested, and not a prewritten command provided by DOS.

You learned the following key points about batch files:

- Batch files can be as simple as one line or as complex as many hundreds of lines.

- Batch files can contain a series of sequentially executed commands or programs, or even other batch files.

- Batch files can be invoked as easily as any DOS command—by simply typing the name of the batch file at the command prompt or selecting it from DOS 4's File System. This allows you to create your own set of specialized add-on DOS commands.

- You can terminate the execution of your batch program by pressing the Break key combination.

- Variable parameters make your batch files very flexible in terms of when and how you can use them. These variables are referred to as %0, %1, %2, %3, and so on through %9.

The next chapter will take your batch-file construction skills one giant step further. You'll learn about the set of specialized subcommands designed to work only within the batch-programming mechanism. These unique commands can be incorporated into any batch file, making DOS comparable to a high-level computer language.

SUBCOMMANDS IN DOS BATCH FILES

BATCH FILES HAVE THEIR OWN SET OF SPECIALIZED support commands, known as *subcommands*. You don't need them to create simple batch files, but you greatly expand your possibilities when you learn them. You'll learn about all of these extra built-in tools in this chapter. Depending on what type of batch program you write, you may need to use one or several subcommands.

Some subcommands will be commonplace in your batch files; for example, you will frequently use ECHO or REM to insert messages both in the batch file itself and on the video screen. You'll use others only occasionally; for example, you'll use PAUSE only for batch files that must allow users sufficient time to read information on the screen. Still others will be used in specific situations only. In this category, you'll see the FOR subcommand, which allows the repetition of operations, the IF subcommand, which provides decision making, and the GOTO subcommand, which manages the flow of control.

In the preceding chapter, you looked at some simple examples of batch files, in which each command was executed successively. DOS also allows you to execute these commands nonsequentially, according to your own specified order. Changing the order of command execution is known as modifying the flow of control, or simply branching.

This chapter deals with elements that make the DOS batch-file feature into a simple but practical high-level programming language. A final section in the chapter discusses the distinction between creating a standard batch-file chain (which allows you to transfer control of execution from one file to another) and emulating true programming subroutines.

The SHIFT subcommand provides the virtually unnecessary capability of running a batch file that needs more than the allowable variable parameters (%0 to %9). Most DOS books make you struggle through the concept of shifting parameters, using trumped-up examples. Since no realistic batch file needs more than a few input parameters, I won't waste your time on such an impractical subcommand.

INCORPORATING MESSAGES INTO BATCH FILES

In the last chapter, you briefly used the ECHO subcommand to suppress the display of the commands themselves while a batch file was processing. ECHO has some other uses. If ECHO is followed by text instead of by ON or OFF, it will print the text. Thus, ECHO can be used to display information on the screen during the execution of a batch file.

To see how this works, create a new batch file, called HELP1.-BAT, containing several ECHO subcommands, each of which contains helpful information for a user (see Figure 15.1). This batch file will explain how the previously created MOVE.BAT file can be used. (The figure contains a few sample lines of text to demonstrate the method of using the ECHO subcommand; the dots at the bottom indicate where you can add additional lines of text.) Running this batch file by typing in

   HELP1

at the DOS prompt results in the screen shown in Figure 15.2.

Notice that the first two commands set ECHO to OFF and clear the screen, so the remaining "echoed" messages appear without your seeing the actual ECHO subcommand for each line. Regardless of whether ECHO is on or off, the textual information on the ECHO line is always displayed. ECHO OFF only suppresses the display of any succeeding DOS commands in the batch file.

One of the command lines that is usually suppressed—and purposely so—is a REM statement. You will see many REM statements in batch-file listings. Here is an example:

   REM This is a simple internal commenting line.
   REM So is this... for the TYPICAL.BAT file

A REM (Remark) statement is used for internal documentation in a batch file. It usually contains notes to the programmer or to the future user of the batch program. Anything from the file name to information about algorithms and techniques will be welcomed by

```
ECHO OFF
CLS
ECHO   The batch file MOVE.BAT is designed to
ECHO   transfer a file(s) from one drive or
ECHO   directory to any other drive/directory.
ECHO   ==========================================
ECHO   MOVE first copies, then deletes the
ECHO   originals.  The general form is:
ECHO        MOVE   source   destination
  .
  .
  .
```

Figure 15.1: The HELP1.BAT file

```
      The batch file MOVE.BAT is designed to
      transfer a file(s) from one drive or
      directory to any other drive/directory.
      ----------------------------------------
      MOVE first copies, then deletes the
      originals.  The general form is:
           MOVE   source   destination

  C>_
```

Figure 15.2: Results of executing the HELP1.BAT file

someone trying to understand the inner workings of a batch program. Nearly all of the remaining batch files in this book will have at least one REM statement containing the name of the batch file itself.

If ECHO is set to OFF, then the REM statements will not be shown on the video screen during program execution. The more complex or obscure your batch-file logic, the more you need to have several REM lines built into it.

INTERRUPTING BATCH FILES DURING EXECUTION

There are two kinds of interruptions in life: permanent and temporary. DOS provides batch-file equivalents to these types of interruptions with the PAUSE subcommand and the Break key combination.

When a PAUSE subcommand is used in a batch file, the execution of the commands in the file stops temporarily, and DOS displays the message "Strike a key when ready...." When you press the Return key or the spacebar (or virtually anything else), the next command in the batch file will execute.

The PAUSE subcommand is not necessary to the functioning of the program, but it has a practical function. Filling the screen with a lot of instructions is a sure way to lose a user's attention. Instead, you can display a little information, pause the display, clear the screen, and display a little more information. This will keep the user alert.

HELP2.BAT, an expanded version of the batch file that you saw in the last section, represents a two-screen help system (see Figure 15.3). This is implemented by inserting the two commands PAUSE and CLS into the middle of the batch file. PAUSE temporarily interrupts the execution of the batch file, prompting you to press any key when you are ready to go on. CLS simply erases the messages you've

> In a batch file like HELP1.BAT, which displays text, it's a good idea to add PAUSE as a final command so that the screen information can be read. Information that is displayed to a user is usually only one part of a more complex batch file; pausing the execution allows the user to read the messages before continuing the program.

```
REM The HELP2.BAT File
ECHO  OFF
CLS
ECHO The batch file MOVE.BAT is designed to
ECHO transfer a file(s) from one drive or
ECHO directory to any other drive/directory.
ECHO .
ECHO MOVE first copies, then deletes the
ECHO originals.  The general form is:
ECHO      MOVE  source  destination
ECHO .
ECHO *******************************************************
ECHO Press Ctrl-BREAK key to terminate these messages, or
PAUSE
CLS
ECHO .
ECHO *******************************************************
ECHO Make sure you have a backup copy of all important files.
ECHO This batch file does an unconditional ERASE of
ECHO all the files requested to be moved.  It does this
ECHO even if the COPY command fails, and the files never
ECHO make it to the destination drive or directory (%%2)
```

Figure 15.3: The HELP2.BAT file

already read, so that you can concentrate on the new messages displayed. When you run the HELP2.BAT program, the results will be like those shown in Figure 15.4.

When a PAUSE subcommand is issued, almost any key will cause the batch-file processing to resume. One exception to this rule is pressing Ctrl-ScrollLock, the Break key combination. If you press this, the

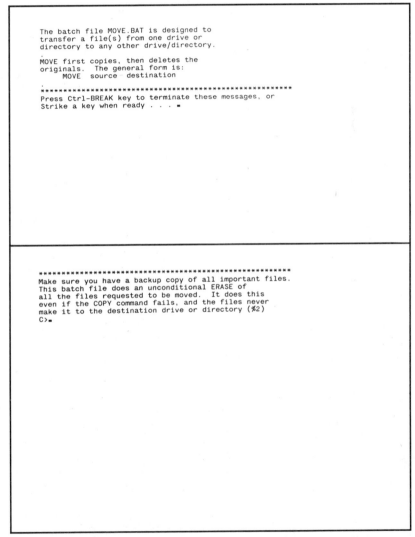

Figure 15.4: A two-screen help system created with PAUSE and CLS

batch file will be interrupted. DOS first displays a ^C on the screen and then asks if you wish to terminate the batch job. Figures 15.5 and 15.6 demonstrate the screen results of your answer. In Figure 15.5, your Y answer causes the batch file to cease immediately and returns control to the DOS prompt. This is a permanent interruption.

Notice in Figure 15.6 that the ^C occurred in the middle of the third ECHO statement's output. Because you answered N, the currently executing statement does not complete, and the batch file continues with the next line. In short, DOS's message gets in the way of normal batch-file output, which is another reason to avoid asking a batch file to continue after you interrupt it.

The Break key combination will also work with DOS commands that have built-in pauses, such as FORMAT and DISKCOPY. When these commands display such messages as "strike ENTER when ready," the Break combination will cancel the command. You may also want to use Break to stop the execution of a batch file that is not working as you desire.

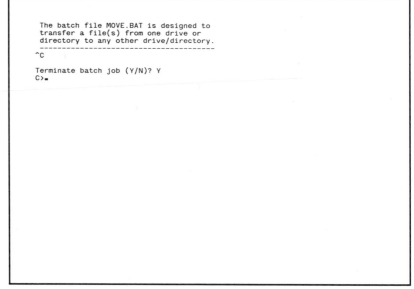

Figure 15.5: Permanent batch-file interruption with the Break key combination

DECISION MAKING IN BATCH FILES

DOS can test the value of certain variables and parameters during the execution of a batch file. Performing this test is known as *decision making,* or *logical testing.* A logical test allows branching within a program, which means that different actions will be performed based on the results of the test.

A branching statement (also called a *conditional* statement) might look like this:

IF Something = Something Else   Do This   Otherwise Do That

A more formal way of stating this is

IF A = B Then Perform Action C   Otherwise Perform Action D

A = B is called a *logical expression.* As in any language, it can stand for such things as Wage = 500 or Lastname = Robbins. If A = B is a true statement, then C will happen. On the other hand, if A = B is false, then action D will take place. This branching ability allows you to create batch files that evaluate circumstances and perform different actions according to the conditions found.

```
    The batch file MOVE.BAT is designed to
    transfer a file(s) from one drive or
    d^C

Terminate batch job (Y/N)? N -----------------------------------------
    MOVE first copies, then deletes the
    originals.  The general form is:
        MOVE  source  destination

C>_
```

Figure 15.6: Continuing a batch file after interrupting its execution

A SAMPLE BRANCHING PROGRAM

To get an idea of the usefulness of branching, let's create a batch file that takes advantage of it and also uses what you've learned already in this chapter. This program's purpose will be to help you to search a disk for a certain file and report if it is there or not.

After you've worked with your computer for a while, you probably will accumulate many diskettes with many files. Once in a while, you'll need to locate one file among those diskettes. Which diskette is usually the big question. You can easily miss the file name on a complete disk directory listing, even if you printed the listing out and kept it with the disk.

A new batch file, LOCATE.BAT, is just the ticket. Type in the LOCATE.BAT file as shown in Figure 15.7. (The line numbers are for your convenience only—don't enter them!) Once you've typed in this batch file, you can simply enter

LOCATE *FileName*

to learn if the file is on the diskette.

Figure 15.8 depicts the step-by-step flow of execution for the branching that occurs in the LOCATE.BAT file you've just entered. The first two commands, ECHO OFF and CLS, are familiar to you by now. The next subcommand is new: the IF subcommand. It is used to test a condition that the computer can evaluate as true or false.

The IF subcommand can be used in three ways:

1. IF EXIST or IF NOT EXIST. This form of IF is used to test if a file exists.

2. IF A == B or IF NOT A == B. This form tests the equality of A and B, where A and B represent character strings. Note that DOS uses == as the symbol for equality. The character strings can be literals or variables. A *literal* (also known as a constant) is any unchanging character string, such as JUDD or END. A variable is one of the changing parameters %0 through %9, which you learned about in Chapter 14. For example, the command

IF %1 == END

The batch program presented here for diskettes can also be used to locate a file in a hard-disk directory.

When you are testing for the equality of groups of characters, as you do with the IF and the FIND subcommands, case matters. If you enter the lowercase letters *end* as the first parameter in IF %1 == END, DOS will evaluate the IF as false. If you enter the uppercase letters *END,* the logical expression will be true.

tests to see if the first variable parameter in the batch-file command, %1 (a variable), is equal to the letters END (a literal). This is the most common use of the IF subcommand.

```
1    ECHO OFF
2    CLS
3    IF NOT EXIST %1 GOTO NOFIND
4    ECHO The file %1 has been located!
5    GOTO END
6    :NOFIND
7    ECHO The file %1 cannot be found.  Look elsewhere.
8    :END
9    ECHO ON
```

Figure 15.7: The LOCATE.BAT file

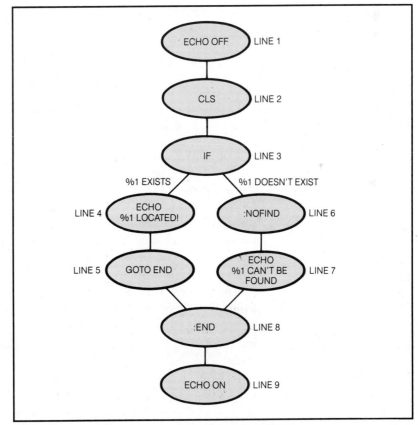

Figure 15.8: Flow of control in the LOCATE.BAT file

3. IF ERRORLEVEL #. This form tests to see if the preceding command has been executed correctly. DOS or any individual application program can set a return code equal to a number from 0 to 255. Usually, a value of 0 means that the preceding command completed successfully; a number greater than 0 indicates a failure, the value indicating the different reasons for that failure. Only DOS commands like BACKUP, FORMAT, and RESTORE will affect this return-code value. (You can, of course, write your own programs to set the return code, but that requires a course in programming and goes beyond the scope of this book.) Note that ERRORLEVEL # means a return code of *# or greater.*

If any of these three DOS commands fail, the error level can be compared to a particular number, #, and different action can be taken depending on the severity of the error. The higher the return code, the more severe the error. The IF statement can control which succeeding section of the batch file receives control, depending on the value of this error level.

In this batch file you are using the IF NOT EXIST form of the IF subcommand to test whether a certain file exists. Line 3 is

IF NOT EXIST %1 GOTO NOFIND

What does GOTO NOFIND mean? The GOTO subcommand tells DOS to continue executing the batch file at a new place. NOFIND is a special placeholder, or label, that you enter into the batch file to indicate that desired location. Where is NOFIND? Look again at Figure 15.7. You will see :NOFIND on line 6. If the file name entered in the batch-file command line as %1 cannot be found on the disk (in other words, does not exist), then batch-file processing jumps from line 3 to line 6. The label line does nothing except facilitate this jumping, so the actual next line executed is on line 7. This branching technique is referred to in programming languages as the *flow of control.*

If, however, the file does exist, then the next command to execute will be the next available one in the batch file, the one on line 4. This is just an ECHO subcommand, which states that the sought-after file has been located:

ECHO The file %1 has been located!

The displayed message will contain the actual file name specified, typed in by you as %1, the first parameter on the command line.

The next line, line 5, is called an *unconditional transfer of control*. It is necessary in this batch-file language to enable the processing sequence to skip over the :NOFIND section of the program. The label :END is again just a placeholder to mark where processing can continue. If the desired file has been located (line 4), then the flow of execution should skip over the :NOFIND section, and the next line of code to be executed would be line 9.

Line 8 is called a *nonexecutable instruction,* because it does not represent any steps that the processor takes. It is simply a label for that place in the program. It can be compared to the address on your house, which is just a label that helps friends and the postal service find their way to you.

Let's go back now to the LOCATE command. To see how it works, try it with a file on a diskette or in a directory. Assuming your DOS operating disk is in drive A,

LOCATE A:chkdsk.com

will produce the message "The file A:chkdsk.com has been located!" The command

LOCATE A:topview.exe

will probably not find a file by that name. It will produce the message "The file A:topview.exe cannot be found. Look elsewhere." If you wanted to search a large directory on your hard disk for the VTREE.COM file, you could enter

LOCATE C:\utility\vtree.com

You might receive the message "The file C:\utility\vtree.com has been located!".

It's easy to see that the task performed by this batch file can be done in other—perhaps simpler—ways. However, you've used an

IF subcommand, a GOTO subcommand, the label mechanism, and variable parameters. That's the main point of this batch file, not the actual job being performed. You can use these tools to make your own batch files, which will do meaningful work for you on your own system.

USING LOOPING AND REPETITION IN BATCH FILES

The FOR subcommand is similar to commands in other programming languages that facilitate repetition. Often, one or more commands in a program need to be repeated, sometimes a fixed number of times and sometimes a variable number of times. In either situation, the FOR subcommand enables you to meet this need.

The general form of the FOR subcommand is

FOR %%*Letter* IN (*Possibilities*) DO *Command*

Letter can be any single alphabetic letter. It is similar to the variable parameters you saw in Chapter 14 (%0, %1, %2, and so on). In this situation, however, double percent-sign variables are used. The % % tells DOS that you are referring to a batch-file variable in the looping FOR statement.

The *Command* in the FOR statement that will be executed repeatedly can change slightly during each repetition. This works similarly to the variable parameter method, which required you to write the batch file originally using %1 or %2 to refer to possible first or second input parameters. This method deferred execution so that when the batch file actually executed, it used the actual values typed in after the batch-file name, instead of using the placeholder % expressions.

In a FOR subcommand, execution is similarly deferred until the command executes. At that time, the *Possibilities* are evaluated, and the *Command* is executed for each possibility. When written into a batch file, this command can represent a more concise form of coding. For example, suppose you have a program called QRTLY.EXE that generates a quarterly business report. This program requires only that you specify the desired quarter for the current fiscal year.

Entering the following at the DOS prompt would produce a report for quarter 3:

> QRTLY 3

At the end of the fiscal year, you might want to generate current copies of the quarterly reports for each quarter. You would enter

> QRTLY 1
> QRTLY 2
> QRTLY 3
> QRTLY 4

and press Return after each line. All four of these successive requests could be replaced in a batch file called REPORTS.BAT with one automatic FOR subcommand, as shown in Figure 15.9.

Using this looping mechanism would not require you to wait for each quarterly report to finish before you requested the next to begin:

FOR is a batch-file subcommand. This means it can only be executed from within a batch file.

> FOR %%A IN (1 2 3 4) DO QRTLY %%A

Your first reaction might be that this is an awfully complicated-looking expression just to save typing in four simple QRTLY report requests. Again, it just demonstrates the technique. If you had a monthly report program called MONTHLY.EXE, you could just as easily request the printing of twelve monthly reports with

> FOR %%A IN (1 2 3 4 5 6 7 8 9 10 11 12) DO MONTHLY %%A

The modified REPORTS file would look like REPORTS2.BAT, shown in Figure 15.10.

```
ECHO OFF
REM The REPORTS.BAT File
REM Produce the Four Quarterly Reports
FOR %%A IN (1 2 3 4) DO QRTLY %%A
ECHO ON
```

Figure 15.9: The REPORTS.BAT file

As you've seen in the general form of the FOR subcommand, there can be only one *Command* parameter executed after the DO portion of the command. It can be a program name, as you've just seen demonstrated, or it can be another DOS command, like DIR or CHKDSK. The following FOR subcommand exemplifies this:

FOR %%A IN (%1 %2 %3 %4) DO DIR %%A

This command would perform a DIR command for each variable parameter (up to four different file names). If this FOR subcommand were in a batch file called HUNT.BAT, as shown in Figure 15.11, you might invoke HUNT in the following manner to determine if any of the specified files were located in the current directory:

HUNT HEART.EXE, LUNGS.EXE, LIVER.COM

The result might look something like Figure 15.12. Even though you've suppressed the display of the DOS commands themselves with ECHO OFF, the remaining output still appears cluttered.

Using a batch subcommand as the object of DO can produce a more concise and attractive result. An IF subcommand can be used to replace the DIR command:

FOR %%A IN (%1 %2 %3 %4) DO IF EXIST %%A ECHO %%A FOUND

```
ECHO OFF
REM The REPORTS2.BAT File
REM Produce the Twelve Monthly Reports
FOR %%A IN (1 2 3 4 5 6 7 8 9 10 11 12) DO MONTHLY %%A
ECHO ON
```

Figure 15.10: The REPORTS2.BAT file

```
ECHO OFF
REM The HUNT.BAT File
FOR %%A IN (%1 %2 %3 %4) DO DIR %%A
ECHO OFF
```

Figure 15.11: The HUNT.BAT file

```
D:\MEDICINE>HUNT HEART.EXE LUNGS.EXE LIVER.COM

D:\MEDICINE>ECHO OFF

 Volume in drive D is DRIVE D
 Directory of  D:\MEDICINE

HEART    EXE    20533 02-23-89  11:34a
        1 File(s)    7714816 bytes free

 Volume in drive D is DRIVE D
 Directory of  D:\MEDICINE

File not found

 Volume in drive D is DRIVE D
 Directory of  D:\MEDICINE

LIVER    COM       87 02-23-89   3:28a
        1 File(s)    7714816 bytes free

D:\MEDICINE>
D:\MEDICINE>
```

Figure 15.12: Executing HUNT.BAT to repeat a DOS command

The results, shown in Figure 15.13, speak for themselves. The desired information about whether the files exist is not obscured by any additional DOS directory information. In this FOR subcommand, the actual command executed by DO is IF EXIST %%A ECHO %%A FOUND.

Note, however, that the ECHO OFF command itself is still displayed. This is because the echoing feature is on until ECHO OFF shuts it off. Only DOS 4 and DOS 3.3 users can surmount this limitation by preceding the command with the @ symbol.

@ECHO OFF

will turn the echoing feature off for all succeeding commands, and the @ symbol will suppress the display of this command as well.

Try out all of the sample batch files in this section to affirm your understanding of the subcommands. In some cases, you will have to change the directory references to references that will work on your system. Either in addition to or in place of the examples in this section, create a new batch file—for example, GYRO.BAT—that will provide extra information to a user about your chosen topics. The batch file could be invoked as follows:

GYRO HEART

This would determine if a text file called HEART.HLP existed. If it did, the screen would clear and the contents of the HEART.HLP file would be displayed. If it did not, the message "No help is available on subject HEART" would be displayed. Create your own sample .HLP text files to test your batch file.

USING BATCH CHAINS AND BATCH SUBROUTINES

Since a batch file can execute any command that otherwise could be entered directly at the DOS prompt, a batch file can invoke another batch file. By simply entering the name of the second batch file, you can pass control from the first to the second file. Execution continues with the instructions in the second batch file and does not return to the first (calling) batch file. This is known as *chaining*. It is

```
C>TYPE HUNT2.BAT
ECHO OFF
REM The HUNT2.BAT File
FOR %%A IN (%1 %2 %3 %4) DO IF EXIST %%A ECHO %%A FOUND
ECHO OFF

C>HUNT2 HEART.EXE LUNGS.EXE LIVER.COM BRAIN.EXE

C>ECHO OFF
HEART.EXE FOUND
LIVER.COM FOUND

C>_
```

Figure 15.13: Subcommands within subcommands

different from the calling procedure familiar to programmers.

Look at the listings of the three batch files in Figures 15.14, 15.15, and 15.16. These three files together demonstrate both the capabilities and the limitations of chaining. Carefully read the steps of each of the three batch files, while looking at the output results in Figure 15.17.

The first batch file executes three simulated instructions and then invokes the second batch file as its last instruction. These simulated instructions take the place of any other successive batch-file commands that you might write. (You should focus on chaining here, rather than on other command lines; the simulated instructions are displayed merely to give you a representative context for the chaining technique.)

After FIRST is done, it passes control to SECOND by invoking as its last instruction the name of the file (SECOND) to which control will be passed. Then batch file SECOND executes another three simulated instructions before passing control to batch file THIRD.

```
ECHO OFF
REM The FIRST.BAT File
ECHO Simulated Instruction 1 in First.bat
ECHO Simulated Instruction 2 in First.bat
ECHO Simulated Instruction 3 in First.bat
SECOND
```

Figure 15.14: The FIRST.BAT file

```
ECHO OFF
REM The SECOND.BAT File
ECHO Simulated Instruction 1 in Second.bat
ECHO Simulated Instruction 2 in Second.bat
ECHO Simulated Instruction 3 in Second.bat
THIRD
ECHO Last Instruction in Second.bat
```

Figure 15.15: The SECOND.BAT file

```
ECHO OFF
REM The THIRD.BAT File
ECHO Simulated Instruction 1 in Third.bat
ECHO Simulated Instruction 2 in Third.bat
ECHO Simulated Instruction 3 in Third.bat
```

Figure 15.16: The THIRD.BAT file

> Proper chaining of batch files requires the new batch-file name to be the last instruction of the preceding batch file in the chain.

THIRD executes its own three simulated instructions before the chain process is complete. However, the line "Last instruction in Second.bat" is never executed, because the third batch file was invoked *in the middle* of the second batch file!

True subroutines provide you with the ability to write modular batch files that perform well-defined task sequences, and to temporarily leave one batch file to execute a sequence *without losing your place* in the first batch file. If you need to run a batch file while in the middle of another batch file, you can do this in two ways. If you are using DOS 3.3 or DOS 4, you can use the CALL subcommand. If you are using an earlier version of DOS, you must invoke the COMMAND.COM program itself. The forms required are

CALL *BatchFileName*

for DOS 3.3 and DOS 4 users, and

COMMAND/C *BatchFileName*

for all earlier versions. Since under most circumstances DOS batch files can only chain, the COMMAND/C version brings into memory a completely separate copy of DOS for the express purpose of running the named batch file.

```
C>FIRST

C>ECHO OFF
Simulated Instruction 1 in First.bat
Simulated Instruction 2 in First.bat
Simulated Instruction 3 in First.bat
Simulated Instruction 1 in Second.bat
Simulated Instruction 2 in Second.bat
Simulated Instruction 3 in Second.bat
Simulated Instruction 1 in Third.bat
Simulated Instruction 2 in Third.bat
Simulated Instruction 3 in Third.bat

C>_
```

Figure 15.17: Batch-file chaining

With either the CALL or COMMAND/C method, when the batch file has executed all its commands, control will be returned to the very next line in the running batch file—the one *following* the CALL or COMMAND/C instruction—and execution will continue from there.

Look again at the THIRD.BAT file shown in Figure 15.16, and then look at FOURTH.BAT, shown in Figure 15.18. You can use these two files and the secondary command processor technique to invoke and run the instructions within the THIRD.BAT file, as shown in Figure 15.19. The results are different from the results of chaining.

Running FOURTH by this method will result in the same first three simulated instructions as with chaining. When those three have executed, control will be transferred to the THIRD batch file, at

```
@ECHO OFF
REM The FOURTH.BAT File
ECHO Simulated Instruction 1 in Fourth.bat
ECHO Simulated Instruction 2 in Fourth.bat
ECHO Simulated Instruction 3 in Fourth.bat
CALL THIRD
ECHO Last Instruction in Fourth.bat
```

Figure 15.18: The FOURTH.BAT file

```
C>FOURTH
Simulated Instruction 1 in Fourth.bat
Simulated Instruction 2 in Fourth.bat
Simulated Instruction 3 in Fourth.bat
Simulated Instruction 1 in Third.bat
Simulated Instruction 2 in Third.bat
Simulated Instruction 3 in Third.bat
Last Instruction in Fourth.bat
C>_
```

Figure 15.19: DOS supports true subroutines

which point its three simulated instructions will execute. However, unlike the previous chaining example, control returns to FOURTH, which can execute its last instruction. If there were another instruction in FOURTH or another hundred instructions, they would then all execute. In this way, sophisticated, structured application environments and systems can be built up by using only DOS commands and the batch-file mechanism.

SUMMARY

In this chapter, you extended your understanding of batch files. You learned about a variety of specialized commands that only work from within batch files. These subcommands provide DOS with the kind of features normally reserved for a high-level computer language:

- Messages can be included for internal documentation with the REM subcommand. You can also include messages to be displayed during the execution of the batch program with the ECHO subcommand.

- All batch-file command lines are displayed on the console as they execute. You can suppress any particular one by preceding it with the @ character in column 1 of the command line (DOS 3.3 and DOS 4 only), or you can suppress all succeeding command lines with the ECHO OFF command.

- Batch files can contain the standard logic seen in most programming languages. Branching is managed by the GOTO subcommand in conjunction with simple labels.

- Decision making is provided with the IF subcommand. DOS allows decisions on whether a file exists or not (EXIST), decisions on whether character strings equal each other or not (= =), and decisions about the severity of command errors (ERRORLEVEL #).

- The FOR subcommand controls the sophisticated features of looping and command repetition.

- You can interrupt your own batch program temporarily with the PAUSE subcommand or permanently with the Break key combination.

- You can implement true programming subroutines by using the CALL subcommand (DOS 3.3 and DOS 4 only) or by invoking a secondary command processor with COMMAND/C (for earlier versions of DOS).

Now that you possess these fundamental batch-file construction skills, the next chapter will make a more advanced user out of you. You will learn many tricks and techniques that will lead you to develop fancy implementations and systems of your own.

SOPHISTICATED BATCH-FILE EXAMPLES

YOU'VE SEEN IN CHAPTER 14 THAT THE PRIMARY ROLE of batch files is to allow you to conveniently group together a collection of DOS commands, other programs, and other batch files. You've also seen how this entire collection of commands can be run by entering the batch-file name with any special parameters at the DOS prompt.

As you've learned in the last two chapters, there are two situations in which you should write batch files:

1. When you have a time-consuming sequence of unattended operations to be performed.

2. When you need to run a complex sequence of commands frequently, and you would like to ensure that they are performed consistently.

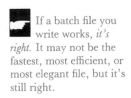 If a batch file you write works, *it's right.* It may not be the fastest, most efficient, or most elegant file, but it's still right.

In this chapter, you will see a wide range of batch files. These examples provide you with usable programs: you can type them in yourself, or you can send for the diskette with the files already on it (see the coupon at the end of this book). These examples will also give you ideas for creating similar programs for your own computer system.

AUTOMATING SYSTEM JOBS

When you turn on your computer and load DOS, DOS scans the root directory of the disk for a batch file called AUTOEXEC.BAT. If it finds that file, it executes the commands within it automatically.

DOS does not supply a default AUTOEXEC.BAT file. However, many application programs do supply one on their system disks. When loading a new application program, be sure that the program's AUTOEXEC.BAT file does not overwrite an existing AUTOEXEC-.BAT file that you carefully created.

The AUTOEXEC-.BAT file must be stored in the root directory of the disk. It will be ignored if it is stored in any other directory.

AUTOEXEC.BAT is a valuable tool. In both diskette and hard-disk systems, it can be used to execute any number of DOS commands or other programs. For example, you can set the time and date if you have a battery-powered clock in your computer, or you can configure your PROMPT and MODE commands for specific serial-port and video-screen requirements. There is no limit to the variations you can make in your AUTOEXEC.BAT file.

Let's take a look at some of these AUTOEXEC.BAT variations. You'll look first at how to load and run a specific program automatically when you power up your computer. Then you'll see how to set up a customized PROMPT command. Finally, you'll explore some possibilities for more complex system setup.

AUTOMATING THE SYSTEM STARTUP

It's easy to add an automatic startup feature to your system disk. As soon as DOS is loaded, the computer will run a particular program. Let's assume you want to run the BASICA program each time you start your system. Since BASICA is totally self-contained, all you need to do is use the COPY command to place a copy of BASICA-.COM on your new system disk.

Assuming your new system disk is on drive B for dual-diskette systems and on drive C for hard-disk systems, you would use the command

    COPY BASICA.COM B:

for a dual-diskette system, or the command

    COPY BASICA.COM C:

for a hard-disk system.

A simple task your AUTOEXEC.BAT file can do is to enter the name of a particular application program you want to execute. The principle shown here will apply to any program that you want to start up automatically when your system boots. For this example, you'd like to invoke BASICA.COM automatically on startup. Use whatever text-editing method you like to create an AUTOEXEC.BAT file containing the one line that invokes the BASICA program:

BASICA

If you'd like to try out this method with another program such as a word processor—say, WP.COM—make sure you copy WP.COM to the new system disk. In this case, your AUTOEXEC.BAT file will contain one line:

WP

Since many application programs include overlay files, you must be sure to copy those files to your new system disk. For instance, suppose your word processor requires a file called WP.OVL. You would need to have that file on the system disk containing your new AUTOEXEC.BAT file.

To see if your new setup will work as planned, restart the computer from your system disk. You can do this in two ways. First, you can turn off the computer, wait a few seconds, and then turn the computer on again. When the disk spins, DOS should be loaded and the program should run automatically.

As an alternative, you can reboot your system by pressing the Ctrl-Alt-Del key combination. This will also restart the computer, and your AUTOEXEC.BAT will be executed. However, it will not perform the same internal hardware and memory checks that occur with an actual startup.

Using Ctrl-Alt-Del is called *warm booting* since the computer has already been turned on. A *cold boot* occurs when you first turn on the computer's power; the same sequence takes place then, with the addition of several internal hardware tests.

Either of these rebooting procedures can be followed with most programs, and any main program can be run automatically at system startup. However, keep in mind that some copy-protected programs have their own instructions for automatic startup.

Don't get casual about the Ctrl-Alt-Del rebooting method. If you are in the middle of running a program like a word processor, a database manager, or a spreadsheet, rebooting may destroy your current working file.

CHANGING THE DEFAULT SYSTEM PROMPT

Changing your default system prompt is often so useful that you might want to have it set automatically when you turn on the computer. You can use the AUTOEXEC.BAT file to accomplish this, as

Using the PROMPT command in the AUTO-EXEC.BAT file changes all primary and secondary command processor prompts, including the DOS 4 command prompt. (Remember that you obtain DOS 4's prompt by pressing Shift-F9 or by selecting Command Prompt from the Start Programs menu.) Conversely, changing the PROMPT from a secondary prompt will only affect that subordinate command prompt; the main DOS prompt will remain unchanged.

There is no limit to the number of command lines you can have in any batch file. However, you should not write batch files with too many commands in them. They become harder to understand, modify, and debug as they get larger.

DOS commands themselves can be executed automatically during startup.

Create an AUTOEXEC.BAT file in the root directory that contains the single line

```
PROMPT $p$g
```

To see how this particular command is activated, reboot.

OTHER POSSIBILITIES WITH AUTOEXEC.BAT

The possibilities are limitless when it comes to adding useful instructions to your AUTOEXEC.BAT file. Just about everything else you'll read about in this chapter could be included in it. For that matter, just about anything you've already learned, from setting the prompt uniquely to initializing function keys, could be included in your startup AUTOEXEC.BAT file.

For example, suppose that you want to simply press the function key F9 or F10 to generate a wide directory listing or a clean screen. As you learned in Chapter 11, the following two commands will provide that setup:

```
PROMPT $e[0;67;"DIR/W";13p
PROMPT $e[0;68;"CLS";13p
```

Include these in your AUTOEXEC.BAT file, and voilà—your wish has become DOS's command. Use the more sophisticated versions of the PROMPT command presented in Chapter 11 if you'd like an even more useful prompt than this.

Use your own judgement and creativity in adding commands to your AUTOEXEC.BAT file. The rest of this chapter contains a host of tips, tricks, and techniques that can be used with batch files. You'll want to include some of these in your AUTOEXEC.BAT file. The next section provides a good example of using batch files in AUTOEXEC.BAT.

CREATING YOUR OWN MENU SYSTEM

It's always helpful to set up a mechanism that makes it easy for you and others to run programs. Hard-disk menu systems are designed to provide that very capability. Of course, you can always buy one; you'll read more about that in Chapter 18. However, an inexpensive way to set up a menu system is to use DOS's batch-file feature. A series of batch files stored on your hard disk can enable anyone to access the programs you have installed. You'll now see one possible design for such a series of batch files.

DOS 4 users can naturally take advantage of the Start Programs menu mechanism, which is already in place. However, using this does require that you conform to the rules set by DOS 4. If you understand and apply the techniques shown in this section, you'll be able to set up a comparable menu structure. Your structure, however, will have unlimited flexibility. You can easily change both the appearance and the functionality of your own batch files.

The first step in creating your own menu system is to create a file that will contain a listing of the programs available on your system. Let's put this display menu into a text file called MENU.SCR, as shown in Figure 16.1.

Remember that nearly everyone designs and programs differently, and that all of the batch files you see here are demonstrations. Feel free to add embellishments or to design the instruction sequences differently.

```
              MENU OF AVAILABLE HARD DISK PROGRAMS

     TO SELECT ONE, TYPE ITS NUMBER AND PRESS <RETURN>


     1  -    INVENTORY MANAGEMENT SYSTEM

     2  -    BUDGET ANALYSIS SYSTEM

     3  -    WORD PROCESSING

     4  -    SYSTEM UTILITIES


     ENTER YOUR CHOICE NOW, PLEASE:
```

Figure 16.1: Menu management file

This file of text can be displayed each time your system boots up. All you must do is write an AUTOEXEC.BAT file containing these two simple commands:

```
CLS
TYPE MENU.SCR
```

To make this menu work, you must create other DOS batch files for each option listed on the menu. For example, to run your inventory management system, you need to create a batch file called 1.BAT. Typing 1 and pressing Return will then execute the commands in that file.

A typical batch file for a menu system would contain a set of actions like the following:

DOS 4 users can enter the same series of commands, separating one command from the next by pressing F4, as a program-startup command sequence (see Chapter 6).

1. Changing the directory to the correct one (for example, C:\DBMS\INVNTORY).

2. Running the program. For example, to run a dBASE IV customized inventory program called INVENT.PF.G, the batch file would execute the command DBASE INVENT.

3. Returning to the root directory after the program has completed.

4. Displaying the menu again, so that the user can make another choice.

Figure 16.2 shows the contents of sample .BAT files that perform these actions for choices 1, 2, and 3 on the menu in Figure 16.1. The 1.BAT file brings up a database-management program, the 2.BAT file brings up a spreadsheet program, and the 3.BAT file brings up a word-processing program. The contents of each of these batch files are almost exactly the same, except that the directory and program have been changed in each.

The fourth choice on your sample menu, SYSTEM UTILITIES, is interesting because it suggests the possiblity of a flexible multilevel menu system. You could create a batch file called 4.BAT that would contain a new screen display, listing several utility choices. The utility operations could be safely nestled inside other batch files, and another entire set of menu choices could be automated.

```
CD \DBMS\INVNTORY
DBASE   INVENT
CD \
TYPE MENU.SCR

------------------

CD \LOTUS
LOTUS
CD \
TYPE MENU.SCR

------------------

CD \WP
WP
CD \
TYPE MENU.SCR
```

Figure 16.2: The 1.BAT, 2.BAT, and 3.BAT files

At this point, you should write your own 4.BAT batch file and any necessary subordinate batch files to complete the menu example. Although you can use your imagination, start off with the following simple tasks:

1. Clear the screen, and display a file of new choices with TYPE. Call this file UTIL.SCR, and give the user these options:

   A. Display the current date and time
   B. Format a new diskette in drive A

   Remember that 1.BAT, 2.BAT, and so on are already used for your main menu, so your utility files will have to be named differently. For example, you might want the two options just presented to be contained in batch files named A.BAT and B.BAT. In fact, you could even create new batch files called 1.BAT, 2.BAT, and so on, but you would have to place them in a separate directory and run them from there.

2. When done, display the main menu again (MENU.SCR).

3. The final step is to create a new AUTOEXEC.BAT file that will start up your menu system automatically when the computer is turned on. Although you may come back throughout

Remember to add REM statements to document all batch files that aren't transparently simple. Use them for your successor, for another programmer who uses your batch file, and for yourself—after all, *you* could be the one who, two months later, tries to figure out why a certain statement was included.

this chapter to change the file, start off with an AUTOEXEC.-BAT file that looks like the one in Figure 16.3. This file contains commands that change the prompt, open a path, clear the screen, and display the menu.

You are now ready to test the menu system you've created. Before you do, let's review the several files that make up your menu system:

- MENU.SCR. This file contains the menu display. It has no DOS function. Its only purpose is to tell the user what options are available on the hard disk.

- AUTOEXEC.BAT. This file executes when the computer is turned on or booted. It opens the path needed for hard-disk operation and displays the menu for the user to read.

- 1.BAT, 2.BAT, 3.BAT, 4.BAT. These files execute the choices listed on the menu. You should create one batch file for each choice.

- If you completed the exercise, you also wrote UTIL.SCR and several other batch files.

To test the entire menu system, reboot your computer. When the computer starts up, it should display your menu. You should test each option on the main menu, as well as each option you programmed into the submenu. Be careful to use a new disk or scratch disk when testing the FORMAT choice on your Utility menu.

```
ECHO OFF
PROMPT $P$G
PATH \;\DBMS;\WP;\LOTUS;\DOS
CLS
TYPE MENU.SCR
```

Figure 16.3: AUTOEXEC.BAT file for hard-disk menu management

IMPROVING PERFORMANCE WITH BATCH FILES

There are many ways to improve performance with batch files. Some of these are ridiculously easy—what's hard is thinking of them at all. In this section, you'll learn a host of simple possibilities for batch files. Since the lines of code are few, you can implement these approaches quickly if you choose.

SIMPLIFYING CONSISTENT SEQUENCES

Most of us are not great typists. Even for those who can speed along, there is great value to be gained in reducing the number of keys to be pressed. In the music world, there is much debate on the value of pressing one button and getting the sound of an entire rhythm section. No such debate rages in the PC world; anything that gets the same result with fewer keypresses receives a broad welcome.

ABBREVIATIONS Any DOS command can be abbreviated to the ultimate in simplicity with a one-line batch file. For example, the CHKDSK command can be shortened to the letter C simply by creating a batch file called C.BAT, and including in it the one instruction

CHKDSK

When you type C at the DOS prompt, the batch file C.BAT will be given control, and its one instruction will be executed as if you had typed it at the DOS prompt.

This technique can also be used for commands that normally take parameters, such as the RENAME or the XCOPY command. You could just as easily create a batch file called R.BAT that only contains the one executable instruction

RENAME %1 %2

When you wanted to use this command, you could type R instead of typing RENAME along with the variables. For instance, if you wanted to rename OLD.TXT to NEW.TXT, you could now type

R OLD.TXT NEW.TXT

DOS would quickly discover that R is a batch file, and the job would be handled through the batch-file invocation of the RENAME command, using the parameters represented as %1 and %2.

If you run your batch files from DOS 4's Start Programs or File System menus, do not bother to abbreviate commands with batch files. Since you do not have to type in the batch-file name, you do not save time by reducing the keystrokes in the name.

This simplification technique can be extended to commands with multiple lines. If you frequently do a CHKDSK on your A and C drives, your version of C.BAT could contain the following lines:

```
CHKDSK A:
CHKDSK C:
```

In this case, you won't even have to type C twice and press Return twice. On the other hand, the C.BAT file will be less flexible for other purposes, since it will always issue the CHKDSK command for two disk drives, A and C.

SHORTHAND NOTATION FOR COMMANDS   Certain commands that perform fixed chores can also be simplified with batch files. For instance, you learned in Chapter 9 how to use the MODE command to manage various aspects of different devices. If your system has both a color and a monochrome monitor, you could use a batch file to invoke the proper version of the MODE command. To switch output to the monochrome monitor, you could enter

```
MODE MONO
```

in a file called MONO.BAT. To switch output to the color monitor using 80 columns with color enabled, you could enter

```
MODE CO80
```

in a file called COLOR.BAT. Then, whenever you needed to switch, you would only have to enter the simple batch name, MONO or COLOR, to obtain the desired result. With this method a user doesn't have to remember (or even know) the actual DOS command or command/parameter sequence that produces a particular result.

Another good use of this technique is turning on the compressed printing mode for your Epson- or IBM-compatible printer, which you learned about in Chapter 8 as well. You could create a batch file called COMPRESS.BAT that contains one line:

```
MODE LPT1: 132
```

You could create another batch file called NORMAL.BAT that would also contain only one line:

MODE LPT1: 80

Anyone could now type COMPRESS at the DOS prompt to send a wide spreadsheet or database information to the printer. When they were done, they could enter the command NORMAL to return the printer to its normal configuration.

Another benefit of this method appears when you acquire new printers at a later date. Only the inside portion of the batch file has to be changed once, and only by one knowledgeable person. Everyone else using the system still only has to remember to type COMPRESS or NORMAL.

REPEATED AUTOMATIC INVOCATION

Any time you need to execute the same command repeatedly, the following technique can come in handy. Perhaps you need to find a text string in a series of files located in different directories; or perhaps you just need to obtain a directory listing of several diskettes successively. This method relies on the fact that %0, as a batch-file variable, represents the actual name of the batch file itself.

Take a look at the CONTENTS.BAT file shown in Figure 16.4. In this batch file, the PAUSE command prompts you to enter a new diskette into drive A and then waits for you to do so (see Figure 16.5).

If you press the Return key at this point, you will receive a directory listing of the diskette you placed in drive A, as shown in the top portion of the figure. However, this is also the point in the batch program at which you can terminate the otherwise unending sequence

Remember that the line numbers in this batch file and in the other files listed in this chapter are there for reference only. If you type in these batch programs for yourself, leave out the line numbers.

```
1   REM   CONTENTS.BAT
2
3   PAUSE Load diskette into drive A:
4   DIR  A: /P
5   %0
```

Figure 16.4: The CONTENTS.BAT file

```
COLORBAR BAS      1427   12-30-85   12:00p
COMM     BAS      4254   12-30-85   12:00p
DEBUG    COM     15799   12-30-85   12:00p
DONKEY   BAS      3572   12-30-85   12:00p
EXE2BIN  EXE      3063   12-30-85   12:00p
LINK     EXE     39076   12-30-85   12:00p
MORTGAGE BAS      6178   12-30-85   12:00p
MUSIC    BAS      8575   12-30-85   12:00p
MUSICA   BAS     13431   12-30-85   12:00p
PIECHART BAS      2180   12-30-85   12:00p
SAMPLES  BAS      2363   12-30-85   12:00p
SPACE    BAS      1851   12-30-85   12:00p
VDISK    LST    136315   12-30-85   12:00p
       18 File(s)     107520 bytes free

C>contents

C>REM  CONTENTS.BAT

C>
C>PAUSE Load diskette into drive A:
Strike a key when ready . . . ^C

Terminate batch job (Y/N)? y
C>_
```

Figure 16.5: Running the CONTENTS.BAT file

by pressing Ctrl-C. If you do not, the batch file will retype its own name and the word "contents," and the batch file will begin to execute again; you will be prompted to enter another diskette.

The key to this repetitive behavior is in line 5 of the listing. The %0 is only a variable parameter that substitutes for the original batch-file name typed at the DOS prompt.

PROGRAM SETUP AND RESTORATION

This section offers different approaches for initiating your own programs. You've already seen a typical small application method in Figure 16.2. In that example, a main program was run (perhaps with initial parameters) after the proper directory was entered. Now let's look at two other times you'll want to consider using batch files.

INVOKING THE SAME SEQUENCE OF PROGRAMS You sometimes perform a recurring series of steps in the computing world. For instance, you may run your word processor (WP.EXE) to create a new document and then, as a matter of course, run your grammar and style checker (STYLE.COM). You may also run a specialized spelling checker (SPELL.EXE) before you rerun your word processor to implement any suggested changes. The sequence, then, is as follows:

1. Word processor runs.

2. Style checker runs.

3. Spelling checker runs.

4. Word processor runs again.

If these programs do not allow parameter passing, you could write a batch file called WRITE.BAT, which would consist of the following lines:

```
WP
STYLE
SPELL
WP
```

On the other hand, many programs now allow you to specify a parameter to indicate the name of a file to be selected. If a program allows such a specification, then a batch file can be even more useful. Suppose you are working on a proposal called PROPOSAL.DOC. Your WRITE.BAT file could do more work if it contained these lines:

```
WP PROPOSAL.DOC
STYLE PROPOSAL.DOC
SPELL PROPOSAL.DOC
WP PROPOSAL.DOC
```

Simply typing WRITE at the DOS prompt would bring you successively through all four program invocations, each one bringing in the specified PROPOSAL file.

Here's another example. You may be working on the Great American Novel, and each chapter you write undergoes the same painstaking care and attention as the rest of your word-processed documents. You can take the simplifying process one step further by using the variable parameter technique. Look at the following batch file:

```
WP CHAPTER%1
STYLE CHAPTER%1
SPELL CHAPTER%1
WP CHAPTER%1
```

If you've named your files CHAPTER1, CHAPTER2, and so on, you can then invoke your four-program sequence by typing at the DOS prompt the chapter number as the parameter:

    WRITE 5

Keep in mind that if your novel has more than nine chapters, you'll have to name them differently so that you don't exceed DOS's maximum limit of eight characters in a file name.

SETUP AND RESTORATION FOR TWO-DRIVES   Some programs assume that the data they use is available on the default disk drive and directory. Since DOS allows you to run a program that isn't in the current drive and directory, you can first switch to the drive or directory containing your data and then run the program. After the program is done, you can change back to your original drive or directory. This is usually the root for hard-disk systems, and drive A for dual-diskette systems. The technique for returning to the root was shown in Figure 16.2. On a dual-diskette system, you can perform a similar sequence of steps.

Figure 16.6 shows a typical configuration, in which programs reside on drive A and data files on drive B. Suppose you want to run a main program called ESTATE.EXE, which is on your program disk and which uses several real estate data files on the data disk in drive B. The following batch file (SWITCH.BAT) will change the default drive to B for the duration of the execution of ESTATE.EXE, and then reset the default drive back to A. DOS will look on B for any files referenced by the ESTATE program.

    REM SWITCH.BAT
    B:
    A:ESTATE
    A:

CHAINING FOR DISKETTE-SWITCHING APPLICATIONS

As you know, any batch file can contain references to other batch files. Now you'll learn how those referenced batch files can also be on

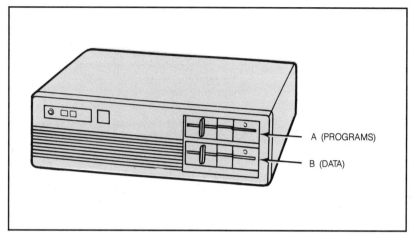

Figure 16.6: Typical configuration for a two-drive operation

different drives. You can use this technique to develop sophisticated multidiskette applications. For example, you could have a batch file called FIRST.BAT on drive A, which has a number of instructions in it, ending with an invocation of a SECOND.BAT file, located on drive B. A segment of the FIRST.BAT file might look like Figure 16.7.

The SECOND.BAT file, which could control the backing up of your files onto a clean diskette, could be located on your data disk. SECOND.BAT might look like Figure 16.8. When control transfers to SECOND.BAT, its first instruction pauses the computer, prompting you to remove the main program diskette from A and replace it with a backup diskette. After performing the XCOPY backup sequence, the batch file pauses again so you can reinsert your original system diskette in drive A.

The last statement in SECOND.BAT is your opportunity to continue the execution chain. This ''last line'' can be the name of another batch file to execute, on either A or B. You can even include

```
Instruction 1
Instruction 2
    .
    .
    .
Last instruction
B:
SECOND
```

Figure 16.7: Segment from FIRST.BAT file

```
PAUSE Place your data backup diskette into drive A:
XCOPY  *.*  A:
PAUSE Replace your original system diskette in drive A:
**** last line ****
```

Figure 16.8: Sample SECOND.BAT file

a variable such as %1 in this last line, transferring it from the original FIRST.BAT file to a THIRD.BAT program. The %1 could also be a command that would be executed as the last instruction of the SECOND.BAT file. In short, the last line in the SECOND.BAT file could contain A:FIRST, which would rerun the original starting program; %1, which would run a command passed from FIRST-.BAT to SECOND.BAT; or the name and location of any other batch file to continue the chain. If your last line uses %1, then of course the FIRST.BAT file should be modified to include a parameter in the final line.

INITIALIZING YOUR RAM DISK

A batch file is an obvious place for the series of commands necessary to set up your RAM disk. If you use the VDISK or RAM-DRIVE options of your CONFIG.SYS file, your RAM disk will already be created. However, some memory boards (like AST boards) come with a program that can initialize a RAM disk whenever you choose. If this is the case on your system, you should invoke the program with a batch file.

Say you have created a RAM disk called D. The following RAMINIT.BAT file could copy programs and files to it—for instance, commonly used batch files like HELP.BAT and frequently used DOS programs like CHKDSK.COM, SORT.EXE, and the command processor COMMAND.COM.

```
COPY HELP.BAT D:
COPY CHKDSK.COM D:
COPY SORT.EXE D:
COPY COMMAND.COM D:
```

You could also set the COMSPEC environment here to tell DOS where to find the command processor. (COMSPEC is a special DOS variable, designed to specify where a copy of COMMAND-.COM can be found. You will learn more about this variable in Chapter 17.)

Finally, you could reset the path to check the RAM disk for referenced files that are not in the default directory:

```
SET COMSPEC = D:\COMMAND.COM
PATH D:\;C:\LOTUS;C:\WP;C:\UTILITY;C:\DOS
```

In Chapter 11, you learned about a wide range of uses for a RAM disk. Placing all of those things in this RAMINIT.BAT file is a good technique, even if you eventually include a reference to RAMINIT-.BAT in your AUTOEXEC.BAT file for automatic initialization of your RAM drive.

If you use this RAM disk method for improving your system's performance, remember to put the RAM disk on your path *before* any other references to directories that may contain the original copies of the files. Then the fast-access RAM copy of the referenced file is located first, before the slower disk-resident version of the same file.

INITIALIZING YOUR COLOR MONITOR

You learned in Chapter 11 how to use the PROMPT command to set up the foreground and background colors on a color monitor. Having to look up or remember the codes can be tedious. This is a perfect opportunity for a batch file. RGB.BAT will expect two parameters, each specifying what colors the monitor should use for the foreground and background. The calling sequence will be

RGB *Foreground Background*

Entering the following sequence at the DOS prompt will cause all future output to appear in blue letters on a white background:

RGB BLUE WHITE

The batch file itself can be seen in Figure 16.9.

Several interesting points are demonstrated in this file:

- There are two major sections in the logical flow. The first section (lines 3–28) controls the setting of the background colors,

```
 1   REM  RGB.BAT
 2
 3   ECHO OFF
 4   IF ARG==ARG%2 GOTO FOREGROUND
 5   GOTO BK%2
 6   :BKBLACK
 7   PROMPT $e[40m
 8   GOTO FOREGROUND
 9   :BKWHITE
10   PROMPT $e[47m
11   GOTO FOREGROUND
12   :BKRED
13   PROMPT $e[41m
14   GOTO FOREGROUND
15   :BKGREEN
16   PROMPT $e[42m
17   GOTO FOREGROUND
18   :BKBLUE
19   PROMPT $e[44m
20   GOTO FOREGROUND
21   :BKMAGENTA
22   PROMPT $e[45m
23   GOTO FOREGROUND
24   :BKCYAN
25   PROMPT $e[46m
26   GOTO FOREGROUND
27   :BKBROWN
28   PROMPT $e[43m
29
30   :FOREGROUND
31   ECHO ON
32   ECHO OFF
33   CLS
34   IF ARG==ARG%1 GOTO DONE
35   GOTO %1
36   :BLACK
37   PROMPT $p$g$e[30m
38   GOTO DONE
39   :WHITE
40   PROMPT $p$g$e[37m
41   GOTO DONE
42   :RED
43   PROMPT $p$g$e[31m
44   GOTO DONE
45   :GREEN
46   PROMPT $p$g$e[32m
47   GOTO DONE
48   :BLUE
49   PROMPT $p$g$e[34m
50   GOTO DONE
51   :MAGENTA
52   PROMPT $p$g$e[35m
53   GOTO DONE
54   :CYAN
55   PROMPT $p$g$e[36m
56   GOTO DONE
57   :BROWN
58   PROMPT $p$g$e[33m
59   :DONE
60   ECHO ON
61   CLS
```

Figure 16.9: RGB.BAT sets foreground and background colors

according to the second color parameter specified after the batch-file name RGB. The second section (lines 30–58) controls the foreground color settings, based on the value of the first parameter on the batch file line.

- This batch file is not case-sensitive, as other batch programs that relied on the IF subcommand would be. In other words, each of the following commands would produce the same result:

  RGB   **BLUE WHITE**
  rgb   blue white

- You can use the IF ARG = = ARG%1 technique to test for the absence of a variable parameter. This IF test will only be true if the variable is missing.

- ECHO ON and OFF, followed by a screen clearing, is necessary between the setting of the foreground and background colors. The foreground prompt must take effect while ECHO is off and before the background color is set.

The overall flow of this program can be seen in Figure 16.10.

SOPHISTICATED BATCH FILES

This section deals with some specific batch files used by experienced DOS users. People's perceptions of advanced subjects differ dramatically; what one person views as sophisticated, another views as old hat. The batch-file techniques presented here are beneficial. If they're new to you, that's all the better. If they're old hat, perhaps you'll learn some new approaches by the manner in which these batch programs are implemented.

CUSTOMIZED SYSTEM HELP SCREENS

Some systems are used by many people at different times. A desirable feature for such a system is customizable help screens. You can use the batch-file mechanism in DOS to easily set up this capability. All it takes is the INFO.BAT file, shown in Figure 16.11.

Once you've installed this batch file in your path, you can use it from any directory. All you need to do is write a text file with an .HLP extension. This file should contain the text information you'd like displayed for anyone requesting help. The user, in turn, will only

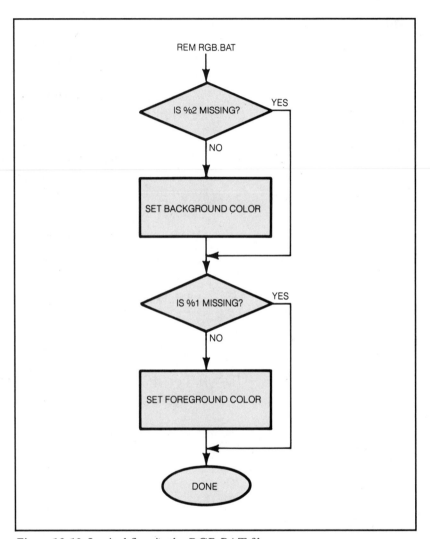

Figure 16.10: Logical flow in the RGB.BAT file

need to run the INFO.BAT file, specifying the first parameter as the topic for which help is desired.

For example, if there is a subject named GOBBLEDY for which you wish to provide users with helpful on-line information, you should place the information in a text file called GOBBLEDY.HLP. Then the user need only enter

INFO GOBBLEDY

In this sample help file, no CLS instruction is executed. It was omitted so that Figures 16.12 and 16.13 could show the entire resulting sequences. If you were to write a similar INFO system for yourself, you might want to insert CLS instructions before lines 5 and 9, the output lines in the INFO.BAT file.

```
 1   REM   INFO.BAT
 2
 3   ECHO OFF
 4   IF EXIST %1.HLP  GOTO OK
 5   ECHO Sorry.  No help available for %1
 6   GOTO END
 7
 8   :OK
 9   TYPE %1.HLP
10   PAUSE
11
12   :END
```

Figure 16.11: Customizable help screens with INFO.BAT

to display the predefined textual information (see Figure 16.12). If help is not available on your system (that is, an .HLP file does not exist for the subject), then a simple message to that effect is given (see Figure 16.13).

The program in Figure 16.11 can be understood quickly by looking at the logic-flow diagram in Figure 16.14. The heart of the batch program begins at line 4, after the initial REM and ECHO OFF statements. If an .HLP file exists for the subject (entered as %1), then the batch file continues executing at line 8. This is really only the

```
C>INFO GOBBLEDY

C>REM   INFO.BAT

C>
C>ECHO OFF
GOBBLEDYGOOK is a specially coined phrase which means wordy and
generally unintelligible jargon.  It is symptomatic of many
computer textbooks.  No one believes that the phrase could
possibly apply to their writings or utterances.

Strike a key when ready . . . ▪
```

Figure 16.12: INFO.BAT makes online help available

```
C>INFO ARRAYS

C>REM  INFO.BAT

C>
C>ECHO OFF
Sorry.  No help available for ARRAYS

C>_
```

Figure 16.13: Screen display when help is not available

label :OK, which is needed by the GOTO statement in line 4. The help information is presented to the user by the TYPE statement in line 9. The PAUSE statement ensures that the user will have time to read the information before anything else appears on the screen or before the screen is cleared.

If no help file exists, the IF statement in line 4 causes line 5 to be executed next. The ECHO statement displays a "Sorry ..." message to the user, and the batch program ends immediately. This is handled by the GOTO statement in line 6, which ensures that none of the instructions between lines 7 and 11 execute.

APPOINTMENT REMINDER SYSTEM

Some computer systems offer the luxury of automatic appointment reminders. In addition, some utility packages like Sidekick permit the entry and retrieval of date-oriented information (however, this is not automatic). The following example can take away the problem of forgetting to check your message or appointment log.

Unless you're very self-disciplined, the easiest way to implement this method begins by including a couple of reminders in your

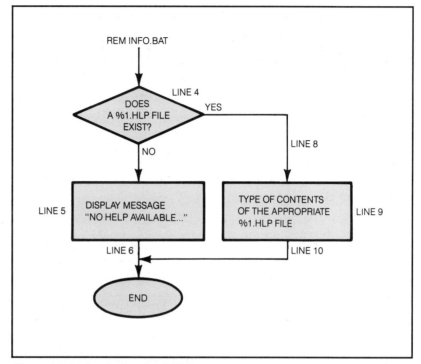

Figure 16.14: Logic flow for INFO.BAT

AUTOEXEC.BAT file. For instance, these three lines should jog your memory:

```
ECHO Remember to enter the following command to
ECHO get your messages for today (or any day).
ECHO TODAY mm-dd-yy
```

When you want to see the message or appointment file for, say, January 1, 1988, you only need to enter

TODAY 01-01-88

The results of this sequence can be seen in Figure 16.15.

The actual batch file that manages this simple operation is shown in Figure 16.16. As you can see, it is only a variation on the help method of the preceding section. The date files are text files, differing only in name and content from the .HLP files.

```
C>TODAY Ø1-Ø1-88

C>REM  TODAY.BAT

C>
C>ECHO OFF
Happy new year!
You probably shouldn't be at work today at all.
However, since you are, don't forget to start writing 1988
        on all your checks, memos, etc.
Also, don't forget the paperwork for the new tech writer
    beginning work tomorrow.

C>TODAY 1/1/88

C>REM  TODAY.BAT

C>
C>ECHO OFF
No messages for 1/1/88

C>■
```

Figure 16.15: Running the TODAY.BAT file

```
 1   REM   TODAY.BAT
 2
 3   ECHO OFF
 4   IF NOT EXIST %1 GOTO ERROR
 5
 6   TYPE %1
 7   GOTO END
 8
 9   :ERROR
10   ECHO No messages for %1
11
12   :END
```

Figure 16.16: The TODAY.BAT file

⊙ The naming convention for date files must be adhered to precisely. If you use dashes, slashes, or even leading zeros to create the text files, then you must also use them when you call up the TODAY.BAT file.

The way in which these text files are used (via the TYPE command) also reflects a similar batch-file approach. With the INFO method, all the files were given an .HLP extension, and their base names reflected the actual topic for which help was desired. In this appointment reminder system, the actual file name is understood (via %1) to be the date itself, a simple enough naming convention. The batch file types out the text file by that precise name. Here, you cannot assume that the batch-file code has the intelligence of the

DOS DATE command; in other words, 01-01-88 could not be replaced by 1/1/88 or any other variation.

The logic flow for this batch file can be found in Figure 16.17. You can see that it is only slightly different from the logic flow in the INFO.BAT file.

One of many additions to this batch file could be the simple addition of the line

DATE %1

just before line 6 (the TYPE instruction). In systems that do not have a battery-powered clock and calendar, the DATE command is usually run when you bring up the system. Since you must enter the date once for your appointment-making system, you can let the batch-parameter mechanism do the work of setting the date as well. Programmers are always looking for ways to reduce user intervention time, system program time, or both. Minor improvements like this will add up dramatically over time.

Remember to erase your older date files when you no longer need them, or they will proliferate quickly.

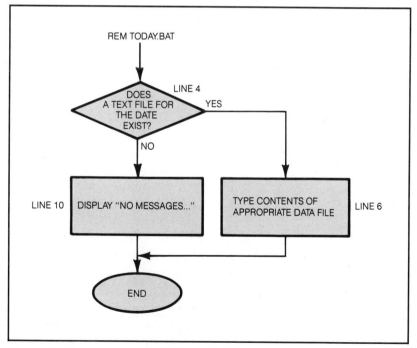

Figure 16.17: Logic flow for TODAY.BAT

BROADCASTING SYSTEM MESSAGES

Yet another variation on the theme of this section can be seen in the ANNOUNCE.BAT file of Figure 16.18. This batch program uses an area in memory called the *DOS environment,* which contains a set of variables and the values assigned to them. The DOS environment always includes the COMSPEC variable and the values you assign to PATH and PROMPT variables, as well as other arbitrarily named variables used by some programs or by the batch files described here.

A little-known technique of referencing DOS environment variables from within batch files allows you to broadcast messages to your system's users. This technique is useful for systems that have a number of different users, with perhaps one primary user. The goal is to have a simple command like

ANNOUNCE

display any and all current system messages for a user (see Figure 16.19).

In this figure, the first line is the key to the technique. You initialize a DOS environment variable (MESSAGE) equal to the name of this week's message file. In this case, the primary system operator only has to make the assignment of WEEK34.TXT to MESSAGE once, usually at the beginning of the day. For the rest of the time that the system is up, simply typing ANNOUNCE at the DOS prompt will display the current message file. Only the system operator needs to know the name of the actual message file, and from week to week, everyone's procedure for displaying system messages remains the same. Even the naming conventions can change, and the system operator is the only one who needs to know it.

```
1   REM ANNOUNCE.BAT
2
3   ECHO OFF
4   ECHO Current System Messages:
5   TYPE %message%
```

Figure 16.18: The ANNOUNCE.BAT file

```
C>SET MESSAGE=WEEK34.TXT

C>TYPE WEEK34.TXT
Messages for Week 34 of FY88:
      Ted Bishop is on vacation.  Susanne Powers will be filling in.
      Next Saturday is the company picnic.  Mary has the tickets.
      Don't forget.  Backup, backup, backup.
      Time cards due on Thursday this week!

C>ANNOUNCE

C>REM ANNOUNCE.BAT

C>
C>ECHO OFF
Current System Messages:
Messages for Week 34 of FY88:
      Ted Bishop is on vacation.  Susanne Powers will be filling in.
      Next Saturday is the company picnic.  Mary has the tickets.
      Don't forget.  Backup, backup, backup.
      Time cards due on Thursday this week!

C>_
```

Figure 16.19: ANNOUNCE.BAT displays all current system messages

This batch program can be modified slightly to allow for recurring messages that don't change from week to week. For instance, you could insert another line before line 5, like

TYPE ALWAYS.TXT

Then the ALWAYS.TXT file could contain any constant that you wished to display always, regardless of the week. This could contain such things as the operator's name and phone number, the service bureau's phone number, the security guard's extension, and so forth.

USING BATCH-FILE SUBROUTINES FOR STATUS TRACKING

Programmers use a variety of techniques for debugging their code. One of those techniques places additional printing statements at critical points in the source code. These are like snapshots. When the execution flow reaches these points, various parameters and variable values are printed out. The current program status can then be assessed and the problem discovered.

Programmers using this technique quickly learned the value of sending these debugging snapshots to a disk file instead. In this way, their program is not slowed down, and normal screen output is not compromised by debugging output.

You can borrow a page from the programmer's book for your own batch-file programming. Your batch files may at times become complicated, especially if you use the multifile technique of chaining. In writing any batch file, consider writing your own SNAPSHOT.BAT file. In a simple implementation, it could consist solely of the following two commands:

```
DIR >> AUDIT.TXT
CHKDSK >> AUDIT.TXT
```

Whenever SNAPSHOP.BAT was invoked, the current directory and disk status would be noted, and the >> redirection symbol would ensure that the AUDIT.TXT file would receive this information. You could later peruse the contents of this "tracking file" at your leisure.

The CALL subcommand in DOS 3.3 and DOS 4 (or the COMMAND/C feature of earlier DOS versions) is also critical to effective use of the snapshot method. You may want to note the current disk directory and memory status at various points during the execution of one of your batch files.

The ANYOLD1.BAT file shown in Figure 16.20 is representative of any batch file you might write; the vertical dots just stand for your own instructions. Some example DOS commands, like COPY, DIR, and ERASE, have been included. The snapshot is taken by inserting a line that runs the SNAPSHOT.BAT file immediately.

In the figure, lines 8 and 18 use the CALL subcommand. If you're using a version of DOS earlier than 3.3, you could just replace the CALL subcommand with the following:

```
COMMAND/C SNAPSHOT
```

This invokes a secondary copy of the command processor, which then runs the SNAPSHOT batch file before continuing with other statements in the batch program you are testing.

When you are creating your batch file, you can insert as many of these secondary command processor lines as you need to assess the

```
REM ANYOLD1.BAT

REM      .
REM      .         Preceding statements in the batch file
REM      .

COPY A:*.DBF  C:\DATABASE
CALL SNAPSHOT anyold1-A


             .
             .    More statements and batch file activity
             .

DIR C:\DATABASE
DIR A:
PAUSE Everything look OK? BREAK, if not.
ERASE A:\*.WK1
CALL SNAPSHOT anyold1-B
```

Figure 16.20: The ANYOLD1.BAT file

actual actions of your batch program. All of the snapshot results will be placed in the AUDIT.TXT file. You can erase this file any time you'd like to clear it out, since the >> redirection parameter will recreate the AUDIT.TXT file if it does not exist. After your batch file is complete and working just the way you want it to, you can remove all of the snapshot lines.

Note the use of the PAUSE command in ANYOLD1.BAT. Since the next command is ERASE, you're giving the user of your batch program a last chance to cancel out the continuation of the batch file. This is made especially useful by the preceding display of the A and C directories in the ANYOLD1 program.

Several creative variations on this method are available to you. Look at the modified SNAPSHOT.BAT file in Figure 16.21. In this version, two additional lines have been added before the DIR and CHKDSK lines. In fact, the DIR and CHKDSK commands are now being executed for both of the disks affected by commands in ANYOLD1.BAT. Line 4 is an add-on utility program that displays the system date and time. It is one of the Norton Utilities (see Chapter 18), and it presents this information in an attractive and readable format.

You could, of course, use DOS's DATE and TIME commands instead of an additional utility, redirecting their output to the AUDIT.TXT file. However, doing this would require you to press the Return key twice. This is because DOS will place its normal

```
1   REM   SNAPSHOT.BAT
2
3   ECHO Snapshot at point %1   >> AUDIT.TXT
4   TM           >> AUDIT.TXT
5   DIR/W  A:    >> AUDIT.TXT
6   CHKDSK A:    >> AUDIT.TXT
7   DIR/W  C:    >> AUDIT.TXT
8   CHKDSK C:    >> AUDIT.TXT
```

Figure 16.21: The SNAPSHOT.BAT file

request for any date and time changes in the AUDIT.TXT file instead of on your video monitor. You won't see the requests, but DOS will wait for your response anyway.

Line 3 represents another useful variation. The AUDIT.TXT file will expand to include many entries, depending on the complexity of your batch file and how often you invoke the CALL instruction. Each entry can be tagged so that it indicates where the snapshot was taken.

Figure 16.22 shows the beginning of the AUDIT.TXT file. The first AUDIT entry sequence is labeled anyold1-A. When the secondary processor begins each time, it runs the SNAPSHOT program, passing the

> Naturally, you can modify the snapshot examples presented here to include any other utility program lines or DOS commands that will provide you with useful information.

```
Snapshot at point anyold1-A
                                    7:34 pm, Wednesday, March 29, 1989
    Volume in drive D is DRIVE D
    Directory of  D:\XYWRITE\DOS400

    .              ..           PRINT     TMP   FRANCE          LABELS    400
APPA-ADD XY    CH17     XY    CH10-13   XY    BUSINESS TXT   CH10-13  IMG
1        BAT   2        BAT   3         BAT   ANNOUNCE BAT   ANYOLD1  BAT
C        BAT   COLOR    BAT   COMPRESS. BAT   CONTENTS BAT   DEMO     BAT
FIRST    BAT   FOURTH   BAT   HELP1     BAT   HELP2    BAT   HUNT     BAT
HUNT2    BAT   INFO     BAT   MONO      BAT   MOVE     BAT   NORMAL   BAT
PARA     BAT   QRTLY    BAT   R         BAT   RAMRUN   BAT   REPORTS  BAT
REPORTS2 BAT   RGB      BAT   SECOND    BAT   SIMPLE   BAT   SNAPSHOT BAT
THIRD    BAT   TODAY    BAT   01-01-88        ANYOLD1  TXT   AUDIT    TXT
CLIENTS  TXT   FIG1-3   TXT   GOBBLEDY  HLP   LIST     TXT   NAMES    TXT
SAMPLE   DTA   SIMPLE2  BAK   F14-02    XY    SIMPLE4  BAK   MOVE4    BAK
DEMO4    BAK   DEMO4    BAT   MOVE4     BAT   CH14-21  XY    SIMPLE4  BAT
F15-12   CAP
        61 File(s)    7716864 bytes free

Volume INSTALL-4-0 created 08-03-1989 12:09p
Volume Serial Number is 0CDB-0951

    1213952 bytes total disk space
-- More --
```

Figure 16.22: Contents of AUDIT.TXT after running ANYOLD1.BAT

first parameter (%1) along. Line 3 accounts for the value of this parameter (anyold1-A) appearing in the output file AUDIT.TXT. You need only type a different string of characters each time you make a CALL entry in a batch file you want to trace through.

TIPS, TRICKS, AND TECHNIQUES

Earlier in this chapter, you used several batch files that will be useful in your system either directly or with slight modification. They represent stand-alone batch files that can provide you and others with useful additional tools, like the customized help screens or the color monitor initialization. This section will present a number of techniques that you can apply to your batch files. The methods can either be used as you see them, or they can be incorporated into the more sophisticated batch programs you may write.

USING RAM DISKS EFFECTIVELY

You learned in Chapter 11 how to initialize a RAM disk. You only needed to include one of the following two lines in your CONFIG.SYS file:

    DEVICE = VDISK.SYS 256

for PC-DOS, or

    DEVICE = RAMDRIVE.SYS 256

for MS-DOS. You've then created a 256K RAM disk (of course, the disk's size can vary according to what you intend to use it for), and you can proceed to transfer the proper files to it.

If you want your RAM disk to run a word processor, you could use the lines

    REM RAMWP.BAT

    CD\PROGRAMS\WORDPROC
    D:
    WP

These examples assume that you have previously transferred the correct main programs, help files, overlays, and so on, to your RAM disk.

```
C:
CD\
```

to create a file called RAMWP.BAT.

Storing the RAMWP.BAT file in your root directory, and assuming your root is on your path, you could switch to rapid RAM-based word processing easily and quickly by simply typing

```
RAMWP
```

If you use this RAM drive technique for running more than one major program (for example, both a word processor and a DBMS), you must have enough space reserved for both. If you do not, you may need to write a separate batch program to copy the required programs to the RAM drive. You can use the IF and EXIST subcommands to check the RAM drive. They will determine what files are needed and whether any existing files need to be erased to make room for the new ones.

You can use the same technique for your database-management program, or for any other program that is slow because of normal disk-access speed. A variation of the RAMWP.BAT file for a database-management system might contain these lines:

```
REM RAMDBMS.BAT

CD\PROGRAMS\DATABASE
D:
DBMS
C:
CD\
```

This batch file also makes the C hard-disk directory the obvious one for containing your document or data files. D, the RAM disk, is made the current drive so that the WP or DBMS program that executes is the one found on the RAM disk. Any references to C alone, with no directory path, will access the files in the current default directory on the C drive (in this case, either PROGRAMS\WORDPROC or PROGRAMS\DATABASE).

CONTROLLING USER ACCESS

Entire books have been written on the subject of password protection. Even more advanced tomes discuss the subject of *resource allocation,* which involves usage as well as access. Resource allocation means controlling access to both the contents of data files and the running of program files. Let's look at a simple but subtle form of password protection that you can implement with DOS alone.

The DOS environment affords you a special password feature. You can initialize a PASSWORD variable at the DOS prompt or in another batch file. For instance, you can enter

SET PASSWORD = EELS

Then the code segment shown in Figure 16.23 must be contained in a batch file to restrict access to only those people who know the password. If PASSWORD was set correctly to EELS before a batch file containing this code was run, then PROGRAM will run. Otherwise, the invalid password message will be echoed, and the batch file will terminate. In short, only those users who know that the password is EELS and set it correctly will be able to run the particular program. The program could be contained in any .EXE or .COM file, and of course, the batch file could properly reset the directory if necessary in the :RUN section.

The password feature can easily be extended by using several DOS environment variables, each containing different passwords. Your batch programs can check for the proper values. For instance, you can have three passwords controlling access to the inventory, personnel, and accounting programs. Doing this might require several blocks of code like the code just seen, and three passwords, PASS1, PASS2, and PASS3, controlling access to INVENTRY-.EXE, PRSONNEL.EXE, and ACCOUNTS.EXE.

You might have a menu system that passes control to three batch files (see Figure 16.24) instead of directly to the three main programs. Only users who properly knew and set the appropriate DOS environment variable would be allowed access to the program they chose

> DOS 4 users can easily establish password protection for any batch file installed on the Start Programs menu (see Chapter 6).

> This password code uses IF statements to check for entry of the password in uppercase and in lowercase. You never know what case a user will enter when he or she tries to run your batch file or menu system.

```
IF %PASSWORD%==EELS GOTO RUN
IF %PASSWORD%==eels GOTO RUN

ECHO Sorry. That's an invalid password.
GOTO END

:RUN
PROGRAM
:END
```

Figure 16.23: Code segment for password protection

from the menu. Notice in the figure that the third password contains digits only, so IF tests for uppercase and lowercase do not have to be performed.

```
            IF %PASS1%==STORE GOTO RUN
            IF %PASS1%==store GOTO RUN

            ECHO Sorry.  That's an invalid password.
            GOTO END

            :RUN
            INVENTRY


            :END

------------------------------------------------

            IF %PASS1%==JOSHUA GOTO RUN
            IF %PASS1%==joshua GOTO RUN

            ECHO Sorry.  That's an invalid password.
            GOTO END

            :RUN
            PRSONNEL

            :END

------------------------------------------------

            IF %PASS1%==1812 GOTO RUN

            ECHO Sorry.  That's an invalid password.
            GOTO END

            :RUN
            ACCOUNTS

            :END
```

Figure 16.24: Three batch files for a multiple password system

SUMMARY

You've come a long way in this book. Not only have you learned a wide variety of commands and DOS features, but you've learned how to knit those features into seamless and sophisticated automatic batch files. This chapter presented the following examples:

- The AUTOEXEC.BAT file offers you a host of useful applications. Besides automating the system startup, you can change the default system prompt and automate anything you wish at power-up time. This ranges from automatically running any DOS command to automatically running add-on utility software packages.

- Batch files can be used to create simple but functional menu systems to drive the most sophisticated application setup.

- Batch files can simplify consistent instruction sequences. Through the use of abbreviations and shorthand notation, you can reduce your typing burden while simultaneously speeding up your system processing.

- The variable parameters allowed in batch files can provide a valuable tool for repeating critical application tasks automatically.

- A batch file quickly and automatically invokes any application program that is nested in its own subdirectory structure. The current directory and DOS path can be set up before program execution and restored afterwards.

- Operations involving multiple disks and diskettes, as well as sophisticated modular batch systems, can easily be developed with batch-file chaining.

- You can make batch files that will prepare and initialize your RAM disk automatically. This increases system efficiency and improves response time.

- Color monitors can be controlled easily through judicious batch-file development. You saw how a single batch file can make short work of setting the foreground and background colors on color screens.

- With batch files, you can create customized help features, as well as an appointment reminder system. You can also broadcast messages to system users. These features can be very useful on systems that involve many people sharing the computer at different times.

- The CALL subcommand (DOS 3.3 and DOS 4 only) or a secondary command processor can be woven into sophisticated applications. You saw how to do this for capturing system status snapshots, which can help you debug and analyze your system.

- You also learned a couple of new tricks for dealing with RAM disks. Batch programs can load main word-processing, spreadsheet, or database programs onto a RAM disk, and then execute the RAM-resident version of the main program using data files from your hard disk.

- The DOS environment can be used with batch files to manage a password-control system.

Congratulations! Now that you are comfortable with batch-file techniques, you can consider yourself an advanced DOS user. However, keep reading. Chapter 17 offers you a chance to learn about advanced DOS commands. Chapter 18 discusses add-on and add-in utility programs, which enhance the power of DOS. They fill in DOS's functional gaps and add new features.

ADVANCED DOS COMMANDS

CHAPTER 17

YOU HAVE NOW LEARNED ALL THE COMMANDS NECessary for using your DOS system effectively. In this chapter, you'll extend your knowledge to include a special advanced set of commands. None of the standard uses of DOS require these commands, but they can help you immeasurably in dealing with special situations. With their help, you can tailor your system to your specific needs and increase the overall efficiency of your applications.

The commands presented in this chapter will allow you to expand the range of ways in which you manage and manipulate files. Others will enable you to use and traverse your directory and disk structures more easily and more quickly. A final group of commands will help you get more mileage from the main DOS controlling program, COMMAND-.COM. And, for DOS 4 users only, you'll learn how to set up your own personalized dialog boxes for the Start Programs menu.

ADVANCED FILE MANIPULATION

A file attribute is something that describes that file. Height is an attribute of a person; disk storage space is an attribute of a file. Another attribute of a file, indicated by the archive bit, is whether it has been changed since the last time it was backed up with the BACKUP command. Yet another attribute, indicated by the read/ write bit, is whether you are allowed to make or delete permanent changes. Several advanced DOS commands have been designed to work specifically with files and attributes such as these.

CHANGING A FILE'S ATTRIBUTES

Most files can be read from and written to; they are said to be *read/write* and to have an attribute of – R. Some files are restricted, only permitting data to be read from them. These files are called *read-only* and have an attribute of + R. In DOS 4's File System, files can be set as *hidden*, which means they can't be used in a command at the command prompt.

ATTRIB, a DOS disk-resident command, is used to change the read/write and archive file attributes. This command can be very useful; since you can change a file's read/write attribute bit to read-only, you can block the deletion of the file. This helps to prevent a file or group of files from being erased or changed accidentally.

Influencing the archive bit allows you to control which files will be backed up. If you are using many temporary files, for example, you can reset their archive bits to 0 (off). Those files will then be ignored by the BACKUP /M and XCOPY /M commands. No backup or copy will take place; as a result, the backup and copy operations for the rest of your files will be faster, and less disk space will be required.

One version of the ATTRIB command affects the attributes of one or more files. A second, simpler version displays the current attributes of one or more files. The format of the command is

ATTRIB *Switches FileNames*

The *Switches* parameter controls the on/off status of the two file attributes. If *Switches* is not specified, the current attribute values of the specified files are displayed. *FileNames* is any standard file name. Wild cards are allowed, as well as drive and path-name prefixes.

Figure 17.1 shows the ATTRIB command applied to the root directory on drive E of a sample system. It indicates that three files have the A bit (archive attribute) set (files EMPLOYEE.DTA, KEYWORKS.EXE, and BBACKIT.EXE), while only one file has the R bit (read/write attribute) set to read-only (EMPLOYEE-.DTA). In general, a file that has no attributes set does not need to be backed up and can be read from or written to with no restrictions.

If read-only status is set, it may not always be obvious why later operations become difficult. Trying to use EDLIN on a read-only file, for example, produces the understandable message "File is READ-ONLY," but trying to erase such a file produces "Access denied," a less than obvious message.

If switches are included, both the archive and read/write attributes can be modified simultaneously with one ATTRIB command. The first switch, which affects the read-write bit, is specified either as + R for read-only or – R for read/write. If the read-only status is set (+ R), then the file may not be deleted or modified in any way.

The second switch affects the archive bit. It is specified either as + A, which sets the archive bit, or – A, which resets the archive bit. The archive bit is normally set whenever a file is rewritten to disk (after it has been changed). When a BACKUP command is issued, it checks the archive bit. If the archive bit is set, BACKUP will back up

```
When ready to return to the DOS Shell, type EXIT then press enter.

IBM DOS Version 4.00
        (C)Copyright International Business Machines Corp 1981, 1988
        (C)Copyright Microsoft Corp 1981-1986

E:\>DIR

 Volume in drive E is PROGRAMS
 Directory of  E:\

EMPLOYEE DTA     22432 07-01-89    1:26p
KEYWORKS EXE     87252 06-22-87    5:13p
BBACKIT  EXE     61440 07-05-89   11:47p
        3 File(s)    347648 bytes free

E:\>ATTRIB *.*
   A    R     E:\EMPLOYEE.DTA
   A          E:\KEYWORKS.EXE
   A          E:\BBACKIT.EXE

E:\>
```

Figure 17.1: Attribute status of sample root files

the file; otherwise, it won't. After BACKUP has scanned a file and either backed it up or not, the archive bit will be reset to 0. Using the – A switch forces the archive bit to be reset, so that a file will be skipped over during a backup. This allows you some measure of control over whether your files will be backed up.

Table 17.1 shows the different states of a file's attributes when different combinations of these two switches are used. Remember that 1 in a binary system indicates that the attribute bit is on, and 0 indicates that it is off.

As you can see in Figure 17.1, you can determine the current status of a file by using the ATTRIB command without switches. Using the switches, however, lets you control those attribute values yourself. If the command

ATTRIB +R – A SAMPLE.TXT

were used to set the read/write attribute to read-only (on), and the archive attribute off, then the command

ATTRIB SAMPLE.TXT

COMMAND	READ/WRITE BIT	ARCHIVE BIT
ATTRIB +R +A SAMPLE.TXT	1	1
ATTRIB +R −A SAMPLE.TXT	1	0
ATTRIB −R +A SAMPLE.TXT	0	1
ATTRIB −R −A SAMPLE.TXT	0	0

Table 17.1: Attribute combinations with the ATTRIB command

would produce the following result:

    R   A:\SAMPLE.TXT

This shows that the read/write bit for the SAMPLE.TXT file is set to read-only, and that the archive bit is not set—no A indicator appeared. Of course, DOS 4 users can use the ATTRIB command at the command prompt. However, DOS 4 also presents a clearer, more powerful way to change a file's attributes with its Change Attributes choice on the File menu. After selecting one or more files from the File area, you can adjust their attributes by using the mouse or keyboard.

When the Change Attribute dialog box appears, you are prompted to specify a global adjustment or a file-by-file adjustment:

    1. Change selected files one at a time
    2. Change all selected files at once

This prompt always appears, even though it is only applicable when you have selected multiple files. After you choose one of the adjustment modes, the Change Attribute window appears (see Figure 17.2).

If you had previously selected choice 1, then this screen reappears for each file so that you can update its attributes individually. If you had previously selected choice 2, then you set all your selected files to the same attributes in one automatic operation.

To set an attribute, keyboard users highlight it, then press the spacebar. Pressing the spacebar when the highlighted attribute is

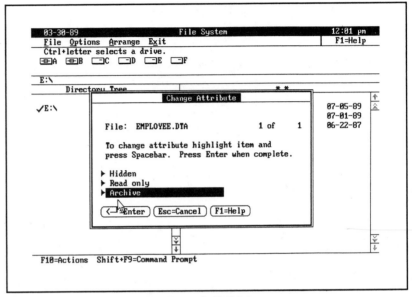

Figure 17.2: Changing file attributes in DOS 4

already set on (as indicated by the triangle symbol to the left of the attribute) deselects it. Mouse users click once on an attribute to select it. Pressing Return, or selecting the Enter pushbutton, will update your selected files.

In this example, I selected the EMPLOYEE.DTA file to demonstrate a DOS 4 feature that is unavailable in earlier DOS versions. When you select the Hidden file attribute, the file becomes invisible to all standard DOS commands—it cannot be accessed at the command prompt (see Figure 17.3).

Only the File System will show the hidden EMPLOYEE.DTA file, premitting you to access it. You can naturally turn off the hidden attribute whenever you want the file to be accessible to all programs and users.

UPDATING SETS OF FILES

If you work with a specific application program (for example, a word processor or a spreadsheet), you might want a backup disk to contain only copies of the most recently modified files. REPLACE allows you to make selective backups of files without using the

```
┌─────────────────────────────────────────────────────────────────┐
│ ┌─────────────────────────────────────────────────────────────┐ │
│ │ When ready to return to the DOS Shell, type EXIT then press enter. │ │
│ │                                                               │ │
│ │ IBM DOS Version 4.00                                          │ │
│ │          (C)Copyright International Business Machines Corp 1981, 1988 │ │
│ │          (C)Copyright Microsoft Corp 1981-1986               │ │
│ │                                                               │ │
│ │ E:\>DIR                                                       │ │
│ │                                                               │ │
│ │   Volume in drive E is PROGRAMS                               │ │
│ │   Directory of  E:\                                           │ │
│ │                                                               │ │
│ │ KEYWORKS EXE      87252  06-22-87    5:13p                    │ │
│ │ BBACKIT  EXE      61440  07-05-89   11:47p                    │ │
│ │          2 File(s)       347648 bytes free                    │ │
│ │                                                               │ │
│ │ E:\>                                                          │ │
│ │                                                               │ │
│ │                                                               │ │
│ │                                                               │ │
│ │                                                               │ │
│ └─────────────────────────────────────────────────────────────┘ │
└─────────────────────────────────────────────────────────────────┘
```

Figure 17.3: Files can be hidden with DOS 4

BACKUP command. It can update the files on the backup disk that were recently changed or newly created on your working disk. It can also ignore any of your older and unchanged files.

The command-prompt format of this command is

REPLACE *Source Destination Switches*

As always, the command may be prefixed by an optional drive and path name indicating where the REPLACE command file is located. *Source* represents the changed or newly created files that are to be written to the destination disk. *Destination* is optional; it specifies the destination drive and path to receive the copies of the specified files. If no destination path is given, the default is the current directory.

The *Switches* parameter represents one or more switches: /A, /P, /R, /S, or /W. Because the REPLACE command is defined primarily by these switches, some of them cannot be used together. Let's use the two directories in Figure 17.4, SOURCE and DEST, to demonstrate the behavior of the REPLACE command with its switches. You can see in Figure 17.4 that the SOURCE directory contains three files, while DEST contains only two. These two are named the

The REPLACE command is simply an advanced, selective version of the COPY command. It is most commonly used when you change versions of DOS and need to update various system files or even an entire DOS directory on your hard disk. You can also use REPLACE to back up your new or modified files at the end of a workday.

Remember that in DOS 4 you can split your screen and work with two directories at once. This is done by selecting Multiple file list from the Arrange menu. You can run a DOS utility or any other utility from one window, while retaining easy and immediate access to your selected files in the other window. That's how I actually ran most of the advanced commands discussed in this chapter.

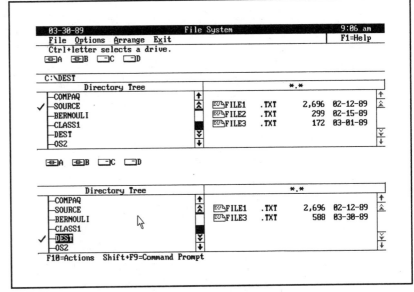

Figure 17.4: Sample directories

same as two files in SOURCE, but one of them (FILE3.TXT) is clearly a more recent version.

The /A switch tells DOS to add files to the destination directory. DOS will only copy source files that are not in the destination directory. The /P (Prompt) switch instructs DOS to pause and ask you if it is all right to copy each file that meets the criteria of *any other* switch that is used.

Let's use the /A and /P switches together. If you issue the command

REPLACE \SOURCE*.* \DEST /A /P

for the files shown in Figure 17.4, the results on your screen will be

Add C:\DEST\FILE2.TXT? (Y/N) Y
Adding C:\DEST\FILE2.TXT

1 file(s) added

The one file in the source directory (FILE2.TXT) that did not already exist by name in the destination directory was selected for replacement.

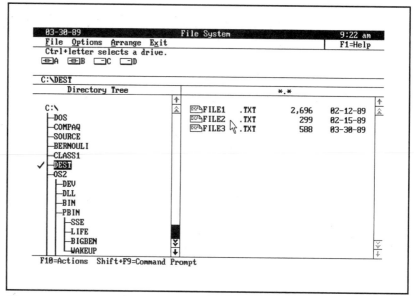

Figure 17.5: Adding files with the REPLACE command

As Figure 17.5 shows, FILE2.TXT was added to the DEST directory; FILE1.TXT and FILE3.TXT were left as they were.

The /R switch overrides the read/write attributes of read-only files on the destination directory. It allows you to replace those read-only files without generating an error message, so you will not be denied the implicit file update performed by REPLACE. This switch should be used with caution, since you or someone else may have set the read/write attribute bit to read-only for a good reason.

The /S switch will only replace or update files, not add new ones. Therefore, it cannot be used with the /A switch. Be careful when you use the /S switch with a wild-card character—it will replace *all* files matching the source specification, including those in any subdirectories of the destination directory. Figure 17.6 shows the results of using the /S switch on the directories shown in Figure 17.4. Entering

REPLACE \SOURCE*.* \DEST /S

tells the computer to use the files in the SOURCE directory to replace any files they match in the DEST directory. Since only

Be careful to enter the source and destination directories in the correct order in your command. Performing a REPLACE backwards could copy your old data over your new versions.

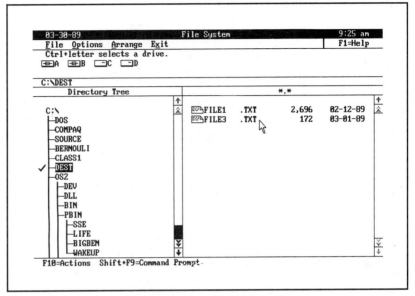

Figure 17.6: Updating matching files with REPLACE

FILE1.TXT and FILE3.TXT are common to both directories, only they are replaced in the DEST directory. Notice that in this example I replaced the FILE3.TXT file that was originally in the DEST directory with a version from the SOURCE directory that was older and smaller. Usually you will be doing the opposite—replacing an older version of a file with a more recent one.

The /W switch tells DOS to pause in order to give you time to insert a new source diskette in a drive before the replacement process begins. For example, you can execute a REPLACE command from a DOS diskette in drive A, replace that disk with the correct source disk, and then proceed to replace files on B with files from the newly inserted source diskette in A.

RESCUING LOST FILES

RECOVER is DOS's "Humpty Dumpty" command—it puts a file or a complete disk back together again. There may be times when something will happen to a file or to a part of the disk containing your file. A file may become unreadable, and access to that file may be denied. (This usually stems from the deterioration of the magnetic disk surface, rather than from the simple attribute modification discussed in the last section.)

The RECOVER command can read a file part by part (actually, disk cluster by disk cluster), skipping over the parts that have gone bad. This command rewrites the file without the bad data and allows you to access what's left. The format to recover specific files is

RECOVER *FileNames*

and the format to recover an entire disk is

RECOVER *DriveName*

Like all DOS commands, RECOVER can be prefixed with a drive and path name to indicate where the disk-resident DOS command file may be found. In the first format, the file names to be recovered can also be prefixed by their directory locations.

Recovering all files on a disk is necessary when the directory or file allocation table of the disk has been damaged. After you use the second version of this command, the directory will be made up of files of the form FILE*nnnn*.REC, where *nnnn* is a number. All of the recovered files will be numbered sequentially in the order in which they were recovered. This is not necessarily the order in which they appeared in the directory before the damage was done.

When you try to recover all files on a disk, you are limited to the maximum number of files that can fit into the root directory of the disk. If your disk has a subdirectory structure that contains more than this maximum, you'll have to invoke RECOVER several times, clearing out the recovered files from the root in between invocations. When you have finished recovering your text files, you will probably need to go through each one and edit the end of the recovered files, since the recovery process is likely to capture meaningless data at the end of the last disk cluster occupied by your original file.

File loss may also be due to corruption of the file allocation table (FAT). Even RECOVER is not likely to help you much in this instance.

RECOVER is not designed to work properly on a network disk. Disengage a disk completely from any network before you try to recover files with this command.

Only try to recover an entire drive when your disk's directory has been damaged completely. RECOVER does not distinguish between normally accessible and inaccessible files, so all files in the directory will be renamed in this format.

IMPROVING DISK AND DIRECTORY REFERENCING

The following commands influence the way that DOS looks at its disk drives and disk directory structures. These commands can be very useful when you are running older programs that make fixed assumptions about drives, when your programs do not contain a changeable path specification, or when a path name simply gets too long. These commands will also make your DOS application references easier and faster.

TREATING DISKS AS DIRECTORIES

JOIN is used to make DOS treat a whole disk drive as if it were a subdirectory on another drive. This extraordinary command allows individual DOS commands to treat files on multiple disk drives as if they were part of one sophisticated directory on a single drive.

There are three versions of the JOIN command. As usual, all of them allow you to precede the command itself with a drive and path name specifying where DOS can find the JOIN.EXE file. Entering JOIN with no parameters at the command prompt will display all the current directory and disk names that have been joined. Entering JOIN with two parameters specifies what directory and drive are to be joined. Entering JOIN with only one parameter (a drive identifier) and the /D switch *disjoins* the drive from a directory to which it had been joined.

The JOIN command can be very helpful when it is used with a directory-management program like XTREE. Each time XTREE switches disks, it determines the amount of space already used and the amount of space still available on the disk. This is time-consuming and can be a burden to power users. JOIN allows you to switch the current directory rather than current drive, which is a significantly faster operation.

Executing the following JOIN command will connect the two drives internally:

```
JOIN F: E:\ACCOUNT
```

This can be read as "Join the entire drive *F* to the E:\ACCOUNT directory." Any disk drive identifier may be substituted for F, and any empty directory of files may be substituted for E:\ACCOUNT. To see how this works, look at Figure 17.7, which shows two disk directory structures. Figure 17.8 shows the new directory structure after this JOIN command was executed. Drive F appears to be a subdirectory on drive E.

When you invoke JOIN with no parameters, DOS will display the results of any joining. The computer will show the joined drives and the directories they have been attached to. For example, entering

```
JOIN
```

produces

```
F: = > E:\ACCOUNT
```

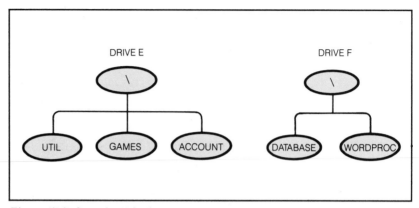

Figure 17.7: Sample disk directory structures

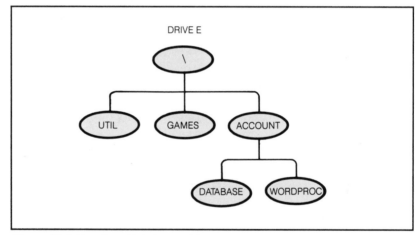

Figure 17.8: Results of joining a disk drive to a directory

This tells you that the root directory of drive F can only be accessed now through the ACCOUNT directory on drive E. In effect, E:\ACCOUNT is the new root directory of drive F, and all of drive F's subdirectories are now subdirectories of E:\ACCOUNT.

When you use the primary form of the JOIN command, in which you specify a drive and a directory to be joined, DOS will simply respond with a new prompt if everything went well. You won't receive any notice that the join was made—and in this case, no news is good news. For example, if ACCOUNT is an empty directory, the command

JOIN F: E:\ACCOUNT

will produce no obvious result.

If the proposed root directory (E:\ACCOUNT) had contained files, you would have received the error message "Directory not empty," and the JOIN command would have failed. Although a proposed root directory *may* have subdirectories and the JOIN command can still be made, any subdirectories in existence will be suppressed temporarily until the drive and directory are disjoined. You won't be able to access any information in that part of your directory structure.

Continuing with this example, if a DIR command is executed on drive E after the join has been made, the remaining amount of disk storage shown will be that of drive E, not of drive F. If anything is saved in the ACCOUNT subdirectory (actually on drive F), then disk storage will be used on drive F, not on E. Thus, it is possible to save in ACCOUNT (drive F) a file that is larger than the apparent amount of disk storage space left. In addition, access to drive F will be denied, so any command using drive F explicitly (such as DIR F:) will generate the error message "Invalid drive specification."

The last version of the JOIN command cancels the effects of a previous JOIN command. You must specify the JOIN command you wish to disengage (there may have been many). The following command would disengage the join just executed in our example:

JOIN F: /D

If the destination drive (that is, the proposed root directory of the JOIN command in question) is omitted, with the intention of undoing all joinings, the error message "Incorrect number of parameters" will appear. Similarly, disjoining a drive that has not been joined will generate the error message "Invalid parameter."

Now let's work through an actual session with the JOIN command. The following sequence shows how to join drive F with the ACCOUNT directory. Use DOS 4's File System to split your screen and check the tree structure of the two disks, as shown in Figure 17.9. You next run the JOIN command to append drive F's root directory to E:\ACCOUNT (see Figure 17.10).

As you can see in Figure 17.11, the former drive F is no longer accessible (only drives A, B, C, D, and E can be switched to). Drive F's tree structure now begins at the ACCOUNT directory on drive E.

TREATING DIRECTORIES AS DISKS

The SUBST (Substitute) command is the opposite of the JOIN command: it will create a new disk drive out of any existing directory. To visualize this, look at Figure 17.8 first and Figure 17.7 next. Starting with one directory structure, you can take a directory (ACCOUNT) and all of its subdirectories and make that directory the root directory of a new drive.

This command is frequently used for running older software packages that cannot reference files in a hierarchical directory structure. By fooling these packages into thinking they are only addressing files on a disk drive, you can still make use of the DOS directory structure for file storage.

The SUBST command comes in handy in another common situation. If you have a hard disk with a directory structure containing many levels of subdirectories, this command allows you to avoid typing long path names. For the same reason, it is useful when you have a program that requests a file name and path but only allows a certain amount of characters to be entered. WordPerfect is an example of this type of program.

Like the JOIN command, SUBST has three versions. The first actually performs a substitution, the second displays all current substitutions, and the third cancels a previous substitution.

Let's look at an example. Specify a directory structure, as shown in Figure 17.12. Then suppose you need to run an older general ledger program that needs the files in ACCOUNT\GL, but the older program does not support paths. You would issue the following command:

    SUBST G: E:\ACCOUNT\GL

This command makes DOS assume there is a disk drive G, and that the

The SUBST command also reduces your typing burden. You can redefine any directory, no matter how deep in your hierarchical structure, as a single-letter drive identifier. All future command references will be shorter, and less liable to contain typing errors.

Since a substituted drive is really only a portion of another drive, don't mistake it for a RAM drive. SUBST offers convenience, not increased performance.

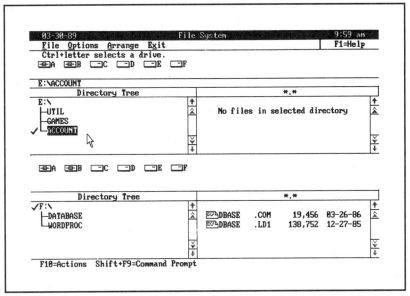

Figure 17.9: Directory trees and listings of drives E and F

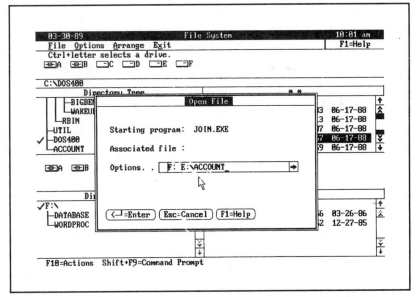

Figure 17.10: Joining drive F to the ACCOUNT directory on drive E

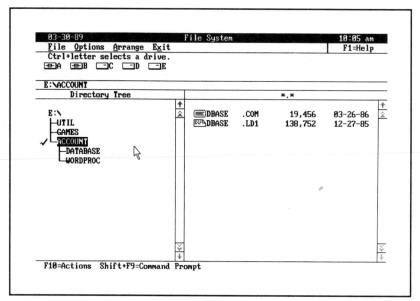

Figure 17.11: New hierarchical structure after a JOIN

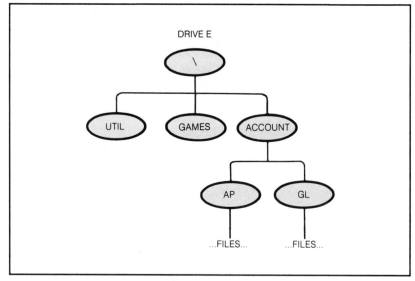

Figure 17.12: Sample directory structure

contents of this drive are the contents of the ACCOUNT\GL subdirectory on drive E. Drive G now includes all of the directory's subdirectories (in this example, however, there are no subdirectories).

Unlike the JOIN command, the SUBST command allows you to access the specified subdirectory directly after the SUBST command has been issued. If you save a file on G (or in the subdirectory), it will also be saved in the subdirectory (or on G), because both access the same part of the disk (see Figure 17.13). In effect, this command opens up another "window" into a directory, and you can access that directory's contents through the window simply by using a drive specifier.

Let's actually use this version of the SUBST command. In Figure 17.14, you can see drive E's directory structure, as well as the three current files found in the GL directory. Notice that there are six accessible drives in this example, identified by the letters A through F. Opening up a second DOS 4 window to run the SUBST.EXE command gives you the screen shown in Figure 17.15. I typed two parameters in the Options field. The first parameter, G:, is the new drive identifier for E:\ACCOUNT\GL, the second parameter.

Once the substitution has taken effect, as seen in Figure 17.16, you

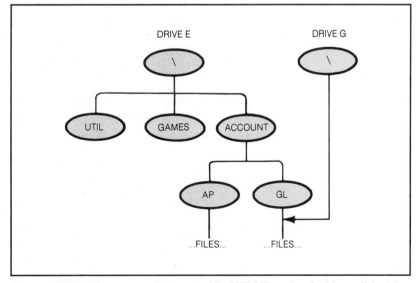

Figure 17.13: Directory references with SUBST and a fictitious disk-drive identifier

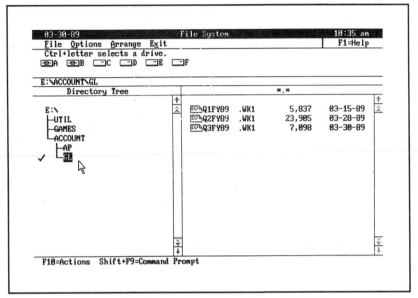

Figure 17.14: Beginning directory structure prior to SUBST

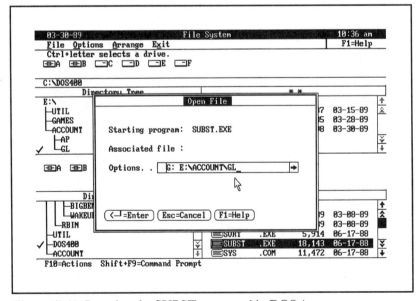

Figure 17.15: Running the SUBST command in DOS 4

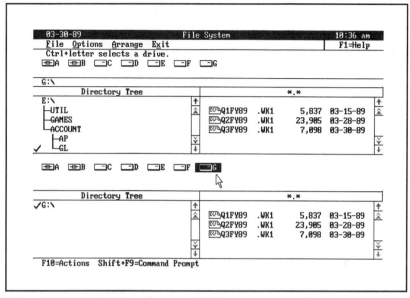

Figure 17.16: SUBST creates a new G drive

can access the three .WK1 files in either of two ways. If you look at the file listing in drive G, you will see the same contents as in the E:\AC-COUNT\GL directory. These files do not actually exist twice. You are simply being given two methods for referencing the individual files.

The second version of SUBST causes all currently active substitutions to be displayed. DOS will show you the created drive identifier and the drive and directory to which it is linked. For example,

```
E:\ > SUBST
G: = > E:\ACCOUNT\GL
```

shows you that drive G is currently being used as a substitute for ACCOUNT\GL on drive E. As a result, the ACCOUNT\GL directory can be accessed normally (on drive E) or through its substitute (on the fictitious drive G).

The final version of SUBST is used to undo a substitution. To undo the SUBST command shown in the previous example, you would type

```
SUBST G: /D
```

By default, DOS only supports drives A through E. In order to create and access drives lettered beyond E, you must include in your CONFIG.SYS file the command LASTDRIVE = *n*, where *n* is the last letter allowed for a drive. For example, LASTDRIVE = Z allows drives labeled A through Z.

The /D switch disjoins, or disassociates, the directory from the fictitious drive G. Trying to use the DIR command on drive G will then
result in an "Invalid drive specification" message.

REROUTING DISK INPUT AND OUTPUT

Some older programs have hard-coded drive references, which
means they are internally frozen, with no way for you to make use of
a hard disk. The ASSIGN command can help you solve this problem. It causes any requests for one drive to be carried out on another
drive. ASSIGN is very useful with older software packages designed
to work only with drives A and B. You can have your files in a directory on your hard disk, and the older program will be tricked into
believing it is accessing the files on a single drive without any hierarchical structures.

You should not use ASSIGN with BACKUP, RESTORE,
LABEL, JOIN, SUBST, or PRINT. These commands act on the
contents of drives and directories; serious problems can result if your
intended destination drive has previously been reassigned to another
drive. As a matter of protection, DOS ignores reassignments when
you invoke the even more dangerous FORMAT, DISKCOPY, and
DISKCOMP commands.

The ASSIGN command has two versions. The first will make or
break assignments, while the second cancels all assignments currently in effect. The first version is the most frequently used:

> **ASSIGN** *DriveX = BigDrive*

In this version, DOS will cause all future references to files and directories on *DriveX* to be treated as if they had been made to *BigDrive*. As
always with DOS external commands, you can prefix the command
name with a drive identifier and a path name.

A simple example of this command is assigning to drive C any references to the files on drive A.

> **ASSIGN** A = C

can be read as "Let the current working directory on drive C handle
everything requested of drive A." When the command DIR A: is

Protect your hard
disk against some
computer viruses. Use
the ASSIGN C = A
method to test new soft-
ware. If a hidden virus
attempts to write to your
hard disk (C) when you
install the software, the
write request will be
rerouted to the scratch
diskette you placed in
drive A. If you then see
that something is wrong,
do not install the infected
program on your hard
disk, where immeasur-
able damage could be
done.

executed, a directory of drive C will appear. To undo ASSIGN commands, use ASSIGN by itself without any drive assignments:

ASSIGN

SPEEDING UP DISK ACCESS

When you have a directory structure that contains many levels of subdirectories, DOS can take a very long time to search for a file or directory. To combat this problem, Microsoft developed the FAST-OPEN command, which maintains a list of the most recently accessed directory and file locations. This means that if you repeatedly reference a directory or file, DOS will be able to locate it more quickly on the disk. The FASTOPEN memory buffer will contain the disk location of that directory or file; DOS can then access it without having to check the disk directory structure itself.

In fact, you can set up a number of memory buffers in DOS 4 for the express purpose of holding file data, rather than just file and directory locations. In this way, when the file is referenced again, the data is retrieved from this so-called *memory cache*. Reading the data from this memory cache at the speed of memory chips is much faster than reading the data from the original sectors on the disk drives.

The general format of this command is

FASTOPEN *Drive: = Size, Buf*

Drive is the drive you want FASTOPEN to work for. You must repeat the *Drive:* and *= Size, Buf* parts of the command for each drive you want FASTOPEN to affect. *Size,* an optional parameter, represents the number of directory or file entries that FASTOPEN will remember. *Buf* represents the number of contiguous memory buffers reserved in memory for storing file data from the most recently referenced files.

Make sure that the FASTOPEN command file is available on the current directory or path. As with all DOS commands, you can precede the command name with the full path name leading to it.

The most common use of the FASTOPEN command is simply to specify the disk drive whose performance you want to improve. For

FASTOPEN cannot be used on a drive defined by the JOIN, SUBST, or ASSIGN command. In addition, it should not be used on network drives.

example, entering

FASTOPEN C:

will enable DOS to remember the last 34 directories and files accessed (the default), and thus be able to go right to them on the disk.

FASTOPEN can only be used once per boot session and reserves 35 bytes per entry. A buffer size of 100 (FASTOPEN C: = 100) would therefore consume about 3500 bytes of memory. It is recommended that *Size* be at least as great as the highest number of levels in the directory structure, so that any file in the directory can be quickly found. In fact, unless you are only working with one file, *Size* should be larger. The default is reasonable, unless you have special usage requirements and perform some actual timing tests.

Using the *Buf* parameter to install a memory cache in your system is one of the most effective steps you can take to improve the performance of your overall DOS 4 system. In DOS 4, you can also add the /X switch if you have expanded memory. Using this switch will carve the memory cache out of expanded memory, freeing up low memory for programs.

COPYING FILES FASTER

A special command called XCOPY (available only in DOS 3.2 and later versions) allows more sophisticated file transfers between disks and directories. You should use it for multifile transfers because it is usually faster than COPY. I also recommend it for transferring files from many different directories, because XCOPY understands better than COPY how to select files located in remote sections of the disk.

The general format of the XCOPY command is

XCOPY *Source Destination Switches*

where *Source* and *Destination* are specified as they are with the COPY command. Using the *Switches* parameter, which represents one or more switches, can greatly expand the range of files to be copied. A simple example of using the XCOPY command is the following:

XCOPY D:\DBASE\ *.* A:

You cannot use XCOPY to transfer multiple files to a printer. It is designed for disk transfers only.

This command will copy all files in the DBASE directory to the disk in drive A. As DOS copies the files, it displays the file names on the screen (see Figure 17.17).

The unique aspect of this command is revealed by the message "Reading source file(s)," which appears after you enter the command. Unlike the COPY command, which reads a single source file and then writes a destination file, the XCOPY command first reads as many source files as possible into available memory. Only then does it stop to write the destination files. Since memory operations occur much more rapidly than disk operations, XCOPY transfers files faster.

SWITCHES FOR THE XCOPY COMMAND You should now take a look at the XCOPY command's switches, in the order of their importance. The most powerful switch is /S, which lets you select files located in the subdirectory structure. As you can see in Figure 17.18, the /S switch directs DOS to look in all subdirectories of the source directory for file names that match your file specification. Using the /S switch with *.BAT enabled DOS to copy the

```
When ready to return to the DOS Shell, type EXIT then press enter.

IBM DOS Version 4.00
        (C)Copyright International Business Machines Corp 1981, 1988
        (C)Copyright Microsoft Corp 1981-1986

C:\DOS400>XCOPY D:\DBASE\*.* A:
Reading source file(s)...
D:\DBASE\ASSIST.HLP
D:\DBASE\COMMAND.COM
D:\DBASE\CONFIG.DB
D:\DBASE\CONFIG.SYS
D:\DBASE\DBASE.COM
D:\DBASE\DBASE.LD1
D:\DBASE\DBASE.MSG
D:\DBASE\DBASEINL.OVL
D:\DBASE\HELP.DBS
D:\DBASE\DBASE.OVL
        10 File(s) copied

C:\DOS400>
```

Figure 17.17: XCOPY reading files into memory and writing destination files

```
When ready to return to the DOS Shell, type EXIT then press enter.

IBM DOS Version 4.00
        (C)Copyright International Business Machines Corp 1981, 1988
        (C)Copyright Microsoft Corp 1981-1986

C:\DOS400>XCOPY \*.BAT A: /S
Reading source file(s)...
\AUTOEXEC.BAT
\COMPAQ\1.BAT
\COMPAQ\2.BAT
\COMPAQ\3.BAT
\OS2\RBIN\HELP.BAT
\OS2\RBIN\NEW-VARS.BAT
\DOS400\AUTOEXEC.BAT
\DOS400\SHELLTXT.BAT
\DOS400\DOSSHELL.BAT
        9 File(s) copied

C:\DOS400>
```

Figure 17.18: Searching all subdirectories for wild-card matches with the /S switch

AUTOEXEC.BAT file in the root, as well as the three .BAT files in the COMPAQ subdirectory, the two .BAT files in the \OS2\RBIN directory, and the three .BAT files in the \DOS400 directory.

If the respective directories do not already exist on the destination disk, DOS automatically creates them for you and then copies the files to them.

You can also control the copying operation by employing the /P switch, which tells DOS to prompt you with each file name that matches the wild-card specification. You can then decide whether each file will be copied.

Look at the sample XCOPY transfer in Figure 17.19, which uses both the /S and the /P switches. In this example, I answered affirmatively (Y) only three times when prompted. XCOPY then copied the three selected files to the destination drive. These files were

\LIST.TXT

\NAMES.TXT

\BERNOULI\BBACKIT.TXT

```
When ready to return to the DOS Shell, type EXIT then press enter.

IBM DOS Version 4.00
          (C)Copyright International Business Machines Corp 1981, 1988
          (C)Copyright Microsoft Corp 1981-1986

C:\DOS400>XCOPY \*.TXT A: /S /P
\FILE1.TXT (Y/N)?N
\FILE3.TXT (Y/N)?N
\JUNK.TXT (Y/N)?N
\LIST.TXT (Y/N)?Y
\NAMES.TXT (Y/N)?Y
\SOURCE\FILE1.TXT (Y/N)?N
\SOURCE\FILE2.TXT (Y/N)?N
\SOURCE\FILE3.TXT (Y/N)?N
\BERNOULI\BBACKIT.TXT (Y/N)?Y
\DEST\FILE1.TXT (Y/N)?N
\DEST\FILE3.TXT (Y/N)?N
\DOS400\TEMP1.TXT (Y/N)?N
\DOS400\TEMP2.TXT (Y/N)?N
       3 File(s) copied

C:\DOS400>
```

Figure 17.19: XCOPY's /P switch prompt

Notice that one of these files (\BERNOULI\BBACKIT.TXT) is in a subdirectory of the root. Since I used the /S switch, XCOPY recreated the same directory structure on the destination disk (assuming it was not there already) and copied the file to the correct subdirectory.

Another important switch, /D, allows you to specify that all files should be copied if their creation dates are the same as or later than the date you give. The form required is /D:*mm-dd-yy* unless you have installed a DOS version with a different date format (see Chapter 12).

The remaining switches are of less practical importance. When you use XCOPY's /A switch, only files that are marked for backup are copied. The files' archive attributes are not changed by this switch. The /M switch also copies the files marked for backup, but it does change their archive attributes to indicate that they have been backed up.

The /V switch performs the same task as it does on the COPY command, requesting the extra read-after-write verification step. The /W switch's only job is to pause briefly and ask you to press any key to begin copying files.

INFLUENCING THE COMMAND PROCESSOR AND ITS ENVIRONMENT

The command processor on your system disk, COMMAND-.COM, is the program that interprets all of the commands you type in from the keyboard. It has been primarily responsible for interpreting all the commands you've learned so far. It takes your command and first scans its own internal command list to see if it can handle your request without going to the disk. If the command is a memory-resident command, then the way in which that command will work is defined somewhere in COMMAND.COM. If it is an external command, COMMAND.COM will check the directory to see if the command file is present. If it is not, and your command is not in a batch file, you will get an error message. However, if it does find the command file, control will be transferred to that file.

Let's look at some examples. TYPE is a resident command used to display the contents of ASCII files. When COMMAND.COM is ready to accept a command, it displays the DOS prompt. Say you type in the command TYPE OUTLINE.TXT. COMMAND-.COM first determines that TYPE is a resident command. It then looks internally for the instructions that tell it what to do when the TYPE command is used. Following these instructions, it gets the file name you typed in and displays the file.

External commands are not really commands at all—each external command request actually runs a program contained in a separate file. These files are called .COM or .EXE files. For example, a file named ASSIGN.COM contains the program that performs an ASSIGN command. Say you issue the command ASSIGN A = B. COMMAND.COM first checks that it is not a resident command. After first checking the current working directory, it will then find the file called ASSIGN.COM somewhere along the specified path and transfer control of the system to that file. When ASSIGN is done assigning, control passes back to COMMAND.COM. Of course, this assumes you've set the path properly (PATH \DOS).

When COMMAND.COM is doing all of this, it must not only access those parts of itself that contain definitions and instructions, but it also must access the DOS environment. This contains user-defined definitions, such as the current path and the last available drive (LASTDRIVE in CONFIG.SYS). The SET command gives you direct control over the contents of the DOS environment.

RENAMING COMMANDS

The SET command is used to change character strings and definitions within the DOS environment. Both you and DOS can set aside named areas of this environment for character strings. You can use them for anything you like—for example, individual path names for future commands, file names for later DOS operations, or variable values used by several batch files.

The SET command with no parameters

```
SET
```

can display the current DOS environment settings. A modified format can erase any existing entry:

```
SET Name =
```

will erase the DOS environment variable *Name*. To create a completely new DOS environment string or to change one that already exists, use the format

```
SET Name = String
```

where *Name* is either a variable name defined by you, or one of the system's predefined names like PROMPT, PATH, LASTDRIVE, or COMSPEC.

Let's take a look at a sample sequence that demonstrates this command. First, you can display the existing DOS environment, which includes all externally defined system defaults and user definitions. For example, issuing the SET command at the DOS prompt:

```
A:\> SET
```

will display the following:

```
COMSPEC = A:\COMMAND.COM
PATH = \
PROMPT = $p$g
LASTDRIVE = Z
FILES = \wordproc\wordperf\files
```

You are limited by default to 127 bytes of total available DOS environment space, although this default may be increased by using the /E switch of the SHELL command (see Chapter 22).

The first four of these environment names are predefined and have special meaning to the system. You've seen all of these except for COMSPEC, which is only modified infrequently, when you've relocated your command processor to some drive or directory other than the root of the boot disk. COMSPEC is usually used when you place COMMAND.COM on a RAM disk to speed up applications that invoke the command processor frequently.

The next version of the SET command will remove an entire string definition from the DOS environment. With the DOS environment defined as just shown, executing the command

```
SET PATH =
```

will clear the value of the PATH variable. If you then execute the SET command, you will see that the PATH variable has been removed:

```
A:\> SET
COMSPEC = A:\COMMAND.COM
PROMPT = $p$g
LASTDRIVE = Z
FILES = \wordproc\wordperf\files
```

The entire path definition has been removed. Asking for the current path at the DOS prompt now will result in a "No Path" message.

The last version of SET will define or modify a DOS environment string. Say you want to replace the path. You can do it in one of two ways: by using the PATH command (see Chapter 6), or by using the SET command. Using the command

```
SET path = \utility
```

would change or create the path definition, as shown here:

```
A:\> set
COMSPEC = A:\COMMAND.COM
PATH = \utility
PROMPT = $p$g
LASTDRIVE = Z
FILES = \wordproc\wordperf\files
```

Notice that the variable name "path" was changed to "PATH," but "utility" stayed in the same case. This is because the case of the DOS environment's character string may have meaning to you and affect how you intend to use it.

Definitions contained in the DOS environment can only be used (that is, actually referred to) by programs or batch files. For example, typing CD FILES at the DOS prompt will not work. You can, however, create a batch file that accesses the DOS environment string FILES:

```
A:\ > COPY CON: TEST.BAT

dir %FILES%
^Z
```

The command dir %FILES% would cause the command processor to look up FILES in the DOS environment and, when found, substitute its definition (in this case, \wordperf\wordproc\files) for %FILES%. Remember, this is *not* available directly from the DOS prompt.

As you can see, the DOS environment can be used by programs and batch files and is a convenient way to pass information to these programs. For example, suppose a program needs a certain file name or path, but for some reason the program does not ask the user directly for this information. (Security reasons often account for this situation.) The path information can be put into the DOS environment, which then can be made inaccessible to the user but readily obtainable from the program.

As you learned in Chapter 16, a leading percent sign indicates a batch variable, while leading and trailing percent signs together indicate a DOS environment string.

CREATING A SECOND COMMAND PROCESSOR

There will be times when it may be useful to create or invoke a second command processor. COMMAND.COM, the first command processor, is invoked when the computer is turned on. It is the part of DOS that takes in, translates, and executes your standard commands. However, invoking a second command processor with COMMAND can give you the ability to execute DOS commands from inside a program (written in BASIC, Pascal, and so on) and then return to that program. This command also allows you to load and customize a command processor that has special functions and abilities or altered command definitions. The COMMAND command has several switches: one to specify the memory residency status of the new command processor, one to name a file to be run on invocation, and one to change the size of the DOS environment.

The general format of this command is

COMMAND *Location Switches*

Location is the optional drive and path where the command processor to be invoked is located. This parameter gives you the ability to prepare and then use a nonstandard or restricted version of a command processor. The *Switches* parameter represents any or all of the optional switches /P, /C *String*, and /E:*xxxxx*.

The new command processor must be named COMMAND.COM as well. Once the new processor is invoked, however, the directory containing the new processor will not become the new root directory. Everything will run as it did before you reassigned the processor, but the processing rules of the new processor will be in effect.

The optional switches define the new processor's environment. The /P (Permanent) switch causes the new command processor to become the primary processor. DOS will assume as initial values all the existing DOS environment variables defined by the prior command processor. You may change any of them, but you will not be able to exit to the previous DOS environment. Without /P, the new DOS environment exists only temporarily, and you can exit from it only by using DOS's EXIT command. This comes in handy if you are using a modified command processor for security reasons.

The /C *String* parameter tells the new processor to execute the command in *String* when it is invoked. If this is left out, the new command processor will be invoked and prompt you for commands. For example, the normal processor that is run every time you start the computer, COMMAND.COM, has a built-in *String* value of AUTOEXEC.BAT, which causes the AUTOEXEC.BAT file to be run when the system starts.

The /E:*xxxxx* parameter can define a new DOS environment size, so that extensive use of the SET command will be permitted. This is only necessary when you begin doing fancy things with your batch files (as you saw in the previous chapter) or your application programs.

For example, suppose you have a command processor in the UTILITY directory, in which the ERASE command has not been defined. You would like 500 bytes of DOS environment, and you would like this processor to supplant the COMMAND.COM processor permanently. The following command will do all of this:

COMMAND \UTILITY /P /E:500

COMMAND is the command name, and UTILITY is the directory containing the new command processor. The /P switch makes the newly active command processor (the secondary command processor) the permanent primary processor, and /E:500 tells the computer to allow half a kilobyte of DOS environmental memory.

Invoking a secondary processor without the /P parameter will cause the DOS environment to appear as in Figure 17.20. You may terminate the secondary processor invoked without /P by using the DOS EXIT command. This will deactivate the secondary DOS environment and reactivate the main processor. On exiting from the secondary processor, the computer will reenter the DOS environment of the first processor. Therefore, any changes you made to the DOS environment variables of the secondary command processor will be lost when you exit to the primary DOS environment.

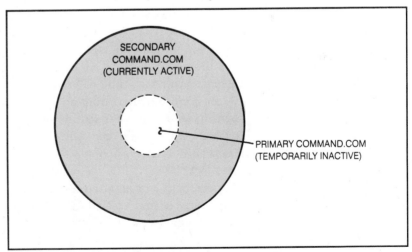

Figure 17.20: Invoking a secondary command processor

While any changes you make to the DOS environment while you are running the secondary processor will be lost when you exit to the primary processor, anything else you have done—such as changing drives and deleting files—will be permanent.

This can come in handy in a number of instances. If necessary, you could even use this command to increase the available DOS environment. Simply reinvoking the original command processor with

```
COMMAND \ /P /E:5000
```

would activate the same processor, but expand the DOS environment to 5000 bytes and make the new processor the primary processor.

You should not invoke a secondary command processor lightly, since each new invocation of COMMAND.COM requires a finite additional amount of physical memory to be allocated. Permanently attaching a secondary processor is better used as a technique for customization or security, rather than for simply expanding the DOS environment.

RUNNING DOS 4 PROGRAMS WITH YOUR OWN DIALOG BOXES

Chapter 6 explains how to run any .EXE, .COM, or .BAT file from the Start Programs menu. As you'll recall, you enter program startup commands (PSCs) to add a new program to a group menu. The sequence of PSC options that you enter during this setup is interpreted and run each time you select the menu choice.

A program-startup command without options is sufficient to run a program, assuming your PATH or APPEND lists are properly set. However, you can also customize your menu choice's dialog box by entering any of the PSC options in the Add or Change Program dialog box when you define the menu choice.

On my system, I added menu choices for the DOS CHKDSK (Check Disk), FORMAT (Format), and LABEL (Label Disk) commands.

For example, look at the customized dialog box in Figure 17.21. This box appeared when I selected Label Disk from my revised DOS Utilities menu. Certain elements of this dialog box are common to all DOS 4 dialog boxes. As you can see in Table 17.2, you can specify your own title, instructions, field names, and the default for the fields.

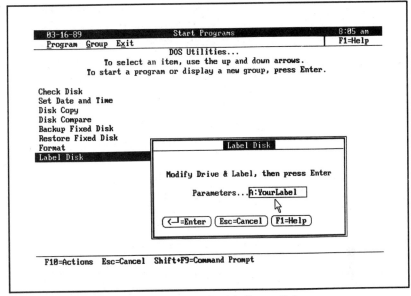

Figure 17.21: Customized dialog box for labeling a disk

Dialog Box Elements	Their Value in Figure 17.21's Dialog Box
The title line	Label Disk
The instruction line	Modify Drive & Label, then press Enter
The prompting message	Parameters...
The entry field contents	A:YourLabel

Table 17.2: Customizable elements in a dialog box

In my example, I specified a meaningful title for the DOS Utilities menu choice and then repeated that title for its dialog box. I also gave instructions to tell the user to enter a drive identifier and a unique disk label in the format shown in the entry field: A:YourLabel.

Table 17.3 contains the extensive set of PSC options that you can use to set up your own dialog box for running a program. I only used

PROGRAM-STARTUP COMMAND OPTIONS	EXPLANATION
[ ]	Displays the default prompt whenever the program is run.
[/T"..."]	Specifies a title line, which can be up to 40 characters and is placed in quotes.
[/I"..."]	Specifies the instruction message, which can be up to 40 characters and is placed in quotes.
[/P"..."]	Specifies the prompting message, which can be up to 20 characters and is placed in quotes.
[/D"..."]	Specifies a default value to display in the entry field. It can be up to 40 characters, and can be typed over by the user.
%n	Specifies a value the user will enter later. This variable must not be enclosed in the standard brackets.
[%n]	Saves for future program use a %n value previously entered in the entry field. It must precede all other options inside the brackets.
[/D"%n"]	Specifies a default value to display in the entry field. This option uses a previously entered value that was saved with the [%n] option.
[/C"%n"]	Saves the %n value entered in the previous run for use as %n again in the current run.
[/L"x"]	Limits the length of the entry field to x, which must be less than 127 (the maximum and default value).

Table 17.3: Options for your program-startup commands (PSCs)

Program-Startup Command Options	Explanation
[/R]	Erases the default values in the entry field when the first key pressed by the user is not a cursor-movement key (e.g. an arrow or the Tab key).
[/M"e"]	Checks that all file names entered refer to existing files before processing the option sequence.
[/F"..."]	Ensures that a file name that is entered inside the quotes refers to an existing file before completing the command. If it does not exist, a beep sounds and the dialog box is redisplayed.
/#	Substitutes the drive letter from which the DOS shell started into the option sequence at this point. This option must be entered outside the brackets.
/@	Substitutes the path from the root directory of the DOS shell drive into the option sequence at this point.

Table 17.3: Options for your program-startup commands (PSCs) (continued)

five of these options to create the dialog box shown in Figure 17.21. Using the Change Program dialog box, I entered these five options after LABEL in the Commands field. (You can see the beginning of the PSC sequence in Figure 17.22.) All options in a PSC must be enclosed in a single pair of brackets. My complete PSC entry is the following:

```
LABEL [/T"Label Disk" /P"Parameters..." /L"13"
/I"Modify Drive & Label, then press Enter"
/D"A:YourLabel"]
```

Don't write all your PSCs in at once. Enter one or two, then test them before entering other PSCs. This makes it easier to identify and solve any problems.

When you first begin to create your own dialog boxes, don't try to enter all the PSC options at once. First, add an entry with one or two optional entries. Make sure they work first, then add other options. This is a technique often used in programming. It minimizes the number of

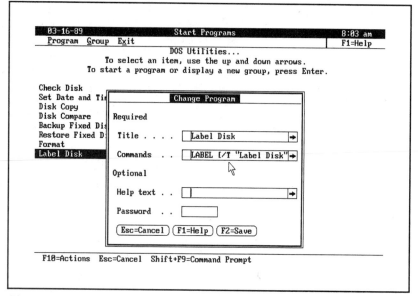

Figure 17.22: Customizing your own utility program dialog box

errors that can creep in and maximizes your ability to quickly identify any resulting problems. Instead of searching through lists of PSC options to find the error, you only have to study one or two.

SUMMARY

You have now mastered some of the most advanced features of DOS. The sophisticated capabilities you've seen in this chapter often lie buried under unreadable documentation. In this chapter, however, you've seen how these advanced features can be used to your advantage.

- The ATTRIB command gives you complete control over the file attributes that govern whether the file can be erased, modified, or backed up.

- Files and entire disks that have become physically damaged can often be recovered with the RECOVER command.

- You can upgrade backups and software easily and quickly by using the REPLACE command.

- Entire disk drives can be seen as only a single directory branch of another disk structure by using the JOIN command.

- The SUBST command allows you to treat an entire directory branch as a separate and unique (but fictitious) disk drive. This is useful with older programs that don't allow directory path references. The ASSIGN command is also useful for hard-coded programs; it lets you reroute disk references.

- Speedier disk access can be obtained with DOS 3.3 and DOS 4's FASTOPEN command, which keeps the disk locations of recently used files and directories in memory. DOS 4 users can also use the FASTOPEN command to create memory caches for file data.

- You can create sophisticated application environments with the SET command, which controls the creation and modification of DOS environment string variables.

- You can exercise control over the command processor itself by invoking a secondary processor with the COMMAND command. This allows unique security and customization possibilities.

- In DOS 4, you can set up your own Start Programs entries and customize the appearance and processing of your dialog boxes.

You now have a complete picture of DOS, and you can see that it is a very useful operating system. However, software developers have created a vast body of new software designed to extend and enhance the power of DOS. The next chapter presents the best examples of add-on and add-in software that you should consider acquiring to make even more effective use of your DOS software.

EXTENDING THE POWER
OF DOS

CHAPTER 18

MICROSOFT SUPPLIES MANY USEFUL PROGRAMS
with your DOS; as with all things, however, there is still room for
improvement. For instance, when you back up hard disks, DOS does
not tell you how many diskettes you will need. In this chapter, you will
learn about a program that provides this feature, and about other programs that "fill the gaps" in DOS's operations.

You will also learn about a number of programs that provide functionality well beyond the current scope of DOS. For example, different
computers often have different disk formats, and different word processors often have different internal file-storage formats. Offices with
several computers and different types of word processors can benefit
from the special-purpose *conversion utilities* that work with DOS.

Because they provide you with added utility features, these programs
are usually known as *utility programs*. Some utility programs are similar to
the external (disk-resident) commands of DOS, like CHKDSK or
FORMAT. You can execute them whenever you choose, as long as
they are accessible in the current directory or on the path. They require
a certain amount of memory to run, but they release it back to DOS
when they are done. Some people refer to these disk-resident enhancement programs as *add-on* utilities.

Other utility programs are similar to the internal commands of
DOS, like DIR or ERASE. This second type of utility is called a
memory-resident or *terminate-and-stay-resident* (*TSR*) program. A memory-
resident program is loaded from disk only once as part of its required
setup phase. It is read into a certain area of memory that will not be
used later by any other program. It then terminates, but stays resident for rapid activation at some later time. Some people refer to
these memory-resident programs as *add-in* utilities.

DOS 4 users must make sure that they purchase third-party utility programs that are compatible with DOS 4. Because of internal design differences, some utilities will work with DOS 4 only, while others will only work with earlier versions of DOS.

Ambitious utility software vendors will always create innova-tive software solutions to hardware problems and software oversights. However, you may not learn of such a product unless the vendor also possesses sufficient marketing skills.

Initiate your memory-resident (TSR) programs before intitating the DOS-SHELL. Otherwise, your system may crash.

Memory-resident
utility programs are
fast; however, the cost for
this responsiveness is that
some of your physical
memory must be allocated
to them. That reduces the
amount remaining for
your main programs and
other memory-resident
software.

Most memory-resident software will do nothing—not even offer a command prompt—until you type a unique key combination, called a *hot key*, to call it into action. For instance, SideKick leaps into action when you press the Ctrl-Alt key combination. Keyworks presents its own menu of options when you summon it with the gray Plus key (usually on the right side of most keyboards). The appealing aspect of these memory-resident programs is that their complete capabilities are instantaneously available when you need them, even during the execution of another program.

In some cases, you can make more than one memory-resident program available simultaneously. If you do load one or more memory-resident programs, however, you should use the CHKDSK command afterwards to see if enough memory is still free to run your main application program.

Back up your data
files before running
any new memory-
resident utility with
existing software to pro-
tect yourself from an
unexpected memory
conflict or a system crash.

Some memory-resident programs and main application programs will not work together, because each will try to use the same area of memory. This can result in many problems, from the memory-resident program or main program simply not working correctly, to having to reboot a frozen system, to having your entire hard disk erased. Check the documentation before you begin to be sure there are no incompatibilities with your current software.

Thousands of utility programs are available on the market today; advertisements for such products appear in the backs of all major PC-oriented magazines. In this chapter you will see how some programs improve the performance of hard disks, while others speed up your keyboard and screen. You'll see utilities designed to enhance your printed output, to organize your desktop functions, and to make hard-disk file management easier. This chapter only selects a few examples in the most useful categories of utility programs; keep in mind that there are many excellent alternatives to the programs presented here.

IMPROVING YOUR HARD-DISK MANAGEMENT

Managing many directories on a hard disk can require great effort and care. However, a class of utility programs can relieve your burdens. In this section, you'll look at Q-DOS II, a hard-disk file manager; PreCursor, a hard-disk menu system; the Norton Utilities, a wide-ranging file and directory support tool; and Back-It, a powerful substitute for DOS's BACKUP and RESTORE commands.

MANAGING YOUR FILES
AND DIRECTORIES WITH Q-DOS II

Q-DOS II makes standard DOS features much easier to use. Many of DOS's functions, such as formatting disks, displaying directories, and listing and copying files, are implemented in Q-DOS II. Those commands that are not directly available in DOS can be executed easily from within Q-DOS II. Figure 18.1 shows the main menu of Q-DOS II.

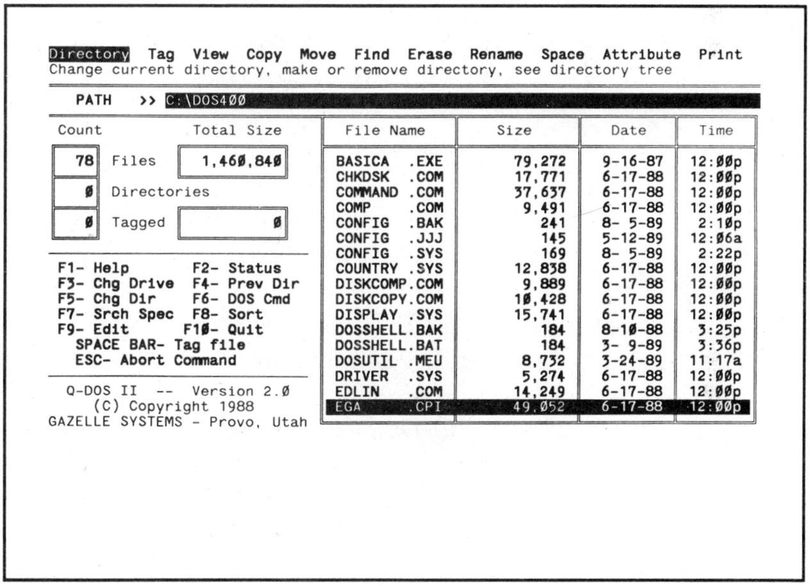

```
 Directory  Tag  View  Copy  Move  Find  Erase  Rename  Space  Attribute  Print
 Change current directory, make or remove directory, see directory tree

     PATH   >>  C:\DOS400

   Count          Total Size        File Name      Size       Date       Time

    78   Files      1,460,840       BASICA  .EXE    79,272    9-16-87    12:00p
                                    CHKDSK  .COM    17,771    6-17-88    12:00p
     0   Directories                COMMAND .COM    37,637    6-17-88    12:00p
                                    COMP    .COM     9,491    6-17-88    12:00p
     0   Tagged          0          CONFIG  .BAK       241    8- 5-89     2:10p
                                    CONFIG  .JJJ       145    5-12-89    12:06a
                                    CONFIG  .SYS       169    8- 5-89     2:22p
  F1- Help       F2- Status         COUNTRY .SYS    12,838    6-17-88    12:00p
  F3- Chg Drive  F4- Prev Dir       DISKCOMP.COM     9,889    6-17-88    12:00p
  F5- Chg Dir    F6- DOS Cmd        DISKCOPY.COM    10,428    6-17-88    12:00p
  F7- Srch Spec  F8- Sort           DISPLAY .SYS    15,741    6-17-88    12:00p
  F9- Edit       F10- Quit          DOSSHELL.BAK       184    8-10-88     3:25p
    SPACE BAR- Tag file             DOSSHELL.BAT       184    3- 9-89     3:36p
    ESC- Abort Command              DOSUTIL .MEU     8,732    3-24-89    11:17a
                                    DRIVER  .SYS     5,274    6-17-88    12:00p
   Q-DOS II  --  Version 2.0        EDLIN   .COM    14,249    6-17-88    12:00p
      (C) Copyright 1988            EGA     .CPI    49,052    6-17-88    12:00p
 GAZELLE SYSTEMS - Provo, Utah
```

Figure 18.1: Q-DOS II's main menu

As you can see from the main menu line at the top of Figure 18.1, Q-DOS II offers you much more convenience in implementing many standard DOS commands. For example, instead of having to type a complete COPY command, specifying file names and path names, you use a more visual technique. You *tag,* or graphically select, which directories and files you want copied and where they should be copied to. You can easily see directories by moving along the directory tree (see Figure 18.2) and pressing Return, which will bring up a sorted list of files that reside in the selected directory.

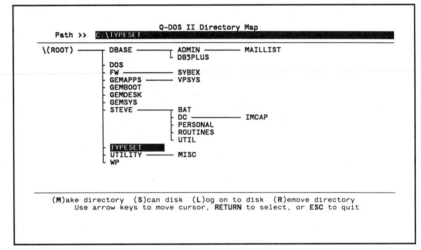

Figure 18.2: Q-DOS II's graphic representation

You can sort directory entries by anything on the entry's line, such as the date or extension. Although you see the files sorted in the Q-DOS II directory window, they will not be physically rearranged on the disk. Although the screens may appear crowded at first glance, they are quite comfortable in actual use.

Q-DOS II is available from

> Gazelle Systems
> 42 North University Avenue, Suite 10
> Provo, Utah 84601
> (800) 233-0383
> (801) 377-1288

SETTING UP MENU SYSTEMS WITH PRECURSOR

A menu program enables you to predefine paths and program names, and to present to a user a simple and familiar list of choices.

No commands need be entered at the DOS prompt, since all required DOS commands will have been incorporated into the menu system setup.

Some users prefer to enter commands at the DOS prompt because they only run one simple application, and they are more comfortable entering individual commands. Others feel that a menu system is too slow or restrictive, or that they simply cannot give up the memory required for the menu program itself. For most users, however, understanding and using DOS at the command level is unnecessary. This is especially true if the operations performed are repetitive and require little variation.

If the set of programs you run on your machine is fairly constant, a menu program can be a definite convenience. It can save you the trouble of changing directories or remembering where a particular program is located on your hard disk. This is particularly convenient in a large office environment, where it may not be feasible to teach all users enough about DOS to enable them to get on with their jobs. A menu system can be set up once by a knowledgeable user, leaving only a simple, one-key selection for individual users.

PreCursor is an excellent menu program. Beyond offering a menu system, it provides most of the key DOS functions on its own special DOS menu. You can do most things from PreCursor that you can do from DOS, without having to remember or know as much about formats and restrictions. The main menu of PreCursor is very cleanly laid out, and shows you exactly what you can do and where to go (see Figure 18.3).

The program is organized into menus and submenus. You can categorize your programs, placing them on different menus by function. By choosing an option, you can execute a DOS program, a batch file, or a DOS command, or you can go to another menu of predetermined choices. The DOS function keys are used to obtain special PreCursor services, such as creating and editing menu screens, initializing program parameters, and setting up passwords (see Figure 18.4).

Menu systems can be set up for a large number of users, and access can be restricted by a powerful password mechanism. Separate passwords can be created for each individual menu choice, as well as for entire menus.

PreCursor is available from

The Aldridge Company
2500 City West Boulevard, Suite 575
Houston, Texas 77042
(713) 953-1940

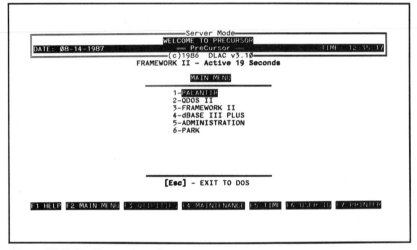

Figure 18.3: PreCursor's main menu

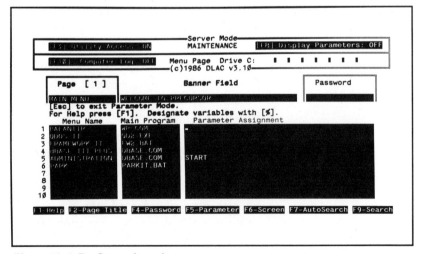

Figure 18.4: PreCursor's maintenance menu

INVESTIGATING DISK CONTENTS WITH THE NORTON UTILITIES

The Norton Utilities is a group of programs designed to increase your control over the data that is actually stored on your disk. For example, you can look at specific parts of the disk and modify the data you find there. You can also recover files that have been accidentally erased, and even recover complete hard disks that have been formatted. Utilities of this kind come in very handy when you've made a major blunder. Even if things are going smoothly, the Norton Utilities can provide you with a greater understanding of how your system is set up, as well as an insider's glimpse into previously inaccessible disk files.

The latest version of the Norton Utilities features a menu-driven system. The system shows you various screens of information. For example, you can see a screen of all the files on the disk, including hidden files, system files, and those that have been deleted but not yet overwritten since their deletion. You can change the attributes of any file, controlling even more attributes than you can with the ATTRIB command in DOS. You are even able to change any individual byte in any file anywhere on the disk. All of this can be displayed when you request file information. For the technical user, detailed data about specific files and the hard disk as a whole is also available on another screen choice.

Included in the Norton Utilities are many individual utility programs that are both easy in form and powerful in function (see Table 18.1). For example, the DS (Directory Sort) program will first display your current directory on the screen. You can then specify how you want to sort the directory's files, using several levels of sorting. The sorted directory is then displayed, and you have your choice of resorting it differently or writing it to the disk.

The main hub of the utilities is the NI (Norton Integrator) program. This program brings information about all of the other Norton programs onto one screen, where you can choose which program to execute. Each program, when highlighted, has a format and functional description displayed on the right side of the screen. At the bottom of the screen is a command line that changes whenever you highlight a different program. It allows you to enter parameters for a

UTILITY NAME	PROGRAM DESCRIPTION
ASK	Creates interactive batch files
BEEP	Controls the computer's speaker
DS	Sorts a directory's file names
DT	Tests disks for physical errors
FA	Sets, resets, and scans file attributes
FF	Finds disk files by name
FI	Assigns and retrieves file comments
FR	Recovers an accidentally formatted hard disk
FS	Lists and totals file sizes
LD	Creates a graphic view of directory structure
LP	Prints files with line numbers and headers
NCD	Allows fast directory navigation
NI	Integrates all utilities for easy selection
NU	Allows detailed disk and file exploration
QU	Allows quick unerase capability
SA	Sets screen colors and attributes
SD	Reorganizes disks to remove fragmentation
SI	Reports system information
TM	Displays time and offers stopwatch capability
TS	Searches text in files and disks
UD	Recovers removed directories
VL	Views, adds, removes, or changes disk labels
WIPEFILE	Completely blanks out file contents
WIPEDISK	Completely blanks out disk contents

Table 18.1: The Norton Utilities, Advanced Edition (4.0)

specific command. The right half of the screen explains the high-lighted command and its possible switches (see Figure 18.5).

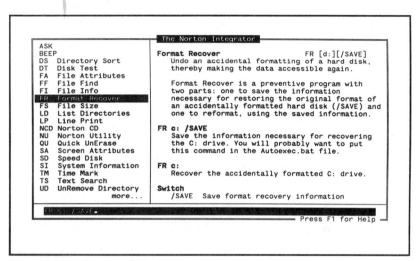

```
                              ┌─ The Norton Integrator ─┐
  ASK
  BEEP                        Format Recover              FR [d:][/SAVE]
  DS   Directory Sort          Undo an accidental formatting of a hard disk,
  DT   Disk Test               thereby making the data accessible again.
  FA   File Attributes
  FF   File Find               Format Recover is a preventive program with
  FI   File Info               two parts: one to save the information
  FR   Format Recover          necessary for restoring the original format of
  FS   File Size               an accidentally formatted hard disk (/SAVE) and
  LD   List Directories        one to reformat, using the saved information.
  LP   Line Print
  NCD  Norton CD              FR c: /SAVE
  NU   Norton Utility          Save the information necessary for recovering
  QU   Quick UnErase           the C: drive. You will probably want to put
  SA   Screen Attributes       this command in the Autoexec.bat file.
  SD   Speed Disk
  SI   System Information     FR c:
  TM   Time Mark               Recover the accidentally formatted C: drive.
  TS   Text Search
  UD   UnRemove Directory     Switch
              more...          /SAVE   Save format recovery information

  ┌ FR c: /SAVE ──────────┐
                                                         Press F1 for Help
```

Figure 18.5: The Norton Integrator menu

The Norton Utilities are available from

Peter Norton Computing, Inc.
2210 Wilshire Boulevard
Santa Monica, California 90403
(213) 453-2361

MAKING BACKUPS WITH BACK-IT

Backups can sometimes get very complicated, especially if you don't want or need to back up an entire disk. They can also take a long time and can be subject to simple mistakes, such as inserting the wrong diskette or forgetting a group of files. Back-It provides a way to back up and restore files easily on your hard disk. You can use it in place of DOS's BACKUP and RESTORE commands.

Back-It's main menu (see Figure 18.6) shows you a well-grouped approach to its chores. The top line provides all desired options. When you are ready to back up, Back-It lets you choose exactly which directories to back up by showing you the directory tree and letting you move around in it, tagging the directories you want or don't want backed up.

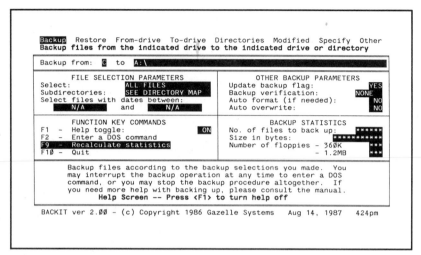

Figure 18.6: Back-It's main menu

The program is very easy to use. It will even tell you how many diskettes you will need for the backup. You move around the menu screen by using the arrow keys. You can select different functions of the program from the menu bar at the top of the screen, and then modify the parameters that accompany a certain function on the main screen. Back-It is fast and truly user-friendly, offering you many additional options such as different standard backup sets, variable levels of data verification, and automatic formatting of target diskettes.

Back-It is available from

> Gazelle Systems
> 42 North University Avenue, Suite 10
> Provo, Utah 84601
> (800) 233-0383
> (801) 377-1288

SPEEDING UP YOUR HARD DISK

If you have a hard-disk system, the efficient operation of the hard disk is crucial to the efficient use of your entire computer system. As the number of files on your hard disk gets larger, the time involved to access a file increases, slowing down your system. There are several reasons for this slowdown.

As you know, when DOS writes a file on the disk, it writes it in groups of sectors called clusters. The number of 512-byte sectors in each cluster does vary by the version of DOS you are using, but the principle of cluster writing creates the speed problem. As an example, let's say that you write a first file to disk, and it uses up a full cluster. Then you write another file to the disk, and it uses up the next (contiguous) cluster. Your disk looks like this:

Cluster	Contents
1	File 1 (first cluster of file 1)
2	File 2 (first cluster of file 2)

Then you go back and double the size of the first file, perhaps by expanding a database or adding a new page of text with your word processor; you then save it again.

Instead of pushing the second file up to make room for the two clusters of the first file, DOS saves the additional information for the first file in cluster 3, leaving cluster 2, which contains the second file, untouched. If you were to expand the second file next, and then add a third file, the disk would look like this:

Cluster	Contents
1	File 1 (first cluster of file 1)
2	File 2 (first cluster of file 2)
3	File 1 (second cluster of file 1)
4	File 2 (second cluster of file 2)
5	File 2 (third cluster of file 2)
6	File 3 (first cluster of file 3)
.	.
.	.
.	.

As you can see, files get broken up as you work on them. The time it takes to move the disk's read/write head can increase dramatically as the number of your files increases and as your files become more and more fragmented. *Fragmentation* occurs when pieces of the same file are stored in nonadjacent clusters on a disk. As this condition evolves, the first half of a file could be on an outside track, whereas the second half could be on an inside track. Head movement across the disk would take a lot more time than it would with sequential clusters.

Reducing or eliminating fragmentation speeds up the disk. The way to do this is to go through the whole disk and rearrange the clusters so that all clusters for every file are contiguous. With a great deal of effort, you can actually do this yourself. All you need to do is to copy all files in all directories onto backup disks, reformat the entire disk, and then rewrite the files back onto the disk. An easier way is to buy VOPT, a utility described in this section.

A less-obvious solution is to cut the disk-access speed. This relieves the symptoms but does not really solve the problem. The memory-resident program Lightning will actually remember disk sector data every time it is used, so that continued access to the same sector will, instead of accessing the disk drive, access a memory *cache* that already has the data in it. In DOS 4, you can simply use the FASTOPEN command with its *Buf* parameter to do the same thing (see Chapter 17). This is much faster than accessing the disk, but does cost you a certain amount of memory for both the Lightning program and the memory cache.

RAPID FILE REORGANIZATION WITH VOPT

VOPT is an interesting package of utilities from Golden Bow Systems. It features a hard-disk optimizer that can optimize a badly fragmented disk in only a few minutes. It is so fast that it can be used in your AUTOEXEC.BAT file to optimize the disk every time you boot up; this takes only a few seconds.

The VOPT program itself is very easy to use: just issue the VOPT command at the prompt, and you have started. First the program uses its own version of CHKDSK to make sure there are no lost clusters or disk errors. Should there be, VOPT will end and you will be instructed to use the DOS command CHKDSK/F to correct the problem. Once this is done, or if no errors are found, optimization is started. Figure 18.7 shows a map of the disk space before optimizing, created by another utility program (VMAP) included on the VOPT diskette.

File sizes and numbers always seem to expand to fill whatever size hard disk you are using. Be sure you take the time to delete older files or early versions of files regularly.

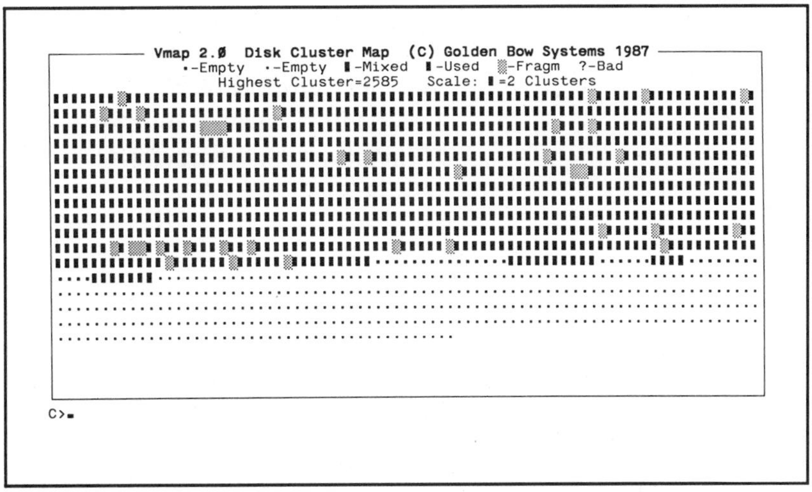

Figure 18.7: VMAP disk-space display before optimizing

The probability of a utility package containing extra utility programs is directly proportional to the pizzazz and usefulness of its first utility.

VOPT itself displays a version of this disk map, which changes during the optimization process. When the process is complete, you are shown statistics about the overall effort, as shown in Figure 18.8. The cluster display is more colorful than necessary, but flair and drama are always attractive in a good program.

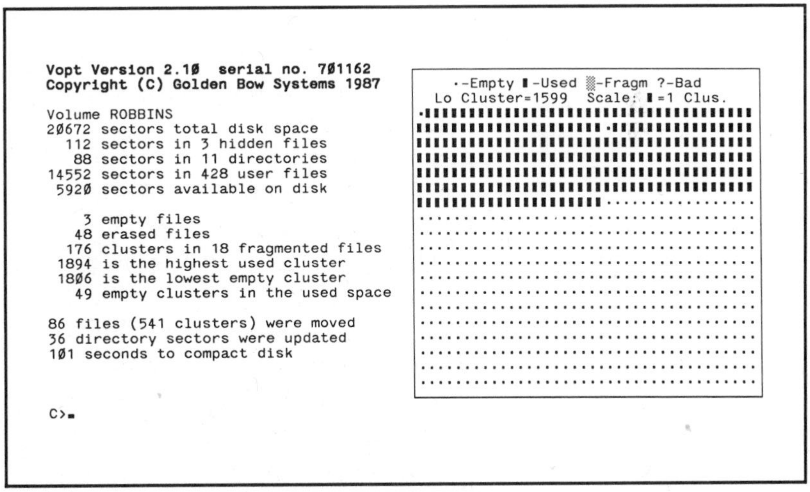

Figure 18.8: VOPT display after optimizing

VOPT is available from

Golden Bow Systems
2870 Fifth Avenue, Suite 201
San Diego, California 92103
(619) 298-9349

INSTALLING A MEMORY CACHE WITH LIGHTNING

The Lightning program remembers the information stored in disk sectors. For example, you may need to access file information contained in disk sectors 1 and 2. The actual data stored in the sectors is placed in a memory buffer, or cache. If you need to access the data again, Lightning locates it in memory, eliminating the need for DOS to access the disk again.

Lightning must be executed only once at the command prompt (or from a batch file), along with all parameters. It then becomes memory-resident, the memory cache is set up, and no further intervention on your part is required. It uses a default memory cache of 60K, but you can expand that (even to extended memory, if it exists in your system). Lightning can also display statistics on speed improvement, by disk, in your system.

Lightning is available from

The Personal Computer Support Group
4540 Belt Way
Dallas, Texas 75244
(214) 351-0564

MAKING ROOM WITHOUT LOSING DATA

Another problem with disks of all sizes is that they can run out of space. This is especially true if you use large databases or manage hundreds or thousands of files. A creative solution to the problem of space availability is to shrink your existing files down to a much smaller size. This is sometimes called *data compression*. When you need to use the files, you can expand them back to their normal size and then compress them again when you're through. This provides extra disk space, and your files are available for use when necessary. The utility program Squish provides this capability for your system.

COMPRESSING DATA WITH SQUISH

Squish is one of those programs that may, with its first use, save you hundreds of dollars in the cost of purchasing a new disk, not to mention reducing the time it takes to create backup diskettes. Files stored by DOS on a disk are usually stored with a lot of unused space. For example, all the blank characters and lines in your word-processing files, and all those empty fields in your database files, take up a lot of unnecessary disk space. In other words, many files are stored inefficiently, taking up more room than is needed on both your hard disk and on your backup diskettes.

To get around this, Squish "runs interference" between your disk drive and DOS. When you save a file, Squish intercepts the request, compressing the file into the least amount of space possible, and then writes the "squished" file to disk. For example, a single Pascal program that originally takes up over 36K can be squished to less than 27K, an improvement of 25 percent.

Squish runs invisibly—that is, you do not know that it is running, but it is there. It has a memory-resident portion (about 40K), which is activated not by a hot key, but by any request to DOS for a task requiring disk access. Squish converts files automatically when you access them; if you save a file, it will be squished automatically. You will never see anything to indicate that it has been compressed except that it will take up less space than it normally would.

To "unsquish" a file, just load it in as usual. Squish will intercept the load command, get the file, decompress it, and send it on to your application. It does all of this in memory, so you don't need to budget extra disk space for decompressed files. Again, there will be no indication that the file is being unsquished, except that it may take slightly longer to load than usual.

Programs that improve system performance typically trade speed for space; that is, if the utility improves speed, you usually have to give up memory space for this improvement. On the other hand, if the utility improves space usage, you usually have to give up operational speed to obtain that benefit.

You can also run Squish for existing files stored on your disk. You may want to do this for a few large files only. When memory-resident, however, Squish can tell the difference between a squished and an unsquished file.

Squish is available from

SunDog Software Corporation
264 Court Street
Brooklyn, New York 11231
(718) 855-9141

ENHANCING YOUR CONSOLE'S POWER

Your console is the most important part of your computer system in that it is the means by which you control the system and by which the system responds to you. Should the keyboard not "feel" right to you, or should you be uncomfortable with its setup or behavior (mushy keys, poor key layout, and so on), it will influence the way you use your system and the amount of time you spend on it. Therefore, it is important that you feel comfortable with the keyboard and the display.

There are many ways to customize the keyboard, making it much more powerful. This means that you can redefine the keys so that more can be done from the keyboard. For example, by using the Keyworks program, you can redefine any key on your keyboard to actually type a different character, word, command, sentence, or paragraph. When you redefine a key into some sort of an instruction set, such as redefining the F3 key to type DIR A: and press Return, you have created your own keyboard macro. (Remember, a macro is a set of instructions that are executed at once, whether the instructions are stored in memory or in a file on the disk.)

Another utility acts on your display. Scroll & Recall gives you the ability to take a second look at any data that has been displayed for you in a line-by-line manner, but has since scrolled off the screen. How many times have you wanted to go backwards to see something that scrolled too quickly off the screen? Or how often have you run a long program that produced results that you didn't write down, and that you'd like to see again?

EXTENDING KEYBOARD POWER WITH KEYWORKS

In many application programs, long sequences of keystrokes are often needed to accomplish something. For instance, many commercial database services require you to connect your computer to theirs through a dial-up telephone connection. You may have to sign on to their computer, enter a password, and then pass through five different levels of menus just to read some news. The keystrokes might be LOGON JUDD 123456 3 2 1 4 5 READ #1. Typing this out every time is a real chore.

To alleviate this, programs like Keyworks have been written to enhance the keyboard by giving key combinations like Alt-F, which normally doesn't do anything, the ability to substitute for a string of keystrokes. By using one of these programs, you can even represent a whole paragraph with one key, and then whenever you hit that key, the paragraph will appear. If you use WordStar or any other program that requires a series of keystrokes to implement certain features, this type of program is for you.

Keyworks is a keyboard macro program with extraordinary versatility. It actually includes a complete programming language. One of the many features of this memory-resident program allows you to directly edit the macros that you have defined. When you select this option, Keyworks goes into full-screen mode, similar to many word processors, allowing you to edit the macros directly. Cut and paste capabilities allow you to create new, complex macros from old ones.

Several other useful capabilities come with Keyworks, such as a way to encrypt confidential disk files for security purposes. Most essential DOS features are implemented as well, enabling you to reproduce DOS commands in a *pop-up* display while other programs are running. (In a pop-up display, all of the screen's contents appear instantaneously, instead of appearing line-by-line as they are written to the screen.) All of Keyworks's features are available from a pop-up system of menus.

Keyworks's menu system is very accessible. You can also use Keyworks to set up your own system of menus and help screens. Although it does take a bit more work than using the PreCursor utility described earlier, Keyworks has more potential power because of its macro language, which is as powerful as many high-level programming languages and allows decision making, looping, and flow-of-control commands.

Keyworks is available from

The Alpha Software Corporation
1 North Avenue
Burlington, Massachusetts 01803
(617) 229-2924

RECALLING FORMER SCREEN OUTPUT WITH SCROLL & RECALL

Scroll & Recall recalls past commands issued at the DOS prompt or other program prompts. It also remembers a variable number of lines that have been shown on the screen but that have been scrolled off the screen. This comes in handy when you are issuing a lot of DOS commands and need to see the exact format of an earlier command. Also, if you need to look back at a computer session or see part of a listing or directory that has scrolled off the screen, this program is for you.

Scroll & Recall is available from

Opt-Tech Data Processing
P.O. Box 678
Zephr Cove, NV 89448
(702) 588-3737

REISSUING PREVIOUS DOS COMMANDS WITH RECOMM

Many commands you issue in DOS are repetitions of commands you issued earlier in the same session. Sometimes you issue the same command several times; other times, you issue a similar command with only minor variations. ReComm is a utility that can instantaneously call back to the DOS prompt any command issued previously. It even saves and recalls command and text sequences from within many application programs.

ReComm has a built-in line editor, so you can use the cursor keys to make any desired edits to the recalled command prior to reissuing it. This means that you can easily correct errors in the last issued DOS command as well. (You merely press Return to reissue the command.)

All of ReComm's activities occur at the bottom of the screen when you call the screen up with a redefinable hot key. Help is also available at the touch of the usual F1 key (see Figure 18.9). Active screens are saved and restored after ReComm has completed its operations.

```
┌─────────────────────────── ReComm Commands ───────────────────────────┐
│ ┌─────────────────────────────────┬────────────────────────────────┐ │
│ │         Cursor Movement         │            Delete              │ │
│ ├─────────────────────────────────┼────────────────────────────────┤ │
│ │ Left arrow       = Left one char│ Del      = Character under cursor│ │
│ │ Right arrow      = Right one char│ Bksp     = Character left of cursor│ │
│ │ Ctrl-left arrow  = Left one word │ Ctrl-Home = To beginning of command│ │
│ │ Ctrl-right arrow = Right one word│ Ctrl-End = To end of command    │ │
│ │ Home             = Start of command                               │ │
│ │ End              = End of command                                 │ │
│ ├─────────────────────────────────┼────────────────────────────────┤ │
│ │         Buffer Control          │            Other               │ │
│ ├─────────────────────────────────┼────────────────────────────────┤ │
│ │ PgUp        = Display previous command│ Enter = Execute displayed command│ │
│ │ PgDn        = Display next command    │ Esc   = Cancel, return to program│ │
│ │ Ctrl-PgUp   = Delete displayed command│ Ins   = Turn insert mode on/off │ │
│ │ Ctrl-PgDn   = Delete all buffer cmds  │ F1    = Turn Help on/off        │ │
│ ├─────────────────────────────────┴────────────────────────────────┤ │
│ │         Alt-=    Enables/disables command capture                 │ │
│ └───────────────────────────────────────────────────────────────────┘ │
│ ┌───────────────────────────────────────────────────────────────────┐ │
│ │ ReComm Version 1.Ø       Computer Options        Press F1 for Help │ │
│ ├───────────────────────────────────────────────────────────────────┤ │
│ │ CHKDSK A: /F                                                       │ │
│ └───────────────────────────────────────────────────────────────────┘ │
└─────────────────────────────────────────────────────────────────────────┘
```

Figure 18.9: ReComm's activity screen with help display

ReComm is available from

Computer Options
198 Amherst Avenue
Berkeley, California 94708
(415) 525-5033

DRESSING UP YOUR PRINTED OUTPUT

So far in this chapter you have seen how you can enhance the console and and disk drives by means of utility programs. You can also enhance your printer. Since it generates the physical output of the work you do, it is very useful to have additional control over it.

For example, if you have a large spreadsheet that stretches over 200 columns and you have only a 9-inch wide printer, you have a problem. The two programs listed here, however, will print your spreadsheet sideways, so it can be as wide as you wish. The Printworks program also allows you to change character sets, styles, fonts, and sizes, which is important if you need to make signs or overhead transparencies, or if you just want to vary the appearance of your typed text.

PRINTING WIDE OUTPUT WITH SIDEWAYS

You may deal with databases containing many fields or with spreadsheets containing many columns. The usual solution to printing all the information is to carefully extract for printing specific portions of the database or spreadsheet, and then tape the printed pieces together.

Sideways is perhaps the best-known program for solving the wide-output problem. This utility prints the extremely wide output sideways on the printed page. In other words, it rotates the output by 90 degrees, giving a whole new sequence of control commands to your printer. This solution usually is reserved for use on dot-matrix printers with continuous-feed paper.

Sideways is available from

Funk Software
22 Third Street
Cambridge, Massachusetts 02142
(617) 497-6339

MODIFYING TYPE SIZES AND STYLES WITH PRINTWORKS

Printworks is another program that allows sideways printing. It also allows you to control a wide range of other printing features. Many printers have built-in hardware that can produce condensed, boldface, and wide characters. Some can also print pica, elite, and even proportionally spaced output characters.

Printworks gives you a full-screen display that presents all the possibilities for customizing your printer. After a required installation phase, you merely select the options you want for your printed output. With Printworks you can also generate your own special fonts and characters, including graphics, foreign, or special characters not available on your keyboard.

Printworks is available from

Phoenix Technologies, LTD.
6600 Kalanianaole Highway
Honolulu, Hawaii 96825
(808) 396-6368

CONVERTING FILE AND DISK FORMATS

There are many programs available that perform the same task—for example, there are many word-processing programs. However, a file from one word processor cannot be moved directly into another word processor, because most word processors make extensive use of special control codes to perform their text formatting. The file must first be converted to a format that the new word processor can understand. Many conversion programs perform this function, although their ability is limited to converting to or from only a very few programs.

Like word processors, some computer systems are not compatible. To load a disk from one operating system into another (from CP/M to DOS, for example, or from DOS to UNIX), you must convert the entire contents of the disk to a format acceptable to the other system. Each operating system writes its files in a certain way at certain places on a disk; in addition, different operating systems use different storage and formatting schemes.

For example, you may be using 5¼'' diskettes, but their different layouts inhibit compatibility. In other cases, you may even be using the same operating system (such as DOS) but have switched to a different machine (from an IBM PC/AT to a Personal System/2, for example). One machine might use 3½'' diskettes, while the other machine might use 5¼'' diskettes. Both can use identical application programs and the same version of DOS, but the data must be converted from one diskette format to another. The following programs offer just this kind of service.

CHANGING DISK SIZES WITH BROOKLYN BRIDGE

The Brooklyn Bridge utility package offers two separate programs. One program runs on a computer with 3½'' diskettes, while the other program runs on a computer with 5¼'' diskettes. This utility package is similar to a communications program, but its purpose is more focused: it allows you to specify file names to be transferred between two different disk drives.

Brooklyn Bridge transfers the specified files between machines by means of cables connecting the required serial ports on each machine. This is an inexpensive and creative solution to the problem of hardware incompatibility.

Brooklyn Bridge is available from

White Crane Systems
6889 Peachtree Ind. Boulevard, Suite 150
Norcross, Georgia 30092
(404) 394-3119

READING DIFFERENT MACHINE FORMATS WITH XENOCOPY-PC

XenoCopy-PC converts the diskette formats of files from various operating system formats. It is no longer as necessary for DOS users as it once was, since fewer and fewer offices have multiple machines with incompatible operating systems. However, if your office still has an old TeleVideo running a CP/M word processor, and various newer IBMs and compatibles running the same word processor, XenoCopy-PC is the right package to own.

XenoCopy-PC pays for itself every time a file written on a TeleVideo must be used by someone using a differently formatted IBM diskette on his or her machine. It is very easy to use, offering a simple menu-selection procedure to specify each of the two incompatible diskette formats.

XenoCopy-PC is available from

XenoSoft
2210 Sixth Street
Berkeley, California 94710
(415) 525-3113

REWRITING WORD-PROCESSING FORMATS WITH R-DOC/X

R-Doc/X is a very handy program to have around when one or more people are using two or more word processors. It converts word-processing files to different formats for use by other word processors. If your office has several people using different word processors, you don't necessarily have to force them to select one for consistency. You also don't have to sacrifice the required time and effort to learn a new word-processing system if you are already comfortable with your current one. Instead, you can just convert it to someone else's word-processing format; they will be able to work on the file as well.

R-Doc/X does a pretty good job of converting files, but there are a few things it cannot understand and hence will not convert properly. Some of these are headers and footers, multicolumn documents, and specific types of tab stops. Therefore, if one of your word processors uses these, you should make sure the conversion will be sufficient before you actually select this program.

R-Doc/X is available from

Advanced Computer Innovations
30 Burncoat Way
Pittsford NY 14534-2216
(716) 454-3188

ORGANIZING YOUR WORK

The best thing to have when you work is organization. If you spend a lot of time on the computer, you know how much of a chore keeping manual records (such as a date book or a phone directory) can become. Having to swing around and look at a clock is also a chore, as is rifling through your drawers or under papers for a calculator. The worst visible signs of wasted effort are those little notes to yourself, scrawled half-legibly on scraps of paper, that multiply over the course of a day.

Computers are good at keeping things straight, so why not give them a few extra tasks? The SideKick program does just that. It should make your life quite a bit easier.

ORGANIZING YOUR DESKTOP WITH SIDEKICK

SideKick is a desktop organizer. Its name derives from the sidekicks of the old West, who were always trusty companions. You can call up SideKick at any time by pressing its hot key, since it is a memory-resident program.

SideKick incorporates many features. Its main menu, shown in Figure 18.10, outlines everything SideKick can do. For example, you can move the menu bar or type in a letter. If you type in the letter N or press F2, you will find yourself in the NotePad section of SideKick, which allows you to type and save notes for yourself or for later inclusion into a file. It is actually a mini-version of a word processor, using a set of control codes similar to that found in WordStar. This feature is useful as a rapid editor for small database programs, as well as for small batch files in DOS.

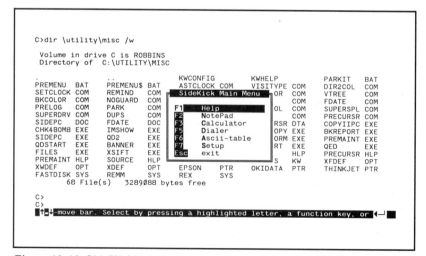

Figure 18.10: SideKick's main menu

You can also access an on-screen calculator, a calendar, and an automatic phone dialer, should you have a modem hooked up. Side-Kick also includes a phone directory that works with the autodialer, and a datebook that can keep track of your appointments.

SideKick is available from

Borland International
4585 Scotts Valley Drive
Scotts Valley, California 95066
(800) 543-7543

SUMMARY

DOS is clearly not the end-all for your computing needs. There are thousands of additional utilities, from hundreds of utility vendors, that can extend the power and capabilities of your disk operating system dramatically. In this chapter you have seen only a few of the many excellent products available to you.

- Hard disks require considerable management. Q-DOS II is a powerful file and directory manager that simplifies hard-disk maintenance.

- If simple but professional menu systems are your goal, you should purchase PreCursor, a program whose primary (but not only) strength is the easy setup of program menus.

- The Norton Utilities is one of the oldest and most respected of the utility packages you can buy for your PC. It's a must-have for all PC owners.

- Back-It extends the range of backup and recovery features offered by DOS's BACKUP and RESTORE commands. A more flexible and powerful alternative, it is a worthy choice for reducing your maintenance effort.

- Speeding up your hard disk can be accomplished in several ways. A disk optimizer like VOPT will reduce head movement during file accesses. A memory cache like Lightning will reduce the number of disk accesses. A file compressor like Squish will shrink the files themselves, so that fewer disk accesses are needed to obtain the same data.

* Several programs enhance the power of your console. Keyworks is an extraordinarily powerful keyboard enhancer. Scroll & Recall is useful for looking back at data already lost from the screen. ReComm saves typing effort during sessions in which you issue the same or similar DOS commands many times.

* Printed output can be dressed up with several programs like Sideways, which prints out extremely wide data files, and Printworks, which prints output in a variety of type styles and sizes.

* Conversions are important because of the multiplicity of computers, disk formats, and software products. Examples of conversion programs are Brooklyn Bridge, which converts different diskette sizes, R-Doc/X, which converts different word-processing formats, and XenoCopy-PC, which converts different diskette formats.

* SideKick is a popular product containing an attractive collection of desktop tools, including a small word processor, a phone dialer, a calendar, and a calculator.

So far, I have taken you from the basic concepts of DOS, disk files, and formats to advanced commands, batch-file programming, and now to add-on and add-in utility programs. You can now perform any computing task with assurance, and do it easily and quickly. You know what commands exist, what the options for batch files are, and what extra utility software exists.

In Part 6, I'll show you how to use DOS in conjunction with other systems.

PART 6

GOING BEYOND

If you are one of those DOS users who want more than DOS alone can provide, Part 6 is for you. Chapter 19 presents Windows, the popular multitasking DOS program by Microsoft, the developers of DOS. It provides an attractive growth path for DOS users who want to run multiple programs at once.

Chapter 20 explains the various methods for surmounting DOS's 640K memory barrier to run application programs. Lastly, Chapter 21 introduces you to OS/2, the advanced operating system that not only breaks the 640K memory barrier but allows sophisticated multitasking as well. You can make a smooth transition to this new operating system by learning how to efficiently run your DOS programs under it.

WINDOWS AND DOS

MICROSOFT WINDOWS OFFERS YOU A GRAPHIC interface to a multitasking DOS operating environment on IBM and compatible personal computers. The Windows operating environment provides an additional layer of control between DOS and applications software to allow you to use your computer's capacity more fully.

Although Windows may appear to be primarily a graphics-interface extension of DOS, it is in fact an enhanced operating environment that permits multitasking and data transfer operations that are difficult to perform under DOS alone.

INTRODUCTION TO WINDOWS

Only those pro-grams designed to operate under Windows can take complete advantage of the special benefits of this windowing environment.

This chapter describes the operation of Windows and some of its utility programs. These programs are all designed specifically to operate under and interface with the Windows environment; they cannot run without Windows. As the number of personal computer systems running Windows grows, more commercial software packages are being introduced, redesigned, or upgraded to operate under or interface with this environment.

This chapter dis-cusses Windows Version 2 and does not attempt to cover all the differences between Versions 1 and 2. If you have the option of buying one version or the other, you will probably find the later one easier to use.

Like DOS 4, the Windows operating environment differs from DOS's command prompt in that it is a completely new visual interface for users. Your connection to the computer and its operations does not require carefully constructed command requests. Instead, the interface consists of full-screen displays controlled by a mouse. All programs and commands are selectable by the mouse, so you are no longer forced to learn and remember the commands. When a selection requires more information, such as additional parameters on a DOS command, Windows prompts you for the additional information in a dialog box.

The Windows environment differs significantly from both DOS's command prompt and DOS 4's shell with its *multitasking* feature. In DOS, you can only run one program at a time. In Windows, multiple programs can run simultaneously. Windows can manage the sharing of the CPU time cycles in a manner similar to the way DOS can enable print spooling to proceed concurrently with a main foreground program. All programs installed under Windows are able to proceed, sharing the CPU under the supervision of the main Windows software.

In fact, Windows itself is simply a program that runs under DOS. Its role, then, is to present a user interface that is easier both to use and to understand, as well as to manage the concurrent running of several programs designed to run under the Windows environment. Unlike a true multitasking environment such as OS/2, which provides its multiprocessing features to all programs running on your computer, Windows provides multitasking ability only to those programs installed within it.

Furthermore, Windows is limited by the standard DOS restrictions (like 640K of memory), and so must multitask its programs within that restrictive memory span. A true multitasking operating system like OS/2 can directly use and allocate much more memory (up to 16Mb) to the various programs sharing both the CPU and the available memory.

WINDOWS AND DOS

Most software packages currently available are designed to run under DOS as stand-alone applications. Most such applications can run under the Windows operating environment, but they generally can make no use of the graphics interface or multitasking capacities of Windows. The primary benefit to be derived from running standard DOS applications under Windows is that you can load and run several of these applications at the same time. Once multiple applications are loaded, you can switch from one to another without first exiting the current application. In addition to reducing the amount of time required to load individual software packages, Windows lets you transfer data between various applications.

RUNNING DOS PROGRAMS UNDER WINDOWS

A particular advantage of programs designed to run under Windows is that they continue to execute, even after you've activated another DOS program.

Although you can load and run several programs simultaneously under the Windows environment, you can directly access only one of these programs, the *active* program or window, at any one time. The program executing in the active window operates in much the same way as any program running under standard DOS. Programs designed to run under Windows continue to run even when they are not in the active window. Standard DOS programs, on the other hand, run only when they are in the active window. When another window is active, these programs suspend execution.

There are two principal ways to switch between different windows, using the keyboard or the mouse. You may press the Alt-Esc key combination one or more times; pressing Alt-Esc switches windows successively. Depending upon how many windows you have, you will activate one after the other, stopping when you have reached the desired one. Alternatively, if your system has a mouse, you can simply move the cursor to any point within the desired window, then click the mouse.

If the desired window is currently represented as an icon at the bottom of your screen, you may select it with the mouse, then select either the Restore or Maximize options from the dialog box that will appear. Windows will then either restore the window to its original size or enlarge it to fill the screen.

MULTITASKING UNDER WINDOWS

Windows affords increased hardware independence to software, and provides users an intuitive graphic interface to DOS. Windows also lets both users and programs more fully utilize the processing capacity of personal computers. The original concept of personal computers ''One user, one machine, one program'' gradually evolved to ''One user, one machine, several RAM-resident utilities, one main program.'' Windows extends this concept the next logical step: to ''One user, one machine, many programs.''

As noted above, multitasking works by sharing the CPU among various programs. It is a form of time sharing. Since the CPU performs its tasks much faster than most peripheral devices (like printers) and certainly much faster than most users can type, there is always time to spare from the processing chip's point of view.

These spare time cycles can be used by other programs, rather than have everything grind to a halt while one program waits for a user to press Return or for a printer to complete a slow I/O operation. This rapid switching from one program to another creates the *appearance* of multiple programs actually running simultaneously. This is not the real case, since there is only one CPU, and it can at any given moment service only one program. But the rapid context switching creates what is commonly called a multitasking or multiprocessing environment.

HARDWARE REQUIREMENTS OF WINDOWS

Version 1.0 of Windows runs on any IBM PC, PC/XT, PC/AT, 386, PS/2, or compatible computer equipped with at least 320K of RAM, two 360K disk drives, and a CGA graphics display. Version 2.0 requires at least one 1.2Mb disk drive. Running Windows on just these minimal configurations, however, is only minimally productive as the environment requires considerable disk activity and CPU processing. In part because of this overhead, a realistic minimum configuration is a PC/AT or compatible computer with 640K of RAM, a 20Mb hard disk, an EGA graphics display, and a mouse pointing device. Windows can also use extended memory (see Chapter 20) to increase operating speed.

INSTALLING WINDOWS

The Windows operating environment and its associated utilities and programs require a significant amount of disk storage space. Version 2.0 is delivered on nine 360K disks. Before you can run Windows on your personal computer, you must install it for your specific hardware configuration.

Installing Windows on your computer is extremely easy. However, be sure *not* to use the DOS command APPEND prior to running the Windows setup procedure; you should temporarily remove this command from use before taking the steps described here.

Regardless of whether you are installing Windows on a dual-diskette or a hard-disk system, the simple instructions begin the same way. Place the Setup diskette into drive A and enter

A:
SETUP

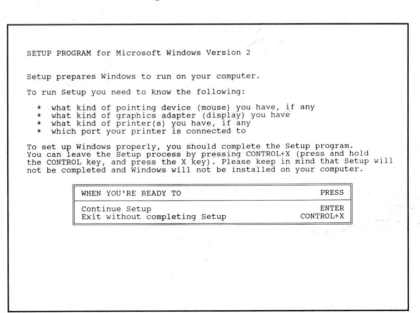

If you place the wrong Windows disk in drive A at any time, Setup merely prompts you again for the correct one.

Microsoft's initialization program takes over, as Figure 19.1 shows, and prompts you for information regarding your particular hardware configuration. This first screen illustrates the type of information you must have to continue with the Windows installation. You must, for example, know enough about your system to tell Setup what kind of mouse, monitor, and printer you are using, and the port to which your printer is connected.

During the actual installation, you are prompted for specific information regarding your individual hardware configuration and you must answer the questions displayed. Press Ctrl-X now to exit from the setup process to determine the answers before continuing or press Return to continue setting up your system.

During the specification of your disk drives, you can install and run the Windows environment from any of the three diskette combinations listed or from a hard disk. The hard-disk option, H, is highlighted as the default choice.

You can run Windows from floppy diskettes, although the program works exceedingly slowly under such a setup. The following example of an installation sequence assumes that you are using a hard disk, choice H in Figure 19.2. Choice H is the default selection.

```
SETUP PROGRAM for Microsoft Windows Version 2

Setup prepares Windows to run on your computer.

To run Setup you need to know the following:

    *  what kind of pointing device (mouse) you have, if any
    *  what kind of graphics adapter (display) you have
    *  what kind of printer(s) you have, if any
    *  which port your printer is connected to

To set up Windows properly, you should complete the Setup program.
You can leave the Setup process by pressing CONTROL+X (press and hold
the CONTROL key, and press the X key). Please keep in mind that Setup will
not be completed and Windows will not be installed on your computer.

    WHEN YOU'RE READY TO                              PRESS
    Continue Setup                                    ENTER
    Exit without completing Setup                 CONTROL+X
```

Figure 19.1: Initial Windows Setup screen

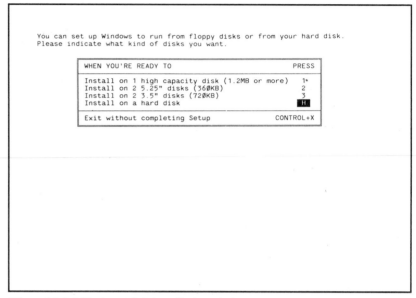

Figure 19.2: Windows disk installation choices

If you select your computer's class and then press Return and find that your computer is not one of the listed IBM, AT&T, or Tandy computers, the compatibility of your system will now be tested.

When selecting the display adapter for your system, you use the cursor keys to highlight the display adapter installed on your computer and then press Return. As is true during the entire setup operation, you can abort the process by typing Ctrl-X.

Windows creates a directory during setup to store all of its support files. As Figure 19.3 shows, the default directory is called WINDOWS, although you can change that name here before Windows actually makes the directory and copies the files from your diskettes to it.

Although the Windows Setup program supports primarily IBM, AT&T, and Tandy computers (see Figure 19.4), in fact, it supports literally hundreds of compatibles as well. You need only select which class of computer you are using.

Once you have identified the general class of your computer, you must specify which of many different display adapters your system uses. Windows supports all of the standard CGA, EGA, and VGA adapters, as well as a host of other popular alternatives, as shown in Figure 19.5.

DOS recognizes many different international keyboards. Chapter 12 discussed the steps required to prepare your DOS for using a different keyboard. You must tell Windows which keyboard layout your system uses. Figure 19.6 lists the choices currently available from Windows.

```
Windows will now be set up on your hard disk in the directory shown
below.

   - If you want to use a different directory and/or drive, use the
     BACKSPACE key to delete the name shown, then type the correct name.

   C:\WINDOWS




              ┌───────────────────────────────────────────────────┐
              │ WHEN YOU'RE READY TO                        PRESS  │
              ├───────────────────────────────────────────────────┤
              │ Continue Setup                              ENTER  │
              │ Exit without completing Setup           CONTROL+X  │
              └───────────────────────────────────────────────────┘
```

Figure 19.3: Setup of Windows default directory

```
Below is a list of computers on which you may set up Windows.

   - Use the DIRECTION (↑,↓) keys to move the highlight to your selection.

   IBM PC, XT, AT (or 100% compatible)
   IBM Personal System/2 Model 25 or 30
   IBM Personal System/2 Model 50, 60, or 80
   AT&T Personal Computer
   Tandy 1000




              ┌───────────────────────────────────────────────────┐
              │ WHEN YOU'RE READY TO                        PRESS  │
              ├───────────────────────────────────────────────────┤
              │ Confirm your choice                         ENTER  │
              │ Exit without completing Setup           CONTROL+X  │
              └───────────────────────────────────────────────────┘
```

Figure 19.4: Computers supported by Windows

```
Please select your display adapter from the following list.

  - Use the DIRECTION (↑,↓) keys to move the highlight to your selection.

  IBM (or 100% compatible) EGA (> 64K) with Enhanced Color Display
  IBM (or 100% compatible) CGA (Color/Graphics Adapter)
  IBM EGA with High-Resolution Monochrome Display
  IBM EGA with Enhanced Color Display (black and white)
  IBM EGA with Enhanced Color Display or PC Color Display (color)
  IBM MCGA (Multi-Color Graphics Array)
  IBM (or 100% compatible) VGA (Video Graphics Array)
  Hercules Adapter with High-Resolution Monochrome Display
  AT&T Color DEB (Display Enhancement Board)
  AT&T Monochrome (Indigenous Display Board)
  Compaq Portable Plasma
  Tandy 1000 Color
  Other (requires disk provided by a hardware manufacturer)


  ┌─────────────────────────────────────────────────────────────┐
  │ WHEN YOU'RE READY TO                              PRESS       │
  ├─────────────────────────────────────────────────────────────┤
  │ Confirm your choice                               ENTER       │
  │ Exit without completing Setup                     CONTROL+X   │
  └─────────────────────────────────────────────────────────────┘
```

Figure 19.5: Windows display adapter options

The default U.S. keyboard is high-lighted, but you can use the cursor keys to select one of the other layouts.

```
Please select your keyboard from the following list.

  - Use the DIRECTION (↑,↓) keys to move the highlight to your selection.

  US keyboard
  AT&T keyboard
  Tandy 1000 keyboard
  British keyboard
  Dutch keyboard
  French keyboard
  German keyboard
  Italian keyboard
  Spanish National keyboard
  Swedish/Finnish keyboard
  Other (requires disk provided by a hardware manufacturer)


  ┌─────────────────────────────────────────────────────────────┐
  │ WHEN YOU'RE READY TO                              PRESS       │
  ├─────────────────────────────────────────────────────────────┤
  │ Confirm your choice                               ENTER       │
  │ Exit without completing Setup                     CONTROL+X   │
  └─────────────────────────────────────────────────────────────┘
```

Figure 19.6: Keyboard layouts known to Windows

Although you can operate Windows without a pointing device, you really shouldn't. The program is designed for use with a mouse, or at least with some form of pointing device such as a trackball or joystick. Figure 19.7 shows the choices available to you during Windows installation.

The choices seen in Figure 19.7 are the most popular pointing devices for Windows use. Using one of these devices facilitates your use of Windows, since software support for them is included in the Windows package.

After you have responded to the various setup screens (Figures 19.1 to 19.7), Setup displays a summary of the key information it gathered from you (see Figure 19.8) and prompts you for confirmation. Press Return if the information is accurate or select any of the answers for correction; Windows will return to the appropriate screen to let you modify your earlier answer.

When you have confirmed your answers, Setup loads several programs (KERNEL.EXE, USER.EXE, MSDOS.EXE, and MSDOSD.EXE). Setup also copies from the Setup diskette to your hard disk a number of necessary files and then prompts you to insert

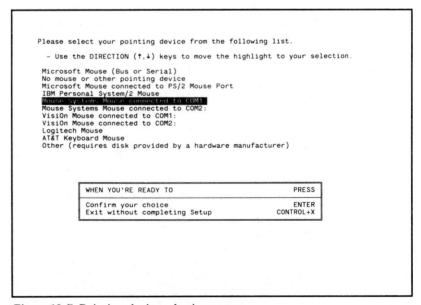

Figure 19.7: Pointing device selection screen

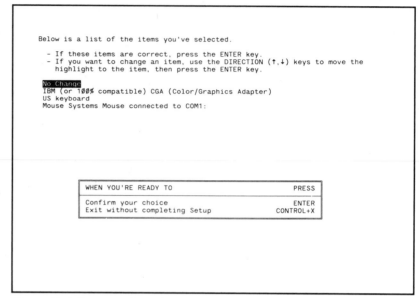

```
Below is a list of the items you've selected.

    - If these items are correct, press the ENTER key.
    - If you want to change an item, use the DIRECTION (↑,↓) keys to move the
      highlight to the item, then press the ENTER key.

    No Change
    IBM (or 100% compatible) CGA (Color/Graphics Adapter)
    US keyboard
    Mouse Systems Mouse connected to COM1:
```

```
  WHEN YOU'RE READY TO                                        PRESS

  Confirm your choice                                          ENTER
  Exit without completing Setup                           CONTROL+X
```

Figure 19.8: Setup confirmation screen

your other Windows diskettes in succession. Figure 19.9 shows the first of several prompt screens.

The first step in the primary setup process loads the main Windows file and overlay instructions. Among other, smaller files, the Windows drivers for your earlier choices are loaded at this time (for the mouse, the keyboard, and so on).

Next, you'll need to install one or more printers or plotters in your Windows configuration. The screen shown in Figure 19.10 prompts you for this step, allowing you to select choice I repeatedly until you have installed all printer and plotter devices. You can then continue with the rest of the installation.

When you choose I, the screen shown in Figure 19.11 appears, presenting a series of output device choices compatible with Windows. Use the cursor-control keys to select the desired device; then press Return. You will then be asked to indicate the port being used for the specified device.

Windows must know the port to which each device used for output is connected. Even though DOS can support more than two serial communications ports, Windows offers only COM1 and COM2 serial support. Figure 19.12 lists the output port selections available.

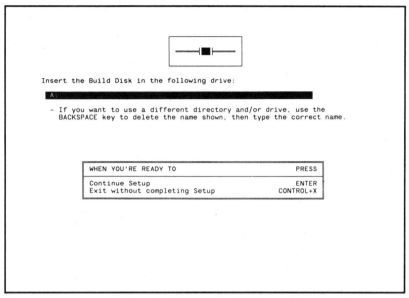

Figure 19.9: Setup requires the Build diskette first.

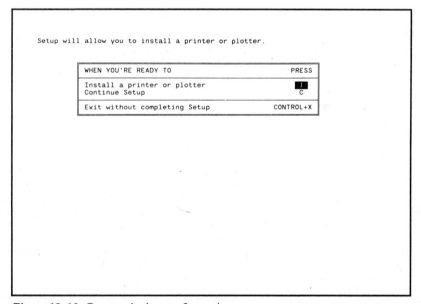

Figure 19.10: Output device configuration

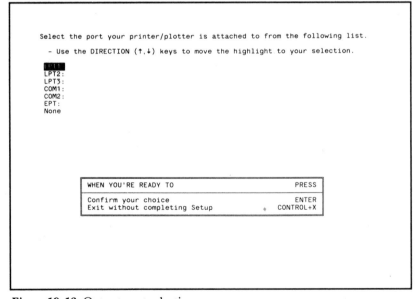

```
Select an output device (printer, plotter, etc.) from the following list.

  - Use the DIRECTION (↑,↓) keys to move the highlight to your selection.

  HP LaserJet Plus [PCL / HP LaserJet]
  HP LaserJet 500+ [PCL / HP LaserJet]
  HP LaserJet Series II [PCL / HP LaserJet]
  HP LaserJet 2000 [PCL / HP LaserJet]
  HP ThinkJet (2225 C-D)
  IBM Color Printer (B/W only)
  IBM Graphics
  IBM Personal Pageprinter [Postscript printer]
  IBM Proprinter [IBM Proprinters]
  IBM Proprinter II [IBM Proprinters]
  IBM Proprinter XL [IBM Proprinters]
  Kyocera F 1010 Laser [PCL / HP LaserJet]
  Linotronic 100/300/500 [Postscript printer]

           (To see more of the list, press the DOWN(↓) key.)

    ┌─────────────────────────────────────────────────────┐
    │ WHEN YOU'RE READY TO          .            PRESS     │
    ├─────────────────────────────────────────────────────┤
    │ Confirm your choice                        ENTER     │
    │ Exit without completing Setup              CONTROL+X │
    └─────────────────────────────────────────────────────┘
```

Figure 19.11: Output device screen

```
Select the port your printer/plotter is attached to from the following list.

  - Use the DIRECTION (↑,↓) keys to move the highlight to your selection.

  LPT1
  LPT2:
  LPT3:
  COM1:
  COM2:
  EPT:
  None




    ┌─────────────────────────────────────────────────────┐
    │ WHEN YOU'RE READY TO                       PRESS     │
    ├─────────────────────────────────────────────────────┤
    │ Confirm your choice                        ENTER     │
    │ Exit without completing Setup          *   CONTROL+X │
    └─────────────────────────────────────────────────────┘
```

Figure 19.12: Output port selections

You must select one of these ports for each printer or plotter you specify during the Windows setup. After this is done, the screen shown in Figure 19.10 will be redisplayed. If you have more than one printer or plotter installed, you can specify it now by selecting I once again and then specifying the port to which the device is connected. When you have finished specifying devices, you can continue with the rest of the Windows setup.

Continuing the Windows setup displays the screen shown in Figure 19.13, which allows you to specify the country for your Windows operation. Just as for DOS (see Chapter 12), selecting one of these countries automatically specifies the currency symbol, separator symbols for the date and time, and other country-specific features used by Windows.

Once this initial configuration is complete, you must load several required Windows utilities into your system. Just as you were prompted to insert the Build diskette into drive A, you now are prompted to insert the Utilities 1 disk (see Figure 19.14). Depending on the hardware you specified as part of your system configuration, you may also be prompted to insert the Utilities 2 and Displays disks, which contain many of the alternative choices for Windows support software.

Windows 2.03 supports 27 country settings.

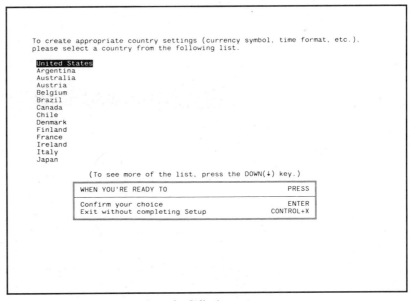

Figure 19.13: Country settings for Windows

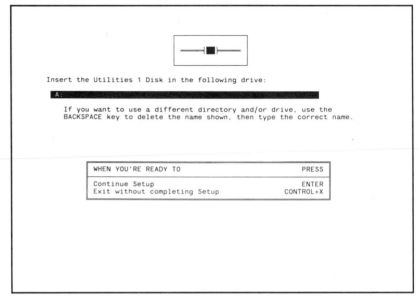

Figure 19.14: Utilities are loaded after Build.

After reading from the Utilities 1 disk, Setup asks for the Fonts (1 and 2) disks. After reading the necessary files from the Fonts disks and copying those files to the \WINDOWS directory, Windows prompts you to insert your Desktop Applications disk.

Pressing Return after placing the Desktop Applications disk into drive A copies the primary desktop application modules (CALC.EXE, CALENDAR.EXE, CARDFILE.EXE, CLOCK.EXE, PAINT-.EXE, NOTEPAD.EXE,and so on) to your \WINDOWS directory.

You are next prompted to insert your Windows Write disk in drive A. In fact, this prompt is misleading; the correct disk to load at this point is labeled Program disk. This disk contains the primary software for the Windows word-processing program, called Write.

You are nearly done with the Windows setup. The screen shown in Figure 19.15 now appears. This screen displays information about the software that was changed after the manuals and documentation were complete. The special files containing this last-minute information are disk resident. Setup tries to make sure that you read this information by including this screen in the installation process.

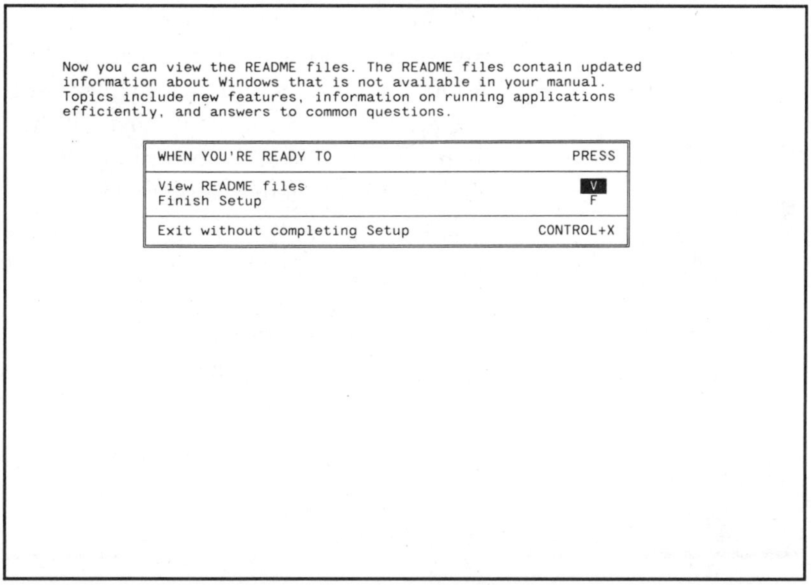

```
Now you can view the README files. The README files contain updated
information about Windows that is not available in your manual.
Topics include new features, information on running applications
efficiently, and answers to common questions.

┌─────────────────────────────────────────────────────────────┐
│ WHEN YOU'RE READY TO                                    PRESS │
├─────────────────────────────────────────────────────────────┤
│ View README files                                        [V] │
│ Finish Setup                                              F   │
├─────────────────────────────────────────────────────────────┤
│ Exit without completing Setup                       CONTROL+X │
└─────────────────────────────────────────────────────────────┘
```

Figure 19.15: README text is part of the setup process.

When you are done viewing the text information, your current directory will be \WINDOWS, and you can begin operating the WINDOWS program by typing WIN. You can later modify the path (perhaps set from AUTOEXEC.BAT) to include \WINDOWS; this will allow you to initiate Windows at any time, regardless of the current drive or directory.

Do not skip the final steps of reading the README files during the setup process. The advice and information contained in those text files may be relevant and even critical to your system. For instance, information about many popular laser printers, and the use of soft fonts on those printers, is contained only in the README files. Additional information about Windows performance and advice regarding system modification for performance and convenience also appears on these important text screens.

The Windows operating environment that results from the initial installation procedure is more than sufficient for a beginning user. From this environment, you can use utility programs and follow printed instructions to modify Windows to accept changes in system hardware and in the use of current hardware.

⊙ Skipping the README information may cause you to be unaware of important Windows information not included in the standard documentation.

You can also have Windows automatically load one or more software applications whenever you load Windows into the computer. Although this may significantly increase the amount of time required to start Windows, you will have all the applications opened in this manner available at the beginning of the Windows session instead of having to load them one by one later.

Because of the way Windows manages memory during multitasking operations, it is more efficient to load programs into the Windows environment by order of decreasing memory requirements (that is, starting with the program with the largest memory requirement first). Although this sequential loading of programs can be performed manually, allowing Windows to do it for you is obviously easier.

> When installing programs under Windows, load those programs requiring the most amount of memory first.

USING WINDOWS

You usually load Windows by entering WIN at the DOS prompt. You can write a simple batch file to set the default drive and directory and to enter the request to DOS to run WIN. When installed on a hard disk, Windows is usually stored in the \WINDOWS subdirectory, so you must either change to that directory or ensure that \WINDOWS is on the path.

Once you have entered the WIN command, by whatever means, Windows displays the Microsoft logo and begins operating. The time required for Windows to become functional depends on the speed of your computer and disk drives and on the number of applications that Windows has been configured to start automatically. When the Windows operating environment is completely set up, a full-screen window similar to the one in Figure 19.16 appears.

Files in the current directory (\Windows) of the current drive (C) are displayed. The default drive is represented by a highlighted icon; the first entry in the directory also is highlighted. Available options include the three main menu choices: File, View, and Special.

The window in Figure 19.16 is for the Windows MS-DOS Executive application program in Version 2. MS-DOS Executive is always available during a Windows session and is used to initiate other applications and perform some DOS disk operations. The use of the MS-DOS Executive will be discussed shortly, but first take a brief look at the areas of the window and the icons on it.

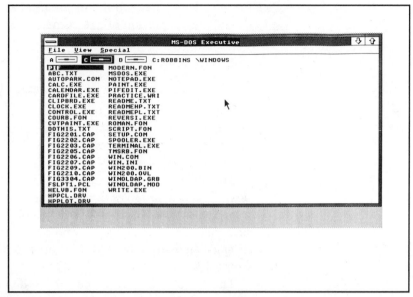

Figure 19.16: Initial Windows Version 2.03 screen display

THE COMPONENTS OF A WINDOWS SCREEN

The standard window in a Windows application has three primary and two secondary (optional) components. The first primary area consists of the top two lines of the window: the title bar and the Command menu. The title bar contains the name of the application and (in Versions 2.X) three icons, one on the left and two on the right. The Command menu displays the names of the commands associated with a particular application (File, View, and Special, in Figure 19.16). The second primary area is the work area, or working window. The third primary area, which appears as a dark or inverse stripe across the bottom of the screen, is the icon display area. Applications that are loaded but not shown in the work area as full or partial windows are displayed here as icons.

Depending on the application, two other components, vertical and horizontal scroll bars, may appear in the window. If present, the vertical scroll bar (see Figure 19.20) appears at the right side of the work area, and the horizontal scroll bar (see Figure 19.41) appears immediately above the icon display area. When displayed, the scroll bars can be used to scroll the work area to display any information that exceeds the number of lines, or the number of characters in a line, of the work area. The scroll bars are used as they are in programs that display only a portion of a document or spreadsheet at a time.

The title bar in Figure 19.16 displays three icons. The two icons that appear on the right side of the title bar, a down arrow and an up arrow, control the display of the associated window. The down arrow, or minimize box, changes the window into an icon. The up arrow, or maximize box, expands the window to a full-screen display. When a window has been maximized to a full-screen display, the up arrow changes to a double up arrow, or window restore box. This box restores the window to its previous display size.

The third icon, on the left side of the title bar, is the Control menu box. This box provides access to the Control menu, which is common to all Windows applications. Choices on this menu control the size, location, display status, and termination of an application and its associated window. They are outlined in the section ''Using the Control Menu.''

The components of the title bar just described are included in Version 2 only; the title bar in Version 1 simply displays the name of the application program. Similar features are available in Version 1, but they are generally less convenient to use.

RUNNING WINDOWS

Windows provides a graphics-oriented interface that allows a user to perform various operations by selecting the appropriate commands from pull-down menus. Displaying a pull-down menu and selecting commands can be accomplished by using a mouse or by entering a series of multikey keyboard commands (which are entered as Alt plus the selected key). The keyboard commands are inconvenient at best and confusing at worst; using a mouse is strongly recommended for users of Windows. The examples in the remainder of this chapter assume the use of a mouse pointing device.

If your cursor is not positioned on one of the Windows icons or on a text choice, it will appear as a small arrow on your screen. This arrow is the mouse pointer. As in DOS 4, to select an icon on a window, you position the pointer on the icon and press mouse button one. When you press the button, either the icon will change color, indicating that it can be moved to another location on the screen, or a pull-down menu will appear.

In Figure 19.17, the Control menu box has been selected, and its menu is displayed because the mouse button has been pushed. If you release the mouse button while the pointer is inside the icon, the menu will remain on screen. If you click the mouse button with the pointer on some empty area of the screen, the menu will disappear. However, if you move the pointer to the Command menu with the mouse button still pressed, the menu command that is touched by the pointer will change its display characteristics (usually to white letters on a colored background) to indicate it has been selected. If you move the pointer off the command, the command will revert to its original display and will not be selected. To execute a command on a menu, select it with the pointer and release the mouse button. If you don't want to execute any of the commands on a menu, move the pointer back to the menu icon or to an empty area of the screen before releasing the mouse button.

This menu appears after you select the horizontal box icon in the upper-left corner of any window. The six controls displayed are available to you for managing any window. From the menu, you can move a window around the screen and adjust its size any way you like. You can replace the entire window with an icon only, expand the window to fill the screen, restore the window to its original size, or close the window.

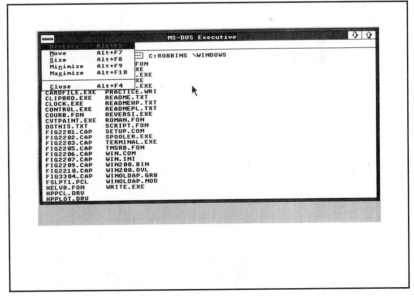

Figure 19.17: The main Control menu

Windows displays commands in a different color, shade, or font if they are invalid or temporarily disabled.

Frequently, one or more of the commands in a pull-down menu will be disabled because they are invalid or meaningless at the time. When a command has been disabled, it is displayed in a different color, shade, or font than valid commands. For example, the Print choice in Figure 19.47, later in this chapter, appears dimmer than the other options. This indicates that it is not a valid choice for the currently selected file. When the pointer touches a disabled command, the display characteristics do not change. If you release the mouse button while it is touching a disabled command, the menu will disappear.

USING THE CONTROL MENU

The Control menu, shown in Figure 19.17, is available in every application designed to operate in the Windows environment. It controls the display of an application window and closes (terminates) an application program. The commands on this menu are as follows:

Restore: Restores window appearance and size to original values. It is also accessible as Alt-F5.

Move: Moves the window to another location on a multiple window display. It is also accessible as Alt-F7.

Size: Adjusts the size of the window in a multiple-window display. It is also accessible as Alt-F8.

Minimize: Closes the active window, reduces it to an icon, and places the icon in display area at the bottom of the screen. It is also accessible as Alt-F9.

Maximize: Expands a window or an icon to the largest possible screen size. It is also accessible as Alt-F10.

Close: Closes a window, terminating the current application program and removing it from the Windows environment. It is also accessible as Alt-F4.

As you can see, each of these commands also can be activated by an Alt-keystroke combination. You can use keystroke commands regardless of whether a pointing device (a mouse) is installed, but pointing is usually easier.

USING MS-DOS EXECUTIVE

MS-DOS Executive is the primary control application in the Windows environment. It is initiated automatically when Windows is loaded into the computer system, and it must remain active as long as Windows is running. MS-DOS Executive performs the following three primary functions:

1. It loads and runs other application programs in Windows.

2. It displays the current disk directory listing.

3. It provides access to DOS disk-control operations such as file COPY, DELETE, and RENAME; disk FORMAT; and subdirectory creation and alteration.

When Windows is first loaded, MS-DOS Executive is the only application window open. If additional applications have been open, they appear as icons in the display area at the bottom of the screen.

Figure 19.16, presented earlier, shows a sample MS-DOS Executive window. The actual directory list and disk drive icons vary between different computer systems. At the top of the work area, a disk drive icon is displayed for each disk drive on the computer system. The icon for the current default disk drive is displayed in inverse video. To the right of the disk icons, the default drive letter, volume label, and current subdirectory path are displayed. Below the disk icons is a directory listing of the files in the current subdirectory. Generally, the first file in the directory listing is displayed in reverse video to mark it as the default selection.

CHANGING THE DEFAULT DISK DRIVE

You can change the default disk drive by positioning the pointer on the icon for the disk drive that is to become the new default drive and then clicking the mouse button once. The icon for the original default disk drive will revert to normal video display, and the new default drive icon will change to reverse-video display. The new default drive letter, volume label, and subdirectory path of the new default drive will then be displayed, as will a directory listing of the files in that subdirectory.

SELECTING A FILE FROM THE DIRECTORY LIST

To change the selected file in the directory list, move the pointer to the file name and click the mouse button once. The previously selected file name will be restored to normal display, and the new file name will display in reverse video.

USING THE MS-DOS EXECUTIVE COMMAND MENU

MS-DOS Executive provides three pull-down menu commands (File, View, and Special) in the Command menu at the top of the window. The functions of the commands available under these three menus are described in the following sections. Position the pointer on a Command menu command and hold down the mouse button; the pull-down menu for that command will be displayed.

With the mouse button still pressed, move the pointer down through the menu. As the pointer passes over a command, the command is selected and displayed in reverse video. If you release the mouse button, the selected command will be performed on the selected file or files in the work area. If additional information or verification is required to complete a command, one or more pop-up windows will appear.

CONTROLLING DOS FILES   Figure 19.18 shows the File command pull-down menu. The command functions available here are performed on the currently selected file shown in the work area. The command functions are as follows:

RUN: Brings an application .COM, .EXE, or .BAT file into the Windows environment and executes it. If a Windows application is to be run, a window will be open for it on the screen. If a standard DOS application is being run, the display screen will revert to normal DOS mode. The application will then run as it normally does under DOS.

LOAD: Loads and executes Windows and standard DOS applications in the Windows environment, but with the applications displayed as icons in the icon display area. No window will be open for the application.

COPY: Copies one or more selected files to another disk or directory. You can copy more than one file at a time by selecting multiple files from the work area directory list. To select more than one file, press and hold the Shift key on the keyboard while pointing to and selecting the files with the mouse.

GET INFO: Displays full directory information for the selected file.

DELETE: Deletes the selected files.

PRINT: Sends one or more ASCII text files to the Windows print spooler.

RENAME: Renames the selected file.

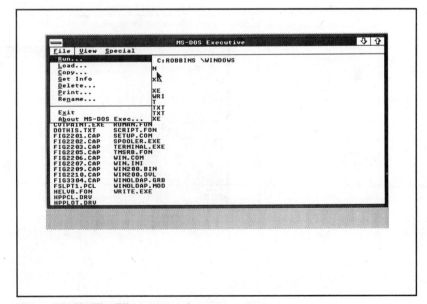

Figure 19.18: The File command menu

This menu lets you perform DOS operations on the files in the displayed directory. You can run a program or batch file, load a program or batch file for later execution, or obtain the equivalents of the DOS commands COPY, ERASE, RENAME, and DIR. If the highlighted file is printable, the PRINT command option is also available.

VIEWING DOS DIRECTORY CONTENTS   Figure 19.19 shows the View command pull-down menu. The command functions available here determine how the file list appears in the work area. Normally, the file name and extension of all files in the current subdirectory are displayed in alphabetical order by file name. By selecting different options, you can organize the file list by date, time, size, or extension. Only program files or files matching a specified naming convention are displayed. The \WINDOWS directory files listed behind the pull-down View window appear in the default short format.

As you can see, check marks indicate the default choice in each of the three categories of this menu. By default, all files appear in name order using the short format, which displays showing only the base name and extension of each file.

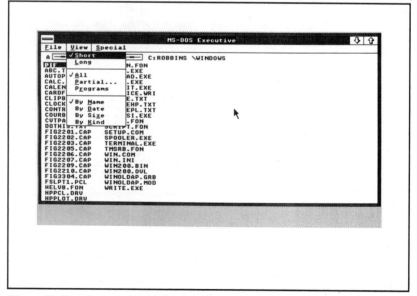

Figure 19.19: The standard View menu

Moving the mouse down the menu to select the long format results in a display similar to Figure 19.20. Notice that a vertical scroll bar appears on the right side of your screen since there are more files in this directory than can be displayed on one screen. The long file-name format (which includes date, time, and size) will remain in effect until you again select the short format.

USING SPECIALIZED DOS COMMANDS   Figure 19.21 shows the Special command pull-down menu. The command functions available from this menu provide access to common DOS operations associated with hard-disk use (formatting new disks, changing or assigning a disk volume label, creating new disk subdirectories, or changing the current subdirectory on a disk drive).

Miscellaneous but important DOS command capabilities are available from this Special menu. The choices here are equivalent to the DOS MD, CD, FORMAT, FORMAT/S, and LABEL commands. The Windows command for ending the Windows session is also available from this menu.

The Special menu also includes the command to terminate a Windows session (End Session). If you select End Session, a window

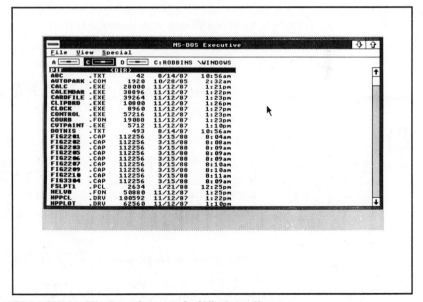

Figure 19.20: The long format of a Windows directory

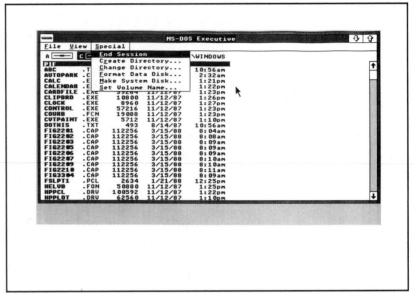

Figure 19.21: The Special menu

appears requesting verification (see Figure 19.22). If you select the
OK icon, Windows closes any open windows. If an open window or
loaded application contains new or modified data that has not been
saved, a dialog box allows you to save or discard that data.

SAVING TIME AND ENERGY WITH WINDOWS APPLICATIONS

This display of
available .EXE
appears when you select
files Programs on the
View menu. Running
any one of these pro-
grams requires only that
you highlight its name
and then press Return.

The Windows directory contains several built-in .EXE files. Most
of these (shown in Figure 19.23) are unique application programs
included with your Windows software. In this section, you'll explore
these useful tools. You can then decide which ones best serve your
own needs.

PERFORMING ON-SCREEN CALCULATIONS

The Calculator application, shown in Figure 19.24, functions as a
standard 10-key calculator. When this application is active, you can

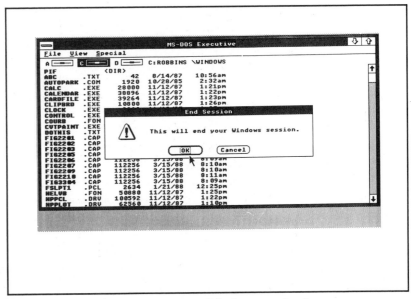

Figure 19.22: Confirmation screen at Windows termination

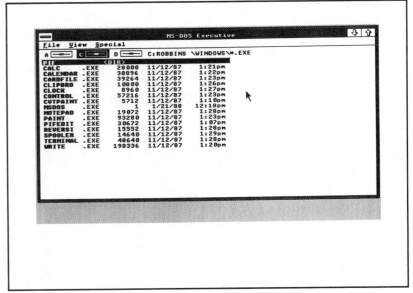

Figure 19.23: .EXE programs included with Windows

use it to perform calculator operations by positioning the pointer over the appropriate key and clicking the mouse button or by typing the appropriate keys on the keyboard. This application also can transfer and receive information from other applications.

The on-screen calculator resembles a pocket calculator. It includes the standard number keys, arithmetic functions, single-value memory location, and a square-root button.

The screen cursor (normally an arrow elsewhere on the screen) appears as a small octagonal symbol. You can move this symbol directly over any of the calculator keys with your mouse. Pressing the mouse button is then equivalent to pressing that key on the keyboard. Calculations proceed as they would on any portable calculator, with intermediate and final numeric results shown in the calculator display window. In Figure 19.24, this window shows a value of 0 and the cursor is located just to the right of the calculation window.

MAINTAINING YOUR APPOINTMENT CALENDAR

Various desktop software packages offer a date and time appointment calendar. Windows offers CALENDAR.EXE, which runs in a

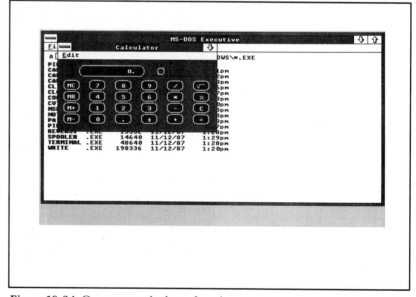

Figure 19.24: On-screen calculator function

window on the desktop. Figure 19.25 shows the initial view of this software facility. Optional settings dictate the size, shape, and contents of each window application when it first appears on the desktop. In this case, the appointment calendar is set to November 15, 1988 (today's date), beginning with 8:00 A.M. and showing one-hour intervals.

The current time and date is displayed, as are the entries for this date, beginning at 8:00 A.M. No appointments have yet been entered on this system for this date. Notice the small icon at the bottom of the screen. It represents the active and available Calculator program, whose desktop window has been minimized by using the Control menu.

MS-DOS Executive also is still available and can be partially seen on the screen. It is said to be in the *background*, since the primary window is running the Calendar program.

In Figure 19.26, I minimized MS-DOS Executive to reduce the visual clutter. This leaves only the window containing the Calendar on the screen, plus the two icons now visible in the display area at the bottom of the screen. The disk represents MS-DOS Executive; the miniature calculator represents the Calculator program.

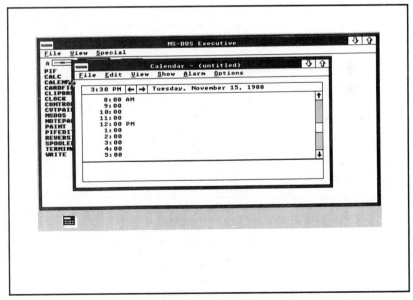

Figure 19.25: Initial window display of the Calendar feature

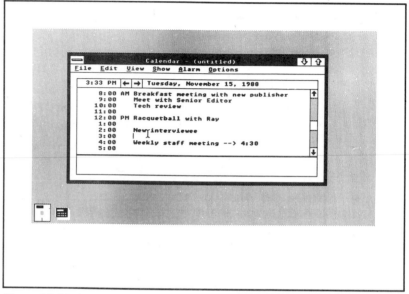

Figure 19.26: A completed appointment calendar

You can make entries for different times on the visible schedule. In Figure 19.26, I made appointments for 8:00, 9:00, 10:00, 12:00, 2:00, and 4:00. The cursor for the next entry is on the 3:00 line. This calendar is completely new and has not yet been named; thus, the file name *untitled* appears on the top title bar.

The Calendar program has six pull-down menus: File, Edit, View, Show, Alarm, and Options. Figure 19.27 displays the pull-down contents of the File menu. This File choice is common across the desktop applications, as are most of the features listed here.

As you can see, you can create new entries or files (New), open existing entries or files (Open), save your current work to a new or already existing file (Save), back up your current work to a uniquely specified file (Save As), print your schedule (Print), or delete files (Remove). You can also always close an application window (Exit) or display information about the application (About ...).

Save is highlighted, indicating that the file will be saved under its current name, SCHEDULE.CAL (shown in the title line at the top of the window).

To save a copy of your appointments schedule under a different name, you select the Save As choice, which displays the screen shown in Figure 19.28. The dialog box shows the current name as the default name and permits you to type over that name with another.

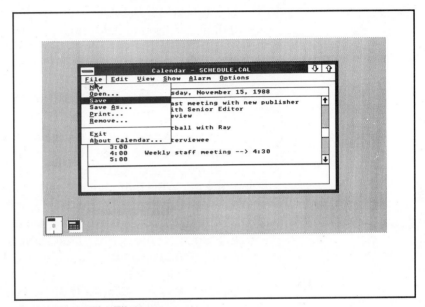

Figure 19.27: The File menu

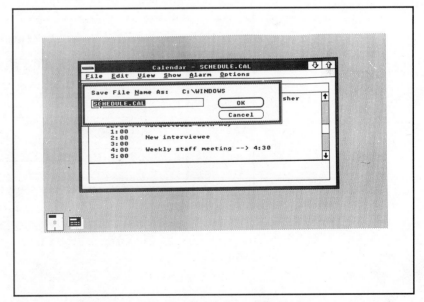

Figure 19.28: Saving a Calendar file under a different name

After entering a new file name in the dialogue box, you need only select OK with your mouse to save the file. Selecting Cancel withdraws your request to save the file at all.

The Edit menu provides a number of standard editing features, including the deletion (cutting) and reinstatement (pasting) capabilities common to most desktop applications. You'll explore these editing capabilities in the context of the next desktop application discussed, the Cardfile.

The View menu lets you display the Calendar by day (as shown in Figure 19.26), or by month (as shown in Figure 19.29).

The entire current month is displayed, with the currently selected day shown in reverse video. The symbols > and < indicate that the selected date is also today's date. Move the cursor with the mouse and then press the button once to select another day.

Notice in Figures 19.28 and 19.29 that the vertical scroll bar is visible. You can use the mouse to move the time or date forward or backward by moving the cursor to the scroll bar and pressing the mouse button. Moving downward in the scroll bar is equivalent to moving forward in time.

You can also move forward or backward using control-key and function-key combinations, as shown in Figure 19.30.

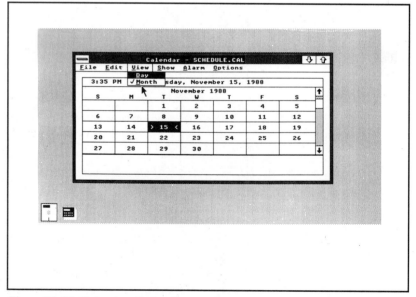

Figure 19.29: Calendar display by month

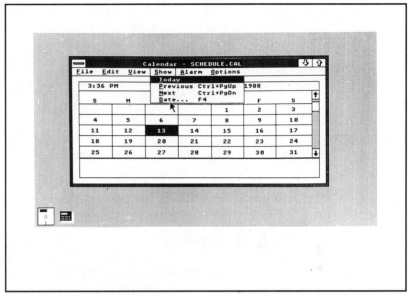

Figure 19.30: The Show menu

No matter what date you are currently working with, you can quickly return to today's date (that is, the system date). You can also move forward (Next) or backward (Previous) by one day, or you can specify a particular date. Each of these choices is available from this mouse-selected pull-down menu or by using the keystrokes Ctrl-PgUp, Ctrl-PgDn, or F4.

Mouse-based software such as Windows usually encourages the use of the intuitive mouse interface, using pull-down menus and mouse button selections. However, for reasons sometimes of speed and personal preference, the software also offers keystroke combinations that provide the same functionality. As Figure 19.30 shows, Windows often displays these keystroke alternatives on the pull-down menu to remind you of them.

Keystroke possibilities are not available once you've pulled down a menu; they are alternatives to the menus.

As you'll learn shortly, you can set an alarm to go off on your computer when a particular appointment time arrives. As Figure 19.31 demonstrates, you can also set the alarm to go off up to 10 minutes in advance of an appointment time. At the specified time, a dialog box will appear or an icon will flash. Figure 19.31 shows the screen when you select the Alarm pull-down menu. In this dialog box, you specify how many minutes (up to 10 minutes) in advance of an appointment the alarm is to go off. You also specify whether the alarm is to be audible (by clicking the sound box and displaying an X) or visible only.

Up to this point, the screen displays have all shown 1-hour intervals using a 12-hour clock and beginning at 8:00 A.M. These settings all are adjustable from the Day Settings choice of the Options menu. Figure 19.32 shows the day settings available to you.

You can set the appointment interval to 15, 30, or 60 minutes by selecting the number with your mouse. Similarly, you can switch between a standard 12-hour clock or a 24-hour format. You can directly enter the starting time for your display in the starting time box.

If you prefer your appointment calendar based on 15-minute intervals rather than 60-minute intervals, you choose this option to change the specification. Naturally, if you use 15-minute intervals, any single screen will display less total time.

When an alarm has been set for a particular appointment, the visual indicator appears as a small bell icon to the left of the appointment time, as seen next to the 3:00 slot in Figure 19.33.

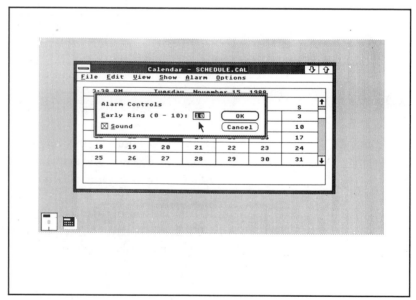

Figure 19.31: Setting the alarm controls

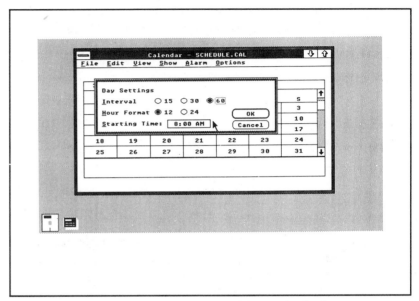

Figure 19.32: Day Settings dialog box, available on the Options menu

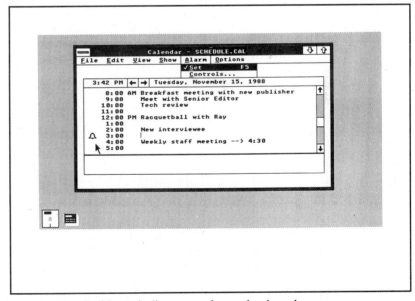

Figure 19.33: Bell icons indicate any alarms that have been set.

An alarm has been set for 3:00 on Tuesday, November 15, so the bell icon appears next to that line on the display. You set alarms by using the Set choice on the Alarm menu. The Controls choice produces the dialog box shown in Figure 19.31.

Scrolling on a particular date is easily accomplished using the cursor keys (up and down arrows) or the vertical scroll bar and the mouse. Figure 19.34 shows the result of scrolling down the day from the range 8:00 A.M. to 5:00 P.M. to the range 2:00 P.M. to 11:00 P.M. To enter new information, position the mouse at the desired time, then press the button once.

BUILDING YOUR OWN SIMPLE DATABASE

Complex database-management systems provide powerful capabilities for managing large amounts of data. The commands and tools available in these DBMS program are often much more than is necessary for many simple files of information. The concept behind the Windows Cardfile program is that much information is easily stored on the equivalent of a 3 × 5-inch card. Thus, with the Cardfile, you create visual cards on your computer screen. When you run the Cardfile

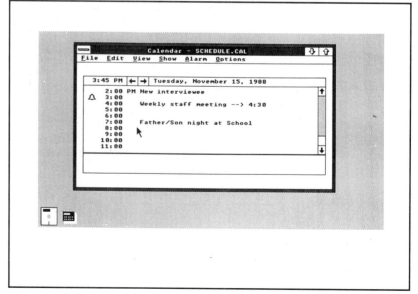

Figure 19.34: Scrolling through the daily time slots

program from MS-DOS Executive, the screen shown in Figure 19.35 appears.

As with the Calendar, you can give each card file a unique file name. Card files are untitled until you enter a name. The first blank card is displayed for your information entry.

As the figure shows, the Cardfile offers five pull-down menus. The first three menus perform functions similar to those they perform in the Calendar program. The Card and Search menus are unique to the Cardfile program. Notice in the figure that the MS-DOS Executive window has been maximized and no longer appears as an icon. However, the Calendar program has been minimized and now appears only as an icon at the bottom of the screen.

When setting up a card file, the first step to take is to give your card a title, or index line. Select Index on the Edit menu, shown in Figure 19.36, to obtain the proper dialog box.

Selecting the Index choice on the Edit menu allows you to give each card a unique title, or index line. The name refers to the method Windows uses internally to store and retrieve individual file cards (via an index into the file).

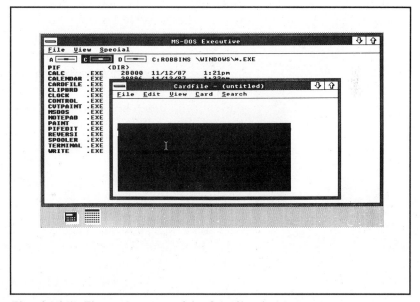

Figure 19.35: First appearance of the Cardfile window

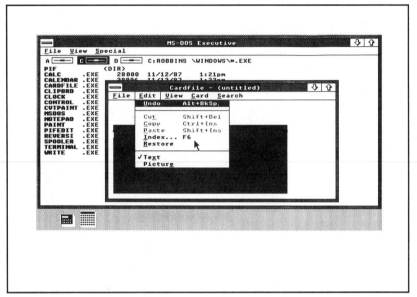

Figure 19.36: The Index choice on the Edit menu

The resulting dialog box, shown in Figure 19.37, allows you to enter a brief title for the card. This *index line* appears at the top of each card on the computer screen. The Cardfile also uses the characters in these index lines to arrange the cards for display. The default arrangement of the cards on your monitor is standard alphabetic order.

The last name is entered first, so that later automatic alphabetizing by the Cardfile program will sort the cards into a logical order. After you enter the index line, the dialog box disappears, and the card is redisplayed with the index line entry appearing as the first line on the card. You can then begin typing any information you would like to appear and be stored on this card. Figure 19.38 shows a completed card entry for Jimmy Beswell, a racquetball opponent of the person keeping this sample card file.

The individual's name is used as the index line, for easy alphabetizing. Notes about each individual's game skills are kept for later reference.

To add additional cards to this simple card file select the Card pull-down menu. As Figure 19.39 shows, you then choose Add (or alternatively press F7) to create a new blank card on your screen.

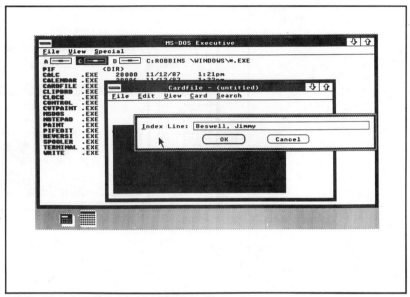

Figure 19.37: Index line entry for the first card in the file

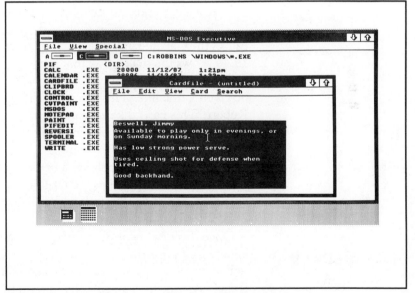

Figure 19.38: First card entry in file of racquetball opponents

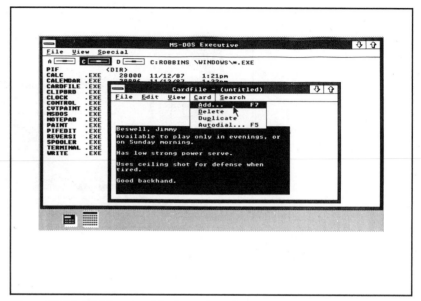

Figure 19.39: Making new blank card entries

You will be asked to give the card a title (index line) before you enter new information on that card. Adding a new card to your file causes the Cardfile program to ask you for the title of the card. Figure 19.40 shows the dialog box that appears.

A new card added after your first one (Beswell, Jimmy) must first be given a title line. This second card is given the index line Kayple, Robert. This card, like all cards, will later be quickly accessible via the Search menu simply by entering the first letters of the index line (in this case, the person's name).

The resulting display shows a new card that is blank except for the index line at the top of the card (see Figure 19.41). The former card is obscured except for the index line (Beswell, Jimmy). You can now enter information for the new current card.

Once this display appears, you can begin typing, and the text will appear on the card.

Figure 19.42 shows the completed second card. All notes about Robert Kayple have been entered onto his card and are visible.

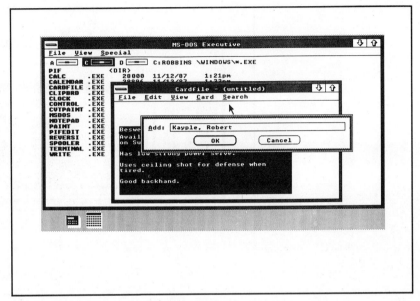

Figure 19.40: Giving title lines to new cards

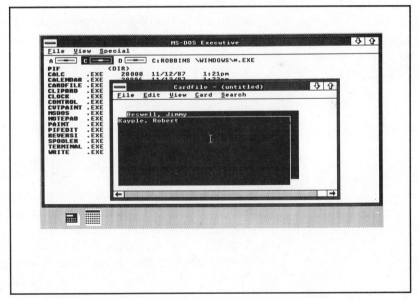

Figure 19.41: Newly added cards at the top of the deck, or file

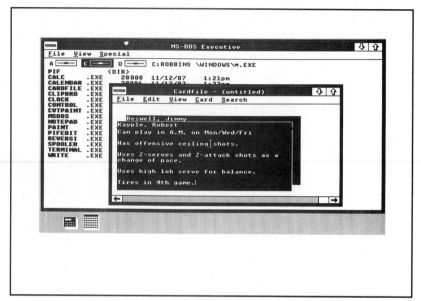

Figure 19.42: Multiple cards with their index lines visible

This card is entered in the card file under the index line Kayple, Robert. The Cardfile program displays the top index line for several cards at a time, so that you can easily select cards with your mouse. Selecting an index line moves its card to the top of the deck, where you can read the card's contents.

You can add other cards by selecting Card/Add. Figure 19.43 shows a deck containing a third racquetball opponent's card. Since all three cards fit on one screen, Windows does not yet need to display a scroll bar.

You can easily add more cards with the Add choice from the Card menu. If more cards were created than fit on one screen, a horizontal scroll bar would appear, allowing you to scroll through the deck from front to back (left to right on the scroll bar).

A useful tool when your card deck becomes much larger is the Search pull-down menu. As you can see in Figure 19.44, you only need to enter the first several characters of the index line to enable the Cardfile program to quickly find a particular card.

The GoTo choice on the Search menu lets you enter several characters from the card's title, or index line. The program quickly finds the specified card and makes it the topmost card on the deck, as the next figure shows.

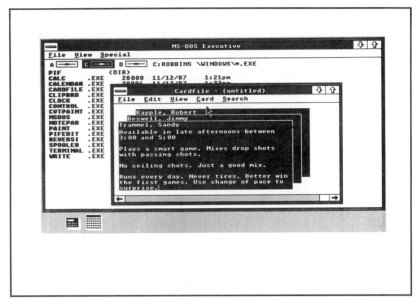

Figure 19.43: Adding cards with the Add choice on the Card menu

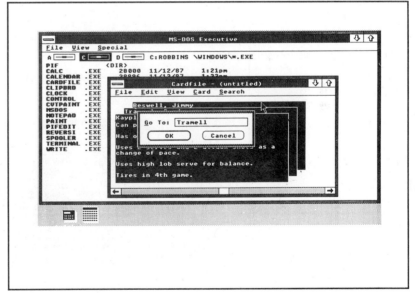

Figure 19.44: Finding a particular card quickly with Go To

At any time you can change the appearance of your card file from its default view of complete cards, as shown so far, to an alternative view displaying only the index lines for the card entries. These two choices appear on the View menu, shown on Figure 19.45.

You can view your card file in two ways: either as a deck of titled cards (the Cards option), or as a list of card titles (the List option). Selecting List displays the screen in Figure 19.46.

Figure 19.46 displays the card file as a list of index lines, or titles, for easy reference. Naturally, more card titles can appear on one screen display in this format than in the alternative format displaying complete cards.

Your card file has a list of titles, or index lines. In this format, you can see more entries on a single screen and thus can easily and quickly select the next card you want to see or modify.

When you're done working on your card file, you will most likely want to save it to a disk file. In fact, you should probably save it earlier than that to ensure that a power failure doesn't cost you a great deal of work. Once you've saved your work, your data will be protected.

Figure 19.47 displays the File menu, including the standard options for creating, opening, and saving files. It also contains useful

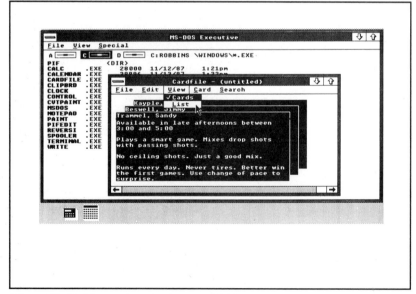

Figure 19.45: Alternative viewing possibilities

choices for printing individual cards (one to a page) and for printing your entire card file (multiple cards per printed page).

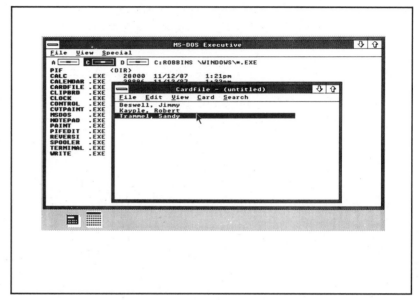

Figure 19.46: Index line listing of your card entries

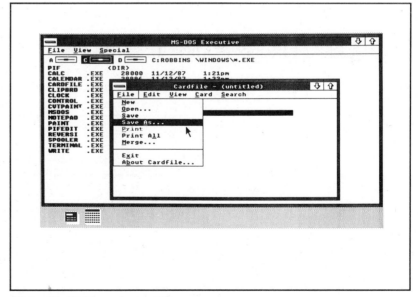

Figure 19.47: The primary File menu

In particular, the printing choices provide you with the ability to print
individual cards, one to a page, and to print several cards on a single
page. All cards are printed with a solid border for easy visual separation.
Figure 19.48 shows a printout of the three cards created in this card file
session. All three cards appear on one page; each card is printed with a
solid border for easy identification and perhaps cutting.

```
Beswell, Jimmy
Available to play only in evenings, or
on Sunday morning.

Has low strong power serve.

Uses ceiling shot for defense when
tired.

Good backhand.



Kayple, Robert
Can play in A.M. on Mon/Wed/Fri

Has offensive ceiling shots.

Uses Z-serves and Z-attack shots as a
change of pace.

Uses high lob serve for balance.

Tires in 4th game.



Trammel, Sandy
Available in late afternoons between
3:00 and 5:00

Plays a smart game. Mixes drop shots
with passing shots.

No ceiling shots. Just a good mix.

Runs every day. Never tires. Better win
the first games. Use change of pace to
surprise.
```

Figure 19.48: Results of selecting Print All from the File menu

One last feature of the Cardfile program is its ability to dial a telephone number. This feature is included in case your cards represent a person or business that you want to call. Selecting the Autodial choice from the Card menu displays the screen in Figure 19.49.

You can enter a phone number in the Dial entry field (for example, 212-234-5476), or you can allow the program to automatically find the phone number on the topmost card in your file. The first phone number, if any, on the topmost card is placed in the Dial entry field. In this dialog box, you can also set the baud rate to 300 or 1200, the port to COM1 or COM2, and the dialing to pulse or tone (touch tone). The selected number is then dialed through your connected modem as soon as you select OK.

Suppose at this time that you have correctly saved your card file as RACQUET. As you can see in Figure 19.49, the formerly untitled card file is now called RACQUET.CRD. The default .CRD extension was added when the file was saved as RACQUET from the File menu.

You can now maximize the MS-DOS Executive window to select the Special menu and end the Windows session. Windows will check to verify that other sessions have had their data updates properly saved. In Figure 19.50, Windows discovered that your calendar entries have not been updated in the file named SCHEDULE.CAL.

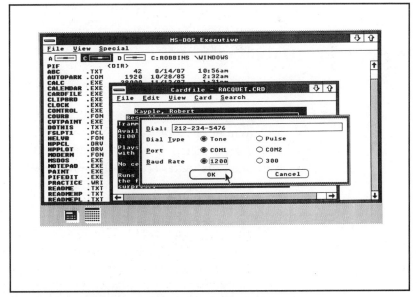

Figure 19.49: Autodial option on the Card menu

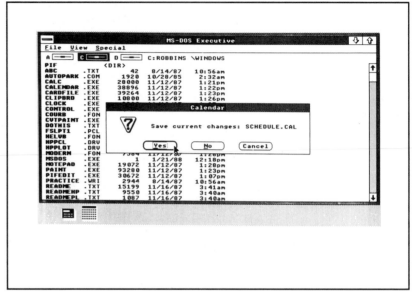

Figure 19.50: Automatic protection against inadvertent data loss

Windows will not allow you to end a session with outstanding data changes that have not been saved to a disk. In this example, you tried to end the session after saving your card file work. Windows discovers that the SCHEDULE.CAL file had not been updated and so provides you the opportunity to correct this possible oversight before you lose your work.

Sophisticated spooling needs can be better met through the features of Windows or OS/2 (see *Essential OS/2*, SYBEX, 1988) than by standard DOS alone.

SPOOLING YOUR OUTPUT INFORMATION

Spooling (see Chapter 8) is even more powerful under Windows than under DOS alone. You can configure Windows to understand several pieces of output hardware (during the Setup procedure) at one time, and because of the multitasking capabilities of Windows, you can just as easily have different output spools, or streams, actively working at the same time. Each separate output device in your system can print files from a different queue of file names. Different programs in your system can be responsible for sending output to each of the output ports and the different devices connected to those ports. Using MS-DOS Executive to run SPOOLER.EXE, you can view and manipulate all of this simultaneous output. The example system in Figure 19.51 has been configured to expect output to LPT1 to actually be connected to an HP LaserJet printer. Also, output to LPT2 will be directed to an HP plotter.

The initial window displays all configured output devices, the ports associated with them, and two pull-down menus: Priority and Queue. This display also indicates whether each queue is actively open for accepting and processing output data (Active), or is paused and temporarily closed to output processing. Notice that MS-DOS Executive is being displayed in a background window, and that the recently used Cardfile program has been minimized and is visible as a new icon at the bottom of the screen.

Since you can have multiple output streams executing simultaneously, Windows provides the Priority pull-down menu (see Figure 19.52) to let you influence which queue(s) achieves better response. No matter how many queues exist, you can specify whether each queue is to receive low or high priority service. Since Windows intercepts CPU timer interrupts and then allocates time to each of the programs running under it (including the spools), a high-priority spool will achieve better output processing performance than will a low-priority spool.

When the Spooler program begins, after Windows itself begins, all configured output devices have separate spools that are open and

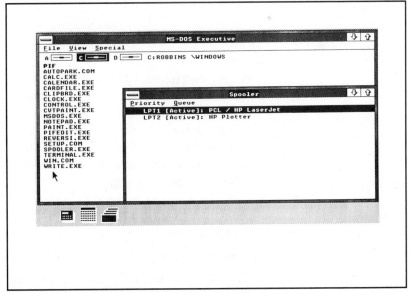

Figure 19.51: Results of executing the SPOOLER.EXE program

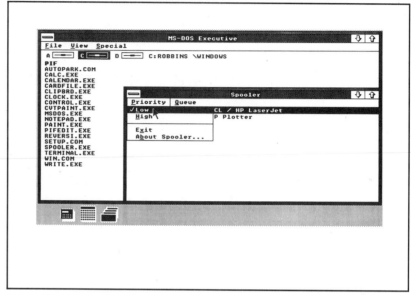

Figure 19.52: The Priority menu of the SPOOLER.EXE

actively queueing output information. Each of the possible file names queued for printing on a particular device is listed in the main SPOOLER window, just below the port and device line shown earlier in Figure 19.51. You can control whether any of these individually queued up file names are to be temporarily paused or canceled completely.

Figure 19.53 shows the Queue menu. Notice that the Terminate option is dimmed, since there is currently no file name in the highlighted queue (HP LaserJet) available for cancellation.

Each queued file can be paused, or halted from printing. When you are ready to continue printing, you must return to this menu and select Resume. Although the Terminate option is not currently available, you can normally use this choice to completely remove (cancel) a print job from a queue.

MAKING NOTES AND PERFORMING OTHER SIMPLE FILE EDITING

Windows lets you manipulate text in several ways. The easiest and simplest mechanism for text manipulation is the Notepad program, shown in Figure 19.54. Notice that before Notepad was run, I minimized the Spooler window; it now appears as a new icon at the bottom of the screen.

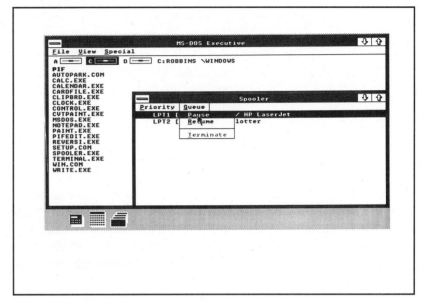

Figure 19.53: The Queue menu

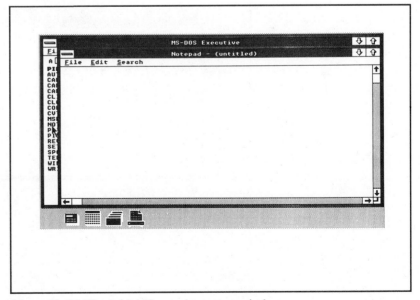

Figure 19.54: The initial Notepad program window

Only three pull-down menus are provided: File, Edit, and Search. Use File to manipulate all the data on the notepad at once, Edit to manipulate individual characters and strings in the file, and Search to locate specific text strings on the Notepad.

When the Notepad program begins, the cursor appears as a blinking vertical bar, as it did in the Cardfile program. You can simply begin typing text onto the Notepad; in fact, you are entering information into the memory-resident portion of what will later become a disk file. Figure 19.55 shows a typical entry sequence.

Typically used for jotting down short and simple notes, the Notepad can be used as a handy programming editor or as a simple, word-wrapping text processor. Note that word wrap is an option, not a default feature.

Although it's not apparent until you enter some text, the default status of the Notepad is line mode. All text stays on a single line until you press the Return key. If you enter more text than can be seen on the screen, the Notepad scrolls the viewing window to the right so you can see your most recently entered characters.

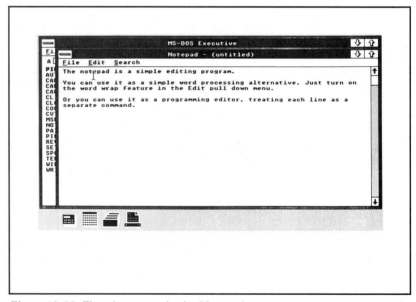

Figure 19.55: First data entry in the Notepad

Programmers can take advantage of the Notepad's simplicity by using it as a convenient programming editor. Computer languages typically work on a line-by-line command basis.

This wide scrolling mode is not the typical way in which the Notepad was designed to work. It is more likely that your text entries will be short notes, and the Notepad will perform the function anticipated by its name of simply storing brief remarks or notes.

The File menu visible in Figure 19.56 works like other file menus discussed so far. Note the vertical scroll bar on the right side of the screen. Windows expects note files to exceed the size of the on-screen window; you can use the vertical scroll bar to move up and down through the file's contents.

You can create a new file to store the Notepad's contents, open an old file and display its contents on the Notepad, save the current Notepad contents to disk, save the contents of the current Notepad in a specifically named alternate file, and send the Notepad's contents to a queue for printing.

Selecting the Edit menu displays the screen in Figure 19.57. Word wrap has been turned on in this figure to allow the Notepad to be used as a simple letter writer; paragraphs flow more easily when word wrap is used. However, note that you cannot yet use the text-manipulation commands (Cut, Paste, Undo, and so on) since you have not selected any text for them to operate on.

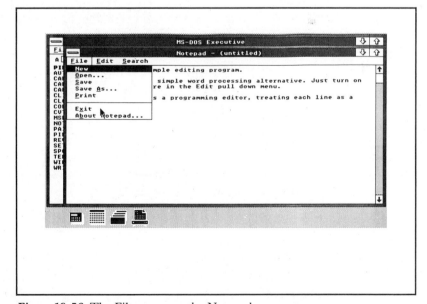

Figure 19.56: The File menu on the Notepad

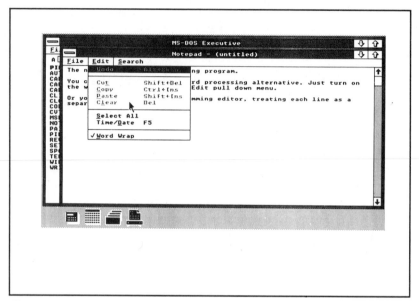

Figure 19.57: The Edit menu of the Notepad

Built into the Windows environment is both a concept and a program called the Clipboard (CLIPBRD.EXE). Whenever data is deleted, copied, or moved around in the Windows environment, a copy of that data is stored in a memory buffer. This buffer is analogous to a clipboard and paper. Unless the paper on the clipboard is actually thrown away, you can retrieve it and restore the data placed on it to its former location, and you can just as easily insert a copy of that data at any other location as well.

In Windows, data that has been highlighted (selected) can be operated on by the Edit menu commands. The data usually is moved temporarily onto the internal Clipboard until you decide what its final disposition will be. In Figure 19.58, the second paragraph on the Notepad has been selected by the mouse. It appears in reverse video behind the Edit menu. Since a text string has been selected and can be acted upon, the formerly dimmed Cut, Copy, and Clear options are now available.

These three options are available because a text string has been selected on the Notepad for manipulation in some way. Cut removes the string from its current location, saving a copy of the string on the Clipboard for later use. Copy leaves the string as it is and where it is,

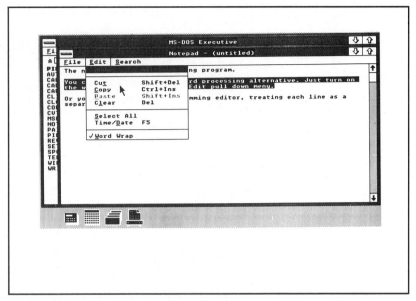

Figure 19.58: The Edit menu shows Cut, Copy, and Clear available

but deposits a copy of it on the Clipboard for later access. Clear erases the text completely; you will be unable to transfer it to another application, although you can use the Undo command to restore the deleted text in this application.

Suppose, for instance, that you had selected Cut in Figure 19.58. The entire second paragraph would have been removed (cut) from its existing location. Since there is now information on the Clipboard, the next time you call up the Edit menu, the Undo and Paste choices will be displayed in normal letters, indicating that they are available as choices.

Figure 19.59 shows the screen after the second paragraph was first cut, the cursor was moved to the end of the notes, and Paste was selected. The paragraph was reinserted (pasted) into the Notepad at the location of the cursor. The net effect in this case was to move the second paragraph from the middle of the document to the end. You could now select Undo to reverse the editing steps. You can use Undo to undo any editing step, whether a cut-and-paste or a simple deletion (clear).

◉ Use the *Undo* choice immediately to correct an error. Waiting until after other operations may nullify Undo's ability to perform its job successfully.

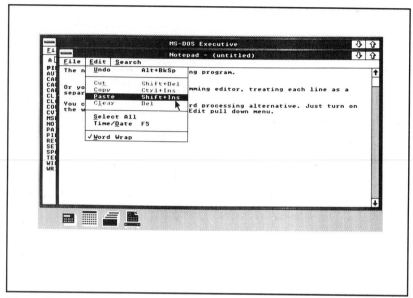

Figure 19.59: Pasting text in a new file location

In this moving operation, the middle paragraph was first cut, then the cursor was moved to the end of the Notepad text, and finally the paragraph was pasted back into the Notepad at the new location.

When your notes become more voluminous, you may need the help offered on the Search menu. As shown in Figure 19.60, you can find any specified character string. When you select Find, a dialog box appears where you can enter the string for which you want the Notepad program to search.

Find was selected to locate occurrences of the string *you* in the document. The first occurrence is displayed in reverse video. You can select Find Next on the Search menu to locate the next occurrence of the string in the text. Case is ignored in the search, so the *You* at the beginning of the next paragraph would be highlighted next.

After each occurrence of the specified string is found, you can press F3 or select Find Next from the Search menu to ask the Notepad program to find the next occurrence of the same string. It's important to realize that the searching begins at the point where the cursor is located and proceeds until the end of the notes is reached. Therefore, you should move the cursor to the top of the file before you issue a search request. When the program can find no more occurrences of the string a dialog box appears (see Figure 19.61).

When searching through an entire file for text, first position the cursor to the top of the file. Searching proceeds from the current cursor location to the end of the file.

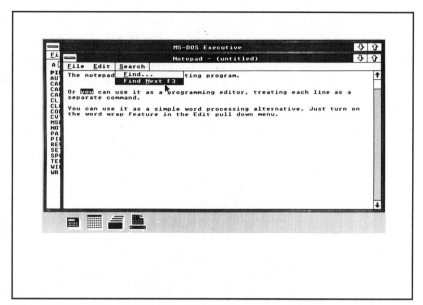

Figure 19.60: Repeated Find requests during a text search

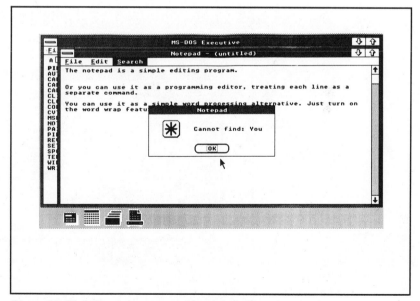

Figure 19.61: When no more matches can be found

CONTROLLING
YOUR WINDOWS CONFIGURATION

When your Windows environment is initially configured, the Setup program asks you to enter a number of important items of information. You can change some of these values at any time by invoking the CONTROL.EXE program (see Figure 19.62).

Three pull-down menus (Installation, Setup, and Preferences) are provided, and the initial display contains the system date and time and a sliding-scale control of the cursor blink rate and the mouse double-click time separation. All of these values can be changed from this window.

You can directly change the system date and time from this window, known as the Control Panel, achieving the same results as when you use the DATE and TIME commands at the DOS prompt. The other features unique to the Control Panel are the cursor blink rate and the time interval between double clicks from your mouse. Notice the word TEST underneath the double-click box.

Some applications require that you double click the mouse button. To distinguish between a double click and two successive yet separate clicks, Windows tests the amount of time that elapses between

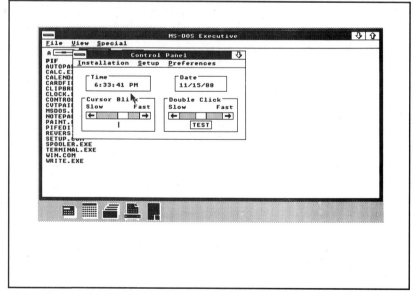

Figure 19.62: The Control Panel as it first appears

the clicks. The scroll bar in the Double Click box allows you to adjust this interval. You can then move the cursor into the TEST box and try to double click the mouse. If Windows recognizes the two clicks as a double click, based on your interval setting, then the word TEST will invert (white on black to black on white or vice versa).

The Control Panel also lets you install or remove printer and font information. Figure 19.63 shows the options available under the Installation pull-down menu.

This Installation menu lets you add or delete printer and font information. Selecting Add brings up a dialog box that lists the various supported devices you can install. Associated driver files are displayed when you select a device for installation.

The printer driver files used during this control function are obtained from the Utilities disk files on your original disks or from the \WINDOWS directory on your installed hard disk. You can also add or remove output fonts to your Windows installation with this menu. Although the minimum required fonts are automatically loaded during setup, you can override the initial settings and add or delete specific font files available to you.

You can review the current output device and port connections by selecting the Printer choice on the Setup menu, shown in Figure 19.64.

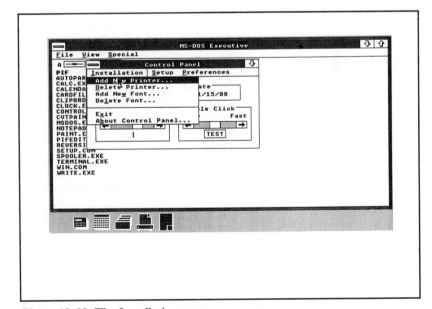

Figure 19.63: The Installation menu

Currently configured printers and plotters are displayed. You can specify the system default printer and adjust its timeout values (in seconds) on this screen. This example shows a maximum 15 seconds wait before Windows will notify you of an offline condition. Also, Windows will wait for 45 seconds for an online printer to print successfully before notifying you of an error.

The Printer choice lets you specify which printer is to be used as the default printer for output from applications designed and configured for Windows operation. Simply move the cursor to the name of the desired printer and click OK. After selecting the default printer, you can enter the printer timeout information in the new dialog box that appears (already visible in Figure 19.64).

A second option on the Setup menu is Connections. Selecting this option results in the display in Figure 19.65, which lists currently configured printers and plotters and the port to which each is connected.

As you select any one of these choices, with the mouse or cursor keys, the port to which that device is connected is highlighted on the right. You can change the port connection by selecting a different port name in the Connection box.

Miscellaneous Windows system values can be set from the Preferences menu, shown in Figure 19.66. The following settings are

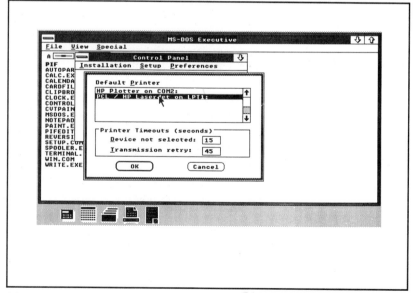

Figure 19.64: The Printer selection on the Setup menu

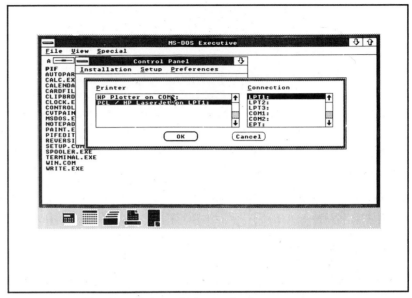

Figure 19.65: The Connections choice on the Setup menu

accessible on this Preferences menu: country settings, mouse speed and click settings, system beep status, window borders, thickness, and color intensity and hues for color monitors.

A dialog box is displayed when you select any of the choices on the Preferences menu, prompting you to clarify your requirements. For example, Figure 19.67 shows the result of selecting Screen Colors from the Preferences menu.

Moving the brightness and color bars to extreme rightmost and leftmost values produces the sharpest contrast between background and foreground. This also reduces the intensity of color on color monitors, however.

You can now determine, on a sliding scale, values to be used for the hue, brightness, and color saturation of all items displayed by Windows. First, you must select which item is to be influenced (such as the menu bar or the screen background). Then you use your mouse to point to different places on the graduated bars for hue, brightness, and color. The Sample window on the right changes appearance to reflect your choices.

All aspects of a Windows display, including the backgrounds of the different portions and the contents of those portions of the screen, can be controlled from this Preferences menu.

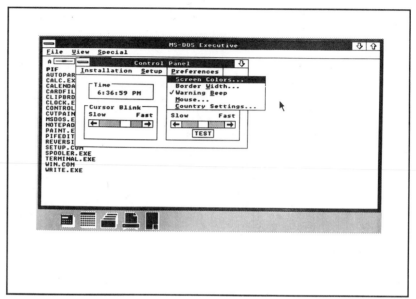

Figure 19.66: The Preferences menu

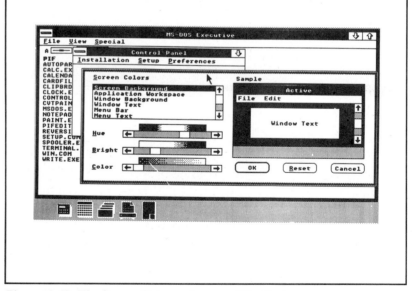

Figure 19.67: The Screen Colors submenu of the Preferences menu

PLAYING REVERSI: HAVING SOME FUN

Microsoft includes a game called Reversi in the Windows desktop applications package. As Figure 19.68 shows, this game looks similar to the more sophisticated game, go; Reversi follows similar rules for moves to capture territory owned by your opponent's pieces (circles).

The object of Reversi is to trap the opponent's circles between your own, thereby turning an opponent's white circles to black, enlarging the territory on the board owned by circles of your color.

At the end of the game, the player owning the most territory wins. The game goes quickly (very quickly, if you play against the computer), and it's both intellectually challenging and fun. It can be more fun if you pull down the Game menu before each of your moves to select the Hint choice. The computer then places the cursor in the best location for your next move. Naturally, do this only for the first game or two to quickly learn how to play the game successfully.

PRODUCING ANALOG CLOCK DISPLAYS

Computers typically display time in digital format. Windows has a program called CLOCK.EXE, however, that displays the time of day in analog format (see Figure 19.69).

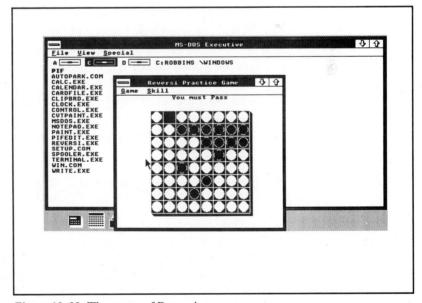

Figure 19.68: The game of Reversi

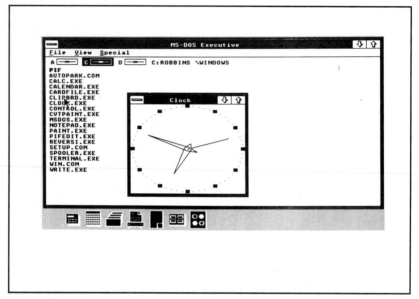

Figure 19.69: A colorful way to tell time when in Windows

This analog display of time shows standard hour and minute
hands and a moving second hand. Notice that the control panel and
the Reversi game have both been minimized to icons at the bottom
of the screen.

This analog clock keeps and displays accurate time, regardless of
where you move it on your screen. You can use the control box menu
(in the upper-left corner of the clock display) to move the clock or to
change the size of the clock. In fact, as Figure 19.70 shows, even if
you minimize the clock to an icon, it continues to keep and display
the correct time. Of course, this is because Windows is a multitasking
environment, and the Clock program continues to run, even though
its visual output appears only in the minimized icon.

ACCESSING THE CLIPBOARD DIRECTLY

When you learned about the Notepad earlier in this chapter, you
learned that any text that is deleted or cut is actually temporarily
stored in a memory-resident buffer called the Clipboard. During
normal use of the other application programs, you never actually see
or manipulate the temporary data stored in this Clipboard.

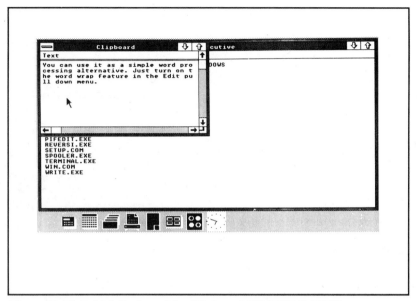

Figure 19.70: Initial display of the Clipboard (CLIPBRD.EXE)

You can run the program CLIPBRD.EXE under Windows to display the current contents of the Clipboard. As Figure 19.70 shows, the Clipboard contains the character string last cut from the Notepad, in Figure 19.58. This cutting could have been undone in the Notepad by selecting Undo from the Edit menu, or this data acquired from the Notepad and now available on the Clipboard could be placed in another application. For example, if you activate the Cardfile application and select the Paste function, the current contents of the Clipboard (the two sentences in Figure 19.70) will be inserted on the top card in the Cardfile.

In this sample session, the contents of the Clipboard were deposited by the Cut command last used from the Notepad application and shown in Figure 19.58.

Suppose, for example, that you minimized the Clipboard and MS-DOS Executive and then restored the Cardfile. Figure 19.71 displays the new screen display. The Clipboard icon appears at the bottom of the screen, and MS-DOS Executive returns to the leftmost position at the bottom of the screen. The Cardfile icon is removed in favor of the real Cardfile display.

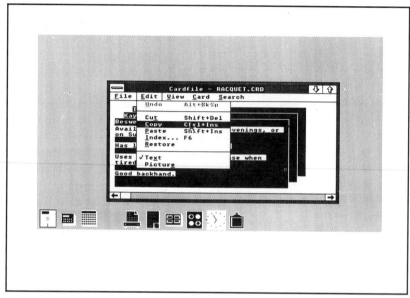

Figure 19.71: Restoring the Cardfile window

Text on one card is first selected. This is followed by the Copy function on the Edit menu. This text is immediately available for pasting into another application because all of it is now on the Clipboard.

If you select all the text information on Jimmy Beswell's card and then pull down the Edit menu, you can then copy that data. This choice leaves the card untouched, but deposits a copy of all the text on the Clipboard, wherever the icon or window representing it happens to be located. However, whatever used to be on the Clipboard is now gone forever.

Figure 19.72 shows the information most recently acquired from the Cardfile now available on the Clipboard (whose window size has been adjusted using the Size choice on the Control menu).

Data on the Clipboard is usually placed there by the Delete, Cut, or Copy commands. The Clipboard immediately reflects the copy operation most recently performed in the Cardfile program (see Figure 19.71). When this occurs, the former contents, shown in Figure 19.70, are discarded.

Once again, remember that you should save your work at regular intervals. In a complex Windows environment containing many simultaneous applications, such as the example you've worked with here, it is easy to forget what data has been saved and what has not.

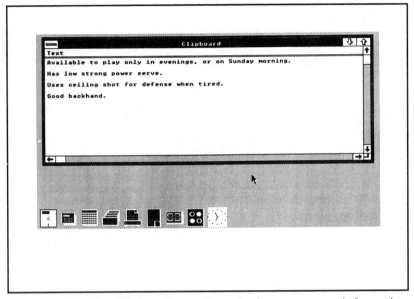

Figure 19.72: The Clipboard contains only the most recent information deposited in it.

Windows will not allow you to end a session (by selecting End Session on the MS-DOS Executive Special menu) without prompting you to save any new data. Figure 19.73 displays one of the prompt boxes displayed by Windows if you forget to save recent updates.

In this case, the Notepad data had previously been saved to a file called TEST1.TXT, but further adjustments during the session have not been saved. Selecting Yes now correctly updates the disk file to reflect these changes. A similar box appears for each application with changes or updates that have not been saved.

SUMMARY

In this chapter, you have learned about the Windows multitasking operating environment. It offers a dramatic step beyond the single-program, command-prompt environment of standard DOS.

- You have seen how to run multiple DOS programs simultaneously under windows.

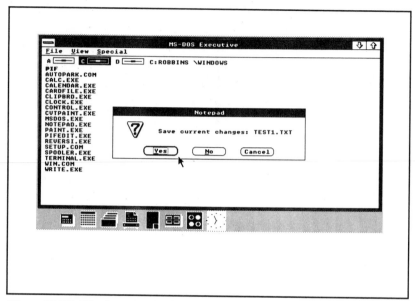

Figure 19.73: Windows reminds you to save your work.

- You have learned the steps necessary to install and configure Windows for your computer system.

- The MS-DOS Executive offers a range of file-management, command-selection, and window-controlling choices.

- Built-in application programs offer a variety of utility capabilities, such as on-screen calculation, appointment calendar maintenance, output spooling, note and text manipulation, and even cutting and pasting operations between utilities.

Now that you've seen how Windows offers you the opportunity for multitasking in DOS, turn to Chapter 20 for a peek behind the scenes. In the next chapter, you'll learn how Windows as well as other advanced DOS programs make use of large amounts of additional memory to break through the DOS 640K memory barrier.

BREAKING THROUGH
THE 640K LIMIT

_____

TWENTY YEARS AGO, SOPHISTICATED PROGRAMS could be (and were) written using computers with as little as 4K of memory. In the early 1980s, users and developers alike marveled at the DOS facility for addressable program space of up to 640K. Times change.

And they continue to change. Within a few years, applications were being written that consumed all of that 640K and begged for more. Spreadsheets frequently displayed a ''memory full'' message as the range of cells and formulas quickly exceeded available space. Integrated packages discovered scarce file space left in memory after all the requisite code to support the multiple applications was loaded.

Users discovered that DOS and their individual application programs didn't always do everything they wanted. Consequently, memory-resident software surged in popularity in the mid-eighties. These packages consumed portions of the 640K memory limit.

Users also wanted easier access to multiple programs. This situation led to various programming solutions, from common data-file formats to conversion programs to simultaneous program execution. Programs such as Desqview and Windows approach this requirement for simultaneity in different ways (see the discussion that follows), but the performance of both still suffers when available memory is limited.

EARLY SOLUTIONS TO MEMORY RESTRICTIONS

Limitations on memory affect programs in two primary ways. In the first case, the program must reference data files that are larger than can fit into what little memory remains after the program itself is loaded. This limitation affects word processors such as WordPerfect and WordStar. In the second case, the program itself requires more memory for its own code routines and logic than is available. This limitation affects more recent and sophisticated DOS programs such as dBASE IV and Framework III. Some programs struggle with both limitations and meet those constraints with the two solutions presented in this section.

REFERENCING LARGE DATA FILES

Databases are often quite large, easily exceeding 640K. In fact, the most common database applications on microcomputers are inventory files and customer or client mailing lists. These files often exceed one megabyte in size. Database programs and word processors don't even fight the constraint; these packages simply spill excess memory requirements right over into disk space.

In essence, then, a large file is maintained on disk; the application program brings into memory only a piece of the file at a time. The application uses this piece and then updates the disk file. Then the program brings another piece of the data file into the memory buffer area to be used by the application program. Most word processors and database managers use this technique (see Figure 20.1).

The solution seen here is implemented when a program must access a data file whose size exceeds available physical memory. A portion of memory (a buffer) within the application program's addressable space is designated to hold the desired portion of the data file. Whichever portion of the data file is being referenced determines at each moment the contents of the memory-resident buffer.

A program can reserve a small data area within its own address space and designate it as an input/output buffer. Depending on what portion of the disk-based data file you reference, the program fills the buffer with the portion of the file containing the desired data.

LOADING LARGE, SOPHISTICATED PROGRAMS

Most popular application software packages contain more instructions and coding sequences than can fit at once into conventional

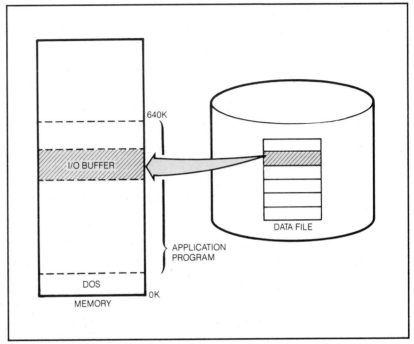

Figure 20.1: Applications can manage their own memory buffers.

DOS memory. Remember that this conventional memory is constrained to 640K, as shown in Figure 20.2.

Conventional memory is limited to 640K and spans both the memory requirements of your DOS version and the needs of your individual application program. Upper memory is accessible to the Intel chips that run DOS, but is used only for special purposes: 128K is reserved for video memory, and the remaining 256K is reserved for read-only memory tasks, primarily the built-in BIOS.

The actual limit of 1Mb is a constraint of the 8086 and 8088 chips from Intel, which construct their memory addresses using 20 bits (2^{20} = 1Mb). IBM PC and PC/XT computers and compatibles are absolutely restricted by the hardware in this way. This is also true for machines using the newer 80286 chip in real mode; the IBM PC/AT and compatibles fall into this category.

Many users do not avail themselves of all the capabilities of programs that offer advanced features. Recognizing this reality is fundamental to this next solution to memory limitation. Figure 20.3

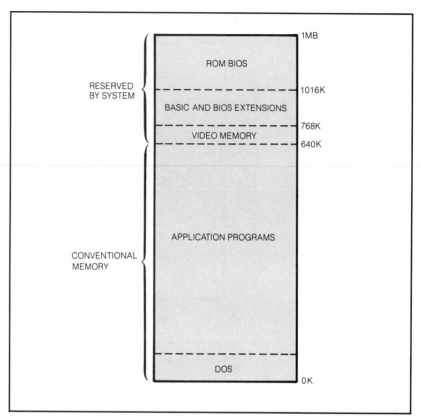

Figure 20.2: Standard DOS memory usage (map)

illustrates how *overlays*, or submodules, provide a solution to the memory-limitation problem.

Memory overlays solve the problem of limited space by splitting program code into a main module and one or more submodules. If the main code, loaded at program startup, does not contain the needed instruction sequence, then the appropriate overlay module containing the required code is loaded into memory. This code overwrites a clearly designated portion of memory called the overlay area.

When designing an application, the program designer can specify that certain routines are always resident. These should be the routines the user will probably want to use most frequently. The designer can place less frequently needed routines in an auxiliary load module, known as an *overlay file*. Some extremely feature-rich

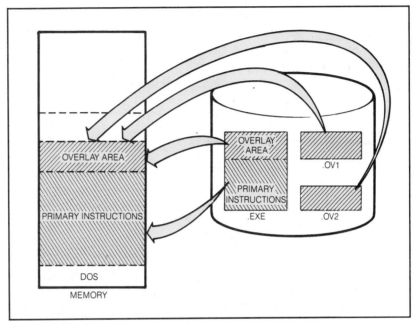

Figure 20.3: Overlay files use the same memory but at different times.

software packages, such as CAD (computer-aided design) programs, often have two or three overlay files.

When the program runs, it determines which feature the user is calling, either via a command prompt or through a menu mechanism. If that particular feature is not supported by the instructions in the portion of the package currently in memory, then the overlay file containing the proper instructional routines is loaded into memory. Typically, a designated portion of memory, called the *overlay area*, is used as the temporary home for these overlay routines.

In this way, an application can contain an unlimited number of features. If loaded at the same time, these features could easily consume hundreds of kilobytes more than can fit into conventional memory. The overlay mechanism ensures that conventional memory is never exceeded, and that when a particular feature is activated, the code to support the feature is loaded.

Overlays are a form of demand loading that works quite successfully for many programs. However, besides the CPU drain, an additional problem of the overlay technique is the designer effort and

The primary disadvantage of using overlays is the extra processing required to load them.

knowledge necessary to split the support routines into separate modules and properly prepare the overlay files.

Overlays were a good first solution to the memory limitation problem. Faster and easier methods have since been developed, although they are not all available to all programs and to all processing chips.

USING EXTENDED MEMORY TO BREAK THE MEMORY BARRIER

The most obvious solution to memory constraints is to increase the amount of memory available in the system. If memory were easily added without limit, then such techniques as those discussed in the previous section would be unnecessary. Entire data files and program files supporting an enormous range of features could, regardless of their size, be easily loaded into memory.

Even though memory is becoming increasingly inexpensive, simply adding memory chips or boards is not the answer. Physical availability of memory on a system is not enough. The processing chip must be able to address that memory, and the operating system must also be able to gain access to the program code and data stored in that memory; the application programs themselves may need to modify their addressing techniques to make effective use of the new addresses located outside of conventional memory.

USING PROTECTED MODE TO EXTEND MEMORY ADDRESSABILITY

The 80286 chip from Intel offers a feature called *protected mode*. Whereas the 8088/8086 chips used 20 bits to construct an address (gaining access to 1 megabyte of memory), this chip uses 24 bits for addressing. Those extra 4 bits allow the protected mode of the chip to directly access 16Mb of memory ($2^4 = 16$), many times that allowed by earlier chips. Figure 20.4 depicts this enhanced feature of the 80286 chip.

The 80286 chip has a split personality. With only a few assembly language instructions, the operating mode of the chip can be changed from real mode to protected mode. In protected mode, the extra

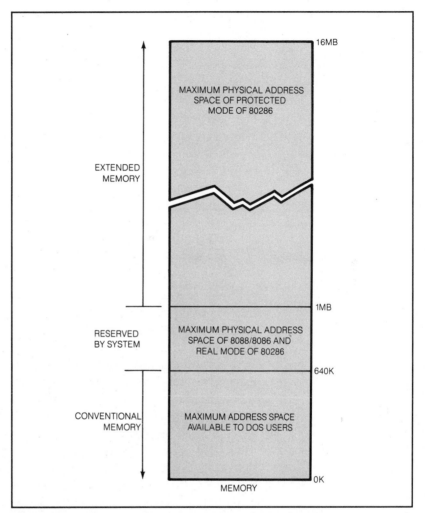

Figure 20.4: 80286 chips can address 16 megabytes of memory.

address lines on the PC/AT and PS/2 computers allow access to 16 megabytes. This extra memory beyond one megabyte is called *extended memory*.

Unfortunately, most software (including DOS itself) has not been adapted to actually use any of the address space beyond one megabyte. However, DOS 3.X and 4 have been able to use this extra memory in the form of a RAM disk (called VDISK in IBM PC-DOS systems). Remember that RAM disks use memory addresses to store files in a special format that emulates the organization and accessibility of a disk drive. This allows disk operations such as online overlay transfers to work at memory speeds rather than at the much slower disk speeds.

With a RAM disk, only RAM disk software knows that the data and file access is actually from memory, not from a real disk drive. In fact, earlier RAM disk drivers often created virtual disks from unused memory locations in the conventional memory space below the 640K limit. In either case, however, you must first copy data files or overlay files from their real disk locations to the RAM disk before any programs can access them. After using the data files, you must remember to copy any changes back to their permanent file locations, typically on your hard disk.

LIMITATIONS OF EXTENDED MEMORY

Extended memory is just a tool. The 80286 chip provides access to that memory, but DOS is limited in its ability to use it. Instruction support in the ROM BIOS is extremely limited, being restricted to determining how much memory is installed and transferring data to and from conventional memory. DOS and the BIOS do not manage this extended memory in any sophisticated way, so it is difficult for multiple programs to use portions of extended memory simultaneously.

DOS still does not directly address the extended-memory locations. The newest IBM operating system, OS/2, from Microsoft and IBM, does introduce a sophisticated memory manager that uses this extended memory directly. See my *Essential OS/2* (SYBEX, 1988) for more information about how this mechanism is implemented.

Certainly, extended memory can be used as more than just an area for large RAM disk operations. That's just what industry leaders proclaimed in 1985 when they announced new standards for memory utilization. These standards, known as the LIM specification, form the basis for the discussion in the next section.

USING EXPANDED MEMORY FOR MORE POWERFUL OPERATIONS

The next creative solution to memory constraints was developed in 1985 by Lotus Development Corporation and Intel. In an attempt to

See Chapter 11 for detailed information about how DOS 4 supports expanded memory with new device drivers.

further stretch the capabilities of the millions of existing microcomputers, these companies announced a new specification for what they called expanded memory. After viewing early presentations of their specifications, Microsoft Corporation joined Lotus and Intel to release the LIM EMS (Lotus-Intel-Microsoft expanded-memory specification 3.2.) This common standard became an overnight hit.

USING BANK SWITCHING TO EXPAND YOUR MEMORY

Like the size of conventional memory, the size of your desk surface is finite. You can assign a central portion of your desk to papers and folders, selected from a potentially unlimited number of files in your file cabinet. You can have a series of relevant papers on your desk, reserving one area for reference folders you get from and return to your file cabinet (see Figure 20.5).

Even though your desktop is physically limited in size, you can use unlimited reference materials by switching among file folders, reserving one portion of your desk as a "switching area." Although your desk may contain a variety of other materials that does not change, you can access 2, 5, or 50 file folders during your own personal information processing, though only one of these folders is open and accessible at any given moment.

Similarly, a computer can reserve a portion of conventional memory as a central "switching area." If this area is analogous to the file folder area in the center of your desk, then any number of similarly sized (or smaller) portions of extended memory can be logically brought into this area. This technique is called *bank switching* (a *bank* of storage addresses in memory is a physically and logically addressable unit). Figure 20.6 depicts this approach to memory expansion.

In the original LIM 3.2 specification, up to 8Mb of expanded memory could be accessed through one 64K reserved lower memory area. This area was typically carved out of an unused area of contiguous memory located in the sparsely used ROM area at the upper end of addressable memory (below 1Mb).

The LIM EMS specification contained many details of expanded-memory management and of the interface between that memory and programs wanting to gain access to it. Many of these details are

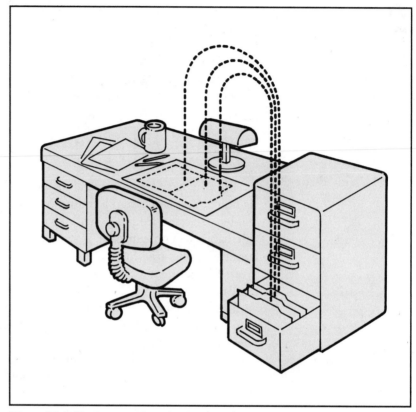

Figure 20.5: Desktop analogy for memory bank switching

embodied in a program called the Expanded Memory Manager
(EMM.SYS), which expanded-memory systems must include as a
device driver in the CONFIG.SYS file.

During system booting, when all device drivers are installed,
EMM.SYS looks for a contiguous, available area of 64K in the
uppermost 256K of memory reserved for ROM programs. When it
finds such an area, EMM.SYS takes control of these addresses and
uses them as a window into the separate expanded-memory locations. IBM PCs and PC/XTs, as well as PC/ATs and PS/2s in real
mode, can address only up to 1Mb; however, these 64K address locations are directly addressable by the processing chip.

When a program wants access to the additional memory locations
in the expanded-memory area, it must make a precisely defined
interrupt call to EMM.SYS that provides the uniform interface to

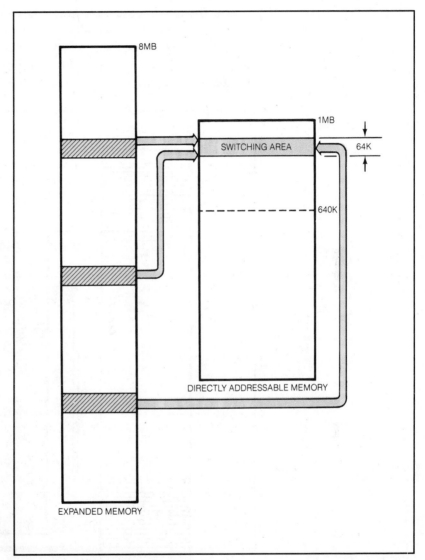

Figure 20.6: The Lotus-Intel-Microsoft expanded-memory specification
(LIM EMS 3.2)

any of those locations. EMM.SYS enables this access by providing a
unique programming handle to each program using expanded memory. These programs can be single-tasking or multitasking programs,
other device drivers, or even written memory-resident programs.

Even though the area reserved by the expanded-memory manager is 64K in size, EMS 3.2 actually called for the banks to be only 16K in size. Hence, as can be seen in Figure 20.7, the EMM must manage the necessary access to up to 8Mb of physical expanded memory through the regimen of switching base addresses in units of 16K.

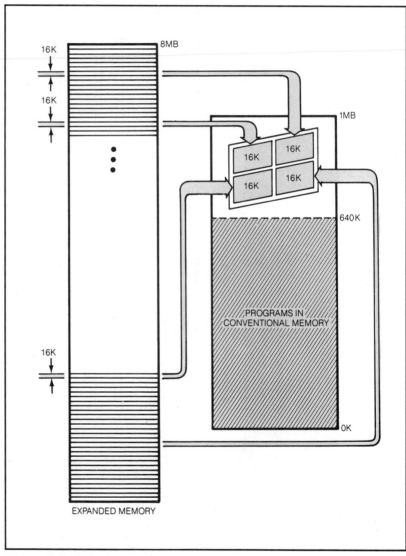

Figure 20. 7: 8Mb of expanded memory is managed 16K at a time.

Conventional memory programs can use this technique to access up to 8Mb of additional expanded memory, according to the original expanded-memory specification 3.2. They do so through software-interrupt calls to the EMM.SYS device driver. EMM.SYS switches banks of 16K memory addresses. The window into these expanded memory pages is provided and maintained by EMM.SYS in a contiguous block of 64K, carved out of the 256K ROM area at the top of the typical 1Mb address space.

All expanded memory is treated as a collection of memory banks, divided into 16K pages. Simple instructions are part of the memory specification, allowing programs to switch new 16K pages into the 64K addressable window or to switch existing pages and their data out of the window and back to expanded-memory locations.

In total, EMM.SYS provides a variety of services to a requesting program, well beyond the standard initialization and output functions of a standard device driver. EMM.SYS also provides information, through software-interrupt 67H, regarding hardware and software module statuses and the current allocation of expanded-memory pages. Diagnostic routines are available, as are routines to manage the actual mapping of logical pages into and out of expanded memory into physical pages in the 64K window.

The LIM EMS specification was the possible groundwork for the next generation of multitasking operating systems. But progress continued in the DOS world with the introduction of new products from industry competitors.

ENHANCING THE EXPANDED-MEMORY SPECIFICATION

AST Research and Quadram are two of the industry leaders in the production of add-on memory boards, and Ashton-Tate is a major producer of personal computer software. Together, these three companies released their own new specifications for expanded-memory use. Their enhanced version of EMS was called EEMS (enhanced expanded-memory specification).

EEMS was more complex than EMS 3.2 and differed in key ways. Whereas EMS located the switching area above the DOS 640K program area, EEMS mapped expanded memory into addressable space anywhere under the 1Mb address limit. This feature allowed

EEMS enabled program code, not just data, to be switched into addressable memory locations below 640K.

easy switching of memory pages that contain addressable code because they could be switched into the lower memory addresses accessible by DOS programs.

EEMS also offered an expanded mapping window. Whereas EMS allowed the mapping of only four 16K logical expanded memory pages into physical memory, EEMS allowed the mapping of 64 logical pages ($64 \times 16K = 1Mb$). EEMS also supported a minimum window size of 16K. In fact, as it turns out, the upper limit on window size was somewhat unrealistic, since much of that 1Mb is needed by DOS, application program code, video buffers, and system ROMs. The new EEMS specification did, however, realistically make available all free space: often as much as 20 logical pages.

EEMS also allowed software specification of mapping areas at runtime. Under EMS 3.2, you had to take great care setting the proper switches and jumpers on the memory boards to specify the mapping area. Additionally, EMS 3.2 required one contiguous 64K memory area. EEMS allowed the use of several areas that are not necessarily physically contiguous.

For a while, it was unclear which of these two heavyweight standards would emerge the winner. Microsoft's Windows used EMS to implement its multitasking strategy, and Quarterdeck's Desqview used EEMS in its more powerful multitasking operating environment. The differing concepts and implementation strategies of these memory specifications made writing programs that run easily under both specifications difficult. In fact, memory boards conforming to one specification do not necessarily work under the other.

EVERYONE WINS WITH THE LIM EMS 4.0 SPECIFICATION

Users of DOS and designers of programs in the DOS environment were gratified in 1987 by the announcement of the latest evolution of the expanded-memory specifications. This latest announcement, variously referred to as LIM 4.0 or EMS 4.0, specifies a new set of developer functions that support much larger DOS application programs, as well as multitasking. These new specifications permit the use of these improved features on all DOS machines, even the seemingly more limited 8088/8086 PC and PC/XT models.

EMS 4.0 incorporates all of the best aspects of the earlier EMS 3.2, as well as the improvements made in EEMS, thus reducing confusion among program developers and setting EMS 4.0 apart as a viable standard for future program growth in the DOS world. The AST/Quadram/Ashton-Tate group has accepted the new standard.

The new standard defines more than twice the number of functions and subfunctions (30 versus 15) contained in EMS 3.2. In addition, accessible expanded memory has been increased from a maximum size of 8Mb to 32Mb. Incorporating some of the EEMS techniques ensures that EMS 4.0 supports the execution of both standard program code as well as TSR (terminate-and-stay-resident) programs in expanded memory.

EMS 4.0 directly supports multitasking. An occasional requirement of programs when they run concurrently with other programs is that they be able to share data. This new standard also defines how, specifically, common data access and sharing can take place.

The developers of EMS 4.0 clearly state that it is not itself a multitasking operating system. It does, however, provide a formidable array of features that allow applications to perform multitasking in expanded memory. A variety of programs, RAM disks, and print spoolers all can run simultaneously in expanded memory.

The new OS/2 system for IBM computers, on the other hand, is a full-blown multitasking operating system, with significantly enhanced features over both DOS and EMS 4.0. However, if your computer does not run OS/2 or you do not upgrade your system to OS/2, EMS 4.0 can breathe new life into your system. New software will undoubtedly be designed, and certainly much old software will be upgraded, to work in this enhanced DOS environment.

As you learned in Chapter 11, DOS 4 supports expanded memory. Two special drivers are available to DOS 4 users to directly support expanded-memory adapters (XMA2EMS.SYS) and to emulate an expanded-memory adapter (XMAEM.SYS). The following section explains how emulation can provide you with expanded-memory capabilities, even when you don't have expanded memory.

SAVING MONEY WITH EXPANDED-MEMORY EMULATORS

If you have no available slots in your IBM PC or PC/XT for a specially designated expanded-memory board, or if you choose to avoid the expense of a new expanded-memory board, several vendors now offer help. This help may be especially relevant if you've already spent money on an AT-type extended-memory board.

Since the expanded-memory specification is device independent, the source of the expanded memory is unimportant to applications using it. Therefore, just as surely as a piece of software can cause memory to be perceived as a RAM disk, so a piece of software can cause a disk to be perceived as memory.

In fact, the same concept can be taken one step further. Expanded-memory-emulation software can adhere to the EMS requirements, providing memory pages not from an expanded memory board, but from any one of the sources shown in Figure 20.8.

The emulation software conforms to the expanded-memory specifications, so the source of the data is irrelevant to an application program making the proper EMS calls. The source could be a standard expanded-memory hardware board, as shown at the top of Figure 20.8, or it could be one of the two sources for emulated expanded memory, as shown at the bottom of the figure.

If your system already includes extended memory, you can configure the emulation software to use that memory as if it were expanded memory. You can use DOS 4's XMAEM.SYS device driver to do this if you have an 80386 machine (see Chapters 11 and 22). Naturally, the drawback of this method is the extra software overhead (which can be considerable) required for the emulated access.

Even if your system has no additional memory installed, you still can run software requiring expanded memory. The emulation routines can create a disk file equal in size to the simulated expanded memory that you need but don't have. The emulator handles the reading and writing of the disk file to obtain the 16K pages needed by the expanded-memory manager. This solution permits you to run software in an expanded-memory environment, albeit at significantly reduced speeds because of the relatively enormous disk input/output overhead.

Although emulation may seem attractive, it has some obvious drawbacks. As pointed out, using it is markedly slower than using expanded memory directly. The overhead for the software emulation is considerable, and if you are using a disk file to emulate expanded memory, the

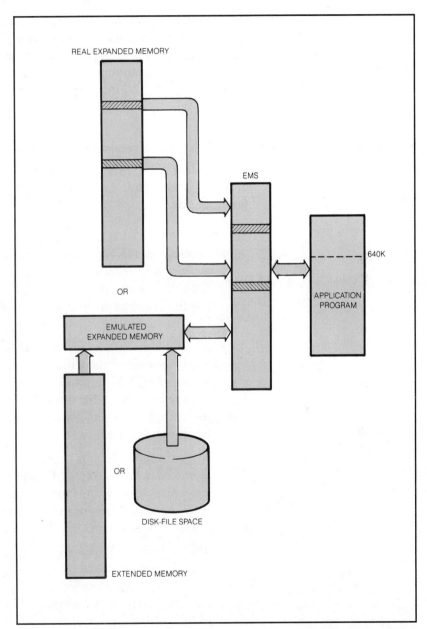

Figure 20.8: Expanded memory can be emulated in either AT-style extended memory or in disk files created just for this purpose.

disk I/O overhead further reduces overall system performance. In addition, emulation software is not always completely compatible with programs designed to run using actual hardware boards. So even if you're willing to endure reduced performance, you still may not be able to run your favorite expanded-memory program.

SUMMARY

You've learned a variety of creative approaches in this chapter, all aimed at surmounting the 640K limit imposed by DOS on application programs.

- Early solutions concentrated on reusing memory within the application's .EXE space. Large amounts of data was managed within internal buffers maintained by the program. Larger amounts of executable code were managed by grouping the instructions into separate overlay files, which would later use the same area of memory, but at different times.

- 80286 chip technology enabled direct addressing of up to 16Mb of extended memory. However, very few programs written for DOS took advantage of this possibility, since it required the special protected mode of the hardware. DOS itself used extended memory only for its RAM disk configuration feature.

- Major industry leaders (Lotus, Intel, and Microsoft) defined a set of specifications (LIM 3.2) for addressing up to 8Mb of expanded memory through small 16K blocks of memory reserved from locations in lower memory (under 1Mb). This is called "bank switching."

- The Enhanced Expanded Memory Specification (EEMS) was created by Ashton-Tate and Quadram to improve the LIM definitions. Both groups of specifications have been collectively grouped and improved in the 1987 announcement of the LIM 4.0 Expanded Memory Specification.

- As an alternative to those unwilling or unable to buy or add expanded memory boards to your computers, you can emulate expanded memory with either extended memory or even disk files. Both of these techniques save money, but have a severe performance impact on your system.

- DOS 4 directly supports the EMS 4.0 specifications with its XMA2EMS.SYS device driver. Furthermore, DOS 4 also provides device-driver support (XMAEM.SYS) for emulating expanded memory in 80386 systems.

Now that you know how to overcome the 640K limit from within DOS, read Chapter 21 to learn how to overcome it by running DOS under OS/2, IBM and Microsoft's newest operating system.

RUNNING DOS PROGRAMS
IN OS/2

OS/2 PROVIDES MANY DRAMATIC IMPROVEMENTS over DOS. The range and nature of these new capabilities are presented in detail in my 1988 book, *Essential OS/2*, from SYBEX. Each of the preceding two chapters in this book presented techniques and programs designed for the DOS arena which provide some of OS/2's standard capabilities. Chapter 19 concentrated on the multitasking capabilities of Windows, and Chapter 20 focused on methods for addressing memory in excess of 640K.

OS/2 features multitasking for all new programs written for its special protected-mode environment. This protected mode is an inherent, but previously little-used capability of the 80286 and 80386 processing chips. OS/2 also features memory management logic which enables programs to address physical memory up to 16Mb, and even enables programs to write code for addressing memory beyond what physically exists; this then is called *virtual memory*.

In this chapter, you'll learn an important OS/2 benefit: you are not required to buy or write completely new programs, because almost all of your DOS programs can run under OS/2. OS/2 can give you the benefits of a dramatically improved operating system, including the enhanced new features, without losing the functionality of your current DOS programs.

The compatibility between DOS and OS/2 is provided through the OS/2 *real mode*, which emulates DOS. Real mode provides an operating environment that allows you to run most of your DOS programs with no changes. This real mode is the portion of OS/2 that only uses the portion of the 80286/80386 chips, also called real mode, that merely acts like a very fast DOS 8088/8086 processing chip. You may sometimes hear this real mode referred to as the DOS Compatability Box.

This chapter also explains the steps necessary to make a smooth transition from DOS to the OS/2 environment including setting up, starting up, and configuring your OS/2 environment to permit DOS programs to run. Additionally, you will learn a number of important distinctions between the two operating environments, and potential obstacles to running DOS programs in OS/2. The chapter examines a broad range of issues, from proper configuration to initial batch file contents to some of the more complex programming issues of OS/2 function calls.

WORKING IN REAL MODE

In order to run DOS programs, you must switch the processing chip from OS/2's protected, multitasking mode to its DOS compatible real mode. When OS/2's protected mode (the normal default mode) starts up, you are presented with one of several possibilities. First, you may see the primary OS/2 control screen which lists all running programs, as well as program and mode possibilities. Second, you may see some main program (perhaps a menu screen) running. Or, you may simply see the normal protected-mode command interpreter prompt, [C:\].

The primary control screen displayed by OS/2 varies according to version. In the first version, OS/2 1.0, the primary screen is called the Session Manager. It is a text screen that lists the currently executing programs, as well as the installed possibilities for new programs. Version 1.1 of OS/2 contains the Presentation Manager, a completely graphic interface based on the technique of multiple windows. One screen window, now called the Task Manager, is devoted to the same role of showing the currently executing OS/2 tasks. A separate window, called Start Programs, facilitates your initiating all possible installed OS/2 tasks. In this chapter, I'll refer to the Task Manager seen in the most current graphic version of OS/2.

If your version of OS/2 does not automatically display the Task Manager, perhaps because someone has configured it in a special way, you can easily display this important management screen. Pressing the Ctrl-Esc key combination displays the Presentation Manager screen (in OS/2 1.1), which gives you access to the Task Manager and Start Programs windows. At this point, you can either start new programs or switch to a running program.

If you want to run a DOS application, the simplest method is to switch to the Task Manager window and use an arrow key to highlight the DOS Command Line choice. Then press the Return key. This moves the processor into real mode and displays the DOS command prompt. The OS/2 CMD.EXE command file interpreter handles all protected-mode OS/2 command requests, while the COMMAND-.COM command line interpreter handles all real-mode command requests. Once you have brought up COMMAND.COM, you can continue as if your machine were running DOS alone. If you've loaded your disk with your applications, set your PATH and your working directory as required to run the DOS program.

If you try to run one of your DOS programs (.EXE or .COM) from the protected mode command prompt, you will receive one of the following two error messages:

If you follow the instructions in this section and get a message saying "Insufficient Memory," don't worry that the 3Mb of RAM you bought aren't enough to run your old program. They are. The next section on configuration explains how to configure your new OS/2 system to understand the different memory requirements of the DOS programs you'll be running in OS/2's real mode.

DOS0191E: The system has detected an unacceptable signature in the file, *Filename.*

or

DOS0193E: The system has detected an unacceptable executable format in file, *Filename.*

OS/2 displays one of these two messages when you try to run a file that is either formatted incorrectly for OS/2, or represents an incorrect version of the program. Under most conditions, you would try to find the correct version of the program. In this case, you are trying to run what you know is the real mode or DOS version of the program. Since the .EXE and .COM files from DOS are unreadable as executable files in OS/2, it is unable to understand the instructions. Any program that was originally compiled, assembled, or prepared to run in DOS mode can be run only in OS/2's real mode. Let's look at some examples.

RUNNING YOUR WORD PROCESSOR

To run a DOS-based word processor on OS/2, you must first switch to real mode and get the familiar C> prompt. In this example, the word processor is located in the WP directory of the C drive. To access it, enter the following commands at the C > prompt:

```
PATH C:\;C:\OS2;C:\WP
CD \WP
WP
```

The first line augments the system search path in order to look for files in the root first, then to search the OS2 directory for any necessary supporting routines (such as the external commands CHKDSK or XCOPY), and lastly to look in the WP directory (where the word processor in this example can be found). The second line performs the standard change directory (CD) request to make the word-processing directory the current default. The final step in real mode asks the COMMAND.COM interpreter to pass control to your version of WP.COM or WP.EXE, depending on which word processor you are using.

RUNNING YOUR DATABASE-MANAGEMENT PROGRAM

Now suppose that you have a database program whose main and support files are located in a directory called DBMS. You want to run your inventory program located in a subdirectory of the DBMS directory called INVNTRY. You want to switch to the INVNTRY subdirectory that contains the inventory database information, but you must still ensure that the principal DBMS files are accessible through the PATH. Use the following sequence of statements in real mode:

```
PATH C:\;C:\OS2;C:\DBMS
APPEND \DBMS
CD \DBMS\INVNTRY
DBASE
```

In this example, your working directory is now the INVNTRY directory. This is where the dBASE.COM program will look for the appropriate database files or create new ones. The PATH command meanwhile ensures that OS/2 knows how to find its appropriate system files in either the root or the OS2 directory. Because of the

PATH command, OS/2 can also find the main dBASE program in the DBMS directory. The APPEND command, on the other hand, enables the system to locate any required overlay files used by the main executable dBASE programs.

RUNNING YOUR SPREADSHEET PROGRAM

Finally, you may wish to run a favorite spreadsheet, like Lotus 1-2-3. All of Lotus's main system files may be located in the LOTUS subdirectory, while all of your budget worksheets are located in a subdirectory called BUDGET, and your accounting worksheets are located in a different subdirectory called ACCOUNTS. Like database managers, sophisticated spreadsheets usually work on an overlay basis. You therefore need the following sequence of steps to run this kind of application in OS/2's real mode:

```
PATH C:\;C:\OS2;C:\LOTUS
APPEND \LOTUS
CD \LOTUS\ACCOUNTS
123
```

As you can see in Figure 21.1, the CD command makes the ACCOUNTS directory the current working directory. To OS/2 this means that your worksheet files will be accessible in that directory. If you want to switch to the BUDGET directory, do so either from within Lotus or modify the CD command before running the 123.EXE program. The PATH and APPEND lines again direct the OS/2 system to find the main 123.EXE program (via PATH), and any subordinate overlay files (via APPEND), in the LOTUS directory.

Most DOS programs will run if you follow the instructions above. As mentioned at the beginning of this section, however, some programs may not run directly because they require more memory than the default number of kilobytes allotted by OS/2 to real mode. If this is the only problem, you'll get an ''Insufficient Memory'' message, and you should follow the guidelines for configuring your system in the next section.

If your program doesn't run in real mode for some other reason, read about potential obstacles in the ''Distinctions and Obstacles''

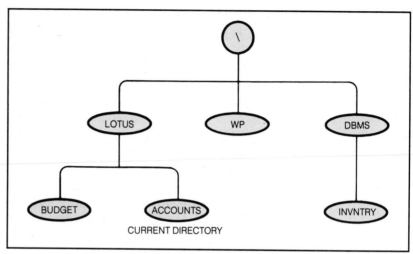

Figure 21.1: Directory structure for real-mode applications

section of this chapter. Your program may use certain system interrupts or DOS-function calls for manipulating hardware that are not allowed in any program in the OS/2 environment, even in real mode. In these cases, you must either find a replacement program or get the errant program rewritten for the OS/2 environment.

CONFIGURING YOUR OS/2 SYSTEM FOR DOS PROGRAMS

Some versions of OS/2 offer a dual boot feature that enables a single hard disk to maintain complete and separate OS/2 and DOS systems. During the bootstrap process, you are asked to choose which of the two systems you want to be the controlling operating system.

In both DOS and OS/2, the system assumes certain default values if you do not specify new ones with a CONFIG.SYS file. In OS/2 as in DOS, there is only one controlling configuration file. However, in some versions of OS/2 from Microsoft, you have the option of installing both DOS and OS/2 on a single hard disk. In this case, a CONFIG.SYS file controls the booting of DOS, while a separate CONFIG.OS2 file oversees the booting of OS/2. If both systems are not installed on the same disk, then CONFIG.SYS becomes the controlling file containing all configuration information.

OS/2 allows you to override any or all of a host of initial values for internal systems parameters. The control you have via this initial file is so much enhanced over DOS that an entire chapter of *Essential OS/2* is entirely devoted to the initial setup conditions now under your control.

This chapter, however, addresses only the minimum required to enable DOS programs to run in real mode. Figure 21.2 shows an example CONFIG.SYS file.

When you first install OS/2, the installation program (INSTAID.EXE) prepares a CONFIG.SYS (or CONFIG.OS2) file such as this one for you. As you can see in line 12, the SHELL command specifies that the DOS COMMAND.COM program will be a permanently resident command interpreter for real-mode instructions (indicated by the /p switch). All of the lines in this prototype CONFIG.SYS file are as they appear during initial installation of OS/2, except lines 13, 18, and 19. Line 13 is essential to DOS programs. During OS/2 initialization, the default is to install a real-mode memory size of 256K (RMSIZE = 256).

```
 1   REM
 2   REM     Prototype Config.sys file for OS/2 when booting off a hard disk
 3   REM
 4   REM
 5   REM     If your system has less than 4Mb of RAM, shrink the size of the
 6   REM     diskcache and the real mode box.  If you are not going to use the
 7   REM     compatibility mode then remove the REM statement from the line that
 8   REM     reads PROTECTONLY=yes
 9   REM
10
11   BUFFERS=50
12   SHELL=Command.com /p /e:512 c:\
13   RMSIZE=640
14   PROTSHELL=Shell.exe Cmd.exe
15   IOPL=yes
16   LIBPATH=C:\
17   MEMMAN=Noswap,move
18   DEVICE=Ansi.sys
19   DEVICE=Hardrive.sys
20
21   REM     The rest of the file contains commented out lines.  Delete the word
22   REM     REM from the begining of the command lines if that feature is needed
23   REM     or wanted.
24
25   REM PROTECTONLY=yes
26   REM DISKCACHE=512
27   REM SWAPPATH=C:
28   REM DEVICE=C:\Com01.sys
29   REM DEVICE=C:\Vdisk.sys 256 512 16
30   REM DEVICE=C:\Pointdd.sys
31
32   REM     Select one of the following drivers:
33   REM     02 - serial, 03 - Bus, 04 - Import
34   REM DEVICE=C:\Mousea02.sys mode=b
35   REM DEVICE=C:\Mousea03.sys mode=b
36   REM DEVICE=C:\Mousea04.sys mode=b
37
38   REM     The following lines enable the Code Page support drivers.
39
40   REM DEVINFO=scr,ega,C:\Viotbl.dcp
41   REM DEVINFO=kbd,us, C:\Keyboard.dcp
42   REM DEVINFO=lpt1,4201,C:\4201.dcp,rom=(437,0)
43   REM CODEPAGE=437,850
```

Figure 21.2: Sample CONFIG.SYS file

If you configure OS/2 to run DOS applications, use the maximum RMSIZE value of 640 to help protect running OS/2 programs from errant DOS programs running at the same time.

At first glance, the RMSIZE parameter enables you to simply tell OS/2 how much of its low memory to reserve for DOS program execution. If you do not use all 640K for the real mode area, OS/2 uses the remainder of these low memory addresses for running OS/2 (protected-mode) programs. Unfortunately, since errant DOS programs have access to all memory addresses below 1Mb, a failed DOS program can adversely affect protected mode programs and data which happen to be occupying low memory addresses. For this reason, you should always configure your OS/2 system (with the RMSIZE parameter) to consume all 640K.

In any event, if your automatically generated configuration file does not allocate enough real-mode memory, you can use your line editor or word processor to change the value in line 13. It is not unusual to use all 640K in real mode for large, demanding programs like computer-aided design programs, or for certain memory-resident utility programs that are run in conjunction with standard software. In this case, the DOS real mode will almost surely need to occupy 640K and you must make sure that your CONFIG.SYS file contains the line

        RMSIZE = 640

OS/2 uses up at least 100K of the low 640K memory locations. DOS programs which formerly required all 640K will not be able to run in OS/2's real mode.

In fact, since OS/2 itself occupies approximately 100K of low memory, you really only have about 540K left for DOS applications running in the real mode. Naturally, then, some DOS applications with extensive DOS memory requirements will not even be able to run in this OS/2 emulation environment (real mode).

Depending on need, applications, and installed hardware, you may also have to add extra lines such as lines 18 and 19. Some application programs, like the PreCursor menu-management application program, require that the ANSI.SYS device driver be added to your CONFIG.SYS file (line 18). It is available at all times in protected mode for OS/2 programming and applications. However, you must load the ANSI.SYS device driver yourself (by including the line DEVICE = ANSI.SYS in your CONFIG.SYS file) if you intend to use special ANSI escape sequences in real mode such as cursor movement, graphics characters, and colors on color monitors. (Read the section on the PROMPT command in Chapter 11 for a full explanation of ANSI escape sequences.)

The last example insertion in this CONFIG.SYS file is seen on line 19: DEVICE = HARDRIVE.SYS. This line is for a system with a nonstandard hard disk installed, and a hard-disk device driver called HARDRIVE.SYS. Your system may have this or other unique installed devices, each of which requires the insertion of a line of this kind:

DEVICE = *drivername*

As you can see in Figure 21.2, there are a number of other sample features that are included as remarks (REM statements). These are suggested additions and you can invoke any of the special configuration parameter situations by removing the REM from the beginning of the desired line (as lines 21 through 23 explain). Read Chapter 9 of *Essential OS/2* for further information on any of these additional commands. If you're only interested in the minimum requirements for running DOS programs at this time, continue to the next section on startup programs and procedures.

CONTROLLING AUTOMATIC STARTUP IN OS/2 REAL MODE

When you first boot up your OS/2 system, the internal setup of OS/2 is completely initialized according to the command requests placed in the CONFIG.SYS file. These commands influence OS/2 and its internal settings one time only. They are acted upon at system bootup, and are not interpreted or acted upon again until the next time you boot up OS/2.

In contrast to this, Figure 21.3 represents the system flow that can be influenced by you at system start. In DOS, the system would automatically run a special startup batch file called AUTOEXEC-.BAT immediately after configuration and before giving you control at the command prompt. OS/2 has a similar mechanism.

In real mode, the same AUTOEXEC.BAT runs with the same results. If you have a file called AUTOEXEC.BAT in the root directory of your boot drive, all of the individual command line entries contained within it will be executed one after the other the first time OS/2 switches to real mode. Just as in DOS systems, all real-mode batch files are

Your AUTO-EXEC.BAT and STARTUP.CMD batch files must reside in the root directory of your boot disk.

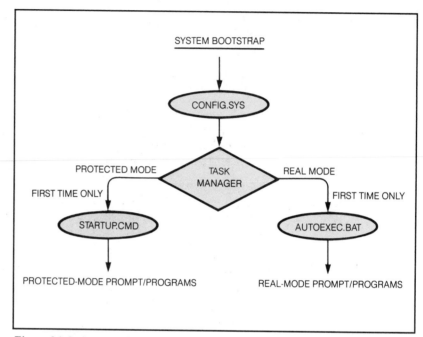

Figure 21.3: Automatic system startup flow

named with a .BAT extension; the AUTOEXEC.BAT allows for this automatic execution of a "batch" of commands. Paralleling this automatic invocation of the AUTOEXEC.BAT file is another batch file called STARTUP.CMD that is automatically invoked the first time OS/2 switches to protected mode. However, unlike the CONFIG.SYS file, which can only be invoked at system startup, both these batch files can be run at any time. As OS/2 is implemented, the processor comes up in protected mode, so the STARTUP.CMD file (if it exists) is run automatically. This is directly comparable to the automatic running of AUTOEXEC.BAT in a DOS system.

The AUTOEXEC.BAT file can be a sequence of commands like those you are familiar with from DOS as shown below:

```
SET COMSPEC = C:\COMMAND.COM
SET PATH = C:\;C:\OS2
PROMPT $n$g
```

The system PATH is set for system files and external command files. The COMSPEC parameter is also set (for clarification only, because C:\COMMAND.COM is the usual default file and directory), which tells OS/2 where it will be able to find the real-mode interpreter (COMMAND.COM). The PROMPT command in the third line initializes the default system prompt to $n (the working drive) followed by $g (a chevron symbol). As you read in Chapter 16, there is no end to the many additions and modifications you can make to this AUTOEXEC.BAT file, allowing a more flexible and utilitarian startup sequence for your system.

You can use this AUTOEXEC.BAT file to tell OS/2 how to access your old DOS files automatically. To do so, look at a copy of your own DOS system AUTOEXEC.BAT file, and then add your own appropriate adjustments or new lines to OS/2's default AUTOEXEC.BAT file. In the simplest case, you can leave the COMSPEC and the PROMPT lines alone. You might adjust the PATH command in your AUTOEXEC.BAT to include reference to the DBMS and LOTUS directories, by changing it as follows:

    SET PATH = C:\;C:\OS2;C:\DBMS;C:\LOTUS

An APPEND line of the following sort tells the system where the overlay files can be found for your application programs:

    APPEND C:\DBMS;C:\LOTUS

At the end of your AUTOEXEC.BAT file, you can pass control to a hard-disk menu-management utility you've already set up by adding the following line:

    PREMENU

This passes control to the main menu program of a hard-disk management package, giving you and other users of your system potential access to all executable DOS programs on your hard disk.

DISTINCTIONS AND OBSTACLES

If you follow the simple guidelines in the previous sections, you should have your old DOS programs up and running in no time. In most cases, it's as simple as adding a couple of lines to the CON-FIG.SYS file and a couple of lines in an AUTOEXEC.BAT file. But life is not always so simple, and certain DOS programs will never run under OS/2. For example, a sophisticated backup system such as Back-It Version 3.0 uses direct memory access (DMA) to achieve very high performance. Data are written to floppy disks at the same time as data are read from the hard disk. This particular program does not work successfully under OS/2, because OS/2 does not allow some of the interrupt-based techniques that are used. However, it can (and probably will) be rewritten using the simultaneous threads technique so that it will run in OS/2.

Some programs can be made to run with slight adjustments to the code, but this requires that you are either able to get into the code to adjust it, or that the programmer can provide you with an upgraded version of the code. In this section, you will learn some of the distinctions that should be considered in attempting to make or rewrite these programs.

Let's take a look first at some of the overlapping issues in the DOS and OS/2 operating environments. Figure 21.4 shows a number of the key distinctions between OS/2 and DOS. It also shows the overlap that allows DOS applications to run in OS/2's real mode.

OS/2 uses the hardware features of the 80286 and 80386 chip for protected-mode operations, and will not run on machines based on 8088 or 8086 chips. DOS, although it will run on the more advanced chips, uses only the real-mode portion of the chip. Because they do not take advantage of any of the advanced hardware operations of the new chips, DOS programs, whether run under DOS directly or in OS/2's real mode, are limited to 640K of addressable memory.

If your program is timer or clock dependent, it will not work properly.

Although they can make direct use of hardware interrupts, DOS programs running under OS/2 cannot participate in protected multitasking. This means that during protected-mode operations, your real-mode DOS program is frozen. It receives no interrupts and does not continue executing, because it receives no CPU service while you are executing in protected mode. In addition, the advanced programming features of *segmentation* and *memory overcommitment* can't be used completely by DOS programs.

Segmentation refers to the partitioning of memory by logical addresses rather than physical addresses, enabling you to run

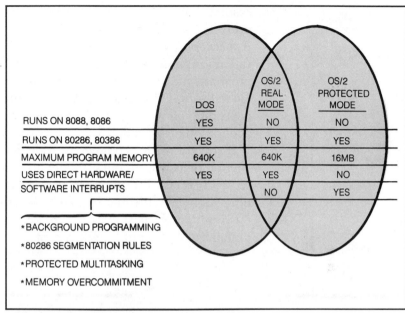

	DOS	OS/2 REAL MODE	OS/2 PROTECTED MODE
RUNS ON 8088, 8086	YES	NO	NO
RUNS ON 80286, 80386	YES	YES	YES
MAXIMUM PROGRAM MEMORY	640K	640K	16MB
USES DIRECT HARDWARE/ SOFTWARE INTERRUPTS	YES	YES	NO
		NO	YES

*BACKGROUND PROGRAMMING

*80286 SEGMENTATION RULES

*PROTECTED MULTITASKING

*MEMORY OVERCOMMITMENT

Figure 21.4: Overlap of OS/2 and DOS features

programs that can reference more memory than actually exists. Virtual memory, through OS/2's sophisticated memory manager, provides the ability to offer more apparent (virtual) memory to a running process than there is physical (actual) memory available. This is called memory overcommitment.

Some DOS programs are version specific and will only run on versions 2.X or 3.X. These may not work under OS/2, because the numbering of versions is different. As well, the set of system calls and returned error values differs from version to version.

Those of you accustomed to programming with interrupts may have written your programs to use interrupt 21H services under DOS. Most of the working but undocumented services through this interrupt are no longer supported by OS/2 real mode. Certain service interrupts that access ROM video services by address won't work either, because the management of interrupt 10 has been dramatically changed in OS/2.

There are many internal distinctions in the methods programmers must use to handle interrupts, manage devices, and code their applications. As a result, Microsoft has defined a special subset of its total

Since interrupt handling has changed drastically under OS/2, older special purpose DOS device drivers will surely not work in the OS/2 environment.

system calls that are designed to work in both real-mode and protected-mode environments. This subset is called the Family **Application Program Interface (FAPI)** of the complete OS/2 Application Programming Interface (API), and is the suggested subset for programs run in both real mode and protected mode. Programs written in this way can also be run on machines using DOS 2.X or 3.X, depending on which actual subset of instructions are chosen by the application programmer.

If you are writing commercial code that you want to run in either environment, you would certainly do well to write it with the FAPI set of functions. It ensures that users will have much greater ease running your code in either operating-system environment, eliminates the drain on physical memory, and enhances the performance and usefulness of the entire OS/2 system.

SUMMARY

One of the first ways you will probably use your OS/2 system is to run your DOS programs. Even if you are using OS/2 primarily for new programs, there will probably be times you will want to run DOS programs. This chapter detailed the steps to take to exploit this attractive functionality of OS/2.

- **Real mode runs DOS** programs in OS/2. OS/2 allows you to reserve (through CONFIG.SYS) a portion of physical memory (up to 640K) for emulating a DOS environment.

- **When you switch to real mode, you can run most existing application programs** and all standard DOS commands, like CD or PROMPT.

- **A CONFIG.SYS file initializes both real-mode and protected-mode operations.** Some configuration commands control initial conditions in real mode, and others control these startup system values in protected mode. To run real-mode programs, the most important command is the RMSIZE parameter, which must be set equal to the number of kilobytes your DOS program requires.

- The first time real mode is entered from the Task Manager, a batch file called AUTOEXEC.BAT executes. All commands within it are assumed to be standard batch-file commands, adhering to standard batch-file processing rules.

- When OS/2 first boots, a batch file called STARTUP.CMD executes in protected mode, enabling you to initialize your working environment for protected-mode operations.

- If no STARTUP.CMD file exists in the root directory of the boot drive, OS/2 starts up with the Presentation Manager screen. A special keystroke, Ctrl-Esc, can bring this special screen into view, regardless of what happens to be running on your OS/2 system.

- The number of overlapping features between OS/2 and DOS explains the compatibility that allows many DOS programs to run in OS/2 real mode. But because DOS and OS/2 are not completely compatible, some DOS programs cannot run at all, while others require rewriting.

Use this book now as a reference. Chapter 22 contains summaries of all the DOS commands with their switches and parameters. The appendices contain additional information about vocabulary, character sets, numbering systems, and configuring your fixed disk. The index should point you to anything you'd like to reread.

PART 7

DOS
COMMAND REFERENCE

Chapter 22 contains a detailed, alphabetized reference to all the DOS commands, parameters, and switches. These include commands that were too specialized to describe in the main body of the book and infrequently used parameters and switches for the more common commands. Refer to Chapter 22 as you read this book to obtain a complete understanding of each command. After you finish reading the book, you can use Chapter 22 anytime you want a quick reference to a command's format and options.

I also included three appendices to make your use of DOS a little easier. Appendix A is a glossary of important computer terms used in this book. Refer to the glossary whenever you run across an unfamiliar term. Appendix B is an extended table of ASCII codes, with an explanation of character sets and numbering systems. Appendix C contains complete instructions for configuring or reconfiguring your hard disk.

DOS PROMPT, BATCH-FILE, AND CONFIGURATION COMMANDS

THIS CHAPTER PROVIDES CAPSULE SUMMARIES OF all DOS 4 commands. The majority of these commands are described in more detail in previous chapters of this book (see the index for specific pages); however, the summaries presented here can be used for quick reference to each of the individual commands.

Some commands not covered previously in this book are only needed occasionally, but are presented here for completeness. All batch-file subcommands and all configuration (CONFIG.SYS) commands are reviewed in this chapter as well.

Each capsule summary begins with a general description of the command, followed by the DOS 4 format or formats and the definitions of the command's switches and parameters. Brackets indicate optional switches and parameters. Vertical bars indicate "either/or" choices. The command's type, and any restrictions on its use, close each command capsule.

APPEND

The APPEND command causes the computer to search a predetermined set of directories for files with extensions other than .COM, .BAT, and .EXE.

Format

[*D:Path*]APPEND[*D1:Path1*][;*D2:Path2*...]
[/X[:ON ¦ OFF]][/PATH:ON ¦ OFF][/E][;]

> *D:Path* is the drive and path where the command file is located if it is not in the current directory. You do not need to specify it after the first time that APPEND is loaded, since it then becomes an internal command.

D1:Path1 is the first drive and directory searched after the default drive and directory.

D2:Path2... is the second drive and directory searched after the default drive and directory, and so on.

/X or /X:ON causes APPEND to act like the PATH command, searching for executable files (.COM, .EXE, .BAT) along the APPEND directory list.

/X:OFF turns off the search feature for executable file extensions. Only files with extensions other than .COM, .EXE, or .BAT are then found.

/PATH:ON forces APPEND to search along its directory list for specified file names, regardless of whether the indicated files have drive or path prefixes.

/PATH:OFF directs APPEND to search for files only when you have omitted a drive or path prefix.

/E stores the paths in the DOS environment. This means that paths can be changed with the SET command.

; used alone nullifies the APPEND command by erasing the path list.

Type

Conventionally, this type of command is precisely called an external, terminate-and-stay-resident (TSR) program. It resides on disk until it is needed, thereby taking up no room in memory. When it is invoked for the first time, it comes into memory. When it is done, however, it does not free the memory space it used. Instead, it continues to reside in memory to be used as needed.

Restrictions

DOS provides a default 128 bytes of memory in which to specify paths. Do not use this APPEND command in conjunction with the APPEND command in the IBM PC Network program or in the IBM PC LAN program.

Unless you specify otherwise, applications that use APPEND to locate files in various disk directories may save modified files in the default directory. Sometimes, this is not the directory they were called from (unless that directory was the default directory). Suppose you edit a file with DOS's line editor, EDLIN. Suppose further that the file to be edited is not in the current directory, but *is* specified in the APPEND path list of directories. If you call the file (say TEST.TXT) by its name only—for example,

EDLIN TEST.TXT

Using a complete path name with EDLIN surmounts a possible bug, minimizes confusion about which file is being edited, and even avoids the need to set up an APPEND path list.

then the edited version of the file will be saved in your current default directory. Clearly, this is a potentially deceptive aspect of the APPEND feature. APPEND gave you access to a data file in one directory, but the changed data is saved in the current directory, not the directory from which the file was retrieved. The solution to this problem is to specify a full path name when referencing the file—for example,

EDLIN \FW\DATA\TEST.TXT

When you then save the file after editing it, it will be saved correctly to the original directory, not the current directory.

ASSIGN

ASSIGN redefines the actual drive identifier that handles specific disk requests.

Format
[*D:Path*]ASSIGN [*SourceD1* = *DestD1*] [*SourceD2* = *DestD2*] [...]

D:Path is the drive and path where the command file is located if it is not in the current directory.

SourceD1 is the original drive to be rerouted.

DestD1 is the drive assigned to handle all of *SourceD1*'s requests.

SourceD2, DestD2, and so on are drives used for other assignments.

Type
External.

Restrictions

Do not use ASSIGN with BACKUP, RESTORE, LABEL, JOIN, SUBST, or PRINT. FORMAT, DISKCOPY, and DISK-COMP ignore ASSIGN.

ATTRIB

The ATTRIB command changes the read/write and archive file attributes. When used with parameters, ATTRIB changes the attributes of a file. When used without parameters, ATTRIB displays the attributes.

Format

[*D:Path*]ATTRIB [+ R ¦ – R][+ A ¦ – A][*FileSpec*][/S]

D:Path is the drive and path where the command file is located if it is not in the current directory.

+ R makes *FileSpec* a read-only file.

– R makes *FileSpec* read/write operations possible.

+ A sets the archive bit of *FileSpec*.

– A resets the archive bit of *FileSpec*.

FileSpec is an optional drive and path, including the file name and extension, of the file that is the object of the command. Wild cards are allowed.

/S causes all files in the directory and its subdirectories to be modified.

Type

External.

BACKUP

BACKUP selectively makes backup copies of specified files.

Format

[*D:Path*]BACKUP *SourceD DestD* [/S] [/M] [/A] [/D:*mm-dd-yy*]
[/T:*hh:mm:ss*] [/L[:*FileSpec*]]

D:Path is the drive and path where the command file is located if it is not in the current directory.

SourceD is the drive and optional file specification to be backed up.

DestD is the drive on which the backup will be made.

/S backs up all subdirectories starting with the directory specified in *SourceD*.

/M backs up only those files that have been changed since the last backup.

/A adds the files that will be backed up to the existing files on *DestD* without overwriting them.

/D:*mm-dd-yy* backs up files changed on or after the date specified (the format of the date depends on the country selected).

/T:*hh-mm-ss* backs up files changed at or after the time specified (the format of the time depends on the country selected).

/L creates a log file, BACKUP.LOG, in the root directory of *SourceD*. When you use /L[:*FileSpec*], you can specify a different name and directory for the log file.

Type
External.

Restrictions

You cannot back up any file that is locked up by a program (write access is denied), even if it is normally available for sharing (read access is approved). Do not use BACKUP when JOIN, SUBST, APPEND, or ASSIGN are in effect. FORMAT must be in the same directory as BACKUP or on the directory path since the DOS 4 version of BACKUP automatically formats the destination diskette by default. Unless you use the /A switch, BACKUP will erase all the files on the destination disk. The target disk will be formatted according to the capacity of the drive. Mismatches in capacity or formatting are not allowed.

BREAK

This command makes programs easier to interrupt. Turning BREAK on makes DOS check for the Ctrl-Break key combination at every system call. The default frequency of checking (when BREAK is OFF) is only to check for Ctrl-Break when the program does any I/O (input/output). For example, if you are compiling a long program and the compiler encounters an error and gets stuck in a loop, you will want to halt execution. Having BREAK set to ON allows you to do this.

Format

BREAK [ON ¦ OFF]

ON enables Ctrl-Break to halt programs.

OFF disables the Ctrl-Break function (this is the default).

Type

Internal.

BUFFERS

This command causes a certain number of file-transfer buffers to be set aside in memory. The greater the value of BUFFERS, the more likely that a data reference to a file will be found quickly in memory.

Format

BUFFERS = x,y /X

x is the number of buffers to be set up. If this command is not specified, DOS will determine the number of buffers automatically, based on the current system memory.

y is the number of look-ahead buffers installed for reading sectors in advance during input operations.

/X directs DOS to use expanded memory, if available, for the DOS buffers reserved by this command.

Type

Configuration.

CALL

CALL allows a true subroutine capability in DOS. When you are executing a batch file, you may sometimes need to run a second batch file and then return to the first batch file at the place where the second file was called. In other words, you may want to run a second batch file without having to completely restart the first one. You use the CALL command to do this.

Format
CALL *FileSpec*

> *FileSpec* is the optional drive and path name, including the file name, of the second batch file to be executed.

Type
Batch, internal.

Restrictions
CALL should not be used to pipe or redirect output. Recursive calls are allowed, but you are responsible for ensuring that you do not create an unending loop.

CHCP

The CHCP command allows you to change the currently loaded code page for all eligible installed devices.

Format
CHCP [*xxx*]

> *xxx* is the code-page number.

Type
Internal.

Restrictions
The corresponding device drivers for the specified code page must be available. NLSFUNC must have been executed before this command. Although the CHCP command is internal, it may need to access the COUNTRY command.

━━━━━━━━━   *CHDIR (CD)*   ━━━━━━━━━

You use CHDIR (or simply CD) at the command prompt to change directories as you move through the directory structure.

Format

C[H]D[IR] [*D:Path*]

> *D:Path* is the optional drive and path that you specify as the default directory.

Type

Internal.

━━━━━━━━━   *CHKDSK*   ━━━━━━━━━

The CHKDSK command checks a disk's formatted size and available memory space. It also indicates the amount of disk space consumed by system files, data files, and bad sectors. The DOS 4 version also reports the volume serial number and information about the disk's allocation units (clusters).

Format

[*D:Path*]CHKDSK [*FileSpec*][/F][/V]

> *D:Path* is the drive and path where the command file is located if it is not in the current directory.

> *FileSpec* is an optional drive and path, including the file name and extension, of the file that is the object of the command. Wild cards are allowed.

> /F allows you to make corrections on the disk.

> /V lists all files and their paths.

Type

External.

Restrictions

CHKDSK will not work on drives created by JOIN or SUBST or on networked drives.

CLS

Sometimes the command-prompt screen becomes cluttered, and you no longer need to see everything that is there. To clear the screen, you can use the CLS command. After erasing the screen, DOS places the cursor in the upper-left corner of the screen.

Format

CLS

Type

Internal.

COMMAND

The COMMAND.COM command processor, invoked when the computer is turned on, is the part of DOS that takes in, translates, and executes commands. Invoking a second command processor enables you to execute DOS commands from inside a program and then return to that program. The COMMAND command also allows you to load a customized command processor that has special functions and abilities or altered command definitions.

Format

COMMAND [*D:Path*][/P [/MSG]][/C *String*][/E:*xxxxx*]

D:Path is the drive and path where the command file is located if it is not in the current directory.

/P makes the new processor the primary processor. Using the DOS 4 /MSG switch directs DOS to retain any text associated with error messages in memory. Normally, DOS stores this text to disk and then reads it in when needed.

/C *String* executes the command represented by the *String* parameter.

/E:*xxxxx* sets the DOS environment size to *xxxxx* bytes.

Type

Internal.

COMP

The COMP command compares two or more files to see if they are the same.

Format

[D:Path]COMP [FileSpec1] [FileSpec2]

> *D:Path* is the drive and path where the command file is located if it is not in the current directory.
>
> *FileSpec1* is the optional drive and path, plus the file names and extensions, of the first set of files to be compared. Wild cards are allowed.
>
> *FileSpec2* is the optional drive and path, plus the file names and extensions, of the second set of files to be compared. Wild cards are allowed.

Type

External.

COPY

The COPY command has three distinct uses, with a different format for each one. You can use it to duplicate files, to access devices, or to concatenate files.

Duplicating files with COPY, using the first format of this command, allows you versatility in moving files around the disk system. Whole directories can be copied and thus moved to another location on another disk. Without COPY, you would never be able to transfer newly purchased programs from diskettes to your hard disk, or copy files to a diskette for another system.

The second format of COPY is especially useful for printing multiple files at once, which cannot be done with the TYPE command. It is also the only way for you to directly send information to a device from DOS.

The third format of the COPY command allows files to be concatenated; that is, ASCII-type files can be added to the end of one another to form one big file.

Copies of read-only files created with COPY will *not* be read-only.

Formats

COPY [/A][/B]*SourceFile* [[/A][/B][*DestFile*][/A][/B][/V]]

COPY [/A][/B]*Source* [/A][/B][*Dest*][/A][/B][/V]

COPY [/A][/B]*SourceFile1* + *SourceFile2*[/A][/B] + ...

[*ConcatFile*][/A][/B][/V]

SourceFile is the drive, path, file name, and extension of the file to be copied.

DestFile is the drive, path, file name, and extension of the file to which *SourceFile* will be copied.

Source and *Dest* can be either device or file specifications, although DOS allows only ASCII files to be read from a device.

SourceFile1 and *SourceFile2* are files to be added together (*SourceFile2* is added to the end of *SourceFile1*, and so on).

ConcatFile is the file that contains the concatenated, or linked, source files.

These switches affect the file immediately preceding them as well as all the following files (until the next time the switch is used).

/A is used with *SourceFile, Source,* or *SourceFile1 + SourceFile2* to read data up to but not including the first Ctrl-Z (end-of-file) character; the file is treated as an ASCII file. This is the default setting for concatenation (format 3).

/A is used with with *DestFile, Dest,* or *ConcatFile* to write a Ctrl-Z character at the end of the file.

/B—the default setting for file duplication (format 1)—is used with *SourceFile, Source,* or *SourceFile1 + SourceFile2* to copy the number of bytes equal to the number of bytes in the file.

/B is used with *DestFile, Dest,* or *ConcatFile* to make sure that no Ctrl-Z character is written at the end of the file.

/V causes DOS to check whether all files were copied successfully. It is used only with transfers to disk files.

Type

Internal.

COUNTRY

Since the format of such things as the date and time may change from country to country, your computer must be able to recognize and adapt to these different formats. The COUNTRY command has provisions for up to 21 country codes, and it will also call up a specified code page.

Format

COUNTRY = *xxx*,[*yyy*] [,*FileSpec*]

> *xxx* is the three-digit international code for the country's telephone system.

> *yyy* is the desired code page; it's only necessary for nondefault values.

> *FileSpec* is the path and name of the file containing the country information; the default is \COUNTRY.SYS.

Type

Configuration.

CTTY

If you have a special system configuration or another workstation connected through one of the auxiliary serial ports (AUX, COM1, COM2, COM3, or COM4), CTTY can change the current input and output device (which is usually the keyboard and screen) to something else. You could, for example, specify a teletype as a console.

Format

CTTY *Device*

> *Device* is any valid device name.

Type

Internal.

Restrictions

The keyboard and monitor will be reset as the main console when you use programs that do not use DOS-function calls. Also, specifying a noninput device such as LPT1 in a CTTY command will hang the system. The computer will try to input data from this port, which cannot be done.

DATE

This command changes the date. Use it either to correct or to simply find out what day of the week a certain date is. DATE also resets a permanent clock's date if you have one.

Format

DATE [*mm-dd-yy* ¦ *dd-mm-yy* ¦ *yy-mm-dd*]

If the *mm-dd-yy* specification is left off, you will be prompted for it. The order of *mm-dd-yy* is dependent on the country you have selected.

mm is the month (01 to 12).

dd is the day (01 to 31).

yy is the year, either 80 to 99, or 1980 to 1999.

Type
Internal.

DEBUG

Although DEBUG is not discussed in the DOS user's manual for DOS 3.3 and later versions, it *is* included on their DOS master disk.

The DEBUG command fixes and changes assembly-language programs. It provides a way to run and test any program in a controlled environment: you can change any part of the program and immediately execute the program without having to reassemble it. You can also run machine-language (object) files directly. Programmers often use this DOS tool to make quick program changes, to test variations, and to rapidly isolate errors in assembly-language code.

Format

[*D:Path*]DEBUG [*FileSpec*] [*Param1*] [*Param2*]

D:Path is the drive and path where the command file is located if it is not in the current directory.

FileSpec is an optional drive and path, including the file name and extension, of the file that is the object of the command.

Param1 and *Param2* are any optional parameters that are needed in order to run *FileSpec*.

Type
External.

DEL

The DEL command removes files from the directory. The files are still physically present on the disk and can be retrieved by using certain non-DOS disk utilities (such as Norton Utilities), but they are not accessible using DOS's directory structure.

Format
DEL *FileSpec[/P]*

> *FileSpec* is an optional drive and path, including the file name and extension, of each file to be deleted. Wild cards are allowed. You can specify only a drive and path, omitting file names, in which case all files in the specified directory are deleted.

> /P prompts you to enter a Y or N for each file that you selected for deletion.

Type
Internal.

Restrictions
You cannot use DEL to delete read-only files or any directories.

DEVICE

The DEVICE command loads a device driver. A driver can be anything from a keyboard-enhancement routine to a RAM-disk specification. DEVICE can be used many times in the CONFIG.SYS file, limited only by how the drivers use the system's memory.

Format
DEVICE = *FileSpec[Switches]*

> *FileSpec* is the optional drive and path, including the file name and extension, of the specified driver file.

> *Switches* are the switches corresponding to the specific driver files.

Type
Configuration.

DIR

You use the DIR command to see what files are on a disk. Without this command, it would be extremely difficult, if not impossible, to operate a computer system of any size.

Format
DIR [*FileSpec*][/P][/W]

All parameters
represented by
FileSpec here are com-
pletely independent of
one another. They can be
used in any combination,
either alone or together,
to limit the directory
listing.

> *FileSpec* is an optional drive and path, including the file name and extension, of the file that is the object of the command.
>
> /P causes the computer to pause the directory listing and prompt you to continue listing the files if the listing is longer than one screen.
>
> /W causes the directory listing to be displayed in a wide format (without listing the file size and date and time of creation or modification), with entries listed horizontally as well as vertically.

Type
Internal.

Restrictions
The DIR command does not list hidden or system files.

DISKCOMP

Unlike the COMP command, which compares two sets of files, the DISKCOMP command compares two diskettes (not hard disks). It is usually invoked to verify a DISKCOPY operation. The DOS 4 version ignores any volume serial number differences between the two disks being compared.

Format
[*D:Path*]DISKCOMP [*D1*:[*D2*:]][/1][/8]

> *D:Path* is the drive and path where the command file is located if it is not in the current directory.

D1 and *D2* are the two drives to be compared. If they are not specified, the default drive will be assumed.

/1 forces the computer to compare the diskettes as if they were single-sided (no matter what they really are).

/8 forces the computer to read and compare only the first eight sectors on each track, even if they are 9- or 15-sector diskettes.

Type
External.

Restrictions
DISKCOMP will not work on a hard disk or with the JOIN, ASSIGN, or SUBST commands.

DISKCOPY

Using the DISKCOPY command lets you quickly copy a diskette with a lot of data on it that would otherwise take forever to copy with the COPY command. DISKCOPY copies the raw data of the source diskette, so if it is a system diskette, the new copy will also be a system diskette. If the source diskette is not a system diskette, then the copy will not be a system diskette either, even if the destination diskette originally was a system diskette. The destination diskette will be an *exact* copy of the first. Note, however, that DOS 4 creates a new volume serial number on the destination disk, displaying this identifier on the screen for you. This command will also format a nonformatted destination diskette during the copying process.

Format
[D:Path]DISKCOPY [SourceD:DestD:][/1]

D:Path is the drive and path where the command file is located if it is not in the current directory.

SourceD is the source drive to be copied.

DestD is the destination drive to be copied to.

/1 forces the computer to copy only the first side of the source diskette to the first side of the destination diskette, as if they were both single-sided, even if they are double-sided.

Type
External.

Restrictions
You cannot use this command with a hard disk. It also does not recognize an assigned or substituted drive, and should not be used with JOIN. DISKCOPY cannot reliably read 160K–360K-sized disks that are formatted in a high-capacity drive, and it will not work with network drives.

DOSSHELL

The DOSSHELL command is new with DOS 4.

The DOSSHELL command enables DOS 4 users to initiate the graphic-shell program from the standard DOS command prompt. It is a simple batch file created during the system installation process.

Format
[*D:Path*]DOSSHELL

D:Path is the drive and path where the command file is located if it is not in the current directory.

Type
External.

Restrictions
Do not enter DOSSHELL at a nested shell prompt (i.e. a secondary command processor invoked from within the shell itself); this will consume unnecessary memory.

ECHO

When you set up a batch file, there are times when you don't want the executing commands to be displayed on the screen. Use the ECHO command to suppress the screen's presentation of executing batch-file commands.

You can use ECHO to send a line of text to the printer or a file; for example, ECHO Hello >LPT1 will cause "Hello" to be printed. To print a character that has some other function, enclose it in double quotation marks; for example, ECHO The ">" symbol is used for redirection will print the entire sentence, rather than erroneously treating the > sign as a redirection operator (see Chapter 13).

Format

ECHO [ON ¦ OFF] [*String*]

ON turns on the display of commands, which is the default.

OFF turns off echoing.

String is an optional message that DOS will display regardless of whether ECHO is ON or OFF.

Type

Batch. However, the ECHO command is internal, and you can run it from the DOS shell or command prompt.

EDLIN

EDLIN is DOS's line editor. Unlike many word processors, it is not a full-screen editor. EDLIN has no formatting commands, and you must change data a line at a time. It is good for modifying short ASCII files and for creating and modifying simple batch files.

Format

[*D:Path*]EDLIN *FileSpec*[/B]

D:Path is the drive and path where the command file is located if it is not in the current directory.

FileSpec is an optional drive and path, including the file name and extension, of the file that is the object of the command.

/B causes EDLIN to load a file containing embedded Ctrl-Z (end-of-file) codes.

Type

External.

ERASE

The ERASE command, which is the same as DEL, removes files from the directory. The files are still physically present on the disk and can be retrieved by using certain non-DOS disk utilities (such as Norton Utilities), but they are not accessible using DOS's directory structure.

Format

ERASE [*FileSpec*][/P]

FileSpec is an optional drive and path, including the file name and extension, of each file to be deleted. Wild cards are allowed. You can specify only a drive and path, omitting file names, in which case all files in the specified directory are deleted.

/P prompts you to enter a Y or N for each file that you selected for deletion.

Type

Internal.

Restrictions

You cannot use ERASE to delete read-only files or any subdirectory that still contains files.

EXE2BIN

 The EXE2BIN command is no longer included with DOS 3.3 or DOS 4.

The EXE2BIN command formally converts executable files to command files. You use file with an .EXE extension as the source file to create a file with a .COM or .BIN extension.

Format

[*D:Path*]EXE2BIN *SourceFile* [*DestFile*]

D:Path is the drive and path where the command file is located if it is not in the current directory.

SourceFile is the drive, path, file name, and extension of the file to be converted; .EXE is the default for the extension.

DestFile is the drive, path, file name, and extension for the converted file; .BIN is the default for the extension. If you do not include this parameter on the command line, the converted file will have the same drive, path, and file name as the source file, but its extension will be .BIN.

Type
External.

Restrictions
SourceFile must be a programmer's object file created with the LINK program. The code and data of the file must be less than 64K.

FASTOPEN

The FASTOPEN command speeds up disk access by maintaining a memory-resident table of the most recently used file and directory names. FASTOPEN also can maintain a memory cache of actual file data from the most recently opened files. These two features can be set up independently for multiple disk drives with one FASTOPEN statement.

Formats
[*D:Path*]FASTOPEN *D1*:[= *Size*][*D2*: = *Size*][...][/X]
[*D:Path*]FASTOPEN *D1*:[= ([*Size*],[*Buf*])][...][/X]

D:Path is the drive and path where the command file is located if it is not in the current directory.

D1, D2 and so on are the drives to which FASTOPEN will be attached.

Size is the number of file or directory entries that FASTOPEN will remember.

Buf is the number of contiguous memory buffers reserved in memory for storing actual file data from the most recently used files.

/X directs FASTOPEN to use expanded memory for its buffer space.

Type
External, TSR.

Restrictions

FASTOPEN will not work when JOIN, SUBST, or ASSIGN are in effect on the drives it is attached to. It also will not work with network drives. Using the /X switch for expanded memory requires that you install the device drivers XMAEM.SYS and XMA2EMS.SYS in your CONFIG.SYS file. The sum of all *Size* parameters cannot exceed 999, and the sum of all *Buf* parameters cannot exceed 999.

FCBS

Only users of Version 1 of DOS need to be concerned with this command. In that version, files were accessed via file-control blocks (FCBs). These are approximately 40-byte sections in memory that tell DOS a file's name and other attributes. The FCBS command allows you to access FCBs.

Format

FCBS = MaxNum,PermNum

> *MaxNum* is the number of FCBs that may be opened concurrently (the default value is 4).

> *PermNum* is the minimum number of FCBs that will remain open when DOS tries to close files automatically (the default value is 0).

Restrictions

If *PermNum* is less than *MaxMun*, DOS can close an FCB without alerting the program that is using the FCB. This can cause major problems.

FDISK

Hard disks can be set up to have more than one type of operating system on them. For example, you can have DOS managing one part of a disk and UNIX managing another. Each of these sections is called a *partition*. You can have from one to four operating-system partitions on a disk (see Appendix C). The DOS 4 FDISK utility is easier to use than those in earlier versions, owing to DOS 4's ability to accept disk-partition sizes in absolute megabyte values or in percentages of available space.

Format

[D:Path]FDISK

All data on your
hard disk will be
destroyed when you
create a new primary
partition with FDISK.

> *D:Path* is the drive and path where the command file is located if it is not in the current directory.

Type

External.

Restrictions

FDISK can only be used on hard-disk systems. A disk must be reformatted logically after being partitioned. FDISK will not work if another process is accessing the disk.

FILES

Just as you can specify the number of buffers to be used by DOS, so can you specify the number of files open at any one time. The FILES command delineates the size of the file-control area in which file *handles* are maintained. Do not set this number any higher than the number of files required to be open by your application program mix, because each file handle requires 48 bytes. This increases the size of DOS, decreasing the remaining available memory for your programs.

Format

FILES = x

When you are
using the FILES
command, keep in mind
that the size of DOS
increases by 48 bytes for
each file beyond the eight
default files.

> *x* is a number between 8 and 255 (8 is the default) specifying the number of files that can remain open at one time.

Type

Configuration.

FIND

The FIND command allows you to search through a file to locate any particular string of text characters.

Format

[*D:Path*]FIND [/V][/C][/N]''*String*'' [*FileSpec*]

> *D:Path* is the drive and path where the command file is located if it is not in the current directory.

> /V causes FIND to display each line not containing *String*.

> /C counts the number of lines containing *String* and shows the total.

> /N shows the relative line number of each line containing *String*.

> *String* is the string of characters to be searched for.

> *FileSpec* is the drive, path, file name, and extension of each file to be searched. Multiple files should be separated by a space.

Type

External.

Restrictions

Wild cards not allowed with this command. FIND will end its search when it encounters Ctrl-Z in a file.

FOR

The FOR command sets up a repeating loop in a batch file. This is useful for repeating an operation with a different parameter a specified number of times.

Format

FOR %%*Var* IN (*ComSet*) DO *Command*

> *Var* is a variable name.

> *ComSet* is the set of values to be used successively by *Command*.

> *Command* is the command to be executed using %%*Var* as a varying parameter (which uses the values given in *ComSet*).

Type

Batch, internal.

Restrictions

The variable name used in a FOR command cannot be a DOS-reserved word.

FORMAT

The FORMAT command prepares a disk for use with DOS.

Format

[*D:Path*]FORMAT *D1*:[/S][/1][/4][/8][/V:*Label*][/B][/N:*xx*][/T:*yy*][/F:*Size*]

D:Path is the drive and path where the command file is located if it is not in the current directory.

D1: is the drive to be formatted.

/S causes a system disk to be created.

/1 causes only one side of a disk to be formatted. Version 1.X of DOS was designed to handle single-sided disks only.

/4 causes a high-capacity drive to format a 360K, double-sided diskette.

/8 formats a disk with 8 sectors instead of 9. Version 1.X of DOS was designed to handle only 8 sectors per track. IBM chose a conservative limit to minimize errors from too much data being stored on one track.

/V:*Label* is a DOS 4 switch that automatically assigns *Label* as your disk label and creates a unique serial number, which is written to the boot sector of the disk being formatted. The serial number is displayed for you at the end of the formatting process. You can later see it as part of the output of other DOS commands such as CHKDSK. Earlier versions of DOS only have a /V switch that has FORMAT prompt you for the entry of a volume label; if /V is not included, then the disk is formatted without a label at all. Since DOS 4 requires volume labels and serial-number identification, you will be prompted for a label if you neglect to specify one with this switch.

/B formats a disk with 8 sectors and leaves room for the hidden system files, but it does *not* transfer the system to the diskette;

thus, you can use the SYS command with the diskette. This is especially useful for the earlier versions, which expect only 8 sectors per track.

/N:*xx* formats a disk with *xx* sectors per track. This parameter is required if you use different types of machines, and you prepare disks on one for use on another.

/T:*yy* formats a disk with *yy* tracks. This parameter is required if you use different types of machines, and you prepare disks on one for use on another.

/F:*Size* offers DOS 4 users an easy way of formatting disks to sizes that are smaller than the nominal capacity of the drive they are being formatted in. You will rarely use this switch unless you have multiple machines with disk drives of different sizes. The /F switch simply provides an easier way to decrease your format size than using the /T and /N switches in tandem.

Type
External.

Restrictions
FORMAT ignores assignments made with ASSIGN. You cannot use the /V switch to format a diskette for DOS 1.1. You must use the /V:*Label* switch in DOS 4 to assign a label to a disk; otherwise, you will be prompted to enter one. A 360K diskette formatted in a high-capacity drive cannot be read reliably in single- or double-density drives. If you need a formatted 360K diskette in another machine, format it in that other machine; it then is reliably written to by a high-capacity drive.

GOTO

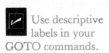
Use descriptive labels in your GOTO commands.

During a batch file's execution, it may become necessary to skip over some commands and execute others in a file. Or it may be necessary to jump back to another point in a file, perhaps for some logical looping. GOTO allows you to transfer execution.

Format

GOTO [:]*Label*

> *Label* is the line identifier used by the batch file to indicate the line to which GOTO will transfer control.

Type

> Batch, internal.

GRAFTABL

It is nice to be able to display the full ASCII range of characters on the screen so that you can see exactly what you are dealing with. If you have a Color Graphics Adapter (CGA), the GRAFTABL command enables you to display the ASCII characters that have codes from 128 to 255. You can select one of five possible code-page groups of these ASCII characters to display.

Format

[*D:Path*]GRAFTABL [437 ¦ 850 ¦ 860 ¦ 863 ¦ 865 ¦ ? ¦ /STATUS]

> *D:Path* is the drive and path where the command file is located if it is not in the current directory.
>
> 437 loads the U.S. code page.
>
> 850 loads the Multilingual code page.
>
> 860 loads the Portuguese code page.
>
> 863 loads the Canadian-French code page.
>
> 865 loads the Norwegian and Danish code page.
>
> ? displays the currently specified code page and all possible code-page options.
>
> /STATUS shows the number of the code page currently in use.

Type

> External.

GRAPHICS

The GRAPHICS command allows you to print your graphics screen by using the Shift-PrtSc key combination. The printing time will depend on what graphics mode you are in.

Format
[*D:Path*]GRAPHICS [*PrinterType* ¦ₔ] [*ProfileFileSpec*]
[/R][/B][/LCD][PB:*Id*]

> *D:Path* is the drive and path where the command file is located if it is not in the current directory.
>
> *PrinterType* is an optional printer-type specification. It can have any of the following values: COLOR1, COLOR4, COLOR8, GRAPHICS, GRAPHICSWIDE, or THERMAL.
>
> *ProfileFileSpec* is the optional drive, path, and file name of a file containing specification data for supported printers.
>
> /R prints a reverse-video image.
>
> /B prints the background color when *PrinterType* is COLOR4 or COLOR8.
>
> /LCD prints an image produced on a liquid crystal display.
>
> /PB:*Id* specifies the size and shape of the printed image. It does this by connecting the GRAPHICS command to one of several possible PrintBox (PB) commands contained within the graphics profile file, whose default is GRAPHICS.PRO.

Type
External, TSR.

IF

Conditional statements play an important role in any type of programming. A conditional statement simply says "Do one thing if a certain condition is true; otherwise, do another thing." This allows branching, or decision making, in your programs.

In most high-level programming languages, conditional statements are defined with the IF command. IF A = B THEN GOTO

:START is executed as "If A equals B, then transfer control to the line labeled :START; otherwise, just go on to the next instruction."

Format

IF [NOT] *Condition Command*

NOT inverts the truth of the condition. If NOT is included, a true condition would be regarded as false, and a false condition as true.

Condition is the criterion for the execution of *Command*. *Condition* can be in one of the following formats:

ERRORLEVEL *Code* is used to determine if the return code of the last program or command that was executed equals *Code* or is greater.

String1 = = *String2* specifies that *String1* must equal *String2* for the condition to be true.

EXIST *FileSpec* causes the condition to be true if the file defined by *FileSpec* resides in the specified directory.

Command is the action (usually a command) that is executed when *Condition* is true or not false.

Type

Batch, internal (acceptable on a DOS 4 shell or command-prompt line).

Restrictions

DOS is case sensitive for *String* values.

INSTALL

The INSTALL command is new with DOS 4.

The INSTALL command lets you install certain memory-resident DOS 4 features when configuring your system.

Format

INSTALL = *[D:Path]FileSpec*

D:Path is the drive and path where the command file is located if it is not in the current directory.

FileSpec is one of the four following DOS 4 internal command files that can be installed in your CONFIG.SYS instead of explicitly invoking the commands later: FASTOPEN.EXE, KEYB.COM, NLSFUNC.EXE, and SHARE.EXE.

Type

Configuration.

JOIN

You use the JOIN command to treat a disk drive and all its contents as if they were a branch of the directory structure on a second drive. The JOIN command has three main formats. The first displays all directory and disk names that have been joined; the second actually performs the joining; and the third disjoins a directory and disk.

Formats

[*D:Path*]JOIN
[*D:Path*]JOIN *DestD SourceD:Path*
[*D:Path*]JOIN /D

D:Path is the drive and path where the command file is located if it is not in the current directory.

DestD is the drive to which a directory will be attached or released.

SourceD:Path is the drive and path of the directory to be joined.

/D unjoins a previously established JOIN.

Restrictions

You can use JOIN only on multidisk systems. You cannot use this command to join a drive created with SUBST.

KEYB

The KEYB command is used to load a new keyboard-translation table for a specific country. There are 21 country codes to choose from.

Formats
[*D:Path*]KEYB [*xx*[,[*yyy*],[*FileSpec*]] [/ID:*iii*]]
[*D:Path*]KEYB *iii*

> *D:Path* is the drive and path where the command file is located if it is not in the current directory.
>
> *xx* is a keyboard code representing a country.
>
> *yyy* is the code page to be used.
>
> *FileSpec* is the drive, path, and file name of the keyboard-definition file (the default is \KEYBOARD.SYS).
>
> /ID:*iii* specifies a particular keyboard code for one of the many different enhanced keyboards.

Type
> External, TSR.

LABEL

LABEL allows you to label your disk volumes electronically. These disk names will appear each time you call up a directory.

Format
[*D:Path*]LABEL [*D1*:][*String*]

> *D:Path* is the drive and path where the command file is located if it is not listed in the current directory.
>
> *D1:* is the drive containing the disk whose label is to be changed or displayed.
>
> *String*, when specified, becomes the label of the disk in D1.

Type
> External.

Restrictions
> You cannot use LABEL with drives that have been substituted or joined.
>
> You cannot use the following characters in a volume label: * ? / \ | . , ; : + = < > [ ] ( ) @ ^.

LASTDRIVE

The LASTDRIVE command allows you to specify up to 26 disk drives for access. If you have several physical disk drives, this command is essential. However, you may choose to partition your hard disk into several logical drives (see Appendix C). In this case, you can cleanly arrange your work and files on different disk drives; this helps you separate projects or files created by different users of the same hardware.

Format

LASTDRIVE = *D*

D is the last accessible drive; the default is E.

Type

Configuration.

Restrictions

If you specify a letter value that is less than the number of drives hooked up to the system, LASTDRIVE will not be accepted. For example, if you specify G as the final drive and have eight drives hooked up to your system, LASTDRIVE will not work—you've assigned seven letters to cover your eight drives.

MEM

 The MEM command is new with DOS 4.

The MEM command displays amounts of total and available memory (low, expanded, and extended). It also displays all currently active programs.

Format

[*D:Path*]MEM [/PROGRAM] [/DEBUG]

D:Path is the drive and path where the command file is located if it is not listed in the current directory.

/PROGRAM lists all current programs along with the standard display of used and available memory.

/DEBUG provides additional information about all system and installed device drivers.

Type
External.

Restrictions
Expanded memory information is only displayed if an appropriate device driver is installed. Extended memory information is only displayed if your system contains more than 1Mb.

MKDIR (MD)

The MKDIR command (or MD for short) creates a new directory, either in the current working directory or at the specified path location in an existing directory tree.

Format
M[K]D[IR] [*D:Path*]

D:Path is the optional drive and path specifying the directory you wish to create.

Type
Internal.

MODE

The MODE command controls and redirects output. There are a great many versions of this command, but they can all be grouped into functional areas.

The two following versions control printers:

Formats
[*D:Path*]MODE LPT*x*: [COLS = *a*] [LINES = *b*] [RETRY = *c*]
[*D:Path*]MODE LPT*x*: = COM*y*

The following MODE command controls serial ports:

Format
[*D:Path*]MODE COM*y*[:]BAUD = *bd* [PARITY = *p*] [DATA = *Dbits*]
[STOP = *Sbits*] [RETRY = *c*]

The next three MODE commands control display screens:

Formats

[*D:Path*]MODE *DisplayType*

[*D:Path*]MODE [*DisplayType*], *Shift* [,T]

[*D:Path*]MODE CON [COLS = a] [LINES = b]

The following version of MODE controls keyboards:

Format

[*D:Path*]MODE CON RATE = r DELAY = d

The remaining MODE commands manage the international language-support features of both printers and monitors:

Format

[*D:Path*]MODE *Device* CODEPAGE PREPARE = ((*CP*)*FileSpec*)

[*D:Path*]MODE *Device* CODEPAGE PREPARE = ((*CPList*)*FileSpec*)

[*D:Path*]MODE *Device* CODEPAGE SELECT = *CP*

[*D:Path*]MODE *Device* CODEPAGE [/STATUS]

[*D:Path*]MODE *Device* CODEPAGE REFRESH

D:Path is the drive and path where the command file is located if it is not in the current directory.

x is a printer number (1, 2, or 3).

COLS $= a$ sets the number of characters per line to x (40 or 80 for controlling displays; 80 or 132 for controlling printers).

LINES $= b$ sets the number of lines per inch to y (6 or 8).

RETRY $= c$ causes the computer to continuously retry accessing the port during time-out errors. The value of c (E, B, or R) directs DOS's response to status requests.

y is a serial-port number (1, 2, 3, or 4).

bd is a baud rate for the COM port (110, 150, 300, 600, 1200, 2400, 4800, 9600, or 19200).

p is a parity value for the COM port; it can be EVEN (the default), ODD, NONE, MARK, or SPACE.

Dbits specifies the number of data bits used. The default is 7 bits.

Sbits specifies the number of stop bits used. The default is one stop bit except when the baud rate is 110; in that case, two stop bits are used as the default.

DisplayType is the display type used. You specify it as 40, 80, BW40, BW80, CO40, CO80, or MONO.

Shift is the direction for a screen shift, either L or R.

T puts a test pattern on the screen for checking the screen alignment when shifting.

CON means that the parameter values of this MODE command apply to the system's display console.

r specifies the keyboard typematic rate (the range is r = 1 to r = 32 representing a rate of 2 – 30 repetitions per second).

d specifies the delay time before auto repeat begins (the range is 1, 2, 3, or 4 representing a delay of ¼, ½, ¾, or 1 second).

Device is a valid device name (CON, LPT1, and so on).

CP is a code-page number (437, 850, 860, 863, or 865).

CPList is a list of code-page numbers.

FileSpec is the file containing the code-page data. Its value is 4201.CPI for the IBM Proprinter, 4208.CPI for the IBM Proprinter X24 and XL24, 5202.CPI for the IBM Quietwriter III Printer, EGA.CPI for EGA displays, or LCD.CPI for the IBM Convertible LCD.

/STATUS displays the active code page and the other available code pages for *Device*.

Type
External, TSR.

MORE

The MORE command is similar to the DIR/P command, which pauses the directory listing after each screenful of data and asks you to press a key to continue. MORE is a filter; that is, data is sent to it, and MORE processes the data and sends it out in a new format. In this case, the filter simply prints the data a screenful at a time and prints " – MORE –" at the bottom of the screen until you press a key.

Format
[*D:Path*]MORE

> *D:Path* is the drive and path where the command file is located if it is not in the current directory.

Type
External.

NLSFUNC

The NLSFUNC command supports international language-support features and code-page switching. It uses the new extended country information provided with DOS 4 (also available in DOS 3.3) to load the part of the keyboard translation table containing the country-specific information.

Format
[*D:Path*]NLSFUNC [*FileSpec*]

> *D:Path* is the drive and path where the command file is located if it is not in the current directory.

> *FileSpec* specifies the location and name of the country-specific code file (the default is \COUNTRY.SYS).

Type
External, TSR.

PATH

The PATH Command sets or resets the sequence of directories (that is, the path) to be searched for executable files.

Format
PATH [*D1:Path1*][;*D2:Path2*...]

> [*D1:Path1*] is the first drive and directory searched.

> [*D2:Path2*...] is the second drive and directory searched, and so on.

Type

Internal.

Restrictions

PATH will not work with data files, overlay files, or other nonexecutable files (see APPEND).

PAUSE

The PAUSE command temporarily halts the execution of a batch file. It also prompts you to strike a key when you are ready to continue.

Format

PAUSE [*String*]

String prints a specified message on the screen before ''Strike any key when ready.''

Type

Batch, internal (acceptable at a DOS command prompt).

PRINT

⊙ The file name is queued, not the file data. Be careful when changing a file's contents after you queue it for printing because DOS will print the changed file, not the version existing when the printing request was made.

The PRINT command invokes, modifies, and adds files to an internal software-based queue. You use queues to send multiple files to be printed in order automatically.

Format

[*D:Path*]PRINT [*Params*][/C][/T][/P][*FileSpec*,...]

D:Path is the drive and path where the command file is located if it is not in the current directory.

Params contains optional switches and parameters that redefine queue characteristics. They are as follows:

/D:*Device* specifies the output device.

/B:*BuffSize* specifies the output buffer's size in bytes.

/U:*BusyTicks* specifies how long the queue will wait each cycle when the printer is too busy to print new data.

/M:*MaxTicks* specifies how much time the queue has to send data to the printer.

/S:*TimeSlice* specifies the number of time divisions.

/Q:*QueueSize* specifies the maximum number of entries in the queue.

/C cancels previous and following entries on the command line.

/T terminates the queue; everything is canceled and stopped.

/P adds previous and following entries on the command line to the queue.

FileSpec, ... is an optional list of the paths and names of files to be queued for printing.

Type

External, TSR.

Restrictions

You cannot use a printer with a printing command other than PRINT while a queue is printing. PRINT cannot be used on a network. Do not remove the disk where the files are located from its drive until the queue has completed printing.

PROMPT

The PROMPT command changes the system prompt to whatever you like. It can display the time, the date, or a simple message. This is useful for finding out which directory you are in before you modify or delete any files.

Format

PROMPT [$*String*][. . .]

$String displays special-purpose entries. Possible values for *String* are shown in Table 22.1.

Type

Internal.

SYMBOL	MEANING
e	The Esc key
p	Current directory of the default drive
g	The > character
n	Default drive identifier
d	System date
t	System time
v	Version number
l	The < character
b	The ¦ character
q	The = character
h	A backspace
_	The carriage-return/line-feed sequence
$	The $ sign

Table 22.1: Special-purpose PROMPT codes (meta symbols)

RECOVER

The RECOVER command lets DOS reconstruct files (either individually or all files on the disk in a given drive) that have become damaged or corrupted.

Formats

[*D:Path*]RECOVER [*D1:Path1*]*SourceFile*
[*D:Path*]RECOVER [*D1*]

D:Path is the drive and path where the command file is located if it is not in the current directory.

D1:Path1 is an optional drive and path where the file *SourceFile* is located.

SourceFile is the file name, with an optional extension, of the file to be manipulated (wild-card characters may be used).

D1 is the drive containing the disk on which all files will be restored.

Type
External.

Restrictions
You cannot use RECOVER on a network disk.

REM

It is often helpful to place comments in your file code, so that if you come back to those files later, you can quickly and easily understand what they contain and how they work. In batch files, this is done with the REM command. The contents of a REM command line are not executed or displayed if ECHO is OFF, but they will be readable if you look at the file itself.

Format
REM *String*

String represents nonexecutable comments.

Type
Batch, internal (acceptable at a DOS command prompt).

Restrictions
Comments may be up to 123 characters long for each REM command. Enclose characters that have special meanings to DOS (such as ¦) in double quotation marks ("¦").

RENAME (REN)

The RENAME command (which can be shortened to REN) performs the very useful function of renaming a file.

Format
REN[AME] *OldFile NewFile*

OldFile is the optional drive and path, including the file name and extension, of the file that will be renamed. Wild cards are allowed.

NewFile is a new file name and extension for *OldFile*. Wild cards are allowed. The *NewFile* parameter does not accept a prefixed drive and path.

Type
Internal.

Restrictions
You cannot use RENAME to give a subdirectory a new name. You cannot specify a drive for the new file name; the renamed file stays in its same location. Thus, you cannot type a drive or a path in front of *NewFile*.

REPLACE

The REPLACE command allows you to easily update a set of files in one directory with another set (usually newer versions) of similarly named files in another directory or drive.

Format
[*D:Path*]REPLACE *SourceFile DestD*[/A][/P][/R][/S][/U][/W]

D:Path is the drive and path where the command file is located if it is not in the current directory.

SourceFile is the identification of the files that will be used to update the other set of files. You must specify the file names, but their extensions, paths, and drives are optional.

DestD is the required drive and optional path of the files to be replaced.

/A adds all files from *SourceFile* that do not currently exist on *DestD* to it.

/P prompts you before replacing a file.

/R replaces only read-only files on *DestD*.

/S replaces files located anywhere in the directory structure when they match the source file names.

/U replaces only files that have older dates and times than their matching source files.

/W waits for you to insert a diskette.

Type

External.

Restrictions

The /A switch is incompatible and cannot be used with either the /S or the /U switch. The entire command line with all of its file specifications and switch entries cannot exceed 63 characters.

RESTORE

The RESTORE command is the reverse of BACKUP: it restores files to the disk and directory from which they were backed up.

Format

**[*D:Path*]RESTORE *SourceD FileSpec*[/S][/P][/B:*mm-dd-yy*]
[/A:*mm-dd-yy*][/M][/N][/L:*hh-mm-ss*][/E:*hh-mm-ss*]**

D:Path is the drive and path where the command file is located if it is not in the current directory.

SourceD is the drive containing the backed-up files to be restored.

FileSpec is the optional drive and path, including the file names and extensions, of the files on *SourceD* to be restored. Wild cards are allowed.

/S restores files in subdirectories of the files specified in *FileSpec*.

/P prompts you before a file is restored if that file has been modified since it was last backed up.

/B:*mm-dd-yy* restores all backed-up files that were last modified on or before *mm-dd-yy*. (*mm-dd-yy* represents a date in months, days, and years.)

/A:*mm-dd-yy* restores all backed-up files that were last modified on or after *mm-dd-yy*.

RESTORE will overwrite files with the same name if they are in the specified directory. Use the /P switch (or the REPLACE command) to avoid rewriting a file.

/M compares the backed-up files and the files on the destination disk; it then restores the files that have been changed or erased since the last backup.

/N restores files that no longer exist on the destination disk.

/L:*hh-mm-ss* restores all files changed since the time specified by *hh-mm-ss*. (*hh-mm-ss* represents time in hours, minutes, and seconds.)

/E:*hh-mm-ss* restores all files changed prior to the time specified by *hh-mm-ss*.

Type
External.

Restrictions
Only files created with BACKUP will be restored. Do not use RESTORE if SUBST, JOIN, or ASSIGN was invoked in a BACKUP operation.

RMDIR (RD)

When you want to delete or remove a directory, you must delete all files or subdirectories in the directory and then use the RMDIR command.

Format
R[M]D[IR] [*D:Path*]

D:Path is the optional drive and path of the directory to be removed.

Type
Internal.

Restrictions
You cannot remove a directory until all files and subdirectories within it have been deleted or removed by a separate operation.

SELECT

In DOS 4, SELECT is a full-screen graphic utility that installs DOS on a new hard or floppy disk. It can also replace an earlier version of DOS. In DOS 3.3 and earlier, SELECT is a more limited command-prompt utility that allows you to install DOS with a particular keyboard layout and country-specific date and time formats.

Format

[*D:Path***]SELECT [[A:¦B:]***DestD***:[***Path***]] *xxx yy***

> *D:Path* is an optional drive and path where the command file is located.
>
> A: or B: is the source drive that contains the command files and country information (A: is the default).
>
> *DestD:Path* is the optional drive and path of the disk to be formatted. The root directory is the default when you do not specify a path. When you do not specify a destination drive, drive B is formatted by default.
>
> *xxx* specifies the country code.
>
> *yy* specifies the keyboard code.

Type

External.

Restrictions

Drives A and B are the only source drives, and the destination drive must not be the same as the source drive. The U.S. keyboard file resides in the computer's memory, so it does not need to be on the source disk. CONFIG.SYS and AUTOEXEC.BAT files are created on *DestD*. High-capacity diskettes must be used in high-capacity drives.

In DOS 4, SELECT is invoked from the graphic interface only. Do not try to use the command prompt to invoke it. The only exception to this is when SELECT is automatically executed during the initial INSTALL process (see Chapter 2).

SELECT uses FORMAT, so anything on the destination disk will be destroyed after this command is used. SELECT may be used on a hard disk, so be careful.

SET

The SET command changes strings and definitions within the DOS environment of your computer. Both you and DOS can use this area of memory set aside for special definitions and defaults.

With SET you can display the current DOS environment, erase the current definition of *Name,* create a new DOS environment string, or change one that already exists.

Format

SET [*Name* = [*Param*]]

> *Name* is a user-specified string used in place of *Param.* It can also contain the DOS environment strings PROMPT, PATH, LASTDRIVE, or COMSPEC.
>
> *Param* is the value given to *Name.*

Type

Internal.

Restrictions

There are only 127 bytes of available DOS environment by default. You can, however, change this limit with the SHELL command's /E switch.

SHARE

The SHARE command loads routines that permit file sharing, allowing you to lock a disk or all or part of a file so that it cannot be used simultaneously by another process.

Format

[*D:Path*]SHARE [/F:*FileMem*][/L:*Locks*]

> *D:Path* is the drive and path where the command file is located if it is not in the current directory.
>
> /F:*FileMem* sets aside the memory to be used for keeping track of file sharing (the default value is 2048 bytes).
>
> /L:*Locks* specifies the number of locks that can be in effect at once (the default value is 20).

Type

External, TSR.

Restrictions

You can load the SHARE command only once. Subsequent attempts at loading will yield an error message. You must reboot your computer to remove a SHARE command.

SHELL

If you are a system programmer or if you have your own command processor, the SHELL command is for you. When DOS loads, SHELL can specify and load your command processor instead of COMMAND.COM. You can also use SHELL with the /E switch to load in the COMMAND.COM file with an expanded DOS environment.

Format

SHELL = *ComFileSpec* [*Params*]

ComFileSpec is the drive, path, and file name of the new command processor.

Params are parameters you use for the specified command processor. For example, if you specify COMMAND.COM for your command processor, you are allowed two parameters:

/E:*xxxx* defines, in bytes, the size of the DOS environment.

/P makes the specified command processor memory resident and causes AUTOEXEC.BAT to be executed after the processor has been loaded.

Type

Configuration.

SHIFT

Batch files often need information from the user—a drive identifier, a file name, a yes-or-no answer, and so on. These temporary values can be put into the variables %0 through %9 and be made available to the batch file when it is run. For those applications that require more than ten variables, Microsoft has developed the SHIFT command. This command simply shifts all of the variables down one number. For example, executing SHIFT would cause the new %0 to equal the old %1, the new %1 to equal the old %2, and so on. The variable %9 could reference a formerly inaccessible eleventh parameter value.

Format

SHIFT

Type

Batch, internal (acceptable at a DOS command prompt).

SORT

The SORT command receives input, sorts it, and then passes it on for display or further manipulation.

Format

[*D:Path*]SORT [/R][/ + *Col*]

> *D:Path* is the drive and path where the command file is located if it is not in the current directory.
>
> /R sorts in reverse alphabetical order.
>
> / + *Col* starts the sorting operation with column *Col* (the default setting is column 1).

Type

External.

STACKS

The STACKS command is intended for very advanced users. It allows you to change the stack resources that are normally defined for you. Stack frames are used for interrupt processing.

Format

STACKS = *n,s*

> *n* specifies the number of stack frames.
>
> *s* specifies the number of bytes in each frame.

Type
Configuration.

SUBST

The SUBST command enables you to access files using either their complete path name or a shorthand notation.

Like the JOIN command, SUBST has three distinct formats for its use. The first displays all of the current substitutions, the second actually performs a substitution, and the third cancels out a substitution.

Formats
[*D:Path*]SUBST
[*D:Path*]SUBST *DestD SourceD*
[*D:Path*]SUBST *Object* **/D**

> *D:Path* is the drive and path where the command file is located if it is not in the current directory.

> *DestD* is the drive to be created to correspond to the source directory (*SourceD*).

> *SourceD* is the directory to be made into drive *DestD*.

> *Object* is the pseudo-drive identifier used as *DestD* and is now to be discarded.

Type
External.

SWITCHES

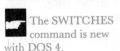
The SWITCHES command is new with DOS 4.

The SWITCHES command restricts the use of an enhanced keyboard to conventional keyboard functions. You use this command to provide compatibility for software not written to understand enhanced keyboard features.

Format
SWITCHES = /K

> /K ensures that conventional keyboard functions are used even though an enhanced keyboard has been installed.

Type

Configuration.

SYS

The SYS command transfers the hidden system files, IBMBIOS-.COM and IBMDOS.COM, from a DOS system disk to a properly prepared target diskette.

Format

[D:Path]SYS DestD:

> *D:Path* is the drive and path where the command file is located if it is not in the current directory.

> *DestD* is the drive the system files will be transferred to.

Type

External.

Restrictions

The root directory of the target disk must have at least two unused file-name entries, and enough space must have been reserved on the target disk to fit the system files.

TIME

You use the TIME command to set the system time at either the DOS 4 shell or command prompt. You can also use it to reset an internal clock. Setting the time comes in very handy when errors occur. For example, you can tell exactly when a file was last written to or changed. It also provides a trail by which a programmer can trace the file-saving flow of a program. I recommend you set the time and date every time you boot up the system. To use this command at DOS 4's graphic shell, you choose DOS Utilities from the main Start Programs screen.

Format

TIME [*hh:mm*[:*ss*[.*xx*]]]

hh is the current hour, in 24-hour format. To translate from 12- to 24-hour if the time is between 1:00 P.M. and 12:00 A.M., add 12 to the hour (for example, 7:45 P.M. = 19:45).

mm is the current number of minutes.

ss is the current number of seconds.

xx is the current number of hundredths of seconds.

Type
Internal.

TREE

The TREE command displays a list of all of your directories and subdirectories and the files they contain. This is especially useful for determining what parts of the directory structure should be pruned. The list shown in DOS versions 3.3X and earlier is textual; it is a graphic representation in DOS 4.

Format

[D:Path]TREE [D:][/F]

D:Path is the drive and path where the command file is located if the file is not in the current directory.

D is the drive identifier of a drive (other than the current one) you want TREE to affect.

/F displays all paths and file names in the directories.

/A is a DOS 4 switch that uses an alternate graphic character set, or code page, for drawing the tree.

Type
External.

TYPE

The TYPE command displays the contents of an ASCII file. ASCII files contain no control codes that would affect the screen display; instead, they appear as straight listings of data.

Using TYPE on a non-ASCII file could display meaningless symbols on your screen. It could also lock up your system entirely. If this happens, you'll need to reboot.

Format

TYPE *FileSpec*

FileSpec is the file name and extension, with an optional drive and path, of the file to be displayed.

Type

Internal.

VER

The VER command displays the current version of DOS in which you are working.

Format

VER

Type

Internal.

VERIFY

The VERIFY command turns the global verify feature of DOS on or off. When it is on, everything written to a file is checked buffer by buffer to ensure the accuracy of the transmission. This is a useful feature, but your system will run more slowly. Use VERIFY ON when you must be completely sure of the validity of the file data being transferred—for example, during BACKUP operations.

Format

VERIFY [ON ¦ OFF]

ON turns the feature on.

OFF turns VERIFY off. This is the default.

Type

Internal.

Restrictions

VERIFY will not work with network disks.

VOL

The VOL command shows you the volume label of the disk contained in a specified drive.

Format

VOL [*D:*]

> *D* is the drive to be checked. You do not need to specify the default drive.

Type

Internal.

XCOPY

The XCOPY command is a modified version of COPY. It does the same thing, only better. Instead of reading and writing files one at a time, XCOPY reads files into a buffer that is equal in size to available memory, and then writes out the contents of the buffer (this is usually several files). XCOPY can be used for a single file or for several different groups of files. You can combine its switches as well.

Format

[*D:Path*]XCOPY [*FileSpec1*][*FileSpec2*][/A][/D:*mm-dd-yy*] [/E][/M][/P][/S][/V][/W]

> *D:Path* is the drive and path where the command file is located if it is not in the current directory.
>
> *FileSpec1* is the necessary drive, path, and file-name specifications for the files to be copied. Wild cards are allowed.
>
> *FileSpec2* is the necessary drive, path, and file-name specifications for the files to be written to. Wild cards are allowed.
>
> /A copies only files with a set archive bit.
>
> /D:*mm-dd-yy* copies only files created or modified on or after the specified date; the dates format depends on the country code.
>
> /E creates corresponding subdirectories on *FileSpec2* before copying is done (even if *FileSpec1* contains no files to transfer).

/M copies files with a set archive bit and resets the archive bit on the source file.

/P prompts you before each file is copied.

/S copies files from all subdirectories within the specified directory in addition to the directory's files. Corresponding subdirectories will be created on *FileSpec2* for all *FileSpec1* directories that contain files.

/V turns VERIFY on during execution of XCOPY only.

/W prompts you to insert different disks before XCOPY executes.

Type
External.

Restrictions
XCOPY will not copy to or from devices. It also will not copy hidden files from the source and will not overwrite existing read-only files in the destination directories.

APPENDICES

APPENDIX *A* *GLOSSARY*

This appendix defines all of the important DOS-related terms used in this book. Although these terms are defined in the text when they are first introduced, the glossary presented here offers concise definitions that will refresh your memory when you read a chapter later in the book, or when you simply can't remember the meaning of a particular term.

action bar   A line at the top of a menu screen that lists the primary actions you can take at that screen.

active partition   The section of a hard disk containing the operating system to be used when the hardware powers up.

allocation unit   *See* cluster.

ANSI driver   A device driver, contained in the ANSI.SYS file, that loads additional support for advanced console features.

application program   A program that performs or replaces a manual function, such as balancing a checkbook or managing inventory.

Application Programming Interface (API)   The set of all OS/2 system service calls, accessible through the standard OS/2 call-return technique.

archive bit   A bit in a file specification used to indicate whether the file in question needs to be backed up.

ASCII   American Standard Code for Information Interchange; the coding scheme whereby every character the computer can access is assigned an integer code between 0 and 255.

assembly language   A symbolic form of computer language used to program computers at a fundamental level.

asynchronous communications   *See* serial communications.

AUTOEXEC.BAT   A batch file executed automatically whenever the computer is booted up.

background task   A second program running on your computer; usually, a printing operation that shares the CPU with your main foreground task.

base name   The portion of a file name to the left of the period separator; it can be up to eight characters long.

BASIC   Beginner's All-purpose Symbolic Instruction Code. A computer language similar to the English language.

batch file   An ASCII file containing a sequence of DOS commands that will execute the commands when you invoke it.

baud rate   The speed of data transmission, usually in bits per second.

binary   A numbering system that uses powers of the number 2 to generate all other numbers.

bit   One-eighth of a byte. A bit is a binary digit, either 0 or 1.

bit mapping   The way a graphics screen is represented in the computer. It usually signifies point-to-point graphics.

booting up   *See* bootstrapping.

boot record   The section on a disk that contains the minimum information DOS needs to start the system.

bootstrapping   When the computer initially is turned on or is rebooted from the keyboard with Ctrl-Alt-Del, it ''pulls itself up by its bootstraps.'' *See also* warm booting, cold booting.

branching   The transfer of control or execution to another statement in a batch file. *See also* decision making.

break key   The control-key combination that interrupts an executing program or command; you activate it by pressing the ScrollLock key while holding down the Ctrl key.

buffer   An area in memory set aside to speed up the transfer of data, allowing blocks of data to be transferred at once.

byte   The main unit of memory in a computer. A byte is an eight-bit binary-digit number. One character usually takes up one byte.

cache   A portion of memory reserved for the contents of recently referenced disk sectors. It facilitates faster reaccess of the same sectors.

case sensitivity   Distinguishing between capital letters and lower-case letters.

chaining   Passing the control of execution from one batch file to another. This represents an unconditional transfer of control.

character set   A complete group of 256 characters that can be used by programs or system devices. It consists of letters, numbers, control codes, and special graphics or international symbols. *See also* code page.

cluster   A group of contiguous sectors on a disk. Also known as an allocation unit, this is the smallest unit of disk storage that DOS can manipulate.

COBOL   A programming language usually used for business applications.

code page   A character set that redefines the country and keyboard information for non-U.S. keyboards and systems.

cold booting   Booting up DOS by turning the computer's power on. *See* bootstrapping.

COMMAND.COM   The command processor that comes with DOS.

command line   The line on which a command is entered. This line contains the command and all of its associated parameters and switches. It may run to more than one screen line, but it is still one command line.

command processor   The program that translates and acts on commands.

command prompt   A visual indicator that an operating system or application program is waiting for input from you.

compressed print   Printing that allows more than 80 characters on a line of output (usually 132 characters, but on newer printers up to 255 characters per line).

computer-aided design (CAD) program   A sophisticated software package containing advanced graphics and drawing features. It is used by engineers, architects, and designers for drawing and design applications.

concatenation   The placing of two text files together in a series.

conditional statement   A statement in a batch file that controls the next step to be executed in the batch file, based on the value of a logical test.

CONFIG.SYS   An ASCII text file containing system configuration commands.

configuration   An initial set of system values, such as the number of buffers DOS will use, the number of simultaneously open files it will allow, and the specific devices that will be supported.

confirmation box   A rectangular window that prompts you to confirm your request. It helps to protect you from making irrevocable errors—for example, when deleting files.

console   The combination of your system's monitor and keyboard.

contiguity   The physical adjacency on a disk of the disk sectors used by a file.

control codes   ASCII codes that do not display a character but perform a function, such as ringing a bell or deleting a character.

control focus   *See* input focus.

copy protection   Special mechanisms contained in diskettes to inhibit the copying of them by conventional commands.

CPU   Central Processing Unit. The main chip that executes all individual computer instructions.

Ctrl-Z   The end-of-file marker.

cursor   The blinking line or highlighting box that indicates where the next keystroke will be displayed or what the next control code entered will affect. *See also* selection cursor.

cutting and pasting   Selecting text from one part of a document or visual display and moving it to another location.

cylinder   Two tracks that are in the same place on different sides of a double-sided disk. It may be extended to include multiple platters. For example, Side 0 Track 30, Side 1 Track 30, Side 2 Track 30, and Side 3 Track 30 form a cylinder.

daisy-wheel printer   A printer that uses circular templates for producing letter-quality characters.

data area   The tracks on a disk that contain user data.

database A collection of data organized into various categories. A phone book is one form of database.

database-management system A software program designed to allow the creation of specially organized files, as well as data entry, manipulation, removal, and reporting for those files.

data bits The bits that represent data when the computer is communicating.

data disk A disk that has been formatted without the /S switch. The disk can contain only data; no room has been reserved for system files.

data stream The transmission of data between two components or computers.

dead key A reserved key combination on international keyboards, which outputs nothing itself but allows the next keystroke to produce an accent mark above or below the keystroke's usual character.

debugging The process of discovering what is wrong with a program, where the problem is located, and what the solution is.

decimal A numbering system based on ten digits.

decision making A point in a batch file at which execution can continue on at least two different paths, depending on the results of a program test. It is also known as logical testing or branching.

default The standard value of a variable or system parameter.

deferred execution In a program or batch file, when execution is delayed until a value for some parameter is finally entered or computed.

delimiter A special character, such as a comma or space, used to separate values or data entries.

destination The targeted location for data, files, or other information generated or moved by a DOS command.

device Any internal or external piece of peripheral hardware.

device driver It is also known as an interrupt handler. A special program that must be loaded to use a device. It adds extra capability to DOS.

device name Logical name that DOS uses to refer to a device.

dialog box   A rectangular window that prompts you to enter data.

digital   A representation based on a collection of individual digits, such as 0's and 1's in the binary number system.

digitizer   A device with a movable arm that can take an image and break it up into small parts, which the computer translates into bits.

directory   A grouping of files on a disk. These files are displayed together and may include access to other directories (subdirectories).

directory tree   The treelike structure created when a root directory has several subdirectories, each of the subdirectories has subdirectories, and so on.

disk drive   A hardware device that accesses the data stored on a disk.

diskette   A flexible, oxide-coated disk used to store data. It is also called a floppy diskette.

disk optimizer   A program that rearranges the location of files stored on a disk in order to make the data in those files quickly retrievable.

disk-resident command   *See* external command.

DOS   Disk Operating System. A disk manager and the program that allows computer/user interaction.

DOS environment   A part of memory set aside to hold the defaults needed in the current environment, such as COMSPEC, PATH, LASTDRIVE, and so on.

DOS prompt   *See* command prompt.

DOS shell   In DOS 4, the graphic interface that lets you use menus, windows, and icons.

dot-matrix printer   A printer that represents characters by means of tiny dots.

double click   Pressing a mouse's button twice in rapid succession.

double-density diskette   A diskette on which magnetic storage material is arranged twice as densely as usual, allowing the storage of twice the usual amount of data. This term generally refers to a 360K, 5¼'' diskette.

drive identifier   A single letter assigned to represent a drive, such as drive A or drive B. It usually requires a colon after it, such as A:.

DRIVER.SYS   A file containing a device driver for an extra external disk drive. Used in the CONFIG.SYS file.

dual tasking   Causing two tasks or programming events to occur simultaneously.

echoing   Displaying on your video monitor the keystrokes you type in.

EDLIN   The DOS line editor.

end-of-file marker   A Ctrl-Z code that marks the logical end of a file.

environment   The context within which DOS interfaces with you and with your commands.

error level   A code, set by programs as they conclude processing, that tells DOS whether an error occurred, and if so, the severity of that error.

expansion cards   Add-on circuit boards through which hardware can increase the power of the system, such as adding extra memory or a modem.

expansion slots   Connectors inside the computer in which expansion cards are placed so that they tie in directly to the system.

extended ASCII codes   ASCII codes between 128 and 255, which usually differ from computer to computer.

extended DOS partition   A hard-disk partition used to exceed the 32Mb, single-disk barrier; it can be divided into logical disk drives.

extended memory   Additional physical memory beyond the DOS 1Mb addressing limit.

extension   The one to three characters after the period following the base name in a file specification.

external buffer   A device, connected to the computer and another device, that acts as a buffer.

external command   A command whose procedures are read from the disk into memory, executed from memory, and then erased from memory when finished.

Family Application Programming Interface (FAPI)   The suggested subset of OS/2 system service calls that enable a developed .EXE program to run under either DOS or OS/2.

file   A collection of bytes, representing a program or data, organized into records and stored as a named group on a disk.

file allocation table (FAT)   A table of sectors stored on a disk, which tells DOS whether a given sector is good, bad, continued, or the end of a chain of records.

file name   The name of a file on the disk. File name usually refers to the base name, but it can include the extension as well.

file version   A term that refers to which developmental copy of a software program is being used or referenced.

filter   A program that accepts data as input, processes it in some manner, and then outputs the data in a different form.

fixed disk   IBM's name for a hard disk.

floppy diskette   *See* diskette.

flow of control   The order of execution of batch-file commands; how the control flows from one command to another, even when the next command to be executed is not located sequentially in the file.

foreground task   The main program running on your computer, as opposed to the less visible background task (usually a printing job).

formatting   The placement of timing marks on a disk to arrange the tracks and sectors for subsequent reading and writing.

fragmentation   A condition in which many different files have been stored in noncontiguous sectors on a disk.

function keys   Special-purpose keys on a keyboard, which can be assigned unique tasks by DOS or by application programs.

gigabyte (Gb)   1024 megabytes.

global characters   *See* wild cards.

graphics mode   The mode in which all screen pixels on a monitor are addressable and can be used to generate detailed images. Contrasts with text mode, which usually allows only 24 lines of 80 characters.

hard disk   A rigid platter that stores data faster and at a higher density than a floppy diskette. It is sealed in an airtight compartment to avoid contaminants that could damage or destroy the disk.

hardware   The physical components of a computer system.

hardware interrupt   A signal from a device to the computer, indicating that an event has taken place.

head   A disk-drive mechanism that reads data from and writes data to the disk.

head crash   Occurs when the head hits the disk platter on a hard disk, physically damaging the disk and the data on it.

help   Helpful textual information. In DOS 4, it is displayed whenever the F1 key is pressed. DOS 4 help text is context dependent, relating directly to whatever item is currently highlighted.

help file   A file of textual information containing helpful explanations of commands, modes, and other on-screen tutorial information. *See also* help.

hexadecimal   A numbering system in base 16. A single eight-bit byte can be fully represented as two hexadecimal digits.

hidden files   Files whose names do not appear in a directory listing. This term usually refers to DOS's internal system files, but can also refer to certain files used in copy-protection schemes.

high-capacity diskette   A 1.2Mb, 5¼'' floppy diskette.

highlighting   Displaying a portion of the screen in reverse video or in a combination of contrasting colors to indicate the choice to be made when you press the Return key.

high-resolution mode   The mode on a video monitor in which all available pixels are used to provide the most detailed screen image possible. On a color monitor, this mode reduces the possible range of colors that can be output.

horizontal landscape   When output to a printer is not done in the usual format, but rather with the wider part of the paper laid out horizontally, as in a landscape picture.

hot key   A key combination used to signal that a memory-resident program should begin operation.

housekeeping   Making sure the directory stays intact and well organized, and that unnecessary files are deleted.

hub   The center hole of a diskette.

IF   A conditional statement in a batch file.

ink-jet printer   A printer that forms characters by spraying ink in a dot pattern. *See* dot-matrix printer.

input focus   The portion of a graphic menu screen that the selection cursor is in. You can switch the input focus among the screen areas by pressing the Tab key or by using the mouse.

interface   The boundary between two things, such as the computer and a peripheral.

internal command   *See* resident command.

interrupt   A signal sent to the computer from a hardware device, indicating a request for service or support from the system.

keyboard translation table   An internal table, contained in the keyboard driver, that converts hardware signals from the keyboard into the correct ASCII codes.

key combination   When two or more keys are pressed simultaneously, as in Ctrl-ScrollLock or Ctrl-Alt-Del.

key redefinition   Assigning a nonstandard value to a key.

kilobyte (K)   1024 bytes.

laser printer   A printer that produces images (pictures or text) by shining a laser on a photostatic drum, which picks up toner and then transfers the image to paper.

LCD   Liquid Crystal Display. A method of producing an image using electrically sensitive crystals suspended in a liquid medium.

letter-quality printer   A printer that forms characters that are comparable to those of a typewriter.

line editor   A program that can make textual changes to an ASCII file, but can only make changes to one line of the file at a time.

line feed   When the cursor on a screen moves to the next line, or when the print head on a printer moves down the paper to the next line.

literal   Something that is accepted exactly as it was submitted.

lockup   The computer will not accept any input and may have stopped processing. It must be warm or cold booted to resume operating.

log file   A separate file, created with the BACKUP command, that keeps track of the names of all files written to the backup diskette(s).

logging on   Signing onto a remote system, such as a mainframe or telecommunications service.

logical   Something that is defined based on a decision, not by physical properties.

logical drives   Disk drives, created in an extended DOS partition, that do not physically exist, but DOS thinks they do. A means for DOS to access a physical disk that has more than 32Mb available.

logical testing   *See* decision making.

look-ahead buffers   512-byte memory buffers used by DOS 4 to read successively positioned disk sectors before those sectors are actually referenced by a program or command, thereby improving performance. They are created by the BUFFERS command.

machine language   The most fundamental way to program a computer, using instructions made up entirely of strings of 0's and 1's.

macro   A set of commands, often memory-resident. When executed, they appear to the program executing them as if they were being entered by you.

medium-resolution mode   The mode on a Color Graphics Adapter in which only 320×200 pixels of resolution are allowed.

megabyte (Mb)   1024 kilobytes.

memory   The circuitry in a computer that stores information. *See also* RAM and ROM.

memory cache   *See* cache.

memory-resident   Located in physical memory, as opposed to being stored in a disk file.

menu   A set of choices displayed in tabular format.

meta symbols   Special single-character codes used by the PROMPT command to represent complex actions or sequences to be included in the DOS prompt.

microfloppy diskette   The 3½" diskette format used in the new Personal System/2 and many other computers.

modem   A device that transmits digital data in tones over a phone line.

monitor   The device used to display images; a display screen.

monochrome   Using two colors only—the background and foreground.

mouse   A device that moves the screen cursor by means of a hand-held apparatus moved along a surface such as a desk. The computer can tell how far and in which direction the mouse is being moved.

mouse pointer   The screen symbol representing the symbolic location of the mouse. When in graphic mode, the mouse pointer is an arrow. When in text mode, it appears as a solid movable rectangle.

multiprocessing   *See* multitasking.

multitasking   When two or more computing applications are executing simultaneously.

multithreading   Simultaneously running multiple independent code sequences (threads) within a single program (task).

national language-support operations   The feature in DOS 3.3 and later versions that supports displays and printers, using a range of code and character groupings.

network   Several computers, connected together, that can share common data files and peripheral devices.

nibble   Four bits, or half a byte.

octal   A numbering system in base 8.

online help   *See* help.

OS/2   Operating System/2. The latest advanced operating system from Microsoft and IBM, which manages computer/user interaction, enhanced-memory features, and multitasking.

operating system   *See* DOS.

overlay files   Files containing additional command and control information for sophisticated and complex programs. An overlay file is usually too large to fit into memory along with the main .EXE or .COM file.

overwriting   Typing or saving new data over what is already there.

parallel communications   Data transmission in which several bits can be transferred or processed at one time.

parameter   An extra bit of information, specified with a command, that determines how the command executes.

parity bit   The bit, added to the end of a sequence of data bits, that makes the total of the data bits and the parity bit odd or even.

partition   The section of a hard disk that contains an operating system. There can be at most four partitions on one hard disk.

Pascal   A programming language used mainly in computer science.

password   A sequence of characters that allows entry into a restricted system or program.

path   The list of disks and directories that DOS will search through to find a command file ending in .COM, .BAT, or .EXE.

peripheral   Any physical device connected to the computer.

piping   Redirecting the input or output of one program or command to another program or command.

pixel   The smallest unit of display on a video monitor—in short, a dot—which can be illuminated to create text or graphics images.

platter   The rigid disk used in a hard-disk drive.

plotter   A device that draws data on paper with a mechanical arm.

port   A doorway through which the computer can access external devices.

Presentation Manager   The windowing interface of OS/2's Version 1.1, which displays executing programs within separate screen windows on the same display monitor.

primary DOS partition   Up to the first 32Mb of a hard disk. Contains the boot record and other DOS information files.

printer   A device that outputs data onto paper using pins (dot matrix), a daisy wheel, ink jets, laser imaging, and so on.

process   *See* task.

program-startup command   Any DOS command (except GOTO) that is included in the Commands field of DOS 4's Add or Change Program dialog boxes. It may also include an option string enclosed in brackets.

protected mode   The principal operating environment of OS/2 that supports multitasking, process protection, and advanced memory management.

public domain   Something not copyrighted or patented. Public domain software can be used and copied without infringing on anyone's rights.

pull-down menu   A vertical list of command choices that appears when you select a choice from an action bar (in DOS 4).

pushbutton   The elliptically shaped symbol in windows that can be selected by a mouse. Selecting it specifies the next operation to be performed.

queue   A series of files waiting in line to be printed.

RAM   Random-Access Memory. The part of the computer's memory to which you have access; it stores programs and data while the computer is on.

RAM disk   An area of RAM that acts as if it were a disk drive. All data in this area of memory is lost when the computer is turned off or warm booted. It is also known as a virtual disk.

range   A contiguous series of values (minimum to maximum, first to last, and so on).

read-after-write verification   An extra level of validity checking, it is invoked with the VERIFY command or the /V switch. It rereads data after writing it to disk, comparing the written data to the original information.

read-only status   A file with this status cannot be updated but can be read.

read/write bit   The bit in a file specification that indicates whether a file can accept changes or deletions, or can only be accessed for reading.

real mode   The single tasking unprotected operating environment that runs old DOS programs under OS/2.

redirection   Causing output from one program or device to be routed to another program or device.

REM statement   A line in a BASIC program containing remarks or comments for program explanation or clarification.

reserved names   Specific words, in a programming language or operating system, which should not be used in any other application context.

resident command   A command located in random-access memory.

resource allocation   Making system facilities available to individual users or programs.

reverse video   Black letters on a white background.

ROM   Read-Only Memory. The section of memory that you can only read from. This contains the basic computer operating system and system routines.

root directory   The first directory on any disk.

scan code   The hardware code representing a key pressed on a keyboard. Converted by a keyboard driver into an ASCII code for use by DOS and application programs.

scrolling   What the screen does when you're at the bottom of it and press Return—all of the lines roll up.

secondary command processor   A second copy of COMMAND-.COM, invoked either to run a batch file or to provide a new context for subsequent DOS commands.

sector   A division of a disk track; usually 512 bytes.

selection cursor   The extended highlighting that indicates that an item or an area of activity can be selected.

serial communications   Data transmission in which data is transferred and processed one bit at a time. It is also known as asynchronous communications.

Session Manager   The OS/2 program that presents a menu of choices enabling you to switch your video display between your DOS program and any of the active OS/2 protected-mode programs.

shareware   Public domain software. *See also* public domain.

snapshot program   A program used in debugging to store the status of system or application program variables.

software   The programs and instruction sets that operate the computer.

software interrupt   A signal from a software program that calls up a routine that is resident in the computer's basic programming. It is also a software signal to the computer that the software program has finished, has a problem, and so on.

source The location containing the original data, files, or other information to be used in a DOS command.

spooling Simultaneous Peripheral Operations On-Line. Using a high-speed disk to store input to or output from low-speed peripheral devices while the CPU does other tasks.

spreadsheet program An electronic version of an accountant's spreadsheet; when one value changes, all other values based on that value are updated instantly.

start bit The bit sent at the beginning of a data stream to indicate that data bits follow.

stop bit The bit sent after the data bits, indicating that no more data bits follow.

string A series of characters.

subcommands Several special commands used only within batch files.

subdirectory A directory contained within another directory or subdirectory. Technically, all directories other than the root directory are subdirectories.

switch A parameter included in DOS commands, usually preceded by the slash (/) symbol, which clarifies or modifies the action of the command.

synchronization The coordination of a sending and receiving device, so that both simultaneously send and receive data at the same rate.

system disk A disk containing the necessary DOS system files for system booting.

task An OS/2 program and the set of system resources that it uses.

text mode The mode in which standard characters can be displayed on a monitor.

thread A logical sequence of code in an OS/2 program. This is the fundamental entity that is assigned CPU time in the OS/2 multitasking environment.

time slice The smallest unit of time managed and assigned by the operating system to programs and other processing activities.

toggle A switch or command that reverses a value from off to on, or from on to off.

track   A circular stream of data on the disk. It is similar to a track on a record, only not spiraling.

TSR   Terminate and Stay Resident. A program that is read into memory the first time it is used and then continues to reside in memory.

utility   A supplemental routine or program designed to carry out a specific operation, usually to modify the system environment or perform housekeeping tasks.

variable parameter   A named element, following a command, that acts as a placeholder; when you issue the command, you replace the variable parameter with the actual value you want to use.

verbose listing   A listing of all files and subdirectories contained on the disk and path specified in the command. It is activated by the CHKDSK command with the /V switch.

vertical portrait   The conventional $8^1/_4$-by-11-inch output for printed information, with the long side of the paper positioned vertically.

virtual disk   *See* RAM disk.

volume label   A name, consisting of up to 11 characters, that can be assigned to any disk during a FORMAT operation or after formatting with the LABEL command.

warm booting   Resetting the computer using the Ctrl-Alt-Del key combination. *See* bootstrapping.

warning box   A rectangular window that warns you of an input error (such as an incorrect password) or a potentially dangerous consequence of a requested operation.

wide directory listing   An alternate output format that lists four columns of file names.

wild cards   Characters used to represent any other characters. In DOS, * and ? are the only wild-card symbols.

word processor   A computerized typewriter. It allows the correction and reformatting of documents before they are printed.

wrapping around   In menus, pressing the down arrow key at the end of a list will move the selection cursor to the top of the list, as if the two ends of the list were attached to each other.

write-protecting   Giving a disk read-only status by covering the write-protect notch.

APPENDIX *B* ASCII CODES

This appendix presents information on how ASCII codes are created, used, and manipulated in DOS. It discusses the different numbering systems used to create these codes, as well as how codes are grouped to form identifiable character sets. Using this information, you can both manage your DOS system more readily and manipulate file data for yourself.

CHARACTER SETS

Just as you use an alphabet and a decimal numbering system, the computer uses its own character and numbering system. DOS maintains, in memory, all of the characters of the English alphabet, including numbers and symbols, as well as some foreign symbols (such as accented vowels). This group of symbols is called a character set. By changing the symbols in this set, you can obtain completely new character sets. This is especially useful for people living in other countries, who have less daily need of U.S. standard characters and who would rather work with their own characters.

ASCII CODES

A character is any letter, number, punctuation symbol, or graphics symbol. In other words, it is anything that can be displayed on a video screen or printed on a printer.

Each character in a character set has a number assigned to it, which is how the computer refers to the various characters in the set. For example, code 65 refers to a capital A, and code 97 refers to a lowercase a. These codes are called ASCII codes (pronounced *"ask-ee codes"*); ASCII stands for American Standard Code for Information Interchange.

Codes 0 through 31 are used as control codes. Displaying one of these codes will cause something to happen instead of causing a symbol to be displayed. For example, displaying code 7 will result in the computer's bell or beeper being sounded. Displaying code 13 will result in a carriage return.

Codes 32 through 127 are ASCII character codes for numbers, letters, and all punctuation marks and symbols. Codes 128 through 255, known as extended ASCII codes, vary from computer to computer. They usually comprise foreign characters, Greek and mathematical symbols, and graphics characters. (Graphics characters consist of small lines and curves that can be used to create geometric patterns.)

DOS has several available ASCII tables, called code pages. The most common is the standard U.S. code page (see Table B.1); the next most common is the Multilingual code page (see Table B.2).

Hex Digits 1st / 2nd	0-	1-	2-	3-	4-	5-	6-	7-	8-	9-	A-	B-	C-	D-	E-	F-
0		►		0	@	P	`	p	Ç	É	á	▓	└	╨	α	≡
1	☺	◄	!	1	A	Q	a	q	ü	æ	í	▒	┴	╤	β	±
2	☻	↕	"	2	B	R	b	r	é	Æ	ó	▓	┬	╥	Γ	≥
3	♥	‼	#	3	C	S	c	s	â	ô	ú	│	├	╙	π	≤
4	♦	¶	$	4	D	T	d	t	ä	ö	ñ	┤	─	╘	Σ	⌠
5	♣	§	%	5	E	U	e	u	à	ò	Ñ	╡	┼	╒	σ	⌡
6	♠	▬	&	6	F	V	f	v	å	û	ª	╢	╞	╓	µ	÷
7	•	↨	'	7	G	W	g	w	ç	ù	º	╖	╟	╫	τ	≈
8	◘	↑	(	8	H	X	h	x	ê	ÿ	¿	╕	╚	╪	Φ	°
9	○	↓	)	9	I	Y	i	y	ë	Ö	⌐	╣	╔	┘	Θ	∙
A	◎	→	*	:	J	Z	j	z	è	Ü	¬	║	╩	┌	Ω	·
B	♂	←	+	;	K	[	k	{	ï	¢	½	╗	╦	█	δ	√
C	♀	∟	,	<	L	\	l	|	î	£	¼	╝	╠	▄	∞	ⁿ
D	♪	↔	-	=	M	]	m	}	ì	¥	¡	╜	=	█	φ	²
E	♫	▲	.	>	N	^	n	~	Ä	Pt	«	╛	╬	█	ε	■
F	☼	▼	/	?	O	_	o	△	Å	ƒ	»	┐	╧	▀	∩	

Table B.1: U.S. ASCII table (code page 437)

Hex Digits 1st / 2nd	0-	1-	2-	3-	4-	5-	6-	7-	8-	9-	A-	B-	C-	D-	E-	F-
0		►		0	@	P	`	p	Ç	É	á	▒	└	ð	Ó	-
1	☺	◄	!	1	A	Q	a	q	ü	æ	í	▓	┴	Ð	ß	±
2	☻	↕	"	2	B	R	b	r	é	Æ	ó	▓	┬	Ê	Ô	=
3	♥	‼	#	3	C	S	c	s	â	ô	ú	│	├	Ë	Ò	¾
4	♦	¶	$	4	D	T	d	t	ä	ö	ñ	┤	─	È	õ	¶
5	♣	§	%	5	E	U	e	u	à	ò	Ñ	Á	┼	ı	Õ	§
6	♠	▬	&	6	F	V	f	v	å	û	ª	Â	ã	Í	µ	÷
7	•	↨	'	7	G	W	g	w	ç	ù	º	À	Ã	Î	þ	¸
8	◘	↑	(	8	H	X	h	x	ê	ÿ	¿	©	└	Ï	Þ	°
9	○	↓	)	9	I	Y	i	y	ë	Ö	®	╣	┌	┘	Ú	¨
A	◙	→	*	:	J	Z	j	z	è	Ü	¬	║	╨	┌	Û	·
B	♂	←	+	;	K	[	k	{	ï	ø	½	┐	╥	█	Ù	¹
C	♀	∟	,	<	L	\	l	¦	î	£	¼	┘	╟	▄	ý	³
D	♪	↔	-	=	M	]	m	}	ì	Ø	¡	¢	=	¦	Ý	²
E	♫	▲	.	>	N	^	n	~	Ä	×	«	¥	╪	Ì	¯	■
F	☼	▼	/	?	O	_	o	△	Å	ƒ	»	┐	□	▀	´	

Table B.2: Multilingual ASCII table (code page 850)

MAPPING ONE CHARACTER SET ONTO ANOTHER

Any device that displays characters has a device driver that literally drives, or controls, the device. When the computer tells a printer to print the letter A, DOS sends the code 65 to the printer driver, which converts the 65 into a series of control codes that will print the A.

For the sake of consistency, computers, printers, and displays all have the same character sets and coding system for ASCII codes 32 through 127. This ensures that when you press a key, the desired character will be displayed, and the same character will be printed by your printer.

The process of matching ASCII codes against characters in a character set is called *mapping*. The following section describes how you map a set of numbers onto a set of characters so that they correspond exactly to each other.

NUMBERING SYSTEMS

Computers use a variety of numbering systems to operate. The most basic numbering system is the binary system, in which there are only two digits, 0 and 1. The digital circuitry used in computers operates by using small voltages that turn magnetic bits on or off. Therefore, 0 and 1 are used to represent the two states of off and on, respectively.

Counting in binary is not difficult, but it does require some adjustment from your standard decimal-numbering scheme. The progression of numbers and their matching decimal conversions are shown in Table B.3.

Chapter 9 contains a detailed explanation of the binary numbering system. The general rule for converting numbers from binary to decimal is to multiply the number in every binary number column by 2 raised to the column-number power. You count column numbers from the right, starting with 0. For the binary number 1101, for example, you would obtain

$$(1 \times 2^0) + (0 \times 2^1) + (1 \times 2^2) + (1 \times 2^3)$$

BINARY	DECIMAL
0	0
1	1
10	2
11	3
100	4
101	5
110	6
111	7
1000	8
1001	9
1010	10

Table B.3: Binary-to-decimal conversion

where any number to the 0 power (2^0 in this case) is defined as equal to 1. This is called *counting in base 2*.

The *decimal* system counts in base 10. Using the same method of converting binary numbers, you can see that breaking down the decimal number 2014 into its component parts works like this:

$$(4 \times 10^0) + (1 \times 10^1) + (0 \times 10^2) + (2 \times 10^3)$$
$$= 4 + 10 + 000 + 2000$$
$$= 2014$$

Another numbering system is called *octal*, or base 8. This system has only eight digits, 0–7. The octal number 701 is converted to base 10 (decimal) by the following computation:

$$(1 \times 8^0) + (0 \times 8^1) + (7 \times 8^2)$$
$$= 1 + 0 + 448$$
$$= 449$$

The last major numbering system in computers is called *hexadecimal*, which counts in base 16. This system has 16 digits in it: 0–9 and A–F, which form the counting sequence 0123456789ABCDEF. To count in this system, you use the same method you use for other numbering systems. The hexadecimal number BA7 translates to decimal as

$$(7 \times 16^0) + (A \times 16^1) + (B \times 16^2)$$

which is equal to

$$7 + (10 \times 16^1) + (11 \times 16^2)$$

which is also equal to

$$7 + 160 + 2816$$
$$= 2983$$

Hexadecimal notation is convenient for byte values because a hexadecimal digit is equivalent to 4 ($2^4 = 16$) binary digits (called a *nibble*) and there are 8 bits ($2^8 = 256$-character set) in a byte. A byte can therefore be represented by two hexadecimal digits.

Table B.4 demonstrates how to count in hexadecimal.

HEXADECIMAL	DECIMAL
0	0
.	.

Table B.4: Hexadecimal-to-decimal conversion

HEXADECIMAL	DECIMAL
.	.
9	9
A	10
B	11
.	.
.	.
F	15
10	16
.	.
.	.
1A	26

Table B.4: Hexadecimal-to-decimal conversion (continued)

Hard disks are usually large enough to contain more than one type of operating system. For example, you can have DOS manage one part of a disk and UNIX manage another. Each of these sections is called a partition. You can have from one to four partitions on a disk.

Partitions make the hard disk, especially a very large one, a more economical investment by allowing you to have up to four completely different computer systems in one set of hardware. However, since the resident systems do not share a common software environment, they cannot share data directly.

DOS 4 can create partitions that are larger than 32Mb.

Two types of partitions can be set up for DOS: a primary DOS partition and an extended DOS partition. The primary DOS partition is the partition that contains DOS and is the first partition on the disk. This is usually the only partition if the hard disk is no larger than 32Mb, which is the maximum partition size in DOS 3.30 and earlier versions. The extended DOS partition is a separate partition that cannot be used for booting, but can be divided into separate logical disk drives. An extended partition helps you access data on a large physical drive more easily. For example, if you are using backup media that is limited to 16Mb (as are some tape drives) or 20Mb (as are some removable hard-disk cartridges), you can back up an entire logical drive to the backup device with just one command.

When you create an extended DOS partition, it is assigned the next logical drive letter. For example, if you have a 60Mb hard-disk drive, you can create a 30Mb primary partition and a 30Mb extended partition. If DOS assigns drive C to the primary partition, the extended partition will be called drive D. You could also subdivide the extended partition into more logical drives (up to the letter Z).

You must create partitions before using a hard-disk drive. You can take the easiest route by simply using the FDISK program to make the entire disk into one primary partition, provided you will only use one operating system. To use multiple operating systems from the same disk, however, you need to leave room for additional partitions and then create those partitions with the other operating system. (Each of these partitions will be a primary partition, but you must designate one as the active partition, the one that will gain control when your system boots up.)

FDISK assigns drive letters to the primary partitions of all physical drives before assigning letters to any logical drives.

Should you install a second hard-disk drive on your system and use FDISK to partition it, its primary partition will become drive D, and all drive identifiers of any logical drives in the first disk's extended partition will be bumped up by one letter. For example, if your first disk has a primary drive C and an extended partition for drive D, then adding a second hard disk will change the former drive D into drive E.

You must always be careful not to lose any existing data on your hard disk during this required partitioning processing. If your disk is already being used and you wish to make a new partition, you will have to first back up all of your data and then run FDISK from a system disk. Then you'll need to reformat your disk before restoring your files to it.

SETTING UP YOUR HARD DISK

In this section, you will learn exactly how to use the FDISK command to partition your disk. This procedure is very important, and it will cause serious damage if done incorrectly. However, when you use FDISK properly, it can make your hard-disk system more efficient.

Any existing data on your disk will be destroyed when you create partitions with FDISK.

The FDISK command requires no arguments and can be easily invoked from DOS 4's File System. After this command creates the appropriate partitions, you must then logically format your hard disks. Any existing data on them will be destroyed when you create partitions with FDISK.

When you first invoke FDISK, the screen will clear and the FDISK Options screen shown in Figure C.1 will appear. As you can see, there are four choices in this initial FDISK screen. If you have a

```
                        IBM DOS Version 4.00
                       Fixed Disk Setup Program
                    (C)Copyright IBM Corp. 1983, 1988

                            FDISK Options

       Current fixed disk drive: 1

       Choose one of the following:

       1. Create DOS Partition or Logical DOS Drive
       2. Set active partition
       3. Delete DOS Partition or Logical DOS Drive
       4. Display partition information


       Enter choice: [1]




       Press Esc to exit FDISK
```

Figure C.1: The FDISK Options menu

system with more than one hard-disk drive, the number in the Current fixed disk drive line will reflect which drive is being partitioned. Also, a fifth option, Select next fixed disk drive, will be displayed on the screen. You can only work on one hard-disk drive at a time, but you can switch from the drive you are working on to another drive. For now, let's assume you have one hard-disk drive.

CREATING A PARTITION

The first option on the FDISK Options menu is to create a DOS partition. Since you are using DOS, and not another operating system like UNIX, you can only create DOS partitions. To put another operating system on the hard disk, you have to use that system's own version of FDISK, which would create its partitions next to DOS's. Choosing the first option to create a DOS partition results in the screen shown in Figure C.2.

Assuming you are starting from scratch, you would select choice 1 to create the primary DOS partition. You will then see the screen shown in Figure C.3. Answering Y at this screen tells DOS to use the

If you plan to use your hard disk to later support another operating system, do not partition the whole disk. Leave some room so that you can later load another system on it.

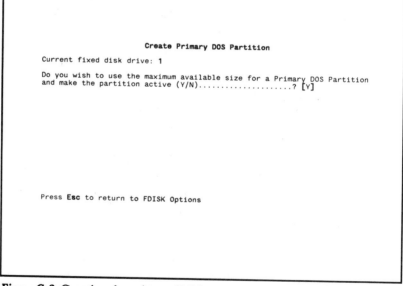

```
                    Create DOS Partition or Logical DOS Drive
        Current fixed disk drive: 1

        Choose one of the following:

        1. Create Primary DOS Partition
        2. Create Extended DOS Partition
        3. Create Logical DOS Drive(s) in the Extended DOS Partition


        Enter choice: [1]



        Press Esc to return to FDISK Options
```

Figure C.2: The Create DOS Partition or Logical DOS Drive menu

```
                        Create Primary DOS Partition
        Current fixed disk drive: 1

        Do you wish to use the maximum available size for a Primary DOS Partition
        and make the partition active (Y/N).....................? [Y]








        Press Esc to return to FDISK Options
```

Figure C.3: Creating the primary DOS partition

whole disk. After making one active partition, DOS then prompts you with the following message:

System will now restart

Insert DOS Install diskette in drive A:
Press any key when ready . . .

Since you just created the partition, there is nothing on the hard disk. The system must be rebooted from your DOS Install diskette, which is one of your original DOS system diskettes. You can now format the entire hard disk as a system disk, just as you would a floppy disk.

On the other hand, if you answer N, another screen will appear and you can then create a smaller partition (see Figure C.4).

There are only two reasons why you would not accept the entire physical disk space for your primary DOS partition. First, you may want to reserve some space on the disk for another operating system. Second, you may want to create additional logical drives for use by DOS. As you can see in Figure C.4, you can define your primary

```
                        Create Primary DOS Partition
        Current fixed disk drive: 1




        Total disk space is   41 Mbytes (1 Mbyte = 1048576 bytes)
        Maximum space available for partition is   41 Mbytes (100%)

        Enter partition size in Mbytes or percent of disk space (%) to
        create a Primary DOS Partition...................................: [  20]

        No partitions defined

        Press Esc to return to FDISK Options
```

Figure C.4: Specifying the size of the primary DOS partition

DOS partition by giving either the number of megabytes or a percentage of the total disk space.

The sample disk I am partitioning in Figure C.4 has a total of 41 megabytes (nominally a 40Mb hard disk). I entered the partition size as an absolute number of 20Mb. The message near to the bottom of the screen, "No partitions defined," shows that I have not yet created any disk partitions. Pressing Return now will create the primary DOS partition and produce the resulting status screen shown in Figure C.5.

This screen tells you that the partition you just created on drive C is a primary DOS partition (PRI DOS) that is 20Mb large, constituting 49% of the entire physical disk. Pressing Esc at this point returns you to the FDISK Options menu.

There can only be one primary DOS partition. When DOS boots up, the system files from this partition are loaded into memory for your operations.

In this example, you have only used 20Mb out of a possible 41, so you can now do one of two things. You can install a non-DOS operating system in the remaining space, or you can create an extended DOS partition and define logical DOS drives in that space. To create an extended DOS partition, you select choice 1 on the FDISK Options menu (see Figure C.1) and then select choice 2 on the Create DOS Partition or Logical DOS Drive menu (see Figure C.2).

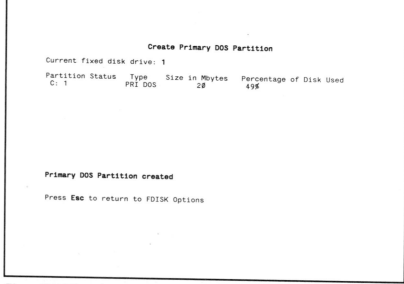

```
                          Create Primary DOS Partition
        Current fixed disk drive: 1

        Partition Status    Type     Size in Mbytes    Percentage of Disk Used
           C: 1            PRI DOS         20                49%




        Primary DOS Partition created

        Press Esc to return to FDISK Options
```

Figure C.5: The primary DOS partition is created.

The screen shown in Figure C.6 then appears, telling you the current partitioning status. In Figure C.6, the maximum available space is 21Mb (51% of the available physical disk). DOS displays the maximum available space in megabytes as the default entry for the extended DOS partition size.

You only need to type in a number on top of the 21 to override the default. In Figure C.6, I entered 51% for the partition's size, leaving no remaining space on this disk for another operating system. I did this to demonstrate that DOS interprets your entry as megabytes if you simply enter a number or as a percentage of the total disk space if you enter a number and a percent sign.

Press Return to enter your size specification. DOS will then display your current disk partition information, including that on the new extended DOS partition (see Figure C.7). Pressing Esc at this screen will return you to the initial FDISK Options menu. You can then create logical drives in your extended partition.

If you select choice 1 on the FDISK Options menu (Figure C.1) and then choice 3 on the Create DOS Partition or Logical DOS Drive menu, DOS tells you that no logical drives have yet been defined in this extended partition (see Figure C.8). You are also told

```
                    Create Extended DOS Partition

    Current fixed disk drive: 1

    Partition Status    Type    Size in Mbytes   Percentage of Disk Used
      C: 1       A     PRI DOS       20               49%



    Total disk space is    41 Mbytes (1 Mbyte = 1048576 bytes)
    Maximum space available for partition is    21 Mbytes ( 51%)

    Enter partition size in Mbytes or percent of disk space (%) to
    create an Extended DOS Partition...............................: [ 51%]



    Press Esc to return to FDISK Options
```

Figure C.6: Creating an extended DOS partition

```
                         Create Extended DOS Partition
         Current fixed disk drive: 1

         Partition Status   Type    Size in Mbytes   Percentage of Disk Used
            C: 1        A    PRI DOS       20              49%
               2             EXT DOS       21              51%




         Extended DOS Partition created

         Press Esc to continue
```

Figure C.7: The status of the hard disk after creating an extended DOS partition

```
               Create Logical DOS Drive(s) in the Extended DOS Partition




         No logical drives defined




         Total Extended DOS Partition size is   21 Mbytes (1 MByte = 1048576 bytes)
         Maximum space available for logical drive is   21 Mbytes (100%)

         Enter logical drive size in Mbytes or percent of disk space (%)...[  15]


         Press Esc to return to FDISK Options
```

Figure C.8: Creating logical drive D in an extended partition

that the extended partition consists of 21Mb, all of which is available for defining logical drives. Your entry on this screen will define the size of the first logical drive. This will become drive D, since the primary DOS partition has been assigned to drive C.

Let's say you enter 15. This creates logical drive D, containing 72% of the available 21Mb in this extended partition. Since all available space in the extended partition has not been used, the resulting screen (see Figure C.9) lets you assign the remaining 6Mb (28%).

You can simply press Return to accept the default assignment of the remaining 6Mb to another logical DOS drive (E). The resulting screen (see Figure C.10) will then contain the completed logical drive information, telling you that all of your extended partition's space has been assigned.

SETTING THE ACTIVE PARTITION

The active partition is the partition that is used to boot the system and is the default partition. Choosing option 2 on the FDISK Options menu presents the screen shown in Figure C.11, which displays your hard

```
              Create Logical DOS Drive(s) in the Extended DOS Partition

Drv Volume Label  Mbytes  System   Usage
D:                   15   UNKNOWN   72%








     Total Extended DOS Partition size is    21 Mbytes (1 MByte = 1048576 bytes)
     Maximum space available for logical drive is    6 Mbytes ( 28%)

     Enter logical drive size in Mbytes or percent of disk space (%)...[    6]

     Logical DOS Drive created, drive letters changed or added

     Press Esc to return to FDISK Options
```

Figure C.9: Creating logical drive E in an extended partition

```
                   Create Logical DOS Drive(s) in the Extended DOS Partition
        Drv Volume Label  Mbytes  System   Usage
        D:                    15  UNKNOWN   72%
        E:                     6  UNKNOWN   28%










           All available space in the Extended DOS Partition
           is assigned to logical drives.
           Press Esc to return to FDISK Options
```

Figure C.10: Final status of your logical DOS drives

```
                              Set Active Partition

          Current fixed disk drive: 1

          Partition Status    Type    Size in Mbytes   Percentage of Disk Used
            C: 1              PRI DOS       20               49%



          Total disk space is    41 Mbytes (1 Mbyte = 1048576 bytes)

          Enter the number of the partition you want to make active...........: [1]




          Press Esc to return to FDISK Options
```

Figure C.11: The Set Active Partition screen

disk's partition information. (Figure C.11 shows the partition status of my hard disk before I created the extended partition.) At this screen, you specify which partition will be the active one.

Typically, you type the number 1 so that the primary DOS partition will have control when your system comes up. However, if you partitioned your disk to include other operating systems, you use the Set active partition choice to make another operating system active the next time the hard disk boots up. Entering a partition number and pressing Return will result in a message that your selected partition has been made active.

DISPLAYING PARTITION INFORMATION

Once you have set up your partitions, you can use choice 4 on the FDISK Options menu to display information about them. This option is useful because you don't have to execute any FDISK functions with it; you can simply look at the information (see Figure C.12).

```
                        Display Partition Information

       Current fixed disk drive: 1

       Partition Status   Type    Size in Mbytes   Percentage of Disk Used
         C: 1       A     PRI DOS       20              49%
            2             EXT DOS       21              51%


       Total disk space is   41 Mbytes (1 Mbyte = 1048576 bytes)


       The Extended DOS Partition contains Logical DOS Drives.
       Do you want to display the logical drive information (Y/N)......?[Y]




       Press Esc to return to FDISK Options
```

Figure C.12: Displaying partition information

The information at the top of the screen is familiar by now. In the bottom half of the screen, DOS also asks you if you want to see information about the defined logical drives. Replying with Y results in a display of all known information about these logical drives (see Figure C.13).

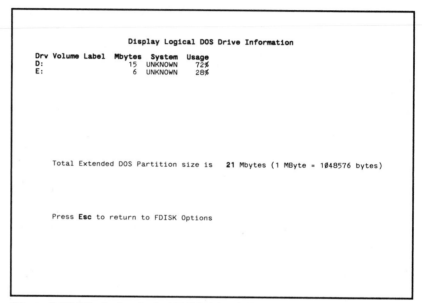

```
                    Display Logical DOS Drive Information

    Drv Volume Label   Mbytes  System   Usage
    D:                     15   UNKNOWN   72%
    E:                      6   UNKNOWN   28%




         Total Extended DOS Partition size is   21 Mbytes (1 MByte = 1048576 bytes)



         Press Esc to return to FDISK Options
```

Figure C.13: Displaying logical DOS drive information

DELETING DOS PARTITIONS

As always, you can revise what you set up in DOS—in this case, your partitions. Selecting choice 3 on the FDISK Options menu produces the Delete DOS Partition or Logical DOS Drive menu (see Figure C.14).

Using this menu, you can delete any of the information you've already set up. You may want to expand or contract other partitions, or you may no longer want to use a partition in the manner you originally designed. In any case, you can only make changes in a certain order. For example, you cannot delete the primary DOS partition without first deleting the extended DOS partition.

```
                    Delete DOS Partition or Logical DOS Drive
        Current fixed disk drive: 1

        Choose one of the following:

        1.   Delete Primary DOS Partition
        2.   Delete Extended DOS Partition
        3.   Delete Logical DOS Drive(s) in the Extended DOS Partition



        Enter choice: [ ]




        Press Esc to return to FDISK Options
```

Figure C.14: The Delete DOS Partition or Logical DOS Drive menu

You also cannot delete an extended DOS partition without first deleting the logical drives in that partition. Trying to delete the extended DOS partition before deleting the drives in it will simply display the current partition information with a message informing you that FDISK can't perform the requested deletion.

Choice 3 in the Delete DOS Partition or Logical DOS Drive menu is probably the first selection you will need to make; you work backward from the order in which you created things. When you select choice 3, a screen containing the logical drive information and the size of the extended DOS partition appears. You are also warned that any data contained in the logical disk drive to be deleted will also be deleted (see Figure C.15).

If you still want to delete the drive, enter its drive identifier. You will then be asked to enter the logical drive's volume label if it has one. You must enter the correct label, otherwise FDISK will not delete the logical drive. If it has no volume label, simply pressing Return will suffice. You will also be asked to explicitly confirm this deletion. Enter Y to do this. If you enter N, the deletion request is ignored, and you are returned to the FDISK Options menu.

```
                Delete Logical DOS Drive(s) in the Extended DOS Partition
     Drv Volume Label  Mbytes  System  Usage
     D:                     9   UNKNOWN  100%




     Total Extended DOS Partition size is    9 Mbytes (1 MByte = 1048576 bytes)

     WARNING! Data in a deleted Logical DOS Drive will be lost.
     What drive do you want to delete..............................? [D]
     Enter Volume Label...............................? [           ]
     Are you sure (Y/N)...............................? [Y]

     Press Esc to return to FDISK Options
```

Figure C.15: Deleting logical DOS drives

Figure C.15 displays the deletion sequence just described for a disk that has a 9Mb extended DOS partition consisting of drive D. Once FDISK deletes the logical drive, it updates the display at the top of the screen. If you have any remaining logical drives in your extended partition, FDISK asks you whether you want to delete another drive. You would then repeat the same procedure to delete other drives. When the last logical drive is deleted, the display indicates which drives have been deleted and informs you that

All logical drives deleted in the Extended DOS Partition.

Pressing Esc at this point will bring you back to the main FDISK Options menu. Now that the logical drives are gone, you can delete the extended DOS partition itself by choosing option 3 on the FDISK Options menu and then option 2 on the Delete DOS Partition or Logical DOS Drive menu. Again, you are shown the partition information display, warned that data will be lost, and asked if you really want to delete the extended DOS partition. If you reply Y, the screen will be updated to show only the primary DOS partition and a message that the extended DOS partition has been deleted. Press Esc to return once again to the FDISK Options menu. You can now delete your primary DOS partition or repartition your hard disk as you see fit.

INDEX

C

M

Selections from
The SYBEX Library

DOS

The ABC's of DOS 4
Alan R. Miller
275pp. Ref. 583-2
This step-by-step introduction to using DOS 4 is written especially for beginners. Filled with simple examples, *The ABC's of DOS 4* covers the basics of hardware, software, disks, the system editor EDLIN, DOS commands, and more.

ABC's of MS-DOS
(Second Edition)
Alan R. Miller
233pp. Ref. 493-3
This handy guide to MS-DOS is all many PC users need to manage their computer files, organize floppy and hard disks, use EDLIN, and keep their computers organized. Additional information is given about utilities like Sidekick, and there is a DOS command and program summary. The second edition is fully updated for Version 3.3.

Understanding DOS 3.3
Judd Robbins
678pp. Ref. 648-0
This best selling, in-depth tutorial addresses the needs of users at all levels with many examples and hands-on exercises. Robbins discusses the fundamentals of DOS, then covers manipulating files and directories, using the DOS editor, printing, communicating, and finishes with a full section on batch files.

MS-DOS Handbook
(Third Edition)
Richard Allen King
362pp. Ref. 492-5
This classic has been fully expanded and revised to include the latest features of MS-DOS Version 3.3. Two reference books in one, this title has separate sections for programmer and user. Multi-DOS partitons, 3 ½-inch disk format, batch file call and return feature, and comprehensive coverage of MS-DOS commands are included. Through Version 3.3.

MS-DOS Power User's Guide, Volume I
(Second Edition)
Jonathan Kamin
482pp. Ref. 473-9
A fully revised, expanded edition of our best-selling guide to high-performance DOS techniques and utilities—with details on Version 3.3. Configuration, I/O, directory structures, hard disks, RAM disks, batch file programming, the ANSI.SYS device driver, more. Through Version 3.3.

MS-DOS Power User's Guide, Volume II
Martin Waterhouse/Jonathan Kamin
418pp, Ref. 411-9
A second volume of high-performance techniques and utilities, with expanded coverage of DOS 3.3, and new material on video modes, Token-Ring and PC Network support, micro-mainframe links, extended and expanded memory, multitasking systems, and more. Through Version 3.3.

DOS User's Desktop Companion
SYBEX Ready Reference Series
Judd Robbins
969 pp. Ref. 505-0
This comprehensive reference covers DOS commands, batch files, memory enhancements, printing, communications and more information on optimizing each user's DOS environment. Written with

step-by-step instructions and plenty of examples, this volume covers all versions through 3.3.

MS-DOS Advanced Programming
Michael J. Young
490pp. Ref. 578-6

Practical techniques for maximizing performance in MS-DOS software by making best use of system resources. Topics include functions, interrupts, devices, multitasking, memory residency and more, with examples in C and assembler. Through Version 3.3.

Essential PC-DOS (Second Edition)
Myril Clement Shaw
Susan Soltis Shaw
332pp. Ref. 413-5

An authoritative guide to PC-DOS, including version 3.2. Designed to make experts out of beginners, it explores everything from disk management to batch file programming. Includes an 85-page command summary. Through Version 3.2.

The IBM PC-DOS Handbook (Third Edition)
Richard Allen King
359pp. Ref. 512-3

A guide to the inner workings of PC-DOS 3.2, for intermediate to advanced users and programmers of the IBM PC series. Topics include disk, screen and port control, batch files, networks, compatibility, and more. Through Version 3.3.

DOS Instant Reference SYBEX Prompter Series
Greg Harvey/Kay Yarborough Nelson
220pp. Ref. 477-1, 4 ¾" × 8"

A complete fingertip reference for fast, easy on-line help:command summaries, syntax, usage and error messages. Organized by function—system commands, file commands, disk management, directories, batch files, I/O, networking, programming, and more. Through Version 3.3.

Hard Disk Instant Reference SYBEX Prompter Series
Judd Robbins
256pp. Ref. 587-5, 4 ¾" × 8"

Compact yet comprehensive, this pocket-sized reference presents the essential information on DOS commands used in managing directories and files, and in optimizing disk configuration. Includes a survey of third-party utility capabilities. Through DOS 4.0.

Understanding Hard Disk Management on the PC
Jonathan Kamin
500pp. Ref. 561-1

This title is a key productivity tool for all hard disk users who want efficient, error-free file management and organization. Includes details on the best ways to conserve hard disk space when using several memory-guzzling programs. Through DOS 4.

OTHER OPERATING SYSTEMS AND ENVIRONMENTS

Essential OS/2 (Second Edition)
Judd Robbins
445pp. Ref. 609-X

Written by an OS/2 expert, this is the guide to the powerful new resources of the OS/2 operating system standard edition 1.1 with presentation manager. Robbins introduces the standard edition, and details multitasking under OS/2, and the range of commands for installing, starting up, configuring, and running applications. For Version 1.1 Standard Edition.

Programmers Guide to the OS/2 Presentation Manager
Michael J. Young
683pp. Ref. 569-7

This is the definitive tutorial guide to writing programs for the OS/2 Presentation Manager. Young starts with basic architecture, and explores every important feature including scroll bars, keyboard and mouse interface, menus and accelerators, dialogue boxes, clipboards, multitasking, and much more.

Programmer's Guide to Windows
(Second Edition)
David Durant/Geta Carlson/Paul Yao
704pp. Ref. 496-8

The first edition of this programmer's guide was hailed as a classic. This new edition covers Windows 2 and Windows/386 in depth. Special emphasis is given to over fifty new routines to the Windows interface, and to preparation for OS/2 Presentation Manager compatibility.

Graphics Programming Under Windows
Brian Myers/Chris Doner
646pp. Ref. 448-8

Straightforward discussion, abundant examples, and a concise reference guide to graphics commands make this book a must for Windows programmers. Topics range from how Windows works to programming for business, animation, CAD, and desktop publishing. For Version 2.

UTILITIES

Mastering the Norton Utilities
Peter Dyson
373pp. Ref. 575-1

In-depth descriptions of each Norton utility make this book invaluable for beginning and experienced users alike. Each utility is described clearly with examples and the text is organized so that readers can put Norton to work right away. Version 4.5.

Mastering SideKick Plus
Gene Weisskopf
394pp. Ref. 558-1

Employ all of Sidekick's powerful and expanded features with this hands-on guide to the popular utility. Features include comprehensive and detailed coverage of time management, note taking, outlining, auto dialing, DOS file management, math, and copy-and-paste functions.

COMMUNICATIONS

Mastering Crosstalk XVI
(Second Edition)
Peter W. Gofton
225pp. Ref. 642-1

Introducing the communications program Crosstalk XVI for the IBM PC. As well as providing extensive examples of command and script files for programming Crosstalk, this book includes a detailed description of how to use the program's more advanced features, such as windows, talking to mini or mainframe, customizing the keyboard and answering calls and background mode.

NETWORKS

The ABC's of Novell Netware
Jeff Woodward
282pp. Ref. 614-6

For users who are new to PC's or networks, this entry-level tutorial outlines each basic element and operation of Novell. The ABC's introduces computer hardware and software, DOS, network organization and security, and printing and communicating over the netware system.

Mastering Novell Netware
Cheryl C. Currid/Craig A. Gillett
500pp. Ref. 630-8

Easy and comprehensive, this book is a thorough guide for System Administrators to installing and operating a microcomputer network using Novell Netware. Mastering covers actually setting up a network from start to finish, design, administration, maintenance, and troubleshooting.

Networking with TOPS
Steven William Rimmer
350pp. Ref. 565-4

A hands on guide to the most popular user friendly network available. This book will walk a user through setting up the hardware and software of a variety of TOPS configurations, from simple two station networks through whole offices. It explains the realities of sharing files between PC compatibles and Macintoshes, of sharing printers and other peripherals and, most important, of the real world performance one can expect when the network is running.

SPREADSHEETS AND INTEGRATED SOFTWARE

Visual Guide to Lotus 1-2-3
Jeff Woodward
250pp. Ref. 641-3

Readers match what they see on the screen with the book's screen-by-screen action sequences. For new Lotus users, topics include computer fundamentals, opening and editing a worksheet, using graphs, macros, and printing typeset-quality reports. For Release 2.2.

The ABC's of 1-2-3 Release 2.2
Chris Gilbert/Laurie Williams
340pp. Ref. 623-5

New Lotus 1-2-3 users delight in this book's step-by-step approach to building trouble-free spreadsheets, displaying graphs, and efficiently building databases. The authors cover the ins and outs of the latest version including easier calculations, file linking, and better graphic presentation.

The ABC's of 1-2-3 Release 3
Judd Robbins
290pp. Ref. 519-0

The ideal book for beginners who are new to Lotus or new to Release 3. This step-by-step approach to the 1-2-3 spreadsheet software gets the reader up and running with spreadsheet, database, graphics, and macro functions.

The ABC's of 1-2-3 (Second Edition)
Chris Gilbert/Laurie Williams
245pp. Ref. 355-4

Online Today recommends it as "an easy and comfortable way to get started with the program." An essential tutorial for novices, it will remain on your desk as a valuable source of ongoing reference and support. For Release 2.

Mastering 1-2-3 Release 3
Carolyn Jorgensen
682pp. Ref. 517-4

For new Release 3 and experienced Release 2 users, "Mastering" starts with a basic spreadsheet, then introduces spreadsheet and database commands, functions, and macros, and then tells how to analyze 3D spreadsheets and make high-impact reports and graphs. Lotus add-ons are discussed and Fast Tracks are included.

Mastering 1-2-3 (Second Edition)
Carolyn Jorgensen
702pp. Ref. 528-X

Get the most from 1-2-3 Release 2 with this step-by-step guide emphasizing advanced features and practical uses. Topics include data sharing, macros, spreadsheet security, expanded memory, and graphics enhancements.

The Complete Lotus 1-2-3 Release 2.2 Handbook
Greg Harvey
750pp. Ref. 625-1

This comprehensive handbook discusses every 1-2-3 operating with clear instructions and practical tips. This volume especially emphasizes the new improved graphics, high-speed recalculation techniques, and spreadsheet linking available with Release 2.2.

The Complete Lotus 1-2-3 Release 3 Handbook
Greg Harvey
700pp. Ref. 600-6

Everything you ever wanted to know about 1-2-3 is in this definitive handbook. As a Release 3 guide, it features the design and use of 3D worksheets, and improved graphics, along with using Lotus under DOS or OS/2. Problems, exercises, and helpful insights are included.

Lotus 1-2-3 Desktop Companion SYBEX Ready Reference Series
Greg Harvey
976pp. Ref. 501-8

A full-time consultant, right on your desk. Hundreds of self-contained entries cover every 1-2-3 feature, organized by topic, indexed and cross-referenced, and supplemented by tips, macros and working examples. For Release 2.

Advanced Techniques in Lotus 1-2-3
Peter Antoniak/E. Michael Lunsford
367pp. Ref. 556-5

This guide for experienced users focuses on advanced functions, and techniques for designing menu-driven applications using macros and the Release 2 command language. Interfacing techniques and add-on products are also considered.

Lotus 1-2-3 Instant Reference Release 2.2 SYBEX Prompter Series
Greg Harvey/Kay Yarborough Nelson
254pp. Ref. 635-9, 4 ¾" × 8"

The reader gets quick and easy access to any operation in 1-2-3 Version 2.2 in this handy pocket-sized encyclopedia. Organized by menu function, each command and function has a summary description, the exact key sequence, and a discussion of the options.

Lotus 1-2-3 Tips and Tricks
Gene Weisskopf
396pp. Ref. 454-2

A rare collection of timesavers and tricks for longtime Lotus users. Topics include macros, range names, spreadsheet design, hardware considerations, DOS operations, efficient data analysis, printing, data interchange, applications development, and more.

Lotus 1-2-3 Instant Reference SYBEX Prompter Series
Greg Harvey/Kay Yarborough Nelson
296pp. Ref. 475-5; 4 ¾" × 8"

Organized information at a glance. When you don't have time to hunt through hundreds of pages of manuals, turn here for a quick reminder: the right key sequence, a brief explanation of a command, or the correct syntax for a specialized function.

Mastering Symphony (Fourth Edition)
Douglas Cobb
857pp. Ref. 494-1

Thoroughly revised to cover all aspects of the major upgrade of Symphony Version 2, this Fourth Edition of Doug Cobb's classic is still "the Symphony bible" to this complex but even more powerful package. All the new features are discussed and placed in context with prior versions so that both new and previous users will benefit from Cobb's insights.

The ABC's of Quattro
Alan Simpson/Douglas J. Wolf
286pp. Ref. 560-3

Especially for users new to spreadsheets, this is an introduction to the basic concepts and a guide to instant productivity through editing and using spreadsheet formulas and functions. Includes how to print out graphs and data for presentation. For Quattro 1.1.

Mastering Quattro
Alan Simpson
576pp. Ref. 514-X

This tutorial covers not only all of Quattro's classic spreadsheet features, but also its added capabilities including extended graphing, modifiable menus, and the macro debugging environment. Simpson brings out how to use all of Quattro's new-generation-spreadsheet capabilities.

Mastering Framework III
Douglas Hergert/Jonathan Kamin
613pp. Ref. 513-1

Thorough, hands-on treatment of the latest Framework release. An outstanding introduction to integrated software applications, with examples for outlining, spreadsheets, word processing, databases, and more; plus an introduction to FRED programming.

The ABC's of Excel on the IBM PC
Douglas Hergert
326pp. Ref. 567-0

This book is a brisk and friendly introduction to the most important features of Microsoft Excel for PC's. This beginner's book discusses worksheets, charts, database operations, and macros, all with hands-on examples. Written for all versions through Version 2.

Mastering Excel on the IBM PC
Carl Townsend
628pp. Ref. 403-8

A complete Excel handbook with step-by-step tutorials, sample applications and an extensive reference section. Topics include worksheet fundamentals, formulas and windows, graphics, database techniques, special features, macros and more.

Excel Instant Reference
SYBEX Prompter Series
William J. Orvis
368pp. Ref.577-8, 4 ¾" × 8"

This pocket-sized reference book contains all of Excel's menu commands, math operations, and macro functions. Quick and easy access to command syntax, usage, arguments, and examples make this Instant Reference a must. Through Version 1.5.

Understanding PFS: First Choice
Gerry Litton
489pp. Ref. 568-9

From basic commands to complex features, this complete guide to the popular integrated package is loaded with step-by-step instructions. Lessons cover creating attractive documents, setting up easy-to-use databases, working with spreadsheets and graphics, and smoothly integrating tasks from different First Choice modules. For Version 3.0.

Mastering Enable
Keith D. Bishop
517pp. Ref. 440-2

A comprehensive, practical, hands-on guide to Enable 2.0—integrated word processing, spreadsheet, database management, graphics, and communications—from basic concepts to custom menus, macros and the Enable Procedural Language.

Mastering Q & A (Second Edition)
Greg Harvey
540pp. Ref. 452-6

This hands-on tutorial explores the Q & A Write, File, and Report modules, and the Intelligent Assistant. English-language command processor, macro creation, interfacing with other software, and more, using practical business examples.

DATABASE MANAGEMENT

The ABC's of Paradox
Charles Siegel
300pp. Ref.573-5

Easy to understand and use, this introduction is written so that the computer novice can create, edit, and manage complex Paradox databases. This primer is filled with examples of the Paradox 3.0 menu structure.

Mastering Paradox
(Fourth Edition)
Alan Simpson
636pp. Ref. 612-X
Best selling author Alan Simpson simplifies all aspects of Paradox for the beginning to intermediate user. The book starts with database basics, covers multiple tables, graphics, custom applications with PAL, and the Personal Programmer. For Version 3.0.

Quick Guide to dBASE:
The Visual Approach
David Kolodney
382pp. Ref. 596-4
This illustrated tutorial provides the beginner with a working knowledge of all the basic functions of dBASE IV. Images of each successive dBASE screen tell how to create and modify a database, add, edit, sort and select records, and print custom labels and reports.

The ABC's of dBASE IV
Robert Cowart
338pp. Ref. 531-X
This superb tutorial introduces beginners to the concept of databases and practical dBASE IV applications featuring the new menu-driven interface, the new report writer, and Query by Example.

Understanding dBASE IV
(Special Edition)
Alan Simpson
880pp. Ref. 509-3
This Special Edition is the best introduction to dBASE IV, written by 1 million-reader-strong dBASE expert Alan Simpson. First it gives basic skills for creating and manipulating efficient databases. Then the author explains how to make reports, manage multiple databases, and build applications. Includes Fast Track speed notes.

Mastering dBASE IV
Programming
Carl Townsend
496pp. Ref. 540-9
This task-oriented book introduces structured dBASE IV programming and commands by setting up a general ledger system, an invoice system, and a quotation management system. The author carefully explores the unique character of dBASE IV based on his in-depth understanding of the program.

dBASE IV User's
Instant Reference
SYBEX Prompter Series
Alan Simpson
349pp. Ref. 605-7, 4 ¾" × 8"
This handy pocket-sized reference book gives every new dBASE IV user fast and easy access to any dBASE command. Arranged alphabetically and by function, each entry includes a description, exact syntax, an example, and special tips from Alan Simpson.

dBASE IV Programmer's
Instant Reference
SYBEX Prompter Series
Alan Simpson
544pp. Ref.538-7, 4 ¾" × 8"
This comprehensive reference to every dBASE command and function has everything for the dBASE programmer in a compact, pocket-sized book. Fast and easy access to adding data, sorting, performing calculations, managing multiple databases, memory variables and arrays, windows and menus, networking, and much more. Version 1.1.

dBASE IV User's
Desktop Companion
SYBEX Ready Reference Series
Alan Simpson
950pp. Ref. 523-9
This easy-to-use reference provides an exhaustive resource guide to taking full advantage of the powerful non-programming features of the dBASE IV Control Center. This book discusses query by example, custom reports and data entry screens, macros, the application generator, and the dBASE command and programming language.

dBASE IV Programmer's
Reference Guide
SYBEX Ready Reference Series
Alan Simpson
1000pp. Ref. 539-5

This exhaustive seven-part reference for dBASE IV users includes sections on getting started, using menu-driven dBASE, command-driven dBASE, multiuser dBASE, programming in dBASE, common algorithms, and getting the most out of dBASE. Includes Simpson's tips on the best ways to use this completely redesigned and more powerful program.

The ABC's of dBASE III PLUS
Robert Cowart
264pp. Ref. 379-1
The most efficient way to get beginners up and running with dBASE. Every 'how' and 'why' of database management is demonstrated through tutorials and practical dBASE III PLUS applications.

Understanding dBASE III PLUS
Alan Simpson
415pp. Ref. 349-X
A solid sourcebook of training and ongoing support. Everything from creating a first database to command file programming is presented in working examples, with tips and techniques you won't find anywhere else.

Mastering dBASE III PLUS:
A Structured Approach
Carl Townsend
342pp. Ref. 372-4
In-depth treatment of structured programming for custom dBASE solutions. An ideal study and reference guide for applications developers, new and experienced users with an interest in efficient programming.

Also:
Understanding dBASE III
Alan Simpson
300pp. Ref. 267-1

Advanced Techniques
in dBASE III PLUS
Alan Simpson
454pp. Ref. 369-4
A full course in database design and structured programming, with routines for inventory control, accounts receivable, system management, and integrated databases.

Simpson's dBASE Tips and
Tricks (For dBASE III PLUS)
Alan Simpson
420pp. Ref. 383-X
A unique library of techniques and programs shows how creative use of built-in features can solve all your needs—without expensive add-on products or external languages. Spreadsheet functions, graphics, and much more.

dBASE III PLUS Programmer's
Reference Guide
SYBEX Ready Reference Series
Alan Simpson
1056pp. Ref. 508-5
Programmers will save untold hours and effort using this comprehensive, well-organized dBASE encyclopedia. Complete technical details on commands and functions, plus scores of often-needed algorithms.

dBASE Instant Reference
SYBEX Prompter Series
Alan Simpson
471pp. Ref. 484-4; 4 ¾" × 8"
Comprehensive information at a glance: a brief explanation of syntax and usage for every dBASE command, with step-by-step instructions and exact keystroke sequences. Commands are grouped by function in twenty precise categories.

Understanding R:BASE
Alan Simpson/Karen Watterson
609pp. Ref.503-4
This is the definitive R:BASE tutorial, for use with either OS/2 or DOS. Hands-on lessons cover every aspect of the software, from creating and using a database, to custom systems. Includes Fast Track speed notes.

Power User's Guide to R:BASE
Alan Simpson/Cheryl Currid/Craig Gillett
446pp. Ref. 354-6
Supercharge your R:BASE applications with this straightforward tutorial that covers system design, structured programming, managing multiple data tables, and more. Sample applications include ready-to-run

mailing, inventory and accounts receivable systems. Through Version 2.11.

Understanding Oracle
James T. Perry/Joseph G. Lateer
634pp. Ref. 534-4
A comprehensive guide to the Oracle database management system for administrators, users, and applications developers. Covers everything in Version 5 from database basics to multi-user systems, performance, and development tools including SQL*Forms, SQL*Report, and SQL*Calc. Includes Fast Track speed notes.

COMPUTER-AIDED DESIGN AND DRAFTING

Visual Guide to AutoCAD
Genevieve Katz
325pp. Ref. 627-8
A visual step-by-step tutorial for AutoCAD beginners, this book gives the reader at a quick glance, the graphically presented information needed to understand and respond to commands. It covers more than 90 commands, from getting started to drawing composites using multiple commands. Through Release 10.

The ABC's of AutoCAD (Second Edition)
Alan R. Miller
375pp. Ref. 584-0
This brief but effective introduction to AutoCAD quickly gets users drafting and designing with this complex CADD package. The essential operations and capabilities of AutoCAD are neatly detailed, using a proven, step-by-step method that is tailored to the results-oriented beginner.

Mastering AutoCAD (Third Edition)
George Omura
825pp. Ref. 574-3
Now in its third edition, this tutorial guide to computer-aided design and drafting with AutoCAD is perfect for newcomers to CADD, as well as AutoCAD users seeking greater proficiency. An architectural project serves as an example throughout.

Advanced Techniques in AutoCAD (Second Edition)
Robert M. Thomas
425pp. Ref. 593-X
Develop custom applications using screen menus, command macros, and AutoLISP programming—no prior programming experience required. Topics include customizing the AutoCAD environment, advanced data extraction techniques, and much more.

AutoCAD Desktop Companion SYBEX Ready Reference Series
Robert M. Thomas
1094pp. Ref.590-5
This is a complete reference work covering all the features, commands, and user options available under AutoCAD Release 10, including drawing basic and complex entities, editing, displaying, printing, plotting, and customizing drawings, manipulating the drawing database, and AutoLISP programming. Through Release 10.

AutoCAD Instant Reference SYBEX Prompter Series
George Omura
390pp. Ref. 548-4, 4 3/4" × 8"
This pocket-sized reference is a quick guide to all AutoCAD features. Designed for easy use, all commands are organized with exact syntax, a brief description, options, tips, and references. Through Release 10.

The ABC's of Generic CADD
Alan R. Miller
278pp. Ref. 608-1
This outstanding guide to computer-aided design and drafting with Generic CADD assumes no previous experience with computers or CADD. This book will have users doing useful CADD work in record time, including basic drawing with the

keyboard or a mouse, erasing and unerasing, making a copy of drawings on your printer, adding text and organizing your drawings using layers.

The ABC's of AutoLISP
George Omura
300pp. Ref. 620-0

This book is for users who want to unleash the full power of AutoCAD through the AutoLISP programming language. In non-technical terms, the reader is shown how to store point locations, create new commands, and manipulate coordinates and text. Packed with tips on common coding errors.

Mastering VersaCAD
David Bassett-Parkins
450pp. Ref. 617-0

For every level of VCAD user, this comprehensive tutorial treats each phase of project design including drawing, modifying, grouping, and filing. The reader will also learn VCAD project management and many tips, tricks, and shortcuts. Version 5.4.

FOR SCIENTISTS AND ENGINEERS

1-2-3 for Scientists and Engineers
William J. Orvis
341pp. Ref. 407-0

Fast, elegant solutions to common problems in science and engineering, using Lotus 1-2-3. Tables and plotting, curve fitting, statistics, derivatives, integrals and differentials, solving systems of equations, and more.

BASIC Programs for Scientists and Engineers
Alan R. Miller
318pp. Ref. 073-3

The algorithms presented in this book are programmed in standard BASIC code which should be usable with almost any implementation of BASIC. Includes statis-

tical calculations, matrix algebra, curve fitting, integration, and more.

Turbo BASIC Programs for Scientists and Engineers
Alan R. Miller
276pp. Ref. 429-1

This practical text develops commonly-needed algorithms for scientific and engineering applications, and programs them in Turbo BASIC. Simultaneous solution, curve fitting, nonlinear equations, numerical integration and more.

Turbo Pascal Programs for Scientists and Engineers
Alan R. Miller
332pp. Ref. 424-0

The author develops commonly-needed algorithms for science and engineering, then programs them in Turbo Pascal. Includes algorithms for statistics, simultaneous solutions, curve fitting, integration, and nonlinear equations.

FORTRAN Programs for Scientists and Engineers (Second Edition)
Alan R. Miller
280pp. Ref. 571-9

In this collection of widely used scientific algorithms—for statistics, vector and matrix operations, curve fitting, and more—the author stresses effective use of little-known and powerful features of FORTRAN.

WORD PROCESSING

Visual Guide to WordPerfect
Jeff Woodward
457pp. Ref. 591-3

This is a visual hands-on guide which is ideal for brand new users as the book shows each activity keystroke-by-keystroke. Clear illustrations of computer screen menus are included at every stage. Covers basic editing, formatting lines, paragraphs, and pages, using the block feature, footnotes, search and replace, and more. Through Version 5.

TO JOIN THE SYBEX MAILING LIST OR ORDER BOOKS
PLEASE COMPLETE THIS FORM

NAME _____ COMPANY _____

STREET _____ STATE _____ ZIP _____

☐ PLEASE MAIL ME MORE INFORMATION ABOUT **SYBEX** TITLES

ORDER FORM (There is no obligation to order)

PLEASE SEND ME THE FOLLOWING:

TITLE	QTY	PRICE
_____	____	____
_____	____	____
_____	____	____
_____	____	____

TOTAL BOOK ORDER   ____ $____

CUSTOMER SIGNATURE _____

SHIPPING AND HANDLING PLEASE ADD $2.00 PER BOOK VIA UPS   _____

FOR OVERSEAS SURFACE ADD $5.25 PER BOOK PLUS $4.40 REGISTRATION FEE   _____

FOR OVERSEAS AIRMAIL ADD $18.25 PER BOOK PLUS $4.40 REGISTRATION FEE   _____

CALIFORNIA RESIDENTS PLEASE ADD APPLICABLE SALES TAX   _____

TOTAL AMOUNT PAYABLE   _____

☐ CHECK ENCLOSED   ☐ VISA
☐ MASTERCARD   ☐ AMERICAN EXPRESS

ACCOUNT NUMBER _____

EXPIR. DATE _____ DAYTIME PHONE _____

CHECK AREA OF COMPUTER INTEREST:

☐ BUSINESS SOFTWARE

☐ TECHNICAL PROGRAMMING

☐ OTHER: _____

OTHER COMPUTER TITLES YOU WOULD LIKE TO SEE IN PRINT:

_____

_____

THE FACTOR THAT WAS MOST IMPORTANT IN YOUR SELECTION:

☐ THE SYBEX NAME

☐ QUALITY

☐ PRICE

☐ EXTRA FEATURES

☐ COMPREHENSIVENESS

☐ CLEAR WRITING

☐ OTHER _____

OCCUPATION

☐ PROGRAMMER   ☐ TEACHER

☐ SENIOR EXECUTIVE ☐ HOMEMAKER

☐ COMPUTER CONSULTANT ☐ RETIRED

☐ SUPERVISOR   ☐ STUDENT

☐ MIDDLE MANAGEMENT ☐ OTHER:

☐ ENGINEER/TECHNICAL _____

☐ CLERICAL/SERVICE

☐ BUSINESS OWNER/SELF EMPLOYED

CHECK YOUR LEVEL OF COMPUTER USE

☐ NEW TO COMPUTERS

☐ INFREQUENT COMPUTER USER

☐ FREQUENT USER OF ONE SOFTWARE
   PACKAGE:
   NAME _____

☐ FREQUENT USER OF MANY SOFTWARE
   PACKAGES

☐ PROFESSIONAL PROGRAMMER

OTHER COMMENTS:

_____
_____
_____
_____
_____
_____
_____

PLEASE FOLD, SEAL, AND MAIL TO SYBEX

SYBEX, INC.
2021 CHALLENGER DR. #100
ALAMEDA, CALIFORNIA USA
94501

SEAL

MASTERING DOS   The Companion Diskette ($19.95)

If you have found *Mastering DOS* to be useful, you will be glad to learn that every one of the batch files in this book is contained in a companion diskette. Save time, energy, and money—and avoid the drudgery of typing these excellent programs—by ordering the *Mastering DOS* Companion diskette now.

An excellent introductory training guide to DOS is also available in audio cassette form. Two cassettes and an accompanying Professional Learning Manual can be your personal aid to quick and easy understanding of DOS.

Use the order form below to order any of the fine products produced by Judd Robbins. Mail today, with complete payment (drawn on a U.S. bank) to Computer Options, P.O. Box 9656, Berkeley, CA 94709.

_____

_____ copies of *Mastering DOS* Companion Diskette, at $19.95 each   _____

_____ copies of *ReComm*, the DOS Command Reissuing Utility,

at $19.95 each _____

_____ copies of *DOS 4 Pull-Down Menu Pocket Reference Card*,

at $6.95 each _____

_____ copies of *Introduction to DOS* Audio Cassette Training,

at $19.95 each _____

_____ Shipping and handling (add $2.50 per item)

_____ California sales tax (please add appropriate amount

for your city/county) _____

TOTAL ORDER: _____

_____
Name

_____
Address

_____
City   State   Zip

_____
Phone

SUMMARY OF DOS COMMANDS*

COMMAND	DESCRIPTION	FORMAT	PAGE
KEYB	Loads in new keyboard translation table and code page	[D:Path]KEYB [xx[,[yyy],[FileSpec]] [/ID:iii]][D:Path]KEYB iii	310
LABEL	Defines or changes existing volume label	[D:Path]LABEL [D1:][String]	642
MEM	Displays total and available memory	[D:Path]MEM [/PROGRAM] [/DEBUG]	643
MKDIR (MD)	Creates a new subdirectory	[D:]Path	128
MODE	Defines attributes for all ports and code pages	[D:Path]MODE LPTx [COLS = a] [LINES = b] [RETRY = c] [D:Path]MODE LPTx: = COMy [D:Path]MODE COMy[:]BAUD = bd [PARITY = p] [DATE = Dbits][STOP = Sbits] [RETRY = c] [D:Path]MODE DisplayType [D:Path]MODE [DisplayType], Shift [,T] [D:Path]MODE CON [COLS = a] [LINES = b] [D:Path]MODE CON RATE = r DELAY = d [D:Path]MODE Device CODEPAGE PREPARE = ((CP)FileSpec) [D:Path]MODE Device CODEPAGE PREPARE = ((CPList)FileSpec) [D:Path]MODE Device CODEPAGE SELECT = CP [D:Path]MODE Device CODEPAGE [/STATUS] [D:Path]MODE Device CODEPAGE REFRESH	222, 307
MORE	Pauses long file displays	[D:Path]MORE	351
NLSFUNC	Loads in routines for code pages and the CHCP command	[D:Path]NLSFUNC [FileSpec]	306
PATH	Defines search list for .EXE, .COM, and .BAT files	PATH [D1:Path1][;D2:Path2...]	149
PRINT	Queues files for printing	[D:Path]PRINT [Params][/C][/T][/P][FileSpec,...]	198
PROMPT	Changes the system prompt	PROMPT [String]	279
RECOVER	Rescues damaged files	[D:Path]RECOVER [D1:Path1]SourceFile [D:Path]RECOVER [D1]	445
RENAME (REN)	Changes the name of a file	REN OldFile NewFile	121

*See Part 7, "DOS Command Reference," for a complete description of commands and their parameters.

SUMMARY OF DOS COMMANDS*

COMMAND	DESCRIPTION	FORMAT	PAGE
REPLACE	Copies, adds, and updates programs	[D:Path]REPLACE SourceFile DestD[/A][/P][/R][/S][/U][/W]	441
RESTORE	Reads backup file back onto disk	[D:Path]RESTORE SourceD FileSpec [/S][/P][/B:mm-dd-yy] [/A:mm-dd-yy][/M][/N][/L:hh-mm-ss][/E:hh-mm-ss]	257
RMDIR (RD)	Deletes empty directories	RD [D:Path]	120
SELECT	Creates a system disk with country information	[D:Path]SELECT [[A: ¦ B:]DestD:[Path]] xxx yy	316
SET	Changes defaults and definitions in DOS environment	SET [Name = [Param]]	463
SHARE	Loads network lock-out routines	[D:Path]SHARE [/F:FileMem][/L:Locks]	656
SORT	Sorts data by column	[D:Path]SORT [/R][/ + Col]	330
SUBST	Makes DOS think a directory is a disk drive	[D:Path]SUBST [D:Path]SUBST DestDSourceD [D:Path]SUBST objectD /D	450
SYS	Transfers hidden system files to another disk	[D:Path]SYS DestD:	660
TIME	Sets the system time	TIME [hh:mm[:ss[.xx]]]	56
TREE	Lists all directories, subdirectories, and files on a disk	[D:Path]TREE [D:][/F]	131
TYPE	Displays the contents of an ASCII file	TYPE FileSpec	107
VER	Displays the current version of DOS	VER	662
VERIFY	Causes DOS to verify everything that is written to disk	VERIFY [ON ¦ OFF]	243

*See Part 7, "DOS Command Reference," for a complete description of commands and their parameters.

SUMMARY OF DOS COMMANDS*

COMMAND	DESCRIPTION	FORMAT	PAGE
VOL	Displays volume label of drive	VOL [*D:*]	663
XCOPY	Copies complete directories, subdirectories, and files	[*D:Path*]XCOPY[*FileSpec1*][*FileSpec2*][/A][/D:*mm-dd-yy*][/E][/M][/P][/S][/V][/W]	458

*See Part 7, "DOS Command Reference," for a complete description of commands and their parameters.

EDLIN COMMANDS*

COMMAND	DESCRIPTION	FORMAT	PAGE
A	Appends lines	[*Num*]A	170
C	Copies lines	[*Line*],[*Line*],*Line*[,*Count*] C	180
D	Deletes lines	[*Line*][,*Line*] D	184
—	Edits line	[*Line*]	177
E	Updates and exits	E	186
I	Inserts lines	[*Line*]I	175
L	Lists lines	[*Line*][,*Line*] L	173
M	Moves lines	[*Line*],[*Line*],*Line* M	179
P	Displays full page	[*Line*][,*Line*]P	173
Q	Aborts and exits	Q	186
R	Replaces globally	[*Line*][,*Line*][?]R[*String*][^Z*NewString*]	183
S	Searches globally	[*Line*][,*Line*][?]S[*String*]	181
T	Merges files	[*Line*]T[*FileSpec*]	171
W	Writes lines	[*Num*]W	172

*See Chapter 7, "Using the DOS Editor," for a complete description of EDLIN commands and their parameters.

CONFIGURATION FILE COMMANDS*			
COMMAND	**DESCRIPTION**	**FORMAT**	**PAGE**
BREAK	Determines when DOS checks for a Ctrl-Break	BREAK = [ON ¦ OFF]	617
BUFFERS	Sets number of buffers	BUFFERS = x,y /x	268
COUNTRY	Specifies date and time formats	COUNTRY = $xxx,[yyy]$ [,$FileSpec$]	294
DEVICE	Loads device drivers into memory	DEVICE = $FileSpec[Switches]$	270
FCBS	Defines how many file control blocks can be used at once	FCBS = $MaxNum,PermNum$	633
FILES	Specifies how many files can be accessed at once	FILES = x	267
INSTALL	Installs specific command files	INSTALL = [$D:Path$]$FileSpec$	378
LASTDRIVE	Specifies the highest drive letter	LASTDRIVE = D	455
SHELL	Specifies location of a different command processor	SHELL = $ComFileSpec$ [$Params$]	657
STACKS	Specifies new stack resources	STACKS = n,s	658
SWITCHES	Restricts an enhanced keyboard to conventional keyboard functions	SWITCHES = /K	659

*See Part 7, "DOS Command Reference," for a complete description of commands and their parameters.